# Decision Technology
## Modeling, Software, and Applications

**Matthew Liberatore**
*Villanova University*

**Robert Nydick**
*Villanova University*

John Wiley & Sons, Inc.

ACQUISITIONS EDITOR          *Beth L. Golub*
MARKETING MANAGER            *Gitti Lindner*
SENIOR PRODUCTION EDITOR     *Caroline Sieg*
DESIGN DIRECTOR              *Maddy Lesure*
ILLUSTRATION EDITOR          *Anna Melhorn*

This book was set in 10/12 Times Roman by Matrix Publishing Services and printed and bound by Hamilton Printing. The cover was printed by Phoenix Color.

This book is printed on acid free paper. ∞

ISBN (Domestic): 0471-41712-2
ISBN(WIE): 0471-42902-3

10 9 8 7 6 5 4 3 2 1

*Dedication*

*To Mary, Kate, Shelly, Chris, and my parents*
*M. J. L.*

*To Sue, Rob, Greg, and my parents*
*R. L. N.*

# Foreword

Every age sets the definition of what one must learn to be considered an educated person of the time. Medieval scholars pondered the seven liberal arts: grammar, dialectic, rhetoric, geometry, arithmetic, music, and astronomy. Most early American colleges set out to train students for the ministry or for service to the state. Many of these academic institutions offered a "broad plan of education" that included a great deal of mathematics, science, government and law. Post World-War II students, especially after the launch of Sputnik, and today's students who have grown up with the Internet, have seen such broad plans to be vague and ever-changing. Universities have become caught up with teaching what is hot and dropping what is not.

What an educated person must know in the 21st Century is somewhat muddled. But, to me, based on the scientific, mathematical, and computational advances of the last half of the 20th century, today's educated person must acquire a knowledge and understanding of what Professors Liberatore and Nydick term *decision technology*.

Decision technology may be viewed as an integration of mathematical theory and computational techniques that combine to form an ever-expanding set of proven decision aids for just about all areas of business, industry and government. Each day you are the beneficiary of decision technology: the supermarket's shelves are stocked with the products you want when you want them; your mutual fund manager decides what to buy or sell and when; your company decides where to locate a new retail outlet; your new house is built on schedule; the time you wait in line at the bank or post office is shorter; your search of the world-wide-web turns up a low-cost airfare for a sudden trip.

Decision making is often a personal and lonely affair. You have choices. You have to decide on whether to take the "road less traveled," or to take the left fork or the right fork along the road of life. You can't fall back on Yogi Berra's advice: "When you come to a fork in the road, take it." The outcome of a road or a fork not taken is never known. Once a decision is made, you have to live with its consequences. You can never claim that your decision was the "best." Although your experiences and judgment help you to make a decision, you will find that the results a decision technology analysis will broaden your view of the road and enable you to make a more confident choice.

Decision technology is a true product of our time. Although based on advanced scientific discoveries, it is distinguished by its use in the everyday world of commerce and industry. Professors Liberatore and Nydick make this clear by describing how four of the main topics of decision technology can improve decision making in a wide range of applications. The four topics—mathematical programming, decision analysis, simulation, and project analysis—cover a major portion of the total field.

The authors have coalesced their many years of teaching and applying decision technology into a text whose material is student friendly and classroom tested. Their pedagogical approach uses software (designed and produced by specialist companies and included in the text's CD) that facilitates the student's ability to put the technology to work. As they note: ". . . the focus of this text is on the application and not on the mathematical details underlying the models."

The educated person of the 21st century must have an understanding of decision technology. Decision technology contributes greatly to the well-being of the U. S. and global economies. A knowledge of decision technology will make you a better employee, a more valued manager, and, a more informed citizen of the world. *Decision Technology* is an excellent guide for your travels along the fork-filled road that leads to the future.

*Saul I. Gass*
*Professor Emeritus*

*Robert H. Smith School of Business*
*University of Maryland*

# Preface

Decision technology is the application of decision-support modeling and computer software to problems in business, government, and other types of organizations. Decision technology is closely related to, and has its origin in, the field of management science. The purpose of this book is to enable advanced undergraduate and graduate students to learn the essentials of modeling with software so that they can create and implement models to support organizational decision making.

This text provides an understanding of the core concepts and ideas underlying the techniques presented so that intelligent decisions can be made concerning how and when specific models and software packages are appropriate. However, the focus of this text is on the application and not on the mathematical details underlying the models. What makes this book different from many others is that we attempt to integrate the discussion of the theory with its application through modeling software. This text's use of Microsoft Project 2002, LINGO, Expert Choice, and Extend Software, instead of spreadsheets, sets it apart from other textbooks.

The text of *Decision Technology* is organized into parts and addresses four of the most important classes of modeling techniques: mathematical programming, decision analysis, simulation, and project analysis. Within each part, an example is covered in detail that provides a solid foundation for building additional models. The text supports the development of modeling skills by emphasizing how the various examples contain components or blocks that can be combined or modified to address other more complex problems.

## SOFTWARE

One or more modeling software packages are applied to various problems within each part of the text. These packages are: LINGO (LINDO Systems Inc. 2001) for mathematical programming; Expert Choice (Expert Choice Inc. 2000) for decision analysis; Extend (Imagine That Inc. 2001), and Stat::Fit (Geer Mountain Software Corporation 2002) for simulation; Microsoft Project 2000 (Microsoft Corporation 2000) for project analysis; and Excel as an interface with LINGO and Extend for data input, model output, and for illustrating project analysis methods. The text is bundled with a CD that contains student versions of LINGO, Expert Choice, Extend, and Microsoft Project 2000. The CD also has a folder that contains all of the model files that are presented in the text.

## INSTRUCTOR FLEXIBILITY

Each part of the text is self-contained, so that the instructor can select the combination and order of the parts in order to meet their teaching needs, whether for a quarter or semester course. In the mathematical programming section, after completing Chapters 2 and 3, those instructors choosing to use the LINGO modeling language would use Chapters 4, 5, and 6 and skip Chapters 7 and 8. Those instructors preferring LINGO's standard algebraic approach would skip Chapters 4, 5, and 6, and cover Chapters 7 and 8. Appendix A: Statistical Concepts, serves as reference material for Part 3: Computer Simulation. Appendix B: Summary Description of All Extend Blocks Used, also provides a useful reference for Part 3. The mathematical prerequisite for this text is a course in algebra. In addition, it is assumed that the student has at least a working knowledge of Windows.

## ANCILLARY TEACHING MATERIALS

The following support materials are available to the adopting instructor from the publisher at:http://www.wiley.com/college/liberatore or by calling (877) 762-2974.

- **Solutions files:** prepared by the authors, includes computer model and Word files for all homework problems in the text.
- **PowerPoint presentation slides**: prepared by the authors, includes an extensive set of charts for all chapters.

# Acknowledgments

W e would like to thank the reviewers who provided helpful comments and suggestions during the development of this manuscript:

Kevin McCarthy, Baker University

John F. Kottas, College of William and Mary

János D. Pintér, Dalhousie University

Neil B. Marks, Miami University

George D. Brower, Moravian College

Issac Gottlieb, Rutgers University

Ron Klimberg, St. Joseph's University

Patrick J. Delaney, United States Military Academy

Hoesein Arsham, University of Baltimore

Barb Downey, University of Missouri-Columbia

We would also like to thank those instructors who class-tested portions of this text.

Colin Benjamin, Florida A & M University

Stuart Boxerman, Washington University

George Brower, Moravian College

Roger Grinde, The University of New Hampshire

Chuhua Kuei, Pace University

Kevin McCarthy, Baker University

Charles Noon, University of Tennessee

Rodrigo Obando, Fairfield University

Jim Patell, Stanford University

Doug Samuelson, The University of Pennsylvania and George Washington University

Janice Winch, Pace University

We would like to offer a special note of thanks to our students who have used preliminary versions of this text during the past several years. These students were drawn from our professional part-time MBA, Executive MBA, and undergraduate programs. Many of these students reported successful applications of the methods to problems within their own organizations. Their feedback has helped to direct this text to meet the needs of today's practicing managers.

We would also like to thank our former student, Jeannette Kelley, for continued interest in our book, suggestions to improve the text and some support materials, and substantial contributions to Chapter 16. We would like to thank Elaine Webster for accepting the challenge and writing a self-contained appendix on statistical concepts.

We offer a special note of appreciation to Expert Choice, Imagine That, LINDO Systems, and Microsoft for allowing us to bundle their software with our text. In particular, we would like to thank our friends Dave Krahl at Imagine That, Mike Jones and Rozann Whitaker at Expert Choice, and Mark Wiley at LINDO Systems for believing in the importance of developing a text that integrates modeling, software, and application.

We also would like to thank Lorraina Raccuia, Editorial Assistant and Caroline Sieg, Senior Production Editor, for their efforts and support during the preparation of this text. We are also indebted to our editor, Beth Golub, for believing in us, sharing in our vision, supporting our efforts, and for having the courage to see this project through to its completion.

# Table of Contents

---

\*Chapter 5 and 6 use the LINGO modeling language approach; Chapters 7 and 8 cover essentially the same material, but use the standard algebraic LINGO approach. Therefore, skip Chapters 5 and 6 *or* 7 and 8 per instruction from your professor. See the Preface for further details.

## Part Four   Project Analysis

# Chapter 1

# Introduction

## DECISION TECHNOLOGY, MANAGEMENT SCIENCE, AND MODELING

### Overview

*Decision technology* is the application of decision-support modeling and computer software to problems in business, government, and other types of organizations. It is a value-added activity dedicated to improving the quality of the decision-making process. The benefits of decision technology include identifying and valuing potential problem solutions and offering penetrating insights into the problem's structure and interrelationships. Knowledge of decision technology is critical—to understand today's and tomorrow's business and industrial worlds one has to have knowledge of how decisions are made and how decision technology can play an important role in supporting the decision-making process.

Decision-aiding models can often be expressed in mathematical terms. For this reason, decision technology is closely related to, and has its origin in, the field of *management science,* also called *operations research.* Management science is a scientific approach to decision making that often uses *mathematical models* to help formulate and solve problems or to gain insight into them. Simply stated, a mathematical model is a representation or an abstraction of a real situation or system. The model does not seek to incorporate every possible factor or relationship present in the real world, but only those needed to adequately address the salient relationships. An example of how a simple model can provide a counterintuitive solution to an interesting problem is given in the appendix at the end of this chapter.

The steps in the modeling process are summarized in Figure 1.1. Problem formulation is critical since it drives the rest of the process, beginning with model development. Interestingly, solving the model is often the easiest part of the process, when performed by a knowledgeable user with good software support. The validation step ensures the adequacy of the "fit" between the model and the reality it seeks to represent. Finally, the modeling effort is completed with its usage or implementation. A successful implementation is one in which the model solution is either directly used by the decision maker, sometimes called a "classic implementation," or one that provides added value through organizational change. Examples of organizational changes include improved coordination and communication patterns, and knowledge creation and dissemination concerning the organization's processes and routines. See Liberatore et al. (2000) for more discussion of classic implementation and modeling and organizational change issues. Lastly, feedback allows the modeler to return to an earlier step in the modeling process to make adjustments as needed.

### Breakeven Example

The following equation is a simple model of total profit (P) for a firm:

$$P = 25x - 200$$

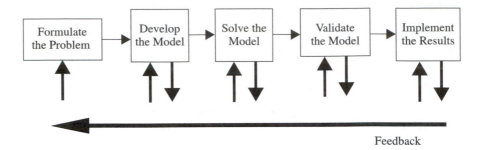

**Figure 1.1** The Steps in
the Modeling Process

where x represents number of units sold, the contribution margin (unit revenue minus variable cost) is $25, and the fixed cost of production is $200. This model shows that as x increases from 10 to 20, P increases from $50 to $300. However, certain factors may have been ignored in the development of this model. Examples include the costs associated with items produced but not sold, some price discounting when a large number of units are sold to one customer, and variable costs changing according to fluctuating materials costs. However, the model may be at a satisfactory level of detail for estimating the breakeven volume for this product (that is, the volume at which the fixed cost is recovered from product contributions).

Specifically, this model indicates that the breakeven volume is 8 (200/25) units. In addition, the model also shows that if the contribution margin were to be decreased by 20%, the breakeven volume would only increase to 10 units (200/(.8 * 25)). The 20% potential decrease may be sufficiently large to include the possible downside factors already mentioned that were ignored in the formulation of this model. As a result, this simple model may be adequate if knowing that the breakeven volume is likely to be in the 8–10 range and is therefore sufficient for the particular decision at hand. The interested reader is referred to Anderson, Sweeney, and Williams (2000), Clauss (1996), and Eppen et al. (1998) for more detailed discussion on modeling activities in management science.

## MODELING TECHNIQUES

Management science is often associated with a body of modeling techniques that find frequent application. This book addresses four of the most important categories of modeling techniques: *mathematical programming, decision analysis, simulation,* and *project analysis.* These four categories were chosen because they are key to the resolution of a wide range of decision problems. We have decided to go into more depth in each of these topics at some sacrifice to the breadth of modeling categories covered. This book is organized into parts, each containing several chapters devoted to each topic. What makes this book different from many others is that we attempt to integrate the discussion of the theory with its application through modeling software. The purpose of this book is to empower students to model a broad range of practical problems.

*Mathematical Programming*   Mathematical programming considers the problem of allocating limited resources among competing activities. These resources could be people, capital, equipment, or materials, whereas the competing activities might be products or services, investments, marketing media, or transportation routes. The objective of mathematical programming is to select the best solution from the set of solutions that satisfy all of the restrictions on the resources. The chapters on mathematical programming cover problems in which the relationships among the factors are either linear or nonlinear, and the factors themselves can take on either continuous or integer values. The reader has the choice of using either the standard algebraic approach or the modeling language approach to study important mathematical programming applications. Commodity flow networks and related problems are not covered. The interested reader is referred to Bazarra, Jarvis, and Sherali (1990), Hillier and Lieberman (2001), and Winston (1995) for coverage of these topics and further discussion of mathematical programming.

*Decision Analysis*   Decision-making methods such as classical decision analysis and the Analytic Hierarchy Process (AHP) provide structure and guidance for thinking systematically about making complex decisions. Examples include which job offer to accept, where to locate a new service facility, and whether a local government should offer a tax amnesty program to increase revenues. Decisions such as these are characterized by uncertainty, conflicting multiple objectives, and differing perspectives of the various affected stakeholders. The chapters in this module focus on the AHP, which uses comparative judgments to analyze decision problems expressed in terms of their goal, decision criteria and alternatives. Readers interested in a more detailed discussion of utility theory or in a discussion of decision trees should consult with Clemen (1996), Samson (1988), and Keeney and Raiffa (1976). Saaty (1996) is a good source for a more in-depth treatment of the AHP.

*Simulation*   Simulation allows the modeling and analysis of complex, real-world systems, when one or more variables or relationships are probabilistic. A simulation model consists of a set of mathematical and logical relationships that describe the operation of the system. Probabilities are used to randomly generate the occurrence of system events, such as arriving customers, and the time needed for system activities, such as a banking transaction. A course of action is evaluated by simulating the operation of the system over an extended period of time. For example, waiting-line or queuing statistics at a bank could be estimated by simulating 1000 days of operation. The chapters in this module focus on process simulations but consider financial simulation as well. Readers interested in obtaining more information about simulation should consult Banks, Carson, and Nelson (1995), Law and Kelton (1991), Pidd (1998), and Thesen and Travis (1991). More details on financial simulation using spreadsheets can be found in Winston (1998). Analytical queuing is not covered in this text, and readers are directed to Gross and Harris (1998), Prabhu (1997), and Kleinrock (1975) for this topic.

*Project Analysis*   A project is a temporary endeavor undertaken to create a unique product or service. Projects are comprised of a set of logically related activities or tasks that lead toward a common goal. Examples include building a warehouse or a ship, developing software or an advertising campaign, and implementing new technologies or work procedures. The chapters in this module focus on determining the project schedule that will allow the project to be completed as quickly as possible, and on analyzing the impact of resource limitations on project completion. Good heuristic (scientific "rule of thumb") procedures are presented to address resource constraints, and to identify the least-cost approach to expedite the project. Other managerial topics such as project organization and control are not addressed here. The interested reader is referred to Meredith and Mantel (2000), Mantel, Meredith, Shafer, and Sutton (2001), Cleland (1999), Kerzner (2000), and Gray and Larson (2000).

Each of the modules addresses the theoretical underpinnings of the models covered. We emphasize understanding key concepts rather than the details of specific algorithms. In each module, one example is covered in detail to provide a solid foundation for building additional models. Also, one or more modeling software packages are applied to various business problems within each module. These packages are: LINGO (LINDO Systems Inc. 2001) for mathematical programming; Extend (Imagine That, Inc. 2001), and Stat::Fit (Geer Mountain Software Corporation 2002) for simulation; Expert Choice (Expert Choice Inc. 2000) for decision analysis; Microsoft Project 2000 (Microsoft Corporation 2000) for project analysis; and Excel as an interface with LINGO and Extend for data input and model output, and for illustrating project analysis methods.

## MODELING SOFTWARE VS. SPREADSHEETS[1]

Electronic spreadsheets are an alternate approach to modeling software. A compelling reason for using spreadsheets is the fact that there are "thirty million users" and that "spreadsheets have overwhelmingly become the analytical vernacular" (Savage 1997, p. 43). Today there are many products and spreadsheet add-ins such as Solver bundled with Excel and What'sBest!, both for optimization; @RISK and Crystal Ball for simulation; and INSIGHT.xla for optimization, decision analysis, and simulation (Savage 1998). These products facilitate the application of management science. In addition, spreadsheet objects, such as one developed for transportation routing, are shipped with roughly a million copies of Excel each year and can be combined with other objects to create additional management science applications (Savage, 1997). All of these are important advantages offered by spreadsheets.

The disadvantages of spreadsheets include their limitations relating to documentability, scalability, and hyperscalability (Savage 1997, 1998). Documentability is the ability to document a spreadsheet model for ongoing maintenance and use by others. Scalability is the ability to change the number of items in a set of the model, for example, the number of products within a production-planning model. Hyperscalability is the ability to add or remove dimensions of the model, such as adding a time dimension to a static production-planning model.

In the past, we have experimented with the use of spreadsheets and have encountered scalability and hyperscalability problems. For example, when we experimented with spreadsheet simulation and the available add-ins, we found that it was difficult for students to address the queuing and process-redesign situations that often occur in practice. One could argue that additional add-ins are needed and perhaps could be developed. However, we want to empower students to model the situations and behaviors that interest them. Visual simulation software packages, such as Extend, do this. Therefore, for model development and pedagogical reasons, we have adopted the use of modeling software for the applications covered in this text (see also Gass, Hirshfeld, and Wasil 2000).

The students' learning curve in using some modeling software packages is steeper than with spreadsheets. Although spreadsheet modeling is initially easy, it quickly becomes difficult to create complex models. In contrast, once the student achieves a certain level of understanding with the modeling software, he or she can easily develop more comprehensive models. In this book we will focus on helping students to learn the essentials of modeling with the software so that they can create and implement their own models.

## BECOMING AN ACTIVE MODELER

Prior to the development of user-friendly modeling software, only specialists generally applied management science techniques such as those mentioned previously. For this reason, the goal of introductory management science courses was to enable students to

---

[1]The remainder of this chapter is largely based on Liberatore and Nydick (1999).

become *intelligent consumers* of management science. Today, while being an intelligent consumer is still important, the goal of decision technology is to empower students to become *active modelers*. This goal is now possible, in part, due to the power, flexibility, and ease of use of modeling software (to be discussed later).

In addition, the focus is now on the application of models and *not* on the mathematical details underlying the models. This does not mean that we can or will ignore the mathematical foundations and important concepts underlying the techniques used. However, our goal is to have enough understanding of the "black box" so we can make intelligent decisions concerning how and when specific models and software packages are appropriate. This results in a paradigm shift: the focus changes from what *could and would* be done with management science to what *can and will* be done with decision technology. The *can and will* comes about primarily by applying decision technology to actual problems faced by organizations. For this reason, project work can be an integral part of the decision-technology course.

## DECISION-TECHNOLOGY PROJECTS

In our experience, many decision-technology applications arise in service-based organizations and address problems in finance and marketing as well as operations. Regardless of origin, a successful implementation occurs if the project genuinely causes a positive change, or demonstrates relevance through positive feedback from management. The journal *Interfaces* is a source of completed management-science and decision-technology applications. Examples of recently completed student projects applying mathematical programming, decision analysis, and simulation follow. Project analysis is not addressed, since this material was recently added to this text.

### Mathematical Programming

Typical mathematical programming projects have focused on job, production, and employee scheduling; transportation and traveling salesperson problems; site location; capital budgeting; menu planning; Markowitz financial portfolio analysis; and financial planning.

1. Many groups applied mathematical programming to job- and staff-scheduling problems. For example, one group developed a model to schedule the generation of circulation lists for bulk mailings. The firm intends to use the model in the upcoming quarter and compare the results with the current manual process. A second group implemented a production-planning and scheduling model. It is being used to suggest line-balancing options and to analyze alternatives for adding a new assembly line. A third project team implemented a model that recommended changing staff assignments across all shifts. In addition, based on the model's recommendations, the firm also added a Saturday shift on a trial basis. A fourth implemented staff-scheduling model supported a request to increase staffing levels at a financial services firm. A fifth implemented staffing model is used to plan weekly staff assignments of health-care professionals for a national leader in physical-rehabilitation services.

2. A major bank holding company whose primary business is credit card lending must determine the proper mix of funding to support operating needs. One student group developed a linear programming model to address this problem and found that their results were within 2% of a forecast generated by an in-house software system. The company's asset/liability group agreed to use the model as a baseline for comparative purposes.

3. Several groups have successfully applied the Markowitz financial portfolio model. One group obtained results similar to those obtained by their bank's proprietary portfolio software. Another group developed a two-phase model in which they used a variety of financial factors to screen potential investments and a Markowitz model to decide on the level of funding for those investments passing the initial screen. Management is considering applying the model. Another project team formed an investment club based on the application of the Markowitz model. They described their approach to the account administrator of another club, who reacted enthusiastically and expressed regret that the students had not joined his club!

4. One group expanded upon the diet-planning model that we developed in class and applied it to an organization of 15 adult communities in three states that serves over 4.4 million meals per year. Additional constraints included limitations on consecutive selection of entrees and meeting a minimum satisfaction level. Management was extremely satisfied with the model's results, but wanted to address how to handle leftovers and how to improve computerization before proceeding with implementation.

5. An unusual and interesting example was an effort to develop a model to minimize the number of transport multiplexes cable television companies will need to meet forecasted demand for a service called near video on demand (NVOD). With NVOD, cable companies compete directly with video rental stores by broadcasting each movie in the offering list several times on related virtual channels. As a result of their modeling efforts, the students made several recommendations on ways to improve the LINGO modeling language, which we sent to LINDO management. LINDO systems' vice president for research and development responded,

> *Their [the student's] suggestions for enhancements to our LINGO package were well thought out and insightful. It is an honor to us to realize that users have taken considerable time and effort to carefully evaluate one of our packages. We'll do our best to see if we can address your students' concern in upcoming releases.*

## Decision Analysis

Typical AHP-based projects have concerned: prioritizing alternatives and resource planning, including product, project, and job selection; employee evaluation systems; facility location; vendor selection; and transport mode or carrier selection.

1. One group used Expert Choice to evaluate and select money-market funds for investing a Fortune 100 company's surplus cash. The evaluation criteria include yield (gross yield and fee), safety (funds ratings, diversification of cash portfolio, and funds age), liquidity (fund asset value and deadline for purchases and redemptions), and the relationship of the fund provider to the company (participation in a revolving credit facility, other business with the company, and the funds sales effort). The group presented the top-rated four funds to the treasurer, who approved the selection and now uses the model to invest the firm's surplus cash, which average $150 million.

2. Several groups have successfully applied AHP to a variety of human-resource-management problems, including redesigning employee-appraisal systems, allocating salary increases, and employee hiring. During the past year, one group tackled the annual evaluation of hourly warehouse employees in a family-owned-and-operated wholesale distribution business. One of the students was a principal

in this business and led the development and testing effort using the AHP ratings approach. After a presentation to the other three principals of the business, the four principals unanimously decided to implement the AHP-based system. A second group developed an Expert Choice model for hiring new employees. The model received positive feedback but could not be immediately implemented because of a large merger. However, the director of professional practices plans to present the model to the merged company.

3. In a number of projects, students have addressed problems in the medical and pharmaceutical fields. For example, several groups have evaluated how to allocate research and development (R&D) resources to competing projects. (Some of these projects are based on the ideas presented in Liberatore (1987).) One of these projects is under consideration by a large pharmaceutical company. Another group project led to further work for one of the group members who successfully implemented an R&D resource allocation method after completing an independent study. This effort also resulted in two publications (Ross and Nydick 1992; Ross and Nydick 1994). In a third project, a group used AHP to evaluate applications for a biomedical research award at a major university. The project was modeled after a project of ours (Liberatore, Nydick, and Sanchez 1992) and was implemented immediately. Another project focused on the selection of surgical residents at a major teaching hospital. This course-related project led to a follow-up independent study project. The resulting selection procedure was implemented and published (Weingarten, Erlich, Nydick, and Liberatore 1997).

4. Another group applied the AHP to evaluate proposals for new projects to support the global food-service business segment of a large international food products firm. The company has tested the model and compared its results with those obtained by the current evaluation process. Based on the favorable results obtained, the company formed an evaluation team to conduct additional testing. In addition, the group recommended adding Expert Choice to the firm's software product suite. It is preparing a report to obtain senior management approval of the model approach and the software purchase.

5. One group used the AHP to evaluate and select investment banks that underwrite securities being structured for the bank's small business clients. The treasury department of this firm decided to run the Expert Choice model in parallel with its current selection process to test the validity of the results. If the findings are favorable, the firm plans to implement the model. In addition, managers asked the group to provide guidance on revising their model for parallel testing by a different business area within the company. In a similar project, another group used the AHP to evaluate a set of growth funds offered by a major mutual-funds investment firm. The firm received the group's results favorably, and the firm is doing additional work to refine the model's criteria and weights. In addition, the company is evaluating the possibility of offering its clients the opportunity to use an AHP-based approach to individually select funds over the World Wide Web.

## Simulation

Typical simulation-based projects have focused on various queuing or waiting line applications. These included call center operations; supermarket, bank, fast food restaurant, and turnpike service systems; and miscellaneous applications such as staffing levels, production capacity planning, and loading-dock performance.

1. One group developed an Extend simulation model to analyze the multistage test procedures for a critical and central component used in launching all digital CATV systems. The four key components simulated are the test procedures for software load, final unit level test, burn-in station, and rework station if the item fails at any previous stage. Given a demand forecast, the group used simulation to determine if there were enough stations at each of the four stages. The group recommended changing from one to two final test stations, from 30 to 35 burn-in slots, and keeping the one software load station and the one rework station. These results were presented to corporate personnel and implemented.

2. Several groups have studied call-center operations, including the operations of a service bureau for customer support; telephone answering for a large medical practice; an auto-attended phone system for a large insurance company; and help desk telephone support. For example, one group used simulation to determine the number of servers needed to staff an on-line technical assistance hot line for a major investment firm. Their model allowed customers to renege and also allowed average interarrival times to vary during the day. The students gathered interarrival data for 22 half-hour periods throughout the day for 19 days, as well as service time and renege data. They analyzed the data using Stat::Fit. Although customers were experiencing long delays in reality, the simulation confirmed that the firm was using the appropriate number of servers, given its targets for average waiting time and reneging. However, the comparison between the actual and simulation results suggested that the available servers might not always be taking calls. Further investigation confirmed that the servers were spending too much time performing non-telephone-support activities. The students recommended ways to correct the problem to managers who said they would consider adjusting the servers' work responsibilities.

3. Another group used simulation to analyze whether a company should open an additional cash-register station as part of the standard design for its new high-volume fast food outlets. Currently this chain, one of the largest in the country, supports only a fixed number of registers in a prototypical store configuration. Coupling the simulation results with an analysis of revenue and operating costs, the group demonstrated that adding a cash register would be profitable. The group presented its recommendations to management.

4. Reengineering a processing system for medical insurance claims was the topic for another group's project. The students used simulation to analyze the performance of the proposed design. Internal consultants independently studied the same problem, arrived at essentially the same results, and drew the same conclusions as the group. In their presentations to management, the students explained that simulation can be used to verify approaches to work-flow problems.

5. Two other groups analyzed the effects of technological change using simulation. The first studied the impact of automatic vehicle information (AVI) systems for use in collecting tolls. AVI systems can process transactions for cars traveling at speeds up to 55 miles per hour whereas manual-attended lane speeds average 2.5 miles per hour. The group considered the performance of different tollbooth plaza configurations, including attended, automatic, AVI systems, and combinations of all three. The students collected interarrival-time and service data from one Pennsylvania Turnpike interchange and obtained operating-cost data from the Transportation Research Board. Based on their analysis, the students recommended a configuration to the Pennsylvania Turnpike Commission.

A second group analyzed a new bank security system, which is designed to stop a group of people from taking control of a bank. Essentially, a customer would enter the first door of a bank, which locks before the second door is opened. A metal detector, similar to those used in airports, is used to scan the customer. If too much metal is detected, the second door remains locked, thus trapping the customer. Otherwise, the second door opens and the customer enters the bank. The security system allows the bank to set the sensitivity of the metal detector. If it is too sensitive, many "innocent" customers would be trapped between the doors. If it is not sensitive enough, the bank could be seized. The student group wanted to investigate the impact of the sensitivity settings on the security system to determine how many customers would be locked between the doors. After multiple model runs, the students presented their results to management, including a recommended sensitivity setting.

## Organizational Feedback

Letters received from company representatives often comment on the value of the course and the completed projects in their respective organizations. A few examples follow.

*I understand the work and personal sacrifices part-time students go through when pursuing a part-time MBA, and it is encouraging to see students' academic pursuits have an immediate impact on their productivity and contribution at work.*

*It became clear very quickly that the coursework and resources offered to MBA students at Villanova, and specifically within this class, is not only thorough but is applicable to today's business environment.*

*It is projects like this one that makes her time and effort away from the office as well as our tuition reimbursement investment worthwhile and beneficial for Kristen, [company name], and myself.*

*I personally appreciate the efforts put forth as a result of this class and feel [company name] has made a beneficial investment.*

*I appreciate this project and effort and am pleased to see that Marty's MBA is paying off sooner rather than later.*

*Even if an approximation, the potential savings outlined in the group's paper of $30,000.00 per year are impressive. I found the results generated from this model to be a very implementable solution.*

*You never cease to amaze me. . . . If the team agrees, we start planning out the next quarter accordingly using the tool. . . . Best case we do 200% of goal and you get a big bonus and another trip to Hawaii. Worst case, we make adjustments as necessary to the plan, nothing lost (at least we actually tried something scientific instead of Tom's dart-board approach). . . . P.S.—Remind me of this proposal next time you need to bail on a sales call because of an MBA class.*

*The group has offered us a solution to a problem that has cost [company name] countless amounts of time and money. . . . In a trial run the auditor scheduling time was reduced from eight hours to two. In addition, each auditor's efficiency was improved noticeably. Travel times were reduced and the number of units audited in one month increased nearly 10%. . . . We hope to present the benefits to our home office in [city name] for company-wide approval. I am confident that upper management will be equally impressed.*

*. . . I have more faith in this method than our traditional spreadsheet models or personal decision making. These results brought up scenarios that we would have never considered*

*before. At the very least this shows that more time needs to be devoted to reviewing conclusions that were made years ago and are taken for granted now as being correct.*

*After reviewing the programming logic for the cup molding process controllers we noted that they were, as you stated, directing raw materials to a primary cup molder in the event of an equal length molding queue. I have instructed the engineers in the plant to reprogram the process controllers to emulate a random material allocation in the event of equal raw material storage in the cup molding staging area. . . . I look forward to seeing you the week of January 18th to review the possibility of simulating the [name omitted] facility.*

*After what I expect to be a successful launch and implementation of this model, I will propose to the Director of the HR that the entire U.S. division of the company utilize the model for 1999 evaluations. In addition, I will propose that the European, Middle-Eastern, African, and Asian regions of [company name] utilize the model with cultural considerations made.*

## SUMMARY

The purpose of decision technology is to improve the quality of decision making in organizations. In this book, we focus on helping students to learn the essentials of decision technology so that they can create and implement their own value-added models. In particular, this chapter provides an introduction to the field of decision technology, which is the application of both decision-support modeling and computer software to problems in business, government, and other types of organizations.

The close relationship between decision technology and management science is discussed. Like management science, decision technology uses mathematical models, which are representations or abstractions of real situations or systems. These models do not seek to incorporate every possible factor or relationship present in the real world, but only those needed to adequately address the salient relationships. We provided an example using a simple breakeven model to illustrate this point.

This chapter also provides a brief overview of the modeling techniques discussed in this book: mathematical programming, decision analysis, simulation, and project analysis. Each of the four modules emphasizes the understanding of key concepts rather than the details of specific algorithms. Each module covers an example in detail to provide a solid foundation for building additional models. Also in each module, one or more modeling software packages are applied to model various business problems.

The advantages and disadvantages of using electronic spreadsheets are discussed, and the reasons given for our decision to use modeling software are presented. In alignment with the purpose and focus of this book, these reasons can be summarized by stating that our goal is to empower students to become active modelers as well as intelligent consumers of decision technology. For this reason, project work can be an integral part of the decision technology course. Short examples of recently completed student projects applying the techniques covered in this book are presented, along with excerpts from letters received from company representatives commenting on the value of completed projects.

## APPENDIX: ANALYTICAL DECISION MAKING VS. INTUITION

Sometimes we cannot rely on our intuition to provide us with the best solution to problems we face. The following example shows how a simple model can help shed light on a problem whose solution is counterintuitive.

Assume that the earth is perfectly round and smooth, and that a string has been placed completely around the equator. Suppose that someone cuts the string, adds 10 feet, and distributes the 10 feet such that the string is equally distant from the earth. Can a mouse crawl under the string?

Many people believe that since we are only adding 10 feet to such a long string (the earth's circumference is over 24,000 miles), the distance that the lengthened string will be above the earth will be negligible. Therefore, using this line of reasoning, it would be impossible for the mouse to crawl under the string. However, the use of a simple model proves otherwise.

We remember that the relationship between circumference (C) and the radius (r) of any sphere is given as:

$$C = 2\pi r \qquad (1)$$

where $\pi$ is the constant equal to 3.14 . . . Now suppose that in equation (1) C is the circumference of the earth expressed in feet, and r is the radius of the earth in feet. This relationship is shown in Figure 1.A.1. Once we add the 10 ft to our string, we

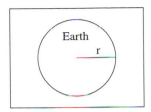

**Figure 1.A.1** Diagram of the Circumference of the Earth and its Radius (r)

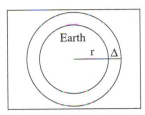

**Figure 1.A.2** Diagram of the Circumference of the Earth and the Circumference of the String with 10 Ft Added

have a new sphere and circumference as shown in Figure 1.A.2. We can use equation (1) to express the relationship between the circumference of our new sphere and its revised radius as:

$$C + 10 = 2\pi(r + \Delta) \qquad (2)$$

where C + 10 is the expanded circumference, and r + $\Delta$ is the revised radius. Here $\Delta$ is the distance of the string above the earth. Since by equation (1), C = $2\pi r$, eliminating C and $2\pi r$ from equation (2) yields:

$$10 = 2\pi\Delta \qquad (3)$$

Solving for $\Delta$ yields $\Delta = 10/2\pi$, or $\Delta = 10/6.28 = 1.59$ ft or 19.10 in. Not only could the mouse crawl under the string, but so could most people!

# REFERENCES

ANDERSON, D. R., D. J. SWEENEY, AND T. A. WILLIAMS, *An Introduction to Management Science: Quantitative Approaches to Decision Making,* 9th ed., Cincinnati, OH, South-Western College Publishing, 2000.

BANKS, J., J. CARSON, AND B. NELSON, *Discrete-Event System Simulation,* 2nd ed., Englewood Cliffs, NJ, Prentice-Hall, 1995.

BAZARRA, M., J. JARVIS, AND H. SHERALI, *Linear Programming and Network Flows,* 2nd ed., New York, Wiley, 1990.

BENNEYAN, J. C. Software Review: "Stat::Fit," *OR/MS Today,* Vol. 25, No. 1, pp. 38–41, 1998.

CLAUSS, F. J., *Applied Management Science and Spreadsheet Modeling,* Belmont, CA, Duxbury Press, Wadsworth Publishing Company, 1996.

CLELAND, D. I., *Project Management: Strategic Design and Implementation,* 3rd ed., New York, McGraw-Hill, 1999.

CLEMEN, R. T., *Making Hard Decisions: An Introduction to Decision Analysis,* 2nd ed., Belmont, CA, Duxbury Press, 1996.

EPPEN, G. D., F. J. GOULD, C. P. SCHMIDT, J. H. MOORE, AND L. R. WEATHERFORD, *Introductory Management Science: Decision Modeling with Spreadsheets.* 5th ed., Upper Saddle River, NJ. Prentice-Hall, 1998.

Expert Choice Inc. Expert Choice 2000, Pittsburgh, PA, 2000.

GASS, S. I., D. S. HIRSHFELD, AND E. A. WASIL, "Model World: The Spreadsheeting of OR/MS," *Interfaces,* Vol. 30, No. 5, pp. 72–81, 2000.

GRAY, C. F., AND E. W. LARSON, *Project Management: The Managerial Process,* New York, Irwin McGraw-Hill, 2000.

Geer Mountain Software Corporation, Stat::Fit, South Kent, CT, 2002.

HILLIER, F. S. AND G. J. LIEBERMAN, *Introduction to Operations Research,* 7th ed., New York, McGraw-Hill, 2001.

Imagine That, Inc. Extend, San Jose, CA, 2001.

KEENEY, R. AND H. RAIFFA, *Decisions with Multiple Objectives,* New York, Wiley, 1976.

KERZNER, H., *Project Management: A Systems Approach to Planning, Scheduling, and Controlling,* 7th ed., New York, Wiley, 2000.

KLEINROCK, L., *Queueing Systems, Vol. I: Theory,* New York, Wiley, 1975.

LAW, A. M. AND W. D. KELTON, *Simulation Modeling and Analysis,* 2nd ed., New York, McGraw-Hill, 1991.

LIBERATORE, M. J., "An Extension of the Analytic Hierarchy Process for Industrial R&D Project Selection and Resource Allocation," *IEEE Transactions on Engineering Management,* Vol. 34, No. 1, pp. 12–18, 1987.

LIBERATORE, M. J., A. HATCHUEL, B. WEIL, AND A. STYLIANOU, "An Organizational Change Perspective on the Value of Modeling," *European Journal of Operational Research,* Vol. 125, pp. 184–194, 2000.

LIBERATORE, M. J. AND R.L. NYDICK, "Breaking the Mold: A New Approach to Teaching the First MBA Course in Management Science," *Interfaces,* Vol. 29, No. 4, pp. 99–116, 1999.

LIBERATORE, M. J., R. L. NYDICK, AND P. SANCHEZ, "The Evaluation of Research Papers (or How To Get An Academic Committee to Agree on Something)," *Interfaces,* Vol. 22, No. 2, pp. 92–100, 1992.

LINDO Systems Inc., LINGO, Chicago, IL, 2001.

MANTEL, S. J., JR., J. R. MEREDITH, S. M. SHAFER, AND M. M. SUTTON, *Project Management in Practice,* New York, Wiley 2001.

Microsoft Corporation, Microsoft Project 2000, Redmond WA, 2000.

MEREDITH, J. R. AND S. J. MANTEL, JR., *Project Management: A Managerial Approach,* 4th ed., New York, Wiley 2000.

PIDD, M., *Computer Simulation in Management Science,* 4th ed., New York, Wiley, 1998.

PRABHU, N. U., *Foundations of Queueing Theory,* Boston, Kluwer Academic Publishers, 1997.

ROSS, M. E. AND R. L. NYDICK, "The Selection of Licensing Candidates in the Pharmaceutical Industry: An Application of the Analytic Hierarchy Process," *The Journal of Health Care Marketing,* Vol. 12, No. 2, pp. 60–65, 1992.

ROSS, M. E. AND R. L. NYDICK, "Structuring the Selection Process of Licensing Candidates in the Pharmaceutical Industry Using the Analytic Hierarchy Process," *Journal of Pharmaceutical Marketing and Management,* Vol. 8, No. 1, pp. 21–36, 1994.

SAATY, T. L., *The Analytic Hierarchy Process: Planning, Priority Setting, Resource Allocation,* Pittsburgh, PA, RWS Publications, 1996.

SAVAGE, S. "Weighing the PROS and CONS of Decision Technology in Spreadsheets," *OR/MS Today,* Vol. 24, No. 1, pp. 42–48, 1997.

SAVAGE, S., *INSIGHT.xla: Business Analysis Software for Microsoft Excel,* Pacific Grove, CA, Duxbury Press, Brooks/Cole Publishing Company, 1998.

SAMSON, D., *Managerial Decision Analysis,* Homewood, IL, Irwin, 1988.

THESEN, A. AND L. TRAVIS, *Simulation for Decision Making,* Belmont, CA, Wadsworth, 1992.

WEINGARTEN, M. S., F. ERLICH, R. L. NYDICK, AND M. J. LIBERATORE, "The Selection of Categorical Surgical Residents Using the Analytic Hierarchy Process," *Academic Medicine,* Vol. 72, No. 5, pp. 400–402, 1997.

WINSTON, W. L., *Introduction to Mathematical Programming: Applications and Algorithms,* Belmont, CA, Duxbury, 1995.

WINSTON, W. L., *Financial Models Using Simulation and Optimization,* Newfield, NY, Palisade Corporation, 1998.

# Chapter 2

# Introduction to Mathematical Programming

## INTRODUCTION

Mathematical programming considers the problem of allocating limited resources among competing activities. These resources could be people, capital, equipment, or materials, whereas the competing activities might be products or services, investments, marketing media, or transportation routes. The objective of mathematical programming is to select the best, or *optimal solution,* from the set of solutions that satisfy all of the restrictions on the resources called *feasible solutions.*

### Examples

There are many applications of mathematical programming in business. Some published examples of mathematical programming applications from *Interfaces* include Camm et al. (1997), Ferrell and Hizlan (1997), Grandzol and Traaen (1995), Koksalan and Sural (1999), Labe, Nagiam, and Spence (1999), Schuster and Allen (1998), and Weigel and Cao (1999). Additional mathematical programming applications drawn from *Interfaces* along with supporting discussion can be found in Assad, Wasil, and Lilien (1992). Mathematical programming can be applied to many activities in an organization as illustrated in the following examples.

- An *operations manager* wishes to determine the most profitable mix of products or services that meets restrictions on labor, materials, and equipment while meeting forecasted demand.
- A *call-center manager* needs to decide how many technicians must be scheduled during each shift so that the forecasted call volume during the day can be met.
- A *financial manager* wishes to find the portfolio that will minimize overall risk while achieving a certain expected return.
- A *marketing manager* must decide how to allocate the advertising budget to different media depending on cost, effectiveness, and mix constraints.
- A *transportation manager* wishes to determine the shortest routes for its delivery vehicles while serving all of its customers.

More in-depth discussion of mathematical programming applications will be given in subsequent chapters. Here we focus on the solution concepts of mathematical programming and their implementation in computer software.

## Components of a Mathematical Program

There are three major components of a mathematical program: decision variables, objective function, and constraints. *Decision variables* are those factors that are controlled by the decision maker. Examples include how many units of each product to produce or ship, the number of people to schedule per shift, and the amount of dollars to allocate to specific investments or advertising media. The *objective function* is a performance measure such as profit, cost, time, or service level that must be optimized (that is, maximized or minimized). Examples include maximizing profit over the product mix and minimizing total delivery time. *Constraints* are restrictions that limit the availability and manner with which resources can be used to achieve the objective. Limitations on available labor, capital, materials, and equipment are constraints. For example, the time available for processing loans may be limited by the number of staff hours available for this activity. However, the number of loans that can be processed is constrained not only by the availability of staff, but also by their skill level and the extent to which the process is automated.

## Assumptions

There are three major classes of mathematical programming problems: linear, integer, and nonlinear. *Linear programming* (LP) makes four key assumptions: linearity, divisibility, certainty, and non-negativity. *Linearity* implies that the objective function and all of the constraints are linear or straight-line relationships. Proportionality and additivity are consequences of the linearity assumption. Proportionality implies that if the production of a given product is doubled, the amount of resources required and the profits earned will also double. Additivity implies that the amount of resources used or profits generated from a given product is independent of the amount of resources used or profits generated from another product. *Divisibility* means that the optimal values of the decision variables may be fractional depending upon the application. For example, the solution to an LP might be to hire 47.35 professionals and 65.79 technicians. *Certainty* requires that the parameters of the LP model are known or can be accurately estimated. Parameters include such factors as per unit profits and costs, amount of available resources, and the quantity of resource units required for producing a good or service. Finally, *non-negativity* simply means that all decision variables must take on positive or zero values.

If we relax the divisibility assumption, decision variables then must take on integer values. This type of mathematical programming is called *integer programming* (IP). If we relax the linearity assumption, the relationships in the objective function and/or constraints may be non-linear. Non-linearity allows for relationships such as substitutability across products and economies of scale. At this point, it is no surprise that this type of mathematical programming is called *non-linear programming* (NLP). Both integer and non-linear programming will be covered in this text. However, we do not relax the certainty assumption, but address it by showing the extent to which the solution of the mathematical programming problem changes as the values of specific parameters change. This process will be addressed in detail in the next chapter and is called *sensitivity analysis*.

## Modeling Process

The process of applying mathematical programming requires the activities of formulation, solution, and interpretation. *Formulation* requires defining the decision variables, objective function, and constraints. In practice, this activity is the most important and difficult part of the process. Later in this chapter and in succeeding chapters we will discuss a variety of model formulations.

The second activity, *solution,* requires determining the optimal values of the decision variables and the objective function. In virtually all practical situations, mathematical programming models are solved using computer software. For example, important solution approaches such as the simplex method developed by Dantzig and the interior point method developed by Karmarkar are incorporated into software. (The interested reader can see Winston (1995) or Hillier and Lieberman (2001) for further discussion about the contributions of these individuals.) To gain insight into the basic ideas behind the solution of mathematical programming problems, we begin our discussion by using a graphical solution approach for LP. We will then extend this approach to the solution of IP and NLP problems. Along the way, we will show how software can be used to solve these problems and also to help us to complete the third activity, the *interpretation* of the results.

## LINEAR PROGRAMMING

### Graphical Solution Using the Corner Point Method

We consider the following simple LP product mix problem. Assume that a firm manufactures alphas and omegas using labor, machine time, and finishing time. Profit for each alpha is \$2.1 and each omega generates a \$3.5 profit. Each alpha requires 10 labor hours, 2 hours of machine time, and 3 hours of finishing time. Each omega requires 14 hours of labor, 20 hours of machine time, and no finishing time. Currently, we have 70 hours of labor, 70 hours of machine time, and 12 hours of finishing time available each day. We would like to determine how many alphas and omegas we should produce to maximize daily profit. The LP formulation of this problem is given as:

```
MODEL:
MAX=2.1*X1+3.5*X2;
10*X1+14*X2<=70;
2*X1+20*X2<=70;
3*X1<=12;
END
```

The term "profit" is being used here in a generic sense: in many situations our objective is to maximize a measure of profit called *contribution margin* (or revenue minus variable costs and expenses). Also note that we are using * to denote multiplication throughout this text to be consistent in how it is represented in our modeling software.

The graphical solution approach requires completing the following steps:

1. Graph the constraints and identify the feasible region.
2. Determine the coordinates of the corner points of the feasible region.
3. Compute the objective function value for each corner point and determine the optimal solution.

We consider each step in turn.

#### 1. Graph the constraints and identify the feasible region.

Since all decision variables must be non-negative, the LP graph is restricted to the first quadrant of a standard two-dimensional plot (also called a Cartesian coordinate system). Because each constraint has a "less than or equal to" sign, its graph is a *region* and not a straight line. However, it is easier to first graph the constraint assuming it is a straight line and then identify the region over which the constraint holds.

We consider the first constraint, $10 * X1 + 14 * X2 <= 70$. The line associated with this constraint is $10 * X1 + 14 * X2 = 70$. A simple approach for graphing this line is to set $X1 = 0$, and then solve for $X2$ to obtain a point on the $X2$ axis. If $X1 = 0$, then

14 * X2 = 70, or X2 = 70/14 = 5. To find the point on the X1 axis, simply reverse the process. If X2 = 0, then 10 * X1 = 70, or X1 = 70/10 = 7. Therefore, the (X1, X2) coordinates of our two points are (0, 5) and (7, 0). Connecting these two points forms a straight line as shown in Figure 2.1. Any (X1, X2) combination that lies on this line will result in the left-hand side of the first constraint being exactly equal to 70. Since our constraint is less than OR equal to 70, we must identify the region that satisfies our constraint.

First, select a point below the line, such as X1 = 2, X2 = 2, and substitute these values into our constraint. We find that 10 * 2 + 14 * 2 = 48 < 70, indicating that this point lies in the feasible region. Now by substituting a point above the line, X1 = 5, X2 = 5, we find that 10 * 5 + 14 * 5 = 120, indicating that this point is not in the feasible region. We conclude that any point on or *below* the line will satisfy this constraint.

The same approach can be applied to the second constraint, 2 * X1 + 20 * X2 <= 7 The (X1, X2) coordinates for the two points on the axis are (0, 3.5) and (35, 0). (Note that (35, 0) is not shown on the graph for scaling reasons.) Any point on or below the line connecting these two points satisfies the second constraint. The third constraint, 3 * X1 <= 12, is a bit different since it does not involve X2. The line corresponding to this constraint is 3 * X1 = 12, so X1 = 4. That is, no matter what the value of X2, X1 always equals 4. This results in a vertical line parallel to the X2 axis at the point X1 = 4. The region covered by the corresponding constraint is the area on the line or to its left.

We are now able to identify the feasible region for our problem. The intersection of the three regions associated with each of these constraints as discussed is the feasible region, shown as the shaded region in Figure 2.1. Any point on the boundary or within the shaded region satisfies all of the constraints.

**2. Determine the coordinates of the corner points of the feasible region.**

The fundamental theorem of linear programming is that an optimal solution always lies at a corner point of the feasible region. Corner points are found on the boundary of the feasible region where two or more lines intersect. An inspection of Figure 2.1 shows that there are five corner points in our problem. It is worthwhile to reflect for a moment on the power and importance of this result. Rather than having to search the boundary *and* the interior of the entire feasible region to find the optimal solution, we only need to check the corner points of the region. It is this result that initially made the solutions of LPs possible.

From Figure 2.1 we see that we can read off the coordinates of some corner points, while the others must be determined by solving two simultaneous equations. The algebra

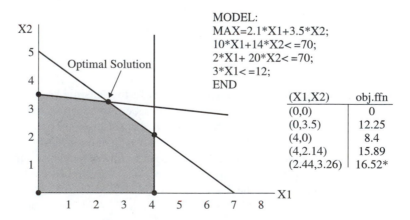

**Figure 2.1** Graph of the Feasible Region and Corner Points for LP Example Problem

**Table 2.1**   Corner Points and Objective Function Values
for LP Example Problem

| (X1, X2) Coordinates | Objective function value<br>2.1 * X1 + 3.5 * X2 |
|---|---|
| (0, 0) | 0 |
| (0, 3.5) | 12.25 |
| (4, 0) | 8.40 |
| (4, 2.14) | 15.89 |
| (2.44, 3.26) | 16.52* |

* Optimal solution.

is left to the interested reader. The five corner points are (0, 0), (0, 3.5), (4, 0), (4, 2.14), and (2.44, 3.26).

### 3.   Compute the objective function value for each corner point and determine the optimal solution.

The last step is to plug the values of the coordinates of each corner point into the objective function and compute the total profit at each point. These calculations are summarized in Table 2.1. As shown in this table, the optimal solution is X1 = 2.44, X2 = 3.26, for the total profit of 16.52.

### Iso-Profit Line Approach

Another approach for identifying the optimal solution is to graph the *iso-profit lines*. To form an iso-profit line, we set the expression for the objective function equal to an *arbitrary* value of profit. For example, we might set 2.1 * X1 + 3.5 * X2 = 14. Therefore, all (X1, X2) combinations lying on this line have a profit of 14. Since we are maximizing profit we wish to move the iso-profit line upward to regions of higher profitability. These additional iso-profit lines must be parallel to the original to preserve the line's slope, which depends on the objective function coefficients and not on the amount of profit. To identify the optimal solution, continue to move the iso-profit upward until it is tangent to the feasible region. If you move the iso-profit line beyond the point of tangency, no

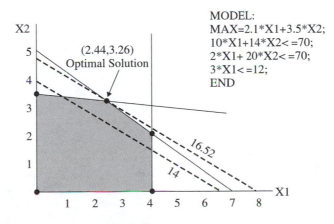

MODEL:
MAX=2.1*X1+3.5*X2;
10*X1+14*X2<=70;
2*X1+ 20*X2<=70;
3*X1<=12;
END

**Figure 2.2** Finding the
Optimal Solution to LP
Example Using the Iso-Profit
Line Approach

points on the iso-profit line will be in the feasible region. As shown in Figure 2.2, the point of tangency is X1 = 2.44, X2 = 3.26. This result represents the same solution that we found by checking the corner points in the previous section.

## Simplex Method Concepts

Many computer software packages use the *simplex method* for solving LP problems. The simplex method systematically searches the corner points until the value of the objective function cannot be improved. In our example problem, the simplex method begins at the origin or (0, 0). As shown in Figure 2.3, the method then moves around the boundary of the feasible region in the direction that provides the largest net gain. Looking at the objective function we see that X2's per unit profit of 3.5 is greater than X1's per unit profit of 2.1. Therefore, the simplex method moves along the X2 axis until it reaches the corner point (0, 3.5) whose objective function value is 12.25.

Next, the simplex method must decide whether to keep moving along the boundary until it hits the next corner point. The portion of the boundary nearest (0, 3.5) is formed by the line 2 * X1 + 20 * X2 = 70. If X1 increases from its current value of 0 to 1 on this boundary line, X2 decreases from 3.5 to (70 − 2(1))/20 or 3.4. As a result, the objective function value changes from 12.25 to 2.1(1) + 3.5(3.4) = 14. That is, we gain 2.1 against a loss of 3.5(.1) = .35 or a net gain of 1.75. Since the increase is positive, the simplex method moves until it reaches the next corner point (2.44, 3.26), which has an objective function value of 16.52.

Should we continue trading off X1 for X2 by moving further along the boundary? The boundary is now formed by the line 10 * X1 + 14 * X2 = 70. If X1 increases from 2.44 to say 3.44, X2 changes from 3.26 to (70 − 10(3.44))/14 = 2.54. In this case we again gain 2.1 for increasing X1 by 1, but lose 3.5(3.26 − 2.54) = 2.52. The net loss is 2.52 − 2.1 = .42, so the simplex method proceeds no further and the optimal solution is reached.

In our example, only three of the five corner points were checked by the simplex method. For larger problems the savings become substantial, and enable problems with thousands of constraints and thousands of decision variables to be solved with relative ease. For additional details on the simplex method, see Dantzig (1998), Anderson, Sweeney, and Williams (2000), Winston (1995), or Hillier and Lieberman (2001).

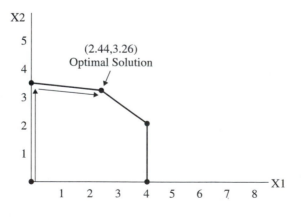

**Figure 2.3** Simplex Solution Path for LP Example

## Karmarkar's Method

A major development in the field of linear programming occurred in the mid-1980s when Narendra Karmarkar of AT&T Bell Laboratories introduced a powerful new solution method for solving large problems. Like the simplex method, Karmarkar's method is an iterative algorithm since it moves from an initial feasible solution to a better feasible solution, and continues until it finds the optimal solution. However, the approach that Karmarkar's method uses to move toward the optimal solution is quite different from the simplex method. Rather than move through the corner points of the feasible region, Karmarkar's method moves through the *interior* of the feasible region. For this reason, Karmarkar's method and related algorithms are called *interior-point algorithms.*

To apply Karmarkar's method, the LP first must be placed in a special form where the objective function is minimized, the right-hand side of the adjusted constraints are all zero, and the sum of the decision variables equals one. Rather than search the corner points of the feasible region, Karmarkar's method uses a transformation from projective geometry that places the current point into the "center" of the feasible region. The algorithm begins in the transformed space by moving in a direction that tends to improve the objective function value while maintaining feasibility. This procedure is repeated until the objective function value is sufficiently close to zero. For further details and an example, see Winston (1995). Further information can also be found in Hillier and Lieberman (2001).

Interior-point methods are now imbedded in some commercial software programs. These methods seem to speed up the computation for certain classes of large linear programming problems. However, the simplex method is still the basis of many commercial LP algorithms. The solution of our LP example using the simplex method as implemented by LINGO will be discussed next.

## LINGO Solution

### Overview

LINGO is a versatile and powerful mathematical modeling software package that allows the user to express problems by using either the standard algebraic format or a set-based modeling language approach (Schrage 2002). It supports the solution of linear, integer, and non-linear programming problems. Decision variables can be entered on either side of the equation and parentheses can be used to group expressions. LINGO supports the use of arithmetic, logical, and relational operators, including division (/) and exponentiation (^). In addition, a variety of built-in mathematical, financial, and probability functions are available to the user. LINGO is a product of LINDO Systems whose web site can be found at: http://www.lindo.com. Once LINGO is opened, the following commands can be used to access an on-line version of the LINGO manual: Select *Help, Help Topics,* "Contents" tab, then select *LINGO User's Manual.* The user is offered an index of the LINGO manual that can also be printed.

Before solving mathematical programming problems in LINGO, we will explain how to change certain default settings. We recommend making these changes the first time that you use your personal copy of LINGO. Select *LINGO, Options* . . . and the "Interface" tab, and then check <u>Terse Output</u> (eliminates unnecessary details) and <u>Send Reports to Command Window</u> (allows the user to view all reports in the same window). You can also increase the <u>Maximum Line Count Limits</u> to allow more output to appear in the *Command Window,* and increase the <u>Width</u> or <u>Page Size Limits</u> to allow longer lines when entering the model. Under the "General Solver" tab, check <u>Allow unrestricted use of primitive</u>

set member names. This option is needed to allow full use of names in all parts of a LINGO model. You must also select the "Prices & Range" option in the Dual Computations box to enable sensitivity analysis. When finished, click on *Save* so that these changes are saved for future use and do not need to be repeated every time you use LINGO.

### Solution of LP Example

When first opening LINGO, your default *Model Window* is labeled "LINGO Model—LINGO1." We now enter the LP example problem in the format shown next into the *Model Window:*

```
MODEL:
MAX=2.1*X1+3.5*X2;
10*X1+14*X2<=70;
2*X1+20*X2<=70;
3*X1<=12;
END
```

Every mathematical programming problem begins with MODEL: and has END as its last statement. Every statement in the body of the model must end with a semicolon, but multiple statements can be placed on the same line as long as each statement ends with a semicolon. The objective function is recognized as following either MAX= or MIN=.

Any LINGO command that processes the information contained in the *Model Window* places output in the *Command Window*. To generate a complete model output, we recommend using the following sequence of commands. First, place a copy of your model in the *Command Window* by selecting *LINGO, Look. . . , OK*. Before completing each of the next three groups of commands, you must click on the *Model Window* to make it active. To solve the model and place the objective function value in the *Command Window,*

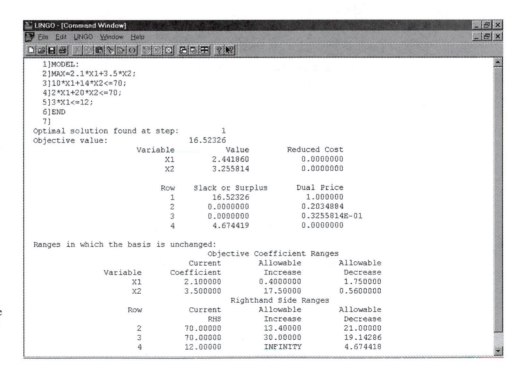

**Figure 2.4** Screen Shot of LINGO's Command Window for LP Example Problem after Executing Suggested Set of Commands

select *LINGO, Solve,* and *Close,* or select the bullseye button on the toolbar. To place the optimal values of the decision variables in the *Command Window,* select *LINGO, Solution, OK,* or select the button to the immediate right of the bullseye. Finally, to place the results of the sensitivity analysis in the *Command Window,* select *LINGO, Range.* The output in the *Command Window* can then be printed or pasted to *Microsoft Word.*

Figure 2.4 is a screen shot of the *Command Window* after executing these commands. Notice that the results of *LINGO, Look. . . , OK.* are the statements found in the *Model Window* preceded by the numbers 1 through 7 followed by right brackets. The numbers 1–7 are simply line numbers and have no other meaning. However, the results of *LINGO, Solution, OK* include <u>rows</u> numbered from 1 to 4. LINGO uses the following convention in numbering rows: the objective function is always row 1, the first constraint is row 2, the second constraint is row 3, and so on. The contents of a LINGO output will be discussed in more detail later.

## INTEGER PROGRAMMING

### Graphical Solution

*Integer programming* (IP) is a variation of linear programming where one or more of the decision variables take on integer values. Integer variables whose values are restricted to 0 or 1 are called *binary variables.* Problems containing both integer variables and variables not restricted to be integer are called *mixed integer programming* (MIP) problems.

We now reconsider our original LP example but add the restriction that both X1 and X2 must be integer valued. This restriction converts our LP into an IP problem. However, there is an important relationship between the solutions of these two problems. The solution to any IP or MIP problem *without* the integer restriction(s) on the decision variables is called the *LP relaxation.* For a maximization problem, the optimal objective function value of the LP relaxation is an *upper bound* on the optimal objective function value of the original IP or MIP problem. The logic for this result is that by adding the restriction that some or all of the decision variables must be integer valued, additional constraints are placed on the original LP problem. Whenever additional constraints are added there are fewer feasible solutions, so we can do no better than before. However, if the solution to the LP relaxation results in integer values for all decision variables, then the optimal solution to the LP relaxation is the optimal solution to the IP problem.

Returning to our problem, the feasible solutions to our IP are shown by the "dots" in Figure 2.5. (There is no dot at (3, 3) because this point violates the first constraint.) As

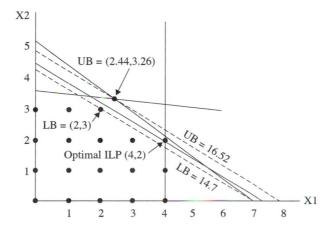

**Figure 2.5** Searching the Gap for the Optimal Solution for IP Example Problem

you recall, the solution of the LP relaxation for our IP is $X1 = 2.44$, $X2 = 3.26$, with an objective function value of 16.52. This value is an upper bound on the optimal objective function value of our IP. However, the LP relaxation solution is not feasible, since it is non-integer.

In the special case where all of the constraints are "less than or equal to" we can find a lower bound that is a feasible integer solution. Simply take the optimal solution values to the LP relaxation and round each of them *down* to their nearest integer. In our example (2.44, 3.26) is rounded down to (2, 3) for an objective function value of 14.7. The interested reader can substitute (2, 3) into the three constraints to verify that they are not violated.

Now we can state an important result. The optimal solution to our IP lies somewhere between the feasible lower bound and the infeasible upper bound. One solution approach is to search the "gap" between the iso-profit lines that pass through the upper and lower bounds. As shown in Figure 2.5, the gap in our problem consists of only one feasible solution, $X1 = 4$, $X2 = 2$, with an objective function value of 15.4. Since this objective function value is greater than that of the feasible lower bound, it is the optimal IP solution. Since we are maximizing profit, if more than one feasible integer solution lies in the gap, the optimal solution is the one that has the largest objective function value.

## Branch and Bound Solution Procedure

Most computer solution approaches for integer programming problems are based on the *branch and bound* algorithm. Branch and bound divides the set of all feasible solutions into smaller subsets or "branches." The algorithm uses various rules to identify the subsets that are most likely to contain the optimal solution and to "prune" those that need not be explored further because they could not possibly contain the optimal solution. After each subset is explored by solving an LP, the upper and lower bounds are adjusted. Eventually the upper and lower bounds converge at the optimal solution. We now apply the branch and bound procedure to our IP example.

We begin by solving the LP relaxation, now called subproblem 1, as before. This subproblem is entered into our branch and bound *tree* given as Figure 2.6. The results of subproblem 1 represent an upper bound on the optimal integer solution. That is, 16.52 is the maximum value that our optimal integer solution can attain. The round down solution of

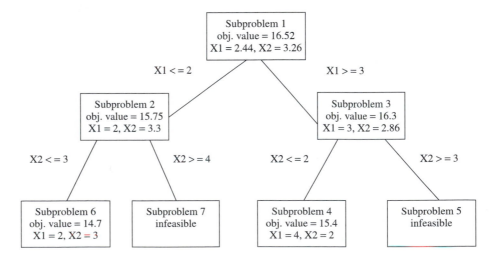

**Figure 2.6** Branch and Bound Tree for IP Example

**Table 2.2**  Lower and Upper Bounds for Branch and Bound IP Example

| After Subproblem(s): | Upper Bound | Lower Bound |
| --- | --- | --- |
| 1 | obj. value = 16.52, X1 = 2.44, X2 = 3.26 | obj. value = 14.7, X1 = 2, X2 = 3 |
| 2, 3 | obj. value = 16.3,  X1 = 3,   X2 = 2.86 | obj. value = 14.7, X1 = 2, X2 = 3 |
| 4, 5 | obj. value = 15.75, X1 = 2,   X2 = 3.3 | obj. value = 15.4, X1 = 4, X2 = 2 |
| 6, 7 | obj. value = 15.4,  X1 = 4,   X2 = 2 | obj. value = 15.4, X1 = 4, X2 = 2 |

X1 = 2, X2 = 3, has an objective value of 14.7 and is a feasible lower bound. This information on upper and lower bounds is entered into our branch and bound summary given as Table 2.2.

Next, we must select a decision variable for *branching*. We consider only those variables that have fractional values in the optimal solution of subproblem 1. Since both X1 and X2 have fractional values, we need a rule to select our branching variable. Many rules are possible, such as selecting the decision variable that is either furthest away from or closest to being integer-valued. Another rule is to select the variable with the smallest subscript. Applying the latter rule indicates that X1 is our branching variable. Since X1 = 2.44 in the LP relaxation and since X1 must be integer-valued in the optimal solution, we create two new subproblems (labeled subproblems 2 and 3) that branch on X1. The first of these subproblems adds the constraint X1 <= 2 to our original problem formulation, while the second adds the constraint X1 >= 3. Note that these two subproblems eliminate the possibility that 2 < X1 < 3, since X1 must be integer-valued. The solutions to these two subproblems are shown in Figure 2.6. An inspection of the results yields a revised upper bound of 16.3 since this is the maximum of the objective values of both LPs. Remember that both LPs together cover all possible cases that remain to be analyzed. Since neither LP yields an optimal integer solution, our lower bound remains at 14.7 as shown in Table 2.2.

Subproblems 2 and 3 can be analyzed further since neither yielded a feasible integer solution nor an infeasible solution. We apply the decision rule that the subproblem that has not been fully analyzed and that possesses the largest objective value should be considered next. Thus, subproblem 3 is selected. Since X2 is the only variable that has a fractional value in the optimal solution of this problem, it is selected as our branching variable. Again, we create two new subproblems (labeled subproblems 4 and 5 in Figure 2.6). We solve these subproblems and continue branching and bounding. After solving subproblems 6 and 7, Table 2.2 shows that the upper and lower bounds are equal, and therefore, we have found the optimal solution.

Some final comments about branch and bound: for MIP problems, only the variables that are integer-valued would be considered for branching. If a variable were binary, the branch values for that variable would be 0 and 1.

## LINGO Solution

The solution of IPs and MIPs in LINGO requires minor modification to an LP model. For example, to make variable Y integer valued in LINGO, add the statement @GIN(Y); before END. Here GIN stands for *General INteger.* This statement allows a variable to take on the values 0, 1, 2, 3, . . . To make Z a binary variable, add @BIN(Z); before END. Here BIN stands for *Binary INteger.* This statement allows a variable to take on only the values of 0 or 1.

Our IP is entered in LINGO as follows:

```
MODEL:
MAX=2.1*X1+3.5*X2;
10*X1+14*X2<=70;
2*X1+20*X2<=70;
3*X1<=12;
@GIN(X1);
@GIN(X2);
END
```

To generate a complete model output, we recommend using the sequence of commands given for LPs, with the exception of the *Range* command, which is not available for integer problems (we will discuss this later). Figure 2.7 is a screen shot of the *Command Window* after executing these commands.

## NON-LINEAR PROGRAMMING

### Graphical Solution

A non-linear programming (NLP) problem is a mathematical program in which at least one of the constraints or the objective function is a non-linear expression. Although linear approximations are often satisfactory, for the most part, we live in a non-linear world. Consider a few examples.

- Doubling the dose of a medicine does not necessarily double its effectiveness.
- Assigning three times as many employees to dig a hole does not necessarily guarantee that the hole will be dug three times as fast.
- Halving the amount of retail display space for a product will not necessarily cut sales in half.

The portfolio problem in finance is an important business application of NLP and will be discussed in detail in Chapters 6 and 8.

```
Command Window                                                      _ □ ✕
    1]MODEL:
 2]MAX=2.1*X1+3.5*X2;
 3]10*X1+14*X2<=70;
 4]2*X1+20*X2<=70;
 5]3*X1<=12;
 6]@GIN(X1);
 7]@GIN(X2);
 8]END
 9]

Optimal solution found at step:          4
Objective value:            15.40000
Branch count:                    1


                Variable          Value        Reduced Cost
                      X1       4.000000           -2.100000
                      X2       2.000000           -3.500000

                     Row    Slack or Surplus       Dual Price
                       1       15.40000             1.000000
                       2       2.000000            0.0000000
                       3       22.00000            0.0000000
                       4      0.0000000            0.0000000
```

**Figure 2.7** Screen Shot of LINGO's Command Window for IP Example Problem after Executing Suggested Set of Commands

In this section we will solve an NLP problem that has a non-linear objective function, two decision variables, and three linear constraints. Because the constraints are linear, we can graph the feasible region just as we did with LP. However, because the objective function is non-linear we are not guaranteed that an optimal solution will always lie at one of the corner points of the feasible region as it does with LP. Unlike LP problems, the optimal solution to an NLP problem can occur at a corner point of the feasible region, a non-corner point along the boundary of the feasible region, or a point in the interior of the feasible region. This implies that searching only corner points may not determine the optimal solution. As a result, the process of searching for the optimal solution is more difficult for an NLP problem than for an LP problem.

Another characteristic of NLP problems that complicates the search for the optimal solution is the presence of local optimal solutions. A *local optimal solution* is the best solution only with respect to feasible solutions close to that point. A *global optimal solution* is the best solution with respect to the complete problem. That is, the global optimal solution is the best of the local optimal solutions.

One might think that a non-optimal corner point in an LP is a local optimum. Suppose that point A is a non-optimal corner point and point B is the optimal corner point. As shown in our discussion of the simplex method, if you move along the boundary of the feasible region even a little distance away from A in the direction of B, the objective function will improve. This means that there does not exist even a small area near A where it is the best point, thereby showing that A cannot be a local optimum.

The difference between local and global optima can be seen by thinking about a mountain climber. After scaling a peak (local optima), the mountain climber might think that the summit (global optima) has been reached. However, there may be other peaks that are higher than the one scaled. This situation is illustrated in Figure 2.8.

The presence of multiple local optimal solutions and a global optimal solution not occurring at a corner point will now be illustrated by the following NLP problem.

```
MODEL:
MAX=100.0004*X2-341.66835*X1+128.1257*X1^2-13.020912*X1^3;
  5*X1+3*X2>=30;
        X2<=8.5;
    -X1+ X2>=3;
END
```

Note that ^ is used for *exponentiation,* that is, raising variables to powers, so X1 ^ 2 is the same as X1 * X1, and X1 ^ 3 is the same as X1 * X1 * X1.

As shown in Figure 2.9, we can solve this NLP problem graphically using essentially the same approach that we used for LP. Since the constraints are linear we can graph the

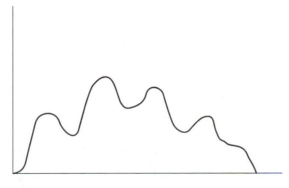

**Figure 2.8** Global vs. Local Optima

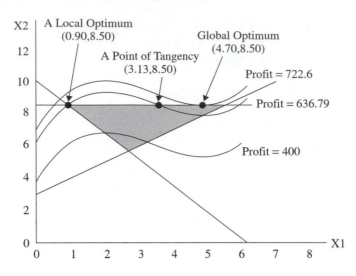

**Figure 2.9** Finding the Local and Global Optimal Solutions to NLP Example Using the Iso-Profit Line Approach

feasible region. Next we use the iso-profit approach to identify the local optimal solutions. Because our objective function is non-linear, the iso-profit functions are curves instead of straight lines. Figure 2.9 shows iso-profit curves with values of 400, 636.79, and 722.6. We see that the local optimal solution of (4.70, 8.50) with an objective function value of 722.6 is also the global optimal solution. This point is not a corner point and is located on the boundary of the feasible region. In addition, there is another local optimal solution at (0.90, 8.50) with an objective function value of 636.79. This solution is a corner point since it is located at the intersection of the lines $X2 = 8.5$ and $5 * X1 + 3 * X2 = 30$.

Figure 2.9 also shows that the iso-profit curve having a value of 636.79 is tangent to the feasible region at a *second point:* $X1 = 3.13$, $X2 = 8.50$. An examination of Figure 2.9 reveals that (0.90, 8.50) is the local optimal solution for all feasible ($X1$, $X2$) until we reach (3.13, 8.50). Feasible points lying to the right of (3.13, 8.50) and above the 636.79 iso-profit curve have higher levels of profit, demonstrating that (0.90, 8.50) is a local, but not a global, optimal solution.

## Gradient Search

Many of the computational methods used to solve NLP problems in practice make use of the vector of partial derivatives of the objective function, known as the *gradient*. Gradient search methods can be compared to a mountain climber successively moving from point A to B, where B appears to be the highest point in the neighborhood of A (a local optimum). That is, gradient methods move in the direction of steepest ascent. The search is continued until the peak is reached, that is, no more improvement in the objective function can be made.

The problem with gradient search methods becomes apparent if we refer to the previous discussion on local and global optima for our example problem. The highest point in the neighborhood of A may be a local optimal solution, but may not be the global optimum. The mountain climber may have reached a peak, but there might be another peak that is higher (Figure 2.8).

The implication is that one must search from different initial solutions to see if several of these converge to the same best solution. Unfortunately, for the general NLP prob-

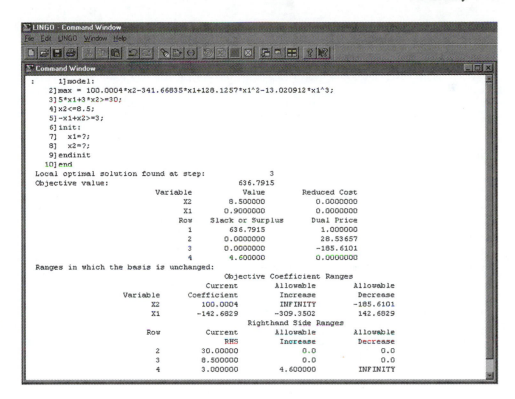

**Figure 2.10** Screen Shot of LINGO's Command Window for NLP Example Problem Using the INIT Command

lem, there are no guarantees that you will find the global optimum. In some cases you may find a series of local optimum. More details about gradient search and other non-linear programming solution methods can be found in Winston (1995) and Pinter (2001).

## LINGO Solution

LINGO uses a gradient search technique to find local optimal solutions. When LINGO is applied to solve our example problem, it will converge to one of the two local optima depending upon where the search is started. The default LINGO initial starting values are zero for each decision variable. Unfortunately, these settings lead to the local optimal solution of (0.90, 8.50) with an objective function value of 636.79. Of course, the only reason we know that this solution is the local, and not the global, optimum is that we already solved this problem graphically!

LINGO allows the user to easily change the starting values for the search by using the INIT command. We recommend using the following format:

```
INIT:
  X1=?;
  X2=?;
ENDINIT
```

When the model is solved, LINGO will prompt the user to enter the specific values for X1 and X2. Figure 2.10 is a screen shot of the *Command Window* after solving our example NLP using INIT. The results shown are based on using X1 = 5 and X2 = 5 as the starting values for X1 and X2. These values also converge to the local optimum of (0.90, 8.50). Unfortunately, the current version of LINGO's non-linear solver is designed to move to quickly to a local optimum. As a result, after trying a variety of initial starting solutions, we were unable to locate the global optimum. This result points to the difficulty of obtaining global optimum solutions in non-linear programming.

## SUMMARY

Mathematical programming considers the problem of allocating limited resources among competing activities. The objective of mathematical programming is to select the optimal solution from the set of feasible solutions. The process of applying mathematical programming requires the activities of problem formulation, solution, and interpretation. This chapter focuses on the solution process. In subsequent chapters we will consider formulation and interpretation issues in more detail.

Specifically, we consider the solution of linear, integer, and non-linear programming problems in this chapter. We begin by using the graphical method to illustrate the key concepts of the solution process for linear programming problems. We then discuss the simplex and Karmarkar's methods, both of which are used in the computer solution of linear programming problems. Next, we employ the graphical method to illustrate how the solution processes of linear and integer programming problems differ. Then we illustrate the application of the branch and bound method for the solution of integer programming problems. In our discussion of non-linear programming problems, we demonstrate that the solution process is characterized by the presence of local and global optima. Again, we use the graphical method to illustrate the solution process, and then discuss gradient search, which is often the basis of computer solution. Throughout this chapter, we demonstrate how the computer software program called LINGO can be applied to solve linear, integer, and non-linear programming problems.

## HOMEWORK PROBLEMS

**2.1** Consider the following linear programming problem (**MP1**):

| maximize | $2 * x1 + 3 * x2$ |
| --- | --- |
| such that: | $1 * x1 + 2 * x2 <= 6$ |
| | $5 * x1 + 3 * x2 <= 15$ |

Provide a printout of the model and the optimal solution using LINGO.

**2.2** Consider the following linear programming problem (**MP2**):

| maximize | $3 * X1 + 3 * X2$ |
| --- | --- |
| such that: | $2 * X1 + 4 * X2 <= 12$ |
| | $6 * X1 + 4 * X2 <= 24$ |

Provide a printout of the model and the optimal solution using LINGO.

**2.3** Consider the following integer programming problem (**MP3**):

| maximize | $5 * X1 + 8 * X2$ |
| --- | --- |
| such that: | $6 * X1 + 5 * X2 <= 30$ |
| | $9 * X1 + 4 * X2 <= 36$ |
| | $1 * X1 + 2 * X2 <= 10$ |

Provide a printout of the model and the optimal solution using LINGO.

**2.4** Consider the following mixed-integer programming problem (**MP4**):

maximize
$$15 * x1 + 12 * x2 + 27 * x3 + 8 * x4 + 20 * x5$$
$$- 50 * y1 - 30 * y2 - 125 * y3$$
such that: $10 * X1 + 8 * X2 <= 30 * Y1;$
$11 * X2 + 7.2 * X3 + 11 * X5 <= 272 * Y2;$
$3 * X1 + 3 * X4 + 2 * X5 <= 124 * Y3;$

Provide a printout of the model and the optimal solution using LINGO if X1 and X3 must be integer valued and Y1, Y2, and Y3 must be 0 or 1.

**2.5** Consider the following non-linear programming problem (**MP5**):
maximize
$$597.235 * X1 \wedge 2 - 287.41 * X1 + 3.89 * X2$$
$$- 12.39 * X1 \wedge 3$$
such that: $X1 + X2 <= 100$
$X1 + X2 >= 13$
$X1 \wedge 2 <= 158$
$X2 <= 17$

Provide printouts of the model and solutions found using the following initial values: X1 = 0, X2 = 0; X1 = 200, X2 = 0; X1 = 0, X2 = 200; and X1 = 200, X2 = 200. What is the best solution that you found?

# REFERENCES

ANDERSON, D. R., D. J. SWEENEY, AND T. A. WILLIAMS, *An Introduction to Management Science: Quantitative Approaches to Decision Making,* 9th ed., Cincinatti, OH, South-Western Publishing, 2000.

ASSAD, A. A., E. A. WASIL, AND G. L. LILIEN, (EDS.), *Excellence in Management Science Practice: A Readings Book,* Englewood Cliffs, NJ, Prentice-Hall, 1992.

CAMM, J. D., T. E. CHORMAN, F. A. DILL, J. R. EVANS, D. J. SWEENEY, AND G. W. WEGRYN, "Blending OR/MS, Judgment and GIS: Restructuring P&G's Supply Chain, *Interfaces,* Vol. 27, No. 1, pp. 128–142, 1997.

DANTZIG, G. B., *Linear Programming and Extensions,* Princeton, NJ, Princeton University Press, 1998 (original hardcover: 1963).

FERRELL, W. G. AND H. HIZLAN, "South Carolina Counties Use a Mixed-Integer Programming-Base Decision Support Tool for Planning Municipal Solid Waste Management, *Interfaces,* Vol. 27, No. 4, pp. 23–34, 1997.

GRANDZOL, J. R. AND T. TRAAEN, "Using Mathematical Programming to Help Supervisors Balance Work Loads, *Interfaces,* Vol. 25, No. 4, pp. 92–103, 1995.

HILLIER, F. S. AND G. J. LIEBERMAN, *Introduction to Operations Research,* 7th ed., New York, McGraw-Hill, 2001.

KOKSALAN, M. AND H. SURAL, "Efes Beverage Group Makes Location and Distribution Decisions for Its Malt Plants," *Interfaces,* Vol. 29, No. 2, pp. 89–103, 1999.

LABE, R., R. NAGIAM, AND S. SPENCE, "Management Science at Merrill Lynch Private Client Group," *Interfaces,* Vol. 29, No. 2, pp. 1–14, 1999.

PINTER, J. D., *Computational Global Optimization in Nonlinear Systems: An Interactive Tutorial,* Atlanta, GA, Lionheart Publishers, 2001.

SCHRAGE, L., *Optimization Modeling with LINGO,* Chicago, LINDO Systems Inc., 2002.

SCHUSTER, E. W. AND S. J. ALLEN, "Raw Material Management at Welsh's, Inc., *Interfaces,* Vol. 28, No. 5, pp. 13–24, 1998.

WEIGEL, D. AND B. CAO, "Applying GIS and OR Techniques to Solve Sears Technician-Dispatching and Home-Delivery Problems, *Interfaces,* Vol. 29, No. 1, pp. 112–130, 1999.

WINSTON, W. L., *Introduction to Mathematical Programming: Applications and Algorithms,* Belmont, CA, Duxbury, 1995.

# Chapter 3

# Mathematical Programming Sensitivity Analysis

## INTRODUCTION

Now that we have an understanding of how mathematical programming problems are solved, we turn to interpreting the results of the solution analysis. *Sensitivity analysis* studies how changes to a mathematical programming model impact the optimal solution. For example, we might like to know what would happen to the optimal solution if the profitability of one of our products increased by $0.50 per unit. We also might like to know what would happen to the optimal solution if 10 more units of one resource became available. Sensitivity analysis is extremely important since the real world is dynamic, and the economic impact of these changes must be evaluated.

For linear and non-linear programming models, sensitivity analysis allows us to study changes without requiring us to resolve the revised problem. For integer programming models, we can make the change to the model and resolve it with LINGO.

## LEGO EXAMPLE

We motivate our discussion of sensitivity analysis by considering an exercise using Legos![1] Assume that we work for a company that manufactures tables and chairs using Legos. Profit for each table is $20 and each chair generates a $16 profit. Assembling two large and two small Legos makes a table. Each chair requires one large and two small Legos. Figure 3.1 shows a picture of an assembled table and chair. Currently, we have six large and eight small Legos available each day.

We would like to determine how many tables and chairs we should produce to maximize daily profit. We could argue that we should produce as many tables as possible since this is the most profitable product. Using the limited resources and assembling as many tables as possible, we see that three tables can be produced that will generate a profit of $60 per day. It could also be argued that as many chairs as possible should be produced since chairs require fewer resources than tables. Once again, by using the large and small Legos, we see that four chairs can be produced for a daily profit of $64. While producing all chairs is better than producing all tables, it may be even better if we produce a combination of tables and chairs. We recommend that you get six small and eight large Legos and through trial and error try to find a combination that produces more daily profit than $64. It is not too hard to figure out that producing two tables and two chairs generates the optimal daily profit of $72.

---

[1]This example is motivated by Pendegraft (1997).

**Figure 3.1** Picture of a Table and a Chair

In the previous chapter we showed how LINGO could be used to solve mathematical programming problems (Schrage 2002). Although we can find the optimal solution through trial and error using the Legos, we also want to determine how the same problem can be solved in LINGO. Figure 3.2 shows the model and output for the Lego problem. This output was generated by the following sequence of commands as discussed in Chapter 2: *Lingo, Look . . . , OK; Lingo, Solve,* and *Close; Lingo, Solution, OK;* and *Lingo, Range.* This model is also in a file called LEGO.LG4. We will now discuss each component of Figure 3.2 in turn.

## The Lego Model

The first part of Figure 3.2 displays the formulation for the Lego problem. The decision variables are labeled as X1 and X2 and refer to the daily production of tables and chairs,

```
:   1]MODEL:
    2]MAX=20*X1+16*X2;
    3]2*X1+1*X2<=6;
    4]2*X1+2*X2<=8;
    5]END
    6]
```

```
Optimal solution found at step:            0
Objective value:                    72.00000
```

| Variable | Value | Reduced Cost |
|---|---|---|
| X1 | 2.000000 | 0.0000000 |
| X2 | 2.000000 | 0.0000000 |

| Row | Slack or Surplus | Dual Price |
|---|---|---|
| 1 | 72.00000 | 1.000000 |
| 2 | 0.0000000 | 4.000000 |
| 3 | 0.0000000 | 6.000000 |

Ranges in which the basis is unchanged:

| | | Objective Coefficient Ranges | |
|---|---|---|---|
| Variable | Current Coefficient | Allowable Increase | Allowable Decrease |
| X1 | 20.00000 | 12.00000 | 4.000000 |
| X2 | 16.00000 | 4.000000 | 6.000000 |

| | | Righthand Side Ranges | |
|---|---|---|---|
| Row | Current RHS | Allowable Increase | Allowable Decrease |
| 2 | 6.000000 | 2.000000 | 2.000000 |
| 3 | 8.000000 | 4.000000 | 2.000000 |

**Figure 3.2** LINGO Model and Output for the LEGO.LG4 Problem

respectively. The objective function indicates that we generate \$20 for each table and \$16 for each chair so that our total profit from producing X1 tables and X2 chairs is 20 * X1 + 16 * X2. The first constraint, 2 * X1 + 1 * X2 <= 6, indicates that if X1 tables are produced and X2 chairs are produced, the total number of large Legos required cannot not exceed the number available. The second constraint, 2 * X1 + 2 * X2 <= 8, limits to eight pieces the number of small Legos used. We now turn to the model output portion of Figure 3.2.

## The Solution

We now begin our review of the output by noting the *Objective value*. We see that the optimal daily profit is \$72. The *Value* column also tells us that we should produce 2 tables (X1) and 2 chairs (X2). The remainder of this section will discuss the other parts of the LINGO output.

## Slack and Surplus

The difference between the available resources and the resources used is defined as either *slack* or *surplus*. There is slack associated with each less than or equal to constraint that represents the amount of unused resource. There is surplus associated with each greater-than-or-equal-to constraint that represents the amount of excess resource above the stated level. Since we have two less-than-or-equal-to constraints—one for large Legos and another for small Legos—we have two slack values and zero surplus values. The *Slack or Surplus* section of the output indicates that the slacks for the optimal solution are zero. This implies that if we produce two tables and two chairs we will use all six large Legos and all eight small Legos. Manually, using six large and eight small Legos, build two tables and two chairs, and convince yourself that you do not have any Legos left over. Mathematically, substitute X1 = 2 and X2 = 2 into the left-hand sides of both resource constraints to find out that all large and small Legos are used with this solution.

Using the six large and eight small Legos, determine out how much slack you would have if you produced three tables. After a bit of manipulation on your part, you will find that you have two unused small Legos. This represents the slack for small Legos *if* three tables are produced. You should also be able to see that you will have two unused large Legos if you produce four chairs.

Now suppose we were required to produce at least one table. That is, we add the constraint X1 >= 1 to our model. Associated with this greater-than-or-equal-to constraint is a surplus variable. It turns out that the original optimal solution of producing two tables and two chairs is still optimal when this additional constraint is included in the formulation. Since we are producing two tables and the constraint indicates that we must produce at least one table, there is one surplus table produced.

## Right-Hand Side Changes

Now we are ready to illustrate the key concepts of sensitivity analysis. What happens if we are not limited to six large and eight small Legos each day? In many situations, we have some control over the amount of resources that are available. If we decide to spend additional money, we might be able to order more Legos from our supplier. If we had more Legos, we might be able to produce a different combination of tables and chairs that generates even more profit than our current optimal solution. Therefore, the issues we wish to address are: what is the economic value of purchasing additional large and small

Legos and what would we do with the additional resources if they were available? With these questions in mind, we would now like to study the economic impact of changing the amount of available resources. In effect, we are studying changes to the right-hand side values of constraints.

We begin by studying the value of one additional large Lego. Return to the Legos once again and build two tables and two chairs using the six large and eight small Legos. If one more large Lego is available, you should realize that if you take apart one of the chairs that uses one large and two small Legos and use the additional large Lego, you can now produce an additional table. The economic impact of this exchange can be evaluated: we lost $16 when we took apart one chair, and gained $20 when we made one additional table. This change results in a net gain of $4. Therefore, with seven large and eight small Legos, we would produce three tables and one chair for a profit of $76. Since the original profit generated from producing two tables and two chairs is $72, we now see that one additional large Lego is worth $4 ($76 − $72). Therefore, we should be willing to spend up to $4 for one additional large Lego.

Note that $4 does not represent the actual cost to acquire an additional Lego. Rather, it represents the *economic value* of an additional unit of this resource. The value of using actual Legos for this exercise is that one can see exactly how the additional large Lego can be used to gain additional profit. Alternatively, we can change the right-hand side (RHS) of the large Lego constraint in LINGO from six to seven and rerun the problem. The result will be the same as we found using the Legos.

If it makes sense to order one additional large Lego from our supplier, then we should determine if it makes sense to order two additional large Legos. Once again, we would have to figure out what we would do with the eighth large Lego. Earlier, we found that with seven large and eight small Legos, we could produce three tables and one chair for a profit of $76. If we have eight large and eight small pieces, we would simply take apart the remaining chair and use the eighth large piece to produce another table. With eight large and eight small Legos, the optimal solution is to produce four tables and zero chairs for a daily profit of $80. Therefore, once again, we see that we would be willing to spend up to $4 for the eighth large Lego. Again, this result can be verified by making the appropriate change in LINGO and rerunning the problem.

We now know that the seventh large Lego is worth $4 and the eighth is worth another $4. Now we want to figure out how much the ninth large Lego is worth. With eight large and eight small pieces we produced four tables and zero chairs. You should be able to see that the ninth large Lego is not worth anything since you do not have any more chairs to take apart. That is, if the ninth large Lego becomes available, you would still produce four tables and zero chairs, implying that the ninth large Lego is slack and therefore has no value. We learned two valuable lessons here, namely that the value of an incremental resource can change, and that slack resources have no value. That is, no matter what the market price is for the ninth large Lego, in our situation it has no economic value.

Thus far we studied what happened to the optimal solution if additional resources became available. We can also study what would happen if *fewer* resources are available. For example, suppose our supplier called to say that they can only provide five large Legos tomorrow. Remember that with six large and eight small pieces available we optimally produce two tables and two chairs. If we only have five large and eight small Legos available, we can take apart one of our two tables and produce a chair out of the pieces that remained. This means that with five large and eight small Legos we would produce one table and three chairs for a daily profit of $68, thus losing $4. It is not a coincidence that one additional large Lego is worth $4 and one fewer large piece costs $4. We will formally study this relationship in the next section.

Let us now look at what would happen if the supplier were only able to provide four large Legos daily. Remember with five large and eight small pieces, we can produce one table and three chairs. If we have four large and eight small Legos available, we take apart the remaining table and make an extra chair. We would therefore produce zero tables and four chairs for a daily profit of $64 and once again lose another $4.

If we analyze what would happen if only three large Legos were available, we see that we have a problem. When we went from five to four large Legos, we simply took apart a table and made a chair out of the pieces. We cannot do this when we downsize from four to three large Legos since we would be producing zero tables. If we have three large and eight small pieces available, we have to take apart one of the chairs but we would not be able to make anything out of the pieces that are left over. As a result, we would end up producing zero tables and three chairs for a profit of $48, thus losing $16 and not the $4 as before. Just as we learned with acquiring additional resources, we now see that the incremental value of reducing resources can change.

If taken together, our results thus far demonstrate the *law of diminishing returns* from economics. The economic value of less than four large Legos is $16 per piece, which then decreases to $4 per Lego up to but not including nine large Legos, and then decreases a second step to $0 for nine or more large Legos. These results are graphically displayed in Figure 3.3.

## Dual Prices and Ranging

This last set of exercises enables us to determine the *dual price* for a resource (large Legos) and the range over which that dual price is valid. The dual price is sometimes called the *shadow price* of a resource. The dual price for a particular constraint is defined as the amount the objective function value will increase (decrease) if the right-hand side value of that constraint is increased (decreased) by one unit. This definition shows that the dual price can be determined for any constraint, whether or not it pertains to resources. The dual price is exactly what we studied when we changed the number of large Legos from four to eight and found that each additional large Lego was worth $4. Since most mathematical programming models of practical importance have many variables and constraints, they cannot be evaluated by a manual process such as the one described above using Legos. Fortunately, the sensitivity analysis information that we developed using this example can be found in the output to a LINGO model.

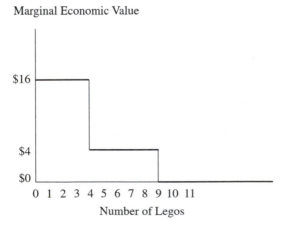

**Figure 3.3** Marginal Economic Value of a Large Lego

The complete output, including sensitivity analysis, for our Lego problem is given as Figure 3.2. LINGO numbers the objective function as row 1, the first constraint (large Legos) as row 2, and the second constraint (small Legos) as row 3. The output indicates that there are three dual prices for the Lego problem. The dual price for row 1 has a value of one and relates to the objective function, and so it can be ignored. Row 2's dual price is 4, meaning that the dual price is $4 for each additional large Lego. This is the same result we found by working with the Legos in the previous section. Similarly, row 3's dual price is 6, meaning that the dual price is $6 for each additional small Lego.

The *Allowable Increase* and *Allowable Decrease* for the *Right-Hand Side Ranges* indicate the amount that the right-hand side of a constraint can be changed without having the dual price change. The allowable increase for large Legos is 2 and coincidentally the allowable decrease is also 2. Since we currently have six large Legos, this means that as long as we have between four (six minus two) and eight (six plus two) large Legos, the dual price of $4 remains valid. As we saw in the Lego exercise in the last section, even though the dual price remains constant between 4 and 8, the optimal values of the decision variables do not. LINGO does not report the changes in the optimal values of the decision variables that are associated with changing the values on the right-hand sides of constraints. However, these changes can be determined by altering the appropriate coefficients and re-running the model.

The allowable increase and allowable decrease for small Legos are 4 and 2, respectively. Since we currently have eight small Legos as long as we have between six (eight minus two) and twelve (eight plus four) small Legos, the dual price of $6 remains valid. Specifically, if we increase (decrease) the amount of small Legos by one, then the objective function increases (decreases) by $6.

Suppose you are provided with two additional small Legos. After some manipulation, you can see that the new optimal solution is to produce one table and four chairs for a profit of $84. In other words, you would be willing to spend up to $12 (84 − 72) for two additional small Legos, so the dual price is $6 (12 ÷ 2). You can continue this exercise to show that the allowable increase for small Legos is 4, while the allowable decrease is 2. Note that dual prices are meaningful if the right-hand side value of one constraint is changed, while all other parameters of the model remain unchanged.

## Changes to the Objective Function Coefficients

Next we consider changes to the objective function coefficients. In this section, we assume that the available resources are fixed. Studying modifications to the objective function coefficients is important since resource costs and product selling prices often change. We need to study these changes to know what impact they have on the optimal solution.

We begin by asking how much the profit of Legos tables would have to increase before we decide to produce more tables. If we produce an additional table, we must give up production of two chairs for a net loss of $12 (20 − 2 ∗ 16). Therefore, the profit of tables must increase by at least $12 before we decide to produce more tables.

We could also ask how much the profit of tables would have to decrease before we decide to produce fewer tables. If we produce one less table, we can only produce one additional chair from the resources freed up for a net loss of $4 (1 ∗ 16 − 20). Therefore, the profit of tables must decrease by at least $4 before we decide to produce fewer tables.

This information can be found in the LINGO output under the objective function coefficient ranges for X1, which represents the number of tables produced (Figure 3.2). The current objective function coefficient for X1 is 20, the allowable increase is 12, and the allowable decrease is 4. These ranges imply that as long as the profit per table remains between \$16 (20 − 4) and \$32 (20 + 12) the optimal solution will be to produce two tables and two chairs. However, even if the change in profit per table remains within this range, total profit will change. For example, suppose that the profit per table increases from \$20 to \$30. Even though the optimal product mix of tables and chairs remains the same, total profit expressed as the objective function value will increase by $2 * \$10 = \$20$.

Now suppose that the profit of tables increases to \$35, which is beyond the allowable increase. Solving the revised problem in LINGO shows that the optimal product mix changes to three tables and zero chairs for a total profit of \$105 (Figure 3.4). Since the profit per table changed to more than \$32, it is now profitable enough to produce an additional table.

When the profit per table is \$35, the allowable decrease for the objective function coefficient for chairs (X2) is infinity. This seemingly strange result is correct: since we are not currently producing any chairs, if the profit per chair decreases by any value, we will still not produce any chairs. Also notice that the allowable increase for the objective function coefficient for chairs is now \$1.50. This means that we would start producing chairs if its objective function coefficient increases by at least \$1.50.

## Reduced Costs

The last part of the output that we need to discuss is the *reduced cost*. When a decision variable has an optimal value of zero, the allowable increase for the objective function coefficient is also called the reduced cost. In general, the reduced cost of a decision variable is equal to the amount the corresponding objective function coefficient would have to change before the optimal value of the decision variable would change from zero to

```
:   1]MODEL:
    2]MAX=35*X1+16*X2;
    3]2*X1+1*X2<=6;
    4]2*X1+2*X2<=8;
    5]END
    6]

 Optimal solution found at step:          1
 Objective value:                    105.0000

                    Variable           Value      Reduced Cost
                          X1        3.000000         0.0000000
                          X2        0.0000000        1.500000

                    Row      Slack or Surplus      Dual Price
                      1         105.0000            1.000000
                      2         0.0000000          17.50000
                      3         2.000000            0.0000000

 Ranges in which the basis is unchanged:

                            Objective Coefficient Ranges
                         Current       Allowable       Allowable
             Variable  Coefficient      Increase        Decrease
                   X1    35.00000       INFINITY        3.000000
                   X2    16.00000       1.500000        INFINITY

                            Righthand Side Ranges
             Row         Current       Allowable       Allowable
                           RHS          Increase        Decrease
              2          6.000000       2.000000        6.000000
              3          8.000000       INFINITY        2.000000
```

**Figure 3.4** LINGO Model and Output for the Lego Problem when Profit per Table is \$35

some positive value. Therefore, the only time that the reduced cost has meaning is when the optimal value of its associated decision variable takes on a value of zero. Effectively, the reduced cost tells us how much the profit per unit would have to increase before we *start* producing that product. In the last section, we saw that the allowable increase for the objective function coefficient tells us how much profit would have to increase before we produce *more* of that product.

Returning to Figure 3.4, we see that we are not producing any chairs and the reduced cost for chairs is $1.50. We also see that the allowable increase for the objective function coefficient for chairs is $1.50. This is not a coincidence. As was mentioned previously, these two values will be the same if the optimal value of the decision variable is zero. Both results indicate that we will start producing chairs if the profitability for chairs increases by at least $1.50 per unit. Now suppose we decide to produce one chair even though it is not optimal to do so under present circumstances. The reduced cost is often called an *opportunity cost* since it indicates that the result of producing one chair will *decrease* the objective function value by $1.50.

If we look at the output from our original model (Figure 3.2), we see that the reduced cost for tables and chairs is zero since we are already producing tables and chairs.

## Alternate Optimal Solutions

Assuming the profitability of tables is $35, what happens if we increase the objective function coefficient of chairs (X2) by *exactly* $1.50? The results are given in Figure 3.5 and show that the optimal value of the objective function is still $105 and the optimal

```
 :    1]MODEL:
      2]MAX=35*X1+17.5*X2;
      3]2*X1+1*X2<=6;
      4]2*X1+2*X2<=8;
      5]END
      6]
```

```
Global optimal solution found at step:          1
Objective value:                        105.0000
```

| Variable | Value | Reduced Cost |
|---|---|---|
| X1 | 3.000000 | 0.0000000 |
| X2 | 0.0000000 | 0.0000000 |

| Row | Slack or Surplus | Dual Price |
|---|---|---|
| 1 | 105.0000 | 1.000000 |
| 2 | 0.0000000 | 17.50000 |
| 3 | 2.000000 | 0.0000000 |

Ranges in which the basis is unchanged:

| | Objective Coefficient Ranges | | |
|---|---|---|---|
| Variable | Current Coefficient | Allowable Increase | Allowable Decrease |
| X1 | 35.00000 | INFINITY | 0.0 |
| X2 | 17.50000 | 0.0 | INFINITY |

| | Righthand Side Ranges | | |
|---|---|---|---|
| Row | Current RHS | Allowable Increase | Allowable Decrease |
| 2 | 6.000000 | 2.000000 | 6.000000 |
| 3 | 8.000000 | INFINITY | 2.000000 |

**Figure 3.5** LINGO Model and Output for the Lego Problem Showing the Presence of Alternate Optimal Solutions

solution is to produce three tables and zero chairs as before (Figure 3.4). However, note that the optimal value of chairs and its reduced cost are *both* zero. That is, since there is no opportunity cost of producing chairs, there must exist another optimal solution involving the positive production of chairs. In fact, producing two tables and two chairs also yields a total profit of 2 * 35 + 2 * 17.5 = $105. However, LINGO converges to only one of the optimal solutions.

To further understand this result we briefly return to the discussion in Chapter 2 about the graphical method. The presence of two optimal solutions implies that the slope of the objective function is the same as the slope of one of the constraints. In this example, the slope of the objective function and the slope of the first constraint are equal, and the iso-profit line is tangent to a *line segment* and not to a point. An interesting implication of this result is that not only are both corner points (3, 0) and (2, 2) optimal, but *any point on the line connecting them* is also optimal. For example, (2.5, 1) is also an optimal (although non-integer) solution.

## Sensitivity Summary

Like dual prices, objective coefficient and reduced cost changes are valid for only one change at a time. There are more complex methods for analyzing the effects of more than one change at a time (Winston, 1995). Also, there are other forms of sensitivity analysis that could be studied. For example, what would happen to the optimal solution if a new constraint were added to the model? What would happen to the optimal solution if a new product were added to the model? What would happen to the optimal solution if one of the constraint coefficients changed? For multiple and more complex changes, we simply recommend rerunning the model after changing the appropriate parameter values. The value of the sensitivity analysis output is that we can obtain a great deal of information about the impact of changes *without* rerunning the model. We will now use the following example to reinforce the sensitivity analysis concepts that we have covered. At the conclusion of this example, we will consider two other situations we have not yet discussed: dual prices for "greater than or equal to" constraints, and output interpretation for minimization problems.

## SENSITIVITY ANALYSIS EXAMPLE: LAWN CARE, INC.

### Concept Review

Lawn Care produces three lawn fertilizers that are composed of nitrate, phosphate, and potash in different proportions. Fertilizer 1 (F1) is 5% nitrate, 5% phosphate, and 10% potash; fertilizer 2 (F2) is 10% nitrate, 10% phosphate, and 5% potash; and fertilizer 3 (F3) is 10% nitrate, 5% phosphate, and 5% potash. Lawn Care currently has 1050 tons of nitrate, 1000 tons of phosphate, and 1580 tons of potash available. The fertilizer profits per ton are $17, $20, and $12, respectively. We assume, for simplicity's sake, that all the fertilizer of each type that can be produced can be sold. The LINGO file for this problem is LAWN.LG4 and the output appears as Figure 3.6.

The decision variables are defined as follows:

$X1$ = number of pounds of F1 produced,

$X2$ = number of pounds of F2 produced, and

$X3$ = number of pounds of F3 produced.

The formulation given in Figure 3.6 shows that the objective function (row 1) seeks to maximize the total profit obtained from the production of the three fertilizers. There is

```
:   1]MODEL:
    2]MAX=17*X1+20*X2+12*X3;
    3]0.05*X1+0.10*X2+0.10*X3<=1050;
    4]0.05*X1+0.10*X2+0.05*X3<=1000;
    5]0.10*X1+0.05*X2+0.05*X3<=1580;
    6]END
    7]

Optimal solution found at step:           1
Objective value:                    300800.0

                    Variable            Value         Reduced Cost
                          X1         14400.00          0.0000000
                          X2         2800.000          0.0000000
                          X3         0.0000000         0.3333332

                         Row    Slack or Surplus       Dual Price
                           1         300800.0           1.000000
                           2         50.00000           0.0000000
                           3         0.0000000          153.3333
                           4         0.0000000          93.33334

Ranges in which the basis is unchanged:

                              Objective Coefficient Ranges
                              Current        Allowable       Allowable
                    Variable  Coefficient    Increase        Decrease
                          X1  17.00000       23.00000        0.9999996
                          X2  20.00000       14.00000        0.9999996
                          X3  12.00000       0.3333332       INFINITY

                              Righthand Side Ranges
                    Row       Current        Allowable       Allowable
                              RHS            Increase        Decrease
                      2       1050.000       INFINITY        50.00000
                      3       1000.000       50.00000        210.0000
                      4       1580.000       420.0000        1080.000
```

**Figure 3.6** LINGO Model and Output for the LAWN.LG4 Problem

one constraint that limits the use and availability of the three active ingredients, namely, nitrate (row 2), phosphate (row 3), and potash (row 4).

Using what we learned in the previous sections on sensitivity analysis, let's interpret the information shown in Figure 3.6. We'll do this by asking the following questions.

***Q1:   How many tons of each fertilizer should Lawn Care produce and what profit will be generated?***   The output indicates that Lawn Care should produce 14,400 tons of F1, 2,800 of F2, and 0 tons of F3 generating a profit of $300,800.

***Q2:   How much of each resource is unused if the optimal solution is implemented?***   The slack tells us that, for the optimal solution, there are 50 unused tons of nitrate (row 2), 0 unused tons of phosphate (row 3), and 0 unused tons of potash (row 4).

***Q3:   Currently the production level of F3 is zero. At what objective function coefficient value would it be beneficial to start producing F3?***   Since the reduced cost of X3 is 0.33, the objective function coefficient for X3 would have to increase from 12 to 12.33 before we would start producing F3.

*Q4:    If the objective function coefficient for X1 increases by $25 per ton will the optimal values of X1, X2, and X3 increase, decrease, or remain unchanged?*    The increase of F1's objective function coefficient of $25 is greater than the allowable increase of $23, thus causing the values of the decision variables and the objective function value to change. Since we are increasing the objective function coefficient of F1, the optimal value of X1 will increase. Since we are currently producing X2 and not X3, increasing production of X1 will result in a decrease in production of X2. The optimal value of X3 may increase or remain at zero.

*Q5:    Suppose that Lawn Care is considering introducing a new fertilizer that uses zero nitrate, zero phosphate, and 20% potash. The new fertilizer will generate a profit of $25 per ton. If additional potash could not be purchased, how much, if any, of the new fertilizer should Lawn Care produce?*    Since additional potash cannot be purchased, any production of F4 will reduce potash availability for F1, F2, and F3. If the right-hand side of potash is reduced by one unit, then the objective function will decrease by $93.33 (the dual price for potash). This ton of potash can be used to produce five tons of F4. Therefore, the profit increases by 5 (25) − 93.33 = 31.67 per ton of potash. This implies that as much F4 as possible should be produced. Since the dual price is constant for 1080 (the allowable decrease), then we should produce at least 5 (1080) = 5400 tons of F4. We say "at least" since you may wish to allocate more than 1080 tons to F4 depending on how the dual price for potash changes. For example, you may wish to rerun the model after reducing the right-hand side of the potash constraint by 1081 to determine the new (and higher) dual price and its range. Using these results, you can determine if additional production of F4 is warranted.

We note that this question also could be solved by defining a new decision variable, X4, to represent the pounds of F4 produced. The term 25 ∗ X4 would be added to the objective function, and .20 ∗ X4 would be added to the left-hand side of the potash constraint (row 4). Again, the value of sensitivity analysis is to quickly obtain information without rerunning the problem.

*Q6:    Suppose that additional phosphate and potash can be secured if needed. Each additional ton of phosphate will cost $135.50. For each additional ton of potash, up to 200, a cost of $92.75 is incurred. Additional tons of potash beyond 200 will cost $89.55 per ton. If only one increase can be made, which additional resource (phosphate or potash), if any, should be secured? How many additional tons should be obtained?*    For phosphate, the dual price equals $153.33/ton, and the allowable increase equals 50 tons. Therefore, the profit increase will be 50 (153.33 − 135.50) = $891.50. For potash, the dual price equals $93.33/ton, and the allowable increase is 420 tons. Therefore, the profit increase will be 200 (93.33 − 92.75) + 220 (93.33 − 89.55) = $947.60. Therefore, potash should be increased by at least 420 tons, subject to the same proviso given in the answer to Q5.

## Adding a "Greater than or Equal to" Constraint

Now we wish to modify the original formulation and add a constraint that places a lower bound on the total number of tons of fertilizer produced:

$$X1 + X2 + X3 >= 17500.$$

We have added this constraint (row 5) in order to discuss the interpretation of a dual price for a "greater than or equal to" constraint. The LINGO output for the revised Lawn Care

```
:    1]MODEL:
     2]MAX=17*X1+20*X2+12*X3;
     3]0.05*X1+0.10*X2+0.10*X3<=1050;
     4]0.05*X1+0.10*X2+0.05*X3<=1000;
     5]0.10*X1+0.05*X2+0.05*X3<=1580;
     6]X1+X2+X3>=17500;
     7]END
     8]
```

```
Global optimal solution found at step:          6
Objective value:                        300500.0
```

| Variable | Value | Reduced Cost |
|---|---|---|
| X1 | 14100.00 | 0.0000000 |
| X2 | 2500.000 | 0.0000000 |
| X3 | 900.0000 | 0.0000000 |

| Row | Slack or Surplus | Dual Price |
|---|---|---|
| 1 | 300500.0 | 1.000000 |
| 2 | 5.000000 | 0.0000000 |
| 3 | 0.0000000 | 160.0000 |
| 4 | 0.0000000 | 100.0000 |
| 5 | 0.0000000 | -1.000000 |

Ranges in which the basis is unchanged:

Objective Coefficient Ranges

| Variable | Current Coefficient | Allowable Increase | Allowable Decrease |
|---|---|---|---|
| X1 | 17.00000 | INFINITY | 1.000000 |
| X2 | 20.00000 | INFINITY | 1.000000 |
| X3 | 12.00000 | 0.3333333 | INFINITY |

Righthand Side Ranges

| Row | Current RHS | Allowable Increase | Allowable Decrease |
|---|---|---|---|
| 2 | 1050.000 | INFINITY | 5.000000 |
| 3 | 1000.000 | 45.00000 | 125.0000 |
| 4 | 1580.000 | 45.00000 | 5.000000 |
| 5 | 17500.00 | 33.33333 | 300.0000 |

**Figure 3.7** LINGO Model and Output for the LAWN. LG4 Problem with Lower Bound Constraint

problem is given as Figure 3.7. Comparing Figures 3.6 and 3.7 shows that total profit has dropped from $300,800 to $300,500, while the total number of tons produced has increased from 17,200 (14,400 + 2,800) to 17,500 (production at the lower bound). The increase in production has led to a different product mix that is on balance less profitable.

The dual price for the lower bound constraint (row 5) is −1, meaning that if the right-hand side of this constraint is increased by one, the objective value will *decrease* by $1. Why is the dual price negative in this situation? As you increase the right-hand side of a "greater than or equal to" constraint, you further restrict the feasible region. Since there are now fewer feasible solutions, your optimal objective value will at best stay the same or decrease.

As a check on the consistency of our results, notice that the allowable decrease for the dual price for the lower bound constraint (row 5) is 300 tons. The interpretation of this result is that for each of the first 300 tons you *remove* from the right-hand side of the lower bound constraint, profit will change by the *negative* of the dual price, or −(−1) = +1. If all 300 units are removed, the new lower bound is 17,200 and profit increases from

$300,500 to $300,500 + $1 * 300 = $300,800, yielding, as expected, the original solution to our problem.

## Interpreting the Output of a Minimization Problem

Now we assume that the objective of the Lawn Care problem is to *minimize cost* rather than to maximize profit. Assume that the constraints are the same as before, except that the lower bound on total tons of fertilizer produced is now 15,000. The objective function coefficients for X1, X2, and X3, are costs of $8, $6, and $7, respectively, and so our objective function is to be minimized. After solving this problem in LINGO we obtain the output given as Figure 3.8.

The optimal solution calls for producing 9,000, 5,000, and 1,000 tons of fertilizers, F1, F2, and F3 respectively, for a total cost of $109,000. We are especially interested in interpreting the dual prices when the objective function is minimized. The dual price for

```
: 1]MODEL:
  2]Min = 8*X1+6*X2+7*X3;
  3]0.05*X1+0.10*X2+0.10*X3<=1050;
  4]0.05*X1+0.10*X2+0.05*X3<=1000;
  5]0.10*X1+0.05*X2+0.05*X3<=1580;
  6]X1+X2+X3>=15000;
  7]END
  8]

Global optimal solution found at step:          7
Objective value:                          109000.0

                  Variable           Value       Reduced Cost
                        X1        9000.000          0.0000000
                        X2        5000.000          0.0000000
                        X3        1000.000          0.0000000

                       Row   Slack or Surplus       Dual Price
                         1        109000.0           1.000000
                         2       0.0000000          20.00000
                         3       0.0000000          20.00000
                         4        380.0000          0.0000000
                         5       0.0000000         -10.00000

Ranges in which the basis is unchanged:

                              Objective Coefficient Ranges
                            Current        Allowable        Allowable
                Variable  Coefficient       Increase         Decrease
                      X1    8.000000        INFINITY         1.000000
                      X2    6.000000        1.000000         INFINITY
                      X3    7.000000        1.000000         1.000000

                              Righthand Side Ranges
                   Row        Current        Allowable        Allowable
                                 RHS          Increase         Decrease
                     2        1050.000        450.0000         50.00000
                     3        1000.000        50.00000         250.0000
                     4        1580.000        INFINITY         380.0000
                     5        15000.00        2533.333         4500.000
```

**Figure 3.8** LINGO Model and Output for the LAWN.LG4 Problem with Lower Bound Constraint and Objective Function to be Minimized

nitrate (row 2) is $20 per ton and is interpreted as follows: if we increase the available tons of nitrate by one, the optimal total cost will *improve* by $20; that is, the objective value will *decrease* by $20. Similarly, the dual price of $-10$ for the lower bound constraint on total production (row 5) translates into a $10 *increase* in the objective value if the right-hand side of the constraint is increased by one ton.

These results lead to a general statement on the sign convention used in LINGO for dual prices. A positive dual price means that increasing the right-hand side of a constraint by one unit will *help* the objective value, that is, increase a maximization objective value or decrease a minimization objective value. A negative dual price will *hurt* the objective value. Increasing the right-hand side of a "less than or equal to" constraint will always either help the objective value or keep it unchanged; increasing the right-hand side of a "greater than or equal to" constraint will always either hurt the objective value or keep it unchanged. For equality constraints, the dual price is not constrained by direction. For further discussion of sensitivity analysis, see Anderson, Sweeney, and Williams (2000), Winston (1995), and Hillier and Lieberman (2001).

## SUMMARY

Sensitivity analysis provides information on how changes to the components of a mathematical programming model impact the optimal solution. A simple product mix problem using Legos was used to motivate our discussion of sensitivity analysis, including the important concepts of dual prices, reduced costs, and range analysis. The dual price is the change in the objective function value if one unit is added to (or taken away from) the right-hand side of a constraint. The range analysis for the dual price indicates how many units can be added to or taken away from the right-hand side of a constraint, yet not change the dual price. The reduced cost is the amount the objective function coefficient of a decision variable would have to improve for the decision variable to assume a positive value in the optimal solution. The objective coefficient ranges indicate how much the objective function coefficient for a decision variable can increase or decrease and the optimal values of the decision variables remain the same. The examples given in this chapter demonstrate how the information provided by sensitivity analysis enhances the value of the modeling process.

## HOMEWORK PROBLEMS

**1.** The HARRIS Company wishes to determine how many of each of three different products they should produce, given limited resources, in order to maximize total profit. The labor and material requirements and the contribution to profit for each of the three products are as follows:

Resource Requirements

|  | Labor (hours/unit) | Materials (pounds/unit) | Profit ($/unit) |
|---|---|---|---|
| Product 1 | 5 | 4 | 3 |
| Product 2 | 2 | 6 | 5 |
| Product 3 | 4 | 3 | 2 |

There are 240 hours of labor available daily for production. The supply of materials is limited to 400 pounds per day. The problem is to determine the quantity to produce of each product in order to maximize total profit.

**(a)** What are the optimal daily production levels for each of the three products?

**(b)** What profit will be obtained from the optimal solution?

**(c)** Is there any unused labor or materials capacity? If so, how much of each capacity exists?

**(d)** How much will the optimal value of the objective function change if the amount of materials available each day increases from 400 to 450? Will the objective function increase or decrease?

**(e)** How much will the value of the objective function change if the amount of labor decreases from 240 to 200? Will the objective function increase or decrease?

**(f)** If the materials cost $0.50/lb, what is the minimum amount of additional materials that should be secured?

**(g)** If the materials contract could be renegotiated so that the profit/unit for product 2 changed from $5 to $8, then what would be the new objective function value and values of the decisions variables?

**(h)** The profit per unit for product 3 is $2, and the production level for product 3 is zero. How much would the profit have to change before it would be profitable to produce product 3?

**2.** GLASSCO produces windows and glass doors and has three plants. Aluminum frames and hardware are made in plant 1, wood frames are made in plant 2, and plant 3 is used to produce the glass and assemble the products. A proposed new product (product 1) is an 8-ft glass door with aluminum framing. A second new product (product 2) is a large (4 × 6 foot) double-hung wood-framed window. Glassco can sell as much of either product as could be produced. The relevant production rate, capacity, and profit information are:

| Plant | Capacity used per unit | | Total Capacity |
|---|---|---|---|
| | Product 1 | Product 2 | |
| 1 | 1 | 0 | 4 |
| 2 | 0 | 2 | 12 |
| 3 | 3 | 2 | 18 |
| Unit Profit | $3 | $5 | |

**(a)** What are the optimal production levels for each type of door?

**(b)** How much profit per minute can Glassco expect if the recommended solution is implemented?

**(c)** How much idle capacity occurs at each plant?

**(d)** If the capacity at plant 3 could be increased at a cost of $1.25 per minute, should this be done? Why?

**(e)** How much will the objective function change if the capacity at plant 2 is increased from 12 to 15? Will the objective function increase or decrease?

**(f)** How much will the objective function change if the capacity at plant 3 is decreased from 18 to 14? Will the objective function increase or decrease?

**(g)** If the capacity at plant 2 could be increased at a cost of $0.80 per minute, what is the minimum amount of additional capacity that should be secured?

**(h)** If the profit for 8-ft doors changed from $3 per door to $5 per door, then what would be the new objective function value? What would the values of the decision variables equal?

**3.** TVCAST produces two types of TV sets, the Alpha and the Omega. There are two production lines, one for each set. The capacity of the Alpha production line is 70 sets per day; the capacity of the Omega line is 50 sets per day. The Alpha set requires one hour of labor; the Omega set requires two hours. Presently, a maximum of 120 hours of labor a day can be assigned to production of the two types of sets. The profit con-

tributions are $20 and $30, respectively, for each Alpha and Omega set.

**(a)** What are the optimal daily production levels of Alphas and Omegas?

**(b)** What profit will be obtained from the optimal solution?

**(c)** Does the firm have any unused production capacity or unused labor capacity? If so, how much unused capacity exists, and where does it exist?

**(d)** How much will the optimal value of the objective function change if the capacity of the Alpha line is increased from 70 to 72? Will the value of the objective function increase or decrease?

**(e)** How much will the value of the objective function change if the capacity of the Omega line is decreased from 50 to 40? Will the value of the objective function increase or decrease?

**(f)** If labor capacity could be expanded by 10 hours per day for a cost of $10 per hour, or if the capacity of the Alpha line could be expanded by 16 sets per day at a cost of $2 per set, which alternative would you choose?

**(g)** What is the current rate of change in the optimal value of the objective function as the capacity of the Alpha line changes? Over what set of values for the capacity of the Alpha line does this rate hold?

**(h)** What happens to the optimal production plan if the profitability of a Omega set increases from $30 to $35? What happens to the optimal value of the objective function?

**(i)** What happens to the optimal production plan and the optimal value of the objective function if the profitability of an Alpha set decreases by $2?

**(j)** What can you say about the optimal value of the objective function if the profitability of a Omega set increases from $30 to $45?

**4.** PANELPINE produces three types of pressed paneling from pine and spruce. The three types of paneling are Western, Old English, and Colonial. Each sheet must be cut and pressed. Each sheet of Western requires five pounds of pine, two pounds of spruce, one hour of cutting, and two hours of pressing. Each sheet of Old English requires four pounds of pine, five pounds of spruce, one hour of cutting, and four hours of pressing. Each sheet of Colonial requires four pounds of pine, two pounds of spruce, two hours of cutting, and two hours of pressing. There are 200 pounds of pine, 160 pounds of spruce, 50 hours of cutting, and 80 hours of pressing available each day. The contribution to profit per sheet is $4 for Western, $10 for Old English, and $8 for Colonial.

**(a)** What are the optimal daily production levels for each type of paneling?

**(b)** What profit will be obtained if the optimal production levels are implemented?

**(c)** What profit would be obtained if 10 Western sheets, 8 Old English sheets, and 2 Colonial sheets are produced each day? Is this production schedule feasible? Why?

**(d)** How much unused pine and spruce resource are available each day? How much unused cutting and pressing capacity are available each day?

**(e)** If spruce wood could be purchased for $3 per pound, should this be done? Why?

**(f)** How much would the objective function change if the cutting capacity is increased from 50 to 60?

**(g)** If the pressing capacity could be increased at a cost of $1.50 per hour, what is the minimum amount of additional resource that should be secured?

**(h)** If the cutting capacity could be increased at a cost of $1 per hour, or the pressing capacity could be increased at a cost of $1.50 per hour, which alternative would you recommend? Defend your answer.

**(i)** The profit per unit for Western paneling is $4, and the production level for Western paneling is zero. How much would the profit have to change before it would be profitable to produce Western paneling?

**(j)** If the profit for Old English changed from $10 per sheet to $15 per sheet, then what would be the new objective function value? What would the values of the decision variables equal? If you cannot answer these questions, state why they cannot be answered.

**5.** SUPERSPORTS Footballs, Inc. manufactures three kinds of footballs: an All-Pro model, a College model, and a High School model. All three footballs require operations in the following departments: cutting and dyeing, sewing, and inspection and packaging. The productivity times and maximum production availabilities are shown below:

| Model | Production Time (minutes) | | |
| --- | --- | --- | --- |
| | Cutting and Dyeing | Sewing | Inspection and Packaging |
| All-Pro | 12 | 15 | 3 |
| College | 10 | 15 | 4 |
| High School | 8 | 12 | 2 |
| Time Available | 300 hours | 300 hours | 150 hours |

Current orders indicate that at least 1000 All-Pro footballs must be manufactured. Supersports realizes a profit of $3 for each All-Pro, $5 for each College, and $3.50 for each High School football.

**(a)** How many of each type of football should be produced?

**(b)** What profit will be obtained if the optimal solution is implemented?

**(c)** Explain why it is not possible to produce 1200 All-Pro, 10 College, and 10 High School footballs. The profit for producing 1200 All-Pro, 10 College, and 10 High School footballs is $3,685, which is less than the optimal profit of $4,000. Explain how a solution that is not possible could result in a suboptimal solution.

**(d)** How much unused time in the cutting and dyeing, sewing, and inspection and packaging departments is available?

**(e)** What would the new objective function value equal if the right-hand side of the fourth constraint were changed to 1001?

**(f)** The profit per unit for High School footballs is $3.50 and the optimal production level is zero. How much would the profit per unit have to change before it would be profitable to produce High School footballs?

**(g)** If workers in the sewing center earn $6 per hour, what is the amount of additional sewing labor time that should be secured? Explain.

**6.** MACRODATA produces two products with the relevant data shown. Each week up to 400 units of raw material can be purchased at a cost of $1.50 per unit. The company employs four workers, who work 40 hours per week (their salaries are considered to be a fixed cost). Workers can be asked to work overtime and are paid $6.00 per hour for overtime. Each week 320 hours of machine time are available. In the absence of advertising, 50 units of product 1 and 60 units of product 2 will be demanded each week. Each dollar spent on advertising product 1 increases the demand for product 1 by 10 units, whereas each dollar spent for product 2 increases the demand for product 2 by 15 units. At most $100 can be spent on advertising.

| | Product 1 | Product 2 |
| --- | --- | --- |
| Selling Price | $15 | $8 |
| Labor Required | 0.75 hour | 0.50 hour |
| Machine Time Required | 1.5 hours | 0.80 hour |
| Raw Material Required | 2 units | 1 unit |

**(a)** How many units of each product should be produced each week? How much overtime should be used each week? How many units of raw material should be purchased each week? How much money should be spent on advertising each product each week?

**(b)** What profit will be obtained if the optimal solution is implemented?

**(c)** If overtime were to cost only $4 per hour, would Macrodata use overtime? Justify your answer.

**(d)** If each unit of product 1 sold for $15.50, would the current basis remain optimal? What would be the new optimal solution value?

**(e)** What is the most that Macrodata should be willing to pay for another unit of raw material? Justify your answer.

**(f)** How much would Macrodata be willing to pay for another hour of machine time?

**(g)** If each worker were required to work 45 hours per week regular time, what would the company's profits be?

**(h)** If each unit of product 2 sold for $10, would the current basis remain optimal? Justify your answer.

## REFERENCES

ANDERSON, D. R., D. J. SWEENEY, and T. A. WILLIAMS, *An Introduction to Management Science: Quantitative Approaches to Decision Making*, 9th ed., Cincinnati, OH, South-Western College Publishing, 2000.

HILLIER, F. S. and G. J. LIEBERMAN, *Introduction to Operations Research,* 7th ed., New York, McGraw-Hill, 2001.

PENDEGRAFT, N., "Lego of My Simplex," *OR/MS Today*, Vol. 24, No. 1, p. 8, 1997.

SCHRAGE, L., *Optimization Modeling with LINGO*, Chicago, LINDO Systems Inc., 2002.

WINSTON, W. L., *Introduction to Mathematical Programming: Applications and Algorithms*, Belmont, CA, Duxbury, 1995.

# Chapter 4

# Mathematical Programming Using the LINGO Modeling Language

## INTRODUCTION

LINGO enables the user to express a mathematical programming problem in a more compact and natural manner than the standard algebraic format (Schrage 2002). For example, the LINGO modeling language can express a series of similar constraints in a single, compact statement. Data can also be represented more naturally as a list or table, and can be read from a spreadsheet, database, or text file. These features simplify the process of updating and expanding models since the data are organized separately from the model formulation. In addition, a set of built-in functions simplifies the expression of complex relationships. LINGO's output can also be sent to a spreadsheet. Starting in this chapter, we illustrate how to use the modeling language through a series of examples (The on-line manual for LINGO and the LINGO "Samples" folder provides additional examples.)

## THE DIET PROBLEM

### Problem Statement

A hospital dietitian must prepare breakfast menus every morning for the hospital's patients. Part of the dietitian's responsibility is to make certain that minimum daily requirements for vitamins A and B are met. At the same time, the menus must be kept at the lowest possible cost. The main breakfast staples providing vitamins A and B are eggs, bacon, and cereal. The (hypothetical) recommended daily allowances (RDAs) for vitamins for males 25–50 years old, and the vitamin contributions for each staple follow in Table 4.1.

The cost of an egg is $0.04, the cost of a bacon strip is $0.03, and a cup of cereal costs $0.02. The dietitian wants to know how much of each staple to serve for breakfast in order to meet the minimum daily vitamin requirements while minimizing total cost. The diet problem is a well-known application of linear programming. For a humorous discussion on the history and personal application of the diet problem, see Dantzig 1990.

As is shown in the previous chapter, we could define our decision variables as

X1 equals the portions of eggs consumed for breakfast,

X2 equals the portions of bacon consumed for breakfast, and

X3 equals the portions of cereal consumed for breakfast,

if we wished to use the standard algebraic approach to solve this problem in LINGO. However, to make our decision variables more descriptive and to demonstrate the relationship between the algebraic and modeling language approaches, we define PORTIONS(EGGS), PORTIONS(BACON), and PORTIONS(CEREAL) as our decision variables. The objec-

**Table 4.1** Vitamin Contribution by Food and Minimum Daily Vitamin Requirements for Diet Problem

| Vitamin | Food | | | Minimum daily RDAs (mg) |
|---------|------|------|--------|---------|
| | Egg | Bacon | Cereal | |
| A | 2* | 4 | 1 | 16 |
| B | 3 | 2 | 1 | 12 |

*in milligrams (mgs)

tive of our LP is to minimize the total cost of breakfast, which equals .04 ∗ PORTIONS (EGGS) + .03 ∗ PORTIONS(BACON) + .02 ∗ PORTIONS(CEREAL). We have one constraint for each vitamin, so that the minimum daily RDAs are met. For vitamin A, this constraint is 2 ∗ PORTIONS(EGGS) + 4 ∗ PORTIONS(BACON) + 1 ∗ PORTIONS (CEREAL) >= 16. A similar constraint is needed for vitamin B. The complete formulation is given as Figure 4.1.

This same problem can be formulated compactly using the LINGO modeling language. For problems with only a few decision variables and a few constraints, there is minimal benefit of using the modeling language. However, suppose we were interested in diet planning for a chain of nursing homes. The presence of many foods and dietary requirements would make understanding, developing, and maintaining the diet model more difficult if it were entered into LINGO in a standard algebraic format. For these reasons, the modeling language is preferred under such circumstances. Additional examples will be given in the next chapter to illustrate the value and power of the modeling language. We choose to start with a simple example in this chapter to illustrate the key ideas and concepts.

## Modeling Steps

We will develop the LINGO modeling language formulation of our diet problem by completing five steps and will discuss each of these steps in turn.

1. Specify the SETS: section of the model, which includes sets, elements, and attributes.

2. Specify the DATA: section of the model by assigning values to attributes.

3. Identify the decision variables as attributes not assigned values in the DATA: section.

4. Formulate the objective function using the @SUM function.

5. Formulate the constraints using the @FOR function.

```
MIN = .04*PORTIONS(EGGS) + .03*PORTIONS(BACON) +
  .02*PORTIONS(CEREAL);
2*PORTIONS(EGGS) + 4*PORTIONS(BACON) + 1*PORTIONS(CEREAL)>=16;
3*PORTIONS(EGGS) + 2*PORTIONS(BACON) + 1*PORTIONS(CEREAL)>=12;

NOTE: Since LINGO would not know how to interpret PORTIONS in this
context, this problem formulation could not be run in LINGO as stated.
If you wish to run the standard algebraic approach for the diet problem,
substitute X1, X2, and X3 for PORTIONS(EGGS), PORTIONS(BACON), AND
PORTIONS(CEREAL), respectively.
```

**Figure 4.1** Statement of the Diet Problem

**Developing the Model**

### 1. Specify the SETS: Section of the Model, Which Includes Sets, Elements, and Attributes

In thinking about modeling the diet problem or any mathematical programming problem, you will often find that related objects of the problem can be placed into groups or *sets*. In a product mix application, some examples of sets might be factories, products, and resources. In delivery scheduling applications, examples of sets might include employees, vehicles, and customers. The members of a set are called *elements*. For example, St. Louis, Philadelphia, and Chicago might be elements of the set of factories.

The characteristics associated with the elements of a set are called *attributes*. For example, each element in the set of products might have attributes such as price and demand, whereas attributes of vehicles might be capacity and cost. Constraints define relationships between attributes, such as demand and capacity. Usually, if a constraint applies to one element of a set, then it will also apply to the other elements. Taken together, sets, elements, and attributes (SEA) are the fundamental building blocks of the LINGO modeling language.

With SEA in mind, we restate our understanding of the diet problem. The basic components, or building blocks, of this problem are the vitamins and the foods. The number of specific vitamins and the number of specific foods affect the dimension or size of the diet problem, in terms of decisions and constraints. We know that each vitamin has a minimum RDA, and that each food has a cost. We would like to know the number of portions of each food to serve during breakfast. The amount of nutrition provided by a food is specific to a vitamin. That is, we must specify both the food *and* the vitamin to gain information about nutrition. Therefore, nutrition is not a basic component of this problem, but depends on foods and vitamins. The total amount of a given vitamin provided during breakfast depends on the number of portions of each food served and the nutritional value of a portion of that food.

From this discussion we conclude that VITAMINS and FOODS are sets. The elements of VITAMINS are A and B, while the elements of FOODS are EGGS, BACON, and CEREAL. An attribute of VITAMINS is their minimum RDAs, or MINIMUMS. The attributes of FOODS are their cost per serving, or COSTS, and the number of portions to be served during breakfast, or PORTIONS.

VITAMINS and FOODS cannot be reduced into more basic sets. Also, knowledge about the attributes of VITAMINS and FOODS does not depend on knowledge of other sets. For these reasons, VITAMINS and FOODS are called *primitive sets*. However, we derive information about nutrition from knowledge of VITAMINS and FOODS. Therefore, NUTRITION is not a primitive set, but is a *derived set*. Specifically, NUTRITION derives its elements from the unique pairs of elements from VITAMINS and FOODS.

We can gain further understanding of the reasons why NUTRITION is a derived set by revisiting Table 4.1. The rows of this table are the elements of VITAMINS and the columns are the elements of FOODS. The *cells* in this matrix are the placeholders for the elements of NUTRITION. The *values* given in the cells are the values of the attribute of NUTRITION that we call MGS, which are the milligrams of each of the VITAMINS in each of the FOODS. Often, it is easy to think of the attributes of derived sets in a matrix format, where the elements of the primitive sets serve as the rows and columns.

Sets of related objects are defined in the SETS: section of a LINGO model. As we will illustrate, this section begins with the keyword SETS: on a line by itself and ends with ENDSETS on a line by itself. Each set, along with its elements and attribute(s) are specified in a separate statement in the main body of the SETS: section. The format for specifying SEA in LINGO is:

```
set_name/ set_elements /: set_attributes;
```

Based on the previous discussion, the SETS: section of the diet problem is:

```
SETS:
 VITAMINS/A, B/: MINIMUMS;
 FOODS/EGGS, BACON, CEREAL/:COSTS, PORTIONS;
 NUTRITION(VITAMINS, FOODS): MGS;
ENDSETS
```

Note that we do not need to specify the elements of the derived set NUTRITION. However, we indicate that NUTRITION is derived from VITAMINS and FOODS.

### 2. Specify the DATA: Section of the Model by Assigning Values to Attributes

We can assign values to the elements of an attribute in the DATA: section of a LINGO model. The purpose of using this section is to separate data from the rest of the model. Placing data in this section simplifies model maintenance and changing problem dimensions. Examples include revising the values for an attribute such as COST or adding values for new COST elements.

This section begins with the keyword DATA: on a line by itself and ends with ENDDATA on a line by itself. Values for the elements of attributes are specified in statements in the main body of the DATA: section. The attributes included in the DATA: section must have been defined in the SETS: section. The recommended format for specifying the values of an attribute in LINGO is:

```
attribute_name = attribute_values;
```

The DATA section for the diet problem is:

```
DATA:
 COSTS = .04, .03, .02;
 MINIMUMS = 16, 12;
 MGS = 2,4,1,
       3,2,1;
ENDDATA
```

Blank spaces or commas are used to separate the attribute values. We will discuss each of these statements in turn.

The three values for COSTS are given in the same order that the elements of the FOODS set appear. This means that EGGS, BACON, and CEREAL cost .04, .03, and .02, respectively. LINGO interprets this data as COSTS(EGGS) = .04, COSTS(BACON) = .03, and COSTS(CEREAL) = .02.

The two values for MINIMUMS are given in the same order that the elements of the VITAMINS set appear. This means that the minimum requirements for vitamins A and B are 16 and 12, respectively. LINGO interprets the data as MINIMUMS(A) = 16, and MINIMUMS(B) = 12.

The six values for MGS depend on LINGO's ordering of the elements in the NUTRITION(VITAMINS,FOODS) derived set. As mentioned previously, the elements of NUTRITION can be represented in a matrix format (see Table 4.1), where the number of VITAMINS is the number of rows and the number of FOODS is the number of columns in the matrix. Since there are two VITAMINS and three FOODS, the MGS data can be represented as a two by three matrix. The rows are the VITAMINS (A and B) and the columns are the FOODS (EGGS, BACON, and CEREAL). As a result, LINGO interprets the data as: MGS(A,EGGS) = 2, MGS(A,BACON) = 4, MGS(A,CEREAL) = 1, MGS(B,EGGS) = 3, MGS(B,BACON) = 2, and MGS(B,CEREAL) = 1.

If NUTRITION were listed in the SETS: section as: NUTRITION(FOODS, VITAMINS), then the appropriate statement in the DATA: section would be

```
MGS = 2,3,
      4,2,
      1,1;
```

In this situation NUTRITION is represented as a three by two matrix, where the elements of FOODS are the rows, and the elements of VITAMINS are the columns.

### 3. Identify the Decision Variables as Attributes Not Assigned Values in the DATA: Section

If an attribute is not assigned a value in the DATA: section, LINGO assumes that the attribute is a decision variable. In our example, the elements of PORTIONS, that is, PORTIONS(EGGS), PORTIONS(BACON), and PORTIONS(CEREAL) are not assigned values and so they are decision variables. For example, if we forgot to specify values for one of our other attributes such as COST in the DATA: section, LINGO would assume that its elements were also decision variables.

### 4. Formulate the Objective Function Using the @SUM Function

An important advantage of using sets is the ability to apply an operation to all members of a set using a single statement. The functions in LINGO that enable you to do this are called *set looping functions*. The @SUM function is an example of a set looping function, and it can be used to compactly express our objective function. The basic form of the @SUM function is

```
@SUM (set_name: expression);
```

*Expression* is a statement of the operation(s) to be performed, such as computing product revenue. The basic idea is that *expression* is evaluated for each element of the set called *set_name*, and the results are summed over all elements. The @SUM produces *one* statement that is evaluated to provide *one* numerical result. This explanation is a bit abstract, but our example will lead to a more concrete explanation.

We begin by expressing our objective function using SEA terminology. We want to MINimize the total cost of the diet, which is obtained by multiplying the COSTS by the PORTIONS for each of the FOODS, and then *SUM*ming over all FOODS. In LINGO:

```
MIN = @SUM(FOODS(J): COSTS(J) * PORTIONS(J));
```

In this example, *set_name* is FOODS, and *expression* is COSTS*PORTIONS. *Expression* only contains attributes; sets should *never* be included. Also, note that "(J)" was added to *set_name* and each term in *expression*, implying some sort of functional relationship. In fact, J is a placeholder that represents the elements of the set FOODS, so it takes on the values EGGS, BACON, and CEREAL. The placeholder must begin with a letter and can include a combination of letters and numbers; the reason for our particular choice will be discussed later. The importance of the placeholder is that the *expression* COSTS(J) * PORTIONS(J) must be evaluated for all values of J. That is, the number of terms in an @SUM *expression* is equal to the number of elements in the *set_name*. These three expressions must then be summed. Therefore LINGO interprets this @SUM statement as

```
COSTS(EGGS)*PORTIONS(EGGS) + COSTS(BACON)*PORTIONS(BACON) +
COSTS(CEREAL)*PORTIONS(CEREAL).
```

Remember that values of COSTS(EGGS), COSTS(BACON), and COSTS(CEREAL) are defined in the DATA: section, and are .04, .03, and .02, respectively. Using this information LINGO further interprets the @SUM as

```
.04*PORTIONS(EGGS) + .03*PORTIONS(BACON) + .02*PORTIONS(CEREAL).
```

### 5. Formulate the Constraints Using the @FOR Function

The @FOR function is another example of a set looping function, and it can be used to compactly express our constraints. The basic form of the @FOR function is:

```
@FOR(set_name: expression);
```

Rather than express each constraint individually, the @FOR function can generate constraints across the elements of *set_name*. The primary advantage of using the @FOR function is that the user enters a constraint only once, and LINGO generates a copy of the constraint FOR each element of *set_name*.

Again, *expression* is a statement of the operation(s) to be performed for each element of *set_name*. If *expression* is a constraint, then LINGO will generate a copy of this constraint FOR each element of the set.

We begin by expressing our constraints using SEA terminology. FOR each of the VITAMINS, we multiply the MGS by the PORTIONS and SUM over all FOODS. The result must be greater than or equal to (>=) the MINIMUMS. In LINGO:

```
@FOR(VITAMINS(I):
  @SUM(FOODS(J): MGS(I,J)*PORTIONS(J))>=MINIMUMS(I));
```

In this example, *set_name* is VITAMINS(I), and *expression* is @SUM(FOODS(J): MGS(I,J) * PORTIONS(J))>=MINIMUMS(I). I is a placeholder that represents the elements of the set VITAMINS, so it takes on the values A and B. Note that J is the placeholder that again represents the elements of FOODS, namely, EGGS, BACON, and CEREAL. Our convention for assigning letters to placeholders is to assign I to the first set mentioned in the SETS: section, J to the second set mentioned, K to the third set, and so on.

At the risk of being repetitive, since VITAMINS is specified as the *set_name*, *the @FOR statement generates one expression FOR each element of the set of VITAMINS.* That is, an expression will be generated "FOR" VITAMIN A and a second expression "FOR" VITAMIN B. The VITAMIN A constraint is generated as follows. First, I is set equal to A. Next, the @SUM function must be evaluated for the case when I is equal to A. LINGO now interprets the @SUM function as

```
@SUM(FOODS(J): MGS(A,J)*PORTIONS(J))>=MINIMUMS(A)
```

The @SUM function is evaluated as before. J takes on the values EGGS, BACON, CEREAL. Therefore LINGO further interprets this @SUM statement as

```
MGS(A,EGGS)*PORTIONS(EGGS) + MGS(A,BACON)*PORTIONS(BACON) +
MGS(A,CEREAL)*PORTIONS(CEREAL).
```

This sum must be greater than or equal to MINIMUMS(A):

```
MGS(A,EGGS)*PORTIONS(EGGS)* + MGS(A,BACON)* PORTIONS(BACON) +
MGS(A,CEREAL)*PORTIONS(CEREAL)>=MINIMUMS(A).
```

Remember that values of MGS(A,EGGS), MGS(A,BACON), MGS(A,CEREAL), and MINIMUMS(A) are defined in the DATA: section and are 2, 4, 1, and 16, respectively. LINGO further interprets the @SUM as:

```
2*PORTIONS(EGGS) + 4*PORTIONS(BACON) + 1*PORTIONS(CEREAL)>=16.
```

The same process is repeated for VITAMIN B, yielding

```
3*PORTIONS(EGGS) + 2*PORTIONS(BACON) + 1*PORTIONS(CEREAL)>=12.
```

## The Complete Model

The complete modeling language formulation of the diet problem is given in a file called DIETA.LG4 and is shown as Figure 4.2. Comments have been added to the model statement to provide additional clarity. All comments begin with an explanation point (!) and end with a semicolon. The solution report after running the LINGO model given in Figure 4.2 is shown as Figure 4.3. *Every* attribute value, even those that are not decision variables, is listed in the solution report. Note that the optimal values of PORTIONS turned out to be integers. That is, we should eat 2 eggs, 3 bacon strips, and 0 cups of cereal each day. This result was not guaranteed since the @GIN (Generalized Integers) command was not specified for each of these variables.

The optimal solution requires serving two portions of eggs, three of bacon, and none of cereal for a total cost of $0.17. Since there are two "greater than or equal to" constraints, the surplus values of zero indicate that the minimum levels for vitamins A and B are being achieved exactly by this solution. Since the dual price for the vitamin B constraint (row 3) is −0.0125, the cost of breakfast will increase by 1.25 cents if the minimum daily requirement for vitamin B is increased by 1 mg. Cereal will not enter into the suggested breakfast unless the cost per portion is decreased by its reduced cost of 5/8 of a cent (i.e., $0.00625).

**Figure 4.2** Complete LINGO Modeling Language Formulation of the Diet Problem

```
MODEL:
 SETS:
  VITAMINS/A, B/ : MINIMUMS;
  FOODS/EGGS, BACON, CEREAL/ : COSTS, PORTIONS;
  NUTRITION(VITAMINS, FOODS) : MGS;
 ENDSETS
! OBJECTIVE FUNCTION;
MIN = @SUM(FOODS(J): COSTS(J)*PORTIONS(J));
! THE MINIMUM DAILY REQUIREMENT CONSTRAINTS;
@FOR(VITAMINS(I):
 @SUM(FOODS(J): MGS(I,J)*PORTIONS(J))>=MINIMUMS(I));
! HERE IS THE DATA;
DATA:
 COSTS = .04, .03, .02;
 MINIMUMS = 16, 12;
 MGS = 2,4,1,
     3,2,1;
ENDDATA
END
```

```
Objective value: 0.1700000
                       Variable            Value        Reduced Cost
                  MINIMUMS( A)           16.00000          0.0000000
                  MINIMUMS( B)           12.00000          0.0000000
                  COSTS( EGGS)      0.4000000E-01          0.0000000
                 COSTS( BACON)      0.3000000E-01          0.0000000
                COSTS( CEREAL)      0.2000000E-01          0.0000000
               PORTIONS( EGGS)           2.000000          0.0000000
              PORTIONS( BACON)           3.000000          0.0000000
             PORTIONS( CEREAL)          0.0000000     0.6250000E-02
                 MGS( A, EGGS)           2.000000          0.0000000
                MGS( A, BACON)           4.000000          0.0000000
               MGS( A, CEREAL)           1.000000          0.0000000
                 MGS( B, EGGS)           3.000000          0.0000000
                MGS( B, BACON)           2.000000          0.0000000
               MGS( B, CEREAL)           1.000000          0.0000000
                           Row    Slack or Surplus        Dual Price
                             1          0.1700000          1.000000
                             2          0.0000000    -0.1250000E-02
                             3          0.0000000    -0.1250000E-01

Ranges in which the basis is unchanged:

                                 Objective Coefficient Ranges
                                   Current       Allowable      Allowable
                  Variable       Coefficient      Increase       Decrease
            PORTIONS( EGGS)     0.4000000E-01  0.5000000E-02  0.2500000E-01
           PORTIONS( BACON)     0.3000000E-01  0.5000000E-01  0.3333333E-02
          PORTIONS( CEREAL)     0.2000000E-01       INFINITY  0.6250000E-02

                                     Righthand Side Ranges
                  Row            Current       Allowable      Allowable
                                    RHS         Increase       Decrease
                    2            16.00000       8.000000       8.000000
                    3            12.00000      12.00000        4.000000
```

**Figure 4.3** Solution Report after Running the LINGO Modeling Language Formulation of the Diet Problem

We can convert the LINGO modeling formulation given in Figure 4.2 to the same algebraic representation of the model given in Figure 4.1. This conversion is accomplished by using the *LINGO*, *Generate* command, selecting *Display model*, and clicking *OK*. Comparing Figures 4.1 and 4.2, we see that the use of natural language helps to clarify the model relationships. A major application of the *LINGO*, *Generate* command is to help debug a LINGO modeling language formulation.

## DIET PROBLEM EXTENSIONS

### Adding a Food

We now present three extensions of the diet problem to illustrate the power of the LINGO modeling language. First, suppose the dietitian has decided to add TOAST to the menu. We assume that a slice of TOAST costs one penny, has 0.1 MGS of VITAMIN A, and 0.8 MGS of VITAMIN B. Three minor modifications of DIETA.LG4 are required to include this new information. In the SETS: section, we add TOAST as an element of FOODS. In the DATA: section, we augment the values for COST to include .01 for TOAST, and the values for MGS to include 0.1 and 0.8 for TOAST. The modified statements are given here and the changes highlighted in bold.

```
FOODS/EGGS, BACON, CEREAL, TOAST/:COSTS, PORTIONS;
COSTS = .04, .03, .02, .01;
MGS = 2,4,1,.1,
        3,2,1,.8;
```

Note that *no* changes were required to the objective function or constraints in order to add the additional food. This LINGO model is in a file called DIETB.LG4.

## Adding Bounds on Portions

Now suppose the dietitian has decided that at least one egg, but no more than two, should be included in the diet, and that no more than two strips of bacon should be eaten. These additional constraints can be added to DIETA.LG4 model by using the @BND function. The @BND function is a variable domain function like @GIN and @BIN. The form of the @BND function is:

```
@BND(lower_bound, variable, upper_bound)
```

This statement limits *variable* to being greater than or equal to *lower_bound* and less than or equal to *upper_bound*. *Variable* is an attribute value. We can express the added constraints as:

```
@BND(1,PORTIONS(EGGS),2);
@BND(0,PORTIONS(BACON),2);
```

The default lower bound for all variables is 0. This LINGO model is in a file called DIETC.LG4.

## Adding a Vitamin

Now suppose the dietitian has decided that a constraint should be added concerning the amount of VITAMIN C obtained from breakfast. Again, three minor modifications of DIETA.LG4 are required to include this new information. In the SETS: section we add C as an element of VITAMINS. We assume that the value of MINIMUMS for VITAMIN C is 10, and that EGGS, BACON, and CEREAL provide, 1, .5, and 3 MGS per PORTION. The modified statements are given here and the changes highlighted in bold. This LINGO model is in a file called DIETD.LG4.

```
VITAMINS/ A, B, C/ : MINIMUMS;
MINIMUMS = 16, 12, 10;
MGS = 2,4,1,
        3,2,1;
        1,.5,3;
```

## WORKING WITH LINGO

There are some important points to remember when working with the LINGO modeling language:

**1.** All statements within model sections must end with a semicolon.

**2.** Comments begin with an exclamation point and end with a semicolon.

**3.** LINGO is not sensitive to case.

**4.** Be careful to match parentheses. Clicking on the space to the right of a parenthesis will highlight it and its match in red. The *File, Match Parenthesis* command (or the

**Table 4.2** Summary of LINGO Modeling Commands Used in This Chapter

| Command | Explanation |
|---|---|
| @SUM(set_name: expression) | *Expression* is evaluated for each element of the set called *set_name*, and the results are summed over all elements. The @SUM produces *one* statement that is evaluated to provide *one* numerical result. |
| @FOR(set_name: expression) | *Expression* is a statement of the operation(s) to be performed for each element of the set called *set_name*. If *expression* is a constraint, then LINGO will generate a copy of this constraint FOR each member of *set_name*. |
| @BND(lower_bound,variable,upper_bound) | This statement limits an attribute called *variable* to being greater than or equal to *lower_bound* and less than or equal to *upper_bound*. |

icon to the left of the *Solve* icon) can be used to toggle between the matched parentheses. For example, if you entered the following statement in LINGO:

```
@FOR(VITAMINS(I):
    @SUM(FOODS(J): MGS(I,J)*PORTIONS(J))>=MINIMUMS(I);
```

and moved the cursor to the right of the parenthesis before VITAMINS, this parenthesis would turn red and you would see that there is no match.

**5.** Debugging a LINGO model is best accomplished by systematically commenting out statements. For example, refer to the Diet Problem model given in Figure 4.2. Now suppose that for the minimum daily requirement constraints, our @FOR expression incorrectly includes VITAMINS(J) instead of VITAMINS(I). You can begin debugging by commenting out all statements except for the first statement in the SETS: section concerning VITAMINS and the corresponding statement in the DATA: section concerning MINIMUMS. Running this model provides a feasible solution. Next, remove the comment relating to FOODS in the SETS: section and COSTS in the DATA: section and rerun, and then do the same for the NUTRITION and MGS statements. Next, remove the comment in front of the objective function. Although LINGO responds with a message that it ran out of memory, no errors are detected in the formulation. This leaves the @FOR statement as being the source of the error. First we check the parentheses as previously described, and then we check to see if we are correctly matching our attributes and sets with the same placeholders. Since MINIMUMS is an attribute of VITAMINS, both of these must have the same placeholder. Given the mismatch, we have identified the source of the error.

The three key LINGO modeling commands covered in this chapter are summarized in Table 4.2.

## SUMMARY

This chapter addressed the use of the LINGO modeling language software to formulate mathematical programming models. The primary advantages of using the modeling language include the ability to express a mathematical programming problem in a more natural and compact manner and to simplify the process of updating and expanding models. We used a simple diet problem as an example to illustrate the steps in developing a modeling language problem formulation. We then considered several modifications of the original problem statement to illustrate the ease at which the modeling language formulation can be adapted. The modeling language formulation of a mathematical programming problem consists of specifying the SETS: and DATA: sections, identifying the decision variables, and formulating the objective function and constraints. The syntax for specifying items in the SETS: section is SEA, or sets, elements, and attributes. Those attributes not specified in the DATA: section are decision variables. The statement of the objective function uses the @SUM set looping function, while groups of identical constraints are formulated using the @FOR set looping function. The @BND command can be used to set lower and upper bounds on attribute values. In the next chapter we will consider a variety of mathematical programming applications using the LINGO modeling language. In developing these applications, we will introduce additional modeling features.

## HOMEWORK PROBLEMS

**1.** POWERS makes four products using three resources. The resource requirements per product are shown below.

|  | Product 1 | Product 2 | Product 3 | Product 4 |
|---|---|---|---|---|
| Resource 1 | 3 | 5 | 2 | 3 |
| Resource 2 | 2 | 1 | 6 | 1 |
| Resource 3 | 3 | 2 | 8 | 6 |

An analyst started to develop a LINGO modeling language formulation for this problem. The SETS section is shown below:

```
SETS:
    PRODUCTS/1..4/: PROFIT, X;
    RESOURCES/1..3/: AVAILABLE;
    COMBINE(PRODUCTS, RESOURCES): RATES;
ENDSETS
```

The analyst began to enter the DATA for this problem as follows:

```
DATA:
    PROFIT = 3, 2, 4, 6;
    AVAILABLE = 150, 267, 201;
ENDDATA
```

**(a)** Write the missing data for the RATES attribute in the correct LINGO modeling language format.

**(b)** Write the LINGO modeling language constraints that make sure that the company does not use more than their available resources.

**(c)** Write the LINGO modeling language objective function that maximizes profit.

**2.** WOODS makes four different products: tables, chairs, cabinets, and desks. They use three resources: wood, labor, and machines. The resource requirements per product are shown below.

|  | Tables | Chairs | Cabinets | Desks |
|---|---|---|---|---|
| Wood | 5 | 2 | 6 | 9 |
| Labor | 3 | 1 | 8 | 5 |
| Machine | 2 | 5 | 4 | 3 |

The company would like to develop a LINGO modeling language formulation for this problem. The SETS section is shown below:

```
SETS:
    PRODUCTS/TABLES, CHAIRS, CABINETS, DESKS/:
    PROFIT, X;
    RESOURCES/WOOD, LABOR, MACHINE/: AVAILABLE;
    COMBINE(PRODUCTS, RESOURCES): RATES;
ENDSETS
```

The analyst began to enter the DATA for this problem as follows:

```
DATA:
    PROFIT = 37, 21, 143, 96;
    AVAILABLE = 332, 290, 175;
ENDDATA
```

**(a)** Complete the DATA section by providing the data for the RATES attribute in the correct LINGO modeling language format.

**(b)** Write the LINGO modeling language constraints that make sure that the company does not use more than their available resources.

**(c)** Write the LINGO modeling language objective function that maximizes profit.

**3.** HUNTER publishes three weekly magazines: *Daily Life, Agriculture Today,* and *Surf's Up.* Publication of one issue of each of the magazines requires the following amounts of production time and paper.

|  | Production (hours) | Paper (pounds) |
|---|---|---|
| *Daily Life* | 0.01 | 0.20 |
| *Agriculture Today* | 0.03 | 0.50 |
| *Surf's Up* | 0.02 | 0.30 |

Each week the publisher has available 120 hours of production time and 3,000 pounds of paper. Total circulation for all three magazines must equal 5,000 issues per week if the company is to keep its advertisers. The selling price per issue is $2.25 for *Daily Life*, $4.00 for *Agriculture Today*, and $1.50 for *Surf's Up*. Based on past sales, the publisher knows that the maximum weekly demand for *Daily Life* is 3,000 issues; for *Agriculture Today* is 2,000 issues; and for *Surf's Up* is 6,000 issues. The production manager would like to know the number of issues of each magazine to produce weekly in order to maximize total sales revenue.

The following SETS section should be used in your model.

```
SETS:
RESOURCES/PRODUCTION, PAPER/:AMOUNTS;
MAGAZINES/DAILYLIFE, AGRICULTURETODAY,
    SURFSUP/:REVENUE, X;
COMBINE(MAGAZINES, RESOURCES):RESCONSUMED;
ENDSETS
```

**(a)** Formulate a LINGO modeling language model that could be used to solve this problem.

**(b)** Solve the model and indicate the optimal values of the objective function and each of the decision variables.

**4.** EASYLOAN Corporation makes five types of loans available to its retail customers. The annual returns (in percent) by type are shown below:

| Type of Loan | Annual Return (Percent) |
|---|---|
| Signature loans | 15 |
| Furniture loans | 12 |
| Automobile loans | 9 |
| Second home mortgage | 10 |
| First home mortgage | 7 |

Legal requirements and company policy place the following limits upon the amounts of the various types of loans: signature loans cannot exceed 10% of the total amount of loans. The amount of signature and furniture loans together cannot exceed 20% of the total amount of loans. First mortgages must be at least 40% of the total mortgages, and at least 20% of the total amount of loans. Second mortgages may not exceed 25% of the total amount of loans.

The company wishes to maximize the revenue from loan interest, subject to the above restrictions. The firm can lend a maximum of $1.5 million. Formulate a LINGO model that could be used to solve this problem. Note that the @FOR command is not needed for this problem. Express your constraints using an algebraic approach with the appropriate attribute names. You may wish to use the @SUM command to simplify the expression of some of the constraints.

# REFERENCES

DANTZIG, G. B., "The Diet Problem," *Interfaces*, Vol. 20, No. 4, pp. 43–47, 1990.

SCHRAGE, L., *Optimization Modeling with LINGO*, Chicago, LINDO Systems Inc., 2002.

WINSTON, W. L., *Introduction to Mathematical Programming: Applications and Algorithms*, Belmont, CA, Duxbury, 1995.

# Chapter 5

# Transportation and Distribution Planning Using the LINGO Modeling Language*

## INTRODUCTION

Mathematical programming has been successfully applied to a variety of important problems in *supply chain* management. These problems address the movement of products across the various links of the supply chain, including suppliers, manufacturers, and customers. In this chapter we will focus on an important subset of supply chain problems, namely transportation and distribution planning. Other supply chain applications such as production scheduling and planning will be discussed in the next chapter. The reason that we consider transportation and distribution planning in a separate chapter is that these problems belong to a special class of mathematical programming problems called *network flow* problems.[1] This common problem structure allows us to apply our building block approach using the LINGO modeling language (Schrage 2002) to successively construct increasingly complex mathematical programming models that address important decisions across the supply chain.

## THE TRANSPORTATION PROBLEM

### Problem Statement

The transportation problem has many practical applications since it addresses the movement of goods between two links in the supply chain, such as the manufacturer and the customer. Usually, the quantities of goods available at the supply and demand locations are known and limited. Often the objective is to minimize the total cost of shipping goods from the supply to the demand locations while meeting demand and not exceeding supply. We begin by formulating the fundamental version of this problem and then extend it through a series of examples.[2]

---

*Chapters 5 and 6 use the LINGO modeling language approach; Chapters 7 and 8 cover essentially the same material but use the standard algebraic LINGO approach. Therefore, skip Chapters 5 and 6 *or* 7 and 8 per instructions from your professor. See the Preface for further details.

[1]Certain classes of network models, such as shortest path, maximum flow, and minimum spanning tree are not covered here. The reader can see Winston (1995) and Hillier and Lieberman (2001) for further information.

[2]Camm et al. (1997) offers an application of transportation and location models that relates closely to material contained in this chapter. Koksalan and Sural (1999) offer another recent location modeling example.

Suppose that a manufacturer ships TV sets from three warehouses (origins) to four retail stores (destinations) each week. Warehouse supplies and demand (in cases) at the retail stores are as follows:

| Warehouse | Supply | Store | Demand |
|---|---|---|---|
| Cincinnati | 200 | New York | 100 |
| Philadelphia | 150 | Chicago | 200 |
| Atlanta | <u>300</u> | Denver | 125 |
| | 650 | Houston | <u>225</u> |
| | | | 650 |

The cost of shipping TV sets by rail from each warehouse to each store differs according to distance. The shipping cost per case of TV sets for each route is:

| | To store | | | |
|---|---|---|---|---|
| From warehouse | NY | CHI | DEN | HOU |
| CIN | $10 | 5 | 12 | 3 |
| PHI | 4 | 9 | 15 | 6 |
| ATL | 15 | 8 | 6 | 11 |

The objective is to determine the amount of TV sets that should be shipped from each warehouse to each store. The network for this problem is given as Figure 5.1. The circles are referred to as *nodes* and the directed line segments connecting the nodes are called *arcs*. Each warehouse and store is represented a node and each possible shipping route (origin–destination pair) is represented by an arc. The supplies and demands are placed next to their respective nodes. The amount of TV sets shipped from the warehouses to the stores represents the flow in the network.

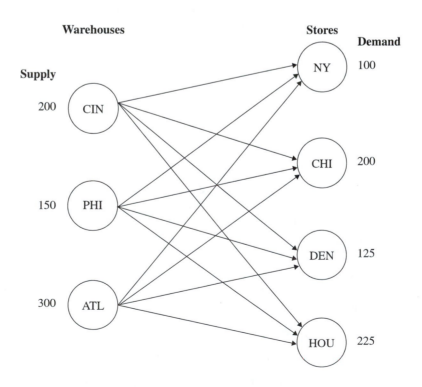

**Figure 5.1** Network Representation of the Transportation Example

## Problem Formulation and Solution

Using the information given about this problem and Figure 5.1, we are now ready to formulate the transportation problem using the LINGO modeling language. We apply the five steps that we used in Chapter 4 to model the diet problem.

### 1. Specify the SETS: Section of the Model, Which Includes Sets, Elements, and Attributes

Since we ship items from warehouses to stores, the two primitive sets for this transportation problem are WAREHOUSES and STORES. The elements of the WAREHOUSES set are CIN, PHI, and ATL and the elements of the STORES set are NY, CHI, DEN, and HOU. We need a derived set that consists of the ROUTES between each of the WAREHOUSES and each of the STORES.

We now need to identify the attributes of each set. We have a SUPPLY for each of the WAREHOUSES and a DEMAND for each of the STORES. We also know the COSTS along each of the ROUTES and we would like to determine the optimal values for the VOLUME to ship along each of the ROUTES. SUPPLY, DEMAND, COSTS, and VOLUME represent the attributes of their respective sets. The complete SETS section using the LINGO modeling language formulation for this problem is:

```
SETS:
  WAREHOUSES/CIN, PHI, ATL/: SUPPLY;
  STORES/NY, CHI, DEN, HOU/: DEMAND;
  ROUTES(WAREHOUSES,STORES): COSTS, VOLUME;
ENDSETS
```

### 2. Specify the DATA: Section of the Model by Assigning Values to Attributes

The data include SUPPLY for each of the WAREHOUSES, DEMAND for each of the STORES, and COSTS for each of the ROUTES. Note that the order of the primitive sets in the derived set ROUTES is WAREHOUSES first, then STORES. Therefore, the first row of COSTS data are those from CIN to the four STORES, followed by the second row of costs from PHI to the four stores, followed by the costs from ATL to the four stores. The complete DATA: section appears as:

```
DATA:
   SUPPLY = 200, 150, 300;
   DEMAND = 100, 200, 125, 225;
   COSTS = 10, 5, 12, 3,
      4, 9, 15, 6,
      15, 8, 6, 11;
ENDDATA
```

### 3. Identify the Decision Variables as Attributes Not Assigned Values in the DATA: Section

Remember that if an attribute is not assigned a value in the DATA: section, LINGO assumes that the attribute is a decision variable. In our example, the elements of VOLUME are not assigned values and so they are decision variables.

### 4. Formulate the Objective Function Using the @SUM Function

The objective for this problem is to MINimize the total cost of transportation, which is obtained by multiplying the COSTS by the VOLUME and SUMming over all ROUTES.

Since we are summing over a derived set, LINGO first sets I equal to CIN, and sets J equal to NY and computes COSTS(CIN,NY) * VOLUME(CIN,NY). LINGO continues with I still equal to CIN, but J cycles through CHI, DEN, and HOU. LINGO then sets I equal to PHI and iterates through the values of J and then does the same for I equal to ATL. The complete objective function for the LINGO modeling language formulation for this problem is:

```
MIN = @SUM(ROUTES(I,J): COSTS(I,J)*VOLUME(I,J));
```

### 5. Formulate the Constraints Using the @FOR Function

This problem is called a *balanced* transportation problem since total warehouse supply and total demand both equal 650. This implies that all demands will be met exactly and all supplies will be fully utilized Therefore, supply constraints are needed to ensure that we ship all of the TV sets that are available at each warehouse. Demand constraints are needed to guarantee that each store receives the exact amount of TV sets that they need. The supply constraints can be stated as follows. FOR each of the WAREHOUSES, we SUM the VOLUME shipped *to* all STORES. Each result must equal the SUPPLY of the corresponding warehouse. The supply constraints for the LINGO modeling language formulation for this problem are:

```
@FOR(WAREHOUSES(I):
  @SUM(STORES(J): VOLUME(I,J))=SUPPLY(I));
```

The demand constraints are expressed as follows. FOR each of the STORES, we SUM the VOLUME shipped *from* all WAREHOUSES. Each result must equal the DEMAND at the corresponding store. The demand constraints for the LINGO modeling language formulation for this problem are:

```
@FOR(STORES(J):
  @SUM(WAREHOUSES(I): VOLUME(I,J))=DEMAND(J));
```

We assume that this company cannot make partial shipments of a case of TV sets. This means that the decision variables must be integer valued. We could state that FOR each of the WAREHOUSES and FOR each of the STORES the VOLUME variables must be specified as General INteger (GIN). These constraints could be specified in LINGO as shown:

```
@FOR(WAREHOUSES(I):
  @FOR(STORES(J):
  @GIN(VOLUME(I,J))));
```

However, this statement is not necessary in our current situation since, if all supplies and demands are integer-valued, the values of our decision variables will also be integer-valued (Winston 1995). We could place an exclamation point in front of this @FOR statement as a reminder that this constraint would be used if some of the supplies and/or demands are not integer-valued.

The complete LINGO model, the algebraic formulation, and the solution for this problem appear in Figure 5.2. The LINGO modeling language formulation is in a file called TRANSA.LG4. As seen in the output that follows, the total shipping cost is $3500. The VOLUME values indicate that the optimal shipments are CIN – CHI: 25; CIN – HOU: 175; PHI – NY: 100; PHI – HOU: 50; ATL – CHI: 175; and ATL – DEN: 125.

Further inspection of the output provides additional insight into the nature of the solution. For example, since the reduced cost of VOLUME(CIN, NY) = 9, the cost of

```
:   1]MODEL:
    2]SETS:
    3]    WAREHOUSES/CIN, PHI, ATL/: SUPPLY;
    4]    STORES/NY, CHI, DEN, HOU/: DEMAND;
    5]    ROUTES(WAREHOUSES,STORES): COSTS, VOLUME;
    6]ENDSETS
    7]
    8]! THE OBJECTIVE;
    9]MIN = @SUM(ROUTES(I,J): COSTS(I,J)*VOLUME(I,J));
   10]
   11]! THE SUPPLY CONSTRAINTS;
   12] @FOR(WAREHOUSES(I):
   13]   @SUM(STORES(J): VOLUME(I,J))=SUPPLY(I));
   14]
   15]! THE DEMAND CONSTRAINTS;
   16] @FOR(STORES(J):
   17]   @SUM(WAREHOUSES(I): VOLUME(I,J))=DEMAND(J));
   18]
   19]! THE STATEMENT BELOW WOULD BE USED IF SOME OF THE SUPPLIES
   20]  AND/OR DEMANDS ARE NOT INTEGER-VALUED;
   21]!@FOR(WAREHOUSES(I):
   22] @FOR(STORES(J):
   23]   @GIN(VOLUME(I,J))));
   24]
   25]! HERE ARE THE DATA;
   26]  DATA:
   27]    SUPPLY = 200, 150, 300;
   28]    DEMAND = 100, 200, 125, 225;
   29]    COSTS = 10, 5, 12, 3,
   30]             4, 9, 15, 6,
   31]            15, 8, 6, 11;
   32]  ENDDATA
   33]END
   34]


MIN   10 VOLUME( CIN, NY) + 5 VOLUME( CIN, CHI) + 12 VOLUME( CIN, DEN)
    + 3  VOLUME( CIN, HOU) + 4 VOLUME( PHI, NY) + 9 VOLUME( PHI, CHI)
    + 15 VOLUME( PHI, DEN) + 6 VOLUME( PHI, HOU)
    + 15 VOLUME( ATL, NY) + 8 VOLUME( ATL, CHI) + 6 VOLUME( ATL, DEN)
    + 11 VOLUME( ATL, HOU)
SUBJECT TO
2] VOLUME( CIN, NY) + VOLUME( CIN, CHI) + VOLUME( CIN, DEN)
    + VOLUME( CIN, HOU) =   200
3] VOLUME( PHI, NY) + VOLUME( PHI, CHI) + VOLUME( PHI, DEN)
    + VOLUME( PHI, HOU) =   150
4] VOLUME( ATL, NY) + VOLUME( ATL, CHI) + VOLUME( ATL, DEN)
    + VOLUME( ATL, HOU) =   300
5] VOLUME( CIN, NY) + VOLUME( PHI, NY) + VOLUME( ATL, NY)
    =   100
6] VOLUME( CIN, CHI) + VOLUME( PHI, CHI) + VOLUME( ATL, CHI)
    =   200
7] VOLUME( CIN, DEN) + VOLUME( PHI, DEN) + VOLUME( ATL, DEN)
    =   125
8] VOLUME( CIN, HOU) + VOLUME( PHI, HOU) + VOLUME( ATL, HOU)
    =   225
END
```

**Figure 5.2** LINGO Output for the Balanced Transportation Problem

```
Global optimal solution found at step:              5
Objective value:                             3500.000

                        Variable            Value      Reduced Cost
                    SUPPLY( CIN)         200.0000         0.0000000
                    SUPPLY( PHI)         150.0000         0.0000000
                    SUPPLY( ATL)         300.0000         0.0000000
                     DEMAND( NY)         100.0000         0.0000000
                    DEMAND( CHI)         200.0000         0.0000000
                    DEMAND( DEN)         125.0000         0.0000000
                    DEMAND( HOU)         225.0000         0.0000000
                 COSTS( CIN, NY)         10.00000         0.0000000
                COSTS( CIN, CHI)         5.000000         0.0000000
                COSTS( CIN, DEN)         12.00000         0.0000000
                COSTS( CIN, HOU)         3.000000         0.0000000
                 COSTS( PHI, NY)         4.000000         0.0000000
                COSTS( PHI, CHI)         9.000000         0.0000000
                COSTS( PHI, DEN)         15.00000         0.0000000
                COSTS( PHI, HOU)         6.000000         0.0000000
                 COSTS( ATL, NY)         15.00000         0.0000000
                COSTS( ATL, CHI)         8.000000         0.0000000
                COSTS( ATL, DEN)         6.000000         0.0000000
                COSTS( ATL, HOU)         11.00000         0.0000000
                VOLUME( CIN, NY)         0.0000000        9.000000
               VOLUME( CIN, CHI)         25.00000         0.0000000
               VOLUME( CIN, DEN)         0.0000000        9.000000
               VOLUME( CIN, HOU)         175.0000         0.0000000
                VOLUME( PHI, NY)         100.0000         0.0000000
               VOLUME( PHI, CHI)         0.0000000        1.000000
               VOLUME( PHI, DEN)         0.0000000        9.000000
               VOLUME( PHI, HOU)         50.00000         0.0000000
                VOLUME( ATL, NY)         0.0000000        11.00000
               VOLUME( ATL, CHI)         175.0000         0.0000000
               VOLUME( ATL, DEN)         125.0000         0.0000000
               VOLUME( ATL, HOU)         0.0000000        5.000000

                             Row   Slack or Surplus     Dual Price
                               1          3500.000        1.000000
                               2         0.0000000        3.000000
                               3         0.0000000        0.0000000
                               4         0.0000000        0.0000000
                               5         0.0000000       -4.000000
                               6         0.0000000       -8.000000
                               7         0.0000000       -6.000000
                               8         0.0000000       -6.000000
```

**Figure 5.2** (*Continued*)

shipping a case of TV sets from CIN to NY would have to improve (decrease) by at least $9 before it would be optimal to ship over this route. However, since COSTS(CIN, NY) = 10, the reduced cost result is telling us that we would only use this shipping route if the cost is $1 per case or less.

Care must be taken in interpreting the impact of the dual variables for the constraints. Since this is a balanced transportation problem, changing one of the supply or demand values in isolation will lead to an infeasible solution. For example, if the supply at Cincinnati is increased from 200 to 201, the demand at one of the stores must also be increased by one unit to maintain feasibility.

## Using Spreadsheets for Data Input and Output

Spreadsheets such as Excel are useful tools for managing large amounts of input data and manipulating and presenting model results. In such situations it may be beneficial to link LINGO to Excel. This will enable LINGO to access all data that is entered in an Excel spreadsheet and then to display the LINGO output in the same spreadsheet. This interface is valuable since data are often stored in spreadsheets and can be easily updated in them.

We recommend using real-time Object Linking and Embedding (OLE) links to Excel. TRANSAOLE.LG4 is the LINGO file that uses OLE to link to an Excel file called TRANSAOLE.XLS. In TRANSAOLE.XLS, we must name all of the data, output, and attribute elements. For example, to name the data in cells C9:C12 as DEMAND in Excel, select *Insert, Name, Define*. Then enter the word DEMAND in the *Names in Workbook:* location. The @OLE statement in LINGO *always* refers to the linked Excel file.

For LINGO to read *all* input data from Excel, we place the following statement in the DATA section:

```
SUPPLY, DEMAND, COSTS = @OLE('TRANSAOLE.XLS');
```

Since the names SUPPLY, DEMAND, and COSTS are the same in LINGO and Excel, they do not have to be stated in the @OLE statement. TRANSAOLE.XLS contains the data that LINGO needs to define SUPPLY, DEMAND, and COSTS. Therefore, these data are being passed *from* Excel *to* LINGO.

To send the output to Excel, we add the following statement to the DATA section:

```
@OLE('TRANSAOLE.XLS') = VOLUME;
```

The values for VOLUME are being exported *from* LINGO *to* Excel. This is the reason that the @OLE statement is on the left-hand side rather the right-hand side (as was the case with the input data). In Excel we defined the locations for VOLUME as cells C20:F22. The total optimal transportation cost is computed in cell B25 in Excel using the following statement:

```
=SUMPRODUCT(VOLUME,COSTS).
```

We can also pass the name of the WAREHOUSES and STORES from Excel to LINGO with the following statements in the SETS section:

```
WAREHOUSES/@OLE('TRANSAOLE.XLS')/: SUPPLY;
STORES/@OLE('TRANSAOLE.XLS')/: DEMAND;
```

In Excel we must define the cell locations for the names of the WAREHOUSES (B4:B6) and STORES (B9:B12). Since the folder containing TRANSAOLE.XLS is not specified, LINGO assumes that this file is in the same folder as TRANSAOLE.LG4. To run this problem we open the Excel file called TRANSAOLE.XLS and the LINGO file called TRANSAOLE.LG4. The LINGO file will read the SUPPLY, DEMAND, and COST data from the Excel spreadsheet. After solving the model in LINGO, the optimal shipment values will be sent from LINGO to Excel, which will then compute the total cost. A screen shot of TRANSAOLE.XLS after LINGO has solved this model is shown as Figure 5.3.

In addition, the @OLE function can be used to pass sensitivity analysis results from LINGO to Excel. These include reduced costs, objective coefficient ranges, slack, dual prices and range analysis for the constraints. The supporting LINGO and Excel files for passing model solution and all sensitivity results from LINGO to Excel are called TRANSAOLE2.LG4 and TRANSAOLE2.XLS, respectively.

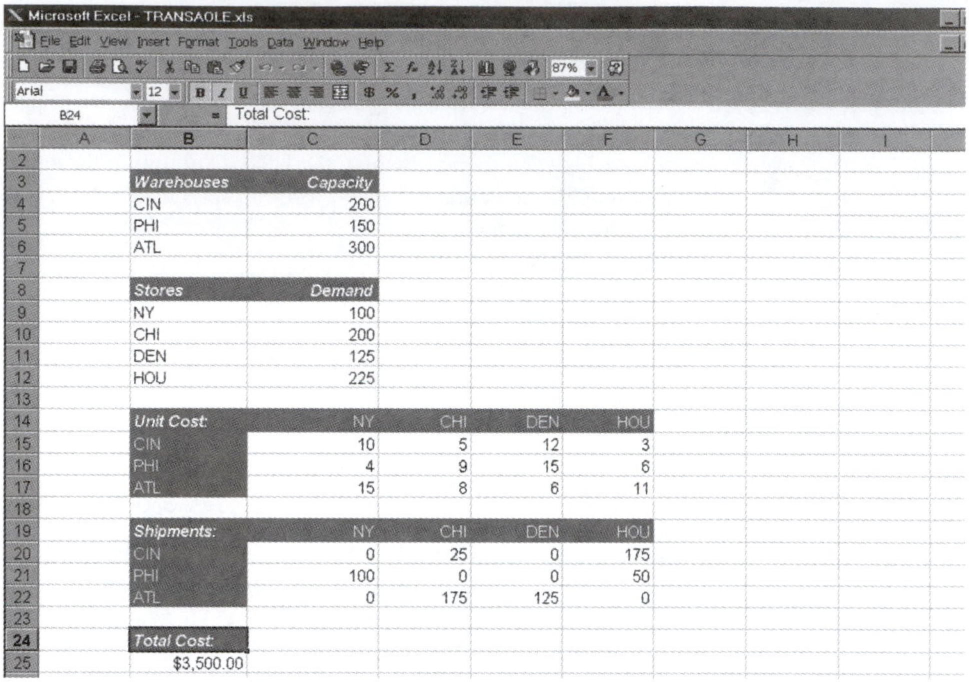

**Figure 5.3** Screen Shot of Excel Spreadsheet Showing Data Input and Model Output

Several modifications of TRANSAOLE.LG4 are required to transform it into TRANSAOLE2.LG4. First, we eliminate the @GIN statement, since range analysis cannot be performed if the decision variables are integer. Second, we add names for the supply and demand constraints by placing constraint names in square brackets after the set name in the @FOR constraints. For example, to name the supply constraints we use the following LINGO command:

```
! THE SUPPLY CONSTRAINTS;
  @FOR(WAREHOUSES(I): [SUPPLYCONSTRAINTS]
  @SUM(STORES(J): VOLUME(I,J))=SUPPLY(I));
```

Since the placeholder I takes on the values CIN, PHI, and ATL, the three supply constraints are labeled SUPPLYCONSTRAINTS(CIN), SUPPLYCONSTRAINTS(PHI), and SUPPLYCONSTRAINTS(ATL), respectively. Third, in the DATA: section we must pass all of the sensitivity results *from* LINGO *to* Excel. For example, the slack values in LINGO for constraints are called the constraint names, such as SUPPLYCONSTRAINTS, and in TRANSAOLE2.XLS the slack values are named SLACKSUPPLY. All of the necessary changes in the DATA: section are given:

```
DATA:
  SUPPLY, DEMAND, COSTS = @OLE('TRANSAOLE2.XLS');
  @OLE( 'TRANSAOLE2.XLS') = VOLUME;
  @OLE( 'TRANSAOLE2.XLS', REDUCEDCOSTS) = @DUAL(VOLUME);
  @OLE( 'TRANSAOLE2.XLS', OBJUP) = @RANGEU(VOLUME);
  @OLE( 'TRANSAOLE2.XLS', OBJDN) = @RANGED(VOLUME);
  @OLE( 'TRANSAOLE2.XLS', DUALDEMAND)= @DUAL(DEMANDCONSTRAINTS);
  @OLE( 'TRANSAOLE2.XLS', DUALSUPPLY)= @DUAL(SUPPLYCONSTRAINTS);
  @OLE( 'TRANSAOLE2.XLS', SLACKDEMAND) = DEMANDCONSTRAINTS;
  @OLE( 'TRANSAOLE2.XLS', SLACKSUPPLY) = SUPPLYCONSTRAINTS;
```

```
        @OLE( 'TRANSAOLE2.XLS', DEMANDUP) = @RANGEU(DEMANDCONSTRAINTS);
        @OLE( 'TRANSAOLE2.XLS', DEMANDDN) = @RANGED(DEMANDCONSTRAINTS);
        @OLE( 'TRANSAOLE2.XLS', SUPPLYUP) = @RANGEU(SUPPLYCONSTRAINTS);
        @OLE( 'TRANSAOLE2.XLS', SUPPLYDN) = @RANGED(SUPPLYCONSTRAINTS);
    ENDDATA
```

A screen shot of TRANSAOL2.XLS containing the sensitivity analysis results after running TRANSAOLE2.LG4 is shown as Figure 5.4. The value "1E+20" in Excel is listed as "infinity" in the LINGO output. Note that the model solution results are the same as those shown in Figure 5.2.

## DIRECT TRANSPORTATION EXTENSIONS

The extensions discussed in this section all maintain the basic structure of the transportation problem as presented in the previous section. The extensions addressed include unbalanced relationships between supply and demand, route restrictions, choice of supply locations, and selection of transportation modes.

| | A | B | C | D | E | F | G |
|---|---|---|---|---|---|---|---|
| 28 | | | | | | | |
| 29 | | Reduced Costs | NY | CHI | DEN | HOU | |
| 30 | | CIN | 9 | 0 | 9 | 0 | |
| 31 | | PHI | 0 | 1 | 9 | 0 | |
| 32 | | ATL | 11 | 0 | 0 | 5 | |
| 33 | | | | | | | |
| 34 | | Objective Function Coefficient Ranges | | | | | |
| 35 | | Upper Limit: | NY | CHI | DEN | HOU | |
| 36 | | CIN | 1E+20 | 1 | 1E+20 | 5 | |
| 37 | | PHI | 9 | 1E+20 | 1E+20 | 1 | |
| 38 | | ATL | 1E+20 | 5 | 9 | 1E+20 | |
| 39 | | | | | | | |
| 40 | | Objective Function Coefficient Ranges | | | | | |
| 41 | | Lower Limit: | NY | CHI | DEN | HOU | |
| 42 | | CIN | 9 | 5 | 9 | 1 | |
| 43 | | PHI | 1E+20 | 1 | 9 | 9 | |
| 44 | | ATL | 11 | 9 | 1E+20 | 5 | |
| 45 | | | | | | | |
| 46 | | Capacity Constraints | | | | | |
| 47 | | | Slack | Dual Price | Upper Limit | Lower Limit | |
| 48 | | CIN | 0 | 3 | 0 | 0 | |
| 49 | | PHI | 0 | 0 | 0 | 0 | |
| 50 | | ATL | 0 | 0 | 0 | 0 | |
| 51 | | | | | | | |
| 52 | | Demand Constraints | | | | | |
| 53 | | | Slack | Dual Price | Upper Limit | Lower Limit | |
| 54 | | NY | 0 | -4 | 0 | 0 | |
| 55 | | CHI | 0 | -8 | 0 | 0 | |
| 56 | | DEN | 0 | -6 | 0 | 0 | |
| 57 | | HOU | 0 | -6 | 0 | 0 | |
| 58 | | | | | | | |

**Figure 5.4** Screen Shot of Excel Spreadsheet Showing Sensitivity Analysis Results

## Unbalanced Problem: Total Supply Greater Than Total Demand

Suppose that PHI actually has 175 TV sets available to ship. In this case total supply across the three warehouses is now 675 TV sets but total demand at the stores is still 650 TV sets. This situation is referred to as an *unbalanced transportation problem*. Since we have 675 TV sets available to ship and we only need 650 TV sets, all of our demand will be satisfied as before. However, across the three warehouses there will be an unused supply of 25 TV sets. The only required modification of our original transportation model (TRANSA.LG4) is to change the supply constraints from equality to "less than or equal to." The LINGO supply constraints become:

```
@FOR(WAREHOUSES(I):
  @SUM(STORES(J): VOLUME(I,J))<=SUPPLY(I));
```

The LINGO modeling language formulation is in a file called TRANSB.LG4. After solving the model, we see that the total shipping cost is still $3500. The VOLUME values indicate that the optimal shipments are CIN – CHI: 25; CIN – HOU: 175; PHI – NY: 100; PHI – HOU: 50; ATL – CHI: 175; and ATL – DEN: 125. These results indicate that 150 units are shipped from PHI, indicating a slack of 25 TV sets at this warehouse. The same result can be found from the slack value of 25 for the PHI supply constraint.

## Unbalanced Problem: Total Demand Greater Than Total Supply

Again referring to the original transportation problem (TRANSA.LG4), suppose that DEN needs 150 TV sets. Now total supply is 650 TV sets but total demand has increased to 675 TV sets. Since we have 650 TV sets available to ship and we need 675 TV sets, all of our supply will be exhausted, however, 25 units of demand will not be satisfied. Similar to the previous unbalanced problem, we change the relational sign in the demand constraints from "equality" to "less than or equal to." The LINGO demand constraints become:

```
@FOR(STORES(J):
  @SUM(WAREHOUSES(I): VOLUME(I,J))<=DEMAND(J));
```

The LINGO modeling language formulation is in a file called TRANSC.LG4. After solving the model, we see that the total shipping cost has decreased from $3500 to $3450. The VOLUME values indicate that the optimal shipments still include CIN – CHI: 25; CIN – HOU: 175; PHI – NY: 100; and PHI – HOU: 50. However, ATL – CHI is now 150 (versus 175) and ATL – DEN is 150 (versus 125). These results show that 25 units of CHI's demand are unmet. The same result can be found from the slack value in CHI's demand constraint. The cost savings occur because the 25 cases were previously shipped from ATL to CHI at a cost of $8 per case, while shipping them to DEN costs $6 per case, for a savings of $50.

## A Restricted Route

Once again, referring to our original formulation (TRANSA.LG4), suppose there is a strike by the shipping company such that the ROUTE from ATL to CHI cannot be used. The original model can be modified to address this situation by simply adding a constraint that guarantees that zero units will be shipped from ATL to CHI. The following constraint can be added anywhere between the SETS: and DATA: sections:

```
VOLUME(ATL,CHI)=0;
```

The LINGO modeling language formulation is in a file called TRANSD.LG4. After solving the model, we see that the total shipping cost has increased to $4375. The significant change in total costs occurred since the ATL – CHI route originally carried 175 TV sets, and now more expensive alternatives must be used. The VOLUME values indicate that the optimal shipments are CIN – CHI: 200; PHI – NY: 100; PHI – HOU: 50; ATL – DEN: 125; and ATL – HOU: 175. We note that an alternate solution approach is to change the cost value from ATL to CHI in the DATA: section to a very large number, say 1000, so that this route will never be used.

## The Warehouse Location Problem

Up to this point we have considered transportation problems that limit the scope of the model to decisions about the volume needed to ship from each warehouse to each store. We would now like to build a model that also considers *where* to locate the warehouses. Interestingly, we can build on the original transportation model (TRANSA.LG4) to accomplish this goal.

For example, suppose that no WAREHOUSES are currently OPEN, but we are considering locating WAREHOUSES in CIN, PHI, and ATL. The fixed cost of constructing each warehouse and the capacities of the WAREHOUSES are shown in the list. Note that total system capacity is greater than total system demand. All other information is the same as in the original transportation problem.

| Warehouses | Fixed Cost | Capacity |
|---|---|---|
| CIN | 125,000 | 300 |
| PHI | 185,000 | 525 |
| ATL | 100,000 | 325 |

Consider the changes that must be made in each component on the LINGO model. In order to model the decision about whether or not to open each warehouse, we define a new attribute for the WAREHOUSES set called OPEN. For each warehouse, OPEN is a binary decision variable that equals 1 if a warehouse is OPEN and 0 if it is not open. FIXEDCOST is also an attribute of WAREHOUSES and represents the fixed cost if a location is OPEN.

```
WAREHOUSES/CIN, PHI, ATL/: CAPACITY, FIXEDCOST, OPEN;
```

The following changes must be made to the objective function and the constraints to complete our model. First, the cost of opening warehouses is obtained by multiplying FIXEDCOST by OPEN and SUMming over all WAREHOUSES. This warehouse cost expression is now added to the shipping cost expression in the objective function.

```
MIN = @SUM(ROUTES(I,J): COSTS(I,J)*VOLUME(I,J))
+@SUM(WAREHOUSES(I): FIXEDCOST(I)*OPEN(I));
```

Second, the existing supply constraints cannot be used since TV sets cannot be shipped from a warehouse if it is not OPEN. Stated another way, we must ensure that nothing is shipped from a warehouse that is not opened. Since the CAPACITY is available only if the warehouse is OPEN, we multiply CAPACITY by OPEN. Therefore, if OPEN is 0, the capacity constraint becomes less than or equal to 0, indicating that nothing will be shipped from that warehouse. If OPEN is 1, the capacity constraint becomes less than or equal to that warehouses capacity and thus becomes equivalent to a supply constraint in TRANSA.LG4.

```
!THE CAPACITY CONSTRAINTS;
 @FOR(WAREHOUSES(I):
   @SUM(STORES(J): VOLUME(I,J))<=CAPACITY(I)*OPEN(I));
```

The third change is to make the OPEN variables binary integers using the @BIN command. This will guarantee that the OPEN variables will equal either 0 or 1.

```
@FOR(WAREHOUSES(I):
 @BIN(OPEN(I)));
```

The DATA: section of the model also needs to be changed since we must add the FIXEDCOST data and the revised CAPACITY data (the latter only to allow alternate warehouse location possibilities).

```
CAPACITY = 300, 525, 325;
FIXEDCOST = 125000, 185000, 100000;
```

The complete LINGO model, the algebraic formulation, and the solution for this problem appear as Figure 5.5. The LINGO modeling language formulation is in a file called TRANSE.LG4. As seen in the output below, the total fixed and shipping costs are $289,100. The OPEN values indicate that warehouses in PHI and ATL are opened, while the VOLUME values indicate that the optimal shipments are PHI – NY: 100; PHI – HOU: 225; ATL – CHI: 200; and ATL – DEN: 125. The slack capacity for the CIN constraint (row 2) is 0, since both the amount shipped out and the available capacity are both 0. The slack value for PHI is 200 (row 3), while the slack for ATL is 0 (row 4) since all of its capacity is used.

## Multimodal Transportation Problem

Again consider TRANSA.LG4, where TV sets are shipped from WAREHOUSES to STORES. We have seen that LINGO uses two-dimensional derived sets (ROUTES) to model shipments. Now assume that the MODE of shipment can be either RAIL or AIR. In a direct generalization, three-dimensional derived sets will be used to incorporate MODE into the model formulation.

We begin by including a set called MODES in the SETS: section of the model. Its attributes are the modes of transportation themselves, namely, RAIL or AIR in our example. We will use K as the placeholder for MODES. Since we now ship TV SETS from WAREHOUSES to STORES using a specific MODE of transportation, we alter the definition of the derived set ROUTES from ROUTES(WAREHOUSES,STORES) to ROUTES(WAREHOUSES,STORES,MODES). An additional (and natural) modification is that any reference to either ROUTES or VOLUME must be changed from (I,J) to (I,J,K). This will guarantee that we loop over all WAREHOUSES (I), all STORES (J), and all MODES (K).

The last change occurs in the DATA: section. In the previous transportation models we had the following cost data.

```
COSTS = 10,  5, 12,  3,
         4,  9, 15,  6,
        15,  8,  6, 11;
```

```
:    1]MODEL:
     2]SETS:
     3]    WAREHOUSES/CIN, PHI, ATL/: CAPACITY, FIXEDCOST, OPEN;
     4]    STORES/NY, CHI, DEN, HOU/: DEMAND;
     5]    ROUTES(WAREHOUSES,STORES): COSTS, VOLUME;
     6]ENDSETS
     7]
     8]! THE OBJECTIVE;
     9]MIN = @SUM(ROUTES(I,J): COSTS(I,J)*VOLUME(I,J))
    10]+@SUM(WAREHOUSES(I): FIXEDCOST(I)*OPEN(I));
    11]
    12]!THE CAPACITY CONSTRAINTS;
    13] @FOR(WAREHOUSES(I):
    14]   @SUM(STORES(J): VOLUME(I,J))<=CAPACITY(I)*OPEN(I));
    15]
    16]! THE DEMAND CONSTRAINTS;
    17] @FOR(STORES(J):
    18]   @SUM(WAREHOUSES(I): VOLUME(I,J))=DEMAND(J));
    19]
    20] @FOR(WAREHOUSES(I):
    21]   @BIN(OPEN(I)));
    22]
    23]! THE STATEMENT BELOW WOULD BE USED IF SOME OF THE CAPACITIES
    24] AND/OR DEMANDS ARE NOT INTEGER-VALUED;
    25]!@FOR(WAREHOUSES(I):
    26] @FOR(STORES(J):
    27] @GIN(VOLUME(I,J))));
    28]
    29]! HERE ARE THE DATA;
    30]  DATA:
    31]    CAPACITY = 300, 525, 325;
    32]    DEMAND = 100, 200, 125, 225;
    33]    COSTS = 10, 5, 12, 3,
    34]            4, 9, 15, 6,
    35]            15, 8, 6, 11;
    36]    FIXEDCOST = 125000, 185000, 100000;
    37]  ENDDATA
    38]END
    39]
```

```
MIN 125000 OPEN( CIN) + 185000 OPEN( PHI) + 100000 OPEN( ATL)
    + 10 VOLUME( CIN, NY) + 5 VOLUME( CIN, CHI)
    + 12 VOLUME( CIN, DEN) + 3 VOLUME( CIN, HOU) + 4 VOLUME( PHI, NY)
    + 9  VOLUME( PHI, CHI) + 15 VOLUME( PHI, DEN)
    + 6  VOLUME( PHI, HOU) + 15 VOLUME( ATL, NY) + 8 VOLUME( ATL, CHI)
    + 6  VOLUME( ATL, DEN) + 11 VOLUME( ATL, HOU)
 SUBJECT TO
 2]- 300 OPEN( CIN) + VOLUME( CIN, NY) + VOLUME( CIN, CHI)
       + VOLUME( CIN, DEN) + VOLUME( CIN, HOU)<=0
 3]- 525 OPEN( PHI) + VOLUME( PHI, NY) + VOLUME( PHI, CHI)
       + VOLUME( PHI, DEN) + VOLUME( PHI, HOU)<=0
 4]- 325 OPEN( ATL) + VOLUME( ATL, NY) + VOLUME( ATL, CHI)
       + VOLUME( ATL, DEN) + VOLUME( ATL, HOU)<=0
 5] VOLUME( CIN, NY) + VOLUME( PHI, NY) + VOLUME( ATL, NY)
       =   100
 6] VOLUME( CIN, CHI) + VOLUME( PHI, CHI) + VOLUME( ATL, CHI)
       =   200
```

**Figure 5.5** LINGO Output for the Warehouse Location Problem

```
7] VOLUME( CIN, DEN) + VOLUME( PHI, DEN) + VOLUME( ATL, DEN)
     = 125
8] VOLUME( CIN, HOU) + VOLUME( PHI, HOU) + VOLUME( ATL, HOU)
     = 225
END
INTE OPEN( CIN)
INTE OPEN( PHI)
INTE OPEN( ATL)
```

Global optimal solution found at step:                           28
Objective value:                                          289100.0
Branch count:                                                    3

| Variable | Value | Reduced Cost |
|---|---|---|
| CAPACITY( CIN) | 300.0000 | 0.0000000 |
| CAPACITY( PHI) | 525.0000 | 0.0000000 |
| CAPACITY( ATL) | 325.0000 | 0.0000000 |
| FIXEDCOST( CIN) | 125000.0 | 0.0000000 |
| FIXEDCOST( PHI) | 185000.0 | 0.0000000 |
| FIXEDCOST( ATL) | 100000.0 | 0.0000000 |
| OPEN( CIN) | 0.0000000 | 124100.0 |
| OPEN( PHI) | 1.000000 | 185000.0 |
| OPEN( ATL) | 1.000000 | 100000.0 |
| DEMAND( NY) | 100.0000 | 0.0000000 |
| DEMAND( CHI) | 200.0000 | 0.0000000 |
| DEMAND( DEN) | 125.0000 | 0.0000000 |
| DEMAND( HOU) | 225.0000 | 0.0000000 |
| COSTS( CIN, NY) | 10.00000 | 0.0000000 |
| COSTS( CIN, CHI) | 5.000000 | 0.0000000 |
| COSTS( CIN, DEN) | 12.00000 | 0.0000000 |
| COSTS( CIN, HOU) | 3.000000 | 0.0000000 |
| COSTS( PHI, NY) | 4.000000 | 0.0000000 |
| COSTS( PHI, CHI) | 9.000000 | 0.0000000 |
| COSTS( PHI, DEN) | 15.00000 | 0.0000000 |
| COSTS( PHI, HOU) | 6.000000 | 0.0000000 |
| COSTS( ATL, NY) | 15.00000 | 0.0000000 |
| COSTS( ATL, CHI) | 8.000000 | 0.0000000 |
| COSTS( ATL, DEN) | 6.000000 | 0.0000000 |
| COSTS( ATL, HOU) | 11.00000 | 0.0000000 |
| VOLUME( CIN, NY) | 0.0000000 | 9.000000 |
| VOLUME( CIN, CHI) | 0.0000000 | 0.0000000 |
| VOLUME( CIN, DEN) | 0.0000000 | 9.000000 |
| VOLUME( CIN, HOU) | 0.0000000 | 0.0000000 |
| VOLUME( PHI, NY) | 100.0000 | 0.0000000 |
| VOLUME( PHI, CHI) | 0.0000000 | 1.000000 |
| VOLUME( PHI, DEN) | 0.0000000 | 9.000000 |
| VOLUME( PHI, HOU) | 225.0000 | 0.0000000 |
| VOLUME( ATL, NY) | 0.0000000 | 11.00000 |
| VOLUME( ATL, CHI) | 200.0000 | 0.0000000 |
| VOLUME( ATL, DEN) | 125.0000 | 0.0000000 |
| VOLUME( ATL, HOU) | 0.0000000 | 5.000000 |

| Row | Slack or Surplus | Dual Price |
|---|---|---|
| 1 | 289100.0 | 1.000000 |
| 2 | 0.0000000 | 3.000000 |
| 3 | 200.0000 | 0.0000000 |
| 4 | 0.0000000 | 0.0000000 |
| 5 | 0.0000000 | -4.000000 |
| 6 | 0.0000000 | -8.000000 |
| 7 | 0.0000000 | -6.000000 |
| 8 | 0.0000000 | -6.000000 |

**Figure 5.5** (*Continued*)

This revised model requires the following cost data:

```
COSTS =  10,8,  5,4,  12,14,  3,4,
          4,6,  9,8,  15,12,  6,5,
         15,17,  8,9,   6,9,  11,8;
```

An inspection of the cost data shows that LINGO requires that the data be entered in pairs. That is, the first two numbers, 10 and 8, represent the per unit shipping cost from CIN to NY using RAIL and AIR, respectively. All other combinations of ROUTES and MODES are handled in the same fashion. The relative simplicity of making this rather significant modification to our base transportation model illustrates the power of the LINGO modeling language.

The complete LINGO model, the algebraic formulation, and the solution for this problem appear as Figure 5.6. The LINGO modeling language formulation is in a file called TRANSF.LG4. As seen in the output below, the total shipping cost is $3425. The VOLUME values indicate that the optimal shipments are CIN – CHI – AIR: 25; CIN – HOU – RAIL: 175; PHI – NY – RAIL: 100; PHI – HOU – AIR: 50; ATL – CHI – RAIL: – 175; and ATL – DEN – RAIL: 125. The reduced costs of the VOLUME variables indicate how much the shipment cost over a given route for a specific mode would have to decrease before it would be economic to use that mode-route combination.

## ASSIGNMENT-BASED TRANSPORTATION EXTENSIONS

The transportation extensions discussed in this section are all based on the assignment problem, which is itself a special class of the transportation problem. We begin with the assignment problem, and then model the traveling salesman and vehicle routing problems.

### Assignment Problem

The assignment problem considers how to assign people to jobs to achieve the lowest time (or cost) solution. For example, we may have five jobs (1 through 5) that need to be completed and five people (Adam, Barb, Chris, Denise, and Ed) who can do the work. We would like to find the optimal set of assignments so that each person does one job and each job is done by one person. Because of varying skill levels, each person requires a different amount of time (or cost) to complete each job. Therefore, the objective is to minimize the total time required to complete all five jobs. The amount of time required for each person to perform each job is given as:

| People | Jobs | | | | |
|--------|----|----|----|----|----|
|        | 1  | 2  | 3  | 4  | 5  |
| ADAM   | 35 | 25 | 22 | 43 | 26 |
| BARB   | 14 | 39 | 25 | 46 | 25 |
| CHRIS  | 15 | 48 | 56 | 21 | 48 |
| DENISE | 32 | 29 | 36 | 30 | 34 |
| ED     | 54 | 46 | 28 | 11 | 57 |

Although the shipping of products from warehouses to stores might seem to be quite different than assigning people to jobs, both problems structurally have much in common. We approach the formulation of the assignment problem by looking at the relationship between these two problems. Looking at the SETS: section, we substitute PEOPLE for WAREHOUSES, JOBS for STORES, TIMES for COSTS, and COMBO for ROUTES. As shown in ASSIGN.LG4 the LINGO modeling language allows numbers to represent the elements of a set rather than specifying names. For example, JOBS/1.. 5/ tells LINGO

```
:    1]MODEL:
     2]SETS:
     3]    WAREHOUSES/CIN, PHI, ATL/: CAPACITY;
     4]    STORES/NY, CHI, DEN, HOU/: DEMAND;
     5]    MODES/RAIL,AIR/;
     6]    ROUTES(WAREHOUSES,STORES,MODES): COSTS, VOLUME;
     7]ENDSETS
     8]
     9]! THE OBJECTIVE;
    10]MIN = @SUM(ROUTES(I,J,K): COSTS(I,J,K)*VOLUME(I,J,K));
    11]
    12]!THE CAPACITY CONSTRAINTS;
    13] @FOR(WAREHOUSES(I):
    14]   @SUM(ROUTES(I,J,K): VOLUME(I,J,K))=CAPACITY(I));
    15]
    16]! THE DEMAND CONSTRAINTS;
    17] @FOR(STORES(J):
    18]   @SUM(ROUTES(I,J,K): VOLUME(I,J,K))=DEMAND(J));
    19]
    20]! THE STATEMENT BELOW WOULD BE USED IF SOME OF THE CAPACITIES
    21]   AND/OR DEMANDS ARE NOT INTEGER-VALUED;
    22]!@FOR(WAREHOUSES(I):
    23] @FOR(STORES(J):
    24]   @FOR(MODES(K):
    25]    @GIN(VOLUME(I,J,K)))));
    26]
    27]! HERE ARE THE DATA;
    28]! The COSTs data are given as a 3X4 paired matrix,
    29]  where the rows are the WAREHOUSES, The columns are
    30]  the STORES, the first number in each pair is the
    31]  RAIL cost, and the second number is the AIR cost;
    32]  DATA:
    33]     CAPACITY = 200, 150, 300;
    34]     DEMAND = 100, 200, 125, 225;
    35]     COSTS = 10,8,    5,4,   12,14,    3,4,
    36]              4,6,    9,8,   15,12,    6,5,
    37]             15,17,   8,9,    6,9,    11,8;
    38]  ENDDATA
    39]END
    40]
```

```
MIN 10 VOLUME( CIN, NY, RAIL) + 8 VOLUME( CIN, NY, AIR)
    + 5 VOLUME( CIN, CHI, RAIL) + 4 VOLUME( CIN, CHI, AIR)
    + 12 VOLUME( CIN, DEN, RAIL) + 14 VOLUME( CIN, DEN, AIR)
    + 3 VOLUME( CIN, HOU, RAIL) + 4 VOLUME( CIN, HOU, AIR)
    + 4 VOLUME( PHI, NY, RAIL) + 6 VOLUME( PHI, NY, AIR)
    + 9 VOLUME( PHI, CHI, RAIL) + 8 VOLUME( PHI, CHI, AIR)
    + 15 VOLUME( PHI, DEN, RAIL) + 12 VOLUME( PHI, DEN, AIR)
    + 6 VOLUME( PHI, HOU, RAIL) + 5 VOLUME( PHI, HOU, AIR)
    + 15 VOLUME( ATL, NY, RAIL) + 17 VOLUME( ATL, NY, AIR)
    + 8 VOLUME( ATL, CHI, RAIL) + 9 VOLUME( ATL, CHI, AIR)
    + 6 VOLUME( ATL, DEN, RAIL) + 9 VOLUME( ATL, DEN, AIR)
    + 11 VOLUME( ATL, HOU, RAIL) + 8 VOLUME( ATL, HOU, AIR)
```

**Figure 5.6** LINGO Output for the Multimodal Transportation Problem

```
  SUBJECT TO
 2] VOLUME( CIN, NY, RAIL) + VOLUME( CIN, NY, AIR)
     + VOLUME( CIN, CHI, RAIL) + VOLUME( CIN, CHI, AIR)
     + VOLUME( CIN, DEN, RAIL) + VOLUME( CIN, DEN, AIR)
     + VOLUME( CIN, HOU, RAIL) + VOLUME( CIN, HOU, AIR) =   200
 3] VOLUME( PHI, NY, RAIL) + VOLUME( PHI, NY, AIR)
     + VOLUME( PHI, CHI, RAIL) + VOLUME( PHI, CHI, AIR)
     + VOLUME( PHI, DEN, RAIL) + VOLUME( PHI, DEN, AIR)
     + VOLUME( PHI, HOU, RAIL) + VOLUME( PHI, HOU, AIR) =   150
 4] VOLUME( ATL, NY, RAIL) + VOLUME( ATL, NY, AIR)
     + VOLUME( ATL, CHI, RAIL) + VOLUME( ATL, CHI, AIR)
     + VOLUME( ATL, DEN, RAIL) + VOLUME( ATL, DEN, AIR)
     + VOLUME( ATL, HOU, RAIL) + VOLUME( ATL, HOU, AIR) =   300
 5] VOLUME( CIN, NY, RAIL) + VOLUME( CIN, NY, AIR)
     + VOLUME( PHI, NY, RAIL) + VOLUME( PHI, NY, AIR)
     + VOLUME( ATL, NY, RAIL) + VOLUME( ATL, NY, AIR) =   100
 6] VOLUME( CIN, CHI, RAIL) + VOLUME( CIN, CHI, AIR)
     + VOLUME( PHI, CHI, RAIL) + VOLUME( PHI, CHI, AIR)
     + VOLUME( ATL, CHI, RAIL) + VOLUME( ATL, CHI, AIR) =   200
 7] VOLUME( CIN, DEN, RAIL) + VOLUME( CIN, DEN, AIR)
     + VOLUME( PHI, DEN, RAIL) + VOLUME( PHI, DEN, AIR)
     + VOLUME( ATL, DEN, RAIL) + VOLUME( ATL, DEN, AIR) =   125
 8] VOLUME( CIN, HOU, RAIL) + VOLUME( CIN, HOU, AIR)
     + VOLUME( PHI, HOU, RAIL) + VOLUME( PHI, HOU, AIR)
     + VOLUME( ATL, HOU, RAIL) + VOLUME( ATL, HOU, AIR) =   225
  END

Global optimal solution found at step:              9
Objective value:                             3425.000
```

| Variable | Value | Reduced Cost |
|---|---|---|
| CAPACITY( CIN) | 200.0000 | 0.0000000 |
| CAPACITY( PHI) | 150.0000 | 0.0000000 |
| CAPACITY( ATL) | 300.0000 | 0.0000000 |
| DEMAND( NY) | 100.0000 | 0.0000000 |
| DEMAND( CHI) | 200.0000 | 0.0000000 |
| DEMAND( DEN) | 125.0000 | 0.0000000 |
| DEMAND( HOU) | 225.0000 | 0.0000000 |
| COSTS( CIN, NY, RAIL) | 10.00000 | 0.0000000 |
| COSTS( CIN, NY, AIR) | 8.000000 | 0.0000000 |
| COSTS( CIN, CHI, RAIL) | 5.000000 | 0.0000000 |
| COSTS( CIN, CHI, AIR) | 4.000000 | 0.0000000 |
| COSTS( CIN, DEN, RAIL) | 12.00000 | 0.0000000 |
| COSTS( CIN, DEN, AIR) | 14.00000 | 0.0000000 |
| COSTS( CIN, HOU, RAIL) | 3.000000 | 0.0000000 |
| COSTS( CIN, HOU, AIR) | 4.000000 | 0.0000000 |
| COSTS( PHI, NY, RAIL) | 4.000000 | 0.0000000 |
| COSTS( PHI, NY, AIR) | 6.000000 | 0.0000000 |
| COSTS( PHI, CHI, RAIL) | 9.000000 | 0.0000000 |
| COSTS( PHI, CHI, AIR) | 8.000000 | 0.0000000 |
| COSTS( PHI, DEN, RAIL) | 15.00000 | 0.0000000 |
| COSTS( PHI, DEN, AIR) | 12.00000 | 0.0000000 |
| COSTS( PHI, HOU, RAIL) | 6.000000 | 0.0000000 |
| COSTS( PHI, HOU, AIR) | 5.000000 | 0.0000000 |
| COSTS( ATL, NY, RAIL) | 15.00000 | 0.0000000 |

**Figure 5.6** (*Continued*)

| | | |
|---|---|---|
| COSTS( ATL, NY, AIR) | 17.00000 | 0.0000000 |
| COSTS( ATL, CHI, RAIL) | 8.000000 | 0.0000000 |
| COSTS( ATL, CHI, AIR) | 9.000000 | 0.0000000 |
| COSTS( ATL, DEN, RAIL) | 6.000000 | 0.0000000 |
| COSTS( ATL, DEN, AIR) | 9.000000 | 0.0000000 |
| COSTS( ATL, HOU, RAIL) | 11.00000 | 0.0000000 |
| COSTS( ATL, HOU, AIR) | 8.000000 | 0.0000000 |
| VOLUME( CIN, NY, RAIL) | 0.0000000 | 8.000000 |
| VOLUME( CIN, NY, AIR) | 0.0000000 | 6.000000 |
| VOLUME( CIN, CHI, RAIL) | 0.0000000 | 1.000000 |
| VOLUME( CIN, CHI, AIR) | 25.00000 | 0.0000000 |
| VOLUME( CIN, DEN, RAIL) | 0.0000000 | 10.00000 |
| VOLUME( CIN, DEN, AIR) | 0.0000000 | 12.00000 |
| VOLUME( CIN, HOU, RAIL) | 175.0000 | 0.0000000 |
| VOLUME( CIN, HOU, AIR) | 0.0000000 | 1.000000 |
| VOLUME( PHI, NY, RAIL) | 100.0000 | 0.0000000 |
| VOLUME( PHI, NY, AIR) | 0.0000000 | 2.000000 |
| VOLUME( PHI, CHI, RAIL) | 0.0000000 | 3.000000 |
| VOLUME( PHI, CHI, AIR) | 0.0000000 | 2.000000 |
| VOLUME( PHI, DEN, RAIL) | 0.0000000 | 11.00000 |
| VOLUME( PHI, DEN, AIR) | 0.0000000 | 8.000000 |
| VOLUME( PHI, HOU, RAIL) | 0.0000000 | 1.000000 |
| VOLUME( PHI, HOU, AIR) | 50.00000 | 0.0000000 |
| VOLUME( ATL, NY, RAIL) | 0.0000000 | 9.000000 |
| VOLUME( ATL, NY, AIR) | 0.0000000 | 11.00000 |
| VOLUME( ATL, CHI, RAIL) | 175.0000 | 0.0000000 |
| VOLUME( ATL, CHI, AIR) | 0.0000000 | 1.000000 |
| VOLUME( ATL, DEN, RAIL) | 125.0000 | 0.0000000 |
| VOLUME( ATL, DEN, AIR) | 0.0000000 | 3.000000 |
| VOLUME( ATL, HOU, RAIL) | 0.0000000 | 4.000000 |
| VOLUME( ATL, HOU, AIR) | 0.0000000 | 1.000000 |

| Row | Slack or Surplus | Dual Price |
|---|---|---|
| 1 | 3425.000 | 1.000000 |
| 2 | 0.0000000 | -3.000000 |
| 3 | 0.0000000 | -5.000000 |
| 4 | 0.0000000 | -7.000000 |
| 5 | 0.0000000 | 1.000000 |
| 6 | 0.0000000 | -1.000000 |
| 7 | 0.0000000 | 1.000000 |
| 8 | 0.0000000 | 0.0000000 |

**Figure 5.6** (*Continued*)

that we have five jobs; however, we have chosen not to name them. This is especially important for sets with many elements.

The decision variables are to ASSIGN PEOPLE to JOBS instead of shipping VOLUME from WAREHOUSES to STORES. The SUPPLY and DEMAND values in the DATA: section are all 1 since each person must do one job and each job is done by one person. The decision variables are binary since we are making one assignment each for people to jobs. The @BIN restriction is not needed, since the optimal values of the decision variables will always take on binary values when the assignment problem is solved as a linear programming problem (see Winston 1995 for further details). These changes show that, in general, an assignment problem is a balanced transportation problem such that all supplies and demands are equal to 1. Of course, unbalanced assignment problems are possible, such as situations where there are more JOBS than PEOPLE, or vice versa.

The complete LINGO model, the algebraic formulation, and the solution for this problem appear as Figure 5.7. As already mentioned, the LINGO modeling language formulation is in a file called ASSIGN.LG4. As seen in the output, the total time to complete all five jobs is 102. The ASSIGN values indicate that the optimal assignments are ADAM to job 3; BARB to job 5; CHRIS to job 1; DENISE to job 2; and ED to job 4. Note that all slack values are 0 since all constraints are "equality."

## Traveling Salesman Problem

The Traveling Salesman Problem (TSP) has frustrated researchers and practitioners because it is an important problem that is simple to state yet extremely difficult to solve. The TSP is concerned with determining the optimal order in which locations should be visited. Specifically, consider a salesman who has a known set of customers who need to be visited and known distances, times, or costs between each pair of customers. The problem is to determine the shortest route that the salesman can take to guarantee that each customer is visited *once and only once* and that the salesman returns to the starting location.

The TSP is also important since it has many applications in addition to routing salesmen. For example, consider a company that uses wire to connect components on a motherboard for a computer. The amount of wire used depends on the location of the components and the order in which the components are connected. Therefore, the company needs all of the components connected but would like to minimize the amount of wire used (see homework problem 4). This problem can be formulated and solved as a TSP problem.

For another TSP problem, consider a company that mixes and sells paint. The problem with mixing paints of varying colors on the same production line is that it takes a different amount of time to clean the machine depending on the order that the paints are mixed. For example, we must spend a lot more time cleaning the machine if we mix black paint followed by white paint compared to the cleaning time required to mix tan paint followed by white paint. We would like to minimize the total time spent cleaning the machine but still mix all the paints that have been ordered (see homework problem 3). This problem can also be formulated and solved as a TSP problem.

Other TSP applications include scheduling jobs on machines, routing telephone calls, and any type of delivery problem. As these examples demonstrate, the TSP is important since it arises so often in our daily lives. We will now discuss the formulation and solution to this problem.

Consider the following example. A soda delivery truck starts at location 1 (L1) and must deliver soda to each of nine other locations before returning to L1. The problem is to determine the order in which the locations should be visited such that the total distance traveled is minimized. The distances between each pair of locations are given in the following table.

|      | L1  | L2  | L3  | L4  | L5  | L6  | L7  | L8  | L9  | L10 |
| ---- | --- | --- | --- | --- | --- | --- | --- | --- | --- | --- |
| L1   | –   | 9   | 11  | 9   | 3   | 12  | 13  | 6   | 11  | 10  |
| L2   | 9   | –   | 4   | 5   | 9   | 4   | 4   | 5   | 18  | 4   |
| L3   | 11  | 4   | –   | 9   | 13  | 2   | 6   | 8   | 19  | 7   |
| L4   | 9   | 5   | 9   | –   | 15  | 11  | 5   | 3   | 15  | 1   |
| L5   | 3   | 9   | 13  | 15  | –   | 14  | 14  | 9   | 11  | 19  |
| L6   | 12  | 4   | 2   | 11  | 14  | –   | 9   | 12  | 20  | 10  |
| L7   | 13  | 4   | 6   | 5   | 14  | 9   | –   | 6   | 22  | 3   |
| L8   | 6   | 5   | 8   | 3   | 9   | 12  | 6   | –   | 10  | 3   |
| L9   | 11  | 18  | 19  | 15  | 11  | 20  | 22  | 10  | –   | 16  |
| L10  | 10  | 4   | 7   | 1   | 19  | 10  | 3   | 3   | 16  | –   |

```
:    1]MODEL:
     2]SETS:
     3]    PEOPLE/ADAM, BARB, CHRIS, DENISE, ED/: SUPPLY;
     4]    JOBS/1..5/: DEMAND;
     5]    COMBO(PEOPLE,JOBS): TIMES, ASSIGN;
     6]END SETS
     7]
     8]! THE OBJECTIVE;
     9]MIN = @SUM(COMBO(I,J): TIMES(I,J)*ASSIGN(I,J));
    10]
    11]!THE SUPPLY CONSTRAINTS;
    12] @FOR(PEOPLE(I):
    13]   @SUM(JOBS(J): ASSIGN(I,J))=SUPPLY(I));
    14]
    15]! THE DEMAND CONSTRAINTS;
    16] @FOR(JOBS(J):
    17]   @SUM(PEOPLE(I): ASSIGN(I,J))=DEMAND(J));
    18]
    19]! HERE ARE THE DATA;
    20]  DATA:
    21]    SUPPLY = 1,1,1,1,1;
    22]    DEMAND = 1,1,1,1,1;
    23]    TIMES  = 35, 25, 22, 43, 26,
    24]             14, 39, 25, 46, 25,
    25]             15, 48, 56, 21, 48,
    26]             32, 29, 36, 30, 34,
    27]             54, 46, 28, 11, 57;
    28]  ENDDATA
    29]END
    30]

MIN    35 ASSIGN( ADAM, 1) + 25 ASSIGN( ADAM, 2) + 22 ASSIGN( ADAM, 3)
    + 43 ASSIGN( ADAM, 4) + 26 ASSIGN( ADAM, 5) + 14 ASSIGN( BARB, 1)
    + 39 ASSIGN( BARB, 2) + 25 ASSIGN( BARB, 3) + 46 ASSIGN( BARB, 4)
    + 25 ASSIGN( BARB, 5) + 15 ASSIGN( CHRIS, 1)
    + 48 ASSIGN( CHRIS, 2) + 56 ASSIGN( CHRIS, 3)
    + 21 ASSIGN( CHRIS, 4) + 48 ASSIGN( CHRIS, 5)
    + 32 ASSIGN( DENISE, 1) + 29 ASSIGN( DENISE, 2)
    + 36 ASSIGN( DENISE, 3) + 30 ASSIGN( DENISE, 4)
    + 34 ASSIGN( DENISE, 5) + 54 ASSIGN( ED, 1) + 46 ASSIGN( ED, 2)
    + 28 ASSIGN( ED, 3) + 11 ASSIGN( ED, 4) + 57 ASSIGN( ED, 5)
 SUBJECT TO
  2] ASSIGN( ADAM, 1) + ASSIGN( ADAM, 2) + ASSIGN( ADAM, 3)
     + ASSIGN( ADAM, 4) + ASSIGN( ADAM, 5) =  1
  3] ASSIGN( BARB, 1) + ASSIGN( BARB, 2) + ASSIGN( BARB, 3)
     + ASSIGN( BARB, 4) + ASSIGN( BARB, 5) =  1
  4] ASSIGN( CHRIS, 1) + ASSIGN( CHRIS, 2) + ASSIGN( CHRIS, 3)
     + ASSIGN( CHRIS, 4) + ASSIGN( CHRIS, 5) =   1
  5] ASSIGN( DENISE, 1) + ASSIGN( DENISE, 2) + ASSIGN( DENISE, 3)
     + ASSIGN( DENISE, 4) + ASSIGN( DENISE, 5) =   1
  6] ASSIGN( ED, 1) + ASSIGN( ED, 2) + ASSIGN( ED, 3) + ASSIGN( ED, 4)
     + ASSIGN( ED, 5) =   1
  7] ASSIGN( ADAM, 1) + ASSIGN( BARB, 1) + ASSIGN( CHRIS, 1)
     + ASSIGN( DENISE, 1) + ASSIGN( ED, 1) =   1
  8] ASSIGN( ADAM, 2) + ASSIGN( BARB, 2) + ASSIGN( CHRIS, 2)
     + ASSIGN( DENISE, 2) + ASSIGN( ED, 2) =   1
```

**Figure 5.7** LINGO Output for the Assignment Problem

```
   9] ASSIGN( ADAM, 3) + ASSIGN( BARB, 3) + ASSIGN( CHRIS, 3)
       + ASSIGN( DENISE, 3) + ASSIGN( ED, 3) =  1
  10] ASSIGN( ADAM, 4) + ASSIGN( BARB, 4) + ASSIGN( CHRIS, 4)
       + ASSIGN( DENISE, 4) + ASSIGN( ED, 4) =  1
  11] ASSIGN( ADAM, 5) + ASSIGN( BARB, 5) + ASSIGN( CHRIS, 5)
       + ASSIGN( DENISE, 5) + ASSIGN( ED, 5) =  1
  END

Global optimal solution found at step:              6
Objective value:                          102.0000
```

|                   Variable | Value | Reduced Cost |
|---------------------------:|:-----:|:------------:|
| SUPPLY( ADAM)              | 1.000000 | 0.0000000 |
| SUPPLY( BARB)             | 1.000000 | 0.0000000 |
| SUPPLY( CHRIS)            | 1.000000 | 0.0000000 |
| SUPPLY( DENISE)           | 1.000000 | 0.0000000 |
| SUPPLY( ED)               | 1.000000 | 0.0000000 |
| DEMAND( 1)                | 1.000000 | 0.0000000 |
| DEMAND( 2)                | 1.000000 | 0.0000000 |
| DEMAND( 3)                | 1.000000 | 0.0000000 |
| DEMAND( 4)                | 1.000000 | 0.0000000 |
| DEMAND( 5)                | 1.000000 | 0.0000000 |
| TIMES( ADAM, 1)           | 35.00000 | 0.0000000 |
| TIMES( ADAM, 2)           | 25.00000 | 0.0000000 |
| TIMES( ADAM, 3)           | 22.00000 | 0.0000000 |
| TIMES( ADAM, 4)           | 43.00000 | 0.0000000 |
| TIMES( ADAM, 5)           | 26.00000 | 0.0000000 |
| TIMES( BARB, 1)           | 14.00000 | 0.0000000 |
| TIMES( BARB, 2)           | 39.00000 | 0.0000000 |
| TIMES( BARB, 3)           | 25.00000 | 0.0000000 |
| TIMES( BARB, 4)           | 46.00000 | 0.0000000 |
| TIMES( BARB, 5)           | 25.00000 | 0.0000000 |
| TIMES( CHRIS, 1)          | 15.00000 | 0.0000000 |
| TIMES( CHRIS, 2)          | 48.00000 | 0.0000000 |
| TIMES( CHRIS, 3)          | 56.00000 | 0.0000000 |
| TIMES( CHRIS, 4)          | 21.00000 | 0.0000000 |
| TIMES( CHRIS, 5)          | 48.00000 | 0.0000000 |
| TIMES( DENISE, 1)         | 32.00000 | 0.0000000 |
| TIMES( DENISE, 2)         | 29.00000 | 0.0000000 |
| TIMES( DENISE, 3)         | 36.00000 | 0.0000000 |
| TIMES( DENISE, 4)         | 30.00000 | 0.0000000 |
| TIMES( DENISE, 5)         | 34.00000 | 0.0000000 |
| TIMES( ED, 1)             | 54.00000 | 0.0000000 |
| TIMES( ED, 2)             | 46.00000 | 0.0000000 |
| TIMES( ED, 3)             | 28.00000 | 0.0000000 |
| TIMES( ED, 4)             | 11.00000 | 0.0000000 |
| TIMES( ED, 5)             | 57.00000 | 0.0000000 |
| ASSIGN( ADAM, 1)          | 0.0000000 | 36.00000 |
| ASSIGN( ADAM, 2)          | 0.0000000 | 0.0000000 |
| ASSIGN( ADAM, 3)          | 1.000000 | 0.0000000 |
| ASSIGN( ADAM, 4)          | 0.0000000 | 38.00000 |
| ASSIGN( ADAM, 5)          | 0.0000000 | 0.0000000 |
| ASSIGN( BARB, 1)          | 0.0000000 | 16.00000 |
| ASSIGN( BARB, 2)          | 0.0000000 | 15.00000 |
| ASSIGN( BARB, 3)          | 0.0000000 | 4.000000 |
| ASSIGN( BARB, 4)          | 0.0000000 | 42.00000 |
| ASSIGN( BARB, 5)          | 1.000000 | 0.0000000 |

**Figure 5.7**  (*Continued*)

| | | |
|---|---|---|
| ASSIGN( CHRIS, 1) | 1.000000 | 0.0000000 |
| ASSIGN( CHRIS, 2) | 0.0000000 | 7.000000 |
| ASSIGN( CHRIS, 3) | 0.0000000 | 18.00000 |
| ASSIGN( CHRIS, 4) | 0.0000000 | 0.0000000 |
| ASSIGN( CHRIS, 5) | 0.0000000 | 6.000000 |
| ASSIGN( DENISE, 1) | 0.0000000 | 29.00000 |
| ASSIGN( DENISE, 2) | 1.000000 | 0.0000000 |
| ASSIGN( DENISE, 3) | 0.0000000 | 10.00000 |
| ASSIGN( DENISE, 4) | 0.0000000 | 21.00000 |
| ASSIGN( DENISE, 5) | 0.0000000 | 4.000000 |
| ASSIGN( ED, 1) | 0.0000000 | 49.00000 |
| ASSIGN( ED, 2) | 0.0000000 | 15.00000 |
| ASSIGN( ED, 3) | 0.0000000 | 0.0000000 |
| ASSIGN( ED, 4) | 1.000000 | 0.0000000 |
| ASSIGN( ED, 5) | 0.0000000 | 25.00000 |

| Row | Slack or Surplus | Dual Price |
|---|---|---|
| 1 | 102.0000 | 1.000000 |
| 2 | 0.0000000 | -26.00000 |
| 3 | 0.0000000 | -25.00000 |
| 4 | 0.0000000 | -42.00000 |
| 5 | 0.0000000 | -30.00000 |
| 6 | 0.0000000 | -32.00000 |
| 7 | 0.0000000 | 27.00000 |
| 8 | 0.0000000 | 1.000000 |
| 9 | 0.0000000 | 4.000000 |
| 10 | 0.0000000 | 21.00000 |
| 11 | 0.0000000 | 0.0000000 |

**Figure 5.7** (*Continued*)

A review of the distance matrix indicates that there may be some similarities between the TSP and the assignment problem. In the TSP, each location must be visited, which is like "demand" in an assignment problem, and each location must be exited, which is like "supply." As in the assignment problem, the demand and supply values are all equal to 1 since we must enter each location once and exit each location once. Unlike the assignment problem, the binary decision variables $X(I,J)$ equal 1 if we visit customer $I$ followed by customer $J$, or they equal 0 if we do not.

Directly applying the assignment problem formulation to our TSP example leads to the LINGO model called TSPSUB.LG4 as shown in Figure 5.8. We note that the distances along the main diagonal of the DIST matrix, that is, 1–1, 2–2, 3–3, and so forth, are all 1000. These large values are entered since we want to prevent these assignments; that is, once we enter a location we must leave that location. The 1000 values ensure that this will happen. (Remember that this same approach was offered to eliminate a route in the transportation problem.)

After solving the model, we find that the total distance traveled is 40. The solution to this problem is $X15 = X27 = X36 = X410 = X51 = X63 = X72 = X89 = X98 = X104 = 1$. However, this solution does not solve our TSP, since each location is not being visited before returning to the original location. For example, this solution indicates that we should travel from location 1 to 5 and from 5 to 1. The movement from 1–5–1 is called a *subtour*. The model solution has five subtours 1–5–1, 2–7–2, 3–6–3, 4–10–4, and 8–9–8 and therefore is not a feasible solution to our TSP problem (see Figure 5.9).

We can successfully address the subtour problem by adding constraints to our formulation that eliminate all possible subtours. For a ten-location problem, we need to add

```
:    1]MODEL:
     2]SETS:
     3]    SUPPLYL/1..10/: SUPPLY;
     4]    DEMANDL/1..10/: DEMAND;
     5]    ROUTES(SUPPLYL, DEMANDL): DIST, X;
     6]END SETS
     7]
     8]! THE OBJECTIVE;
     9]MIN = @SUM(ROUTES(I,J): DIST(I,J)*X(I,J));
    10]
    11] @FOR(SUPPLYL(I):
    12]   @SUM(DEMANDL(J): X(I,J))=SUPPLY(I));
    13]
    14] @FOR(DEMANDL(J):
    15]   @SUM(SUPPLYL(I): X(I,J))=DEMAND(J));
    16]
    17]@FOR(SUPPLYL(I):
    18] @FOR(DEMANDL(J):
    19]  @BIN(X(I,J))));
    20]
    21]! HERE IS THE DATA;
    22]  DATA:
    23]    SUPPLY = 1 1 1 1 1 1 1 1 1 1;
    24]    DEMAND = 1 1 1 1 1 1 1 1 1 1;
    25]    DIST = 1000 9 11 9 3 12 13 6 11 10
    26]            9 1000 4 5 9 4 4 5 18 4
    27]            11 4 1000 9 13 2 6 8 19 7
    28]            9 5 9 1000 15 11 5 3 15 1
    29]            3 9 13 15 1000 14 14 9 11 19
    30]            12 4 2 11 14 1000 9 12 20 10
    31]            13 4 6 5 14 9 1000 6 22 3
    32]            6 5 8 3 9 12 6 1000 10 3
    33]            11 18 19 15 11 20 22 10 1000 16
    34]            10 4 7 1 19 10 3 3 16 1000;
    35]  ENDDATA
    36]END
    37]
```

**Figure 5.8** LINGO Model for the Assignment Formulation of the TSP

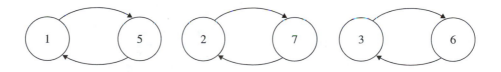

**Figure 5.9** Subtours of the TSP Example Resulting from the Assignment Formulation

constraints to eliminate 2, 3, 4, and/or 5 location subtours. What about the other possibilities? A one-location subtour cannot exist since we put 1000s along the main diagonal, as mentioned. Now consider the possibility of an eight-location subtour. If such a subtour exists, there must also exist a two-location subtour. However, the possibility of an eight-location subtour is eliminated if we add constraints to eliminate all possible two-location subtours.

We now consider the form of the constraints necessary to eliminate two-location subtours. For example, for a subtour involving locations 1 and 2, the subtour-breaking constraint is X12 + X21 <= 1. This constraint allows us to travel from location 1 to location 2 (X12 = 1), **or** from location 2 to location 1 (X21 = 1), but not in both directions since the left-hand side of the constraint would then be 2. Unfortunately, this type of constraint must be repeated for all combinations of 2 out of the 10 locations and would require 45 constraints (10!/2!8!). For three-location subtours involving locations 1, 2, and 3, two additional constraints are needed: X12 + X23 + X31 <= 2 and X13 + X32 + X21 <= 2. There are 240 of these constraints (2 * 10!/3!7!). The total number of subtour-breaking constraints increases greatly when subsets of four and five locations are considered.

Now consider practical problems where the total number of locations to be visited is not 10, but 20, 50, or even more. In some situations, mathematical programming software such as LINGO is unable to converge to the optimal solution in a reasonable amount of time. LINGO's speed can sometimes be improved by selecting _LINGO_, _Option,_ "General Solver" tab, and increasing the _Generator Memory Limit (MB)_ from 4 to 8 or greater, depending upon the total amount of RAM available to you. For larger problems, sometimes the best we can hope for is to run LINGO for a "long" time and then click _Interrupt Solver_ to identify a feasible solution.

An example of a TSP algorithm that includes other forms of the subtour-breaking constraints is given in the file TSP.LG4 that is provided in the samples folder within the LINGO folder. The LINGO modeling language formulation of our example is based on this file and is found in TSPSODA.LG4, which appears as Figure 5.10. There are three

**Figure 5.10** LINGO Output for the TSP Problem

```
:   1] MODEL:
    2] ! Traveling Salesman Problem;
    3] SETS:
    4] CITY / 1.. 10/: U; ! U( I) = sequence no. of city;
    5] LINK( CITY, CITY):
    6]      DIST, ! The distance matrix;
    7]        X; ! X( I, J) = 1 if we use link I, J;
    8] ENDSETS
    9]DATA:   ! Distance matrix, it need not be symmetric;
   10]  DIST = 0 9 11 9 3 12 13 6 11 10
   11]         9 0 4 5 9 4 4 5 18 4
   12]         11 4 0 9 13 2 6 8 19 7
   13]         9 5 9 0 15 11 5 3 15 1
   14]         3 9 13 15 0 14 14 9 11 19
   15]         12 4 2 11 14 0 9 12 20 10
   16]         13 4 6 5 14 9 0 6 22 3
   17]         6 5 8 3 9 12 6 0 10 3
   18]         11 18 19 15 11 20 22 10 0 16
   19]         10 4 7 1 19 10 3 3 16 0;
   20]ENDDATA
   21]
```

```
22]! The model:Ref. Desrochers & Laporte, OR Letters, Feb. 91;
23]  N = @SIZE( CITY);
24]  MIN = @SUM( LINK: DIST * X);
25]  @FOR( CITY( K):
26]   ! It must be entered;
27]   @SUM( CITY( I)| I #NE# K: X( I, K)) = 1;
28]   ! It must be departed;
29]   @SUM( CITY( J)| J #NE# K: X( K, J)) = 1;
30]   ! The weak form of the subtour breaking constraints;
31]   ! These are not very powerful for large problems;
32]   @FOR( CITY( J)| J #GT# 1 #AND# J #NE# K:
33]      U( J) >= U( K) + X ( K, J) -
34]      ( N - 2) * ( 1 - X( K, J)) +
35]      ( N - 3) * X( J, K); );
36]   );
37]  ! Make the X's 0/1;
38]  @FOR( LINK: @BIN( X););
39]  ! For the first and last stop we know...;
40]  @FOR( CITY( K)| K #GT# 1:
41]     U( K) <= N - 1 - ( N - 2) * X( 1, K);
42]     U( K) >= 1 + ( N - 2) * X( K, 1);   );
43] END
44]

Objective value:                    52.00000
Branch count:                          15

                    Variable         Value      Reduced Cost
                     U( 1)        0.0000000        0.0000000
                     U( 2)        9.000000         0.0000000
                     U( 3)        7.000000         0.0000000
                     U( 4)        4.000000         0.0000000
                     U( 5)        1.000000         0.0000000
                     U( 6)        8.000000         0.0000000
                     U( 7)        6.000000         0.0000000
                     U( 8)        3.000000         0.0000000
                     U( 9)        2.000000         0.0000000
                     U( 10)       5.000000         0.0000000

                    Variable         Value      Reduced Cost
                    X( 1, 5)       1.000000         3.00000
                    X( 2, 1)       1.000000         9.000000
                    X( 3, 6)       1.000000         2.000000
                    X( 4, 10)      1.000000         1.000000
                    X( 5, 9)       1.000000        11.000000
                    X( 6, 2)       1.000000         4.000000
                    X( 7, 3)       1.000000         6.000000
                    X( 8, 4)       1.000000         3.00000
                    X( 9, 8)       1.000000        10.00000
                    X( 10, 7)      1.000000         3.000000
```

**Figure 5.10** (*Continued*)

LINGO modeling features that we wish to briefly address. First, the statement N = @SIZE(CITY); sets N equal to the number of elements in the attribute CITY. This is a convenient way of setting up a model in which you want to change the number of elements in an attribute but do not want to make additional changes in the body of the model that involve the number of cities as a parameter.

Second, a "conditional qualifier" is used to limit the membership of the set CITY in several @FOR and @SUM statements. In line 27 of Figure 5.10, the conditional qualifier:

```
I NE K: X(I,K)
```

allows us to exclude X variables such as X(1,1) that loop back to the same location after leaving it. Third, no placeholders are used in the objective function expression. LINGO has no problem processing this expression, since DIST and X are both attributes of LINK.

We illustrate how the presence of subtours violate the subtour-breaking constraints contained in TSPSODA.LG4. First, consider the subtour 2–7–2. We can express the subtour-breaking constraints that involve locations 2–7 (K = 2, J = 7) and 7–2 (K = 7, J = 2) by applying the constraint (taken from the TSPSODA.LG4) for both of these cases:

```
U(J)>=U(K) + X (K, J) - (N - 2)*(1 - X(K, J)) + (N - 3)*X(J, K);
```

After grouping terms we obtain:

```
-9*X(2,7) - 7*X(7,2) - U(2) + U(7)>=-8
-7*X(2,7) - 9*X(7,2) + U(2) - U(7)>=-8
```

Adding both constraints together yields the same type of restriction previously shown to break up two-location subtours:

```
X(2,7) - X(7,2)<=1.
```

Using the same reasoning we eliminate all two-location subtours in this formulation. Now consider the subtour 2–7–4–2. Using the same approach, we express the subtour-breaking constraints that involve locations 2–7 (K = 2, J = 7), 7–4 (K = 7, J = 4), and 4–2 (K = 4, J = 2) as shown:

```
-9*X(2,7) - 7*X(7,2) - U(2) + U(7)>=-8
-7*X(4,7) - 9*X(7,4) + U(4) - U(7)>=-8
-7*X(2,4) - 9*X(4,2) + U(2) - U(4)>=-8
```

For the 2–7–4–2 subtour to occur, X(2,7) = X(7,4) = X(4,2) = 1. Since we have already shown that two-location subtours cannot occur, it must be that X(7,2) = X(4,7) = X(2,4) = 0. Plugging these values into the three previous equations and adding the results yields $-27>=-24$, a contradiction. Using similar arguments, one should be convinced that the constraints given in the TSPSODA.LG4 formulation will eliminate all subtours of any size.

We wish to explain the results of solving TSPSODA.LG4. We have given an abbreviated form of the solution output immediately after the LINGO modeling language formulation. We restricted the output to *LINGO, Solution* by specifying "Attribute or Row Name" first as X and then as U. In addition, we checked the box "Nonzeros only" for the X attribute so that it would be easier to determine the optimal tour. The objective function value tells us that the total distance traveled for this solution is 52. The X values that equal 1 are X(1,5), X(2,1), X(3,6), X(4,10), X(5,9), X(6,2), X(7,3), X(8,4), X(9,8), and X(10,7). These values indicate that the suggested tour is 1–5–9–8–4–10–7–3–6–2–1, as shown in Figure 5.11.

The same tour can be identified by looking at the U values, which give the sequence of each visited location. Since we always start at location 1, its U value is 0. The next location visited will have a U value of 1, then 2, and so on up to 9. The optimal U values are U(1) = 0, U(2) = 9, U(3) = 7, U(4) = 4, U(5) = 1, U(6) = 8, U(7) = 6, U(8) = 3, U(9) = 2, and U(10) = 5. An inspection of the optimal U values verifies the tour we've

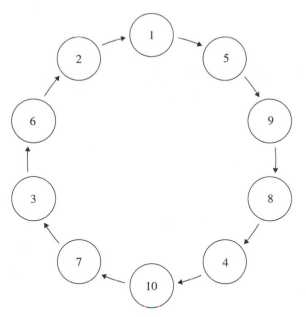

**Figure 5.11** An Optimal Tour of the TSP Example

described. We note that there can be alternate optimal solutions to the TSP problem. For our example, 1–5–2–6–3–7–10–4–8–9–1 is also an optimal solution.

## Vehicle Routing Problem

The next logical extension is to generalize the TSP so that more than one salesman can be deployed. This problem is known as the Vehicle Routing Problem (VRP). Specifically, consider a company that has a fleet of vehicles, each with a fixed capacity. Assume that these vehicles all start at a common depot (location 1) and must return to the depot after visiting seven customers (locations 2 through 8). Each customer has a certain demand that can be satisfied by a vehicle as long as that vehicle's capacity is not exceeded. Each customer's demand can be satisfied by any vehicle. Therefore, the first decision is to determine what vehicles should be assigned to what customers. Once this is known we must determine the order that the customers are visited by each vehicle. The objective is to minimize the total distance traveled by all vehicles.[3]

We will now discuss the VRP model that is provided in the samples folder within the LINGO folder. This model is in a file called VROUTE.LG4. The LINGO formulation and an abbreviated output appear as Figure 5.12.

An inspection of this model formulation shows its relationship with the TSP. The objective is the same as that in the TSP, and constraints are required to make sure that a vehicle enters every location and then leaves it. Unlike the TSP, these constraints must make sure that sufficient vehicle capacity is available if another location is added to a given vehicle tour. We will not further explain the constraints; however, we want to make

---

[3]Weigel and Cao (1999) discuss a vehicle routing application related to the one presented here, except that delivery "time windows" are included in the formulation.

```
 :   1]MODEL:
     2]
     3]! The Vehicle Routing Problem (VRP);
     4]
     5] SETS:
     6]  ! Q(I) is the amount required at city I,
     7]    U(I) is the accumulated delivers at city I ;
     8]    CITY/1..8/: Q, U;
     9]
    10]  ! DIST(I,J) is the distance from city I to city J
    11]    X(I,J) is 0-1 variable: It is 1 if some vehicle
    12]    travels from city I to J, 0 if none;
    13]    CXC( CITY, CITY): DIST, X;
    14] ENDSETS
    15]
    16] DATA:
    17]  ! city 1 represent the common depo;
    18]   Q = 0   6   3   7   7   18   4   5;
    19]
    20] ! distance from city I to city J is same from city
    21]   J to city I distance from city I to the depot is
    22]   0, since the vehicle has to return to the depot;
    23]
    24]  DIST = ! To City;
    25]! Chi  Den Frsn Hous   KC   LA Oakl Anah   From;
    26]    0  996 2162 1067  499 2054 2134 2050!Chicago;
    27]    0    0 1167 1019  596 1059 1227 1055!Denver;
    28]    0 1167    0 1747 1723  214  168  250!Fresno;
    29]    0 1019 1747    0  710 1538 1904 1528!Houston;
    30]    0  596 1723  710    0 1589 1827 1579!K.City;
    31]    0 1059  214 1538 1589    0  371   36!L.A.;
    32]    0 1227  168 1904 1827  371    0  407!Oakland;
    33]    0 1055  250 1528 1579   36  407    0;!Anaheim;
    34]
    35] ! VCAP is the capacity of a vehicle ;
    36]   VCAP = 18;
    37] ENDDATA
    38]
    39] ! Minimize total travel distance;
    40]   MIN = @SUM( CXC: DIST * X);
    41]
    42] ! For each city, except depot....;
    43]   @FOR( CITY( K)| K #GT# 1:
    44]
    45] ! a vehicle does not travel inside itself,...;
    46]    X( K, K) = 0;
    47]
    48] ! a vehicle must enter it,... ;
    49]    @SUM( CITY( I)| I #NE# K #AND# ( I #EQ# 1 #OR#
    50]    Q( I) + Q( K) #LE# VCAP): X( I, K)) = 1;
    51]
    52] ! a vehicle must leave it after service ;
    53]    @SUM( CITY( J)| J #NE# K #AND# ( J #EQ# 1 #OR#
    54]    Q( J) + Q( K) #LE# VCAP): X( K, J)) = 1;
    55]
    56] ! U( K) is at least amount needed at K but can't
    57]   exceed capacity;
    58]    @BND( Q( K), U( K), VCAP);
```

**Figure 5.12** LINGO
Output for the Vehicle
Routing Problem

```
59]
60] ! If K follows I, then can bound U( K) - U( I);
61]   @FOR( CITY( I)| I #NE# K #AND# I #NE# 1:
62]   U( K)>=U( I) + Q( K) - VCAP + VCAP *
63]    ( X( K, I) + X( I, K)) - ( Q( K) + Q( I))
64]    * X( K, I);
65]   );
66]
67] ! If K is 1st stop, then U( K) = Q( K);
68]   U( K)<=VCAP - ( VCAP - Q( K)) * X( 1, K);
69]
70] ! If K is not 1st stop...;
71]   U( K)>=Q( K)+ @SUM( CITY( I)|
72]   I #GT# 1: Q( I) * X( I, K));
73]   );
74]
75] ! Make the X's binary;
76]   @FOR( CXC: @BIN( X));
77]
78] ! Minimum no. vehicles required, fractional
79]   and rounded;
80]   VEHCLF = @SUM( CITY( I)| I #GT# 1: Q( I))/ VCAP;
81]   VEHCLR = VEHCLF + 1.999 -
82]   @WRAP( VEHCLF - .001, 1);
83]
84] ! Must send enough vehicles out of depot;
85]   @SUM( CITY( J)| J #GT# 1: X( 1, J)) >= VEHCLR;
86] END
87]
```

```
Global optimal solution found at step:        147
Objective value:                         5732.000
Branch count:                                   5

          Variable            Value        Reduced Cost
          X( 1, 2)         1.000000          996.0000
          X( 1, 5)         1.000000          499.0000
          X( 1, 6)         1.000000        0.0000000
          X( 2, 8)         1.000000          1055.000
          X( 3, 7)         1.000000          168.0000
          X( 4, 1)         1.000000        0.0000000
          X( 5, 4)         1.000000          710.0000
          X( 6, 1)         1.000000        0.0000000
          X( 7, 1)         1.000000        0.0000000
          X( 8, 3)         1.000000          250.0000
```

**Figure 5.12** (*Continued*)

sure that you understand its optimal solution. After solving the model, we find that the total distance traveled for this solution is 5732. Capacity (VCAP) for each vehicle is 18. Demand (Q) for the seven customers (in locations 2 through 8) is 6, 3, 7, 7, 18, 4, and 5, respectively.

The binary decision variables X(I,J) equal 1 if *some* vehicle travels from I to J and 0 if no vehicles travel from I to J. The solution values for the decision variables are X(1,2) = X(1,5) = X(1,6) = X(2,8) = X(3,7) = X(4,1) = X(5,4) = X(6,1) = X(7,1) = X(8,3) = 1. This means that vehicle 1 leaves the depot (location 1) and visits customers in the following order: 1–2–8–3–7–1. Since customers 2, 8, 3, and 7 have demand of 6, 5, 3, and

4, respectively, the capacity of 18 is not exceeded. Vehicle 2 leaves the depot (location 1) and visits customers in the following order: 1–5–4–1. Since customers 5 and 4 each have demand of 7, the capacity of vehicle 2 is not exceeded. Vehicle 3 leaves the depot (location 1) and visits customer 6: 1–6–1. Customer 6 has a demand of 18 so the capacity for vehicle 3 is not exceeded.

## SUMMARY

In this chapter we applied the LINGO modeling language to formulate the transportation problem and a variety of extensions. We began by modeling the transportation problem, which addresses the shipment of product from origins to destinations, to minimize total shipping costs. Next, we showed how Excel can be used to interface with LINGO to manage data input and output. Then we modeled a series of direct extensions of the transportation model, including unbalanced problems, restricted routes, warehouse location, and choice of transportation mode.

We consider a second group of extensions that are based on the assignment problem, which is itself a special class of transportation problem having all supply and demands equal to one. After formulating and solving the assignment problem, we show that the possibility of subtours prevents the use of the this problem to directly solve the traveling salesman problem (TSP). We then showed how subtour-breaking constraints can be added to the formulation, and then offered a modeling language formulation. The last application considered was the vehicle routing problem, which allows multiple routes to be traversed by a vehicle with limited capacity.

The modeling language and the spreadsheet interface for input and output make transportation and distribution planning using mathematical programming accessible to a broad range of users. The LINGO software package fully supports all of the features and applications of mathematical programming discussed in this chapter.

## HOMEWORK PROBLEMS

**1.** ZENDIR is in the process of planning for new production facilities and developing a more efficient distribution system. At present they have one plant at St. Louis with a capacity of 30,000 units. Because of increased demand, management is considering four potential new sites: Grand Rapids, Denver, Toledo, and Kansas City. The transportation table summarizes the projected plant capacities (in 1,000s), the cost per unit of shipping from each plant to each destination, and the demand forecasts (in 1,000s) over the next year.

| | Destinations | | | Capacities |
|---|---|---|---|---|
| **Plant Sites** | **Providence** | **Atlanta** | **Houston** | **(in 1,000s)** |
| Grand Rapids | 5 | 2 | 3 | 10 |
| Toledo | 4 | 3 | 4 | 20 |
| Denver | 9 | 7 | 5 | 30 |
| Kansas City | 10 | 4 | 2 | 40 |
| St. Louis | 8 | 4 | 3 | 30 |
| Demand (in 1,000s) | 30 | 20 | 20 | |

Suppose that the fixed costs of constructing the new plants, in thousands, are

| | |
|---|---|
| Grand Rapids | $175 |
| Toledo | $300 |
| Denver | $375 |
| Kansas City | $500 |

**(a)** Develop a model to minimize the total cost of plant construction and distribution of goods.

**(b)** Modify the formulation in part (a) to account for the policy restriction that one plant, but not two, must be located in Grand Rapids or in Toledo.

**(c)** Modify the formulation in part (a) to account for the policy restriction that one plant at most can be located in Denver or Kansas City.

**2.** The ROCKWELL School system has three junior high schools that serve the needs of five neighborhood areas. The capacities of the various schools are:

| School | Capacity (Max. enrollment) |
|---|---|
| A | 4,000 |
| B | 3,000 |
| C | 2,000 |
| Total | 9,000 |

The size (number of junior high school students) and ethnic mix of each neighborhood are:

| Neighborhood | # of students | % minority students |
|---|---|---|
| 1 | 2,100 | 30 |
| 2 | 2,400 | 80 |
| 3 | 1,300 | 20 |
| 4 | 800 | 10 |
| 5 | 1,600 | 20 |
| Total | 8,200 | |

The distances (in miles) from each neighborhood to each school are:

**TO: SCHOOL**

| | | A | B | C |
|---|---|---|---|---|
| | 1 | 1.2 | 0.8 | 1.3 |
| From | 2 | 0.4 | 2.0 | 2.2 |
| Neighborhood | 3 | 2.6 | 0.5 | 1.6 |
| | 4 | 1.4 | 0.7 | 2.0 |
| | 5 | 2.4 | 3.0 | 0.2 |

A judge has ruled that no junior high school in the city can have more than 50% nor less than 30% minority enrollment. Assume that students bused from each neighborhood have the same ethnic mix as the whole neighborhood. You wish to devise a busing plan that will minimize the total number of student miles bused yet meet the judge's integration requirements, and at the same time guarantee that no student is bused more than 2.5 miles. Formulate a model that could be used to solve this problem.

**3.** B. A. MCDUFF and Sons has received an order for varying amounts of 5 different colors of paints. The problem is that the order in which the jobs are performed affects the total costs. This is due to the fact that if a dark color is scheduled after a light color, the costs to clean the equipment are less than if a light color is scheduled after a dark color. McDuff has estimated the cleaning costs for each pair of color sequences. These costs are shown in the table.

Color 1 is a rush order and must be scheduled first. In addition, after the 5 jobs have been finished, the paint manufacturer has also scheduled a job for color 1. Determine the order that the jobs should be scheduled.

| | | | COLOR | | |
|---|---|---|---|---|---|
| | **1** | **2** | **3** | **4** | **5** |
| COLOR 1 | – | 130 | 107 | 115 | 105 |
| COLOR 2 | 101 | – | 104 | 106 | 108 |
| COLOR 3 | 127 | 144 | – | 117 | 128 |
| COLOR 4 | 112 | 155 | 127 | – | 143 |
| COLOR 5 | 133 | 158 | 108 | 103 | – |

**4.** CYNEX is a computer chip manufacturer that must route wiring for its new product. There are five pins on the printed circuit board. These five items must be connected in such a way that a complete circuit of wiring exists. The distances (in millimeters) between each pair of items is shown in the table. Determine a solution to this circuit layout problem.

| | | | PIN | | |
|---|---|---|---|---|---|
| | **1** | **2** | **3** | **4** | **5** |
| PIN 1 | – | 16 | 12 | 6 | 4 |
| PIN 2 | 16 | – | 9 | 8 | 14 |
| PIN 3 | 14 | 10 | – | 1 | 18 |
| PIN 4 | 5 | 11 | 2 | – | 22 |
| PIN 5 | 3 | 17 | 19 | 29 | – |

## REFERENCES

CAMM, J. D., T. E. CHORMAN, F. A. DILL, J. R. EVANS, D. J. SWEENEY, and G. W. WEGRYN, "Blending OR/MS, Judgment and GIS: Restructuring P&G's Capacity Chain, *Interfaces*, Vol. 27, No. 1, pp. 128–142, 1997.

HILLIER, F. S., and G. J. LIEBERMAN, *Introduction to Operations Research*, 7th ed., New York, McGraw-Hill, 2001.

KOKSALAN, M. and H. SURAL, "Efes Beverage Group Makes Location and Distribution Decisions for Its Malt Plants," *Interfaces*, Vol. 29, No. 2, pp. 89–103, 1999.

SCHRAGE, L., *Optimization Modeling with LINGO*, Chicago, Lindo Systems Inc., 2002.

WEIGEL, D. and B. CAO, "Applying GIS and OR Techniques to Solve Sears Technician-Dispatching and Home-Delivery Problems," *Interfaces*, Vol. 29, No. 1, pp. 112–130, 1999.

WINSTON, W. L., *Introduction to Mathematical Programming: Applications and Algorithms*, Belmont, CA, Duxbury, 1995.

# Chapter 6

## Scheduling, Finance, and Marketing Applications Using the LINGO Modeling Language*

## INTRODUCTION

In the previous chapter we addressed the application of mathematical programming to transportation and distribution planning. As mentioned in Chapter 2, mathematical programming continues to be successfully applied to a variety of decision-making problems. In this chapter we present important applications using the LINGO modeling language (Schrage 2002) that are grouped into three areas: scheduling, finance, and marketing. Nearly all of these examples were selected on the basis of the applications that our students found useful in their applied projects. A few, such as the retail space allocation example, were selected to illustrate some important aspects of the modeling process. Additional examples can be found in many sources, including Anderson, Sweeney, and Williams (2000), Assad, Wasil, and Lilien (1992), and in the journal *Interfaces*.

## SCHEDULING APPLICATIONS

### A Staff Scheduling Problem

Mathematical programming can be used to address many different types of staff scheduling problems. Such problems abound in practice since many businesses must schedule employees to perform various tasks where demand for these services varies over time. Examples include staffing call centers, assigning workers to shifts in a restaurant, and allocating staff in a service center. An approach for modeling these problems is illustrated in the following scheduling example.

International Airlines is in the process of finalizing an on-line reservations system. To staff this system, telephone operators will need to be available during the day to meet forecasted demand. The following are the forecasts for operators over the ten time periods each day:

---

*Chapters 5 and 6 use the LINGO modeling language approach; Chapters 7 and 8 cover essentially the same material but use the standard algebraic LINGO approach. Therefore, skip Chapters 5 and 6 *or* 7 and 8 per instructions from your professor. See the Preface for further details.

| Period | Time | Operators needed |
|--------|------|:----------------:|
| 1 | 6 a.m.–8 a.m. | 3 |
| 2 | 8 a.m.–10 a.m. | 12 |
| 3 | 10 a.m.–12 noon | 13 |
| 4 | 12 noon–2 p.m. | 10 |
| 5 | 2 p.m.–4 p.m. | 12 |
| 6 | 4 p.m.–6 p.m. | 10 |
| 7 | 6 p.m.–8 p.m. | 6 |
| 8 | 8 p.m.–10 p.m. | 5 |
| 9 | 10 p.m.–12 midnight | 4 |
| 10 | 12 midnight–2 a.m. | 3 |

However, telephone operators are scheduled on a shift basis. International Airlines plans to staff six shifts, of which two are split shifts. The shift times are as follows:

| Shift | Times |
|-------|-------|
| 1 | 6 a.m.–2 p.m. |
| 2 | 8 a.m.–4 p.m. |
| 3 | 10 a.m.–6 p.m. |
| 4 | 6 p.m.–2 a.m. |
| 5 | 10 a.m.–1 p.m. & 4 p.m.–8 p.m. |
| 6 | 8 a.m.–11 a.m. & 5 p.m.–9 p.m. |

The objective of this problem is to minimize the total daily payroll cost while assigning operators to shifts in order to meet demand during each time period. The daily pay rate for the first four shifts is $56, however, since the fifth and sixth shifts are split, the pay rate is $70 per day.

Using the information given about this problem, we are now ready to formulate this scheduling problem using the LINGO modeling language. We apply the five steps that we used in Chapter 4 to model the diet problem.

### 1. Specify the SETS: Section of the Model, which Includes Sets, Elements, and Attributes

We have two primitive sets for this problem: PERIODS and SHIFTS. The elements of these sets are simply the 10 PERIODS and the 6 SHIFTS. We have one derived set which we call MATCHES. This set determines whether a PERIODS demand is satisfied during a SHIFT, that is, if there is a "match." DEMAND for operators is an attribute of PERIODS, while COST and PEOPLE (that is, the number of operators hired) are attributes of SHIFTS. The attribute for the MATCHES set is called YESNO. This attribute is needed to specify the matches between PERIODS and SHIFTS. The complete SETS: section using the LINGO modeling language formulation for this problem is

```
SETS:
  PERIODS / 1..10/: DEMAND;
  SHIFTS / 1..6/: COST, PEOPLE;
  MATCHES (PERIODS,SHIFTS): YESNO;
ENDSETS
```

### 2. Specify the DATA: Section of the Model by Assigning Values to Attributes

The data for DEMAND is given in Figure 6.1 for each of the 10 time periods. The 6 values of COST are 56 for the first 4, and 70 for the last 2. The YESNO values are either 0 or 1 and indicate whether a PERIODS demand is satisfied by a SHIFT.

|  |  |  | SHIFTS | DEMAND |
|---|---|---|---|---|
|  |  |  | 1 2 3 4 5 6 |  |
|  |  | 1 (6 a.m.–8 a.m.) | 1 0 0 0 0 0 | 3 |
| P |  | 2 (8 a.m.–10 a.m.) | 1 1 0 0 0 1 | 12 |
| E |  | 3 (10 a.m.–12 p.m.) | 1 1 1 0 1 0 | 13 |
| R |  | 4 (12 p.m.–2 p.m.) | 1 1 1 0 0 0 | 10 |
| I |  | 5 (2 p.m.–4 p.m.) | 0 1 1 0 0 0 | 12 |
| O |  | 6 (4 p.m.–6 p.m.) | 0 0 1 0 1 0 | 10 |
| D |  | 7 (6 p.m.–8 p.m.) | 0 0 0 1 1 1 | 6 |
| S |  | 8 (8 p.m.–10 p.m.) | 0 0 0 1 0 0 | 5 |
|  |  | 9 (10 p.m.–12 a.m.) | 0 0 0 1 0 0 | 4 |
|  |  | 10 (12 a.m.–2 a.m.) | 0 0 0 1 0 0 | 3 |

Note: The 0 and 1 entries in the matrix above are the YESNO data values.

**Figure 6.1** Matrix Showing the Format of the YESNO data and DEMAND for PERIODS

Figure 6.1 also contains a matrix that represents the format of the YESNO data. For example, the values in the first column indicate that shift 1 helps to satisfy DEMAND during PERIODS 1, 2, 3, and 4. To understand why this is so, look at the times for the first four PERIODS (6–8, 8–10, 10–12, and 12–2) and remember the time for the first shift (6–2). This first shift completely covers these four time PERIODS.

Next we note that row 4 (period 4) and column 5 (shift 5) entry is 0. This may be potentially confusing since shift 5 works from 10:00 to 1:00 and period 4 goes from 12:00 to 2:00. This shift covers the first hour of the period but not the second. It should be clear that the YESNO value must be 0 since shift 5 workers go home at 1:00 and thus cannot help to satisfy demand during the second hour of period 4. We assume then that a value of 1 in YESNO indicates that the given shift *completely* covers the time period in question.

The complete DATA: section is

```
DATA:
 DEMAND = 3,12,13,10,12,10,6,5,4,3;
 COST = 56,56,56,56,70,70;
 YESNO = 1,0,0,0,0,0,
         1,1,0,0,0,1,
         1,1,1,0,1,0,
         1,1,1,0,0,0,
         0,1,1,0,0,0,
         0,0,1,0,1,0,
         0,0,0,1,1,1,
         0,0,0,1,0,0,
         0,0,0,1,0,0,
         0,0,0,1,0,0;
ENDDATA
```

### 3. Identify the Decision Variables as Attributes Not Assigned Values in the DATA: Section

Remember that if an attribute is not assigned a value in the DATA: section, LINGO assumes that the attribute is a decision variable. In our example, the values of PEOPLE are not assigned and so they are decision variables.

### 4. Formulate the Objective Function Using the @SUM Function

The objective for this problem is to MINimize the total cost of staffing each day, which is obtained by multiplying the COSTS by the PEOPLE and SUMming over all SHIFTS. The objective function for the Lingo modeling language formulation for this problem is:

```
MIN = @SUM(SHIFTS(J): COST(J)*PEOPLE(J));
```

### 5. Formulate the Constraints Using the @FOR Function

Now we are ready to express the demand constraints. FOR each of the PERIODS, we multiply YESNO by the PEOPLE and SUM over all SHIFTS. The result must be greater than or equal to the DEMAND. To better understand how this constraint works, let us consider the constraint for period 3. Looking at the third row of the matrix given in Figure 6.1, we multiply the YESNO value in that row by the value of PEOPLE corresponding to the shift in that particular column and sum to obtain

```
1*PEOPLE(1)+1*PEOPLE(2)+1*PEOPLE(3)+0*PEOPLE(4)+1*PEOPLE(5)+0*PEOPLE(6)
```

This sum is the total number of operators that will be available during period 3, and must be *greater than or equal* to period 3's DEMAND of 13 operators.

We do not set these constraints as equalities since it may not be possible to find integer values of PEOPLE that *exactly* meet all constraints. For example, you may need to schedule staff to meet a high level of demand in the first period, but if demand drops in the second period, you may be left with excess capacity. In fact, if you change the relational sign to equality and solve the resulting problem in LINGO, no feasible solution will be found. However, using the relational sign of greater than or equal to for the constraints will yield an optimal solution that minimizes total cost in such a way that the best combination of PEOPLE is found. All constraints will be met while some will be exceeded only if no feasible lower cost solution can be found.

Since we have 10 demand constraints, we can label them for ease of reading the LINGO output by using [PERIODDEMAND] as shown in the @FOR constraint. The demand constraints for the LINGO modeling language formulation for this problem are:

```
@FOR(PERIODS(I): [PERIODDEMAND]
 @SUM(SHIFTS(J): YESNO(I,J)*PEOPLE(J))>=DEMAND(I));
```

We do not need to use the @GIN command to make sure that the values of PEOPLE are integer since the demands in our example are integers:

```
!@FOR(SHIFTS(J):
 @GIN(PEOPLE(J)));
```

The complete LINGO model, the algebraic formulation, and an abbreviated solution for this problem appear in Figure 6.2. We restricted the output to *LINGO, Solution* by specifying "Attribute or Row Name" as PEOPLE, then PERIODDEMAND. The LINGO modeling language formulation is in a file called AIRLINE.LG4. The objective function value indicates that the total staffing cost is $1526 per day. By looking at the values for PEOPLE, we find that we should hire 9, 3, 9, 5, 1, and 0 PEOPLE during the six SHIFTS, respectively. The value of 9 in the "Slack or Surplus" column for PERIODDEMAND[3] indicates a surplus of 9 operators will occur during period 3. This result can be also be obtained by recalling the DEMAND constraint for period 3 and then plugging in the optimal values PEOPLE to find that 22 operators are available, whereas DEMAND(3) equals 13.

```
  :    1]MODEL:
       2]SETS:
       3]    PERIODS / 1..10/: DEMAND;
       4]    SHIFTS / 1..6/: COST, PEOPLE;
       5]    MATCHES (PERIODS,SHIFTS): YESNO;
       6]ENDSETS
       7]
       8]! THE OBJECTIVE;
       9]MIN = @SUM(SHIFTS(J): COST(J)*PEOPLE(J));
      10]
      11]!THE DEMAND CONSTRAINTS;
      12] @FOR(PERIODS(I): [PERIODDEMAND]
      13]    @SUM(SHIFTS(J): YESNO(I,J)*PEOPLE(J))>=DEMAND(I));
      14]
      15]!@FOR(SHIFTS(J):
      16]    @GIN(PEOPLE(J)));
      17]
      18]! HERE IS THE DATA;
      19]   DATA:
      20]    DEMAND = 3,12,13,10,12,10,6,5,4,3;
      21]    COST = 56,56,56,56,70,70;
      22]    YESNO = 1,0,0,0,0,0,
      23]            1,1,0,0,0,1,
      24]            1,1,1,0,1,0,
      25]            1,1,1,0,0,0,
      26]            0,1,1,0,0,0,
      27]            0,0,1,0,1,0,
      28]            0,0,0,1,1,1,
      29]            0,0,0,1,0,0,
      30]            0,0,0,1,0,0,
      31]            0,0,0,1,0,0;
      32]    ENDDATA
      33]
      34]END
      35]

MIN    56 PEOPLE( 1) + 56 PEOPLE( 2) + 56 PEOPLE( 3) + 56 PEOPLE( 4)
       + 70 PEOPLE( 5) + 70 PEOPLE( 6)
SUBJECT TO
PERIODDEMAND( 1)] PEOPLE( 1) >=  3
PERIODDEMAND( 2)] PEOPLE( 1) + PEOPLE( 2) + PEOPLE( 6) >=  12
PERIODDEMAND( 3)]
PEOPLE( 1) + PEOPLE( 2) + PEOPLE( 3) + PEOPLE( 5) >=  13
PERIODDEMAND( 4)] PEOPLE( 1) + PEOPLE( 2) + PEOPLE( 3) >=  10
PERIODDEMAND( 5)] PEOPLE( 2) + PEOPLE( 3) >=  12
PERIODDEMAND( 6)] PEOPLE( 3) + PEOPLE( 5) >=  10
PERIODDEMAND( 7)] PEOPLE( 4) + PEOPLE( 5) + PEOPLE( 6) >=  6
PERIODDEMAND( 8)] PEOPLE( 4) >=  5
PERIODDEMAND( 9)] PEOPLE( 4) >=  4
PERIODDEMAND( 10)] PEOPLE( 4) >=  3
END
```

**Figure 6.2** LINGO Output for the Staff Scheduling Problem

```
Global optimal solution found at step:           7
  Objective value:                        1526.000
  Branch count:                                  0

              Variable           Value        Reduced Cost
              PEOPLE( 1)       9.000000          0.00000
              PEOPLE( 2)       3.000000          0.00000
              PEOPLE( 3)       9.00000           0.00000
              PEOPLE( 4)       5.000000          0.00000
              PEOPLE( 5)       1.0000000         0.00000
              PEOPLE( 6)       0.000000          0.00000

                   Row     Slack or Surplus      Dual Price
       PERIODDEMAND( 1)       6.0000000         0.0000000
       PERIODDEMAND( 2)       0.0000000       -56.0000000
       PERIODDEMAND( 3)       9.000000          0.0000000
       PERIODDEMAND( 4)      11.00000           0.0000000
       PERIODDEMAND( 5)       0.000000          0.0000000
       PERIODDEMAND( 6)       0.0000000       -56.0000000
       PERIODDEMAND( 7)       0.0000000       -14.0000000
       PERIODDEMAND( 8)       0.0000000       -42.0000000
       PERIODDEMAND( 9)       1.000000          0.0000000
       PERIODDEMAND( 10)      2.000000          0.0000000
```

**Figure 6.2** (*Continued*)

## Production Scheduling

Many companies must determine production schedules for their products. For example, a car manufacturer must determine their monthly production schedule so that they meet their target demand levels. A soda bottling plant must also determine how many bottles of each size soda to produce. These problems are examples of a mathematical programming area called production scheduling. Consider the following example.

International Products, Inc. must decide on its production schedule for the next four months. It has contracted to supply a special part for the months of October, November, December, and January at the rates of 12,000, 10,000, 15,000, and 17,000 units, respectively. The company can produce each part at a cost of $6 during regular time or $9 during overtime. Monthly production capacity is 10,000 and 6,000 units during regular and overtime, respectively. A maximum of 2,000 units can be stored per month at a cost of $0.50 per unit. There are 1,000 units in inventory at the end of September and there must be 500 units in inventory at the end of January. International Products can overproduce during some months and store the excess to help satisfy future demand during later months. They would like to determine the production schedule that will minimize total costs while meeting demand. The LINGO formulation is again developed using our five-step approach.

### 1. Specify the SETS: Section of the Model, which Includes Sets, Elements, and Attributes

The two primitive sets for this problem are PRODUCTION and MONTHS. The elements of PRODUCTION are regular time (REG) and overtime (OVER), and the elements of MONTHS are SEP, OCT, NOV, DEC, and JAN. The derived set called COMBINATIONS indicates that PRODUCTION can occur during each of the MONTHS. The attribute of the PRODUCTION set is the production costs (PRODCOST). The MONTHS set has two attributes: the DEMAND for each month and the INVENTORY for each month. The attribute of the COMBINATIONS set is called X, and represents the amount produced during REG and OVER for each of the MONTHS. The complete SETS: section using the LINGO modeling language formulation for this problem is shown.

```
SETS:
  PRODUCTION/REG, OVER/: PRODCOST;
  MONTHS/SEP, OCT, NOV, DEC, JAN/: DEMAND, INVENTORY;
  COMBINATIONS(PRODUCTION, MONTHS): X;
ENDSETS
```

### 2. Specify the DATA: Section of the Model by Assigning Values to Attributes

The data include PRODCOST for REG and OVER, and DEMAND for the five MONTHS. Note that a 0 is entered for SEP demand since this value will not be needed in our formulation. The DATA: section is

```
DATA:
  PRODCOST = 6,9;
  DEMAND = 0,12000,10000,15000,17000;
ENDDATA
```

### 3. Identify the Decision Variables as Attributes that are not Assigned Values in the DATA: Section

The attribute X represents the decision variables, since it specifies the number of units produced by type of PRODUCTION during each MONTH.

### 4. Formulate the Objective Function Using the @SUM Function

The objective is to MINimize the SUM of the total production costs plus the inventory costs. Since we are not interested in determining September's (J=1) production and inventory levels, we use conditional qualifiers to eliminate these terms from our sums. Conditional qualifiers such as

```
| J #GT # 1
```

can be used to limit the membership of sets in any set looping function. Note that the parameter HCOST is specified as .5 within the body of the model. The objective function is shown.

```
MIN = @SUM(COMBINATIONS(I,J)| J #GT# 1: PRODCOST(I)*X(I,J))+
        @SUM(MONTHS(J)| J #GT# 1 : HCOST*INVENTORY(J));
```

### 5. Formulate the Constraints Using the @FOR Function

Constraints are needed to make sure that DEMAND is satisfied for each of the MONTHS. These constraints also compute the ending INVENTORY for each of the MONTHS. This group of constraints is based on the following relationship:

starting inventory + production − demand = ending inventory

In our formulation, the ending inventory of the previous month, INVENTORY (J − 1) is the starting inventory for the next month J. Therefore, the starting inventory for month J, or INVENTORY (J − 1), plus the production during month J, or X(REG,J) + X(OVER,J), equals the total amount of product available to satisfy DEMAND during month J. The difference between the total amount of product available and the DEMAND is equal to the inventory at the end of month J, or INVENTORY (J). Again, we eliminate month 1 (SEP) since we are not interested in planning its production and inventory levels. These constraints are

```
@FOR(MONTHS(J)|J #GT# 1:
  INVENTORY(J-1) + @SUM(PRODUCTION(I): X(I,J))-DEMAND(J)
  =INVENTORY(J));
```

The ending inventory levels for SEP and JAN are specified:

```
INVENTORY(SEP)=1000;
INVENTORY(JAN)=500;
```

The @BND command is used to set lower and upper bounds on the monthly INVENTORY, and REG and OVER production levels (note the use of the conditional qualifier):

```
@FOR(MONTHS(J)| J #GT# 1:
  @BND(0,INVENTORY(J),2000));
@FOR(MONTHS(J)| J #GT# 1:
  @BND(0,X(REG,J),10000));
@FOR(MONTHS(J)| J #GT# 1:
  @BND(0,X(OVER,J),6000));
```

The production levels must be specified as integer-valued:

```
@FOR(COMBINATIONS(I,J): @GIN(X));
```

The LINGO modeling language formulation is in a file called INTER.LG4. The model, algebraic formulation, and abbreviated solution appear in Figure 6.3. The objective function value indicates that the minimum total cost is $362,750. By looking at the values for the decision variables (X(REG,OCT), X(REG,NOV), X(REG,DEC), X(REG,JAN), X(OVER,OCT), X(OVER,NOV), X(OVER,DEC), and X(OVER,JAN)), we find that we should produce 10,000 units each month (excluding September) during regular time, 1,000 units during October's overtime, 500 during November's overtime, and 6,000 units each during December and January's overtime.

# FINANCIAL APPLICATIONS

## The Portfolio Problem

Today many companies, and even individuals, are concerned about how they invest their money. One approach for selecting a portfolio of investments is to specify an acceptable minimum expected return and to find a portfolio with the minimum variance that attains this expected return. By varying the minimum acceptable expected return the investor may obtain and compare several desirable portfolios. This approach is called the Markowitz Portfolio Model and will be studied here. More details on this problem can be found in Luenberger (1998), and an application is discussed in Labe, Nigam, and Spence (1999).

Data can be collected over time to compute the expected returns of each investment and the variance of the portfolio. The variance of the portfolio is the sum of the variances of the individual investments *plus* a measure of how each pair of investments tend to move together. To compute the total variance of a portfolio, we must determine the *covariance matrix* of the investments comprising the portfolio.

```
MODEL:
SETS:
    PRODUCTION/REG, OVER/: PRODCOST;
    MONTHS/SEP, OCT, NOV, DEC, JAN/: DEMAND, INVENTORY;
    COMBINATIONS(PRODUCTION, MONTHS): X;
ENDSETS

! THE OBJECTIVE;
MIN = @SUM(COMBINATIONS(I,J)| J #GT# 1: PRODCOST(I)*X(I,J))+
        @SUM(MONTHS(J)| J #GT# 1 : HCOST*INVENTORY(J));

!SET HOLDING COST PARAMETER;
HCOST=0.5;

!THE DEMAND CONSTRAINTS;
 @FOR(MONTHS(J)|J #GT# 1:
    INVENTORY(J-1) + @SUM(PRODUCTION(I): X(I,J)) -
DEMAND(J)=INVENTORY(J));

!SET BEGINNING AND ENDING INVENTORY LEVELS;
INVENTORY(SEP)=1000;
INVENTORY(JAN)=500;

!SET BOUNDS FOR INVENTORY AND PRODUCTION LEVELS;
@FOR(MONTHS(J)| J #GT# 1:
  @BND(0,INVENTORY(J),2000));

@FOR(MONTHS(J)| J #GT# 1:
  @BND(0,X(REG,J),10000));

@FOR(MONTHS(J)| J #GT# 1:
@BND(0,X(OVER,J),6000));

!REQUIRE PRODUCTION LEVELS TO BE INTEGER-VALUED;
@FOR(COMBINATIONS(I,J): @GIN(X));

! HERE ARE THE DATA;
  DATA:
    PRODCOST = 6, 9;
    DEMAND = 0, 12000, 10000, 15000, 17000;
  ENDDATA
END

MIN  6 X( REG, OCT) + 6 X( REG, NOV) + 6 X( REG, DEC) + 6 X( REG, JAN)
+ 9 X( OVER, OCT) + 9 X( OVER, NOV) + 9 X( OVER, DEC)
+ 9 X( OVER, JAN) + .5 INVENTORY( OCT) + .5 INVENTORY( NOV)
+ .5 INVENTORY( DEC)
 SUBJECT TO
 3]  X( REG, OCT) + X( OVER, OCT) - INVENTORY( OCT) =  11000
 4]  X( REG, NOV) + X( OVER, NOV) + INVENTORY( OCT) - INVENTORY( NOV)
      =  10000
 5]  X( REG, DEC) + X( OVER, DEC) + INVENTORY( NOV) - INVENTORY( DEC)
      =  15000
 6]  X( REG, JAN) + X( OVER, JAN) + INVENTORY( DEC) =  17500
 END
```

**Figure 6.3** LINGO Output for the Production Scheduling Problem

```
GIN X( REG, SEP)
SUB X( REG, OCT)        10000.000
GIN X( REG, OCT)
SUB X( REG, NOV)        10000.000
GIN X( REG, NOV)
SUB X( REG, DEC)        10000.000
GIN X( REG, DEC)
SUB X( REG, JAN)        10000.000
GIN X( REG, JAN)
GIN X( OVER, SEP)
SUB X( OVER, OCT)        6000.000
GIN X( OVER, OCT)
SUB X( OVER, NOV)        6000.000
GIN X( OVER, NOV)
SUB X( OVER, DEC)        6000.000
GIN X( OVER, DEC)
SUB X( OVER, JAN)        6000.000
GIN X( OVER, JAN)
SUB INVENTORY( OCT)      2000.000
SUB INVENTORY( NOV)      2000.000
SUB INVENTORY( DEC)      2000.000

Global optimal solution found at step:              1
Objective value:                            362750.0
Branch count:                                       0

                      Variable         Value      Reduced Cost
                  X( REG, SEP)      0.0000000         0.0000000
                  X( REG, OCT)      10000.00          7.000000
                  X( REG, NOV)      10000.00          6.500000
                  X( REG, DEC)      10000.00          6.000000
                  X( REG, JAN)      10000.00          5.500000
                 X( OVER, SEP)      0.0000000         0.0000000
                 X( OVER, OCT)      1000.000          10.00000
                 X( OVER, NOV)      500.0000          9.500000
                 X( OVER, DEC)      6000.000          9.000000
                 X( OVER, JAN)      6000.000          8.500000
              INVENTORY (SEP)      1000.000          0.0000000
              INVENTORY (OCT)      0.0000000         0.5000000
              INVENTORY (NOV)      500.0000          0.5000000
              INVENTORY (DEC)      1500.000          0.5000000
              INVENTORY (JAN)      500.0000          0.0000000
```

**Figure 6.3**  (*Continued*)

Consider the following problem. Suppose an investor has gathered return rates for three investments over the last six months as shown:

| | Rates | | |
|---|---|---|---|
| **Periods** | **I1** | **I2** | **I3** |
| 1 | 0.07 | 0.14 | 0.05 |
| 2 | 0.05 | −0.07 | 0.06 |
| 3 | 0.02 | 0.05 | 0.03 |
| 4 | 0.04 | 0.14 | 0.07 |
| 5 | 0.12 | 0.02 | 0.10 |
| 6 | 0.08 | 0.19 | 0.06 |

The investor wants to invest $100 (in thousands) and would like a portfolio return of at least 6.5%. In addition, for diversification reasons, at least $50 (in thousands) must be placed in investments 1 and/or 2. The investor wishes to determine the amount that should be placed in each of the three investments to minimize the total variance of the portfolio while achieving the minimum expected return and diversification constraints. Our formulation using the five-step approach proceeds as follows.

### 1. Specify the SETS: Section of the Model, which Includes Sets, Elements, and Attributes

Our primitive sets include the investment alternatives (INVESTS) and the number of time PERIODS over which return data are available. The elements of INVESTS are I1, I2, and I3, and the elements of PERIODS are 1 through 6. The attributes of INVESTS are the expected investment return as computed by LINGO (RBAR) and the amount invested (X). The set RETURNS is derived from knowledge of INVESTS and PERIODS. The monthly return data (RATES) is an attribute of RETURNS. Since we are computing the values in the covariance matrix within our LINGO model, an intermediate result called ERRORS (described below) is required. ERRORS is also an attribute of RETURNS, as shown. The values of the covariance matrix itself are contained in an attribute V of the derived set COVAR. Since there is one covariance term for every combination of investments, COVAR is a three by three matrix derived from INVESTS, that is, COVAR(INVESTS, INVESTS). The complete SETS section is given here.

```
SETS:
  INVESTS /I1, I2, I3/ : RBAR, X;
  PERIODS /1..6/;
  RETURNS(INVESTS,PERIODS): RATES, ERRORS;
  COVAR(INVESTS,INVESTS): V;
ENDSETS
```

### 2. Specify the DATA: Section of the Model by Assigning Values to Attributes

The data consist of the investment return data (RATES) over the six months, and are entered into LINGO as

```
DATA:
RATES = 0.07,0.05,0.02,0.04,0.12,0.08,
    0.14,-0.07,0.05,0.14,0.02,0.19,
    0.05,0.06,0.03,0.07,0.10,0.06;
ENDDATA
```

### 3. Identify the Decision Variables as Attributes that Are Not Assigned Values in the DATA: Section

The amounts placed in each investment (X) are the decision variables. Note that RBAR, ERRORS, and V are not data and are not decision variables. Their values are *calculated* within the LINGO model.

### 4. Formulate the Objective Function Using the @SUM Function

The objective is to minimize the total variance of the portfolio. The values in the covariance matrix indicate the degree of variation between every pair of investments. Each covariance value must be weighted by the amount placed in *both* of the investments contributing to this value.[1] The objective then sums over all possible combinations of investments:

```
MIN=@SUM (COVAR(I,K): V(I,K)*X(I)*X(K));
```

### 5. Formulate the Constraints Using the @FOR Function

Using the RETURN data we need to compute RBAR and V. First we compute RBAR as the average of each investment's return data:

|  | Rates | | |
|---|---|---|---|
| **Periods** | **I1** | **I2** | **I3** |
| 1 | 0.07 | 0.14 | 0.05 |
| 2 | 0.05 | −0.07 | 0.06 |
| 3 | 0.02 | 0.05 | 0.03 |
| 4 | 0.04 | 0.14 | 0.07 |
| 5 | 0.12 | 0.02 | 0.10 |
| 6 | 0.08 | 0.19 | 0.06 |
| RBAR | 0.063333 | 0.078333 | 0.061667 |

Next, we compute the terms of the covariance matrix V. You may remember from statistics that we can compute the covariance matrix using a two-step procedure. First, we compute the ERRORS for each investment, which are defined as RATES minus RBAR. Note that there are six terms (J = 1, 2, . . . , 6) for each of the three investments forming a six by three matrix.

| **RATES(I1,J)-RBAR(I1)** | **RATES(I2,J)-RBAR(I2)** | **RATES(I3,J)-RBAR(I3)** |
|---|---|---|
| 0.006667 | 0.061667 | −0.011667 |
| −0.013333 | −0.148333 | −0.001667 |
| −0.043333 | −0.028333 | −0.031667 |
| −0.023333 | 0.061667 | 0.008333 |
| 0.056667 | −0.058333 | 0.038333 |
| 0.016667 | 0.111667 | −0.001667 |

Second, we take each pair of investments and *cross multiply* the error terms for corresponding periods and then average the result. Each average is a term in the covariance matrix. Since we are taking all combinations of pairs, the result is a three by three matrix. That is, the cross-terms in the matrix are I1–I1, I1–I2, I1–I3, I2–I1, I2–I2, I2–I3, I3–I1, I3–I2, and I3–I3. We can now summarize the total variance of our investment return data as a covariance matrix, V. The variances of the individual investment returns appear along the main diagonal of the matrix. Also, the matrix is symmetrical across the main diagonal, so for example, V(I1,I2) = V(I2,I1).

| Covariance Matrix V | | | |
|---|---|---|---|
|  | **I1** | **I2** | **I3** |
| I1 | 0.001022 | 0.000122 | 0.000544 |
| I2 | 0.000122 | 0.007714 | −0.000247 |
| I3 | 0.000544 | −0.000247 | 0.000447 |

---

[1]More details on the mathematics related to determining the expression for the variance of the portfolio can be found in Luenberger (1998) or Winston (1995).

We now set our two problem parameters: an investment AMOUNT equal to $100 and a Portfolio RETurn (PRET) equal to 6.5%. Setting these values as parameters allows us to easily rerun our model. The sum over X must equal AMOUNT, and the sum placed in investments 1 and 2 in total must be at least 50% of AMOUNT. The @SIZE command is used to specify the number of PERIODS as a parameter, again to minimize the changes necessary to rerun the model.

Note that the default assumption in LINGO is that all variables not specified in the model are non-negative. Looking at the values of ERRORS and V shows that negative values can occur. Therefore, the @FREE command must be used to allow the elements of ERRORS and V to be negative. All of the constraints are shown.

```
N = @SIZE(PERIODS);
@FOR(INVESTS(I):
RBAR(I) = @SUM (PERIODS(J): RATES(I,J))/N;);

@FOR( INVESTS(I):
 @FOR (PERIODS(J):
  ERRORS (I,J)=RATES(I,J)-RBAR(I)));
@FOR(INVESTS(I):
 @FOR (INVESTS(K):
  V (I,K) = @SUM (PERIODS(J): ERRORS(I,J)* ERRORS(K,J))/N));
AMOUNT=100;
PRET=.065;
@SUM (INVESTS(I): X(I)) = AMOUNT;
X(I1)+X(I2)>=.5*AMOUNT;

@SUM(INVESTS(I): RBAR(I)*X(I))>=PRET*AMOUNT;
@FOR(RETURNS(I,J): @FREE (ERRORS));
@FOR(COVAR(I,J): @FREE (V));
```

Note that since the objective function is non-linear of order two and the constraints are linear, the Markowitz portfolio selection is an example of a *quadratic programming problem*.

```
:   1]MODEL:
    2]!MARKOWITZ PORTFOLIO MODEL;
    3]
    4]SETS:
    5]   INVESTS /I1, I2, I3/ : RBAR, X;
    6]   PERIODS /1..6/;
    7]   RETURNS(INVESTS,PERIODS): RATES, ERRORS;
    8]   COVAR(INVESTS,INVESTS): V;
    9]ENDSETS
   10]
   11]!N IS DEFINED SO THAT THE PROBLEM CAN BE GENERALIZED TO INCLUDE
MORE DATA;
   12]N = @SIZE(PERIODS);
   13]
   14]! COMPUTE THE AVERAGE RETURN FOR EACH INVESTMENT;
   15]@FOR(INVESTS(I):
   16]   RBAR(I) = @SUM (PERIODS(J): RATES(I,J))/N;);
   17]
   18]!COMPUTE THE ERROR TERMS FOR EACH INVESTMENT, DEFINED AS INDIVIDUAL
RETURNS
   19] MINUS THE AVERAGE RETURN;
```

**Figure 6.4** LINGO Output for the Portfolio Problem

```
20]@FOR(INVESTS(I):
21]   @FOR (PERIODS(J):
22]    ERRORS (I,J)=RATES(I,J)-RBAR(I)));
23]
24]!COMPUTE THE TERMS OF THE COVARIANCE MATRIX BY CROSS-MULTIPLYING
THE ERROR
25] TERMS FOR EACH PAIR OF INVESTMENTS AND AVERAGING THE RESULTS;
26]@FOR(INVESTS(I):
27] @FOR (INVESTS(K):
28]    V (I,K) = @SUM (PERIODS(J): ERRORS(I,J)* ERRORS(K,J))/N));
29]
30]!THE OBJECTIVE FUNCTION SEEKS TO MINIMIZE THE TOTAL VARIANCE OF
THE PORTFOLIO
31] WHICH IS OBTAINED BY MULTIPLYING EACH COVARIANCE TERM BY THE
DECISION
32] VARIABLES ASSOCIATED WITH THAT TERM;
33][OBJ] MIN=@SUM (COVAR(I,K): V(I,K)*X(I)*X(K));
34]
35]!WE SET THE TOTAL AVAILABLE INVESTMENT AND THE MINIMUM RETURN;
36]AMOUNT=100;
37]PRET=.065;
38]
39]!WE WISH TO INVEST ALL AVAILABLE FUNDS;
40][BUD] @SUM (INVESTS(I): X(I)) = AMOUNT;
41]
42]!WE MUST INVEST AT LEAST HALF OF OUR FUNDS IN INVESTMENTS 1 AND 2;
43][MIX] X(I1)+X(I2)>=.5*AMOUNT;
44]
45]!WE MUST OBTAIN AN EXPECTED TOTAL RETURN THAT MEETS OUR MINIMUM;
46][RET] @SUM(INVESTS(I): RBAR(I)*X(I))>=PRET*AMOUNT;
47]
48]!SINCE THE ERRORS AND COVARIANCE TERMS CAN BE NEGATIVE, WE USE
49] THE FREE COMMAND;
50]@FOR( RETURNS(I,J): @FREE (ERRORS));
51]@FOR( COVAR(I,J): @FREE (V));
52]
53]DATA:
54]RATES = 0.07,0.05,0.02,0.04,0.12,0.08,
55]    0.14,-0.07,0.05,0.14,0.02,0.19,
56]    0.05,0.06,0.03,0.07,0.10,0.06;
57]ENDDATA
58]
59]END

MIN    ? X( I3) + ? X( I2) + ? X( I1)
SUBJECT TO
BUD]  X( I3) + X( I2) + X( I1) =  100
MIX]  X( I2) + X( I1) >=  50
RET]  .0616667 X( I3) + .0783333 X( I2) + .0633333 X( I1) >=  6.5
END

Local optimal solution found at step:         6
Objective value:                      5.935185

                   Variable        Value      Reduced Cost
                     X( I1)     33.33333      0.0000000
                     X( I2)     16.66667      0.0000000
                     X( I3)     50.00000      0.0000000
```

**Figure 6.4** (*Continued*)

The complete LINGO model, the algebraic formulation, and an abbreviated solution for this problem appear in Figure 6.4. Note that the algebraic formulation of the objective function that was generated by the model has question marks in it. This does not mean that LINGO is confused! However, it is LINGO's way of displaying non-linear relationships when the *Generate* command is used.

The LINGO modeling language formulation is in a file called MARK.LG4. The objective function value tells us that the total portfolio variance is 5.935. By looking at the values for the three investments (X(1), X(2), and X(3)), we find that we should invest $33,333, $16,667, and $50,000, in I1, I2, and I3, respectively.

## Capital Budgeting Problem and Extensions

### The Capital Budgeting Problem

Capital budgeting problems are also concerned with investment decisions. However, capital budgeting problems focus on how investment decisions made over a planning horizon impact future profitability. Consider the following example. Apex, Inc. can invest in a variety of projects that over the next four years have varying capital requirements. Faced with limited resources, Apex must select the optimal mix of projects. It is assumed that the projects are independent of one another in terms of capital required and returns received. The estimated present values (PV) of the projects, the capital requirements, and the available capital funds by year follow.

| Project | PV | Capital Required ($000) Per Year | | | |
| | | 1 | 2 | 3 | 4 |
| --- | --- | --- | --- | --- | --- |
| Plant Expansion | 90 | 15 | 20 | 20 | 15 |
| Warehouse Expansion | 40 | 10 | 15 | 20 | 5 |
| New Machinery | 10 | 10 | 0 | 0 | 4 |
| New Product Research | 37 | 15 | 10 | 10 | 10 |
| Available capital funds | | 40 | 50 | 40 | 35 |

The LINGO formulation using our five-step procedure is as follows.

### 1. Specify the SETS: Section of the Model, which Includes Sets, Elements, and Attributes

The sets for this problem are PROJECTS and YEARS. The elements of PROJECTS and YEARS are simply the four projects and the four years. The derived set COMBINE indicates the capital requirements for each project during each year. The attributes of the PROJECTS set are the estimated present values (PV) and a binary variable, X, indicating whether or not a project is funded. That is, if X is equal to 1, we fund the project and if X is 0, we do not fund the project. The attribute for YEARS is the available capital (FUNDS), while the attribute for COMBINE is the capital requirements (CAPREQ). The SETS: section is given as

```
SETS:
  PROJECTS / 1..4/: X, PV;
  YEARS / 1..4/: FUNDS;
  COMBINE(PROJECTS,YEARS): CAPREQ;
ENDSETS
```

## 2. Specify the DATA: Section of the Model by Assigning Values to Attributes

The data include the present values, or PV, for each project, the FUNDS available each year, and the capital requirements or CAPREQ, for each project for each year as given here.

```
DATA:
  PV = 90,40,10,37;
  FUNDS = 40,50,40,35;
  CAPREQ = 15,20,20,15,
           10,15,20,5,
           10,0,0,4,
           15,10,10,10;
ENDDATA
```

## 3. Identify the Decision Variables as Attributes Not Assigned Values in the DATA: Section

Since the X values are not assigned in the DATA: section, they are the decision variables, as expected.

## 4. Formulate the Objective Function Using the @SUM Function

The objective of our capital budgeting problem is to maximize the PV over all projects (X) as shown.

```
MAX = @SUM(PROJECTS(I): PV(I)*X(I));
```

## 5. Formulate the Constraints Using the @FOR Function

A constraint for each year indicates that the total amount of capital consumed by funded projects cannot exceed the available FUNDS for that year. We also specify that the decision variables (X) are binary integer (@BIN). The constraints are

```
@FOR(YEARS(J):
  @SUM(PROJECTS(I): CAPREQ(I,J)*X(I))<=FUNDS(J));
@FOR(PROJECTS(I):
  @BIN(X(I)));
```

The LINGO modeling language formulation is in a file called APEX.LG4. The model, algebraic formulation, and abbreviated solution appear in Figure 6.5. The objective function value indicates that the optimal total present value is $140. By looking at the values for the four binary investment variables (X(1), X(2), X(3), and X(4)), we find that the values of the first three are 1, and the value of the fourth is 0. Therefore, we should invest in projects 1, 2, and 3. The slack value of 15 for AVAILABLEFUNDS (2) indicates that $15 of the available capital during year 2 is not consumed by the optimal mix of funded projects.

### Extensions of the Capital Budgeting Problem

We now consider three extensions to this problem that define special relationships among the decision variables. All of these extensions can be applied to other mathematical programming problems where the decision variables take on binary values. The first variation is called a "multiple choice constraint." Suppose that in addition to the original warehouse expansion project, X(2), Apex is considering two additional warehouse expansion projects,

```
:   1]MODEL:
    2]SETS:
    3]  PROJECTS / 1..4/: X, PV;
    4]  YEARS / 1..4/: FUNDS;
    5]  COMBINE(PROJECTS,YEARS): CAPREQ;
    6]END SETS
    7]
    8]! THE OBJECTIVE;
    9]MAX = @SUM(PROJECTS(I): PV(I)*X(I));
   10]
   11]!THE AVAILABLE FUNDS CONSTRAINTS;
   12] @FOR(YEARS(J): [AVAILABLEFUNDS]
   13]  @SUM(PROJECTS(I): CAPREQ(I,J)*X(I))<=FUNDS(J));
   14]
   15]!MAKE ALL X VARIABLES 0/1;
   16]@FOR(PROJECTS(I):
   17]  @BIN(X(I)));
   18]
   19]! HERE IS THE DATA;
   20]  DATA:
   21]    PV = 90,40,10,37;
   22]    FUNDS = 40,50,40,35;
   23]    CAPREQ = 15,20,20,15,
   24]             10,15,20,5,
   25]             10,0,0,4,
   26]             15,10,10,10;
   27]  ENDDATA
   28]
   29]END
   30]
```

```
MAX    90 X(1) + 40 X(2) + 10 X(3) + 37 X(4)
SUBJECT TO
AVAILABLEFUNDS(1)] 15 X(1) + 10 X(2) + 10 X(3) + 15 X(4) <=  40
AVAILABLEFUNDS(2)] 20 X(1) + 15 X(2) + 10 X(4) <=  50
AVAILABLEFUNDS(3)] 20 X(1) + 20 X(2) + 10 X(4) <=  40
AVAILABLEFUNDS(4)] 15 X(1) + 5 X(2) + 4 X(3) + 10 X(4) <=  35
END
INTE    4
```

```
Optimal solution found at step:          4
Objective value:                  140.0000
Branch count:                         0
```

| Variable | Value | Reduced Cost |
|---|---|---|
| X(1) | 1.000000 | -90.00000 |
| X(2) | 1.000000 | -40.00000 |
| X(3) | 1.000000 | -10.00000 |
| X(4) | 0.0000000 | -37.00000 |

| Row | Slack or Surplus | Dual Price |
|---|---|---|
| AVAILABLEFUNDS(1) | 5.000000 | 0.0000000 |
| AVAILABLEFUNDS(2) | 15.00000 | 0.0000000 |
| AVAILABLEFUNDS(3) | 0.0000000 | 0.0000000 |
| AVAILABLEFUNDS(4) | 11.00000 | 0.0000000 |

**Figure 6.5** LINGO Output for the Capital Budgeting Problem

X(5) and X(6). Suppose that one of the warehouses must be expanded because of increased demand, but there is not sufficient demand to allow expansion of more than one of these three warehouses.

The following additional multiple choice constraint is needed to model this situation:

$$X(2) + X(5) + X(6) = 1$$

Since the sum of three binary variables must exactly equal 1, two must be 0 and one must be 1. Thus, this equation guarantees that exactly one warehouse expansion project is accepted.

We can slightly change the situation just described by stating that we want to expand at *most* one warehouse. The difference between this problem and the last one is that it is now acceptable to not expand any warehouses. Therefore, we replace the equals in the previous constraints with a "less than or equal to" sign:

$$X(2) + X(5) + X(6) <= 1$$

This constraint guarantees that at most one warehouse expansion project is accepted.

The second extension that we consider is called "K out of N alternatives." Suppose that we must accept two of the three warehouse projects. Using the same logic as in the previous examples, the sum of the three binary variables must exactly equal 2.

$$X(2) + X(5) + X(6) = 2$$

This constraint will guarantee that exactly two warehouse expansion projects are accepted. If we require that no more than two of the projects be selected, the constraint would be

$$X(2) + X(5) + X(6) <= 2$$

The third extension that we will discuss is called "conditional constraints." Suppose that we want to model a situation in which the acceptance of one project is conditional upon the acceptance of another project. Specifically, suppose we cannot expand the warehouse, X(2), unless the plant, X(1), is expanded. Many students find that this type of constraint is difficult to model. It sometimes helps to use if–then statements to map out the possibilities. For example, this conditional constraint can be interpreted as follows: if X(1) = 0, then X(2) = 0 and if X(1) = 1, then X(2) = 0 or 1. With this information in mind it is easier to then develop the constraint for this condition:

$$X(2) <= X(1)$$

The modeler should always check that the suggested constraint satisfies the stated conditions. In the current case, if X(1) equals zero, the constraint simplifies to X(2) <= 0, which means that X(2) must equal zero. If X(2) equals one, the constraint simplifies to X(2) <= 1, which means that X(2) can equal zero or one. We see that both conditions are satisfied with this constraint.

If the condition were changed to require that the warehouse expansion be accepted if the plant expansion project is accepted and vice versa, then the constraint would be

$$X(2) = X(1)$$

This constraint implies that whatever value X(1) assumes, X(2) must assume the same value. In plain English, if we do *not* expand the plant (X(1) = 0), then we *cannot* expand the warehouse (X(2) = 0). If we *do* expand the plant (X(1) = 1), then we *must* expand the warehouse (X(2) = 1).

## MARKETING APPLICATIONS

### Media Selection

Marketing managers often have to decide how to allocate an advertising budget to various advertising media. Alternative media include television, radio, newspapers, magazines, and direct mail. Media effectiveness relates to the number of potential customers reached, the quality of the media exposure, and the frequency of exposure. Restrictions relate to available advertising budget and media availability and mix policies.

Consider the following example in which the Weston company wishes to decide how to best allocate its weekly advertising budget to promote its new floor care product. Weston's advertising department has collected the following data concerning the available media:

| Advertising Media | $ Cost/Ad | Reach/Ad | Quality/Ad | Max Slots | Min Slots |
|---|---|---|---|---|---|
| Daytime TV | 1000 | 10000 | 60 | 14 | 5 |
| Daytime Radio | 550 | 7000 | 35 | 21 | 5 |
| Daily Newspaper | 600 | 5000 | 45 | 7 | 2 |

Daytime TV and Radio are 30-second slots and Daily Newspaper signifies a one-half page advertisement. The reach is the estimated audience size for each ad, and quality is Weston's assessment of the relative value of one advertisement in each of the media. Weston wishes to maximize exposure quality, while reaching at least 100,000 potential customers and remaining within their weekly advertising budget of $20,000. The LINGO formulation of this problem using the five-step procedure follows.

### 1. Specify the SETS: Section of the Model, which Includes Sets, Elements, and Attributes

The only primitive set needed in this formulation is MEDIA, with elements TV, RADIO, and PRINT. The attributes include the number of advertising SLOTS assigned to each of the MEDIA, the COST, REACH, and QUALITY for each advertisement, and WESTON's maximum (MAXSLOTS) and minimum (MINSLOTS) number of advertisements allowed for each MEDIA. The complete SETS: section is shown here.

```
SETS:
MEDIA/TV,RADIO,PRINT/:SLOTS,COST,REACH,QUALITY,MAXSLOTS,
MINSLOTS;
ENDSETS
```

### 2. Specify the DATA: Section of the Model by Assigning Values to Attributes

The data for COST, REACH, QUALITY, MAXSLOTS, and MINSLOTS are specified in the DATA: section as

```
DATA:
COST=1000,550,400;
REACH=10000,7000,5000;
MAXSLOTS=14,21,7;
MINSLOTS=5,5,2;
QUALITY=60,35,45;
ENDDATA
```

### 3. Identify the Decision Variables as Attributes that are not Assigned Values in the DATA: Section

The decision variables are the number of SLOTS to allocate on a weekly basis to each of the advertising media.

### 4. Formulate the Objective Function Using the @SUM Function

The objective is to maximize the total exposure QUALITY obtained from all of the advertising SLOTS that are funded. The LINGO formulation of the objective function is

```
MAX=@SUM(MEDIA(I):SLOTS(I)*QUALITY(I));
```

### 5. Formulate the Constraints Using the @FOR Function

The @BND function is applied to set the constraints for the minimum (MINSLOTS) and maximum (MAXSLOTS) numbers of SLOTS for each of the MEDIA. The @GIN function is needed to specify that the values of SLOTS are integer. Two @SUM based constraints are needed to enforce the budget and customer target constraints. The values for BUDGET and CUSTARGET are set as parameters to increase the flexibility of the model. The complete constraints section of the model is shown here.

```
@FOR(MEDIA(I):
 @BND(MINSLOTS(I),SLOTS(I),MAXSLOTS(I)));
@FOR(MEDIA(I):@GIN(SLOTS(I)));
@SUM(MEDIA(I):COST(I)*SLOTS(I))<=BUDGET;
@SUM(MEDIA(I):REACH(I)*SLOTS(I))>=CUSTARGET;
BUDGET=20000;
CUSTARGET=100000;
```

The complete LINGO model, the algebraic formulation, and the solution for this problem appear as Figure 6.6. The LINGO modeling language formulation is in a file called WESTON.LG4. The optimal solution is to fund six TV, 20 RADIO, and seven PRINT advertisements each week for a total quality exposure of 1375. An alternate formulation of this problem is to set a minimum quality exposure level and then maximize total reach. The details for making the changes are left to the reader.

## Floor Space Allocation

Periodically, a department store will reallocate its floor space among its departments. One approach is to approximate the average profit per square meter per year for each department as a linear function of the allocated space. The objective is to find the allocation that maximizes total profit. Like the portfolio problem, the floor space allocation problem is another member of the class of NLP problems called quadratic programs.

Consider the following example where a store has two departments called NONAME and DESIGNER. The department managers were asked to give two estimates of the yearly profit per square meter as a function of the minimum and maximum number of square meters allocated, as shown here.

|  | **Noname** | | **Designer** | |
| --- | --- | --- | --- | --- |
|  | **Sq M Space** | **$/Sq M/Year** | **Sq M Space** | **$/Sq M/Year** |
| Min Space | 9 | $12,000 | 12 | $15,000 |
| Max Space | 50 | 5,000 | 45 | 4,000 |

```
 :   1]MODEL:
     2]SETS:
     3]MEDIA/TV,RADIO,PRINT/:SLOTS,COST,REACH,QUALITY,MAXSLOTS,MINSLOTS;
     4]ENDSETS
     5]MAX=@SUM(MEDIA(I):SLOTS(I)*QUALITY(I));
     6]@FOR(MEDIA(I):
     7]   @BND(MINSLOTS(I),SLOTS(I),MAXSLOTS(I)));
     8]@FOR(MEDIA(I):@GIN(SLOTS(I)));
     9][BUD] @SUM(MEDIA(I):COST(I)*SLOTS(I))<=BUDGET;
    10][RCH] @SUM(MEDIA(I):REACH(I)*SLOTS(I))>=CUSTARGET;
    11]BUDGET=20000;
    12]CUSTARGET=100000;
    13]DATA:
    14]COST=1000,550,400;
    15]REACH=10000,7000,5000;
    16]MAXSLOTS=14,21,7;
    17]MINSLOTS=5,5,2;
    18]QUALITY=60,35,45;
    19]ENDDATA
    20]END

MAX    60 SLOTS( TV) + 35 SLOTS( RADIO) + 45 SLOTS( PRINT)
SUBJECT TO
BUD] 1000 SLOTS( TV) + 550 SLOTS( RADIO) + 400 SLOTS( PRINT)
     <= 20000
RCH] 10000 SLOTS( TV) + 7000 SLOTS( RADIO) + 5000 SLOTS( PRINT)
     >= 100000
END
SLB SLOTS( TV)         5.000
SUB SLOTS( TV)        14.000
GIN SLOTS( TV)
SLB SLOTS( RADIO)      5.000
SUB SLOTS( RADIO)     21.000
GIN SLOTS( RADIO)
SLB SLOTS( PRINT)      2.000
SUB SLOTS( PRINT)      7.000
GIN SLOTS( PRINT)

Global optimal solution found at step:          13
Objective value:                          1375.000
Branch count:                                    5
                        Variable          Value       Reduced Cost
                        SLOTS( TV        6.000000        -60.00000
                   SLOTS( RADIO)         20.00000        -35.00000
                   SLOTS( PRINT)         7.000000        -45.00000
```

**Figure 6.6** LINGO Output for the Media Selection Problem

Assume that there are a total of 65 square meters to be allocated. Furthermore, each department will be allocated neither less than the minimum space nor more than the maximum space. Management wishes to decide how to allocate space to maximize total profit. The application of the five-step method proceeds as follows.

### 1. Specify the SETS: Section of the Model, which Includes Sets, Elements, and Attributes

The only primitive set needed in this formulation is DEPARTS, with elements NONAME and DESIGNER. The attributes include the minimum and maximum space (MINSP and

MAXSP, respectively) and profit (MINPR and MAXPR), respectively. The attribute SPACE represents the amount of floor space allocated to each department. In addition, RPROFIT is the rate of profit change between the MINSP and MAXSP and is computed in the model (as shown). The complete SETS: section is

```
SETS:
  DEPARTS/NONAME, DESIGNER/:MINSP,MAXSP,MINPR,MAXPR,RPROFIT,SPACE;
ENDSETS
```

### 2. Specify the DATA: Section of the Model by Assigning Values to Attributes

The data for MINSP, MAXSP, MINPR, and MAXPR are given in the DATA: section

```
DATA:
  MINSP = 9,12;
  MAXSP = 50,45;
  MINPR = 5000,4000;
  MAXPR = 12000,15000;
ENDDATA
```

### 3. Identify the Decision Variables as Attributes not Assigned Values in the DATA: Section

The decision variables are the amount of SPACE to allocate to each department.

### 4. Formulate the Objective Function Using the @SUM Function

We assume that profit per square meter is linear between the minimum and maximum space (MINSP and MAXSP) allocated to a department. Therefore, the rate of profit change per square meter called RPROFIT equals the change in profit divided by the change in allocated space, or (MAXPR − MINPR)/(MINSP − MAXSP). As shown in Figure 6.7 for the NONAME department, RPROFIT = (12000 − 5000)/(9-50) = −170.73 per square meter for each square meter allocated over a MINSP of 9. That is, if ten meters of SPACE are allocated to the NONAME department, the profit *per square meter* would be $12,000 − 170.73 = $11,829.37. Therefore, profit per square meter for NONAME is the maximum profit per square meter ($12,000) minus 170.73 times the amount of space allocated over the minimum of 9. This relationship can be represented as

$$12000 + (-170.73)(SPACE(NONAME) - 9)$$

Substituting the various LINGO attribute names in the equation, we obtain:

$$MAXPR + RPROFIT (SPACE(NONAME)-MINSP(NONAME)).$$

Total profit is obtained by multiplying profit per square meter by SPACE for each department and then adding the result. Since total profit per square meter is a function of

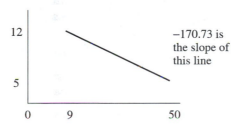

**Figure 6.7** Determining the Rate of Change for Profit per Meter for the NONAME Department

```
:    1]MODEL:
     2]SETS:
     3] DEPARTS/NONAME, DESIGNER/:MINSP,MAXSP,MINPR,MAXPR,RPROFIT,SPACE;
     4]ENDSETS
     5]
     6]!CALCULATE RATE OF CHANGE OF PROFIT/SQ M BETWEEN MINSP AND MAXSP;
     7]!NOTE THAT RPROFIT WILL BE NEGATIVE;
     8]  @FOR(DEPARTS(I):[RTS]
     9]    RPROFIT(I)=(MAXPR(I)-MINPR(I))/(MINSP(I)-MAXSP(I)));
    10]
    11]!THE MAXPR PER SQ M IS REDUCED BY EVERY SQ M ALLOCATED OVER THE
    MINSP,
    12]  AT A RATE OF RPROFIT;
    13]!THEREFORE, TOTAL PROFIT = THE SPACE ALLOCATED TO A DEPARTMENT *
    14]   (MAXPR + RPROFIT * (THE AMOUNT OF SPACE OVER THE MINSP) );
    15][OBJ] MAX = @SUM(DEPARTS(I):
    16]   SPACE(I)*(MAXPR(I)+RPROFIT(I)*(SPACE(I)-MINSP(I))));
    17]
    18]SPACE(NONAME)+SPACE(DESIGNER)=65;
    19]
    20]!SET THE BOUNDS FOR SPACE PER DEPARTMENT, RPROFIT WILL BE NEGATIVE;
    21]  @FOR(DEPARTS(I):
    22]    @BND(MINSP(I),SPACE(I),MAXSP(I));
    23]     @FREE(RPROFIT(I)););
    24]
    25]!HERE IS THE DATA;
    26]DATA:
    27]    MINSP = 9,12;
    28]    MAXSP = 50,45;
    29]    MINPR = 5000,4000;
    30]    MAXPR = 12000,15000;
    31]ENDDATA
    32]
    33]END

 MAX  - ? SPACE( DESIGNER) - ? SPACE( NONAME)
 SUBJECT TO
 4] SPACE( DESIGNER) + SPACE( NONAME) =  65
 END
 SLB SPACE( DESIGNER)    12.000
 SUB SPACE( DESIGNER)    45.000
 SLB SPACE( NONAME)       9.000
 SUB SPACE( NONAME)      50.000


 Local optimal solution found at step:            20
 Objective value:                          537949.3

                 Variable            Value          Reduced Cost
           SPACE( NONAME)         37.56452        0.6731370E-05
          SPACE( DESIGNER)        27.43548        0.0000000


                      Row    Slack or Surplus          Dual Price
             AVAILABLESPACE        0.0000000            709.6767
```

**Figure 6.8** LINGO Output for the Floor Space Allocation Problem

SPACE and is multiplied by SPACE, the result is a quadratic objective function. The objective function for the LINGO modeling language formulation is

```
MAX = @SUM(DEPARTS(I):
  SPACE(I)*(MAXPR(I)+RPROFIT(I)*(SPACE(I)-MINSP(I))));
```

### 5. Formulate the Constraints Using the @FOR Function

The computation of RPROFIT using the @FOR function is included in the constraint section of the model. The sum of the SPACE allocated across all DEPARTS equal the space available. The @BND function is used to specify the MINSP and MAXSP for each DEPARTS. Since RPROFIT can be negative, the @FREE command is needed. Note that the @BND and @FREE statements are included under one @FOR statement. The constraints section of the formulation is

```
@FOR(DEPARTS(I):
  RPROFIT(I)=(MAXPR(I)-MINPR(I))/(MINSP(I)-MAXSP(I)));
 SPACE(NONAME)+SPACE(DESIGNER)=65;
  @FOR(DEPARTS(I):
   @BND(MINSP(I),SPACE(I),MAXSP(I));
   @FREE(RPROFIT(I));););
```

The LINGO modeling language formulation is in a file called DSTORE.LG4. The model, algebraic formulation, and solution appear in Figure 6.8. The objective function value indicates that the optimal total profit is $537,949.30. By looking at the values for the decision variables (SPACE(NONAME) and SPACE(DESIGNER)), we find that we should allocate 37.56 square meters to the NONAME department and 27.44 square meters to the DESIGNER department.

## KEY LINGO COMMANDS

Having completed our discussion of mathematical programming using the LINGO modeling language, we summarize the key Lingo modeling commands used in the past three chapters in Table 6.1.

**Table 6.1**  Summary of Key LINGO Modeling Commands

| Command | Explanation |
| --- | --- |
| @SUM (set_name: expression) | *Expression* is evaluated for each element of the set called *set_name*, and the results are summed over all elements. The @SUM produces *one* statement that is evaluated to provide *one* numerical result. |
| @FOR(set_name: expression) | *Expression* is a statement of the operation(s) to be performed for each element of the set called *set_name*. If *expression* is a constraint, then LINGO will generate a copy of this constraint FOR each member of *set_name*. |
| @BND(lower_bound,variable,upper_bound) | This statement limits an attribute called *variable* to being greater than or equal to *lower_bound* and less than or equal to *upper_bound*. |
| @FREE(variable_name) | This statement allows *variable_name* to assume negative values. LINGO's default setting is that all variable values are non-negative. |
| @SIZE(set_name) | This statement returns the number of elements in *set_name*. It is used to help make models more data independent and easier to modify. |
| set_name\|expression | This is called a "conditional qualifier" and is used to limit the elements of *set_name* in @FOR or @SUM statements. LINGO evaluates *expression* (such as J #GT# 1) and determines which elements are included. |

## SUMMARY

In this chapter we present selected applications of mathematical programming in scheduling, finance, and marketing. At the end of the chapter we summarize the key LINGO modeling commands used in these applications. The specific applications that we address are staff and production scheduling, Markowitz portfolio selection, capital budgeting, media mix, and retail floor space allocation. Each of these applications is formulated using the LINGO modeling language. Many of the applications presented have been applied in practice by our students. Others are presented to illustrate specific modeling issues. Components of the models presented can be combined with others to develop an even broader set of potential applications. The examples contained in this and previous chapters demonstrate the value that mathematical programming can provide for improved decision making.

## HOMEWORK PROBLEMS

**1.** The NORTHSHORE Bank is working to develop an efficient work schedule for full-time and part-time tellers. The schedule must provide for efficient operation of the bank including adequate customer service, employee breaks, and so on. On Fridays the bank is open from 9:00 a.m. to 7:00 p.m. The number of tellers necessary to provide adequate customer service during each hour of operation is summarized here.

| Time | 9–10 | 10–11 | 11–12 | 12–1 | 1–2 | 2–3 | 3–4 | 4–5 | 5–6 | 6–7 |
|------|------|-------|-------|------|-----|-----|-----|-----|-----|-----|
| # of Tellers | 6 | 4 | 8 | 10 | 9 | 6 | 4 | 7 | 6 | 6 |

Each full-time employee starts on the hour and works a four-hour shift, followed by one hour for lunch and then a three-hour shift. Part-time employees work one four-hour shift beginning on the hour. Considering salary and fringe benefits, full-time employees cost the bank $15 per hour ($105 per day), and part-time employees cost the bank $8 per hour ($32 per day).

**(a)** Formulate and solve a LINGO model that can be used to develop a schedule that will satisfy customer service needs at a minimum employee cost.

**(b)** After reviewing the solution to part a, the bank manager has realized that some additional requirements must be specified. Specifically, she wants to ensure that one full-time employee is on duty at all times and that there is a staff of at least five full-time employees. Revise your model to incorporate these additional requirements, and solve for the optimal solution.

**2.** You have just purchased a kit from PLYDECK to build a wooden deck adjacent to your patio. The directions indicate that you will need, among other things, 27 two-ft pieces of 2 × 4 boards, 10 three-ft boards, and 15 four-ft pieces. The kit has instructed you to purchase eight-ft long boards, and then cut them to the desired length. The kit indicates that 20 such boards are required for your addition, and that the boards should be cut according to the following patterns:

| Number of boards | Pattern |
|------------------|---------|
| 7 | 2 2 2 2 |
| 2 | 4 4 |
| 11 | 3 4 |

You believe that it is possible to find a solution that uses less than 20 boards. Formulate a LINGO model that could be used to find the minimum number of boards needed to build the deck.

*Hint:* To solve this problem you must consider other cutting patterns. The other patterns are: 4,2,2; 3,2,2; 3,3,2.

**3.** NOVASTAR has been developing four possible new product lines. Management must now make a decision as to which of these four products actually will be produced and at what levels of production. The company would like to find the most profitable product mix. The one-time start-up cost and the marginal net revenue from each unit produced are given here.

| | Product | | | |
|---|---|---|---|---|
| | **1** | **2** | **3** | **4** |
| **Startup Cost** | $50,000 | $40,000 | $70,000 | $60,000 |
| **Marginal Revenue** | $70 | $60 | $90 | $80 |

Management has imposed the following policy constraints:

1. No more than two of the products can be produced.

2. Product 3 can be produced only if either product 1 or 2 is produced. Similarly, product 4 can be produced only if either product 1 or 2 is produced.

In addition, 2000 units at most of each product can be produced, and total demand for all products is 3500. Formulate a LINGO model for this problem.

**4.** M&M Associates want to choose among a series of new investment alternatives. The potential investment alternatives, the net present value of the future stream of returns, the capital requirements, and the available capital funds over the next 3 years are summarized here.

**(a)** Develop a LINGO model for maximizing the net present value.

| Alternative | Net Present Value | Capital Requirements | | |
|-------------|-------------------|----------|--------|--------|
| | | **Year 1** | **Year 2** | **Year 3** |
| Limited plant expansion | 4,000 | 3,000 | 1,000 | 4,000 |
| Extensive plant expansion | 6,000 | 2,500 | 3,500 | 3,500 |
| Test market new product | 10,500 | 6,000 | 4,000 | 5,000 |
| Advertising campaign | 4,000 | 2,000 | 1,500 | 1,800 |
| Basic research | 8,000 | 5,000 | 1,000 | 4,000 |
| Purchase new equipment | 3,000 | 1,000 | 500 | 900 |
| Capital funds available | | 10,500 | 7,000 | 8,750 |

**(b)** Assume that only one of the plant expansion projects can be implemented. Modify your formulation from part a.

**(c)** Suppose that if the test marketing of the new product is carried out, then the advertising campaign must also be conducted. Modify your formulation from part b to reflect this situation.

**5.** CLUTCHCARGO has three compartments in its plane for storing cargo: front, center, and back. These compartments have capacity limits on both weight and space, as summarized:

| Compartment | Weight capacity (tons) | Volume capacity (cu ft.) |
|---|---|---|
| FRONT | 12 | 7,000 |
| CENTER | 18 | 9,000 |
| BACK | 10 | 5,000 |

The weight of the cargo in the respective compartments must be the same proportion of that compartment's weight capacity to maintain the balance of the airplane. For example, if six tons of cargo are assigned to the front, then nine must be assigned to the center and five to the back. The following four cargoes have been offered for shipment on an upcoming flight as space becomes available:

| Cargo | Weight (tons) | Volume–Weight Conversion (cu ft/ton) | Profit ($/ton) |
|---|---|---|---|
| 1 | 20 | 500 | 220 |
| 2 | 16 | 700 | 280 |
| 3 | 25 | 600 | 250 |
| 4 | 13 | 400 | 200 |

Any portion of each of these cargoes can be accepted. The objective is to determine how much (if any) of each cargo should be accepted and how to distribute each shipment among the compartments to maximize the total profit for the flight. Note that the volume–weight conversion factor means that, for example, if 10 tons of cargo 1 are stored in the plane, then it will occupy 5,000 cubic feet of volume. Formulate a LINGO model that could be used to solve this problem.

**6.** GRILLMEISTER produces a natural gas (NG) and a propane gas (PG) grill. If they charge a price p1 for NG and p2 for PG, they can sell q1 of the NG and q2 of the PG grills, where $q1 = 4000 - 10p1 + p2$, and $q2 = 2000 - 9p2 + 0.8p1$. Manufacturing an NG grill requires 2 hours of labor and 3 burner elements. A PG grill uses 3 hours of labor and 1 burner element. At present, 5,000 hours of labor and 4,500 burner elements are available. Formulate a LINGO model that will maximize Grill Meister's revenue. Note that the price/quantity relationships should be entered as constraints.

**7.** TRUCKCO is trying to determine where they should locate a single warehouse. The positions in the X–Y plane (in miles) of their four customers and the number of shipments made annually to each customer appears in the table. TruckCo wants to locate the warehouse to minimize the total distance trucks must travel from the warehouse to the four customers. Formulate a model to help TruckCo solve this problem. *Note:* set up your problem to minimize the sum of the squared distances along both the X- and Y-axes from the four customers to the warehouse. You may wish to draw a two-dimensional grid to help set up this problem. There are no constraints for this problem.

| Customer | X-Coordinate | Y-Coordinate | # of Shipments |
|---|---|---|---|
| 1 | 5 | 10 | 200 |
| 2 | 10 | 5 | 150 |
| 3 | 0 | 12 | 200 |
| 4 | 12 | 0 | 300 |

# REFERENCES

Anderson, D. R., Sweeney, D. J., and T. A. Williams, *An Introduction to Management Science: Quantitative Approaches to Decision Making*, 9th ed., Cincinatti, OH, South-Western Publishing, 2000.

Assad, A. A., Wasil, E. A., and Lilien, G. L. (eds.), *Excellence in Management Science Practice: A Readings Book*, Englewood Cliffs, NJ, Prentice-Hall, 1992.

Labe, R., R. Nigam, and S. Spence, "Management Science at Merrill Lynch Private Client Group," *Interfaces*, Vol. 29, No. 2, pp. 1–14, 1999.

Luenberger, D. G., *Investment Science*, New York, Oxford University Press, 1998.

Schrage, L., *Optimization Modeling with LINGO*, Chicago, Lindo Systems Inc., 2002.

Winston, W. L., *Introduction to Mathematical Programming: Applications and Algorithms*, Belmont, CA, Duxbury, 1995.

# Chapter 7

# Transportation and Distribution Planning Using LINGO's Standard Algebraic Approach[*]

## INTRODUCTION

Mathematical programming has been successfully applied to a variety of important problems in *supply chain* management. These problems address the movement of products across the various links of the supply chain, including suppliers, manufacturers, and customers. In this chapter we will focus on an important subset of supply chain problems, namely, transportation and distribution planning. Other supply chain applications such as production scheduling and planning will be discussed in the next chapter. The reason that we consider transportation and distribution planning separately is that these problems belong to a special class of mathematical programming problems called *network flow* problems.[1] This common problem structure allows us to apply our building block approach using LINGO (Schrage 2002) to successively construct increasingly complex mathematical programming models that address important decisions across the supply chain.

## THE TRANSPORTATION PROBLEM

### Problem Statement

The transportation problem has found many practical applications because it addresses the movement of goods between two links in the supply chain, such as the manufacturer and the customer. Usually, the quantities of goods available at the supply and demand locations are known and limited. The objective is often to minimize the total cost of shipping goods from the supply to the demand locations yet still meeting demand and not exceeding supply. We begin by formulating the fundamental version of this problem and then extend it through a series of examples.[2]

---

[*]Chapters 5 and 6 use the LINGO modeling language approach; Chapters 7 and 8 cover essentially the same material but use the standard algebraic LINGO approach. Therefore, skip Chapters 5 and 6 *or* 7 and 8 per instructions from your professor. See the Preface for further details.

[1]Certain classes of network models, such as shortest path, maximum flow, and minimum spanning tree are not covered here. The reader can see Winston (1995) and Hillier and Lieberman (2001) for further information.

[2]Camm et al. (1997) offers an application of transportation and location models that relates closely to material contained in this chapter. Koksalan and Sural (1999) offer another recent location modeling example.

Suppose that a manufacturer ships TV sets from three warehouses (origins) to four retail stores (destinations) each week. Warehouse capacities and demand (in cases) at the retail stores are as follows:

| Supply | | Demand | |
|---|---|---|---|
| Warehouse 1 | 200 | Store 1 | 100 |
| Warehouse 2 | 150 | Store 2 | 200 |
| Warehouse 3 | 300 | Store 3 | 125 |
| | 650 | Store 4 | 225 |
| | | | 650 |

The cost of shipping TV sets by rail from each warehouse to each store differs according to distance. The shipping cost per case of TV sets for each route is given here.

| | To | | | |
|---|---|---|---|---|
| From | Store 1 | Store 2 | Store 3 | Store 4 |
| Warehouse 1 | $10 | 5 | 12 | 3 |
| Warehouse 2 | 4 | 9 | 15 | 6 |
| Warehouse 3 | 15 | 8 | 6 | 11 |

The objective is to determine the amount of TV sets that should be shipped from each warehouse to each store. The network for this problem is given as Figure 7.1. The circles are referred to as *nodes* and the directed line segments connecting the nodes are called *arcs*. Each warehouse and store are represented as nodes, while each possible shipping route (origin-destination pair) is represented by an arc. The supplies and demands are placed next to their respective nodes. The amount of TV sets shipped from the warehouses to the stores represents the flow in the network.

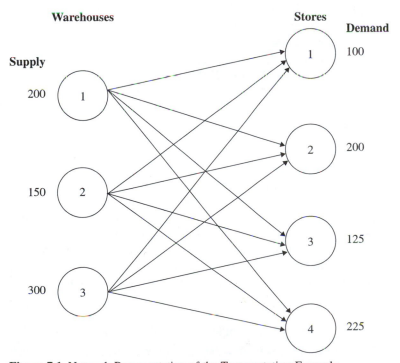

**Figure 7.1** Network Representation of the Transportation Example

## Problem Formulation and Solution

Using the information given about this problem and Figure 7.1, we are now ready to formulate the transportation problem using LINGO. From Chapter 2 we know that developing a mathematical programming problem requires first identifying the decision variables and then formulating the objective function and the constraints. Each of these three steps is described as follows.

### 1. Identify and Define the Decision Variables

The decision variables in this problem represent the number of TV sets (in cases) that we ship from the each of the warehouses to each of the stores. Since we have four stores and three warehouses there are twelve possible shipping routes, and therefore, twelve decision variables. To make it easier to keep track of the identity of each decision variable, we use the following approach for labeling them:

XIJ = number of TV sets (in cases) that are shipped from warehouse I to store J, where

I is the index for the warehouses, and takes on the values 1, 2, 3, and

J is the index for the stores, and takes on the values 1, 2, 3, 4.

### 2. Formulate the Objective Function

The objective for this problem is to minimize the total cost of transportation, which is obtained by multiplying the shipping cost by the amount of TV sets shipped over a given route and then summing over all routes. Since it costs \$10 to ship a unit of 100 TV sets from warehouse 1 to store 1, it costs $10 * X11$ to ship X11 units over this route. Following the same approach for the other eleven routes we obtain the following expression for the objective function. Note that the ! is used to insert a comment into LINGO.

```
!OBJECTIVE FUNCTION;
MIN = 10*X11+5*X12+12*X13+ 3*X14+
       4*X21+9*X22+15*X23+ 6*X24+
      15*X31+8*X32+ 6*X33+11*X34;
```

### 3. Formulate the Constraints

This problem is called a *balanced* transportation problem since total warehouse supply and total demand both equal 650. This implies that all demands will be met exactly and all supplies will be fully utilized. Therefore, supply constraints are needed to ensure that we ship all of the TV sets that are available at each warehouse. Demand constraints are needed to guarantee that each store receives the exact amount of TV sets needed. The supply constraints can be stated: For each warehouse the amount of TV sets shipped *to* all stores must equal the supply of the warehouse. From Figure 7.1 we see that there are four arcs *leaving* warehouse 1. The sum of the amount of TV sets shipped over these four arcs or routes must equal warehouse 1's supply. For warehouse 1 this constraint is:

```
X11+X12+X13+X14=200; !SUPPLY CONSTRAINT FOR WAREHOUSE 1;
```

The remaining two supply constraints are expressed in a similar way:

```
X21+X22+X23+X24=150; !SUPPLY CONSTRAINT FOR WAREHOUSE 2;
X31+X32+X33+X34=300; !SUPPLY CONSTRAINT FOR WAREHOUSE 3;
```

The demand constraints are expressed as follows. For each store the amount of TV sets shipped *from* all warehouses must equal the demand of the store. From Figure 7.1 we see that there are three arcs *entering* store 1. The sum of the amount of TV sets shipped over these three arcs or routes must equal store 1's demand. For store 1 this constraint is:

```
X11+X21+X31=100;  !DEMAND CONSTRAINT FOR STORE 1;
```

The remaining three demand constraints are expressed in a similar way:

```
X12+X22+X32=200;  !DEMAND CONSTRAINT FOR STORE 2;
X13+X23+X33=125;  !DEMAND CONSTRAINT FOR STORE 3;
X14+X24+X34=225;  !DEMAND CONSTRAINT FOR STORE 4;
```

We assume that this company cannot make partial shipments of a case of TV sets. This means that the decision variables must be integer valued. We could use @GIN constraints of the form:

```
@GIN(X1);
```

for each of our twelve decision variables. However, this is not necessary in our current situation since if all supplies and demands are integer-valued, the values of our decision variables will also be integer valued (Winston 1995).

The complete LINGO model and the solution for this problem appears in Figure 7.2. The LINGO model is in a file called TRANSAS.LG4. As seen in the figure's output, the total shipping cost is $3500. The optimal shipments are as follows: warehouse 1 ships 25 cases to store 2 and 175 cases to store 4; warehouse 2 ships 100 cases to store 1 and 50 cases to store 4; and warehouse 3 ships 175 cases to store 2 and 125 cases to store 3.

Further inspection of the output provides additional insight into the nature of the solution. For example, since the reduced cost of X11 equals 9, the cost of shipping a hundred TV sets from warehouse 1 to store 1 would have to improve (decrease) by at least $9 before it would be optimal to ship over this route. Since the cost of shipping a case of TV sets over this route is 10, the reduced cost result indicates that we would only use this shipping route if the cost is $1 per case or less.

Care must be taken in interpreting the impact of the dual variables for the constraints. Since this is a balanced transportation problem, changing one of the supply or demand values in isolation will lead to an infeasible solution. For example, if the supply at warehouse 1 is increased from 200 to 201, the demand at one of the stores must also be increased by one unit to maintain feasibility.

## DIRECT TRANSPORTATION EXTENSIONS

The extensions discussed in this section all maintain the basic structure of the transportation problem as presented in the previous section. The extensions addressed include unbalanced relationships between supply and demand, route restrictions, choice of supply locations, and selection of transportation modes.

### Unbalanced Problem: Total Supply Greater than Total Demand

Suppose that warehouse 2 actually has 175 TV sets available to ship. In this case total supply across the three warehouses is now 675 TV sets yet total demand at the stores is still 650 TV sets. This situation is referred to as an *unbalanced transportation problem.* Since we have 675 TV sets available to ship and we only need 650 TV sets, all of our demand will be satisfied as before. However, across the three warehouses there will be an

```
:  1]MODEL:
   2]!OBJECTIVE FUNCTION;
   3]MIN=10*X11+5*X12+12*X13+ 3*X14+
   4]      4*X21+9*X22+15*X23+ 6*X24+
   5]     15*X31+8*X32+ 6*X33+11*X34;
   6]!CONSTRAINTS;
   7]X11+X12+X13+X14=200;!SUPPLY CONSTRAINT FOR WAREHOUSE 1;
   8]X21+X22+X23+X24=150;!SUPPLY CONSTRAINT FOR WAREHOUSE 2;
   9]X31+X32+X33+X34=300;!SUPPLY CONSTRAINT FOR WAREHOUSE 3;
  10]X11+X21+X31=100;!DEMAND CONSTRAINT FOR STORE 1;
  11]X12+X22+X32=200;!DEMAND CONSTRAINT FOR STORE 2;
  12]X13+X23+X33=125;!DEMAND CONSTRAINT FOR STORE 3;
  13]X14+X24+X34=225;!DEMAND CONSTRAINT FOR STORE 4;
  14]END
  15]

Global optimal solution found at step:          5
Objective value:                        3500.000

            Variable           Value      Reduced Cost
                 X11       0.0000000          9.000000
                 X12       25.00000          0.0000000
                 X13       0.0000000          9.000000
                 X14       175.0000          0.0000000
                 X21       100.0000          0.0000000
                 X22       0.0000000          1.000000
                 X23       0.0000000          9.000000
                 X24       50.00000          0.0000000
                 X31       0.0000000          11.00000
                 X32       175.0000          0.0000000
                 X33       125.0000          0.0000000
                 X34       0.0000000          5.000000

                 Row  Slack or Surplus        Dual Price
                   1       3500.000          1.000000
                   2       0.0000000          3.000000
                   3       0.0000000          0.0000000
                   4       0.0000000          0.0000000
                   5       0.0000000         -4.000000
                   6       0.0000000         -8.000000
                   7       0.0000000         -6.000000
                   8       0.0000000         -6.000000
```

**Figure 7.2** LINGO Output for the Balanced Transportation Problem

unused supply of 25 TV sets. The only required modification of our original transportation model (TRANSAS.LG4) is to change the supply constraints from equality to "less than or equal to." The LINGO supply constraints become:

```
X11+X12+X13+X14<=200;
X21+X22+X23+X24<=175;
X31+X32+X33+X34<=300;
```

The LINGO model is in a file called TRANSBS.LG4. After solving the model, we see that the total shipping cost is still $3500. The optimal shipments are as follows: warehouse 1 ships 25 cases to store 2 and 175 cases to store 4; warehouse 2 ships 100 cases to store 1 and 50 cases to store 4; and warehouse 3 ships 175 cases to store 2 and 125 cases to store 3.

These results indicate that 150 cases are shipped from warehouse 2, indicating a slack of 25 TV sets at this warehouse. The same result can be found from the slack value of 25 for warehouse 2's supply constraint.

## Unbalanced Problem: Total Demand Greater than Total Supply

Again referring to the original transportation problem (TRANSAS.LG4), suppose that store 3 needs 150 TV sets. Now total supply is 650 TV sets while total demand has increased to 675 TV sets. Since we have 650 TV sets available to ship and we need 675 TV sets, all of our supply will be exhausted; however, 25 cases of demand will not be satisfied. Similar to the previous unbalanced problem, we change the relational sign in the demand constraints from "equality" to "less than or equal to." The LINGO demand constraints become:

```
X11+X21+X31<=100;
X12+X22+X32<=200;
X13+X23+X33<=150;
X14+X24+X34<=225;
```

The LINGO model is in a file called TRANSCS.LG4. After solving the model, we see that the total shipping cost has decreased from $3500 to $3450. The optimal shipments are as follows: warehouse 1 continues to ship 25 cases to store 2 and 175 cases to store 4; warehouse 2 continues to ship 100 cases to store 1 and 50 cases to store 4; however, warehouse 3 now ships 150 (versus 175) cases to store 2 and 150 (versus 125) cases to store 3. These results show that 25 cases of store 2's demands are unmet. The same result can be found from the slack value in store 2's demands constraint. The cost savings occurs because the 25 cases were previously shipped from warehouse 3 to store 2 at a cost of $8 per case, while shipping them to store 3 costs $6 per case, for a savings of $50.

## A Restricted Route

Once again, referring to our original formulation (TRANSAS.LG4), suppose there is a strike by the shipping company such that the route from warehouse 3 to store 2 cannot be used. The original model can be modified to address this situation by simply adding a constraint that guarantees that zero cases will be shipped from warehouse 3 to store 2:

```
X32=0;
```

The LINGO model is in a file called TRANSDS.LG4. After solving the model, we see that the total shipping cost has increased to $4375. The significant change in total costs occurred since the warehouse 3–store 2 route original carried 175 TV sets, and now more expensive alternatives are required to make up for its unavailability. The optimal shipments are as follows: warehouse 1 ships 200 cases to store 2; warehouse 2 ships 100 cases to store 1 and 50 cases to store 4; and warehouse 3 ships 125 cases to store 3 and 175 cases to store 4. We note that an alternate solution approach is to change the shipping cost value from warehouse 3 to store 2 to a very large number, say 1000, so that this route will never be used.

## The Warehouse Location Problem

Up to this point we have considered transportation problems that limit the scope of the model to decisions about the amount of product to ship from each warehouse to each store. We would now like to build a model that also considers *where* to locate the warehouses. Interestingly, we can build on the original transportation model (TRANSAS.LG4) to accomplish this goal.

For example, suppose that no warehouses are currently open, but we are considering placing warehouses at locations 1, 2, and 3. The fixed cost of constructing each warehouse and the capacities of the warehouses are shown in the following list. Note that total system capacity is greater than total system demand. All other information is the same as in the original transportation problem.

|              | Fixed Cost | Capacity |
| ------------ | ---------- | -------- |
| warehouse 1  | 125,000    | 300      |
| warehouse 2  | 185,000    | 525      |
| warehouse 3  | 100,000    | 325      |

Consider the changes that must be made to our original transportation model concerning the decision variables, objective function, and the constraints. In order to model the decision about whether or not to open each warehouse, we define new binary decision variables YI, I = 1, 2, 3. For each warehouse I, YI equals 1 if it is open and 0 if it is not open. Since our total cost now includes both the fixed costs of opening warehouses as well as the total shipping cost, we must add some additional terms to our objective function. The cost of opening warehouses is obtained by multiplying the fixed cost of opening warehouse I by YI and then summing over all warehouses I. Our new objective function is:

```
MIN=10*X11+5*X12+12*X13+ 3*X14+
    4*X21+9*X22+15*X23+ 6*X24+
   15*X31+8*X32+ 6*X33+11*X34+
   125000*Y1+185000*Y2+100000*Y3;
```

Second, the existing supply constraints cannot be used since TV sets cannot be shipped from a warehouse if it is not open. Stated another way, we must ensure that nothing is shipped from a warehouse that is not opened. Since the capacity is available only if the warehouse is open, we multiply the warehouse capacity by YI. Therefore, if YI is 0, the capacity constraint becomes less than or equal to 0, indicating that nothing will be shipped from that warehouse. If YI is 1, the capacity constraint becomes less than or equal to that warehouse's capacity and thus becomes equivalent to a supply constraint in TRANSAS.LG4.

```
X11+X12+X13+X14<=300*Y1;!CAPACITY CONSTRAINT FOR WAREHOUSE 1;
X21+X22+X23+X24<=525*Y2;!CAPACITY CONSTRAINT FOR WAREHOUSE 2;
X31+X32+X33+X34<=325*Y3;!CAPACITY CONSTRAINT FOR WAREHOUSE 3;
```

The third change is to make the YI variables binary integers using the @BIN command. This will guarantee that the YI variables will equal either 0 or 1.

```
@BIN(Y1);
@BIN(Y2);
@BIN(Y3);
```

The complete LINGO model and the solution for this problem appear in Figure 7.3. The LINGO model is in a file called TRANSES.LG4. As seen in the figure's output, the

```
:    1]MODEL:
     2]!OBJECTIVE FUNCTION;
     3]MIN=10*X11+5*X12+12*X13+ 3*X14+
     4]     4*X21+9*X22+15*X23+ 6*X24+
     5]    15*X31+8*X32+ 6*X33+11*X34+
     6]    125000*Y1+185000*Y2+100000*Y3;
     7]!CONSTRAINTS;
     8]X11+X12+X13+X14<=300*Y1;!CAPACITY CONSTRAINT FOR WAREHOUSE 1;
     9]X21+X22+X23+X24<=525*Y2;!CAPACITY CONSTRAINT FOR WAREHOUSE 2;
    10]X31+X32+X33+X34<=325*Y3;!CAPACITY CONSTRAINT FOR WAREHOUSE 3;
    11]X11+X21+X31=100;!DEMAND CONSTRAINT FOR STORE 1;
    12]X12+X22+X32=200;!DEMAND CONSTRAINT FOR STORE 2;
    13]X13+X23+X33=125;!DEMAND CONSTRAINT FOR STORE 3;
    14]X14+X24+X34=225;!DEMAND CONSTRAINT FOR STORE 4;
    15]@BIN(Y1);
    16]@BIN(Y2);
    17]@BIN(Y3);
    18]END
    19]

Global optimal solution found at step:           28
Objective value:                           289100.0
Branch count:                                     3

                Variable            Value        Reduced Cost
                     X11        0.0000000            9.000000
                     X12        0.0000000            0.0000000
                     X13        0.0000000            9.000000
                     X14        0.0000000            0.0000000
                     X21         100.0000            0.0000000
                     X22        0.0000000            1.000000
                     X23        0.0000000            9.000000
                     X24         225.0000            0.0000000
                     X31        0.0000000            11.00000
                     X32         200.0000            0.0000000
                     X33         125.0000            0.0000000
                     X34        0.0000000            5.000000
                      Y1        0.0000000            124100.0
                      Y2         1.000000            185000.0
                      Y3         1.000000            100000.0

                     Row   Slack or Surplus          Dual Price
                       1          289100.0            1.000000
                       2         0.0000000            3.000000
                       3          200.0000            0.0000000
                       4         0.0000000            0.0000000
                       5         0.0000000           -4.000000
                       6         0.0000000           -8.000000
                       7         0.0000000           -6.000000
                       8         0.0000000           -6.000000
```

**Figure 7.3** LINGO Output for the Warehouse Location Problem

total fixed and shipping costs are $289,100. Since Y2 = Y3 = 1, warehouses 2 and 3 are opened. The optimal shipments are as follows: warehouse 2 ships 100 cases to store 1 and 225 cases to store 4, and warehouse 3 ships 200 cases to store 2 and 125 cases to store 4. The slack capacity for warehouse 1 is 0 (row 2), since both the amount shipped out and the available capacity are both 0. The slack capacity for warehouse 2 is 200 (row 3), while the slack for warehouse 3 (row 4) is 0 since all of its capacity is used.

## Multimodal Transportation Problem

Again consider TRANSAS.LG4, where TV sets are shipped from warehouses to stores. Now assume that the mode of shipment can be either rail or air. By generalizing the definition of our decision variables, we can incorporate the transportation mode into the model formulation. We now define

XIJK = number of TV sets (in cases) that are shipped from warehouse I to store J by transportation mode K, where

I is the index for the warehouses, and takes on the values 1, 2, 3,

J is the index for the stores and takes on the values 1, 2, 3, 4, and

K is the index for transportation modes and takes on the values 1, 2.

Since we have two transportation modes instead of one, we have doubled the number of decision variables and doubled the number of terms that appear in the objective function and in each of the constraints. Wherever XIJ appears we replace it with XIJ1 + XIJ2. Since the cost to ship from a warehouse to a store depends on the mode, we need additional cost data to modify our objective function. We assume that the original data is comprised of shipping costs by rail. The shipping cost data by rail/air are summarized here.

|  | To | | | |
| --- | --- | --- | --- | --- |
| From | Store 1 | Store 2 | Store 3 | Store 4 |
| warehouse 1 | $10/8 | 5/4 | 12/14 | 3/4 |
| warehouse 2 | 4/6 | 9/8 | 15/12 | 6/5 |
| warehouse 3 | 15/17 | 8/9 | 6/9 | 11/8 |

The complete LINGO model and the solution for this problem appear as Figure 7.4. The LINGO model is in a file called TRANSFS.LG4. As seen in the output below, the total shipping cost is $3425. The optimal shipments are as follows: warehouse 1 ships 25 cases to store 2 by mode 2 and 175 cases to store 4 by mode 1; warehouse 2 ships 100 cases to store 1 by mode 1 and 50 cases to store 4 by mode 2; and warehouse 3 ships 175 cases to store 2 by mode 1 and 125 cases to store 3 by mode 1. The reduced costs of the decision variables indicate how much the shipment cost over a given route for a specific mode would have to decrease before it would be economic to use that mode-route combination.

## ASSIGNMENT-BASED TRANSPORTATION EXTENSIONS

The transportation extensions discussed in this section are all based on the assignment problem, which is itself a special class of the transportation problem. We begin with the assignment problem, and then model the traveling salesman and vehicle routing problems.

```
 1]MODEL:
 2]!OBJECTIVE FUNCTION;
 3]MIN=10*X111+ 8*X112+5*X121+4*X122+12*X131+14*X132+ 3*X141+4*X142+
 4]     4*X211+ 6*X212+9*X221+8*X222+15*X231+12*X232+ 6*X241+5*X242+
 5]    15*X311+17*X312+8*X321+9*X322+ 6*X331+ 9*X332+11*X341+8*X342;
 6]!CONSTRAINTS;
 7]X111+X112+X121+X122+X131+X132+X141+X142=200;!CAPACITY FOR WAREHOUSE
1;
 8]X211+X212+X221+X222+X231+X232+X241+X242=150;!CAPACITY FOR WAREHOUSE
2;
 9]X311+X312+X321+X322+X331+X332+X341+X342=300;!CAPACITY FOR WAREHOUSE
3;
10]X111+X112+X211+X212+X311+X312=100;!DEMAND FOR STORE 1;
11]X121+X122+X221+X222+X321+X322=200;!DEMAND FOR STORE 2;
12]X131+X132+X231+X232+X331+X332=125;!DEMAND FOR STORE 3;
13]X141+X142+X241+X242+X341+X342=225;!DEMAND FOR STORE 4;
14]END
```

```
Global optimal solution found at step:          9
Objective value:                        3425.000
```

| Variable | Value | Reduced Cost |
|---|---|---|
| X111 | 0.0000000 | 8.000000 |
| X112 | 0.0000000 | 6.000000 |
| X121 | 0.0000000 | 1.000000 |
| X122 | 25.00000 | 0.0000000 |
| X131 | 0.0000000 | 10.00000 |
| X132 | 0.0000000 | 12.00000 |
| X141 | 175.0000 | 0.0000000 |
| X142 | 0.0000000 | 1.000000 |
| X211 | 100.0000 | 0.0000000 |
| X212 | 0.0000000 | 2.000000 |
| X221 | 0.0000000 | 3.000000 |
| X222 | 0.0000000 | 2.000000 |
| X231 | 0.0000000 | 11.00000 |
| X232 | 0.0000000 | 8.000000 |
| X241 | 0.0000000 | 1.000000 |
| X242 | 50.00000 | 0.0000000 |
| X311 | 0.0000000 | 9.000000 |
| X312 | 0.0000000 | 11.00000 |
| X321 | 175.0000 | 0.0000000 |
| X322 | 0.0000000 | 1.000000 |
| X331 | 125.0000 | 0.0000000 |
| X332 | 0.0000000 | 3.000000 |
| X341 | 0.0000000 | 4.000000 |
| X342 | 0.0000000 | 1.000000 |

| Row | Slack or Surplus | Dual Price |
|---|---|---|
| 1 | 3425.000 | 1.000000 |
| 2 | 0.0000000 | -3.000000 |
| 3 | 0.0000000 | -5.000000 |
| 4 | 0.0000000 | -7.000000 |
| 5 | 0.0000000 | 1.000000 |
| 6 | 0.0000000 | -1.000000 |
| 7 | 0.0000000 | 1.000000 |
| 8 | 0.0000000 | 0.0000000 |

**Figure 7.4** LINGO Output for the Multimodal Transportation Problem

## Assignment Problem

The assignment problem considers the problem of how to assign people to jobs to achieve the lowest time (or cost) solution. For example, we may have five jobs that need to be completed and five people who can do the work. We would like to find the optimal set of assignments such that each person does one job and each job is done by one person. Because of varying skill levels, each person requires a different amount of time (or cost) to complete each job. Therefore, the objective is to minimize the total time required to complete all five jobs. The amount of time required for each person to perform each job is given here.

| | | | Jobs | | |
|---|---|---|---|---|---|
| People | 1 | 2 | 3 | 4 | 5 |
| 1 | 35 | 25 | 22 | 43 | 26 |
| 2 | 14 | 39 | 25 | 46 | 25 |
| 3 | 15 | 48 | 56 | 21 | 48 |
| 4 | 32 | 29 | 36 | 30 | 34 |
| 5 | 54 | 46 | 28 | 11 | 57 |

Although the shipping of products from warehouses to stores might seem to be quite different than assigning people to jobs, both problems structurally have much in common. We approach the formulation of the assignment problem by looking at the relationship between these two problems: we substitute people for warehouses, jobs for stores, and times for costs.

The decision variables assign people to jobs instead of shipping product from warehouses to stores. The capacity and demand values in the assignment problem are all 1s since each person must do one job and each job is done by one person. The decision variables are binary since we are making one assignment each for person to one job. That is,

XIJ = 1 if person I is assigned to job J,
    0, otherwise

Note that the @BIN restriction is not needed, since the optimal values of the decision variables will always take on binary values when the assignment problem is solved as a linear programming problem (see Winston 1995). These changes show that, in general, an assignment problem is a balanced transportation problem such that all supplies and demands are equal to 1. Of course, unbalanced assignment problems are possible, such as situations where there are more jobs than people, or vice versa.

The complete LINGO model and the solution for this problem appear as Figure 7.5. The LINGO model is in a file called ASSIGNS.LG4. As seen in the figure's output, the total time to complete all five jobs is 102. The optimal values of the decision variables indicate that the optimal assignments are person 1 to job 3, person 2 to job 5, person 3 to job 1; person 4 to job 2, and person 5 to job 4. Note that all slack values are 0 since all constraints are "equality."

## Traveling Salesman Problem

The traveling salesman problem (TSP) has frustrated researchers and practitioners because it is an important problem that is simple to state yet extremely difficult to solve. The TSP is concerned with determining the optimal order in which locations should be visited. Specifically, consider a salesman who has a set of customers who need to be visited and

```
:    1]MODEL:
     2]!OBJECTIVE FUNCTION;
     3]MIN=35*X11+25*X12+22*X13+43*X14+26*X15+
     4]    14*X21+39*X22+25*X23+46*X24+25*X25+
     5]    15*X31+48*X32+56*X33+21*X34+48*X35+
     6]    32*X41+29*X42+36*X43+30*X44+34*X45+
     7]    54*X51+46*X52+28*X53+11*X54+57*X55;
     8]!CONSTRAINTS;
     9]X11+X12+X13+X14+X15=1;!PERSON 1 IS ASSIGNED;
    10]X21+X22+X23+X24+X25=1;!PERSON 2 IS ASSIGNED;
    11]X31+X32+X33+X34+X35=1;!PERSON 3 IS ASSIGNED;
    12]X41+X42+X43+X44+X45=1;!PERSON 4 IS ASSIGNED;
    13]X51+X52+X53+X54+X55=1;!PERSON 5 IS ASSIGNED;
    14]X11+X21+X31+X41+X51=1;!JOB 1 IS ASSIGNED;
    15]X12+X22+X32+X42+X52=1;!JOB 2 IS ASSIGNED;
    16]X13+X23+X33+X43+X53=1;!JOB 3 IS ASSIGNED;
    17]X14+X24+X34+X44+X54=1;!JOB 4 IS ASSIGNED;
    18]X15+X25+X35+X45+X55=1;!JOB 5 IS ASSIGNED;
    19]END
```

```
Global optimal solution found at step:           6
Objective value:                          102.0000

              Variable            Value          Reduced Cost
                   X11        0.0000000             36.00000
                   X12        0.0000000            0.0000000
                   X13         1.000000            0.0000000
                   X14        0.0000000             38.00000
                   X15        0.0000000            0.0000000
                   X21        0.0000000             16.00000
                   X22        0.0000000             15.00000
                   X23        0.0000000             4.000000
                   X24        0.0000000             42.00000
                   X25         1.000000            0.0000000
                   X31         1.000000            0.0000000
                   X32        0.0000000             7.000000
                   X33        0.0000000             18.00000
                   X34        0.0000000            0.0000000
                   X35        0.0000000             6.000000
                   X41        0.0000000             29.00000
                   X42         1.000000            0.0000000
                   X43        0.0000000             10.00000
                   X44        0.0000000             21.00000
                   X45        0.0000000             4.000000
                   X51        0.0000000             49.00000
                   X52        0.0000000             15.00000
                   X53        0.0000000            0.0000000
                   X54         1.000000            0.0000000
                   X55        0.0000000             25.00000

                   Row   Slack or Surplus           Dual Price
                     1         102.0000             1.000000
                     2        0.0000000            -26.00000
                     3        0.0000000            -25.00000
                     4        0.0000000            -42.00000
                     5        0.0000000            -30.00000
                     6        0.0000000            -32.00000
                     7        0.0000000             27.00000
                     8        0.0000000             1.000000
                     9        0.0000000             4.000000
                    10        0.0000000             21.00000
                    11        0.0000000            0.0000000
```

**Figure 7.5** LINGO Output for the Assignment Problem

127

the distances, times, or costs between each pair of customers is known. The problem is to determine the shortest route that the salesman can take to guarantee that each customer is visited *once and only once* and that the salesman returns to the starting location.

The TSP is also important since it has many applications in addition to routing salesman. For example, consider a company that uses wire to connect components on a motherboard for a computer. The amount of wire used depends on the location of the components and the order in which the components are connected. Therefore, the company needs all of the components connected but would like to minimize the amount of wire used (see homework problem 4). This problem can be formulated and solved as a TSP problem.

For another TSP problem, consider a company that mixes and sells paint. The problem with mixing paints of varying colors on the same production line is that it takes a different amount of time to clean the machine depending on the order that the paints are mixed. For example, we must spend a lot more time cleaning the machine if we mix black paint followed by white paint compared to the cleaning time required to mix tan paint followed by white paint. We would like to minimize the total time spent cleaning the machine but still mix all the paints that have been ordered (see homework problem 3). This problem can also be formulated and solved as a TSP problem.

Other TSP applications include scheduling jobs on machines, routing telephone calls, and any type of delivery problem. As these examples demonstrate, the TSP is important since it arises so often in our daily lives.

Consider the following example. A soda delivery truck starts at location 1 (L1) and must deliver soda to each of nine other locations before returning to L1. The problem is to determine the order in which the locations should be visited such that the total distance traveled is minimized. The distances between each pair of locations are given in the following table.

|      | L1 | L2 | L3 | L4 | L5 | L6 | L7 | L8 | L9 | L10 |
|------|----|----|----|----|----|----|----|----|----|-----|
| L1   | –  | 9  | 11 | 9  | 3  | 12 | 13 | 6  | 11 | 10  |
| L2   | 9  | –  | 4  | 5  | 9  | 4  | 4  | 5  | 18 | 4   |
| L3   | 11 | 4  | –  | 9  | 13 | 2  | 6  | 8  | 19 | 7   |
| L4   | 9  | 5  | 9  | –  | 15 | 11 | 5  | 3  | 15 | 1   |
| L5   | 3  | 9  | 13 | 15 | –  | 14 | 14 | 9  | 11 | 19  |
| L6   | 12 | 4  | 2  | 11 | 14 | –  | 9  | 12 | 20 | 10  |
| L7   | 13 | 4  | 6  | 5  | 14 | 9  | –  | 6  | 22 | 3   |
| L8   | 6  | 5  | 8  | 3  | 9  | 12 | 6  | –  | 10 | 3   |
| L9   | 11 | 18 | 19 | 15 | 11 | 20 | 22 | 10 | –  | 16  |
| L10  | 10 | 4  | 7  | 1  | 19 | 10 | 3  | 3  | 16 | –   |

A review of the distance matrix indicates that there may be some similarities between the TSP and the assignment problem. In the TSP, each location must be visited, which is like demand in an assignment problem, and each location must be exited, which is like supply. As in the assignment problem, the demand and supply values are all equal to 1 since we must enter each location once and exit each location once. Unlike the assignment problem, the binary decision variables XIJ equal 1 if we visit customer I followed by customer J, or 0 if we do not.

Directly applying the assignment problem formulation to our TSP example leads to the LINGO model called TSPSUBS.LG4 as shown in Figure 7.6. We note that the distances along the main diagonal of the DIST matrix, that is 1–1, 2–2, 3–3, and so forth, are all 1000. These large values are entered since we want to prevent these assignments; that is, once we enter a location we must leave that location. The 1000 values ensure that

```
MODEL:
MIN=1000*X11+9*X12+11*X13+9*X14+3*X15+12*X16+13*X17+
    6*X18+11*X19+10*X110+9*X21+1000*X22+4*X23+5*X24+9*X25+
    4*X26+4*X27+5*X28+18*X29+4*X210+11*X31+4*X32+1000*X33+
    9*X34+13*X35+2*X36+6*X37+8*X38+19*X39+7*X310+9*X41+5*X42+
    9*X43+1000*X44+15*X45+11*X46+5*X47+3*X48+15*X49+X410+
    3*X51+9*X52+13*X53+15*X54+1000*X55+14*X56+14*X57+9*X58+
    11*X59+19*X510+12*X61+4*X62+2*X63+11*X64+14*X65+1000*X66+
    9*X67+12*X68+20*X69+10*X610+13*X71+4*X72+6*X73+5*X74+14*X75+
    9*X76+1000*X77+6*X78+22*X79+3*X710+6*X81+5*X82+8*X83+3*X84+
    9*X85+12*X86+6*X87+1000*X88+10*X89+3*X810+11*X91+18*X92+
    19*X93+15*X94+11*X95+20*X96+22*X97+10*X98+1000*X99+16*X910+
    10*X101+4*X102+7*X103+X104+19*X105+10*X106+3*X107+3*X108+
    16*X109+1000*X1010;
!CONSTRAINTS!
!EACH LOCATION MUST BE EXITED;
 X11+X12+X13+X14+X15+X16+X17+X18+X19+X110=1;
 X21+X22+X23+X24+X25+X26+X27+X28+X29+X210=1;
 X31+X32+X33+X34+X35+X36+X37+X38+X39+X310=1;
 X41+X42+X43+X44+X45+X46+X47+X48+X49+X410=1;
 X51+X52+X53+X54+X55+X56+X57+X58+X59+X510=1;
 X61+X62+X63+X64+X65+X66+X67+X68+X69+X610=1;
 X71+X72+X73+X74+X75+X76+X77+X78+X79+X710=1;
 X81+X82+X83+X84+X85+X86+X87+X88+X89+X810=1;
 X91+X92+X93+X94+X95+X96+X97+X98+X99+X910=1;
 X101+X102+X103+X104+X105+X106+X107+X108+X109+X1010=1;
!EACH LOCATION MUST BE VISITED;
X11+X21+X31+X41+X51+X61+X71+X81+X91+X101=1;
X12+X22+X32+X42+X52+X62+X72+X82+X92+X102=1;
X13+X23+X33+X43+X53+X63+X73+X83+X93+X103=1;
X14+X24+X34+X44+X54+X64+X74+X84+X94+X104=1;
X15+X25+X35+X45+X55+X65+X75+X85+X95+X105=1;
X16+X26+X36+X46+X56+X66+X76+X86+X96+X106=1;
X17+X27+X37+X47+X57+X67+X77+X87+X97+X107=1;
X18+X28+X38+X48+X58+X68+X78+X88+X98+X108=1;
X19+X29+X39+X49+X59+X69+X79+X89+X99+X109=1;
X110+X210+X310+X410+X510+X610+X710+X810+X910+X1010=1;
END
```

**Figure 7.6** LINGO Model for the Assignment Formulation of the TSP

this will happen. (Remember that this same approach was offered to eliminate a route in the transportation problem.)

After solving the model, we find that the total distance traveled is 40. The solution to this problem is X15 = X27 = X36 = X410 = X51 = X63 = X72 = X89 = X98 = X104 = 1. However, this solution does not solve our TSP, since each location is not being visited before returning to the original location. For example, this solution indicates that we should travel from location 1 to 5 and from 5 to 1. The movement from 1–5–1 is called a *subtour*. The model solution has five subtours 1–5–1, 2–7–2, 3–6–3, 4–10–4, and 8–9–8 and therefore is not a feasible solution to our TSP problem (see Figure 7.7).

We can successfully address the subtour problem by adding constraints to our formulation that eliminate all possible subtours. For a ten-location problem, we need to add constraints to eliminate 2, 3, 4, and/or 5 location subtours. What about the other possibilities? A one-location subtour cannot exist since we put 1000s along the main diagonal,

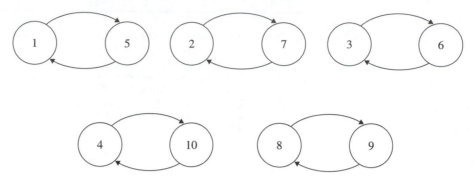

**Figure 7.7** Subtours of the TSP Example Resulting from the Assignment Formulation

as mentioned. Now consider the possibility of an eight-location subtour. If such a subtour exists, there must also exist a two-location subtour. However, the possibility of an eight-location subtour is eliminated if we add constraints to eliminate all possible two-location subtours.

We now consider the form of the constraints necessary to eliminate two-location subtours. For example, for a subtour involving locations 1 and 2, the subtour-breaking constraint is X12 + X21 <= 1. This constraint allows us to travel from location 1 to location 2 (X12 = 1), *or* from location 2 to location 1 (X21 = 1), but not in both directions since the left-hand side of the constraint would then be 2. Unfortunately, this type of constraint must be repeated for all combinations of 2 out of the 10 locations and would require 45 constraints (10!/2!8!). For three-location subtours involving locations 1, 2, and 3, two additional constraints are needed: X12 + X23 + X31 <= 2 and X13 + X32 + X21 <= 2. There are 240 of these constraints (2 * 10!/3!7!). The total number of subtour-breaking constraints increases greatly when subsets of four and five locations are considered.

Now consider practical problems where the total number of locations to be visited is not 10, but 20, 50, or even more. In some situations, mathematical programming software, such as LINGO is unable to converge to the optimal solution in a reasonable amount of time. LINGO's speed can sometimes be improved by selecting *LINGO, Option,* "General Solver" tab, and increasing the *Generator Memory Limit (MB)* from four to eight or greater, depending upon the total amount of RAM available to you. For larger problems, sometimes the best we can hope for is to run LINGO for a "long" time and then click *Interrupt Solver* to identify a feasible solution.

An example of a TSP algorithm using the LINGO modeling language (see Chapter 5) that includes other forms of the subtour-breaking constraints is given in the file TSP.LG4 that is provided in the "samples" folder within the LINGO folder. The algebraic formulation of our example is based on this file and is found in TSPSODAS.LG4, which appears in Figure 7.8. Note that our algebraic formulation of the TSP can not easily be modified for problems of varying sizes and data values. In such cases we recommend the use of the LINGO modeling language version of our example called TSPSODA.LG4.

We illustrate how the presence of subtours violates the subtour-breaking constraints contained in TSPSODAS.LG4. First, consider the subtour 2–7–2. We can express the subtour-breaking constraints that involve locations 2–7 (K = 2, J = 7) and 7–2 (K = 7, J = 2) by applying the constraint (taken from the TSP.LG4) for both of these cases:

```
UJ>=UK + XKJ - ( N - 2)*( 1 - XKJ) + ( N - 3)*XJK;
```

```
:     1]MODEL:
      2]MIN=1000*X11+9*X12+11*X13+9*X14+3*X15+12*X16+13*X17+
      3]    6*X18+11*X19+10*X110+9*X21+1000*X22+4*X23+5*X24+9*X25+
      4]    4*X26+4*X27+5*X28+18*X29+4*X210+11*X31+4*X32+1000*X33+
      5]    9*X34+13*X35+2*X36+6*X37+8*X38+19*X39+7*X310+9*X41+5*X42+
      6]    9*X43+1000*X44+15*X45+11*X46+5*X47+3*X48+15*X49+X410+
      7]    3*X51+9*X52+13*X53+15*X54+1000*X55+14*X56+14*X57+9*X58+
      8]    11*X59+19*X510+12*X61+4*X62+2*X63+11*X64+14*X65+1000*X66+
      9]    9*X67+12*X68+20*X69+10*X610+13*X71+4*X72+6*X73+5*X74+14*X75+
     10]    9*X76+1000*X77+6*X78+22*X79+3*X710+6*X81+5*X82+8*X83+3*X84+
     11]    9*X85+12*X86+6*X87+1000*X88+10*X89+3*X810+11*X91+18*X92+
     12]    19*X93+15*X94+11*X95+20*X96+22*X97+10*X98+1000*X99+16*X910+
     13]    10*X101+4*X102+7*X103+X104+19*X105+10*X106+3*X107+3*X108+
     14]    16*X109+1000*X1010;
     15]!CONSTRAINTS!
     16]!EACH LOCATION MUST BE EXITED;
     17] X11+X12+X13+X14+X15+X16+X17+X18+X19+X110=1;
     18] X21+X22+X23+X24+X25+X26+X27+X28+X29+X210=1;
     19] X31+X32+X33+X34+X35+X36+X37+X38+X39+X310=1;
     20] X41+X42+X43+X44+X45+X46+X47+X48+X49+X410=1;
     21] X51+X52+X53+X54+X55+X56+X57+X58+X59+X510=1;
     22] X61+X62+X63+X64+X65+X66+X67+X68+X69+X610=1;
     23] X71+X72+X73+X74+X75+X76+X77+X78+X79+X710=1;
     24] X81+X82+X83+X84+X85+X86+X87+X88+X89+X810=1;
     25] X91+X92+X93+X94+X95+X96+X97+X98+X99+X910=1;
     26] X101+X102+X103+X104+X105+X106+X107+X108+X109+X1010=1;
     27]!EACH LOCATION MUST BE VISITED;
     28]X11+X21+X31+X41+X51+X61+X71+X81+X91+X101=1;
     29]X12+X22+X32+X42+X52+X62+X72+X82+X92+X102=1;
     30]X13+X23+X33+X43+X53+X63+X73+X83+X93+X103=1;
     31]X14+X24+X34+X44+X54+X64+X74+X84+X94+X104=1;
     32]X15+X25+X35+X45+X55+X65+X75+X85+X95+X105=1;
     33]X16+X26+X36+X46+X56+X66+X76+X86+X96+X106=1;
     34]X17+X27+X37+X47+X57+X67+X77+X87+X97+X107=1;
     35]X18+X28+X38+X48+X58+X68+X78+X88+X98+X108=1;
     36]X19+X29+X39+X49+X59+X69+X79+X89+X99+X109=1;
     37]X110+X210+X310+X410+X510+X610+X710+X810+X910+X1010=1;
     38]!SUBTOUR BREAKING CONSTRAINTS;
     39]!LOCATION 1;
     40]-9*X12-7*X21-U1+U2>=-8;
     41]-9*X13-7*X31-U1+U3>=-8;
     42]-9*X14-7*X41-U1+U4>=-8;
     43]-9*X15-7*X51-U1+U5>=-8;
     44]-9*X16-7*X61-U1+U6>=-8;
     45]-9*X17-7*X71-U1+U7>=-8;
     46]-9*X18-7*X81-U1+U8>=-8;
     47]-9*X19-7*X91-U1+U9>=-8;
     48]-9*X110-7*X101-U1+U10>=-8;
     49]!LOCATION 2;
     50]-9*X23-7*X32-U2+U3>=-8;
     51]-9*X24-7*X42-U2+U4>=-8;
     52]-9*X25-7*X52-U2+U5>=-8;
     53]-9*X26-7*X62-U2+U6>=-8;
     54]-9*X27-7*X72-U2+U7>=-8;
     55]-9*X28-7*X82-U2+U8>=-8;
     56]-9*X29-7*X59-U2+U9>=-8;
     57]-9*X210-7*X510-U2+U10>=-8;
```

**Figure 7.8** LINGO Output for the TSP Problem

```
 58]!LOCATION 3;
 59]-7*X23-9*X32+U2-U3>=-8;
 60]-9*X34-7*X43-U3+U4>=-8;
 61]-9*X35-7*X53-U3+U5>=-8;
 62]-9*X36-7*X63-U3+U6>=-8;
 63]-9*X37-7*X73-U3+U7>=-8;
 64]-9*X38-7*X83-U3+U8>=-8;
 65]-9*X39-7*X93-U3+U9>=-8;
 66]-9*X310-7*X103-U3+U10>=-8;
 67]!LOCATION 4;
 68]-7*X24-9*X42+U2-U4>=-8;
 69]-7*X34-9*X43+U3-U4>=-8;
 70]-9*X45-7*X54-U4+U5>=-8;
 71]-9*X46-7*X64-U4+U6>=-8;
 72]-9*X47-7*X74-U4+U7>=-8;
 73]-9*X48-7*X84-U4+U8>=-8;
 74]-9*X49-7*X94-U4+U9>=-8;
 75]-9*X410-7*X104-U4+U10>=-8;
 76]!LOCATION 5;
 77]-7*X25-9*X52+U2-U5>=-8;
 78]-7*X35-9*X53+U3-U5>=-8;
 79]-7*X45-9*X54+U4-U5>=-8;
 80]-9*X56-7*X65-U5+U6>=-8;
 81]-9*X57-7*X75-U5+U7>=-8;
 82]-9*X58-7*X85-U5+U8>=-8;
 83]-9*X59-7*X95-U5+U9>=-8;
 84]-9*X510-7*X105-U5+U10>=-8;
 85]!LOCATION 6;
 86]-7*X26-9*X62+U2-U6>=-8;
 87]-7*X36-9*X63+U3-U6>=-8;
 88]-7*X46-9*X64+U4-U6>=-8;
 89]-7*X56-9*X65+U5-U6>=-8;
 90]-9*X67-7*X76-U6+U7>=-8;
 91]-9*X68-7*X86-U6+U8>=-8;
 92]-9*X69-7*X96-U6+U9>=-8;
 93]-9*X610-7*X106-U6+U10>=-8;
 94]!LOCATION 7;
 95]-7*X27-9*X72+U2-U7>=-8;
 96]-7*X37-9*X73+U3-U7>=-8;
 97]-7*X47-9*X74+U4-U7>=-8;
 98]-7*X57-9*X75+U5-U7>=-8;
 99]-7*X67-9*X76+U6-U7>=-8;
100]-9*X78-7*X87-U7+U8>=-8;
101]-9*X79-7*X97-U7+U9>=-8;
102]-9*X710-7*X107-U7+U10>=-8;
103]!LOCATION 8;
104]-7*X28-9*X82+U2-U8>=-8;
105]-7*X38-9*X83+U3-U8>=-8;
106]-7*X48-9*X84+U4-U8>=-8;
107]-7*X58-9*X85+U5-U8>=-8;
108]-7*X68-9*X86+U6-U8>=-8;
109]-7*X78-9*X87+U7-U8>=-8;
110]-9*X89-7*X98-U8+U9>=-8;
111]-9*X810-7*X108-U8+U10>=-8;
112]!LOCATION 9;
113]-7*X29-9*X92+U2-U9>=-8;
114]-7*X39-9*X93+U3-U9>=-8;
```

**Figure 7.8** (*Continued*)

```
115]-7*X49-9*X94+U4-U9>=-8;
116]-7*X59-9*X95+U5-U9>=-8;
117]-7*X69-9*X96+U6-U9>=-8;
118]-7*X79-9*X97+U7-U9>=-8;
119]-7*X89-9*X98+U8-U9>=-8;
120]-9*X910-7*X109-U9+U10>=-8;
121]!LOCATION 10;
122]-7*X210-9*X102+U2-U10>=-8;
123]-7*X310-9*X103+U3-U10>=-8;
124]-7*X410-9*X104+U4-U10>=-8;
125]-7*X510-9*X105+U5-U10>=-8;
126]-7*X610-9*X106+U6-U10>=-8;
127]-7*X710-9*X107+U7-U10>=-8;
128]-7*X810-9*X108+U8-U10>=-8;
129]-7*X910-9*X109+U9-U10>=-8;
130]!CONSTRAINTS FOR FIRST AND LAST STOP;
131]8*X12+U2<=9;
132]-8*X21+U2>=1;
133]8*X13+U3<=9;
134]-8*X31+U3>=1;
135]8*X14+U4<=9;
136]-8*X41+U4>=1;
137]8*X15+U5<=9;
138]-8*X51+U5>=1;
139]8*X16+U6<=9;
140]-8*X61+U6>=1;
141]8*X17+U7<=9;
142]-8*X71+U7>=1;
143]8*X18+U8<=9;
144]-8*X81+U8>=1;
145]8*X19+U9<=9;
146]-8*X91+U9>=1;
147]8*X110+U10<=9;
148]-8*X101+U10>=1;
149]@BIN(X11);@BIN(X12);@BIN(X13);@BIN(X14);
150]@BIN(X15);@BIN(X16);@BIN(X17);@BIN(X18);
151]@BIN(X19);@BIN(X110);@BIN(X21);@BIN(X22);
152]@BIN(X23);@BIN(X24);@BIN(X25);@BIN(X26);
153]@BIN(X27);@BIN(X28);@BIN(X29);@BIN(X210);
154]@BIN(X31);@BIN(X32);@BIN(X33);@BIN(X34);
155]@BIN(X35);@BIN(X36);@BIN(X37);@BIN(X38);
156]@BIN(X39);@BIN(X310);@BIN(X41);@BIN(X42);
157]@BIN(X43);@BIN(X44);@BIN(X45);@BIN(X46);
158]@BIN(X47);@BIN(X48);@BIN(X49);@BIN(X410);
159]@BIN(X51);@BIN(X52);@BIN(X53);@BIN(X54);
160]@BIN(X55);@BIN(X56);@BIN(X57);@BIN(X58);
161]@BIN(X59);@BIN(X510);@BIN(X61);@BIN(X62);
162]@BIN(X63);@BIN(X64);@BIN(X65);@BIN(X66);
163]@BIN(X67);@BIN(X68);@BIN(X69);@BIN(X610);
164]@BIN(X71);@BIN(X72);@BIN(X73);@BIN(X74);
165]@BIN(X75);@BIN(X76);@BIN(X77);@BIN(X78);
166]@BIN(X79);@BIN(X710);@BIN(X81);@BIN(X82);
167]@BIN(X83);@BIN(X84);@BIN(X85);@BIN(X86);
168]@BIN(X87);@BIN(X88);@BIN(X89);@BIN(X810);
169]@BIN(X91);@BIN(X92);@BIN(X93);@BIN(X94);
170]@BIN(X95);@BIN(X96);@BIN(X97);@BIN(X98);
171]@BIN(X99);@BIN(X910);@BIN(X101);@BIN(X102);
```

**Figure 7.8** (*Continued*)

```
172]@BIN(X103);@BIN(X104);@BIN(X105);@BIN(X106);
173]@BIN(X107);@BIN(X108);@BIN(X109);@BIN(X1010);
174]END
175]
176]

Global optimal solution found at step:          863
Objective value:                           52.00000
Branch count:                                    25

                        Variable          Value    Reduced Cost
                            X15       1.000000        3.000000
                            X26       1.000000        4.000000
                            X37       1.000000        6.000000
                            X48       1.000000        3.000000
                            X52       1.000000        9.000000
                            X63       1.000000        2.000000
                           X710       1.000000        3.000000
                            X89       1.000000        10.00000
                            X91       1.000000        11.00000
                           X104       1.000000        1.000000
                             U2       2.000000        0.0000000
                             U3       4.000000        0.0000000
                             U4       7.000000        0.0000000
                             U5       1.000000        0.0000000
                             U6       3.000000        0.0000000
                             U7       5.000000        0.0000000
                             U8       8.000000        0.0000000
                             U9       9.000000        0.0000000
                            U10       6.000000        0.0000000
```

**Figure 7.8** (*Continued*)

After grouping terms we obtain:

```
-9*X27 - 7*X72 - U2 + U7>=-8
-7*X27 - 9*X72 + U2 - U7>=-8
```

Adding both constraints together yields the same type of constraint previously shown to break up two-location subtours:

```
X27 - X72 <=1
```

Using the same reasoning one can see that all two-location subtours are eliminated in this formulation. Now consider the subtour 2–7–4–2. Using the same approach, we express the subtour-breaking constraints that involve locations 2–7 ($K = 2$, $J = 7$), 7–4 ($K = 7$, $J = 4$), and 4–2 ($K = 4$, $J = 2$) as shown:

```
-9*X27 - 7*X72 -U2 + U7>=-8
-7*X47 - 9*X74 +U4 - U7>=-8
-7*X24 - 9*X42 + U2 - U4>=-8
```

For the 2–7–4–2 subtour to occur, $X27 = X74 = X42 = 1$. Since we have already shown that two-location subtours cannot occur, it must be that $X72 = X47 = X24 = 0$. Plugging these values into the three equations above and adding the results yields: $-27 >= -24$, which is a contradiction. Using similar arguments, one should be convinced that the constraints given in the TSPSODAS.LG4 formulation will eliminate all subtours of any size.

We wish to explain the results of solving TSPSODAS.LG4. We have given an abbreviated form of the solution output after the LINGO formulation in Figure 7.8. We restricted the output to *LINGO, Solution* by checking the box "Nonzeros only" so that it would be easier to determine the optimal tour. The output for the constraints is not needed so it is omitted. The objective function value tells us that the total distance traveled for this solution is 52. The X values that equal 1 are X15, X26, X37, X48, X52, X63, X710, X89, X91, and X104. These values indicate that the suggested tour is 1–5–2–6–3–7–10–4–8–9–1 as shown in Figure 7.9.

The same tour can be identified by looking at the U values, which give the sequence in which each location is visited. Since we always start at location 1, its U value is 0. The next location visited will have a U value of 1, then 2, and so on up to 9. The optimal U values are $U(1) = 0$, $U(2) = 2$, $U(3) = 4$, $U(4) = 7$, $U(5) = 1$, $U(6) = 3$, $U(7) = 5$, $U(8) = 8$, $U(9) = 9$, and $U(10) = 6$. An inspection of the optimal U values verifies the previously given tour. Note that there can be alternate optimal solutions to the TSP problem. For our example, 1–5–9–8–4–10–7–3–6–2–1 is also an optimal solution.

## Vehicle Routing Problem

The next logical extension is to generalize the TSP so that more than one salesman can be deployed. This problem is known as the vehicle routing problem (VRP). Specifically, consider a company that has a fleet of vehicles, each with a fixed capacity. Assume that these vehicles all start at a common depot (location 1) and must return to the depot after visiting seven customers (locations 2 through 8). Each customer has a certain demand that can be satisfied by a vehicle as long as that vehicle's capacity is not exceeded. Each customer's demand can be satisfied by any vehicle. Therefore, the first decision is to determine what vehicles should be assigned to what customers. Once this is known we must

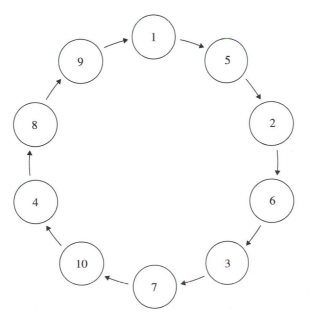

**Figure 7.9** An Optimal Tour of the TSP Example

determine the order that the customers are visited by each vehicle. The objective is to minimize the total distance traveled by all vehicles.[3]

A VRP model called VROUTE.LG4 is provided in the "samples" folder within the LINGO folder. The interested reader can use the *Lingo, Generate, Display Model* command to obtain the algebraic formulation of this model. An inspection of this model formulation shows its relationship with the TSP: the objective is the same as that in the TSP, and constraints are required to make sure that a vehicle enters every location and then leaves it. Unlike the TSP, these constraints must make sure that sufficient vehicle capacity is available if another location is added to a given vehicle tour. The binary decision variables X(I,J) equal 1 if *some* vehicles travel from I to J and 0 if no vehicles travel from I to J. For further details, please see the discussion on the VRP in Chapter 5.

---

[3]Wiegel and Cao (1999) discuss a vehicle routing application related to the one presented here, except that delivery "time windows" are included in the formulation.

## SUMMARY

In this chapter we formulate the transportation problem as well as a variety of extensions and solve them using LINGO. We begin by modeling the transportation problem, which addresses the amount of product shipment from origins to destinations that will minimize total shipping costs. Next we model a series of direct extensions of the transportation model, including unbalanced problems, restricted routes, warehouse location, and choice of transportation mode. We consider a second group of extensions that are based on the assignment problem, which is itself a special class of transportation problem having all supply and demands equal to one. After formulating and solving

the assignment problem, we show that the possibility of subtours prevents the use of the this problem to directly solve the traveling salesman problem (TSP). We then show how subtour-breaking constraints can be added to the formulation, and offer a mathematical programming formulation. The last application that is briefly considered is the vehicle routing problem (VRP), which allows multiple routes to be traversed by a vehicle with limited capacity. The LINGO software package fully supports all of the applications of mathematical programming discussed in this chapter.

## HOMEWORK PROBLEMS

**1.** ZENDIR is in the process of planning for new production facilities and developing a more efficient distribution system. At present they have one plant at St. Louis with a capacity of 30,000 units. But because of increased demand, management is considering four potential new sites: Grand Rapids, Denver, Toledo, and Kansas City. The transportation table summarizes the projected plant capacities (in 1,000s), the cost per unit of shipping from each plant to each destination, and the demand forecasts (in 1,000s) over the next year.

| Plant Sites | Destinations | | | Capacities (in 1,000s) |
|---|---|---|---|---|
| | Providence | Atlanta | Houston | |
| Grand Rapids | 5 | 2 | 3 | 10 |
| Toledo | 4 | 3 | 4 | 20 |
| Denver | 9 | 7 | 5 | 30 |
| Kansas City | 10 | 4 | 2 | 40 |
| St. Louis | 8 | 4 | 3 | 30 |
| Demand (in 1,000s) | 30 | 20 | 20 | |

Suppose that the fixed costs of constructing the new plants, in 1000s, are

| | |
|---|---|
| Grand Rapids | $175 |
| Toledo | $300 |
| Denver | $375 |
| Kansas City | $500 |

**(a)** Develop a model to minimize the total cost of plant construction and distribution of goods.

**(b)** Modify the formulation in part a to account for the policy restriction that one plant, but not two, must be located in Grand Rapids or in Toledo.

**(c)** Modify the formulation in part a to account for the policy restriction that at most one plant can be located in Denver or Kansas City.

**2.** The ROCKWELL School system has three junior high schools that serve the needs of five neighborhood areas. The capacities of the various schools are:

| School | Capacity (Max. enrollment) |
|--------|---------------------------|
| A | 4,000 |
| B | 3,000 |
| C | 2,000 |
| Total | 9,000 |

The size (number of junior high school students) and ethnic mix of each neighborhood are as shown:

| Neighborhood | # of students | % minority students |
|--------------|---------------|---------------------|
| 1 | 2,100 | 30 |
| 2 | 2,400 | 80 |
| 3 | 1,300 | 20 |
| 4 | 800 | 10 |
| 5 | 1,600 | 20 |
| Total | 8,200 | |

The distances (in miles) from each neighborhood to each school are shown in the following table.

A judge has ruled that no junior high school in the city can have more than 50% nor less than 30% minority enrollment. Assume that students bused from each neighborhood have the same ethnic mix as the whole neighborhood. You wish to devise a busing plan that will minimize the total number of student miles bused yet still adhere to the judge's integration requirements, and at the same time guarantee that no student is bused more than 2.5 miles. Formulate a model that could be used to solve this problem.

| | | TO: SCHOOL | | |
|--|--|-----------|--|--|
| | | A | B | C |
| | 1 | 1.2 | 0.8 | 1.3 |
| | 2 | 0.4 | 2.0 | 2.2 |
| **FROM** | 3 | 2.6 | 0.5 | 1.6 |
| **NEIGHBORHOOD** | 4 | 1.4 | 0.7 | 2.0 |
| | 5 | 2.4 | 3.0 | 0.2 |

**3.** B. A. MCDUFF and Sons has received an order for varying amounts of 5 different colors of paints. The problem is that the order in which the jobs are performed affects the total costs. This is due to the fact that if a dark color is scheduled after a light color, the cost to clean the equipment is less than if a light color is scheduled after a dark color. McDuff has estimated the cleaning costs for each pair of color sequences. These costs are shown here.

| | COLOR | | | | |
|--|--|--|--|--|--|
| | 1 | 2 | 3 | 4 | 5 |
| COLOR 1 | – | 130 | 107 | 115 | 105 |
| COLOR 2 | 101 | – | 104 | 106 | 108 |
| COLOR 3 | 127 | 144 | – | 117 | 128 |
| COLOR 4 | 112 | 155 | 127 | – | 143 |
| COLOR 5 | 133 | 158 | 108 | 103 | – |

Color 1 is a rush order and must be scheduled first. In addition, after the 5 jobs have been finished, the paint manufacturer has also scheduled a job for color 1. Determine the order that the jobs should be scheduled.

**4.** CYNEX is a computer chip manufacturer that must route wiring for its new product. There are five pins on the printed circuit board. These five items must be connected in such a way that a complete circuit of wiring exists. The distances (in millimeters) between each pair of items is shown. Determine a solution to this circuit layout problem.

| | PIN | | | | |
|--|--|--|--|--|--|
| | 1 | 2 | 3 | 4 | 5 |
| PIN 1 | – | 16 | 12 | 6 | 4 |
| PIN 2 | 16 | – | 9 | 8 | 14 |
| PIN 3 | 14 | 10 | – | 1 | 18 |
| PIN 4 | 5 | 11 | 2 | – | 22 |
| PIN 5 | 3 | 17 | 19 | 29 | – |

# REFERENCES

Camm, J. D., T. E. Chorman, F. A. Dill, J. R. Evans, D. J. Sweeney, and G. W. Wegryn, "Blending OR/MS, Judgment and GIS: Restructuring P&G's Capacity Chain, *Interfaces*, Vol. 27, No. 1, pp. 128–142, 1997.

Hillier, F. S., and G. J. Lieberman, *Introduction to Operations Research*, 6th ed., New York, McGraw-Hill, 2001.

Koksalan, M. and H. Sural, "Efes Beverage Group Makes Location and Distribution Decisions for Its Malt Plants," *Interfaces*, Vol. 29, No. 2, pp. 89–103, 1999.

Schrage, L., *Optimization Modeling with LINGO*, Chicago, Lindo Systems Inc., 2002.

Weigel, D. and B. Cao, "Applying GIS and OR Techniques to Solve Sears Technician-Dispatching and Home-Delivery Problems, *Interfaces*, Vol. 29, No. 1, pp. 112–130, 1999.

Winston, W. L., *Introduction to Mathematical Programming: Applications and Algorithms*, Belmont, CA, Duxbury, 1995.

# Chapter 8

# Scheduling, Finance, and Marketing Applications Using LINGO's Standard Algebraic Approach*

## INTRODUCTION

In the previous chapter we addressed the application of mathematical programming to transportation and distribution planning. As mentioned in Chapter 2, mathematical programming continues to be successfully applied to a variety of decision-making problems. In this chapter we present important applications using LINGO (Schrage 2002) that are grouped into three areas: scheduling, finance, and marketing. Nearly all of these examples were selected on the basis of the applications that our students found useful in their applied projects. A few, such as the retail space allocation example, were selected to illustrate some important aspects of the modeling process. Additional examples can be found in many sources, including Anderson, Sweeney, and Williams (2000), Assad, Wasil, and Lilien (1992), and in the journal *Interfaces*.

## SCHEDULING APPLICATIONS

### A Staff Scheduling Problem

Mathematical programming can be used to address many different types of staff scheduling problems. Such problems abound in practice since many businesses must schedule employees to perform various tasks where demand for these services varies over time. Examples include staffing call centers, assigning workers to shifts in a restaurant, and allocating staff in a service center. An approach for modeling these problems is illustrated in the following scheduling example.

International Airlines is in the process of finalizing an on-line reservations system. To staff this system, telephone operators will need to be available during the day to meet

---

*Chapters 5 and 6 use the LINGO modeling language approach; Chapters 7 and 8 cover essentially the same material but use the standard algebraic LINGO approach. Therefore, skip Chapters 5 and 6 *or* 7 and 8 per instructions from your professor. See the Preface for further details.

forecasted demand. The following are the forecasts for operators over the ten time periods each day:

| Period | Time | Operators needed |
|--------|------|------------------|
| 1 | 6 a.m.–8 a.m. | 3 |
| 2 | 8 a.m.–10 a.m. | 12 |
| 3 | 10 a.m.–12 noon | 13 |
| 4 | 12 noon–2 p.m. | 10 |
| 5 | 2 p.m.–4 p.m. | 12 |
| 6 | 4 p.m.–6 p.m. | 10 |
| 7 | 6 p.m.–8 p.m. | 6 |
| 8 | 8 p.m.–10 p.m. | 5 |
| 9 | 10 p.m.–12 midnight | 4 |
| 10 | 12 midnight–2 a.m. | 3 |

However, telephone operators are scheduled on a shift basis. International plans to staff six shifts, of which two are split shifts. The shift times are as follows:

| Shift | Times |
|-------|-------|
| 1 | 6 a.m.–2 p.m. |
| 2 | 8 a.m.–4 p.m. |
| 3 | 10 a.m.–6 p.m. |
| 4 | 6 p.m.–2 a.m. |
| 5 | 10 a.m.–1 p.m. & 4 p.m.–8 p.m. |
| 6 | 8 a.m.–11 a.m. & 5 p.m.–9 p.m. |

The objective of this problem is to minimize the total daily payroll cost while assigning operators to shifts in order to meet demand during each time period. The daily pay rate for the first four shifts is $56, however, since the fifth and sixth shifts are split, the pay rate is $70 per day.

Using the information given about this problem, we are now ready to formulate this scheduling problem using LINGO. From Chapter 2 we know that developing a mathematical programming problem requires first identifying the decision variables, and then formulating the objective function and the constraints. Each of these three steps is described as follows.

### 1. Identify and Define the Decision Variables

The decision variables in this problem are the number of operators scheduled during each shift. We let $XI$ = the number of operators scheduled during shift I, I = 1, 2, 3, 4, 5, 6.

### 2. Formulate the Objective Function

The objective for this problem is to minimize the total cost of staffing each day, which is obtained by multiplying the cost of each shift by the number of operators scheduled during that shift and then summing over all shifts. Since it costs $56 for each person scheduled during shifts 1 through 4 and $70 for each person scheduled during shifts 5 and 6, we obtain the following expression for the objective function:

```
!OBJECTIVE FUNCTION;
MIN=56*X1+56*X2+56*X3+56*X4+70*X5+70*X6;
```

Note that the ! is used to insert a comment into LINGO.

### 3. Formulate the Constraints

Now we are ready to discuss the demand constraints. Simply put, the total number of operators scheduled to work during each period must meet or exceed the demand for workers in that period. To formulate these constraints we must first determine which shifts are working during each period. This can be easily determined by forming the matrix given as Figure 8.1. This matrix shows if there is a "match" between shift coverage and a particular period. A match is indicated by a value of 1, otherwise a 0 is shown.

For example, the values in the first column indicate that shift 1 helps to satisfy the demand during the first four periods only. To understand why this is so, look at the times for the first four periods (6–8, 8–10, 10–12, and 12–2) and remember the time for the first shift (6–2). This first shift completely covers these 4 time periods.

We note that the row 4 (period 4) and column 5 (shift 5) entry is a 0. This may be potentially confusing since shift 5 works from 10:00 to 1:00 and period 4 goes from 12:00 to 2:00. This shift covers the first hour of the period but not the second. It should be clear that the coverage must be set to 0 since shift 5 workers go home at 1:00 and thus cannot help to satisfy demand during the second hour of period 4. We assume then that a value of 1 in the matrix indicates that the given shift *completely* covers the time period in question.

For example, to obtain the demand constraint for the third period, look at the third row of the matrix given as Figure 8.1. Multiple the entries in this row by the value of XI corresponding to the shift associated with the particular column and sum to obtain:

```
1*X1+1*X2+1*X3+0*X4+1*X5+0*X6>=13, or
X1+X2+X3+X5>=13
```

where 13 is the total number of operators that are needed during period 3.

We do not set these constraints as equalities since it may not be possible to find integer values of the number of operators that *exactly* meet all constraints. For example, you may need to schedule staff to meet a high level of demand in the first period, but if demand drops in the second period, you may be left with excess capacity. In fact, if you change the relational sign to equality and solve the resulting problem in LINGO, no feasible solution will be found. However, using the relational sign of "greater than or equal to" for the constraints will yield an optimal solution that minimizes total cost in such a way that the best combination of operators is found. All constraints will be met while some will be exceeded only if no feasible lower cost solution can be found.

The complete LINGO model and the solution for this problem appear in Figure 8.2. The LINGO model is in a file called AIRLINES.LG4. We do not need to use the @GIN

|  |  | SHIFTS | DEMAND |
|---|---|---|---|
|  |  | 1 2 3 4 5 6 |  |
|  | 1 (6 a.m.–8 a.m.) | 1 0 0 0 0 0 | 3 |
| P | 2 (8 a.m.–10 a.m.) | 1 1 0 0 0 1 | 12 |
| E | 3 (10 a.m.–12 p.m.) | 1 1 1 0 1 0 | 13 |
| R | 4 (12 p.m.–2 p.m.) | 1 1 1 0 0 0 | 10 |
| I | 5 (2 p.m.–4 p.m.) | 0 1 1 0 0 0 | 12 |
| O | 6 (4 p.m.–6 p.m.) | 0 0 1 0 1 0 | 10 |
| D | 7 (6 p.m.–8 p.m.) | 0 0 0 1 1 1 | 6 |
| S | 8 (8 p.m.–10 p.m.) | 0 0 0 1 0 0 | 5 |
|  | 9 (10 p.m.–12 a.m.) | 0 0 0 1 0 0 | 4 |
|  | 10 (12 a.m.–2 a.m.) | 0 0 0 1 0 0 | 3 |

**Figure 8.1** Matrix Showing the Match Between Periods and Shift Coverage and Period Demand

```
  :   1]MODEL:
      2]!OBJECTIVE FUNCTION;
      3]MIN=56*X1+56*X2+56*X3+56*X4+70*X5+70*X6;
      4]!CONSTRAINTS;
      5]X1>=3;!PERIOD 1'S DEMAND;
      6]X1+X2+X6>=12;!PERIOD 2'S DEMAND;
      7]X1+X2+X3+X5>=13;!PERIOD 3'S DEMAND;
      8]X1+X2+X3>=10;!PERIOD 4'S DEMAND;
      9]X2+X3>=12;!PERIOD 5'S DEMAND;
     10]X3+X5>=10;!PERIOD 6'S DEMAND;
     11]X4+X5+X6>=6;!PERIOD 7'S DEMAND;
     12]X4>=5;!PERIOD 8'S DEMAND;
     13]X4>=4;!PERIOD 9'S DEMAND;
     14]X4>=3;!PERIOD 10'S DEMAND;
     15]END
     16]
```

```
Global optimal solution found at step:            14
Objective value:                            1526.000
Branch count:                                      0

            Variable           Value        Reduced Cost
                  X1        9.000000            0.00000
                  X2        3.000000            0.00000
                  X3        9.000000            0.00000
                  X4        5.000000            0.00000
                  X5        1.0000000           0.00000
                  X6        0.000000            0.00000

                 Row   Slack or Surplus        Dual Price
                   1        1526.000            1.000000
                   2        6.0000000           0.0000000
                   3        0.0000000         -56.0000000
                   4        9.000000            0.0000000
                   5        11.00000            0.0000000
                   6        0.0000000           0.0000000
                   7        0.0000000         -56.0000000
                   8        0.0000000         -14.0000000
                   9        0.0000000         -42.0000000
                  10        1.000000            0.0000000
                  11        2.000000            0.0000000
```

**Figure 8.2** LINGO Output for the Staff Scheduling Problem

command to make sure that the values of our decision variables are integer since the demands in our example are integers:

The objective function value indicates that the total staffing cost is $1526 per day. By looking at the values for the decision variables, we find that we should hire 3, 8, 10, 5, 0, and 1 operators during the six shifts, respectively. The value of 8 in the "Slack or Surplus" column for period 3's demand (row 4 in the output) indicates a surplus of 8 operators will occur during period 3. This result can be also be obtained by recalling the demand constraint for period 3 given above and then plugging in the optimal values of the XI to find that 21 operators are available, while demand equals 13.

## Production Scheduling

Many companies must determine production schedules for their products. For example, a car manufacturer must determine their monthly production schedule so that they meet their target demand levels. A soda bottling plant must also determine how many bottles of each size soda to produce. These problems are examples of a mathematical programming area called production scheduling. Consider the following example.

International Products, Inc. must decide on its production schedule for the next four months. It has contracted to supply a special part for the months of October, November, December, and January at the rates of 12,000, 10,000, 15,000, and 17,000 units, respectively. The company can produce each part at a cost of $6 during regular time or $9 during overtime. Monthly production capacity is 10,000 and 6,000 units during regular and overtime, respectively. A maximum of 2,000 units can be stored per month at a cost of $0.50 per unit. There are 1,000 units in inventory at the end of September and there must be 500 units in inventory at the end of January. International Products can overproduce during some months and store the excess to help satisfy future demand during later months. They would like to determine the production schedule that will minimize total costs while meeting demand. The LINGO formulation is again developed using our three-step approach.

### 1. Identify and Define the Decision Variables

The decision variables in this problem represent the number of units produced in regular time and overtime during the months October, November, December, and January. We let $XIJ$ = number of units produced by production type I during month J, where I = 1 (regular time), 2 (overtime), and J = 2, 3, 4, 5, for October, November, December, and January. We also need decision variables for inventory since these must be determined as well: $IJ$ = inventory at the end of month J.

### 2. Formulate the Objective Function

The objective for this problem is to minimize the sum of regular time and overtime production costs plus the inventory costs. Since we are not interested in determining September's (J = 1) production and inventory levels, these terms are not included. The expression for the objective function is:

```
!OBJECTIVE FUNCTION;
MIN=6*X12+6*X13+6*X14+6*X15+9*X22+9*X23+9*X24+9*X25+
    .5*I2+.5*I3+.5*I4+.5*I5;
```

### 3. Formulate the Constraints

Constraints are needed to make sure that the demand is satisfied for each of the months. These constraints also compute the ending inventory for each month. This group of constraints is based on the following relationship:

$$\text{starting inventory} + \text{production} - \text{demand} = \text{ending inventory}$$

In our formulation, the ending inventory of the previous month (J–1) is the starting inventory for the next month (J). Therefore, the starting inventory for month J plus the

```
:   1]MODEL:
    2]!OBJECTIVE FUNCTION;
    3]MIN=6*X12+6*X13+6*X14+6*X15+9*X22+9*X23+9*X24+9*X25+
    4].5*I2+.5*I3+.5*I4+.5*I5;
    5]!CONSTRAINTS;
    6]!INVENTORY BALANCE BY MONTH;
    7]X12+X22+I1-I2=12000;
    8]X13+X23+I2-I3=10000;
    9]X14+X24+I3-I4=15000;
   10]X15+X25+I4-I5=17000;
   11]!INITIAL AND ENDING INVENTORY CONDITIONS;
   12]I1=1000;
   13]I5=500;
   14]!UPPER BOUNDS ON INVENTORY LEVELS;
   15]I2<=2000;
   16]I3<=2000;
   17]I4<=2000;
   18]!UPPER BOUND ON REGULAR PRODUCTION;
   19]X12<=10000;
   20]X13<=10000;
   21]X14<=10000;
   22]X15<=10000;
   23]!UPPER BOUND ON OVERTIME PRODUCTION;
   24]X22<=6000;
   25]X23<=6000;
   26]X24<=6000;
   27]X25<=6000;
   28]@GIN(X12);@GIN(X13);@GIN(X14);@GIN(X15);
   29]@GIN(X22);@GIN(X23);@GIN(X24);@>GIN(X25);
   30]@>GIN(I2);@GIN(I3);@GIN(I4);
   31]END
   32]

Global optimal solution found at step:              1
Objective value:                            362750.0
Branch count:                                      0
                         Variable        Value      Reduced Cost
                              X12     10000.00         6.000000
                              X13     10000.00         6.000000
                              X14     10000.00         6.000000
                              X15     10000.00         6.000000
                              X22     1000.000         9.000000
                              X23     500.0000         9.000000
                              X24     6000.000         9.000000
                              X25     6000.000         9.000000
                               I2    0.0000000         0.5000000
                               I3     500.0000         0.5000000
                               I4     1500.000         0.5000000
                               I5     500.0000         0.0000000
                               I1     1000.000         0.0000000
```

**Figure 8.3** LINGO Output for the Production Scheduling Problem

regular and overtime production during month J equals the total amount of product available to satisfy the demand during month J. The difference between the total amount of product available and the demand equals the inventory at the end of month J. Again, we eliminate month 1 (September) since we are not interested in planning its production and inventory levels. The starting inventory for September (I1) and the ending inventory requirement for January (I5) are also specified, as well the upper bounds on the inventory levels for October, November, and December. After moving the demand to the right-hand side and moving ending inventory to the left, the inventory balance constraints are:

```
X12+X22+I1-I2=12000;
X13+X23+I2-I3=10000;
X14+X24+I3-I4=15000;
X15+X25+I4-I5=17000;
I1=1000;
I5=500;
I2<=2000;
I3<=2000;
I4<=2000;
```

Upper bounds must also be placed on regular and overtime production each month as shown:

```
X12<=10000;
X13<=10000;
X14<=10000;
X15<=10000;

X22<=6000;
X23<=6000;
X24<=6000;
X25<=6000;
```

Finally, regular, overtime, and inventory variables must be specified as general integer using the @GIN command.

The LINGO model is in a file called INTERS.LG4 and the formulation and abbreviated solution appear in Figure 8.3. The objective function value indicates that the minimum total cost is $362,750. By looking at the values for the decision variables we find that we should produce 10,000 units each month (excluding September) during regular time, 1,000 units during October's overtime, 500 units during November's overtime, and 6,000 units each during December and January's overtime.

## FINANCIAL APPLICATIONS

### The Portfolio Problem

Today many companies, and even individuals, are concerned about how they invest their money. One approach for selecting a portfolio of investments is to specify an acceptable minimum expected return and to find a portfolio with the minimum variance that attains this expected return. By varying the minimum acceptable expected return the investor may obtain and compare several desirable portfolios. This approach is called the Markowitz Portfolio Model and will be studied here. More detains on this problem can be found in Luenberger (1998), and an application is discussed in Labe, Nigam, and Spence (1999).

Data can be collected over time to compute the expected returns of each investment and the variance of the portfolio. The variance of the portfolio is the sum of the variances of the individual investments *plus* a measure of how each pair of investments tend to move together. To compute the total variance of a portfolio, we must determine the *covariance matrix* of the investments comprising the portfolio.

Consider the following problem. Suppose an investor has gathered return rates for three investments over the last six months as shown:

| | Rates | | |
|---|---|---|---|
| **Periods** | **I1** | **I2** | **I3** |
| 1 | 0.07 | 0.14 | 0.05 |
| 2 | 0.05 | −0.07 | 0.06 |
| 3 | 0.02 | 0.05 | 0.03 |
| 4 | 0.04 | 0.14 | 0.07 |
| 5 | 0.12 | 0.02 | 0.10 |
| 6 | 0.08 | 0.19 | 0.06 |

The investor wants to invest $100 (in thousands) and would like a portfolio return of at least 6.5%. In addition, for diversification reasons, at least $50 (in thousands) must be placed in investments 1 and/or 2. The investor wishes to determine the amount that should be placed in each of the three investments to minimize the total variance of the portfolio while achieving the minimum expected return and diversification constraints. Our formulation using the three-step approach proceeds as follows.

## 1. Identify and Define the Decision Variables

The decision variables in this problem are the amounts of money to be placed in each of the three investments. We let $XI$ = amount of money placed in investment I and I = 1, 2, 3.

## 2. Formulate the Objective Function

The objective is to minimize the total variance of the portfolio. The values in the covariance matrix indicate the degree of variation between every pair of investments. Here we let $VIJ$ = the covariance between investments I and J. Each covariance value must be weighted by the amount placed in *both* of the investments contributing to this value.[1] Since there are three investments there are nine terms in the covariance matrix.

Using the investment return data, the covariance terms can be computed as described next. We begin by computing the average of each investment's return data as follows.

| | Rates | | |
|---|---|---|---|
| **Periods** | **I1** | **I2** | **I3** |
| 1 | 0.07 | 0.14 | 0.05 |
| 2 | 0.05 | −0.07 | 0.06 |
| 3 | 0.02 | 0.05 | 0.03 |
| 4 | 0.04 | 0.14 | 0.07 |
| 5 | 0.12 | 0.02 | 0.10 |
| 6 | 0.08 | 0.19 | 0.06 |
| Average | 0.063333 | 0.078333 | 0.061667 |

---

[1] More details on the mathematics related to determining the expression for the variance of the portfolio can be found in Luenberger (1998) or Winston (1995).

Next, we compute the terms of the covariance matrix. You may remember from statistics that we can compute the covariance matrix using a two-step procedure. First, we compute the errors for each investment, which are defined as the investment returns minus the average return. Note that there are six terms for each of the three investments.

**Error Terms**

| I1 returns–average return | I2 returns–average return | I3 returns–average return |
|:---:|:---:|:---:|
| 0.006667 | 0.061667 | −0.011667 |
| −0.013333 | −0.148333 | −0.001667 |
| −0.043333 | −0.028333 | −0.031667 |
| −0.023333 | 0.061667 | 0.008333 |
| 0.056667 | −0.058333 | 0.038333 |
| 0.016667 | 0.111667 | −0.001667 |

Second, we take each pair of investments and *cross multiply* the error terms for corresponding periods and then average the result. Each average is a term in the covariance matrix. Since we are taking all combinations of pairs, the result is a three by three matrix. That is, the cross terms in the matrix are I1–I1, I1–I2, I1–I3, I2–I1, I2–I2, I2–I3, I3–I1, I3–I2, and I3–I3. The variances of the individual investment returns appear along the main diagonal of the matrix. Also, the matrix is symmetric across the main diagonal, so for example V12 = V21. Therefore, rather than including the V21 term in the objective function, we *double* the V12 term.

**Covariance Matrix**

| | I1 | I2 | I3 |
|:---|:---:|:---:|:---:|
| I1 | 0.001022 | 0.000122 | 0.000544 |
| I2 | 0.000122 | 0.007714 | −0.000247 |
| I3 | 0.000544 | −0.000247 | 0.000447 |

The objective function then sums over all possible combinations of investments as shown.

```
V11*X1*X1+2*V12*X1*X2+2*V22*X2*X2+
      2*V13*X1*X3+2*V23*X2*X3+V33*X3*X3
```

We now substitute the covariance values into this expression to obtain the final form of our objective function:

```
MIN=0.001022*X1*X1+2*0.000122*X1*X2+0.007714*X2*X2+
      2*0.000544*X1*X3+2*-0.000247*X2*X3+0.000447*X3*X3;
```

### 3. Formulate the Constraints

There are three constraints in our formulation. First, the average portfolio return must be at least 6.5% of $100 or 6.5:

```
.0633333*X1+.0783333*X2+.0616667*X3>=6.5;
```

Second, the sum of the total amount invested must equal the total amount available:

```
X1+X2+X3=100;
```

Third, the sum placed in investments I1 and I2 must be at least 50% of the amount available, or 50:

```
X1+X2>=50;
```

```
MODEL:
!OBJECTIVE FUNCTION - MINIMIZE TOTAL VARIANCE OF PORTFOLIO;
MIN=0.001022*X1*X1+2*0.000122*X1*X2+0.007714*X2*X2+
    2*0.000544*X1*X3+2*-0.000247*X2*X3+0.000447*X3*X3;
!CONSTRAINTS;
X1+X2+X3=100;!TOTAL AMOUNT AVAILABLE MUST BE INVESTED;
X1+X2>=50;!INVESTMENT MIX REQUIREMENT;
.0633333*X1+.0783333*X2+.0616667*X3>=6.5;!ACHIEVE MINIMUM
  EXPECTED RETURN;
END

 Local optimal solution found at step:          6
 Objective value:                5.933056

                       Variable          Value       Reduced Cost
                             X1       33.33333          0.0000000
                             X2       16.66667          0.0000000
                             X3       50.00000          0.0000000
```

**Figure 8.4** LINGO Output for the Portfolio Problem

Since the objective function is nonlinear of order two, and the constraints are linear, Markowitz portfolio selection is an example of a *quadratic programming problem*. The LINGO model for this problem is in a file called MARKS.LG4. The problem formulation and an abbreviated solution for this problem appear in Figure 8.4. The objective function value indicates that the total portfolio variance is 5.933. By looking at the values for the three investments (X1, X2, and X3), we find that we should invest $33,333, $16,667, and $50,000, in I1, I2, and I3, respectively.

## Capital Budgeting Problem and Extensions

### The Capital Budgeting Problem

Capital budgeting problems are also concerned with investment decisions. However, capital budgeting problems focus on how investment decisions made over a planning horizon impact future profitability. Consider the following example. Apex, Inc. can invest in a variety of projects that have varying capital requirements over the next four years. Faced with limited resources, Apex must select the optimal mix of projects. It is assumed that the projects are independent of one another in terms of capital required and returns received. The estimated present values (PV) of the projects, the capital requirements, and the available capital funds by year follow.

| Project | PV | Capital Required Per Year | | | |
|---|---|---|---|---|---|
| | | 1 | 2 | 3 | 4 |
| **Plant Expansion** | 90 | 15 | 20 | 20 | 15 |
| **Warehouse Expansion** | 40 | 10 | 15 | 20 | 5 |
| **New Machinery** | 10 | 10 | 0 | 0 | 4 |
| **New Product Research** | 37 | 15 | 10 | 10 | 10 |
| **Available Capital Funds** | | 40 | 50 | 40 | 35 |

Our formulation using the three-step approach proceeds as follows.

### 1. Identify and Define the Decision Variables

The decision variables in this problem are whether or not a project is funded. We let $XI = 1$ if project I is funded or $XI = 0$ if project I is not funded, where $I = 1, 2, 3, 4$.

### 2. Formulate the Objective Function

The objective of our capital budgeting problem is to maximize the present value over all projects as shown:

```
MAX=90*X1+40*X2+10*X3+37*X4;
```

### 3. Formulate the Constraints

A constraint for each year indicates that the total amount of capital consumed by funded projects cannot exceed the available funds for that year. We also specify that the decision variables (XI) are binary integer (@BIN). The constraints are shown:

```
15*X1+10*X2+10*X3+15*X4<=40;
20*X1+15*X2+10*X4<=50;
20*X1+20*X2+10*X4<=40;
15*X1+5*X2+4*X3+10*X4<=35;
@BIN(X1); @BIN(X2); @BIN(X3); @BIN(X4);
```

The LINGO model is in a file called APEXS.LG4. The model and abbreviated solution appear in Figure 8.5. The objective function value indicates that the optimal total pre-

```
:   1]MODEL:
    2]!OBJECTIVE FUNCTION - MAX PV OVER ALL PROJECTS;
    3]MAX=90*X1+40*X2+10*X3+37*X4;
    4]!CONSTRAINTS;
    5]15*X1+10*X2+10*X3+15*X4<=40;!CAPITAL CONSTRAINT FOR YEAR 1;
    6]20*X1+15*X2+10*X4<=50;!CAPITAL CONSTRAINT FOR YEAR 2;
    7]20*X1+20*X2+10*X4<=40;!CAPITAL CONSTRAINT FOR YEAR 3;
    8]15*X1+5*X2+4*X3+10*X4<=35;!CAPITAL CONSTRAINT FOR YEAR 4;
    9]@BIN(X1); @BIN(X2); @BIN(X3); @BIN(X4);
   10]END

Global optimal solution found at step:              0
Objective value:                           140.0000
Branch count:                                      0

            Variable           Value        Reduced Cost
                  X1        1.000000           -90.00000
                  X2        1.000000           -40.00000
                  X3        1.000000           -10.00000
                  X4        0.0000000          -37.00000

                 Row   Slack or Surplus          Dual Price
                   1        140.0000            1.000000
                   2        5.000000            0.0000000
                   3        15.00000            0.0000000
                   4        0.0000000           0.0000000
                   5        11.00000            0.0000000
```

**Figure 8.5** LINGO Output for the Capital Budgeting Problem

sent value is \$140. By looking at the values for the four binary investment variables (X1, X2, X3, and X4), we find that the values of the first three are 1 and the value of the fourth is 0. Therefore, we should invest in projects 1, 2, and 3. The slack value of 15 for row 3 indicates that \$15 of the available capital during year 2 is not consumed by the optimal mix of funded projects.

## 4. Extensions of the Capital Budgeting Problem

We now consider three extensions to this problem that define special relationships among the decision variables. All of these extensions can be applied to other mathematical programming problems where the decision variables take on binary values. The first variation is called a "multiple choice constraint." Suppose that in addition to the original warehouse expansion project, X2, Apex is considering two additional warehouse expansion projects, X5 and X6. Suppose that one of the warehouses must be expanded because of increased demand, but there is not sufficient demand to allow expansion of more than one of these three warehouses.

The following additional multiple choice constraint is needed to model this situation:

$$X2 + X5 + X6 = 1$$

Since the sum of three binary variables must exactly equal 1, two must be 0 and one must be 1. Thus this equation guarantees that exactly one warehouse expansion project is accepted.

We can slightly change the situation just described by stating that we want to expand at *most* one warehouse. The difference between this problem and the last one is that it is now acceptable to not expand any warehouses. Therefore, we replace the equals in the previous constraints with a "less than or equal to" sign:

$$X2 + X5 + X6 <= 1$$

This constraint guarantees that at most one warehouse expansion project is accepted.

The second extension that we consider is called "K out of N alternatives." Suppose that we must accept two of the three warehouse projects. Using the same logic as in the previous examples, the sum of the three binary variables must exactly equal 2.

$$X2 + X5 + X6 = 2$$

This constraint will guarantee that exactly two warehouse expansion projects are accepted. If we require that no more than two of the projects be selected, the constraint would be

$$X2 + X5 + X6 <=2$$

The third extension that we will discuss is called "conditional constraints." Suppose that we want to model a situation in which the acceptance of one project is conditional upon the acceptance of another project. Specifically, suppose we cannot expand the warehouse, X2, unless the plant, X1, is expanded. Many students find that this type of constraint is difficult to model. It sometimes helps to use if–then statements to map out the possibilities. For example, this conditional constraint can be interpreted as follows: if X1 = 0, then X2 = 0 and if X1 = 1, then X2 = 0 or 1. With this information in mind it is easier to then develop the constraint for this condition:

$$X2 <= X1$$

The modeler should always check that the suggested constraint satisfies the stated conditions. In the current case, if X1 equals zero, the constraint simplifies to X2 <= 0, which means that X2 must equal zero. If X2 equals one, the constraint simplifies to X2 <= 1, which means that X2 can equal zero or one. We see that both conditions are satisfied with this constraint.

If the condition were changed to require that the warehouse expansion be accepted if the plant expansion project is accepted and vice versa, then the constraint would be

$$X2 = X1$$

This constraint implies that whatever value X1 assumes X2 must take on the same value. In plain English, if we do *not* expand the plant (X1 = 0), then we *cannot* expand the warehouse (X2 = 0). If we *do* expand the plant (X1 = 1), then we *must* expand the warehouse (X2 = 1).

## MARKETING APPLICATIONS

## Media Selection

Marketing managers often have to decide how to allocate an advertising budget to various advertising media. Alternative media include television, radio, newspapers, magazines, and direct mail. Media effectiveness relates to the number of potential customers reached, quality of the media exposure, and the frequency of exposure. Restrictions relate to available advertising budget and media availability and mix policies.

Consider the following example in which the Weston company wishes to decide how to best allocate its weekly advertising budget to promote its new floor care product. Weston's advertising department has collected the following data concerning the available media:

| Advertising Media | $ Cost/Ad | Reach/Ad | Quality/Ad | Max Slots | Min Slots |
|---|---|---|---|---|---|
| Daytime TV | 1000 | 10000 | 60 | 14 | 5 |
| Daytime Radio | 550 | 7000 | 35 | 21 | 5 |
| Daily Newspaper | 600 | 5000 | 45 | 7 | 2 |

Daytime TV and Radio have 30-second slots and Daily Newspaper has a one-half page advertisement. The reach is the estimated audience size for each ad, and quality is Weston's assessment of the relative value of one advertisement in each of the media. Weston wishes to maximize exposure quality, while reaching at least 100,000 potential customers and remaining within their weekly advertising budget of $20,000. Our formulation using the three-step approach proceeds as follows.

### 1. Identify and Define the Decision Variables

The decision variables are the number of slots to allocate on a weekly basis to each of the advertising media. We let XI = number of slots for advertising media I, I = 1, 2, 3, where media 1, 2, and 3 are daytime TV, daytime radio, and daily newspaper, respectively.

### 2. Formulate the Objective Function

The objective of our media selection problem is to maximize the total exposure quality obtained from all of the advertising slots that are funded as shown below:

```
MAX=60*X1+35*X2+45*X3;
```

### 3. Formulate the Constraints

Constraints are needed to make sure that the budget is not exceeded and the customer target is met. Also, constraints set the minimum and maximum number of advertising slots for each of the advertising media. The @GIN function is needed to specify that the values of XI are integer. The complete constraints section of the model is shown:

```
1000*X1+550*X2+400*X3<=20000;!BUDGET;
10000*X1+7000*X2+5000*X3>=100000;!REACH;
!MIN AND MAX SLOTS BY MEDIA;
X1>=5;
X1<=14;
X2>=5;
X2<=21;
X3>=2;
X3<=7;
@GIN(X1); @GIN(X2); @GIN(X3);
```

The complete LINGO model and the solution for this problem appear in Figure 8.6. The Lingo model is in a file called WESTONS.LG4. The optimal solution is to fund six TV,

```
:    1]MODEL:
     2]!OBJECTIVE - MAX EXPOSURE QUALITY;
     3]MAX=60*X1+35*X2+45*X3;
     4]!CONSTRAINTS;
     5]1000*X1+550*X2+400*X3<=20000;!BUDGET;
     6]10000*X1+7000*X2+5000*X3>=100000;!REACH;
     7]!MIN AND MAX SLOTS BY MEDIA;
     8]X1>=5;
     9]X1<=14;
    10]X2>=5;
    11]X2<=21;
    12]X3>=2;
    13]X3<=7;
    14]@GIN(X1); @GIN(X2); @GIN(X3);
    15]END
    16]

Global optimal solution found at step:            17
Objective value:                           1375.000
Branch count:                                     6

                Variable            Value        Reduced Cost
                      X1         6.000000           -60.00000
                      X2         20.00000           -35.00000
                      X3         7.000000           -45.00000

                     Row   Slack or Surplus          Dual Price
                       1          1375.000            1.000000
                       2          200.0000           0.0000000
                       3          135000.0           0.0000000
                       4          1.000000           0.0000000
                       5          8.000000           0.0000000
                       6          15.00000           0.0000000
                       7          1.000000           0.0000000
                       8          5.000000           0.0000000
                       9         0.0000000           0.0000000
```

**Figure 8.6** LINGO Output for the Media Selection Problem

20 radio, and seven newspaper advertisements each week for a total quality exposure of 1375. An alternate formulation of this problem is to set a minimum quality exposure level and then maximize total reach. The details for making the changes are left to the reader.

## Floor Space Allocation

Periodically, a department store will reallocate its floor space among its departments. One approach is to approximate the average profit per square meter per year for each department as a linear function of the allocated space. The objective is to find the allocation that maximizes total profit. Like the portfolio problem, the floor space allocation problem is another member of the class of NLP problems called quadratic programs.

Consider the following example where a store has two departments called Noname and Designer. The department managers were asked to give two estimates of the yearly profit per square meter as a function of the minimum and maximum number of square meters allocated, as shown.

|  | Noname | | Designer | |
|---|---|---|---|---|
|  | Sq M Space | $/Sq M/Year | Sq M Space | $/Sq M/Year |
| Min Space | 9 | $12,000 | 12 | $15,000 |
| Max Space | 50 | 5,000 | 45 | 4,000 |

Assume that there are a total of 65 square meters to be allocated. Furthermore, each department will be allocated neither less than the minimum space nor more than the maximum space. Management wishes to decide how to allocate space to maximize total profit. Our formulation using the three-step approach proceeds as follows.

### 1. Identify and Define the Decision Variables

The decision variables are the amount of space (in square meters) to allocate to each department. We let XI = amount of space allocated to department I, and I = 1, 2, where departments 1 and 2 are Noname and Designer, respectively.

### 2. Formulate the Objective Function

We assume that the profit per square meter is linear between the minimum and maximum space allocated to a department. Therefore, the rate of profit change per square meter equals the change in profit divided by the change in allocated space. As shown in Figure 8.7 for the Noname department, the profit change per square meter is $(12000 - 5000)/(9 - 50) = -170.73$ per square meter for each square meter allocated over the minimum space allocation of 9. That is, if 10 meters of space are allocated to the Noname department, the profit *per square meter* would be $12,000 - 170.73 = $11,829.37.

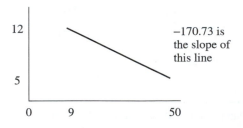

**Figure 8.7** Determining the Rate of Change for Profit per Meter for the Noname Department

Therefore, the profit per square meter for Noname is the maximum profit per square meter ($12,000) minus 170.73 times the amount of space allocated over the minimum of 9. This relationship can be represented as

$$12000 - 170.73 * (X1 - 9).$$

The profit change per square meter for the Designer department = $(15000 - 4000)/(12 - 45) = -333.33$ per square meter. Therefore its profit per square meter is

$$15000 - 333.33 * (X2 - 12).$$

Total profit is obtained by multiplying the profit per square meter by XI for each department and adding the result. Since total profit per square meter is a function of XI and is multiplied by XI, the result is a quadratic objective function. The objective function for this model is

```
MAX = (12000 - 170.73*(X1 - 9))*X1+(15000 - 333.33*(X2 - 12))*X2;
```

### 3. Formulate the Constraints

The sum of the space allocated across both departments must equal the space available. Also, constraints set the minimum and maximum amount of space that can be allocated to each of the departments. The constraints section of the formulation is given as:

```
X1+X2=65;!AVAILABLE SPACE;
!MIN AND MAX SPACE ALLOWED;
X1>=9;
X1<=50;
X2>=12;
X2<=45;
```

```
:   1]MODEL:
    2]!OBJECTIVE -MAX TOTAL PROFIT;
    3]MAX = (12000 - 170.7317*(X1 - 9))*X1+((15000 - 333.3333*(X2 -
          12))*X2);
    4]!CONSTRAINTS;
    5]X1+X2=65;!AVAILABLE SPACE;
    6]!MIN AND MAX SPACE ALLOWED;
    7]X1>=9;
    8]X1<=50;
    9]X2>=12;
   10]X2<=45;
   11]END

Local optimal solution found at step:          21
Objective value:                          537949.3

                Variable            Value         Reduced Cost
                      X1         37.56452            0.0000000
                      X2         27.43548            0.0000000

                     Row   Slack or Surplus         Dual Price
                       1         537949.3            1.000000
                       2        0.0000000            709.6775
                       3         28.56452            0.0000000
                       4         12.43548         0.1074142E-04
                       5         15.43548            0.0000000
                       6         17.56452            0.0000000
```

**Figure 8.8** LINGO Output for the Floor Space Allocation Problem

The LINGO model is in a file called DSTORES.LG4. The model and solution appear in Figure 8.8. The objective function value indicates that the optimal total profit is $537,949.30. By looking at the values for the decision variables we find that we should allocate 37.56 square meters to the Noname department (X1) and 27.44 square meters to the Designer department (X2).

## SUMMARY

In this chapter we present selected applications of mathematical programming in scheduling, finance, and marketing. The specific applications that we address are staff and production scheduling, Markowitz portfolio selection, capital budgeting, media mix, and retail floor space allocation. Each of these applications is formulated using LINGO. Many of the applications presented have been applied in practice by our students.

Others are presented to illustrate specific modeling issues. Components of the models presented can be combined with others to develop an even broader set of potential applications. The examples contained in this and previous chapters demonstrate the value that mathematical programming can provide for improved decision making.

## HOMEWORK PROBLEMS

**1.** The NORTHSHORE Bank is working to develop an efficient work schedule for full-time and part-time tellers. The schedule must provide for efficient operation of the bank including adequate customer service, employee breaks, and so on. On Fridays the bank is open from 9:00 A.M. to 7:00 P.M. The number of tellers necessary to provide adequate customer service during each hour of operation is summarized here.

| Time | 9–10 | 10–11 | 11–12 | 12–1 | 1–2 | 2–3 | 3–4 | 4–5 | 5–6 | 6–7 |
|------|------|-------|-------|------|-----|-----|-----|-----|-----|-----|
| # of Tellers | 6 | 4 | 8 | 10 | 9 | 6 | 4 | 7 | 6 | 6 |

Each full-time employee starts on the hour and works a four-hour shift, followed by one hour for lunch and then a three-hour shift. Part-time employees work one four-hour shift beginning on the hour. Considering salary and fringe benefits, full-time employees cost the bank $15 per hour ($105 per day), and part-time employees cost the bank $8 per hour ($32 per day).

**(a)** Formulate and solve a LINGO model that can be used to develop a schedule that will satisfy customer service needs at a minimum employee cost.

**(b)** After reviewing the solution to part a, the bank manager has realized that some additional requirements must be specified. Specifically, she wants to ensure that one full-time employee is on duty at all times and that there is a staff of at least five full-time employees. Revise your model to incorporate these additional requirements, and solve for the optimal solution.

**2.** You have just purchased a kit from PLYDECK to build a wooden deck adjacent to your patio. The directions indicate that you will need, among other things, 27 two-ft pieces of 2 × 4 boards, 10 three-ft boards, and 15 four-ft pieces. The kit has instructed you to purchase eight-foot long boards, and then cut them to the desired length. The kit indicates that 20 such boards are required for your addition, and that the boards should be cut according to the following patterns:

| Number of boards | Pattern |
|------------------|---------|
| 7 | 2 2 2 2 |
| 2 | 4 4 |
| 11 | 3 4 |

You believe that it is possible to find a solution that uses less than 20 boards. Formulate a LINGO model that could be used to find the minimum number of boards needed to build the deck. *Hint:* To solve this problem you must consider other cutting patterns. The other patterns are: 4,2,2; 3,2,2; 3,3,2.

**3.** NOVASTAR has been developing four possible new product lines. Management must now make a decision as to which of these four products actually will be produced and at what levels of production. The company would like to find the most profitable product mix. The one-time start-up cost and the marginal net revenue from each unit produced are given here.

| | Product | | | |
|---|---|---|---|---|
| | **1** | **2** | **3** | **4** |
| **Start-up Cost** | $50,000 | $40,000 | $70,000 | $60,000 |
| **Marginal Revenue** | $70 | $60 | $90 | $80 |

Management has imposed the following policy constraints:

1. No more than two of the products can be produced.

2. Product 3 can be produced only if either product 1 or 2 is produced. Similarly, product 4 can be produced only if either product 1 or 2 is produced.

In addition, 2000 units at most of each product can be produced, and total demand for all products is 3500. Formulate a LINGO model for this problem.

**4.** M&M Associates want to choose among a series of new investment alternatives. The potential investment alternatives, the net present value of the future stream of returns, the capital requirements, and the available capital funds over the next three years are summarized here.

| Alternative | Net Present Value | Capital Requirements | | |
|---|---|---|---|---|
| | | Year 1 | Year 2 | Year 3 |
| Limited plant expansion | 4,000 | 3,000 | 1,000 | 4,000 |
| Extensive plant expansion | 6,000 | 2,500 | 3,500 | 3,500 |
| Test market new product | 10,500 | 6,000 | 4,000 | 5,000 |
| Advertising campaign | 4,000 | 2,000 | 1,500 | 1,800 |
| Basic research | 8,000 | 5,000 | 1,000 | 4,000 |
| Purchase new equipment | 3,000 | 1,000 | 500 | 900 |
| Capital funds available | | 10,500 | 7,000 | 8,750 |

**(a)** Develop a LINGO model for maximizing the net present value.

**(b)** Assume that only one of the plant expansion projects can be implemented. Modify your formulation from part a.

**(c)** Suppose that if the test marketing of the new product is carried out, then the advertising campaign must also be conducted. Modify your formulation from part b to reflect this situation.

**5.** CLUTCHCARGO has three compartments in its plane for storing cargo: front, center, and back. These compartments have capacity limits on both weight and space, as summarized:

| Compartment | Weight capacity (tons) | Volume capacity (cu ft) |
|---|---|---|
| FRONT | 12 | 7,000 |
| CENTER | 18 | 9,000 |
| BACK | 10 | 5,000 |

The weight of the cargo in the respective compartments must be the same proportion of that compartment's weight capacity to maintain the balance of the airplane. For example, if six tons of cargo are assigned to the front, then nine must be assigned to the center and five to the back. The following four cargoes have been offered for shipment on an upcoming flight as space becomes available:

| Cargo | Volume-Weight | | |
|---|---|---|---|
| | Weight (tons) | Conversion (cu ft/ton) | Profit ($/ton) |
| 1 | 20 | 500 | 220 |
| 2 | 16 | 700 | 280 |
| 3 | 25 | 600 | 250 |
| 4 | 13 | 400 | 200 |

Any portion of each of these cargoes can be accepted. The objective is to determine how much (if any) of each cargo should be accepted and how to distribute each shipment among the compartments to maximize the total profit for the flight. Note that the volume–weight conversion factor means that, for example, if 10 tons of cargo 1 are stored in the plane, then it will occupy 5,000 cubic feet of volume. Formulate a LINGO model that could be used to solve this problem.

**6.** GRILLMEISTER produces a natural gas (NG) and a propane gas (PG) grill. If they charge a price $p1$ for NG and $p2$ for PG, they can sell $q1$ of the NG and $q2$ of the PG grills, where $q1 = 4000 - 10p1 + p2$, and $q2 = 2000 - 9p2 + 0.8p1$. Manufacturing an NG grill requires two hours of labor and three burner elements. A PG grill uses three hours of labor and one burner element. At present, 5,000 hours of labor and 4,500 burner elements are available. Formulate a LINGO model that will maximize GrillMeister's revenue. Note that the price/quantity relationships should be entered as constraints.

**7.** TRUCKCO is trying to determine where they should locate a single warehouse. The positions in the X–Y plane (in miles) of their four customers and the number of shipments made annually to each customer appears in the table. TruckCo wants to locate the warehouse to minimize the total distance trucks must travel from the warehouse to the four customers. Formulate a model to help TruckCo solve this problem. *Note:* set up your problem to minimize the sum of the squared distances along both the X- and Y-axes from the four customers to the warehouse. You may wish to draw a two-dimensional grid to help set up this problem. There are no constraints for this problem.

| Customer | X-Coordinate | Y-Coordinate | # of Shipments |
|---|---|---|---|
| 1 | 5 | 10 | 200 |
| 2 | 10 | 5 | 150 |
| 3 | 0 | 12 | 200 |
| 4 | 12 | 0 | 300 |

## REFERENCES

Anderson, D. R., D. J. Sweeney, and T. A. Williams, *An Introduction to Management Science: Quantitative Approaches to Decision Making*, 9th ed., Cincinnati, OH, South-Western Publishing, 2000.

Assad, A. A., E. A. Wasil, and G. L. Lilien, (eds.), *Excellence in Management Science Practice: A Readings Book*, Englewood Cliffs, NJ, Prentice-Hall, 1992.

Labe, R., R. Nigam, and S. Spence, "Management Science at Merrill Lynch Private Client Group," *Interfaces*, Vol. 29, No. 2, pp. 1–14, 1999.

Luenberger, D. G., *Investment Science*, New York, Oxford University Press, 1998.

Schrage, L., *Optimization Modeling with LINGO*, Chicago, Lindo Systems, 2002.

Winston, W. L., *Introduction to Mathematical Programming: Applications and Algorithms*, Belmont, CA, Duxbury, 1995.

# Chapter 9

# Introduction to Decision Making

## INTRODUCTION

Decision-making methods, such as classical decision analysis and the Analytic Hierarchy Process (AHP), provide structure and guidance for thinking systematically about making complex decisions. Consider three examples from personal, business, and government settings:

Which job offer should I accept?

Where should my company locate a new service facility?

Should my local government offer a tax amnesty program to increase revenues?

Decisions such as these are characterized by uncertainty, conflicting multiple objectives, and differing perspectives of the various affected stakeholders. For example, in deciding which job offer to accept, an individual might consider salary, location, growth potential, benefits, and corporate culture. Significant uncertainty may be related to all of these decision factors, or what we call criteria, but especially to growth potential and culture. Since no job offer will likely be the best across all criteria, trade-offs must be made. For example, one offer might be preferred in terms of salary, growth potential, and benefits, whereas another might be preferred with respect to location and corporate culture. In addition, the perspective of an unattached individual might be quite different than that of an individual whose partner is already working in a given location. Decision-making methods can help stakeholders to better understand the effect of uncertainty and to clarify the trade-offs across criteria.

It is important to be clear at the outset that recommendations offered by decision-making methods should not be blindly accepted. For example, consider the problem of deciding which job offer to accept. Suppose that job A is recommended. Upon further reflection, you might decide to select job B because one of the criteria is so overwhelmingly important to you that it sways your decision. Another possibility is the presence of some other criterion that you did not initially include in your analysis but now realize its importance, which again leads to a decision that is different than the recommended one. If one of these situations occurs, this does not necessarily mean that the analysis was flawed or of no value. Rather, we suggest that the process and its results should be viewed as an important, but not the only, source of information for making decisions. An analysis is only as good as our ability to capture those judgments and values that represent the most important aspects of the problem.

It is important to distinguish between a good decision and a good outcome. Decision-making methods can improve your chances for a good outcome and reduce your chances for an unpleasant one. Unfortunately, even the best analysis can lead to an unpleasant or unexpected outcome. For example, location might be a major criterion that leads you to select a certain job. However, two months after beginning work the company unexpectedly decides to relocate to an area that would have been your *last* choice. The important point is that a good analysis cannot guarantee a good outcome!

## CLASSICAL DECISION ANALYSIS

### Expected Monetary Value

We begin our discussion with a brief consideration of classical decision analysis. Our purpose is to present the key ideas and limitations of the classical approach, and to serve as a lead-in to the AHP. Our discussion of classical decision analysis begins with the following example. Suppose that you inherited the lottery shown as Figure 9.1.

What amount makes you indifferent between selling the lottery or keeping the lottery and playing? Obviously you would sell the lottery if someone offered you $1000. Most people would also sell if they were offered $999 or $998. Few people would sell the lottery if they were only offered $1 or $2 for it. Somewhere in between $1000 and $0 is an individual's indifference point. There is no wrong or right answer—several factors affect your indifference point.

If you are an expected monetary value (EMV) decision maker then your indifference point for this lottery is $500. The EMV is a long-run weighted average, and is computed by multiplying the probability of an event by its monetary outcome and then summing over all possible events:

$$EMV = \Sigma(P_i)(X_i)$$

where $P_i$ = probability of event i, and $X_i$ = payoff of event i.

For the above lottery:

$$EMV = (0.50)(1000) + (0.50)(0) = \$500.$$

Most of us would sell the lottery for less than $500. The problem is that EMV does not consider the decision-maker's attitude toward *risk*. Many factors influence your risk attitude, including wealth and personal beliefs. The next three examples will further illustrate how your attitude toward risk influences your decisions.

**Example 1:** Choose one of the following: A1: $100,000 gift, tax free, for sure; A2: Flip a fair coin; if heads then receive $0, if tails then receive a $250,000 tax free gift.

**Example 2:** Choose one of the following: B1: $1000 loss; B2: 0.006 chance of a $100,000 loss and 0.994 chance of no loss.

**Example 3:** Choose one of the following: C1: $10,000 gift, tax free, for sure; C2: $2^N$ cents, where N is the number of coin flips until the first tails occurs.

For each of these examples, which alternative do you prefer? Most people would choose A1, B1, and C1. However, EMV decision makers would prefer A2, B2, and C2.

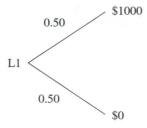

**Figure 9.1** Lottery with a 50% Chance of Winning $1000, and a 50% Chance of Winning $0

Example 1 is like a situation in a lawsuit where a settlement has been offered. If you settle, you receive $100,000 (alternative A1), whereas, if you take the suit to trial, you have a 50/50 chance of winning nothing or $250,000 (alternative A2). Although the expected value of going to trial is $125,000, many people would take the sure thing and avoid any risk.

Example 2 is like purchasing insurance. You can pay a premium of $1000 (alternative B1) or you could accept the risk of a low probability of a high loss event (alternative B2). Although the expected value of B2 is a $600 loss, which is better than a $1000 loss, again most people purchase insurance in such situations and would thus prefer B1.

Example 3 is known as the St. Petersburg Paradox. The EMV computations follow. Most people believe that there is a higher probability that the first tail will occur sooner rather than later. The mathematics reveals a different story. The EMV of the St. Petersburg Paradox is:

| Number of Flips Until First Tail (N) | Probability of N Flips Until First Tail | Payoff | Result |
|---|---|---|---|
| 1 | $(1/2)^1$ | $2^1$ | T |
| 2 | $(1/2)^2$ | $2^2$ | HT |
| 3 | $(1/2)^3$ | $2^3$ | HHT |
| 4 | $(1/2)^4$ | $2^4$ | HHHT |

and so on, leading to

$$\text{EMV} = (1/2)^1 * 2^1 + (1/2)^2 * 2^2 + (1/2)^3 * 2^3 + (1/2)^4 * 2^4 + \cdots$$

$$= 1 + 1 + 1 + 1 + \ldots$$

$$= \text{infinity!}$$

The EMV of this lottery is infinity, which is clearly better than $10,000! However, we have never met anyone who would choose the lottery over a sure $10,000!

These lotteries illustrate the limitations of applying EMV across the board as a decision-making criterion. Each example represents a one-time decision, whereas, EMV is a long-run average. Also, our lottery example demonstrates that people differ in their attitude toward risk.

## Utility Theory

One approach for measuring an individual or group's attitude toward risk is to express their preferences using a utility function. A utility function converts a specific dollar amount or another quantitative measure such as market share to a utility measure. Therefore, it attempts to measure the amount of "pleasure" that one receives from a specific dollar amount. Von Neumann and Morgenstern (1944) argued that people maximize expected utility and not EMV. In a given situation, an individual or group may be risk neutral, risk averse, or risk seeking. Recall the first lottery example in Figure 9.1 that describes a 50/50 chance of winning $0 or $1000. Those who value the lottery at $500 are risk-neutral EMVers. Those who value the lottery at less than $500 are risk averse and those that value the lottery at more than $500 are risk seeking. If X is an amount of money, then a utility function U(X) converts $X into a utility value measure called utils. Returning to our original lottery, people may receive a different amount of pleasure from $500, but everyone receives the same amount of pleasure from the same amount of utils. The utility curve for a risk-averse person or group is upward sloping and concave, as shown in Figure 9.2.

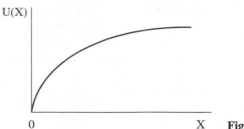

U(X)

0                                 X     **Figure 9.2** A Concave Utility Function

Utility functions can be estimated by developing a series of indifference points be-tween receiving an amount with certainty or playing a lottery. Reconsider the lottery in Figure 9.1 that has a 50/50 chance of winning $0 or $1000. We can establish a utility function for this lottery over the range of $0 to $1000 as follows:

1. Set anchor utility values: $U(1000) = 1$ and $U(0) = 0$.

2. Suppose you are indifferent between receiving $300 or keeping the lottery ticket. This implies that:
   $U(300) = EU(\text{playing lottery}) = .5 * U(1000) + .5 * U(0) = 0.5$, where EU (playing lottery) is the expected utility of playing the lottery.

3. Other points on the utility curve can be defined by finding indifference values for other lotteries.
   a. Consider the lottery of a 50/50 chance of winning $1000 or $300. Suppose you are indifferent for $400. Then,
      $U(400) = EU(\text{lottery}) = .5 * U(1000) + .5 * U(300) = 0.75$
   b. Consider the lottery of a 50/50 chance of winning $300 or $0. Suppose you are indifferent for $50. Then,
      $U(50) = EU(\text{lottery}) = .5 * U(300) + .5 * U(0) = 0.25$

Using these points, the utility curve shown in Figure 9.3 can be drawn. If a decision maker had several decision criteria to consider, he or she might develop utility curves for each of these or one function that combines all. An approach for applying the concepts of util-ity in situations where there are multiple decision criteria or attributes is called multi-attribute utility theory (MAUT). For additional information about the theory and applica-tion of MAUT, the interested reader is referred to Keeney and Raiffa, (1976), Samson, (1988), and Clemen (1996).

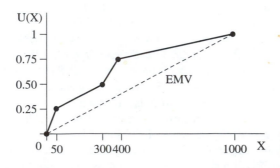

**Figure 9.3** Estimated Piecewise Concave Utility Curve

## Utility in Practice

There are several issues with utility theory that must be addressed in practice.

**1.** It is assumed that decision makers are perfectly consistent in their beliefs about utility. From the utility curve that we just estimated, we know that U(50) = 0.25, U(300) = 0.50, and U(400) = 0.75. This implies that U(300) = 2 * U(50), U(400) = 1.5 * U(300), so U(400) = 3 * U(50). This might be acceptable in some cases, but consider the following example. Suppose we have estimated a utility curve for market share. From the curve, we find that: U(30%) = 2 * U(20%) and U(20%) = 1.5 * U(15%). Utility theory requires us to believe that U(30%) = 3 * U(15%). In fact, when considering this comparison, we might believe that U(30%) is four or even five times larger than U(15%). Individuals are not always perfectly consistent in their judgments but this does not mean that they are illogical!

**2.** The use of lotteries to determine a utility curve is artificial since individuals are asked to make hypothetical choices and use this information to solve real problems. For example, individuals are not contending with lotteries when they are deciding how to value the differences in market share.

**3.** Utility functions must be anchored on a fixed scale. What happens when phenomena must be evaluated that are outside the range of the scale? Returning to our original lottery problem, what happens if we increase the value of winning the lottery from $1000 to $2000? We cannot extrapolate the curve since it was defined on a $0 to $1000 scale.

**4.** Utility curves can only be developed if numbers can be assigned to the relevant criteria. How would you develop a utility curve to measure intangible and highly subjective criteria? For example, how would you create a utility curve to measure the style of a car?

For these and other reasons, managers often make decisions that are inconsistent with the maximization of expected utility. That is, expected utility often is not *descriptive* of actual decision-making behavior, even though it is appealing from a *prescriptive* point of view.

## ANALYTIC HIERARCHY PROCESS

### Background

#### Overview

The AHP is an alternate approach to the maximization of expected utility and has grown in popularity as a useful decision support methodology. An article in *Fortune* (Palmer 1999) has highlighted the contribution of AHP developer Dr. Thomas Saaty. We will show how the AHP successfully addresses the limitations of expected utility previously discussed. In addition, we will show how the AHP can be successfully implemented in practice using the software package called Expert Choice.

The AHP (Saaty 1977, 1994, 1996) is a decision-making method for prioritizing alternatives when multicriteria must be considered. It is an approach for structuring a problem as a hierarchy or set of integrated levels. AHP problems are usually structured in at least three levels:

*The goal*, such as selecting the best car to purchase,

*The criteria*, such as cost, safety, and appearance,

*The alternatives*, namely the cars themselves.

This hierarchy for purchasing the best car is given as Figure 9.4.

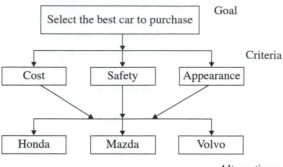

**Figure 9.4** AHP Hierarchy for Car Purchase Decision

An AHP analysis begins by measuring the extent to which each alternative achieves each of the criteria. Next, we determine the relative importance of the criteria in meeting the goal. Finally, we synthesize the results of the two analyses to compute the relative importance of the alternatives in meeting the goal.

Managerial judgments drive the AHP approach. The AHP *never* requires you to make an absolute judgment or assessment: you would never be asked to directly evaluate the cost of a car. AHP *does* require you to make a relative assessment between *two* items at a time. That is, AHP uses a *ratio scale* of measurement. For example, AHP would ask you to make a relative assessment of the cost of car A compared to the cost of car B. Specifically, the question would be: How much better (or worse) is car A compared to car B? The pairwise comparison between cars A and B might tell us that car A gets 65% of the cost weight, whereas car B gets 35% of the cost weight. Individual judgments, such as comparing the relative cost of two cars, are called *pairwise comparisons*.

The basis for these judgments can be objective or subjective information. For example, appearance might be a subjective criterion used to compare two cars. In this situation, the pairwise comparison could be based on the decision-maker's subjective judgment about the appearance of the two cars. However, as discussed, the cars can also be compared on cost. This objective information could be used as a basis for a pairwise comparison based on the actual cost of the cars.

Consistency of judgments can also be measured and is important when three or more items are being compared. Suppose a basketball, soccer ball, and softball are being compared. We may judge the basketball to be twice as large as the soccer ball and the soccer ball to be three times as large as the softball. If we are perfectly consistent, we judge the basketball to be six times as large as the softball. AHP does not *require* perfect consistency, however, it does provide a measure of consistency. We will discuss consistency in more detail in Chapter 10.

### AHP Applications

Fortune 500 companies and other organizations such as Corning, John Deere, the U.S. State Department, and Toronto Hydro have applied the AHP in complex decision-making settings (Palmer 1999). The AHP also has been successfully applied to a variety of evaluation, selection, and resource allocation problems. A partial list includes R&D projects (Liberatore 1987) and research papers (Liberatore, Nydick, and Sanchez 1992); vendors (Nydick and Hill 1992), transport carriers (Liberatore and Miller 1995), and site locations (Hedge and Tadikamalla 1990); product formulation (Liberatore and Nydick 1990) and pharmaceutical licensing (Ross and Nydick 1992); capital budgeting and strategic planning (Liberatore, Monahan, and Stout 1992); and surgical residents (Weingarten, Erlich, Nydick, and Liberatore 1997), and medical treatment (Dolan, Isselhardt, and Cappuccio 1989, and Dolan and Bordley 1993). Sources of references on applications can be found in Zahedi (1986), Golden, Wasil, and Harker (1989), Vargas and Zahedi (1993), and Wasil and Golden (1991). In the following sections we illustrate the applicability of the AHP through a discussion of two thought-provoking examples.

## Consumer Testing Services

Consumer testing services prepare evaluations for services and products, such as self-propelled lawn mowers. They consider a variety of criteria, including bagging, mulching, discharging, handling, and ease of use. Based on their evaluations, they determine an overall score for each mower.

Would you make your lawn mower purchasing decision based solely on the testing services' overall scores? Probably not! Although some of the information presented in these reports will be very helpful, several additional questions come to mind when interpreting their final results and scores. For example, how did the testing service determine the relative importance of each criterion? That is, did they weight bagging and mulching equally or did they place more weight on one of them? Even if you knew how they weighted these criteria, an individual consumer might choose to weight them differently based on their own personal preferences. For example, cost might be the most important criterion for a young couple, safety might be more important during the time when the couple's children mow the lawn, yet ease of use might rise to the top as the couple moves toward their retirement years. Are there other criteria that are important to you? For example, some people might consider the working conditions and compensation for those people involved with assembling the lawn mowers. Have you ever thought about these issues while reading any of these consumer testing magazines? As we will see later, the AHP can successfully address all of these issues.

## The AHP and Sports

Many individuals are concerned, and sometimes obsessed about, sports rankings and ratings. Golden and Wasil (1987) applied the AHP to rank outstanding season, career, and single-event records across sports. For example, according to them the top three season records of all time are: Babe Ruth, 1920: .847 slugging average; Joe DiMaggio, 1944: 56 game hitting streak; and Wilt Chamberlain, 1961–1962: 50.4 points per game scoring average. The top three career records are: Johnny Unitas, 1956–1970: touchdown passes in 47 consecutive games; Babe Ruth, 1914–1935: .690 slugging average; and Walter Payton, 1975–1986: 16,193 rushing yardage. The top three single-event records are: Wilt Chamberlain, 1962: 100 points scored; Norm Van Brocklin, 1951: 554 passing yards; and Bob Beamon, 1968: 29′ 2.5″ long jump.

Do you agree with these results? Arriving at an answer is not trivial since we are comparing records *across* different sports. Therefore, we must select criteria that can be applied to *all* sports. Golden and Wasil used the following criteria in their study: duration of record—years record has stood, years expected to stand; incremental improvement—percent better than previous record; and other record characteristics—glamour, purity (single person vs. team).

Did the Golden and Wasil article end all arguments about what are the greatest sports records of all times? Absolutely not! In bars and living rooms across the country, people still argue about sports and always will. The AHP provides a methodology for structuring the debate. Different criteria and different judgments could produce different results.

We offer one final comment about sports. In reading the sports pages prior to a professional football game, we often read discussions of how well teams match-up across different positions. For example, the wide receivers of one team may be compared to the defensive backs of the opponent. These match-ups are often used to predict a winner. "Match-ups" is a pairwise comparison concept!

Our culture is obsessed with quantitative rankings of all sorts of things including products and services, sports teams, and universities. There are a number of questions concerning what criteria are selected, how they are measured and combined to form an overall score or ranking, and how much meaning we can attribute to scores and rankings. We do not know if the organizations providing these rankings have carefully considered these issues when publishing their results. Several well-known ratings and rankings are discussed and critically analyzed on a web site at:

http://www.expertchoice.com/annie.person.

### Apples, Oranges, and Pairwise Comparisons

The discussion of how to compare records from different sports recalls a saying from childhood:

*You can't compare apples and oranges. All you get is mixed fruit!*

After the discussion about comparing sports records, do you still believe this statement? We hope not! What criteria might *you* use when comparing apples and oranges? There is a vast set of criteria that one might consider. These criteria may change depending upon time of day or season of year. Some examples are taste, texture, smell, ripeness, juiciness, nutrition, shape, weight, color, and cost. We are sure that you can you think of others!

The point is that people are often confronted with choices like the choice between apples and oranges. Their choice is based on some psychological assessment as to the set of relevant criteria and their importance, and how well the alternative choices or courses of action achieve each criterion. The AHP is ideally suited to help individuals make such choices.

## SUMMARY

In this chapter we have seen that decision analysis provides structure and guidance to complex decision-making processes. We have provided an overview of the classical decision analysis and showed how utility theory can express attitudes toward risk. We have illustrated how to estimate utility functions using lotteries and pointed out some limitations of applying utility theory in practice.

The AHP is offered as an alternative decision-making process. This method has been successfully applied to a variety of evaluation, selection, and resource allocation problems. The AHP structures decision-making problems in at least three levels: goal, criteria, and alternatives. Judgments are expressed in the form of pairwise comparisons. The synthesis of the problem hierarchy results in final alternative weights that are ratio-scaled.

In the next two chapters we illustrate how the AHP can be used in many different environments to improve the decision-making process. The next chapter provides a detailed example of the basics of the AHP; the one that follows offers a validation exercise and covers issues such as multilevel hierarchies, the ratings approach, and group decision making. Together these two chapters provide a complete picture of the Analytic Hierarchy Process.

# REFERENCES

Clemen, R.T., *Making Hard Decisions*. 2nd ed. Belmont, CA, Duxbury Press, 1996.

Dolan, J. G., B. Isselhardt, and J. Cappuccio, "The Analytic Hierarchy Process in Medical Decision Making: A Tutorial." *Medical Decision Making*, Vol. 9, 1989, pp. 40–50.

Dolan, J. G. and D. R. Bordley, "Involving Patients in Complex Decisions About Their Care: An Approach Using the Analytic Hierarchy Process." *Journal of General Internal Medicine*, Vol. 8, 1993, pp. 204–209.

Golden, B. L. and E. A. Wasil, "Ranking Outstanding Sports Records." *Interfaces*, Vol. 17, No. 5, 1987, pp. 32–42.

Golden, B. L., E. A. Wasil, and P. T. Harker (eds.), *The Analytic Hierarchy Process*. New York, Springer-Verlag, 1989.

Hedge, G. G. and P. R. Tadikamalla, "Site Selection for a 'Sure Service Terminal.'" *European Journal of Operational Research*, Vol.48, No. 1, 1990, pp. 77–80.

Keeney, R. L. and H. Raiffa, *Decisions with Multiple Objectives: Preferences and Value Tradeoffs*. New York, Wiley, 1976.

Liberatore, M. J., "An Extension of the Analytic Hierarchy Process for Industrial R&D Projects Selection and Resource Allocation." *IEEE Transactions on Engineering Management*, Vol. 34, No. 1, 1987, pp. 12–18.

Liberatore, M. J. and R. L. Nydick, "An Analytic Hierarchy Approach for Evaluating Product Formulations." In *Computer Aided Formulation: A Manual for Implementation*, A. H. Bohl (ed.). New York, VCH Publishing Company, 1990, pp. 179–194.

Liberatore, M. J., R. L. Nydick, and P. M. Sanchez, "The Evaluation of Research Papers (or How to Get an Academic Committee to Agree on Something)." *Interfaces*, Vol. 22, No. 2, 1992, pp. 92–100.

Liberatore, M. J., T. F. Monahan, and D. E. Stout, "A Framework for Integrating Capital Budgeting Analysis with Strategy." *The Engineering Economist*, Vol. 38, No. 1, Fall 1992, pp. 31–43.

Liberatore, M. J., and T. Miller, "A Decision Support Approach for Transport Carrier and Mode Selection." *Journal of Business Logistics*, Vol. 16, No. 2, 1995, pp. 85–115.

Nydick, R. L. and R. Hill, "Using the Analytic Hierarchy Process to Structure the Vendor Selection Procedure." *The Journal of Purchasing and Materials Management*, Vol. 28, No. 2, 1992, pp. 31–36.

Palmer, B. "Click Here for Decision," *Fortune*, 10 May 1999, pp. 153–156.

Ross, M. E. and R. L. Nydick, "The Selection of Licensing Candidates in the Pharmaceutical Industry: An Application of the Analytic Hierarchy Process." *The Journal of Health Care Marketing*, Vol. 12, No. 2, 1992, pp. 60–65.

Saaty, T. L., "A Scaling Method for Priorities in Hierarchical Structures." *Journal of Mathematical Psychology*, Vol. 15, No. 3, 1977, pp. 234–281.

Saaty, T. L., "How to Make a Decision: The Analytic Hierarchy Process." *Interfaces*, Vol. 24, No. 6, 1994, pp. 19–43.

Saaty, T. L., *The Analytic Hierarchy Process*. Pittsburgh, PA: RWS Publications, 1996.

Samson, D., *Managerial Decision Analysis*. Homewood, IL: Irwin, 1988.

Vargas, L. G. and F. Zahedi, "Special Issue on the Analytic Hierarchy Process." *Mathematical and Computer Modelling*, Vol. 17, Nos. 4–5, 1993.

Von Neumann, J. and O. Morgenstern, *Theory of Games and Economic Behavior*. Princeton, Princeton University Press, 1944.

Wasil, E. A. and B. L. Golden (eds.), "Public Sector Applications of the Analytic Hierarchy Process." *Socio-Economic Planning Sciences*, Vol. 25, No. 2, 1991.

Weingarten, M. S., F. Erlich, R. L. Nydick, and M. J. Liberatore, "A Pilot Study of the Use of the Analytic Hierarchy Process for the Selection of Surgery Residents." *Academic Medicine*, Vol. 72, No. 5, 1997, pp. 400–402.

Zahedi, F., "The Analytic Hierarchy Process: A Survey of the Methods and Its Applications." *Interfaces*, Vol. 16, No. 4, 1986, pp. 96–108.

# Chapter 10

# The Analytic Hierarchy Process Using Expert Choice

## APPLYING THE AHP USING EXPERT CHOICE
## CAR PURCHASE EXAMPLE

In the previous chapter, we discussed various decision support aids including expected value, utility theory, and the analytic hierarchy process (AHP). We explained how the AHP offers certain important advantages in decision-making situations characterized by multiple and often conflicting criteria. In this chapter, we discuss the theory and application of the AHP using a motivating example (Saaty 1977, 1994, 1996). After completing this example, you should have a good understanding of the basics of the AHP approach and its application through decision support software. There are a variety of PC-based AHP packages such as HIPRE3+ (www.hut.fi/Units/SAL/Downloadables/hpdemo.html), Criterium (www.infoharvest.com), and Expert Choice (www.expertchoice.com). We will use the most popular package, Expert Choice, which has extensive capabilities for modeling, editing, and sensitivity analysis—a true decision support tool.

### Building the Hierarchy

A couple is trying to make a decision about which car they should purchase. They have decided to focus on three criteria: cost, safety, and appearance. They have narrowed their alternatives to three specific cars—a Honda, a Mazda, and a Volvo—and would now like to evaluate them. The AHP hierarchy, consisting of the goal, the criteria, and the alternatives can now be easily entered into Expert Choice.

After launching Expert Choice, select the *File, New* option, and after selecting a destination folder, enter a file name such as CARS. (Expert Choice adds the AHP file extension.) Next, enter a description for your goal, such as, "Select the best car." To enter the criteria, for example, cost, safety, and appearance, use the *Edit* and *Insert Child* of Current Node commands. When entering criteria the goal must be highlighted. After entering all criteria use the Esc key or simply hit the Enter key an extra time. To add the alternatives, for example, Honda, Mazda, and Volvo, select the *Edit, Alternative,* and *Insert* commands. You can also use the "Add Alternative" button in the upper right-hand corner of the model window. This sequence of commands must be repeated to enter each alternative. Additional details can be found in the Expert Choice tutorial provided with the software. The AHP hierarchy, as shown in Expert Choice, appears as Figure 10.1. Note that there are no weights for cost, safety, and appearance, since no pairwise comparisons have been entered into the model.

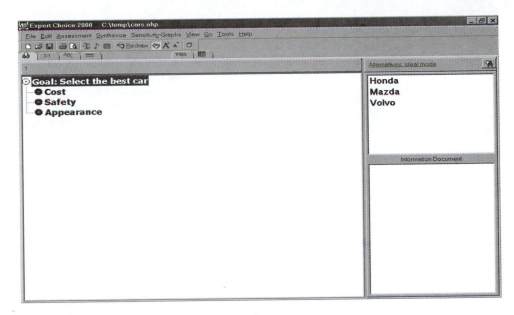

**Figure 10.1** AHP Hierarchy for the Car Selection Problem

## Analyzing the Hierarchy

To analyze the car hierarchy complete the following three stages:

1. Determine the *priorities* or weights of the alternatives for each criterion.
2. Determine the weights of the criteria in achieving the goal.
3. Determine the overall weight of each alternative in achieving the goal. This is accomplished by combining the results of the first two stages and is called *synthesis*.

To complete the first stage the couple can base their judgments on the following (hypothetical) performance information shown in Table 10.1. It is important to note that, when an individual or group provides pairwise comparisons, they should be based on data to the extent possible.

## Entering and Processing the Cost Judgments

The couple begins the process by entering judgments in the form of *pairwise comparisons* between each pair of cars for the cost criterion. In this example, these pairwise comparisons should be based on the couple's judgments concerning the relative costs of the three cars. Remember that the costs of the three cars are $22,000, $28,500, and $33,000,

**Table 10.1**   Hypothetical Data for Car Selection Example

| Car | Cost | Safety* | Appearance |
|---|---|---|---|
| Honda | $22,000 | Average | Sporty |
| Mazda | $28,000 | Above Average | Slick |
| Volvo | $33,000 | Excellent | Dull |

*Safety Rating from a consumer testing service: the higher the number, the safer the car.

respectively. There are many scales that could be used to elicit their judgments. The scale shown in Table 10.2 is the standard one-to-nine developed by Saaty (1994). As Table 10.2 indicates, items that are close and nearly indistinguishable can be compared using a comparison between 1 and 2 (rounded to a single decimal point). Expert Choice also allows the user to enter any pairwise comparison between 1 and 9 rounded to one decimal place.

Since there are three cars that are being pairwise compared, there is a total of nine judgments that are needed. These nine judgments can be entered into a three-by-three pairwise comparison matrix. We begin by comparing the Honda to the Honda. Since the Honda is equally preferred to itself, using the AHP scale, we enter a 1 (equal importance) in the first row, first column entry of the matrix as shown in Table 10.3. The other entries along the main diagonal of the matrix are also 1 since each car is equally preferred to itself.

Now suppose that the couple believes that the Honda ($22,000) is equally to moderately preferred to the Mazda ($28,500) with respect to cost. This implies that the row 1, column 2 entry of the matrix should be a 2. Some people might argue that the Honda should be 1.295 times better than the Mazda (that is, 28,500/22,000). However, if you recall our discussion in the previous chapter about lotteries and preferences, most people do not value lotteries according to expected value. Risk-averse individuals value them less than the expected value, while risk-seeking people value them more. Similarly, for some individuals, $28,500 is significantly greater than $22,000, implying a pairwise comparison greater than 1.295. Other individuals may perceive virtually no difference between the two costs, implying a judgment somewhere between 1 and 1.295. Expert Choice has an *Assessment, Direct* mode in which the cost values could be entered and Expert Choice would simply compute a ratio, such as 1.295, and use it as the pairwise comparison. However, since preferences are rarely linear, in general we do not recommend this option.

Continuing with our example, if the couple judges that the Honda is 2 times better than the Mazda, this implies that the Mazda ($28,500) is one-half as good as the Honda ($22,000). This means that its *reciprocal judgment*, (1/2), should be placed in the row 2,

**Table 10.2**   Standard 1–9 AHP Measurement Scale

| Intensity of Importance | Definition | Explanation |
|---|---|---|
| 1 | Equal importance | Two activities contribute equally |
| 3 | Moderate importance | Experience and judgment slightly favor one activity over another |
| 5 | Strong importance | Experience and judgment strongly favor one activity over another |
| 7 | Very strong | An activity is favored very strongly over another |
| 9 | Extreme importance | The evidence favoring one activity over another is of the highest possible order of affirmation |
| 2, 4, 6, 8 | For compromise | Sometimes one needs to interpolate a compromise judgment numerically because there is no good word to describe it |
| 1.1–1.9 | For tied activities | When elements are close and nearly indistinguishable; moderate is 1.3 and extreme is 1.9 |
| Reciprocals of above | If activity A has one of the above numbers assigned to it when compared with activity B, then B has the reciprocal value when compared to A | For example, if the pairwise comparison of A to B is 3.0, then the pairwise comparison of B to A is 1/3 |

**Table 10.3**    Cost Pairwise Comparison Matrix

| Cost | | Honda | Mazda | Volvo |
|---|---|---|---|---|
| (22K) | Honda | 1 | 2 | 4 |
| (28.5K) | Mazda | 1/2 | 1 | 2 |
| (33K) | Volvo | 1/4 | 1/2 | 1 |

column 1 entry of the matrix. Suppose the couple judges the Mazda ($28,500) to be equally to moderately preferred to the Volvo ($33,000). This requires that a 2 be placed in the row 2, column 3 entry of the matrix, and its reciprocal (1/2) be placed in the row 3, column 2 entry.

Assuming perfect consistency of judgments, we would conclude that the Honda ($22,000) is 4 times (that is, moderately to strongly) preferred to the Volvo ($33,000). (We will relax this assumption later.) We would then enter a 4 in the row 1, column 3 entry of the matrix, and its reciprocal (1/4) would be placed in the row 3, column 1 entry. The matrix would now be complete, as shown in Table 10.3.

The weights for each car with respect to cost can now be computed by Expert Choice. A numerical procedure is used, and involves raising the pairwise comparison matrix to powers that are successively squared each time. The row sums are then calculated and normalized. The computer is instructed to stop when the difference between these sums in two consecutive calculations is smaller than a prescribed value. For further details the interested reader can go to Expert Choice's home page and can select Software, Software Downloads, and the AHP Slideshow Demo Download to obtain a presentation on the theory behind the AHP.

We now illustrate a simple three-step procedure that provides a generally good approximation to the computational procedure used in Expert Choice. The process can be summarized in the following steps.

1. Sum the elements in each column of the original matrix.
2. Divide each element in the original matrix by its column sum. This results in the adjusted matrix.
3. Compute the row averages—these are the weights.

These steps are illustrated now for the cost matrix.

***Step 1: Sum the Elements in Each Column of the Original Matrix***    The results of this step are shown in Table 10.4.

**Table 10.4**    Cost Pairwise Comparison Matrix and Column Sums

| Cost | | Honda | Mazda | Volvo |
|---|---|---|---|---|
| (22K) | Honda | 1 | 2 | 4 |
| (28.5K) | Mazda | 1/2 | 1 | 2 |
| (33K) | Volvo | 1/4 | 1/2 | 1 |
| **Column Totals** | | 7/4 | 7/2 | 7 |

**Table 10.5**   Adjusted Cost Pairwise Comparison Matrix

| Cost | | Honda | Mazda | Volvo |
|---|---|---|---|---|
| (22K) | Honda | 4/7* | 4/7 | 4/7 |
| (28.5K) | Mazda | 2/7 | 2/7 | 2/7 |
| (33K) | Volvo | 1/7 | 1/7 | 1/7 |

*This entry is obtained by dividing the Honda entry in the original matrix (1) by the Honda column total (7/4).

**Step 2: Divide Each Element in the Original Matrix by Its Column Sum. This Results in the Adjusted Matrix**   The adjusted matrix is shown as Table 10.5.

The process of dividing each column element by the column sum is called *normalization*. Essentially, this step places the elements in each column on the same footing. After normalization, the elements in each column sum to one. For example, for the third column, judgments totaling 7 were made. The Honda received 4 of 7 (that is, 57.1% of the weight), the Mazda received 2 of 7 (that is, 28.6% of the weight), and the Volvo received 1 of 7 (that is, 14.3% of the weight). Similar comparisons can be made for the other two columns. Notice that no variation is seen across the rows of the adjusted matrix because the judgments are perfectly consistent.

**Step 3: Compute the Row Averages—These Are the Weights**   The adjusted matrix with the car weights for the cost criterion is shown as Table 10.6.

The results in Table 10.6 show that with respect to cost, the Honda receives the highest weight with a score of 0.571, the Mazda receives the second highest score of 0.286, and the Volvo has the lowest score of 0.143. Note that these weights sum to 1.00.

Why do we need to compute the row averages if the three entries are the same in each row? As mentioned previously, the only reason the entries were the same is that the couple was perfectly consistent in their judgments. As will be discussed in the next section, if we are not perfectly consistent, there will be differences in entries across the rows of the adjusted matrix. Since each of the row entries in the adjusted matrix can be viewed as an estimate of the true row weight, we simply average these values to obtain our best estimate.

The process of entering pairwise comparisons into Expert Choice and obtaining the weights is straightforward. To enter the pairwise comparisons for the cost criterion, first highlight the cost node in the hierarchy. Next, select the Pairwise Numerical comparisons button (3:1). This button appears on the top left-hand side of the toolbar to the right of the Model View button. After selecting the Pairwise Numerical Comparisons button, the screen given as Figure 10.2 appears.

**Table 10.6**   Adjusted Cost Pairwise Comparison Matrix and Weights

| Cost | | Honda | Mazda | Volvo | Weights Row Average |
|---|---|---|---|---|---|
| (22K) | Honda | 4/7 | 4/7 | 4/7 | 0.571 |
| (28.5K) | Mazda | 2/7 | 2/7 | 2/7 | 0.286 |
| (33K) | Volvo | 1/7 | 1/7 | 1/7 | 0.143 |
| | | | | **Total** | 1.000 |

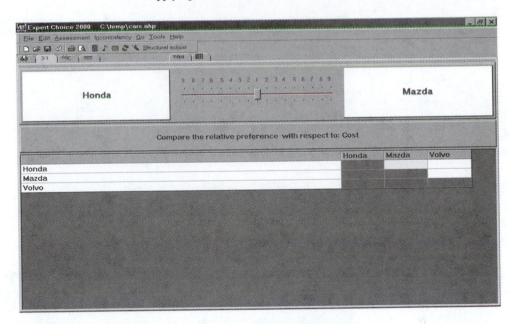

**Figure 10.2** Pairwise Numerical Comparisons Screen for the Cost Criterion

Sliding the bar between Honda and Mazda to the left so that it rests on the 2 indicates that the Honda is two times better than the Mazda when considering the cost criterion. If the Mazda were 2 times better than the Honda, the bar would be slid to the 2 on the right. The other pairwise comparisons are entered in a similar fashion. The screen given as Figure 10.3a is the result after all cost pairwise comparisons are entered: Honda to Mazda (2), Mazda to Volvo (2), and Honda to Volvo (4).

Notice that the pairwise comparison matrix shown by Expert Choice displays only three entries. Expert Choice automatically assumes that there are 1's along the main diagonal and adds the necessary reciprocals of the judgments entered. For example, since Honda is 2.0 times more preferred than the Mazda with respect to cost, Expert Choice automatically assumes that the Mazda is one-half as preferred to the Honda with respect to cost. In general, if n items are being compared, then a total of $n(n - 1)/2$ judgments should be entered into Expert Choice. As n increases, the number of required judgments is much less than $n \wedge 2$, which is the total number of pairwise comparisons in the full matrix.

There are other buttons that allow the user to switch to different modes for entering pairwise comparisons. The Pairwise Verbal Comparisons (ABC) and the Pairwise Graphical Comparisons (the button that looks like a bar graph) are used for such purposes. The only difference between these comparison modes is how the pairwise comparison questions are displayed. In the numerical mode the comparisons use a 1–9 numerical scale, whereas the verbal comparisons use the equal, moderate, strong, very strong, and extreme scale. These verbal comparisons are then converted to 1, 3, 5, 7, and 9 numerical values. These numerical values are then used for computational purposes. The graphical mode uses the same numerical scale but shows the user a visual comparison based on the length of two bars. Figure 10.3b shows the graphical pairwise comparisons for the cost criterion. Our experience indicates that many people are most comfortable with this mode since they can see a pie chart that provides a good idea of the relative differences between the items being compared. Ultimately, the user can select whatever mode they prefer.

Once all pairwise comparisons are entered, the user will be asked if the judgments should be recorded. Simply click Yes and you will be taken back to Model View where

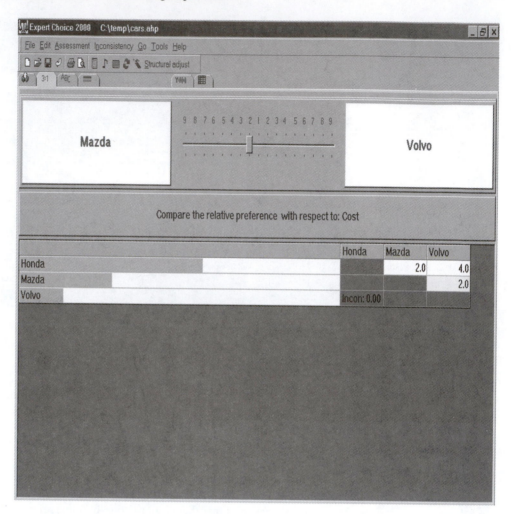

**Figure 10.3a** Numerical Comparisons Screen with the Three Judgments Entered for the Cost Criteria

the weights for the cars, with respect to the cost criterion, are displayed. Expert Choice screen shots for Verbal and Graphical modes as well as the Model View displaying the weights are shown as Figures 10.4 through 10.6, respectively. Notice in Figure 10.4, we have indicated that the Honda to Mazda pairwise comparison for cost is somewhere between Equal and Moderate, that is, twice as preferred. The bars in Figure 10.5 indicate that the Honda is judged to be twice the size as the Mazda for cost, that is, twice as pre-

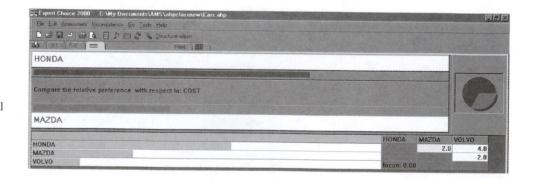

**Figure 10.3b** Graphical Numerical Comparison Screen with Three Judgments for the Cost Criterion

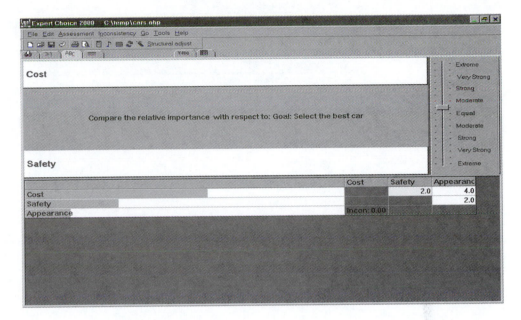

**Figure 10.4** Verbal Comparison Screen Showing that the Honda is Twice as Preferred as the Mazda for the Cost Criterion

ferred. Remember, you can always select the Model View to see the complete hierarchy and any weights that have been computed. Figure 10.6 shows that the computed cost weights for Honda, Mazda, and Volvo are 0.571, 0.286, and 0.143, respectively.

## Inconsistency of Judgments

When we compared the cars with respect to cost, Expert Choice shows the inconsistency in Figure 10.3a by reporting that the inconsistency ratio (Incon:) = 0.0. If the inconsistency ratio is greater than one order of magnitude, that is, greater than 0.10, then some revision of judgment may be required. To assist in this process, Expert Choice has an

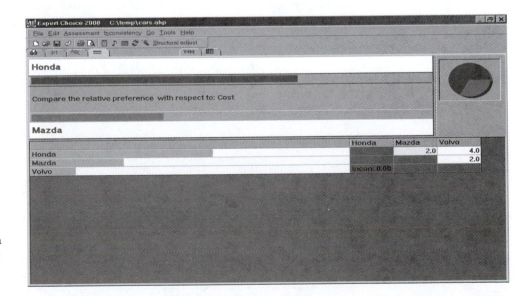

**Figure 10.5** Graphical Comparison Screen Showing that the Honda is Twice as Preferred as the Mazda for the Cost Criterion

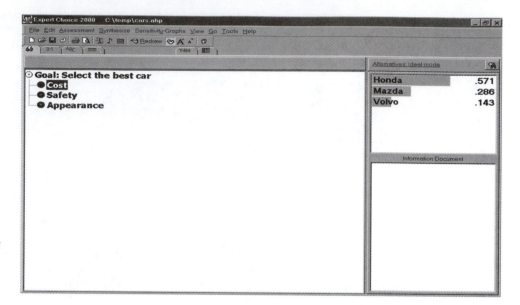

**Figure 10.6** Model View and Weights (Priorities) for the Three Cars with Respect to Cost

*Inconsistency* option (within any Pairwise Comparison mode) to identify the most inconsistent judgments, in order.

In actual practice, inconsistency in judgments often occurs. Inconsistency may result from problems of estimation, errors between the comparisons, or a natural inconsistency in the comparisons. One example of natural inconsistency is in a sporting contest. If team A is twice as likely to beat team B, and if team B is three times as likely to beat team C, this does not necessarily imply that team A is six times as likely to beat team C. This inconsistency may result because of the way that the teams "match-up" overall. The point is not to stop inconsistency from occurring, but rather to make sure that the level of inconsistency remains within some reasonable limit.

Let us study how a change in judgment about cost affects the car weights. Suppose the couple decides to change their comparison of Mazda to Volvo from a 2 to a 3. Remember that this changes the comparison for Volvo to Mazda from (1/2) to (1/3). As a result of these changes, the judgments are now somewhat inconsistent. The new matrix and computations of the weights using the three steps are shown in Tables 10.7 through 10.9.

***Step 1: Sum the Elements in Each Column of the Original Matrix***

***Step 2: Divide Each Element in the Original Matrix by its Column Sum. This Results in the Adjusted Matrix***

**Table 10.7** Cost Pairwise Comparison Matrix and Column Sums: Inconsistent Judgments Case

| Cost | | Honda | Mazda | Volvo |
|---|---|---|---|---|
| (22K) | Honda | 1 | 2 | 4 |
| (28.5K) | Mazda | 1/2 | 1 | 3 |
| (33K) | Volvo | 1/4 | 1/3 | 1 |
| **Column Totals** | | 7/4 | 10/3 | 8 |

**Table 10.8**  Adjusted Cost Pairwise Comparison Matrix: Inconsistent Judgments Case

| Cost | | Honda | Mazda | Volvo |
|------|------|-------|-------|-------|
| (22K) | Honda | 4/7 | 6/10 | 4/8 |
| (28.5K) | Mazda | 2/7 | 3/10 | 3/8 |
| (33K) | Volvo | 1/7 | 1/10 | 1/8 |

***Step 3: Compute the Row Averages—These Are the Weights***    The results in Table 10.9 show that with respect to cost, the Honda receives the highest weight with a score of 0.557, the Mazda receives the second highest score of 0.320, and the Volvo has the lowest score of 0.123. The inconsistency resulted in some changes in the original weights of 0.571, 0.286, and 0.143. Since we altered the Mazda-to-Volvo judgment from a 2 to a 3, the weight for the Mazda increased while the weight for the Volvo decreased. Also, notice that the entries in the rows of the adjusted cost pairwise comparison matrix (Table 10.8) now vary across each row. Essentially, inconsistency measures the degree of variation across the rows.

To make this pairwise comparison change in Expert Choice from the Model View screen, highlight the cost node and select any Pairwise Comparisons mode. We illustrate this change with the Numerical Pairwise Comparisons mode. Highlight the Mazda-to-Volvo cell, slide the comparison bar to the left from 2 to 3, and select the Model View and record the judgments to see the new weights. The screens showing the (slightly) inconsistent judgments and the new weights appear as Figures 10.7 and 10.8, respectively. Notice that the weights of 0.558, 0.320, and 0.122 for the Honda, Mazda, and Volvo, respectively, are slightly different than the weights computed above using the three-step procedure. This difference is not due to rounding, but reflects the difference between the three-step procedure and the exact computational procedure when the judgments are not perfectly consistent. The differences in weights between these two methods tend to increase as the level of inconsistency increases. For the revised set of judgments we note that the inconsistency ratio is 0.02. For the remainder of this chapter, we will use the weights obtained from Expert Choice only.

The weights can also be used to measure the effectiveness of the cars. Prior to doing the AHP analysis we knew that, with respect to cost, Honda was first ($22,000), Mazda was second ($28,500), and Volvo was third ($33,000). The ranking of the cars after completing the AHP analysis is the same, as expected. However, the AHP provides more information than a simple ordinal ranking. It provides information on *how much better* one car is compared to another based on the pairwise comparison. For example, based on our results, we determined that the Honda is 1.74 (0.558/0.320) times better than the Mazda, and the Honda is 4.57 times better than the Volvo. One could question why the Honda to

**Table 10.9**  Adjusted Cost Pairwise Comparison Matrix and Weights: Inconsistent Judgments Case

| Cost | | Honda | Mazda | Volvo | Weights Row Average |
|------|------|-------|-------|-------|----------------------|
| (22K) | Honda | 4/7 | 6/10 | 4/8 | 0.557 |
| (28.5K) | Mazda | 2/7 | 3/10 | 3/8 | 0.320 |
| (33K) | Volvo | 1/7 | 1/10 | 1/8 | 0.123 |

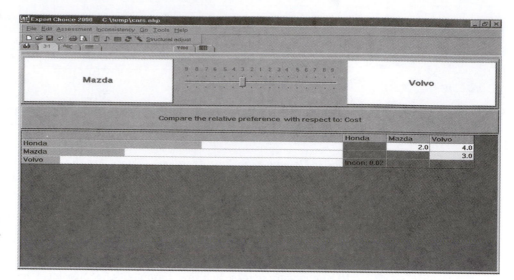

**Figure 10.7** Inconsistent Pairwise Comparisons for the Cars with Respect to Cost

Mazda ratio is 1.74 and not the original judgment of 2. The reason for this difference is the inconsistency across all three judgments in the matrix.

## Remaining Computations for the Car Example

The cars must be pairwise compared for the safety criterion and then for the appearance criterion. The Expert Choice screen shots showing the pairwise comparisons and the results of the calculations of the weights for safety and appearance appear as Figures 10.9 through 10.12, respectively. The safety pairwise comparisons are all inverted, that is, for each comparison, the bar was moved to the right. This means that, for safety, the Mazda is two times more preferred than the Honda, the Volvo is five times more preferred than the Honda, and the Volvo is four times more preferred than the Mazda. The couple based their judgments about safety on the safety ratings given in the previous hypothetical data chart. Note that the safety rating of Volvo (Excellent) is higher than the safety ratings of the Mazda (Above Average) and the Honda (Average). If you were viewing Figure 10.9

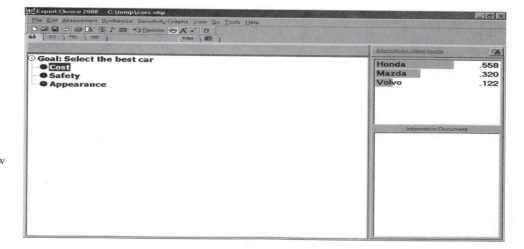

**Figure 10.8** Model View and Weights (Priorities) for the Three Cars with Respect to Cost: Inconsistent Judgments Case

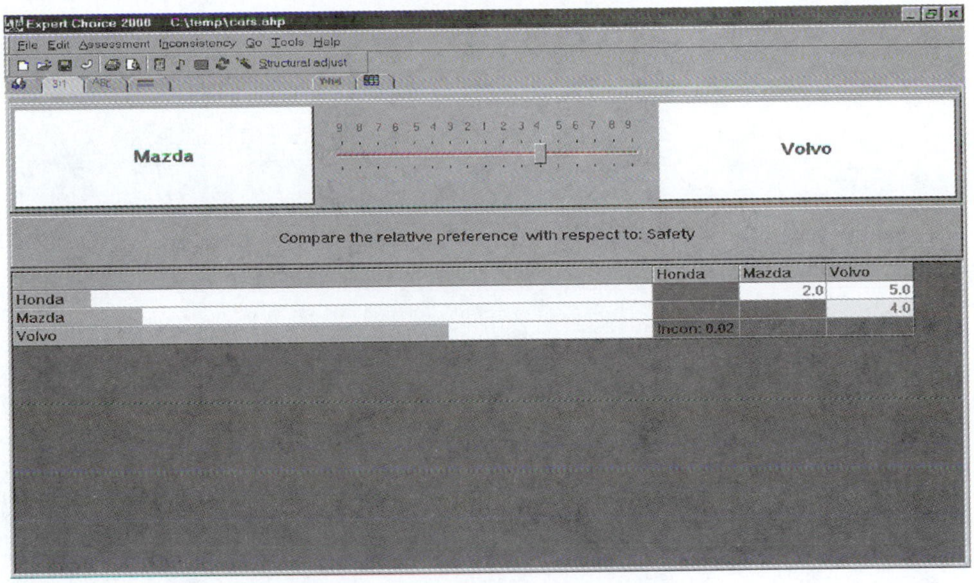

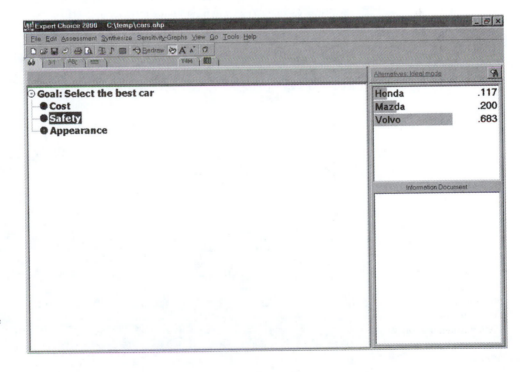

**Figure 10.9** Numerical Comparison Screen with the Three Judgments Entered for the Safety Criterion

in color, you would see that the color of each judgment is no longer black but red. This *inverted* judgment represents how much more important or preferred the column alternative is to the row alternative. When the judgment number is black, it represents how much more important or preferred the row is to the column alternative. Remember that the wording always correctly reflects the direction of the comparison.

Next we enter the pairwise comparisons for the cars with respect to the appearance criterion (Figures 10.11 and 10.12). The couple must agree on how much they prefer a

**Figure 10.10** Model View and Weights (Priorities) for the Three Cars with Respect to Safety

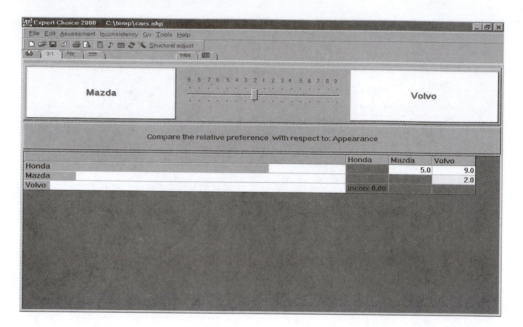

**Figure 10.11** Numerical Comparison Screen with the Three Judgments Entered for the Appearance Criterion

sporty appearance to a slick appearance, and so forth. As mentioned in the previous chapter, Expert Choice can incorporate criteria that measure how well alternatives achieve intangible and highly subjective criteria such as appearance. Once the appearance and safety judgments are entered, the first stage of analyzing the AHP car hierarchy is now complete.

The second stage requires obtaining judgments relating the importance of the criteria in achieving the goal. These judgments are entered in a similar fashion as the alternative pairwise comparisons that we have already explained. These pairwise comparisons and the resulting weights are shown in Figures 10.13 and 10.14. Notice that there are no data to

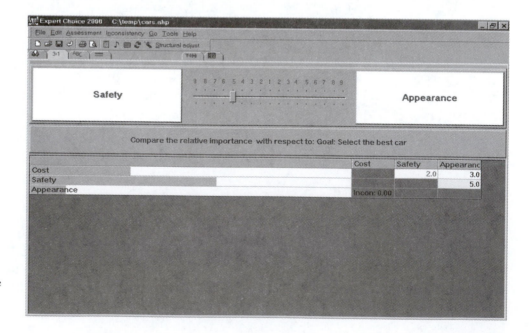

**Figure 10.12** Model View and Weights (Priorities) for the Three Cars with Respect to Appearance

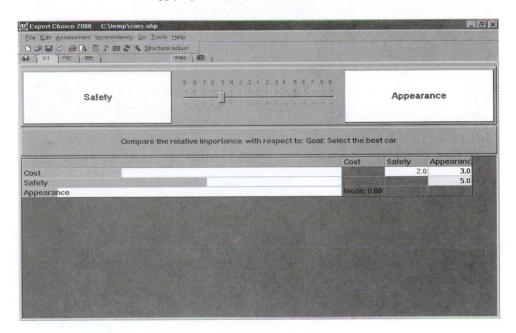

**Figure 10.13** Numerical Comparison Screen with the Three Judgments Entered for the Criteria

support these judgments since they are purely a reflection of the couple's preferences. Assume that the couple judged safety to be twice as important as cost, cost three times as important as appearance, and five times as important as appearance.

The third and last stage is to compute the overall weights for each car in achieving the couple's goal of selecting the best car for them. The car weights for the cost, safety, and appearance criteria, and the criteria weights can be found in Figures 10.8, 10.10, 10.12, and 10.14, respectively. These weights are summarized in Table 10.10.

Using the information in Table 10.10, the final weight for each car is computed by multiplying each criterion weight by the car weight for the given criterion and then sum-

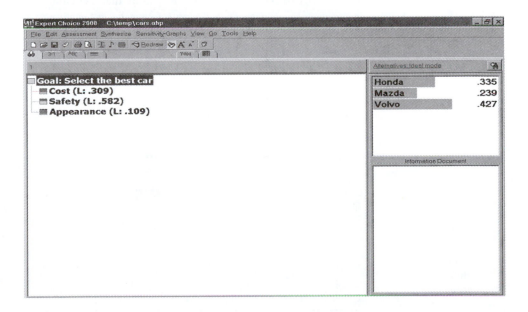

**Figure 10.14** Model View and Weights (Priorities) for the Three Criteria

**Table 10.10** Criteria Weights and Car Weights for Each Criterion Obtained from Expert Choice

| | Criteria | | |
|---|---|---|---|
| | Cost | Safety | Appearance |
| | 0.309 | 0.582 | 0.109 |
| **Cars** | | | |
| Honda | 0.558 | 0.117 | 0.761 |
| Mazda | 0.320 | 0.200 | 0.158 |
| Volvo | 0.122 | 0.683 | 0.082 |

ming over all criteria. This is nothing more than computing a weighted average. The computational results are shown in Table 10.11.

Table 10.11 illustrates the difference between *local* and *global* weights in the AHP. For example, with respect to the cost criterion, the local weights for the Honda, Mazda, and Volvo are 0.558, 0.320, and 0.122, respectively, and sum to one. The global weights for these cars, with respect to cost, are computed by multiplying the cost criterion weight (0.309) by the local weights. The global weights are 0.173, 0.099, and 0.038, respectively, for the three cars. Therefore, the global weights for three cars with respect to cost sum to the cost criterion's weight of 0.309.

These weighted average calculations, called *synthesis,* are shown in Expert Choice after all pairwise comparisons are entered and when you are in the Model View and the goal is highlighted. At this time, the Distributive mode (above the alternatives window) should be selected. The difference between the Distributive and Ideal modes of Synthesis will be discussed later. The resulting Expert Choice screen shot is shown as Figure 10.15.

The final weights provide a measure of the relative performance of each alternative. It is important to properly interpret the meaning of these results. For example, when taking all of the pairwise comparisons into consideration, the results show that the Volvo is ranked first, the Honda second, and the Mazda third. In addition, the couple seems to prefer the Volvo 1.37 (0.444/0.324) times more than the Honda and 1.91 (0.444/0.232) times more than the Mazda. We can only make the latter statements because all of our judgments are pairwise comparisons, meaning that they are ratio-scaled numbers.

Should the couple buy the Volvo? The AHP provides a method to elicit and process the necessary judgments for decision-making. The results should be used as an aid in the decision-making process and should not and cannot replace the decision maker. They also can be used to support further discussion of the decision-making problem and might lead to revision of judgments. This iterative process is quite normal and should even be

**Table 10.11** Computation of Global Car Weights and Final Car Weights

| Cars/Criteria | Cost | Safety | Appearance | Final Car Weights |
|---|---|---|---|---|
| **Honda** | (0.558)(0.309) | (0.117)(0.582) | (0.761)(0.109) | |
| | 0.173 | 0.068 | 0.083 | 0.324 |
| **Mazda** | (0.320)(0.309) | (0.200)(0.582) | (0.158)(0.109) | |
| | 0.099 | 0.116 | 0.017 | 0.232 |
| **Volvo** | (0.122)(0.309) | (0.683)(0.582) | (0.082)(0.109) | |
| | 0.038 | 0.397 | 0.009 | 0.444 |
| **Criteria weights** | 0.309 | 0.582 | 0.109 | 1.000 |

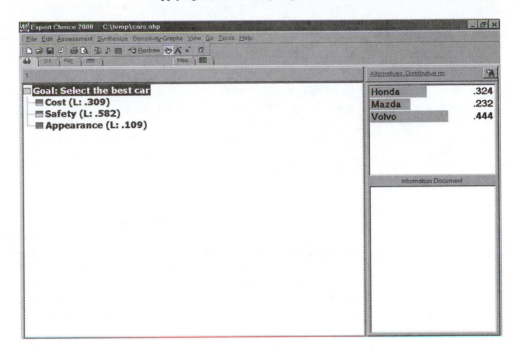

**Figure 10.15** Final Weights for the Three Cars Using Distributive Synthesis

encouraged. As a result, the AHP can help to facilitate communication between different individuals or groups, such as the couple in our case. This dialogue can help to generate consensus and to improve decision making.

## Distributive vs. Ideal Synthesis

The process used in the previous section for computing the weighted averages for the alternative cars is called *distributive synthesis*. Distributive synthesis works well when there is a fixed amount of a resource that must be distributed to a fixed set of alternatives. For example, suppose the distributive synthesis weights of three alternative projects are 0.5, 0.3, and 0.2, and your available funds are $100. These results can be used to distribute the $100 in direct proportion to their weights, yielding shares of $50, $30, and $20, respectively. However, adding the same or nearly identical copies of one of the projects dilutes this project's share of the $100 because the pot is fixed and the weights of all alternatives are normalized so that they sum to one.

Why is this fact about distributive synthesis important in practice? In some cases after completing an AHP analysis using distributive synthesis, we are more interested in the ranking of the alternatives than in their final weights. In such situations we may wish to consider an additional alternative after completing the initial analysis. It is possible that a *rank reversal* could occur in this situation. For example, our results show that the cars are ranked as Volvo, Honda, and Mazda. If another Volvo is added that is similar to our original Volvo, it is possible that the Honda will be ranked higher than the original Volvo. The reason for this rank reversal is that the second Volvo is getting more of its weight from the original Volvo than from the Honda and the Mazda.

A good example of rank reversal occurred in the 1988 presidential election when Ross Perot entered the race. Many experts believed that Perot took away more votes from George Bush than he did from Bill Clinton. It could be argued that George Bush would have won the election if Ross Perot had never entered the race.

**Table 10.12**    Computation of the Ideal Weights for the Car Example

| Criteria/Cars | Honda | Mazda | Volvo |
|---|---|---|---|
| **Cost** | (.558/.558) * .309 = .309 | (.320/.558) * .309 = .177 | (.122/.558) * .309 = .068 |
| **Safety** | (.117/.683) * .582 = .100 | (.200/.683) * .582 = .170 | (.683/.683) * .582 = .582 |
| **Appearance** | (.761/.761) * .109 = .109 | (.158/.761) * .109 = .023 | (.082/.761) * .109 = .012 |
| **Initial ideal weights** | 0.518 | 0.370 | 0.662 |
| **Final ideal weights (normalized)** | 0.518/1.550 = 0.335 | 0.370/1.550 = 0.239 | 0.662/1.550 = 0.427 |

In most cases this rank reversal is not acceptable since either the original Volvo is better than the Honda or it is not, and this is independent of whether the second Volvo exists or not. As just mentioned, distributive synthesis should be used when there is a fixed amount of resources that must be distributed to a fixed set of alternatives. The distributive mode should *not* be used if preservation of rank is important to you and additional alternatives might be added before your decision is implemented. *Ideal Synthesis* should be used in such circumstances to prevent rank reversal.

The ideal mode of synthesis gives the full weight of the criterion to the alternative that ranks highest under that criterion. The other alternatives are given a portion of the criterion weight based on their local weight. Table 10.12 summarizes the computation of the initial ideal weights and the normalization of these weights to obtain the final ideal weights. Since the initial ideal weights do not sum to one, normalization is accomplished by dividing the initial ideal car weights by the sum of these weights (1.550). These are the ideal weights reported in Expert Choice and are shown in the screen shot as Figure

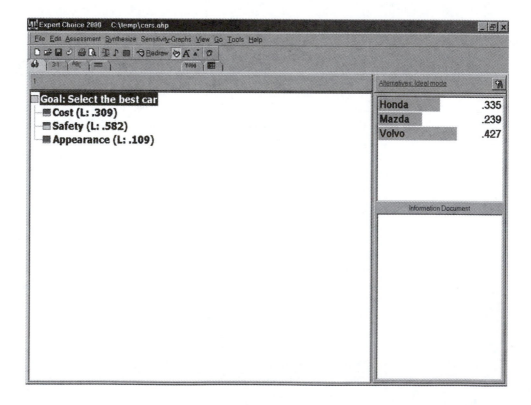

**Figure 10.16** Final Weights for the Three Cars Using Ideal Synthesis

10.16. Note that when analyzing a fixed set of alternatives, the final alternative weights will be different depending upon whether distributive or ideal synthesis is used. However, the rankings of these alternatives will always be the same in this situation.

## Sensitivity Analysis

Sensitivity analysis is an important aspect of any decision-making process. Often decision makers want to know whether small changes in their judgments will appreciably affect the final weights and rankings of the alternatives. If the model's outcomes are found to be sensitive to small changes in a particular judgment, the decision maker may desire to carefully review the sensitive judgment in order to validate the results. Also, sensitivity analysis allows the user to play "what if" games with the model to better understand the model's relationships and inherent trade-offs.

From the main menu in Expert Choice, select Sensitivity-Graphs to show how the final weights and the rankings of the alternatives will change if some or all of the criteria weights are changed. Sensitivity analysis can also be performed from nodes farther down in the hierarchy if the model has more than three levels. (See discussion on multilevel hierarchies in the next chapter.) There are five graphical sensitivity analysis modes available in Expert Choice: Performance, Dynamic, Gradient, Head-to-Head, and 2D. The first three show how a change in a criterion weight affects the final weights of the alternatives. The last two show how the alternatives perform with respect to any two criteria. These five modes can be summarized as follows:

*Performance:* places all sensitivity information on a single chart with horizontal line graphs for the alternatives linked to vertical bars for the criteria

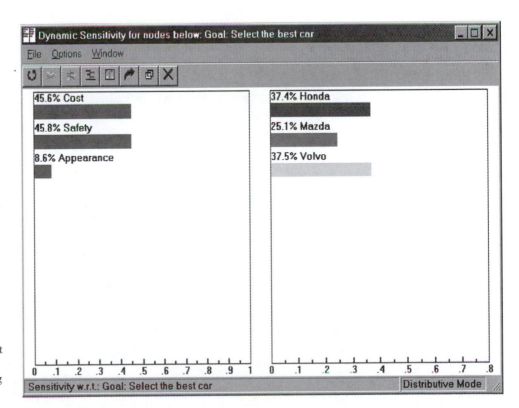

**Figure 10.17** Dynamic Sensitivity Analysis Showing the Cost Weight that Would Result in the Volvo and Honda Having the Same Final Weight

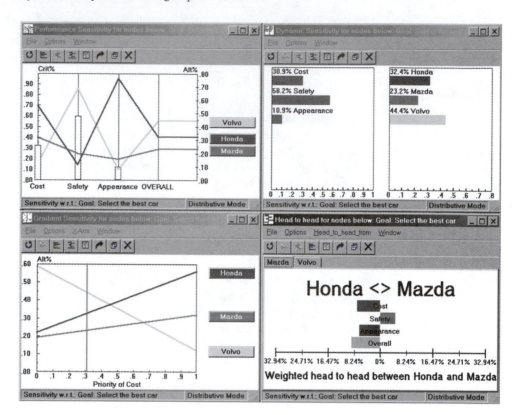

**Figure 10.18** Display of Four Sensitivity Analyses Options in Expert Choice

*Dynamic:* two sets of dynamically linked horizontal bar graphs: one for criteria and one for alternatives

*Gradient:* a line graph that shows how the weights of the alternatives vary according to the weight assigned to a specific criterion (Use the *X-Axis* option to change the selected criterion.)

*Head-to-Head:* a graph that shows the differences between any two alternatives for any criterion

*2D:* shows how well the alternatives perform with respect to any two criteria

An important use of sensitivity analysis is to determine how much a given criterion weight must change before there is a change in the rankings of the two highest alternatives. This type of breakeven analysis can be easily accomplished in Expert Choice. For example, to display the dynamic sensitivity mode choose Dynamic from the Sensitivity-Graphs option on the taskbar of the main Expert Choice screen. Once in this mode, we drag the cost criterion bar from 30.9% to approximately 45.9% as shown in Figure 10.17. At this cost weight the Volvo and the Honda will both have the same and highest final weight. Based on this result, we see that the final rankings are relatively *insensitive* to a change in the cost criterion weight because this weight had to be increased by almost 50% to lead to a change in the alternative rankings. The sensitivity analysis that we are performing is from the distributive mode. The results will be different if you are in the ideal mode. Four of the sensitivity modes can be displayed simultaneously as shown in Figure 10.18. To display them select Sensitivity-Graphs and Open Four Graphs.

## SUMMARY

This chapter discusses the application of the AHP and Expert Choice using a motivating example of a couple trying to decide which car to purchase. We show how to build and analyze the hierarchy, enter and process all pairwise comparison judgments, and compute final alternative weights using an approximation procedure and Expert Choice. We also discuss the differences between the distributive and ideal mode and this application. Sensitivity analysis is used to show whether a small change in judgments appreciably affects the final weights and rankings of the alternatives. In the next chapter we turn our attention to the extensions of the AHP.

## HOMEWORK PROBLEMS

**1.** TRAINOR Corporation is trying to figure out where to locate a new service center. There is only one criterion: proximity to their customers. Management developed the following pairwise comparison matrix:

|        | City 1 | City 2 | City 3 |
|--------|--------|--------|--------|
| City 1 | 1      | 5      | 7      |
| City 2 | 1/5    | 1      | 3      |
| City 3 | 1/7    | 1/3    | 1      |

**(a)** Determine the priorities for the three cities using Expert Choice.

**(b)** For the TRAINOR problem, are the judgments consistent? Explain.

**2.** SAMUELS Market Research Corporation wanted to evaluate three new bottled water products. There is only one criterion that is being considered: taste. The following judgments were obtained:

A is moderately more preferable than B.
A is equally to moderately more preferable than C.
B is strongly more preferable than C.

**(a)** Determine the priorities for the bottled waters with respect to the taste criterion using Expert Choice.

**(b)** For the SAMUELS problem, compute the inconsistency ratio. Are the judgments consistent? Explain.

**3.** HARLING Equipment needs to select a new VP of Operations. The two possible candidates are Lance Adams and Sara Powell, and the criteria thought to be most relevant in the selection are leadership ability (L), problem solving skills (P), and interpersonal skills (I). The following pairwise comparison matrices were obtained:

| Criterion | L   | P   | I   |     | Leadership | Adams | Powell |
|-----------|-----|-----|-----|-----|------------|-------|--------|
| L         | 1   | 1/3 | 1/4 |     | Adams      | 1     | 4      |
| P         | 3   | 1   | 2   |     | Powell     | 1/4   | 1      |
| I         | 4   | 1/2 | 1   |     |            |       |        |

| Problem Solving | Adams | Powell |     | Interpersonal | Adams | Powell |
|-----------------|-------|--------|-----|---------------|-------|--------|
| Adams           | 1     | 1/3    |     | Adams         | 1     | 2      |
| Powell          | 3     | 1      |     | Powell        | 1/2   | 1      |

Determine the overall priority for each of the candidates using Expert Choice.

**4.** BRAXTON Associates was considering the purchase of a new mobile phone for their corporate limousine. They considered three different systems that varied in terms of price (P), sound quality (Q), and features (F). The following pairwise consistency matrices were developed:

| Criterion | P   | Q   | F   |     | Price | A   | B   | C   |
|-----------|-----|-----|-----|-----|-------|-----|-----|-----|
| P         | 1   | 3   | 4   |     | A     | 1   | 4   | 2   |
| Q         | 1/3 | 1   | 3   |     | B     | 1/4 | 1   | 1/3 |
| F         | 1/4 | 1/3 | 1   |     | C     | 1/2 | 3   | 1   |

| Quality | A   | B   | C   |     | Features | A   | B   | C   |
|---------|-----|-----|-----|-----|----------|-----|-----|-----|
| A       | 1   | 1/2 | 1/4 |     | A        | 1   | 4   | 2   |
| B       | 2   | 1   | 1/3 |     | B        | 1/4 | 1   | 1   |
| C       | 4   | 3   | 1   |     | C        | 1/2 | 1   | 1   |

Determine an overall priority for each mobile phone using Expert Choice.

**5.** TEMPO Corp. is trying to rank the overall performance of three vendors (V1, V2, V3) using the AHP. The three evaluation criteria are COST, SERVICE, and RELIABLE. The necessary pairwise comparison data are given below:

| Criteria with Respect to Goal | | | |
|----------|------|---------|----------|
|          | Cost | Service | Reliable |
| COST     | 1    | 2       | 3        |
| SERVICE  |      | 1       | 2        |
| RELIABLE |      |         | 1        |

**Vendors with
Respect to Cost**

|     | V1  | V2  | V3  |
| --- | --- | --- | --- |
| V1  | 1   | 3   | 4   |
| V2  |     | 1   | 2   |
| V3  |     |     | 1   |

**Vendors with
Respect to Service**

|     | V1  | V2  | V3  |
| --- | --- | --- | --- |
| V1  | 1   | 1/3 | 1/2 |
| V2  |     | 1   | 3   |
| V3  |     |     | 1   |

**Vendors with
Respect to Reliable**

|     | V1  | V2  | V3  |
| --- | --- | --- | --- |
| V1  | 1   | 2   | 1/3 |
| V2  |     | 1   | 1/7 |
| V3  |     |     | 1   |

**(a)**   Determine the overall priorities of each of the three vendors using Expert Choice. Which vendor is the most preferred?

**(b)**   For the Tempo problem, which pairwise comparison matrix is the most inconsistent? Give a reason to support your answer.

**(c)**   For the Tempo problem, perform a sensitivity analysis to determine what COST weight would result in V1 and V2 having the same priority. Also find the COST weight for which the priorities of V1 and V3 are the same. With these results in mind, are the final rankings of the three vendors sensitive to the weight of COST?

**6.**   XENOX must purchase an expensive piece of equipment for use in their mailroom operation. They would like to use the AHP to help them make their selection. They have identified two criteria: financial factors and quality factors. For the financial factors, two subcriteria exist: initial cost and cost to operate. For the quality factors, two subcriteria exist: reliability and durability. Two alternatives are being considered.

The following judgments have been made. Xenox has decided that the financial factors are twice as important as the quality factors. The cost to operate is three times more important than the initial cost. Reliability is twice as important as durability.

Alternative 1 is twice as good as alternative 2 with respect to initial cost, but alternative 2 is three times as good as alternative 1 with respect to cost to operate. Alternative 1 is three times as good as alternative 2 with respect to reliability, but alternative 2 is twice as good as alternative 1 with respect to durability.

**(a)**   Compute the final weights for each alternative. Based on this analysis, which alternative would you recommend? Explain.

**(b)**   Perform sensitivity analysis to determine what durability weight would result in the two alternatives being equally preferred.

# REFERENCES

Saaty, T. L., "A Scaling Method for Priorities in Hierarchical Structures." *Journal of Mathematical Psychology*, Vol. 15, No. 3, 1977, pp. 234–281.

Saaty, T. L., "How to Make a Decision: The Analytic Hierarchy Process." *Interfaces*, Vol. 24, No. 6, 1994, pp. 19–43.

Saaty, T. L., *The Analytic Hierarchy Process*. Pittsburgh, PA, RWS Publications, 1996.

# Chapter 11

# Extensions of the Analytic Hierarchy Process Using Expert Choice

## INTRODUCTION

In the previous chapter, we discussed the theory and application of the AHP using a car purchase decision as a motivating example. We also showed how AHP models can be developed and analyzed using Expert Choice. In this chapter, we use a validation exercise to demonstrate the process of making pairwise comparisons in practice. We will also discuss several extensions to the basic AHP, including multilevel hierarchies, ratings models, and group decision making. The topics discussed in this chapter illustrates the true power and practicality of the AHP (Saaty 1977, 1994, 1996).

## AHP VALIDATION EXERCISE

Can pairwise comparisons accurately reflect an individual's judgments? If the AHP is applied to a situation where objective measures exist, can it lead to accurate results? We now turn our attention to these issues by considering an exercise that demonstrates the validity of the results provided by Expert Choice. Specifically, this exercise shows that the AHP can process subjective judgments and derive estimates that are very close to known values. Suppose we wish to make judgments on the relative sizes of the areas of five shapes in order to determine the percentage each shape contributes to the total area. For example, the results might indicate that one shape is 30% of the total areas of the five shapes. Of course, we could use plane geometry to compute the exact areas. Yet, the AHP, using a *subjective* method of assessing relative areas, can provide estimates that are very close to the actual values. The five shapes are shown in Figure 11.1.

Within Expert Choice, your shapes model should have two levels. The first is the goal, namely to estimate the relative areas of the five shapes. The second level is the alternatives, that is, the five shapes themselves. Note that there is only one criterion, relative area, so there is no need to have a separate level for criteria in this hierarchy. Since there are five shapes that must be pairwise compared concerning their relative areas, a total of ten judgments (5(4)/2) are required.

We also note that the numerical, verbal, or graphical modes can be used for these pairwise comparisons. We have found that the accuracy of the final estimates is not adversely affected by the mode that is used. Interestingly, you never need to explicitly use any numerical judgments to estimate the relative area of these five shapes!

Once the ten judgments are entered and recorded, the weights represent the relative areas of the five shapes. We have found that nearly every student is able to accurately

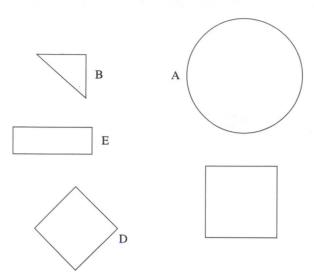

**Figure 11.1** The Five Shapes for the AHP Validation Exercise

estimate the relative areas of these shapes. Usually if this is not the case on the first try, the inconsistency ratio is much higher than 0.10. This high inconsistency is often caused by the bar being slid the wrong way for one of the judgments. After this correction is made, the inconsistency drops dramatically, and the accuracy of the estimates improves. For comparison purposes, we provide the actual relative size of the five shapes: Circle A: 0.471; Triangle B: 0.050; Square C: 0.234; Diamond D: 0.149; and Rectangle E: 0.096. How close were you?

## STRUCTURING MULTILEVEL HIERARCHIES

We now turn our attention to multilevel hierarchies. The structure of the car hierarchy, which we discussed in the previous chapter, is rather straightforward, consisting of a goal, three criteria, and three alternatives. However, it is not unusual for a decision maker to have a problem with many more criteria and alternatives, as well as additional levels. We summarize several key points that should be considered when structuring hierarchies.

Saaty (1996) recommends limiting the hierarchy to nine levels with no more than nine items per level. This is based on the psychological result that people can consider 7 +/− 2 items simultaneously (Miller, 1956). Remember that if ten items must be pairwised compared, a total of 45 judgments (10(9)/2) are required. Generally, decision makers find it difficult to make such a large number of judgments related to one criterion. In addition, it is much more difficult to maintain an acceptable consistency level as the number of comparisons increases. Therefore, if ten or more items must be pairwise compared, it is recommended that they be grouped into categories, thus creating an additional level in the hierarchy.

Let us now return to our car evaluation problem. After brainstorming, suppose the couple identified ten specific evaluation factors. For example, exterior color and styling, interior color and styling, layout of dashboard, location of cup holders, and cargo space might be grouped as subcriteria under an appearance criterion. As a second example, subcriteria such as purchase price, operating costs, insurance cost, and maintenance costs might be grouped under a cost criterion. On the other hand, the couple might decide that there is only one measure of safety that is of interest to them. As we can see, it is not necessary to have subcriteria under each criterion. Therefore, the AHP hierarchies need not be balanced.

The hierarchy we have just described would now have four levels: goal, criteria, subcriteria, and alternatives. To enter this model into Expert Choice you would enter the goal, criteria, and alternatives as before. To enter the cost subcriteria, highlight the cost criterion, use the *Edit* and *Insert Child of Current Node* commands, and enter subcriteria in the same manner in which you entered criteria. The same process must be repeated when entering the appearance subcriterion. If you do not see all levels of the hierarchy, simply select the *View* and *Expand All* commands. Alternatively, if many subcriteria are entered at one time in a brainstorming session, they can be dragged and dropped under the desired criterion. The complete hierarchy is shown as Figure 11.2 and the model is given in the file called CARMULTI.AHP.

It is important to note that the alternatives must be pairwise compared with respect to each subcriterion. Each group of subcriteria must be pairwise compared to determine their importance in achieving the criterion they support. As usual, the criteria must be pairwise compared to determine their importance in achieving the goal. After processing the pairwise comparison matrices, we obtain criteria and subcriteria weights and alternative weights for each subcriterion. Synthesizing the hierarchy requires computing a weighted average of the alternative weights with respect to each subcriterion using the global subcriteria weights.

We have often found it necessary to give a better idea about how multilevel hierarchies work in practice. Think of criteria weights as slices of a pie, that is, the more important the criterion, the bigger the slice of pie. Since subcriteria are defined for a specific criterion, taking the slice of the criterion pie and dividing it into additional slices determines subcriterion weights.

All of this effort might sound like a lot of work, and one might ask if anyone would really go to all this trouble. This question is easy to answer: Yes, if the decision is im-

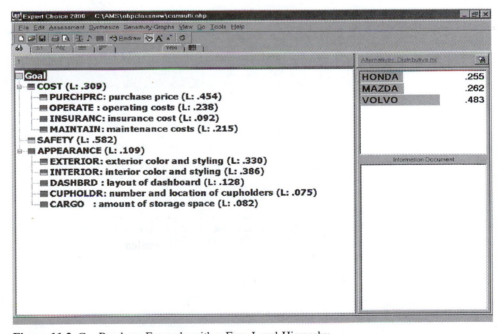

**Figure 11.2** Car Purchase Example with a Four-Level Hierarchy

portant enough. You might not use the AHP to decide what brand of paper clips to purchase, but it is difficult to complain about the time required to go through the process when you are using it to decide what heart surgeon the hospital will hire. The latter is a very important decision and one that has tremendous impact on many lives.

A hierarchy originally structured in three levels might also need to be expanded to additional levels if some of the items on the same level of the hierarchy are not comparable in importance. This means that the relative importance of items on a given level should be within one order of magnitude, or a factor of ten. For example, in considering criteria for deciding which project to fund, someone might initially list a variety of market criteria such as initial market size, five-year projected compounded growth rate, and relative market share. However, they may only be interested in one financial criterion such as net present value (NPV). Because of the importance of NPV as a decision criterion, it may not be comparable to any of the three market criteria *individually*. For this reason, the individual market criteria should not be on the same level of the hierarchy as NPV. These market criteria might be included on a level below a market criterion, since market criteria *collectively* might be judged to be comparable to NPV.

We now display two additional examples of multilevel hierarchies using Expert Choice. The necessary pairwise comparisons were not entered. The first example is a vendor selection problem for a particular type of cable. This model is based on a student project that was submitted to upper management. The criteria, subcriteria, and alternatives appear as Figures 11.3. This model is given in the file called VENDOR.AHP.

The second example of a multilevel hierarchy is a site selection problem for a new office complex of a major insurance company. This model is also based on a student project and was reviewed with interest by the real estate consultant. The criteria, subcriteria, and alternatives appear as Figure 11.4. This model is given in the file called SITE.AHP. Note that there are many multilevel models found in the "samples" folder in Expert Choice. A few models of special interest include Improve Beltway Traffic.AHP, National Health Plans.AHP, Patent Application.AHP, TQM–Baldrige Competition.ahp, and Venture Capital Evaluation.ahp.

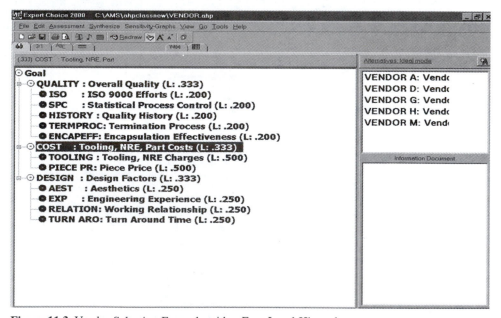

**Figure 11.3** Vendor Selection Example with a Four-Level Hierarchy

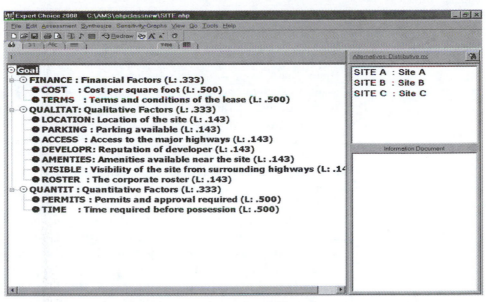

**Figure 11.4** Site Selection Example with a Four-Level Hierarchy

## THE AHP RATINGS APPROACH

### Conventional Versus AHP Ratings and Scoring Methods

We saw in the last section that multilevel hierarchies are needed when there are many criteria. What happens when there are many alternatives? The AHP ratings approach is appropriate in situations where a large number of alternatives must be evaluated. Consider the problem of evaluating employee performance: if 50 employees must be evaluated, then 1,225 (50(49)/2) pairwise comparisons would be required for *each* criterion! Clearly the standard AHP approach is impractical under such conditions.

The AHP ratings approach differs from the conventional AHP in that a series of ratings are associated with each criterion. For example, in evaluating an employee's organizational skills, a manager could rate the employee as Excellent, Very Good, Good, Fair, or Poor. A very important point about ratings scale intensities is that they must be defined. For example, it is not enough to say that an employee has excellent organizational skills. It is crucial to define what excellent means and how it is attained. We recommend that these ratings intensities and their definitions be discussed and agreed upon by the appropriate individuals.

Pairwise comparisons are needed to determine the relative importance of each ratings scale category (also called an *intensity*). For example, with respect to the organizational skill criterion, how much more preferable is an Excellent rating compared to a Very Good rating? Notice that the answer to this pairwise comparison question might be quite different if we changed the criterion from organizational skills to implementation skills. In fact, you may decide to use different intensities for each criterion. It is also important to understand that alternatives are not pairwise compared in a rating model, rather alternatives are rated for each criterion.

Ratings models are a part of everyday life. Consider the process of assigning grades to students in any course. Since an A is assigned a score of 4.00 and a C is assigned a score of 2.00 when computing the GPA, it follows that an A is twice as good as a C in a

GPA computation. We never met a student who agreed with this! Do you? The problem is that letter grades are really ordinal measures, that is ranks, but they are used in GPA calculations as ratio-scaled numbers. The letter grade problem can be illustrated further by the following simple example. Although a 91 is only two points higher than an 89, assigning an A worth 4.00 quality points to the 91 and assigning a B worth 3.00 quality points to the 89 means that the 91 is really 1.33 (4.00/3.00) times better than the 89 in a GPA computation! This problem and many others like it are discussed at Expert Choice's web site at www.expertchoice.com. Click on AHP, then the Annie H. Person link to read about this problem and other problems with ranking methods and systems.

Along the same lines, many organizations use non-AHP based ratings or scoring models for evaluation. For example, in evaluating carpet suppliers, a residential construction company might assign the values 3, 1, 2 for cost, support, and quality, respectively. Typically, they could assign 5, 4, 3, 2, and 1 to ratings of excellent, very good, good, fair, and poor, respectively. Suppose supplier A is judged to be good in cost, excellent in support, and good in quality. Supplier A would then be assigned a score of $3 * 3 + 1 * 5 + 2 * 3 = 20$. Assume that supplier B is judged to be excellent in cost, fair in support, and very good in quality. Supplier B's score would be $3 * 5 + 1 * 2 + 2 * 4 = 25$. Can we say that supplier B is 1.25 times (25/20) or 25% better than supplier A? Absolutely not!

The problem with such scoring models is that the numbers assigned as criteria weights and as intensity weights are not necessarily ratio-scaled. If all of these numbers are not ratio-scaled, then ratio-scaled comparisons between supplier total scores are meaningless. In this situation, ratio-scale measurement assumes, for example, that cost is 3 times (3/1) more important than support, and that an excellent rating is 1.25 times (5/4) better than a very good rating for each criterion. This is rarely, if ever, the case for such scoring systems! The AHP is preferred to conventional scoring approaches because it applies ratio-scale measurement throughout the evaluation process.

## Applying the AHP Ratings Approach Using Expert Choice: Carpet Supplier Evaluation Example

The previously mentioned carpet supplier evaluation problem can also be modeled in Expert Choice using the ratings approach. The goal and criteria (and possibly subcriteria) are entered in a ratings model in the same fashion that they were entered in a standard AHP model. Criteria (and possibly subcriteria) pairwise comparisons are also performed. At this point, the criteria (and possibly subcriteria) weights are known. Figure 11.5 shows a sample hierarchy, where the criteria are cost, support, and quality. Notice that the alternatives do not appear in this figure since they are not part of the hierarchy. The pairwise comparisons that were entered are cost to support: 4; support to quality: 1/3; and cost to quality: 2. These pairwise comparisons result in criteria weights for cost, support, and quality of 0.558, 0.122, and 0.320, respectively. These values are also shown in Figure 11.5.

The next step is to enter the rating scale intensities. To accomplish this, select the Data Grid button on the toolbar. This button looks like a spreadsheet. To enter the rating scale intensities for the first criterion, highlight a cell in the first criteria column and select the *Formula Type* and *Ratings* commands. You can now enter each rating scale intensity in the Intensity Name column. In our example we will use Excellent, Very Good, Good, Fair, and Poor. When finished, select the *Assess* command. You can now enter the pairwise comparisons for the rating scale intensities. As shown in Figure 11.6, an excellent rating is judged to be 2 times better than a very good rating when the cost criterion is considered. After recording all judgments, select the *Close* command. Figure 11.7 shows the results of this process (before the *Close* command is executed) as the intensities and their weights are displayed.

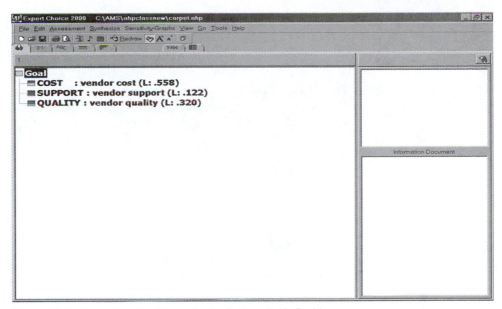

**Figure 11.5** Carpet Supplier Hierarchy for Ratings Scale Problem

It is important for you to understand how the priorities are computed. Rating scale intensities are computed similarly to ideal synthesis without the normalization step. All local intensity weights are divided by the largest intensity weight. In our example, the local weights for each ratings scale intensity are 0.419, 0.263, 0.160, 0.097, and 0.062. (These weights are not displayed, but are computed by Expert Choice based on the ratings scale pairwise comparisons that were entered (see Figure 11.6).) The next step is to divide each score by the largest weight (0.419). The adjusted weights are 1.000, 0.627, 0.382, 0.232, and 0.148 and are displayed in Figure 11.7.

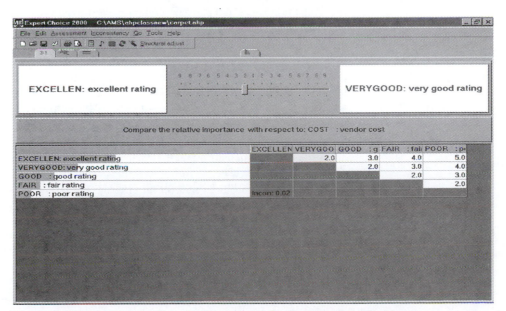

**Figure 11.6** Rating Intensity Pairwise Comparisons for Carpet Supplier Problem

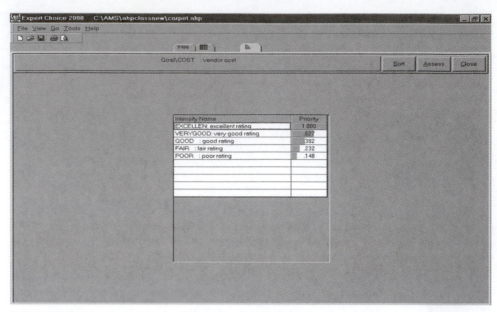

**Figure 11.7** Rating Intensities for Carpet Supplier Problem for Cost Criterion

At this point we have entered the rating scale intensities and their pairwise comparisons for the cost criterion. We must now consider the intensities and their pairwise comparisons for the support and quality criteria and make a decision. The intensities and their pairwise comparisons could be the same for all criteria or they could vary by criteria. If the rating scale intensities are not the same for all criteria, highlight a cell in the second criteria column (support) and repeat the process described. For example, the decision maker may choose to use exceptional, acceptable, and unacceptable as intensities for the support criterion.

If the intensities and pairwise comparisons are the same for all criteria, then we would copy the intensities and pairwise comparisons for the Cost criterion to the other two criteria, as outlined next. First, select the Formulas Grid button. This button looks like $Y = f(X)$. It is possible that this button will not appear on the toolbar. If it does not appear, select the Model View button and then select the Data Grid button. To copy the intensities and pairwise comparisons (from the cost criterion) to the other criteria (support and quality), highlight the Ratings cell in the Type column of the cost criterion and select the *Edit* and *Copy Formula* commands. Next, highlight the Ratings cells for the support and quality criteria and select the *Edit* and *Paste Formula* commands. You have now copied all of the ratings intensities and their pairwise comparisons from the cost criterion to the support and quality criteria. In our example, we will assume that all intensities and pairwise comparisons are the same for all criteria.

We are now ready to enter the alternatives and their corresponding ratings. Although we indicated that the ratings model should only be used if there are more than nine alternatives, for simplicity and to illustrate the process we show an example with only five alternatives. To begin, select the Data Grid button. Remember that alternatives are never entered in the hierarchy for a ratings model. To enter the first alternative, highlight the first cell in the Alternative column and enter each alternative in turn. When you are finished entering alternatives, highlight the cell corresponding to the first alternative (row 1) and the cost criterion (column 1). When you highlight this cell, the intensities and their weights will appear on the screen (Figure 11.8).

The decision maker can now select the desired intensity for Supplier A for the Cost criterion. If an excellent rating is chosen, the decision maker simply clicks in the Excellent location and that intensity appears in the Cost column for Supplier A. The adjusted intensity weight selected by the evaluator is multiplied by the criterion weight and the result is added to the total score. For example, if we select an Excellent rating for cost, then the adjusted intensity weight (1.000) times the cost weight (0.558) or the full cost weight (0.558) is added to the total score. On the other hand, if we select a Good rating for cost, then the adjusted intensity weight (0.382) times the cost weight (0.558) or a pro-rated portion of the cost weight (0.213) is added to the total score.

The desired ratings intensities are chosen for all criteria and for all alternatives. The next step is to select the _View_ and _Totals column_ commands to see the final scores for each alternative. To sort, highlight any final weight and select the _Edit_ and _Sort_, _Descending_ commands. These results are shown in the ratings spreadsheet for five suppliers given as Figure 11.9. The model is given in a file called CARPET.AHP.

Since ratio-scale measurements have been used throughout the AHP ratings process, we can now state that Supplier B is 1.722 (0.787/0.457) times better than Supplier A. This statement cannot be made using the simple scoring approach previously discussed. The scores produced by the AHP ratings method are a form of absolute measurement. That is, regardless of how many additional alternatives are evaluated, the total scores of alternatives previously evaluated do not change.

An example of a ratings model hierarchy using subcriteria was developed for an employee evaluation system. This model is based on a student project that utilized the actual criteria in an organization's evaluation system. The model was presented and favorably evaluated by the company's human resource department. Part of the hierarchy appears as Figure 11.10, and the model is in the file called EMPEVAL.AHP. In viewing this file, we note that the company decided that all criteria are weighted equally, but there are

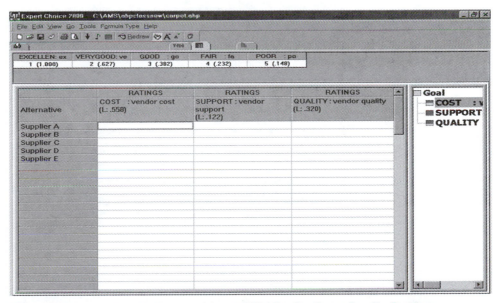

**Figure 11.8** Alternatives, Rating Intensities, and Weights for Carpet Supplier Problem

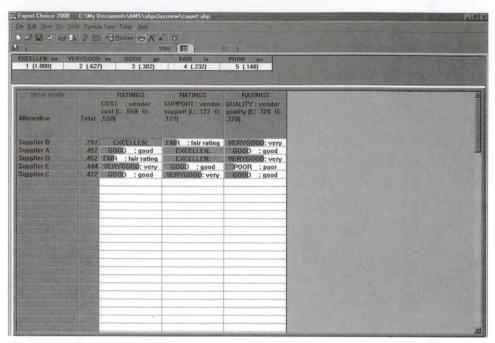

**Figure 11.9** Final Alternative Weights for Carpet Supplier Problem

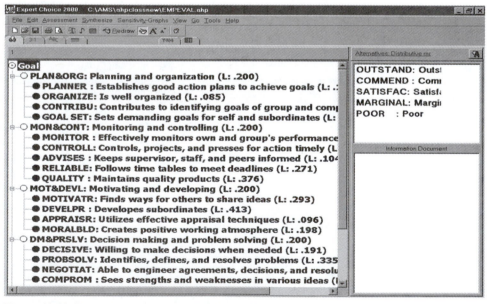

**Figure 11.10** Hierarchy for Employee Evaluation Problem

significant differences in the subcriteria weights. Other ratings model files, such as Coast Guard Officer Evaluations.AHP, Employee Evaluation.AHP, Graduate School Admissions.AHP, Ice Cream Site.AHP, Prioritization of Research Projects.AHP, Resource Allocation–Activity Level.AHP, Resource Allocation–Discrete Alternative.AHP, and Resource Allocation–Northeast Fisheries Center.AHP, can be found in the samples folder of your version of Expert Choice.

## GROUP DECISION MAKING

Up to this point, we have not looked explicitly at differences between individual and group decision making using the AHP. How did the couple arrive at their combined judgments in the original car selection problem? There are many ways of applying the AHP to support a group decision-making process. The simplest approach is to have all participants who are involved in the decision discuss, debate, and eventually agree on each pairwise comparison entry. This approach is often preferred; however, time or distance constraints may make this approach impractical.

Alternatively, the group could agree on the structure of the hierarchy and then each individual could enter their own judgments in separate copies of the model. The results could then be summarized and used as a basis to reach a consensus or to allow the participants to revise their judgments. Another approach is to create a hierarchy where the first level under the goal would consist of the participants in the decision process. The importance of the individuals in making the decision could be determined by pairwise comparisons, resulting in equal or different weights assigned to each participant. The criteria and alternatives would be placed under each individual. The criteria may even differ across individuals. The final weights of the alternatives reflect the weighted judgments of all participants.

The final approach is to achieve consensus *mathematically*. In this situation, participants provide their own judgments for each pairwise comparison. For example, suppose two participants are asked to compare cost to safety. If judgments are provided of 9/1 and 1/9, they must be averaged somehow. The arithmetic mean would produce a value of 4.56. Does this result accurately reflect the average of the judgments? Since both individuals are at opposite ends of the scale, we would expect the combined judgment to be that cost and safety are equal, or an average of 1.00.

The *geometric mean* produces this result since it is more suited to averaging ratio-scaled numbers than the arithmetic mean. In general, if there are n individuals that provide judgments, the geometric mean is defined as the $n^{th}$ root of the product of the n judgments. For our example, the geometric mean is the square root of the product of 9/1 and 1/9, or 1.00. If in comparing cost to safety the judgments of three individuals are 2, 4, and 8, their consensus judgment is the cube root of 2 * 4 * 8 or the cube root of 64, which is 4. We note that the geometric mean results enable the user to take reciprocals, where the arithmetic mean does not. For example, the cube root of 2 * 4 * 8 is 4 while the cube root of (1/2) * (1/4) * (1/8) is ¼.

Expert Choice has a powerful way of managing the entire group decision-making process.[1] Expert Choice achieves consensus mathematically by computing all needed

---

[1]The group decision-making capabilities described in the remainder of this section are not available with the version of Expert Choice provided with this text. However, these features are available with other versions of the software. See www.expertchoice.com for further details.

geometric means. The process begins by having the group brainstorm and agree on a hierarchy. We must indicate that this is a group model by selecting the *Go* and *Participants Table* commands. Next, we select *Edit*, and *Group Enable*, followed by *Edit*, *Add N Participants*, and enter the number of participants. At this point, we can click on any participant to change their name, enter any demographic information, and enter a password. The last step in this phase is to select the *File* and *Close* commands.

At this point, there are N participants and a facilitator. The facilitator acts as the leader and may enter judgments, if desired. When a group model is opened, you must respond with either the facilitator's name or the name of one of the participants. The facilitator has access to all information, but participants only have access to their information.

We will use the car purchase example to illustrate the group decision making process within Expert Choice. Suppose a husband and wife agree that cost, safety, and appearance are the three relevant criteria. Suppose they further agree that a Honda, Mazda, and Volvo are the alternatives that they would consider purchasing. Figure 11.11 shows the participant's table for this problem.

As mentioned earlier, when this model is opened, you will be asked for the participant's name or the name of the facilitator. To successfully open the model you must respond with "facilitator," "husband," or "wife." This model can be used in several ways: Expert Choice allows group models to be stored on a network or web page. This means that the facilitator, husband, or wife can access the file and enter the desired pairwise comparisons. The facilitator can enter pairwise comparisons for any participant, but a participant can only enter their own comparisons. If the facilitator opens the model, the participant's drop-down list appears on the toolbar as shown in Figure 11.12. (This drop-down list does not appear if the model is opened by one of the participants.) If the facilitator wants to enter pairwise comparisons for a participant, that participant is chosen and pairwise comparisons are entered as usual. As mentioned earlier, a participant can also enter their own pairwise comparisons if they are given access to the model file.

After all pairwise comparisons have been entered, the judgments must be combined. This is accomplished by selecting Combined from the Participants drop-down list. Next,

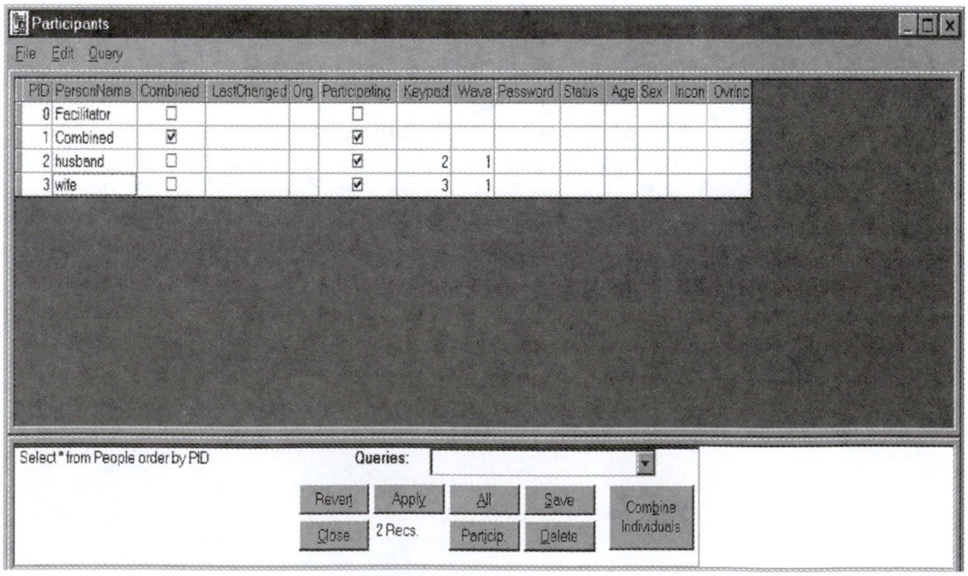

**Figure 11.11** Participants Table for Group Car Purchasing Problem

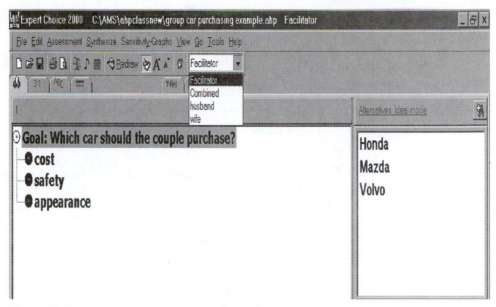

**Figure 11.12** Hierarchy for Facilitator for Group Car Purchasing Problem

the *Assessment*, *Combine Participants' Judgments/Data*, *Entire Hierarchy*, and *Both* commands are selected. This command sequence combines all judgments by computing the necessary geometric means. Figures 11.13 and 11.14 show criteria pairwise comparisons for the husband and wife, respectively. Figures 11.15 and 11.16 show the combined pairwise comparisons and criteria weights for these combined judgments.

We can now interpret the information provided in these figures. Figure 11.14 indicates that the husband believes that cost is 2 times more important than safety, while

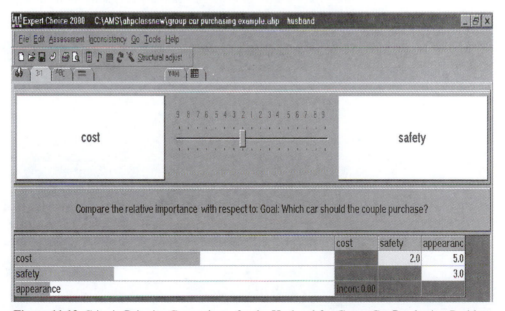

**Figure 11.13** Criteria Pairwise Comparisons for the Husband for Group Car Purchasing Problem

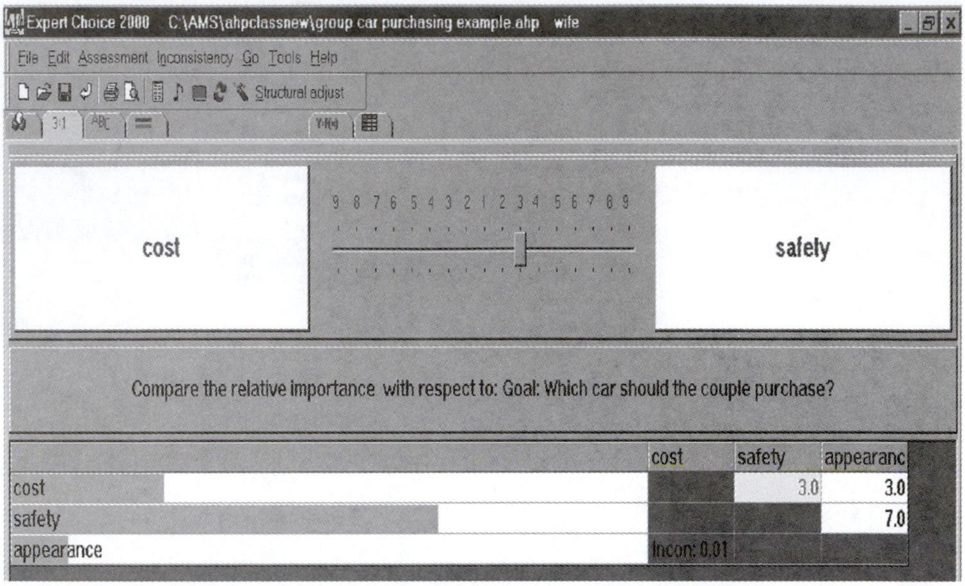

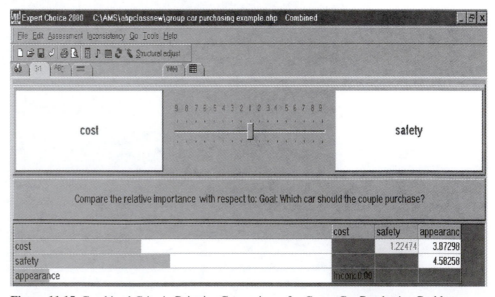

**Figure 11.14** Criteria Pairwise Comparison for the Wife for Group Car Purchasing Problem

Figure 11.15 shows that the wife believes that cost is one-third as important as safety. The geometric mean of these two judgments is the square root of 2 times (1/3), which is 0.81650. Since this number is less than one, the combined judgments indicate that safety is 1/0.81650 or 1.22474 times more important than cost, as shown in Figure 11.15. The judgments for the two other criteria are combined in a similar fashion. These judgments indicate that the couple believes that cost is 3.87298 (that is, the square root of 5 times 3) times more important than appearance and that safety is 4.58258 (that is, the square root of 3 times 7) times more important than appearance. These combined judgments can be processed to compute the criteria weights, as shown in Figure 11.16.

**Figure 11.15** Combined Criteria Pairwise Comparisons for Group Car Purchasing Problem

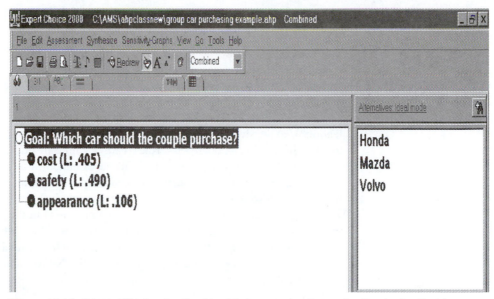

**Figure 11.16** Criteria Weights for Combined Judgments for Group Car Purchasing Problem

Next, the couple must provide pairwise comparisons for the cars for each criterion. These judgments should be combined as shown above so that the final weights for each car can be computed. These final combined car weights appear in Figure 11.17 and in a file called group car purchasing example.ahp. As shown, Expert Choice provides a useful tool to manage the group decision-making process.

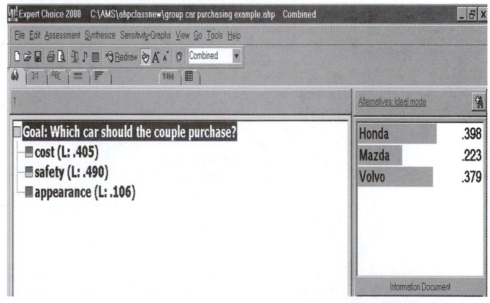

**Figure 11.17** Final Weights for Combined Judgments for Group Car Purchasing Problem

## CASE STUDY: HEALTH TECHNOLOGY ASSESSMENT[2]

We have learned a great deal about using the AHP as a decision-support tool. In this section we share some of our experiences so that you can understand some of the practical issues involved with implementing the AHP. Although we have used the AHP in a wide variety of settings, we will now discuss our experiences with a mid-sized suburban tertiary care teaching hospital.

Specifically, there was a need to perform a health technology assessment for the selection of expensive neonatal ventilators for a new women's health addition to the hospital. The hospital is a 500+ bed tertiary care teaching institution in the suburbs of one of the top 10 U.S. cities (by population). It was founded in the early 1900s, and has been one of the few successful independent health systems in the region. The hospital enjoys many thriving specialized services, including a large In-Vitro Fertilization (IVF) program. The hospital has one of the largest obstetrics programs in the area, and in the year 2000 there were approximately 4400 deliveries. Of these, there were 425 admissions to the 25-bed Neonatal Intensive Care Unit (NICU), which also includes transfers from other area hospitals. The IVF program contributes to the NICU admissions as well, as some of these parents are older, higher-risk couples who have a greater tendency toward high-risk pregnancies. Newborn children are often referred to as neonates in the hospital setting, to help distinguish their special physiological condition and needs from more stable babies and children.

Due to the growing IVF, birthing, and general women's health issues, the hospital has purchased a nearby piece of land to build a new women's health hospital. The neonatal ventilator is one critical device that the hospital needed to evaluate. Neonatal ventilators are, in fact, quite unique. The small size of premature babies (as small as 0.5 kg, or about 1 pound), presents many demanding electromechanical requirements. For example, the tiny premature infant's lungs are often incompletely developed and may be quite stiff and fragile. Neonatal ventilators must be able to accurately deliver rapid, tiny puffs of precisely blended air and oxygen. An infant's lungs may only be the size of an adult's small finger, and any over-inflation may result in either rupturing the lungs or blocking the blood that the heart is trying to pump through the lungs.

Ventilators that can be used for neonates range in price from around $18,000 to nearly $40,000, and each manufacturer and model has widely differing features. Also, the ventilators have a significant life-cycle cost of ownership due to supplies and maintenance requirements, which can dwarf the initial purchase price. The hospital could need to purchase as many as 24 or more units for the new NICU. When combined with 5–10 year life cycle costs of supplies, maintenance, and repairs, the purchasing decision for 24 neonatal ventilators rapidly becomes a million-dollar commitment. In addition, competent clinical and technical training and support is needed for a decade or more for safe and effective patient care, so the staffing factors are very significant. Because of these investment consequences, the clinical engineering and respiratory therapy departments were called upon for their participation in this study.

An overview of this study's process follows. There were two senior department directors identified for this project's interdisciplinary team: the Respiratory Therapy Director's department provides the routine clinical staffing to support the patients; and the Clinical Engineering Director's department evaluates, installs, inspects, repairs, and maintains the devices. Before meeting with the directors, we produced a simplistic hierarchy

---

[2]The remainder of this section is largely based on Sloane, Liberatore, Nydick, Luo, and Chung (2002).

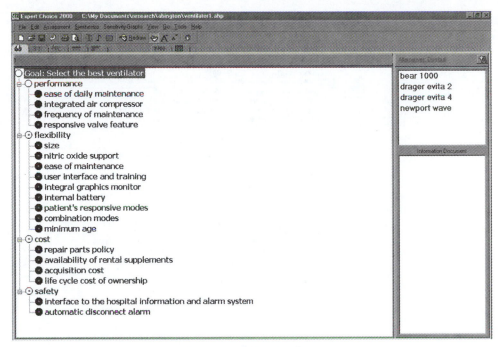

**Figure 11.18** Initial Hierarchy for Selecting the Best Ventilator

for the selection of neonatal ventilators. We believed that this was important since both directors had no prior experience with the AHP. Our hierarchy had four criteria and several subcriteria for each criterion (Figure 11.18).

We next met with both directors and explained the AHP. We asked each person to study the part of the hierarchy that most impacted their work. They could change any part of the hierarchy, either adding or deleting criteria or subcriteria. These brainstorming sessions were critical to the success of the project: It took five iterations and resulted in the hierarchy shown in Figure 11.19. (We note that Figure 11.19 was created using the following commands: *File*, *Print Preview*, *File*, *Save as Word Document,* creates a file that can then be opened in Word. The benefit of using these commands is that the entire hierarchy can be displayed in one figure.)

Expert Choice has useful drag and drop features that allow the user to delete subcriteria or move them from one part of the hierarchy to another. Essentially, we would enter as many subcriteria as we could identify into Expert Choice and then move them to the appropriate criteria. At one point we found it easier to brainstorm using Word. After entering many subcriteria in Word, it was easy to copy from Word and paste these factors into Expert Choice as subcriteria. This was accomplished by copying the subcriteria into the clipboard in Word. Next the goal is highlighted in Expert Choice, and the user selects the *Edit*, and *Paste Children from Clipboard* commands.

We also had a discussion on how cost should be handled in the hierarchy. We decided to leave it in the hierarchy, but another strategy would have been to omit cost completely and basically have a benefits hierarchy. After completing the AHP the alternative scores would represent benefits scores, and could then be used in a cost/benefit analysis to help make the final decision. However, the directors decided that they wanted cost to be directly represented and measured in the hierarchy.

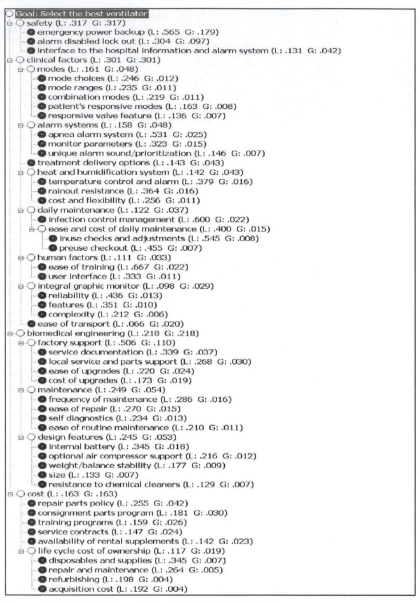

○ Goal: Select the best ventilator
├─ ○ safety (L: .317  G: .317)
│   ├─ ● emergency power backup (L: .565  G: .179)
│   ├─ ● alarm disabled lock out (L: .304  G: .097)
│   └─ ● interface to the hospital information and alarm system (L: .131  G: .042)
├─ ○ clinical factors (L: .301  G: .301)
│   ├─ ○ modes (L: .161  G: .048)
│   │   ├─ ● mode choices (L: .246  G: .012)
│   │   ├─ ● mode ranges (L: .235  G: .011)
│   │   ├─ ● combination modes (L: .219  G: .011)
│   │   ├─ ● patient's responsive modes (L: .163  G: .008)
│   │   └─ ● responsive valve feature (L: .136  G: .007)
│   ├─ ○ alarm systems (L: .158  G: .048)
│   │   ├─ ● apnea alarm system (L: .531  G: .025)
│   │   ├─ ● monitor parameters (L: .323  G: .015)
│   │   └─ ● unique alarm sound/prioritization (L: .146  G: .007)
│   ├─ ● treatment delivery options (L: .143  G: .043)
│   ├─ ○ heat and humidification system (L: .142  G: .043)
│   │   ├─ ● temperature control and alarm (L: .379  G: .016)
│   │   ├─ ● rainout resistance (L: .364  G: .016)
│   │   └─ ● cost and flexibility (L: .256  G: .011)
│   ├─ ○ daily maintenance (L: .122  G: .037)
│   │   ├─ ● infection control management (L: .600  G: .022)
│   │   └─ ○ ease and cost of daily maintenance (L: .400  G: .015)
│   │       ├─ ● inuse checks and adjustments (L: .545  G: .008)
│   │       └─ ● preuse checkout (L: .455  G: .007)
│   ├─ ○ human factors (L: .111  G: .033)
│   │   ├─ ● ease of training (L: .667  G: .022)
│   │   └─ ● user interface (L: .333  G: .011)
│   ├─ ○ integral graphic monitor (L: .098  G: .029)
│   │   ├─ ● reliability (L: .436  G: .013)
│   │   ├─ ● features (L: .351  G: .010)
│   │   └─ ● complexity (L: .212  G: .006)
│   └─ ● ease of transport (L: .066  G: .020)
├─ ○ biomedical engineering (L: .218  G: .218)
│   ├─ ○ factory support (L: .506  G: .110)
│   │   ├─ ● service documentation (L: .339  G: .037)
│   │   ├─ ● local service and parts support (L: .268  G: .030)
│   │   ├─ ● ease of upgrades (L: .220  G: .024)
│   │   └─ ● cost of upgrades (L: .173  G: .019)
│   ├─ ○ maintenance (L: .249  G: .054)
│   │   ├─ ● frequency of maintenance (L: .286  G: .016)
│   │   ├─ ● ease of repair (L: .270  G: .015)
│   │   ├─ ● self diagnostics (L: .234  G: .013)
│   │   └─ ● ease of routine maintenance (L: .210  G: .011)
│   └─ ○ design features (L: .245  G: .053)
│       ├─ ● internal battery (L: .345  G: .018)
│       ├─ ● optional air compressor support (L: .216  G: .012)
│       ├─ ● weight/balance stability (L: .177  G: .009)
│       ├─ ● size (L: .133  G: .007)
│       └─ ● resistance to chemical cleaners (L: .129  G: .007)
└─ ○ cost (L: .163  G: .163)
    ├─ ● repair parts policy (L: .255  G: .042)
    ├─ ● consignment parts program (L: .181  G: .030)
    ├─ ● training programs (L: .159  G: .026)
    ├─ ● service contracts (L: .147  G: .024)
    ├─ ● availability of rental supplements (L: .142  G: .023)
    └─ ○ life cycle cost of ownership (L: .117  G: .019)
        ├─ ● disposables and supplies (L: .345  G: .007)
        ├─ ● repair and maintenance (L: .264  G: .005)
        ├─ ● refurbishing (L: .198  G: .004)
        └─ ● acquisition cost (L: .192  G: .004)

**Figure 11.19** Final Hierarchy to Select the Best Ventilator

We next had to focus on how the alternatives would be compared. After consideration of the relatively large number of bottom-level criteria in the final model (46), and the potential number of alternative neonatal ventilators that could be considered (as many as a dozen or more), pairwise comparing the alternatives was judged to be infeasible. As a result, we chose the AHP rating system.

The directors created and defined meaningful rating scale intensities for each criterion to describe the possible performance the alternatives could achieve. Even more importantly, they defined each rating scale intensity. This was critical when the ventilators were evaluated for each intensity since it was understood what performance was required to achieve each rating.

The weights for the rating categories themselves were created by pairwise comparison as will be discussed. As examples, several of the resulting rating terms, descriptions, and final weights are provided in Figure 11.20. This table also helps to illustrate why the rating system makes the results easier to interpret by other clinical, technical, and administrative staff. For example, other hospital staff can readily grasp the meaning of "simple" daily maintenance requirements, and can also reasonably interpret the comparable weight (29%) that would be given to a "very intensive" alternative.

After all parties agreed that the hierarchy represented their views of what was important in the decision process, it was time to provide pairwise comparisons. Each director provided pairwise comparisons for their part of the hierarchy, which worked for all but the pairwise comparisons for the criteria. In this case, both directors worked together to reach a consensus for each pairwise comparison.

The directors found that it was helpful to rank the criteria, subcriteria, and rating scale intensities from Most Important or Preferred to Least Important or Preferred. The benefit of doing this is that the directors could focus on the pairwise comparison only and they did not have to worry about the direction of the preference. This greatly helped with inconsistency. Both directors also felt most comfortable with the graphical pairwise comparison mode since it visually represents the relative differences between the items being compared.

| Criteria category | Ratings and descriptions | Weight |
|---|---|---|
| Daily maintenance requirements: Pre-use checkout | "Simple"—easy to reliably learn and quick to perform | 1.0 |
| | "Somewhat intensive"—takes time to learn and perform well | .76 |
| | "Very intensive"—likely to be complex and time consuming | .29 |
| Alarm disable lockout | "Very flexible"—many alternatives can be configured | 1.0 |
| | "Limited"—only a few modes are available | .68 |
| | "None"—no lockout is provided | .28 |
| Responsive Valve Feature | "Excellent"—unusually sensitive response | 1.0 |
| | "Adequate"—should meet most of our neonates' needs | .49 |
| | "Limited"—not likely to meet some of the hospital's needs | .1 |
| Factory support: Service documentation | "Excellent"—current materials readily available for purchase | 1.0 |
| | "Limited availability"—restrictions are placed on who can buy current and/or complete documentation | .40 |
| | "None"— significant material is limited to manufacturer's employee use only | .09 |
| Training program | "2 Staff training"—Training for at least 2 hospital staff is free | 1.0 |
| | "1 Staff training"—Training for only 1 hospital staff is free | .53 |
| | "No staff training"—All training must be paid separately | .19 |

**Figure 11.20** Sample Criterion Ratings, Descriptions, and Weights

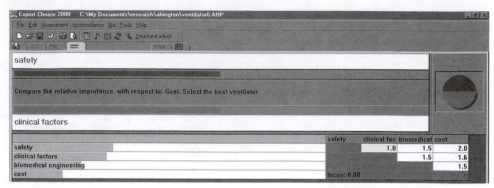

**Figure 11.21** The Criteria Pairwise Comparisons and the Corresponding Weights

One final step in the process was to show each director the pairwise comparison screen after the weights were computed. An example for the criteria pairwise comparisons is shown as Figure 11.21. Notice that the weights are visually depicted as shaded bars where each criteria name appears. From this we can not only see that safety is more important than clinical factors, but the shaded bars indicate that these two criteria are relatively close in importance. We gave the directors an opportunity to make changes if they did not feel comfortable with these differences. Expert Choice allows the user to move the bar if desired. For example, if a director believed that the safety weight should be higher, we could drag Safety's bar to the right. Expert Choice would then determine the individual pairwise comparisons that would produce the desired weights. It is important to note that this should be done to slightly adjust the weights only if necessary and should not be used to determine the weights initially.

The purpose of this case study is to show the true power and flexibility of the AHP and Expert Choice. In addition, there are other examples of AHP models in the "samples" folder of your version of Expert Choice. The AHP seems straightforward and intuitive and to a certain extent it is. However, it is based on the theory of ratio-scale measurement using pairwise comparisons and is capable of capturing the attitudes and beliefs of decision makers in important business situations. It is our hope that the last three chapters have convinced you that the AHP is an effective decision-support tool that can be used to help individuals and groups make decisions.

## SUMMARY

We began this chapter using a validation exercise to demonstrate the process of making pairwise comparisons in practice. Using subjective judgments, we were able to develop estimates of the relative areas of five figures that are very close to their actual values. We then discussed issues related to structuring multi-level hierarchies, including guidelines for determining the number of items and levels, and the effective use of additional levels for such items as subcriteria. Next, we considered situations where a large number of alternatives need to be evaluated. We discussed the use of standard scoring approaches and showed how the AHP can incorporate the scoring of alternatives. An important benefits of the AHP rating or scoring approach is the consistent use of ratio-scaled measurement throughout the eval-

uation process. We then turned to the differences between individual and group decision making using the AHP and discussed why the geometric mean is used to average multiple judgments. We also illustrated Expert Choice's capabilities in supporting group decision making. We concluded with additional suggestions for improving the application of the AHP in practice, using a case study in health technology assessment.

As seen in three chapters, the AHP offers many benefits to support complex decision-making processes. It provides a natural way to elicit managerial judgments and has the important advantage of being able to measure the degree of inconsistency in judgments. Since it is easy to use, many managers will be comfortable with the decision process and its results. In particular, the process of structuring the hierarchy allows broad participation in the decision-making process and often leads to agreement on the relevant criteria, thus minimizing the effects of politics and hidden agendas. The software package Expert Choice fully supports all of the features and applications of the AHP discussed in the decision analysis chapters.

## HOMEWORK PROBLEMS

**1.** OPAQUE Corp. is trying to evaluate five vendors using the AHP ratings method. The three evaluation criteria are COST, QUALITY, and SERVICE. The pairwise comparison data are summarized:

### Criteria with Respect to Goal

|         | Cost | Quality | Service |
|---------|------|---------|---------|
| Cost    | 1    | 2       | 3       |
| Quality |      | 1       | 2       |
| Service |      |         | 1       |

Opaque has decided to use five rating categories for each of the three criteria. The rating categories are: excellent (EXCEL), above average (AAVER), average (AVER), below average (BAVER), and poor (POOR). The same set of pairwise comparisons for the relative importance of the rating categories will be used for each of the criteria:

### Rating Categories

|       | EXCEL | AAVER | AVER | BAVER | POOR |
|-------|-------|-------|------|-------|------|
| EXCEL | 1     | 2     | 4    | 6     | 9    |
| AAVER |       | 1     | 2    | 7     | 8    |
| AVER  |       |       | 1    | 5     | 9    |
| BAVER |       |       |      | 1     | 4    |
| POOR  |       |       |      |       | 1    |

Five vendors are to be evaluated and have been rated as follows:

| Vendor | Cost  | Quality | Service |
|--------|-------|---------|---------|
| V1     | EXCEL | BAVER   | BAVER   |
| V2     | AAVER | AAVER   | AAVER   |
| V3     | BAVER | EXCEL   | EXCEL   |
| V4     | AAVER | BAVER   | BAVER   |
| V5     | AVER  | AAVER   | AAVER   |

**(a)** Determine the overall priorities or scores of each of the five vendors using Expert Choice. Which vendor has the highest score?

**(b)** For the OPAQUE problem, do the vendor scores sum to one? Explain.

**(c)** Which pairwise comparison matrix is the most inconsistent? Give a reason to support your answer.

**(d)** Suppose COST and QUALITY are equally important in vendor selection. Does the ranking of the five vendors change? Are the rankings of the vendors sensitive to changing this judgment? Support your answer with appropriate analysis.

**2.** CARR, Inc. is trying to select an office supply vendor. Four vendors are being considered and the criteria are COST (cost of supplies), RESPOND (the average amount of time needed to respond to a request), and DAMAGE (the average dollar amount of damaged goods per shipment). Carr has collected the following pairwise comparison information:

### Criteria

|         | Cost | Respond | Damage |
|---------|------|---------|--------|
| Cost    | 1.0  | 2.0     | 4.0    |
| Respond |      | 1.0     | 1.5    |
| Damage  |      |         | 1.0    |

In addition, Carr has decided to use the RATINGS approach to evaluate each of the vendors with respect to each of the criteria. The same ratings scale and weights will be used for all criteria. The pairwise comparison matrix for the ratings is:

### Ratings Ratings Pairwise Comparison Matrix

|       | Excel | VGood | Good | Fair | Poor |
|-------|-------|-------|------|------|------|
| EXCEL | 1.0   | 1.5   | 3.0  | 4.0  | 9.0  |
| VGOOD |       | 1.0   | 1.5  | 2.5  | 7.0  |
| GOOD  |       |       | 1.0  | 2.0  | 5.0  |
| FAIR  |       |       |      | 1.0  | 3.0  |
| POOR  |       |       |      |      | 1.0  |

The ratings intensities for the four vendors are:

|    | Cost  | Respond | Damage |
|----|-------|---------|--------|
| V1 | VGOOD | VGOOD   | VGOOD  |
| V2 | EXCEL | VGOOD   | FAIR   |
| V3 | VGOOD | EXCEL   | GOOD   |
| V4 | FAIR  | EXCEL   | EXCEL  |

**(a)** List the four vendors in rank order and state their overall weights.

**(b)** Management has decided to use a *single* criterion, ON-TIME (percentage of deliveries that arrive on-time), instead of the three criteria used in part a. Management also decided to use the following pairwise comparisons for the vendors instead of the rating approach.

### On-Time Pairwise Comparison Matrix

|    | V1  | V2  | V3  | V4  |
|----|-----|-----|-----|-----|
| V1 | 1.0 | 1.5 | 1/2 | 1.0 |
| V2 |     | 1.0 | 1/4 | 1/2 |
| V3 |     |     | 1.0 | 2.5 |
| V4 |     |     |     | 1.0 |

Based on the ON-TIME pairwise comparison data only, list the four vendors in rank order and state their overall weights. Assume that only these four vendors are being considered now or in the future.

**(c)**   Management concludes that the results in parts a and b *both* have merit and that each should have equal weight in their final decision. That is, they wish to obtain a final ranking of the four vendors where the results from part a have 50% of the weight, and the results from part b have 50% of the weight. Since only four vendors will ever be considered now or in the future, the *final weights must sum to one*. Briefly describe your approach for computing the final weights, list the four vendors in rank order, and state their overall weights. You may not need to use Expert Choice to answer this question.

**3.**   TIERNEY Enterprises is trying to decide how it will invest its capital in three building projects. Only three distinct projects are being considered now or in the future: P1, P2, and P3. P1 is single family homes development, P2 is a townhouse development, and P3 is a condominium development.

The criteria are as follows:

PRICE: the expected selling price per unit,
SIZE: the number of units in each development,
LOCATION: the quality of the location,
SCHOOLS: the quality of the school system.

Tierney has collected the following pairwise comparison information:

|          | **Criteria** | | | |
|----------|-------|------|----------|---------|
|          | **Price** | **Size** | **Location** | **Schools** |
| Price    | 1.0   | 1.5  | 2.0      | 4.0     |
| Size     |       | 1.0  | 2.0      | 2.0     |
| Location |       |      | 1.0      | 1.6     |
| Schools  |       |      |          | 1.0     |

|    | **Price** | | |
|----|------|------|------|
|    | **P1** | **P2** | **P3** |
| P1 | 1.0  | 4.0  | 3.0  |
| P2 |      | 1.0  | 1.0  |
| P3 |      |      | 1.0  |

|    | **Size** | | |
|----|------|------|------|
|    | **P1** | **P2** | **P3** |
| P1 | 1.0  | 1/2  | 1.0  |
| P2 |      | 1.0  | 3.0  |
| P3 |      |      | 1.0  |

|    | **Location** | | |
|----|------|------|------|
|    | **P1** | **P2** | **P3** |
| P1 | 1.0  | 1/4  | 1/4  |
| P2 |      | 1.0  | 1/2  |
| P3 |      |      | 1.0  |

|    | **Schools** | | |
|----|------|------|------|
|    | **P1** | **P2** | **P3** |
| P1 | 1.0  | 1/2  | 1/5  |
| P2 |      | 1.0  | 1/3  |
| P3 |      |      | 1.0  |

**(a)**   List the three projects in rank order and state their overall weights.

**(b)**   Which pairwise comparison matrix is the most inconsistent? State a reason for your answer. Are any of the pairwise comparison matrices perfectly consistent? Explain.

**(c)**   What minimum value of the PRICE weight would lead to the top two projects being ranked equally? Based on your results, would you say that the top ranking is sensitive to a change in the PRICE weight? Explain.

**(d)**   Unexpectedly, management wishes to consider a fourth development (P4). P4 is another single family homes development. The additional pairwise comparison information is as follows:

|    | **Price** | **Size** | **Location** | **Schools** |
|----|------|------|----------|---------|
|    | **P4** | **P4** | **P4** | **P4** |
| P1 | 1.0  | 1.0  | 1.0  | 1.0  |
| P2 | 1/3  | 3.0  | 5.0  | 2.0  |
| P3 | 1/3  | 1.0  | 5.0  | 6.0  |
| P4 | 1.0  | 1.0  | 1.0  | 1.0  |

Resolve the problem as in part a and list the four projects in rank order and state their overall weights.

**(e)**   Compare the rankings obtained in parts a and d. What happened with the addition of P4? Looking at the available data, can you offer an explanation as to why this occurred?

**(f)**   How can the situation addressed in part e be avoided within Expert Choice? Describe your approach, and indicate the revised set of weights and rankings for parts a and d.

**4.**   JACKSON Industries has one production facility located at their corporate headquarters in Lancaster. They have two additional offices in Hershey and York. Increased demand has resulted in Jackson deciding to add a new production facility in either Hershey or York. Jackson does not anticipate considering any other sites in the future. The executive committee has agreed to use the AHP to help them make this decision. They also agreed that the relevant criteria are: Proximity to customers (LOCATION), Construction costs (COSTS), and Impact on the community (SOCIAL). The executive committee has also decided on the following pairwise comparisons for the alternatives.

For LOCATION, Hershey is 2 times more preferred than York. For COST, York is 3 times more preferred than Hershey. For SOCIAL, York is 4 times more preferred than Hershey.

The executive committee decided to ask the management group in Hershey to provide pairwise comparisons for the criteria. That pairwise comparison matrix is:

|          | Location | Cost | Social |
|----------|----------|------|--------|
| Location | 1        | 8    | 2      |
| Cost     |          | 1    | 5      |
| Social   |          |      | 1      |

**(a)** Enter this problem into Expert Choice using the pairwise comparisons from the executive committee in Lancaster and the management group in Hershey. List the two locations in rank order and state their overall weights. Which location is most preferred?

**(b)** Next, the executive committee decided to ask the management group in York to provide pairwise comparisons for the criteria. That pairwise comparison matrix is:

|          | Location | Cost | Social |
|----------|----------|------|--------|
| Location | 1        | 1/2  | 5      |
| Cost     |          | 1    | 1/2    |
| Social   |          |      | 1      |

Enter this problem into Expert Choice using the pairwise comparisons from the executive committee in Lancaster and the management group in York. List the two locations in rank order and state their overall weights.

**(c)** You should find that the rankings are different for parts a and b. The executive committee decided to combine the pairwise comparisons made by the Hershey and York management groups by computing the geometric mean.

Enter this problem into Expert Choice using the pairwise comparisons from the executive committee in Lancaster and the geometric means computed from the pairwise comparisons provided by the management groups in Hershey and York. List the two locations in rank order and state their overall weights.

**(d)** Would you recommend that the results from parts a, b, or c be implemented or would you recommend that further analysis be done? If you recommend further analysis, what suggestions would you make to the executive committee of Jackson? Explain.

**5.** GOURMETFOODS.COM is trying to decide what web design company to use. They have identified three relevant criteria: creativity, stability, and maintenance. There are only three web design finalists that are being considered now or in the future. For simplicity we will refer to these vendors as alpha, beta, and gamma. The vice-president of marketing has asked two of her managers, Julie and Bill, to help in the analysis.

Julie has provided the following pairwise comparisons.

|            | Creativity | Stability | Maintenance |
|------------|------------|-----------|-------------|
| Creativity |            | 2         | 5           |
| Stability  |            |           | 3           |

**Creativity**

|       | Alpha | Beta | Gamma |
|-------|-------|------|-------|
| Alpha |       | 3    | 5     |
| Beta  |       |      | 2     |

**Stability**

|       | Alpha | Beta | Gamma |
|-------|-------|------|-------|
| Alpha |       | 1/4  | 1/7   |
| Beta  |       |      | 1/2   |

**Maintenance**

|       | Alpha | Beta | Gamma |
|-------|-------|------|-------|
| Alpha |       | 1/3  | 2     |
| Beta  |       |      | 4     |

Bill has provided the following pairwise comparisons.

|            | Creativity | Stability | Maintenance |
|------------|------------|-----------|-------------|
| Creativity |            | 3         | 2           |
| Stability  |            |           | 4           |

**Creativity**

|       | Alpha | Beta | Gamma |
|-------|-------|------|-------|
| Alpha |       | 1/3  | 1/5   |
| Beta  |       |      | 5     |

**Stability**

|       | Alpha | Beta | Gamma |
|-------|-------|------|-------|
| Alpha |       | 1/3  | 7     |
| Beta  |       |      | 1/3   |

**Maintenance**

|       | Alpha | Beta | Gamma |
|-------|-------|------|-------|
| Alpha |       | 1/4  | 3     |
| Beta  |       |      | 5     |

**(a)** For Julie's pairwise comparisons, list the three vendors in rank order and state their overall weights.

**(b)** Which of Julie's pairwise comparison matrix is the most inconsistent? Explain.

**(c)** For Julie's judgments, perform a sensitivity analysis to determine what maintenance weight would result in the two highest ranked vendors having the same final weights. Are the final rankings of the two highest ranked vendors sensitive to the weight of maintenance? Explain.

**(d)** For Bill's pairwise comparisons, list the three vendors in rank order and state their overall weights.

**(e)** For the combined pairwise comparisons, list the three vendors in rank order and state their overall weights.

**(f)** Comment on the quality of the recommendation provided in part e. Would you recommend that these weights be used to make a recommendation? Explain your answer.

**(g)** It is important to the vice-president that Julie and Bill both have input into the decision process. How would you recommend changing what was done so that input from Julie and Bill is meaningful? Explain your answer.

## REFERENCES

Miller, G. A., "The Magical Number 7 +/−2: Some Limits on Our Capacity for Processing Information." *Psychological Review,* Vol. 63, 1956, pp. 81–97.

Saaty, T. L., "A Scaling Method for Priorities in Hierarchical Structures." *Journal of Mathematical Psychology*, Vol. 15, No. 3, 1977, pp. 234–281.

Saaty, T. L., "How to Make a Decision: The Analytic Hierarchy Process." *Interfaces*, Vol. 24, No. 6, 1994, pp. 19–43.

Saaty, T. L., *The Analytic Hierarchy Process.* Pittsburgh, PA, RWS Publications, 1996.

Sloane, E. B., M. J. Liberatore, R. L. Nydick, W. Luo, and Q. B. Chung, "Using the Analytic Hierarchy Process as a Clinical Engineering Tool to Facilitate Iterative Multidisciplinary Health Technology Assessment, 2002, (Working Paper).

# Chapter 12

# Introduction to Computer Simulation

## INTRODUCTION

Simulation provides the user with *flexibility* to evaluate the performance of a wide variety of systems. A simulation model consists of a set of mathematical and logical relationships that describe the operation of the system. Specifically, simulation allows the modeling and analysis of complex, real-world systems, when one or more variables or relationships are probabilistic. A simulation model evaluates a course of action by modeling the operation of the system over an extended period of time. For example, waiting line or queuing statistics at a bank could be estimated by simulating 1000 days of operation.

Unlike mathematical programming, which is an example of a *prescriptive* model, simulation is an example of a *descriptive* model. However, as we will see simulation can test a series of complex policies for cost/benefit analysis. Comparing simulation to other modeling techniques is like comparing a moving picture to a snapshot. Because of the power and flexibility of simulation it is one of the most frequently used decision-technology methods. Some examples of simulation applications include Everett (1996), Lee and Elcan (1996), Mullens and Toleti (1996), Savory and Saghi (1997), Trippi (1996), and Watson (1997).

Statistical concepts, including sampling, descriptive statistics, and probability distributions are applied in this chapter. Students wishing to obtain a fuller understanding of these topics are referred to Appendix A: Statistical Concepts.

## APPLICATION EXAMPLE: ADDING A SECOND SERVICE BAY

Consider a decision faced by Quik Lube, a limited automotive repair shop. They would like to know if it is beneficial to add another service bay to their operation. There are a variety of factors that must be considered when making this decision. These include several categories of uncertain events, such as the rate at which customers arrive, the amount of time required for service, and the amount of time a customer will wait in line before leaving. Quik Lube must also consider the profit generated by the different types of services offered, such as oil and filter changes, brake repairs, and muffler installations.

One output of Quik Lube's simulation model might be the expected profit that they will reap if another bay is added. Besides a single best estimate of profit, simulation can also provide a measure of the range and variability of profit that might occur. In addition, simulation can also provide measures of Quik Lube's performance, such as the average amount of time that customers wait for service. Before a final decision can be made, the simulation results in both improved profit performance and altered customer service levels must be weighed against the cost associated with constructing, maintaining, and operating the new service bay. Since some of the factors are uncertain, Quik Lube might run a series of cases to determine the conditions favoring the addition of the service bay. These runs can be viewed as a form of sensitivity analysis.

## Advantages Of Simulation

There are three major advantages of modeling a decision problem using simulation. First, simulation is a flexible modeling tool that can handle complex relationships with relative ease. Returning to our Quik Lube example, one such relationship might be that there are a limited number of parking spaces for cars to wait. Another example is the observation that Quik Lube's customers are impatient, and are only willing to wait ten minutes for service before they leave.

Second, simulation models are easy to explain and understand. For example, a flow diagram can be drawn to illustrate the various process flow steps associated with the arrival, waiting, service, and exiting of Quik Lube's customers. These diagrams help to simplify the explanation of the modeling relationships. Third, simulation can be accomplished in a variety of computing environments through the use of different types of software packages. For example, some users still prefer to code their simulation models in general-purpose programming languages such as C++, Basic, and Fortran. Others may prefer to work in a spreadsheet environment and use Excel. Also a variety of special purpose simulation packages are available, such as

Arena—http://www.arenasimulation.com/, (Kelton, et al. 1998)

Automod—http://www.autosim.com/simulation/automod.asp

Extend—http://www.imaginethatinc.com, (Imagine That, Inc. 2000)

Flexsim ED—http://www.taylor-ed.com/

GPSS—http://www.wolverinesoftware.com/products.htm, (Banks, et al. 1995)

Promodel—http://www.promodel.com/

Simul8—http://www.SIMUL8.com

SLX—http://www.wolverinesoftware.com/products.htm

Witness—http://www.lanner.com/corporate/technology/witness.htm

Some vendors use simulation software packages to create industry specific products such as Contact Center (www.rockwellsoftware.com) based on Arena, and Supply Chain Builder (http://www.simulationdynamics.com/Sc/index.htm) based on Extend.

## Classes Of Simulation Models

There are two classes of simulation models: *discrete event* and *continuous*. In discrete event simulation, a change in the system being simulated ("the simulated world") occurs only when an event happens. The simulation time clock advances based on the occurrence of the *next event*. In the Quik Lube example, the next events in the simulated world are the arrival of a car, the beginning of a service, or the completion of a service. At each of these times the status of Quik Lube's simulated world changes. For example, the number of cars waiting in line changes when a car arrives and joins the line.

In continuous simulation, the system changes continuously over time. Time advances in a *fixed increment* and the behavior of the system is updated during each increment. For

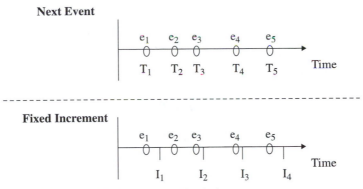

**Figure 12.1** Time Mechanisms for Simulation

example, simulating the flight of an airplane on autopilot is continuous since factors, such as the aircraft's position or velocity, can change continuously over time. If the time fixed increment is 0.05 seconds, changes in flight information during this interval are used to automatically adjust the flight plan. The difference in the occurrence of events (e's) and the time when these events affect the simulation time clock (T's or I's) is shown in Figure 12.1.

Discrete event simulation is often used to analyze process flows, such as those in a supermarket, a discrete parts manufacturing process, or a bank. Continuous simulation works well in continuous flow manufacturing applications, such as petrochemicals, or in financial cash-flow analysis. We will focus on the use of discrete event simulation, but will cover continuous simulation using a financial example.

## MONTE CARLO SIMULATION

### The Use of Random Numbers in Simulation

Suppose that we want to simulate the performance of Quik Lube. We need to define probability distributions that describe the time between customer arrivals, called the *interarrival time*, and how long service takes, called the *service time*. This is always accomplished by gathering and then analyzing relevant data. Assume that we have gathered interarrival time data and their relative frequency of occurrence (or probability) as shown in Table 12.1.

Using this information, we want to generate a sequence of interarrival times for Quik Lube's customers. Clearly these times must be random, but the chance that a given interarrival time will occur must correspond to its probability. The process of generating a sequence of random values or a *sample* from a probability distribution is called *Monte*

**Table 12.1**  Interarrival Times and Probabilities for Quik Lube

| Interarrival time | Probability |
|---|---|
| 5 | 0.15 |
| 10 | 0.35 |
| 15 | 0.50 |

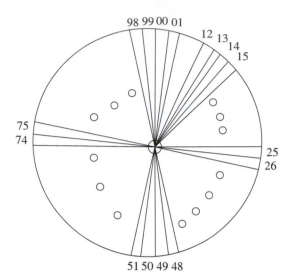

**Figure 12.2** A Roulette Wheel for Generating Random Values in Monte Carlo Simulation

*Carlo simulation.* To understand how Monte Carlo simulation works, consider a roulette wheel with 100 identical slots as shown in Figure 12.2. Since each slot has the same chance of occurrence on the spin of the wheel, we can partition the slots according to the probabilities given and link the results of a spin with an interarrival time. The slots linked to a specific interarrival time form a *random interval*. The relationship between the interarrival time, probability of occurrence, and random intervals for the Quik Lube example are shown in Table 12.2. For example, if we spin the roulette wheel and the ball lands in slot 74, an interarrival time of 15 minutes is generated.

Unless you happen to have a roulette wheel in your back pocket, a simpler procedure is needed. A table of random digits first prepared in 1955 by, whom else, the Rand Corporation (1983) can be used. An excerpt from the book appears as Table 12.3. What does it mean for these digits to be random? Every digit in the table is equally likely to be 0 through 9 and the patterns of random digits do not repeat. This table can be used at any starting point, and in blocks of 1, 2, 3, or more digits. For simplicity, we will start using this table by selecting numbers from the upper left-hand corner and moving from left to right.

Suppose we want to generate a random sample of 20 interarrival times. Since our probabilities have two significant digits, we use blocks of two random digits from Table 12.3. Since the first two digits are 6 and 3, according to Table 12.2, a 63 corresponds to an interarrival time of 15 minutes. Each value randomly generated from a probability distribution is called a *trial*. The results of 20 trials appear in Table 12.4.

Based on the results of the 20 trials, we might conclude that the expected interarrival time is the average, or mean, of the results of the 20 trials, or 10.25. However, using the

**Table 12.2** Interarrival Times, Probabilities, and Random Intervals for Quik Lube

| Interarrival time | Probability | Random interval |
|---|---|---|
| 5 | 0.15 | 00–14 |
| 10 | 0.35 | 15–49 |
| 15 | 0.50 | 50–99 |

**Table 12.3**   Table of Random Digits

| | | Random Digits | | | | |
|---|---|---|---|---|---|---|
| 63271 | 59986 | 71744 51102 | 15141 80714 | 58683 | 93108 | 13554 79945 |
| 88547 | 09896 | 95436 79115 | 08303 01041 | 20030 | 63754 | 08459 28364 |
| 55957 | 57243 | 83865 09911 | 19761 66535 | 40102 | 26646 | 60147 15702 |
| 46276 | 87453 | 44790 67122 | 45573 84358 | 21625 | 16999 | 13385 22782 |
| 55363 | 07449 | 34835 15290 | 76616 67191 | 12777 | 21861 | 68689 03263 |
| 69393 | 92785 | 49902 58447 | 42048 30378 | 87618 | 26933 | 40640 16281 |
| 13186 | 19431 | 88190 04588 | 38733 81290 | 89541 | 70290 | 40113 08243 |
| 17726 | 28652 | 56836 78351 | 47327 18518 | 92222 | 55201 | 27340 10493 |
| 36520 | 64465 | 05550 30157 | 82242 29520 | 69753 | 72602 | 21756 54935 |
| 81628 | 36100 | 39254 56835 | 37636 02421 | 98063 | 89641 | 64953 99337 |
| 84649 | 38968 | 75215 75498 | 49539 74240 | 03466 | 49292 | 36401 45525 |
| 63291 | 11618 | 12613 75055 | 43915 26488 | 41116 | 64531 | 56827 30825 |
| 70502 | 53225 | 03655 05915 | 37140 57051 | 48393 | 91322 | 25653 06543 |
| 06426 | 24771 | 59935 49801 | 11082 66762 | 94477 | 02494 | 88215 27191 |
| 20711 | 55609 | 29430 70165 | 45406 78484 | 31639 | 52009 | 18873 96927 |

This table is reproduced with permission from The Rand Corporation, *A Million Random Digits*, The Free Press, New York, 1955 and 1983.

original probability information from Table 12.1, we see that the true expected inter-arrival time is:

$$\text{Expected interarrival time} = (.15)(5) + (.35)(10) + (.50)(15) = 11.75.$$

The true expected interarrival time and its simulated average differ because the simulated average is based on the results of a sample of interarrival times. We know from statistics that the simulation average will approach the expected value as we increase the number of trials. So if we took 200 samples, instead of 20, it would be more likely (but not guaranteed!) that the simulated average would be closer to the true expected interarrival time.

**Table 12.4**   Generating 20 Trials for Interarrival Times Using Random Digits

| Random digits | Interarrival time | Random digits | Interarrival time |
|---|---|---|---|
| 63 | 15 | 15 | 10 |
| 27 | 10 | 14 | 5 |
| 15 | 10 | 18 | 10 |
| 99 | 15 | 07 | 5 |
| 86 | 15 | 14 | 5 |
| 71 | 15 | 58 | 15 |
| 74 | 15 | 68 | 15 |
| 45 | 10 | 39 | 10 |
| 11 | 5 | 31 | 10 |
| 02 | 5 | 08 | 5 |

Upon further examination of the results from Table 12.4, we observe that an inter-arrival time of 5 occurred in 6 out of 20 trials or 30% of the time. However, in Table 12.1 we see that an interarrival time of 5 has a 15% chance of occurrence, much lower than the simulated result. Similar comparisons can be made for the other interarrival times. Again the reason for any difference between the simulated and the expected results is the small sample size for our simulation. These differences are important, because as we will discuss later, sample-size issues affect the precision of our estimates of key simulation results, such as waiting time in line.

## Spreadsheet Simulation

We said before that few people have a roulette wheel in their back pockets. We also believe that few people carry around a book of random digits. For this reason, we can simplify the generation of random numbers by using *pseudo-random number generators* available on all computers. Pseudo-random number generators use formulas that generate a long series of integers before the sequence repeats itself. Programming languages have built-in pseudo-random number generators, such as Rnd(1) in BASIC. For further discussion on generating random numbers and values from probability distributions see Law and Kelton (2000) and Banks et al. (2001).

Electronic spreadsheets have the capability to generate pseudo-random numbers between 0 and 1. For example, the =RAND() function in Excel returns a random number between 0 and 1: press F9 to generate a new random number. We recommend that you set the spreadsheet to manual calculation mode so that new random values will be generated only when F9 is pressed. This is accomplished by using the *Tools, Options, Commands, Calculations, Tab,* and *Manual* buttons.

The same Quik Lube simulation that we accomplished using random digits can be done in Excel using the =VLOOKUP and =RAND() commands. An Excel screenshot showing the use of the =VLOOKUP command and the results of 9 of the 20 trials appears as Figure 12.3. For example, a random number of 0.2175901 was generated in cell B14 for the first trial. You can think of this as a spin of a roulette wheel of 22. Using the formula given in cell C14 this random number produced an interarrival time of 10 minutes. The formula given in cell C14 is: =VLOOKUP(+B14,$A$8:$B$11,2). The =VLOOKUP command works as follows. The $A$8:$B$11 block is the location of the cumulative probabilities and the interarrival times. If the random number from B14 is less than 0.15 (a probability of 0.15), then the interarrival time is 5. If the random number is less than 0.50 but greater than or equal to 0.15 (a probability of 0.35), then the time is 10. If the random number is less than 1.00 but greater than or equal to 0.50 (a probability of 0.50), then the time is 15. The 0 in B11 can be any number because this cell will never be used since a random number exactly equal to 1.00 is never generated. The 2 in the =VLOOKUP command indicates that the interarrival times are located in the second column of the $A$8:$B$11 block. To generate the additional trials, simply copy cells B14 and C14 to B15 through C33.

Within Excel it is easy to augment this spreadsheet to include basic performance statistics about the simulated trials, such as average and standard deviation. These values can be compared to the true population mean and standard deviation, as can be seen in a file called QUIK.XLS.

Using several probability distributions we can build additional types of models in Excel. Usually in these models, we must use some additional Excel commands, such as =IF, =MAX, and =MIN. Consider the following example of a service technician for a major refrigerator appliance manufacturer who is trained to service two refrigerators, the Alpha and the Beta. Past data have indicated that approximately 60% of the technician's

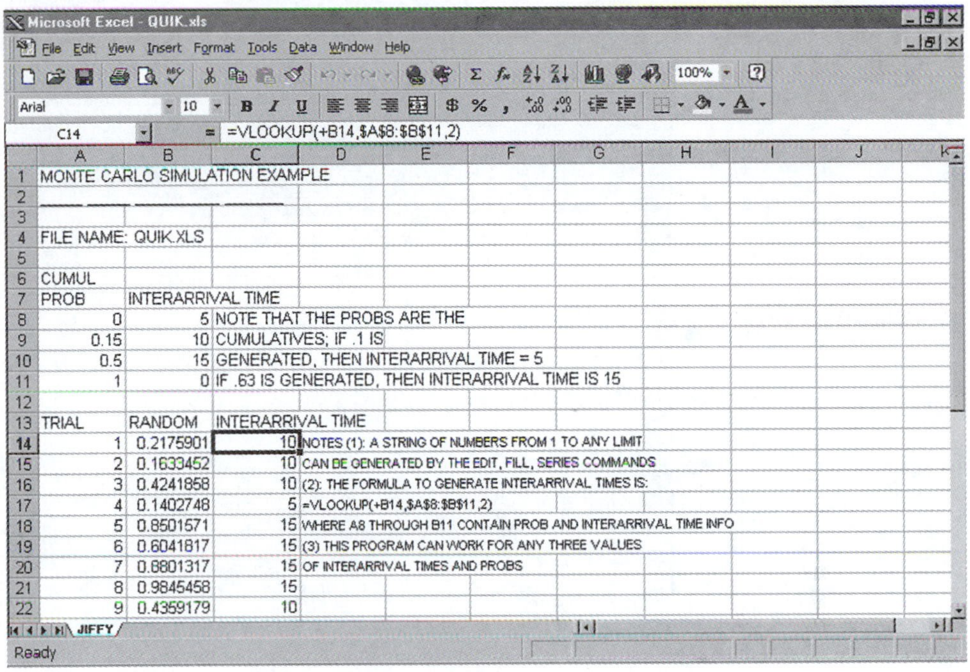

**Figure 12.3**  Screen Shot of an Excel Spreadsheet for Quik Lube Simulation

service calls are for the Alpha while 40% are for the Beta. The service time distributions for the two models are shown in Table 12.5. We want to develop an Excel spreadsheet to simulate 20 service calls and determine the total service time spent.

Three lookup tables are required to set up this problem in Excel. The first is used to determine the type of refrigerator requiring service (Alpha or Beta). The second and third tables determine the service time for the Alpha and Beta, respectively. An =IF command is used to select the appropriate service time table depending on whether an Alpha or Beta call was generated. This simulation is in a file called FRIDGE.XLS.

In the next chapter we will study the process of building simulation models of queuing or waiting-line processes where customers arrive, wait in line, receive service, and exit. It is possible to build waiting-line simulation models in Excel, however, the Excel skills required can be considerable. For example, the process of keeping track of customers as they move through the system may not be straightforward. An example of the most basic of these queuing models is given in a file called QSINGLE.XLS (based on Hesse 1989). A screen shot of this model appears as Figure 12.4. Additional examples of

**Table 12.5**  Service Time Distributions for Alpha and Beta Refrigerators

| Alpha | | Beta | |
|---|---|---|---|
| Time (minutes) | Relative frequency | Time (minutes) | Relative frequency |
| 25 | 0.50 | 20 | 0.40 |
| 30 | 0.25 | 25 | 0.40 |
| 35 | 0.15 | 30 | 0.10 |
| 40 | 0.10 | 35 | 0.10 |

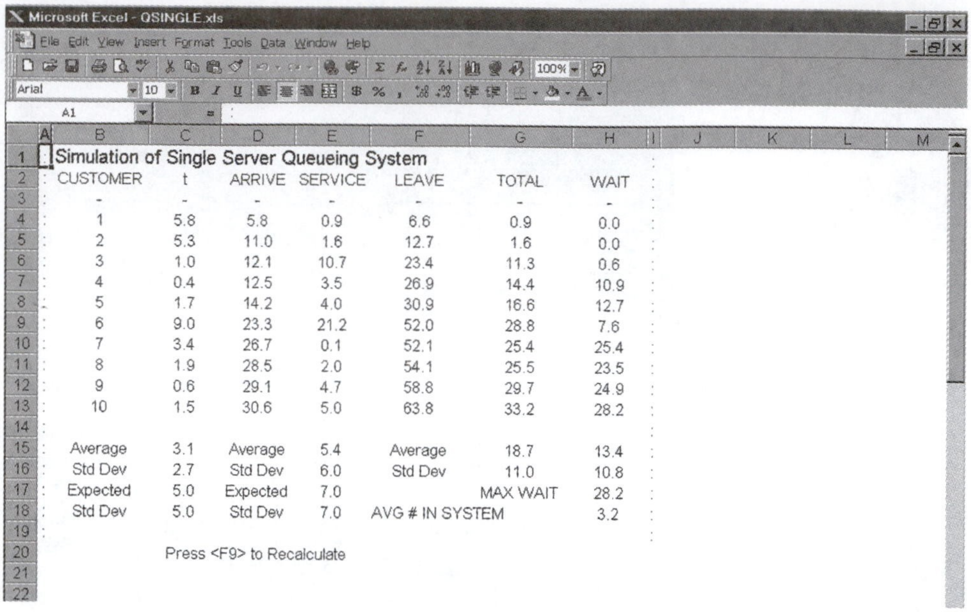

Simulation of Single Server Queueing System

| CUSTOMER | t | ARRIVE | SERVICE | LEAVE | TOTAL | WAIT |
|---|---|---|---|---|---|---|
| - | - | - | - | - | - | - |
| 1 | 5.8 | 5.8 | 0.9 | 6.6 | 0.9 | 0.0 |
| 2 | 5.3 | 11.0 | 1.6 | 12.7 | 1.6 | 0.0 |
| 3 | 1.0 | 12.1 | 10.7 | 23.4 | 11.3 | 0.6 |
| 4 | 0.4 | 12.5 | 3.5 | 26.9 | 14.4 | 10.9 |
| 5 | 1.7 | 14.2 | 4.0 | 30.9 | 16.6 | 12.7 |
| 6 | 9.0 | 23.3 | 21.2 | 52.0 | 28.8 | 7.6 |
| 7 | 3.4 | 26.7 | 0.1 | 52.1 | 25.4 | 25.4 |
| 8 | 1.9 | 28.5 | 2.0 | 54.1 | 25.5 | 23.5 |
| 9 | 0.6 | 29.1 | 4.7 | 58.8 | 29.7 | 24.9 |
| 10 | 1.5 | 30.6 | 5.0 | 63.8 | 33.2 | 28.2 |
| | | | | | | |
| Average | 3.1 | Average | 5.4 | Average | 18.7 | 13.4 |
| Std Dev | 2.7 | Std Dev | 6.0 | Std Dev | 11.0 | 10.8 |
| Expected | 5.0 | Expected | 7.0 | | MAX WAIT | 28.2 |
| Std Dev | 5.0 | Std Dev | 7.0 | AVG # IN SYSTEM | | 3.2 |

Press <F9> to Recalculate

**Figure 12.4** Screen Shot of an Excel Spreadsheet for a Single Server Simulation

Excel-based simulation models can be found in Appendix 13.1 in Anderson, Sweeney, and Williams (2000).

The process of developing spreadsheet-based simulation models becomes more manageable when spreadsheet add-ins are used, such as those available from INSIGHT.xla (Savage 1998). However, as discussed in the first chapter of this book, we found that it was difficult for students to address the queuing and process-redesign situations that often occur in practice using spreadsheets since the needed add-ins may not be available. As we will see in the next chapter, visual simulation software packages such as Extend equip the student with the flexibility and power needed to model complex queuing systems with relative ease.

## GAME SHOW SIMULATION

### The Monte Hall Problem and Solution

We will now present an interesting and counterintuitive problem that will demonstrate how simulation can help to shed light on relevant issues. Craig F. Whitaker addressed a seemingly innocent question to the "Ask Marilyn" column in *Parade Magazine* (vos Savant 1990). "Suppose you're on a game show, and you're given the choice of three doors: behind one door is a car; behind the others are goats. You pick a door, say No. 1, and the host, who knows what's behind the doors, opens another door, say No. 3, which has a goat. He then says to you, "Do you want to pick door number 2? Is it to your advantage to switch your choice?" The game show referred to is "Let's Make a Deal," a popular television show hosted by Monte Hall in the 1970s. So Monte wants to know: do you want to switch?

Most people think it makes no difference to switch since there are two doors left, and behind one is a goat and the other a car, so there must be a 50-50 chance of getting the car. Marilyn vos Savant's answer to the Monte Hall Problem was: "Yes, you should switch. The first door has a one-third chance of winning but the second door has a two-thirds chance." Not convinced? Consider the following argument. Suppose you adopt a switching strategy.

There are two possible cases to consider. In the first case, the car is in fact behind the first door. If you switch, you lose. The chance of this case occurring is 1/3. In the second case, the car is *not* behind the first door. The chance of this case occurring is 2/3. In this case, the host must open either door 2 or door 3 to reveal a goat. If the host opens door 3 to reveal the goat, then the car must be behind door 2. If the host opens door 2 to reveal the goat, then the car must be behind door 3. Therefore, regardless of whether the host opens door 2 or door 3 under case 2, if you switch, you win. This argument implies that the probability of switching and winning is 2/3, while the probability of not switching and winning is 1/3.

Marilyn's correct answer is counterintuitive. Some people believe that it does not make any difference if you switch since two doors remain unopened. What they forget is the fact that revealing a goat behind one door provides important information to the contestant. For other people one of the difficulties in reaching the correct solution is having a clear understanding of what assumptions are being made. One of the key issues we have stressed throughout the book is the importance of clearly stating your assumptions before attempting the problem solution. In the Monte Hall Problem, key assumptions include (1) the car has an equally likely chance of being behind each door; (2) the car is more valuable than the goat! (the car is not an old wreck and the goat is not a prize-winning breeder); and (3) the position of the car will not change once the game begins. In particular, your decision to switch may change if a different set of assumptions hold (Bohl, Liberatore, and Nydick 1995). For example, if the car can move once a door has been opened, then it makes no difference if you switch or not.

## Understanding the Solution Using Simulation

If we follow these three assumptions, we can use simulation to help us better understand this problem and its solution. Rather than create a computer-based simulation model for the Monte Hall Problem (we leave this as an exercise), we refer the reader to a web site located at: http://www.stat.sc.edu/~west/javahtml/LetsMakeaDeal.html. (This address is case sensitive.)

In this applet, the computer plays the role of the host. The user is asked to pick a door by clicking the mouse on one of the three doors. After the initial choice, the computer reveals an empty door by displaying a picture of a donkey. The user has the choice of staying with his/her initial selection or switching to the remaining door. The computer keeps track of the number of times the game is played with the switching and not-switching strategies and the number of times the game is won with each strategy. By following a switching strategy over 20 or more trials, the results of playing this simulation game should convince even the most skeptical individual that Marilyn's counterintuitive solution is correct. We hope that this example and the others that follow it will convince you that simulation is a powerful approach for solving important and practical problems that are faced in business, government, and everyday life.

## SUMMARY

In this chapter we have discussed how simulation enables the modeling of complex situations where one or more of the factors are probabilistic. We began by describing the advantages of simulation and the differences between discrete event and continuous simulation models. We discussed the process of Monte Carlo simulation, including the generation of random and pseudo-random numbers. We also illustrated how spreadsheets can be used to build simulation models, and have pointed out the limitations of this approach. We now turn our attention to simulation using a powerful commercial software package called Extend. In the next chapter, we will show the process of building queuing simulations that model the processes of generating arrivals, entering the arrivals into queues, servicing the arrivals, and exiting them from the system. Our intent is to show how Extend can be used more easily than roulette wheels, tables of random numbers, or Excel to simulate complex business situations involving randomness.

## HOMEWORK PROBLEMS

**1.** VECO is building a new generator for its Rosemont plant. Even with good maintenance procedures, the generator will have periodic failures or breakdowns. Historical figures for similar generators indicate that the relative frequency of failures during a year is as follows:

| Number of Failures | 0 | 1 | 2 | 3 |
|---|---|---|---|---|
| Relative Frequency | 0.80 | 0.15 | 0.04 | 0.01 |

Assume that the useful lifetime of the generator is 25 years. Use a spreadsheet simulation to estimate the number of breakdowns that will occur in the 25 years of operation. Is it common to have five or more consecutive years of operation without a failure?

**2.** A child goes door-to-door selling raffle tickets as a fundraising effort for his DELCO Little League baseball team. If the child sees the woman of the house, there is a 15% chance of selling tickets. If the child convinces the woman of the house to buy tickets, the relative frequency distribution for the number of tickets bought is as follows:

| Number of Tickets | 1 | 2 | 3 |
|---|---|---|---|
| Relative Frequency | 0.60 | 0.30 | 0.10 |

On the other hand, if the man of the house answers the door, the child's chances of making a sale are 25%. In addition, the relative frequency distribution for the number of tickets sold is as follows:

| Number of Tickets | 1 | 2 | 3 | 4 |
|---|---|---|---|---|
| Relative Frequency | 0.10 | 0.40 | 0.30 | 0.20 |

The child's coach has found that no one answers the door at about 30% of the houses contacted. However, of the people who do answer the door, 80% are women and 20% are men. The cost of each ticket is $2.

**(a)** Using a spreadsheet simulation, show the house-by-house results for 25 calls.

**(b)** What is the total amount raised for the 25 calls?

**(c)** Based on your results from part b, how many tickets should the child expect to sell by calling on 100 houses per day? What is the child's expected daily sales?

**3.** The RADNOR newsstand orders 250 copies of the *New York Times* daily. Primarily due to weather conditions, the demand for newspapers varies from day to day. The probability distribution of the demand for newspapers is as follows:

| Number of Newspapers | 150 | 175 | 200 | 225 | 250 |
|---|---|---|---|---|---|
| Relative Frequency | 0.10 | 0.30 | 0.30 | 0.20 | 0.10 |

The newsstand makes a 15-cent profit on every paper sold, but it loses 10 cents on every paper unsold by the end of the day. Use 10 days of simulated results in a spreadsheet to determine whether the newsstand should order 200, 225, or 250 papers per day. What is the average daily profit the newsstand can anticipate based on your recommendation?

## REFERENCES

Anderson, D. R., D. J. Sweeney, and T. A. Williams, *An Introduction to Management Science: Quantitative Approaches to Decision Making*, 9th ed., Cincinnati, OH, South-Western College Publishing, pp. 633–639, 2000.

Banks, J., J. S. Carson, B. L. Nelson, and D. M. Nichol, *Discrete-Event Simulation*, 3rd ed., NJ, Prentice-Hall, 2001.

Banks, J., J. S. Carson, and J. N. Sy, *Getting Started with GPSS/H*, 2nd Ed., Annandale, VA, Wolverine Software Corporation, 1995.

Bohl, A. H., M. J. Liberatore, and R. L. Nydick, "A Tale of Two Goats . . . and a Car, or the Importance of Assumptions in Problem Solutions," *Journal of Recreational Mathematics*, Vol. 27, No. 1, pp. 1–9, 1995.

Everett, J. E., "Iron Ore Handling Procedures Enhance Export Quality," *Interfaces*, Vol. 26, No. 6, pp. 82–94, 1996.

Hesse, R., "Spreadsheet Queuing," *Decision Line*, Vol. 20, No. 3, p. 9, 1989.

Imagine That, Inc., *Extend User's Guide*, San Jose, CA, 2000.

Kelton, W. D., R. P. Sadowski, and D. A. Sadowski, *Simulation with Arena*, MA, McGraw-Hill, 1998.

Law, A. M. and W. D. Kelton, *Simulation Modeling Analysis*, 3rd ed., NY, McGraw-Hill, 2000.

Lee, Y. and A. Elcan, "Simulation Modeling for Process Reengineering in the Telecommunications Industry," *Interfaces*, Vol. 26, No. 3, pp. 1–9, 1996.

Mullens, M. A. and R. Toleti, "A Four-Day Study Helps Home Building Move Indoors," *Interfaces*, Vol. 26, No. 4, pp. 13–24, 1996.

The Rand Corporation, *A Million Random Digits*, New York, The Free Press, 1955 and 1983.

Savage, Sam, *INSIGHT.xla: Business Analysis Software for Microsoft Excel*, Duxbury Press, Pacific Grove, CA, Brooks/Cole Publishing Company, 1998.

Savory, P. and G. Saghi, "Simulating Queue Scheduling Policies for a Spacecraft Simulator," *Interfaces*, Vol. 27, No. 5, pp. 1–8, 1997.

Trippi, R. R., "The AIM Game: Learning Investment Management Principles Through Monte Carlo Simulation, *Interfaces*, Vol. 26, No. 3, pp. 66–76, 1996.

vos Savant, M.O., "Ask Marilyn," *Parade Magazine*, September 9, 1990, p 13.

Watson, E. F., "An Application of Discrete-Event Simulation for Batch-Process Chemical-Plant Design," *Interfaces*, Vol. 27, No. 6, pp. 35–50, 1997.

# Chapter **13**

# Introduction to Process Simulation Using Extend

## QUEUING SIMULATION

### Introduction to Queuing

The last chapter introduced the concept of computer simulation. We discussed the process of Monte Carlo simulation using roulette wheels, tables of random numbers, and spreadsheets. We also discussed the limitations of spreadsheets for process simulation. In this chapter, we show how a visual simulation package called Extend can be used for process simulation. We introduce Extend by simulating a simple process, waiting in line in a retail bank.

Waiting in line is a part of everyday life that most of us would like to avoid or at least minimize. In fact, one study on time management found that most people spend five years of their lives waiting in lines and six months sitting at traffic stops (*New York Times*, 1988). Another study reports that Americans spend 37 billion hours a year waiting in lines (*Washington Post*, 1992). People not only physically wait in restaurants, banks, and supermarkets, but they also wait to have their telephone calls answered in a call center or for files to be downloaded from the Internet. Besides people waiting, jobs and materials wait to be processed in a manufacturing facility; telephone calls wait to be routed; customers wait for power to be restored after a storm; and ships and rail cars wait to be unloaded.

In analyzing the performance of any waiting line or *queuing* system, we will see that there is a fundamental trade-off between the cost of providing service and the amount of waiting time. Adding waiters in restaurants and work centers in factories is one method for reducing waiting time, but it may come with a significant increase in cost. Business process redesign can sometimes lead to reduced waiting without an operating cost increase. Simulation models can explore the performance of queuing systems when the number of servers or the process design itself changes. These issues will be discussed in more detail in future chapters.

Many changes that most of us take for granted and yet have impacted our everyday lives happened because of a desire to improve the performance of queuing systems. Some examples include offering incentives to shift demand to off-peak periods, changing from multiple to single lines in a bank to reduce the variance of the average waiting time, entertaining customers while in line, placing mirrors near elevator doors, and using technology in place of people (for example, ATM machines). Other specific changes that help to reduce waiting time are express checkout lines, optical scanners, paying tolls in one direction only, left turning lanes, right turn on red (*after stopping!*), credit cards and now speed passes at service station pumps. See the *New York Times* (1988) for additional discussion about more ways of overcoming long waiting times.

The formal analysis of the performance of queuing systems, called queuing theory, began in 1908 with the work of the Danish telephone engineer A. K. Erlang. Since that time, mathematical queuing models have been developed for many situations (see for example, Gross and Harris 1997). However, these models cannot easily handle all of the subtleties found in many practical situations. For this reason simulation is often preferred over mathematical analysis.

We note that statistical concepts, including sampling, discrete and continuous probability distributions, goodness-of-fit tests, and confidence intervals, are applied in this chapter. Students wishing to obtain a fuller understanding of these topics are referred to Appendix A: Statistical Concepts.

## QUEUING SIMULATION WITH EXTEND: A BANKING EXAMPLE

### Introduction

We will use a banking example and Extend to illustrate how to simulate queuing systems. Extend is a powerful, leading-edge, visual simulation software package that empowers the user to develop dynamic models of real-life processes (ImagineThat, Inc. 2001). Extend's web site can be visited at http://www.imaginethatinc.com. When needed, upgrades can also be downloaded at this site. When Extend LT is launched a worksheet with sample models will automatically open. If you wish, you may turn off this feature by selecting the *Edit* and then the *Preferences* commands, then in the dialog box of the "Model" tab simply delete the Default Model demo.mox and click OK.

### Extend Blocks

We begin with a brief overview of Extend before discussing the banking example. Simulation models in Extend are built using *blocks*. Each of Extend's blocks specifies an action or process. Information comes into a block and is processed by the program in the block. The programming language is transparent since users simply retrieve the needed blocks. A given block then transmits information to the next block in the simulation. These blocks are linked to form a model; for example, blocks can be used to generate arrivals, place arrivals in a queue, provide service, and exit. Additional blocks keep track of time, provide random service times, and plot statistics such as, the queue length and queue waiting time. After completing our initial banking example, we will introduce additional blocks and modeling features to illustrate key simulation concepts and additional applications. A summary description of all blocks used in this book is given in Appendix B.

Blocks are stored in *libraries* in Extend's Libraries folder. If an Extend model is opened, the required libraries are automatically opened. When a new model is created, you must open the required libraries using the *Library, Open Library* commands. We recommend that you configure Extend so that it automatically opens commonly used libraries. First select the *Edit* and then the *Preferences* commands. Then in the dialog box of the Libraries tab enter the following libraries in the Preload libraries location: *Discrete Event.lix*, *Generic.lix*, *Plotter.lix*, *Statistics.lix*, *Optimization.lix*, *Quick Blocks.lix*, and *Mfg.lix* (manufacturing). It is also possible to select *Library*, *Discrete Event.lix*, and *Open Library Window* to display all of the blocks in the discrete event library. You may want to do this since discrete event blocks are frequently used to build queuing simulation models. This window can be moved to the right of the model window for easy access.

Extend models are composed of *connected* blocks. There are four types of connectors: *item input*, *item output*, *value input*, and *value output*. Item input and output con-

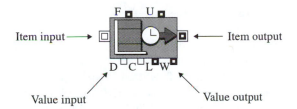

**Figure 13.1** Extend's *Activity, Multiple* Block Illustrating the Four Types of Connectors

nectors are used to move the items (for example, customers or products) from one block to another. Value input and output connectors are used to pass parameters between blocks. The *Activity, Multiple* block (found in *Discrete Event.lix, Activities*) shown in Figure 13.1 illustrates all four types of connectors. This block is used to determine the service time and to set the number of servers for a specific activity (such as a retail banking transaction), and will be discussed in more detail later. Filled-in connectors (F, U, L, and W) are value output connectors, and white connectors (D and C) are value input connectors. For example, the D connector represents the delay or service time (value input) for a *specific* item or customer, while the W connector represents the waiting time for items leaving the queue.

Each Extend block has a dialog box for setting parameters and viewing outputs. Double clicking on the block accesses its dialog box. Figure 13.2 shows a sample dialog box for the *Activity, Multiple* block. Tabs are used to organize the information in each dialog box. In particular, Figure 13.2 shows the result of clicking on the Activity tab. This screen allows the user to set the Delay (that is, service time) and Maximum number in activity (that is, number of servers). Other tabs will be discussed later.

## Banking Problem Overview

The banking problem that we want to simulate is an example of a single server, or *single channel*, queuing system. We will model this problem using discrete event simulation. For simplicity we assume that customers (called *items* in Extend) randomly arrive at a retail bank that has one teller (server) and a single first-in-first-out (FIFO) queue. We do not differentiate between types of services, such as making deposits, withdrawals, or account

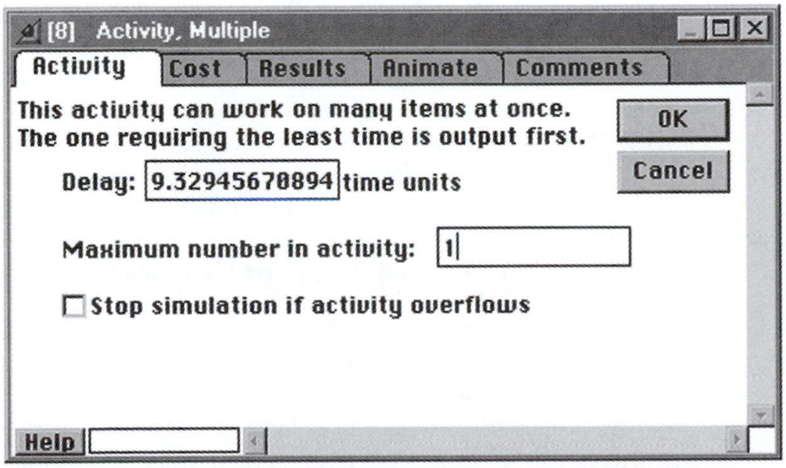

**Figure 13.2** Screen Shot of a Dialog Box for Extend's *Activity, Multiple* Block

inquiries. We also assume that the time for this single service is random. After receiving service the customer exits the bank.

Extend's blocks can represent the four key activities of this queuing system: a customer arrives, enters the queue, receives service, and then exits. When first opening Extend, your default model window is labeled Model-1.mox. As you follow this discussion, you can build your own banking model in Extend. After your model is completed, compare it to the one contained in a file called BANK1T.mox. We now consider in turn each of the activities needed to build the banking model.

## Generating Arrivals

The *Generator* block is found in the *Discrete Event.lix* library and the *Generators* submenu, and is used to generate arriving customers, also called *arrivals*. Select the *Discrete Event.lix* library, the *Generators* submenu and the *Generator* block to place a copy of this block in your active model window. Alternatively, you can click and drag the *Generator* icon from the *Discrete Event.lix* library window to your active model window.

In many queuing situations arrivals occur randomly; we cannot predict the exact time of an arrival. *Probability distributions* can provide good descriptions of arrival patterns. This information can be used to form a *discrete probability distribution* such as the one used in the Quik Lube example in the previous chapter. Alternatively, interarrival time data can be collected and fitted to a *continuous probability distribution*.

## Applying Stat::Fit to Interarrival Time Data

A variety of continuous distributions are built into Extend's *Generator* block. If interarrival time data are collected, a package such as Stat::Fit (Geer Mountain Software Corporation 2002) can be used to determine which distribution is appropriate to use based on goodness-of-fit tests, such as Chi Squared, Kolmogorov Smirnov, and Anderson Darling (Law and Kelton 2000). We illustrate how to use Stat::Fit to find the best fitting probability distribution for 100 interarrival times stored in an Excel file called RANTIME.XLS.

Begin by copying the 100 interarrival time data points from the RANTIME.XLS file to the clipboard in Excel. Open Stat::Fit, select *File*, *New*, *Edit*, *Paste*, and click on the Auto::Fit button. Select continuous distributions and assigned bound. Stat::Fit will automatically assign the Lowest Allowed Value. After clicking OK, Stat::Fit provides a series of fitted probability distributions (along with their parameters) ranked in order of best to worst fit. As shown in Figure 13.3, the best fit for the data is an *exponential distribution* with a minimum value of 0 and a *mean interarrival time* of 2.86. Notice that the exponential and the Erlang distributions have the same rank because an Erlang whose second parameter is 1 is identical to an exponential distribution. (We will discuss the Erlang in more detail later.) Figure 13.3 also shows a comparison graph of the actual interarrival times versus the fitted exponential distribution. This plot was obtained by clicking on the exponential distribution in the Auto::Fit window.

We also use this example to validate the accuracy of Stat::Fit. In reality, we randomly generated the 100 data points from an exponential distribution with a mean of 3.00. (See Law and Kelton 2000 for a discussion of procedures for generating random values for

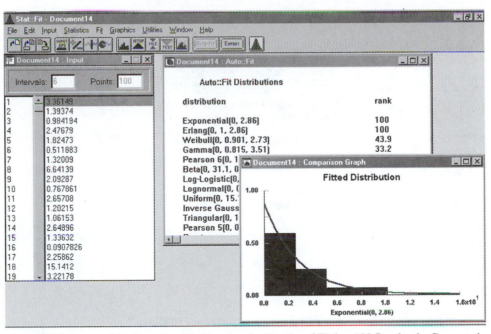

**Figure 13.3** Screen Shot from Stat::Fit Showing the Results of Fitting 100 Randomly Generated Interarrival Times

probability distributions.) The difference between the estimated mean of 2.86 provided by Stat::Fit and the actual mean of 3.00 is once again due to the small sample size. However this difference is minimal and demonstrates the value and accuracy of using Stat::Fit to fit sample data. We recommend collecting a minimum of 30 observations before using Stat::Fit. In practice when developing an Extend model, the user would enter the probability distribution and the estimated mean provided by Stat::Fit, that is, an exponential with a mean of 2.86. For mathematical simplicity, we will use an exponential distribution with a mean interarrival time of 3.00 to model the customer arrival process.

Returning to Extend, we can now specify the interarrival time probability distribution in our generator block. Double-click on the *Generator* block to open up the dialog box, click on the Items tab, then click on the box to the right of Distribution. The user is then presented with a choice of probability distributions as shown in Figure 13.4. Simply click on Exponential, then enter 3.00 in the box to the right of (1) Mean =. If a different distribution were specified, the user may need to specify additional parameters. For example, if the normal distribution is selected, the user must supply the mean and standard deviation.

Based on the results of previous research, we know that the shapes of some distributions are related to certain arrival processes. The choice of the exponential distribution for modeling interarrival times in our banking simulation was not an arbitrary one. The exponential distribution is often used to model interarrival times in business processes, service industries, and queuing.

Figure 13.5 is an Extend graph of an exponential distribution with a mean interarrival time of 3.00 minutes based on a plot of 20,000 randomly generated interarrival times (trials). This plot was obtained by setting the N items for N = location to 20000 and clicking the Plot button in the Items tab of the *Generator* block. This plot shows that the exponential distribution is skewed to the right, so it is more likely that the interarrival times

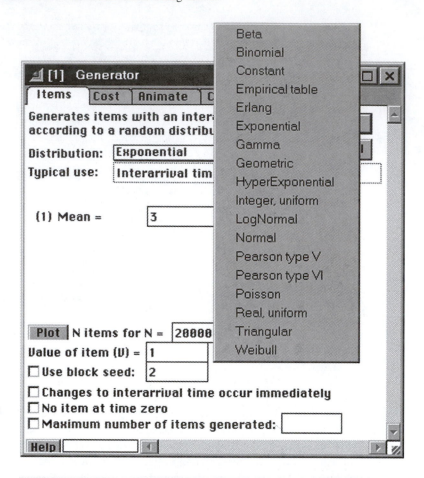

**Figure 13.4** Screen Shot of the Dialog Box for the *Generator* Block after Selecting the Items Tab and Distribution

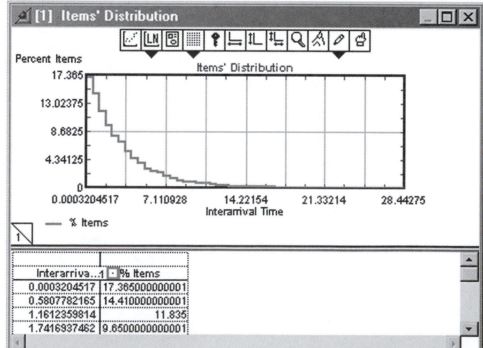

**Figure 13.5** Screen Shot of an Exponential Interarrival Time Distribution Plot with a Mean of 3 Based on 20,000 Randomly Generated Values, from the *Generator* Block Items Tab

will be less than 3 minutes than greater than 3 minutes, and that there is a small chance of very long interarrival times. Earlier we recommended that at least 30 observations be collected and entered into Stat::Fit for evaluation. These 30 observations should not be confused with the 20,000 items plotted. This 20,000 is an arbitrary number that was used to ensure a smooth plot. Note that the Stat::Fit and Extend graphs are, as expected, similar.

It is important to understand the relationship between the mean interarrival time and the *mean arrival rate* since these are sometimes confused in practice. Simply stated, since our mean interarrival time is 3 minutes, then our mean arrival rate is 20 customers per hour. Using conventional (and convenient) queuing theory notation, the mean arrival rate ($\lambda$) is the reciprocal of the mean interarrival time ($1/\lambda$). This relationship between mean interarrival time and mean arrival rate holds for any probability distribution. In our example, since ($1/\lambda$) = 3 minutes/arrival, then $\lambda$ = 1/3 arrival/minute, or $\lambda$ = [1/3 arrival/minute] $*$ 60 minutes/hour = 20 arrivals/hour. In Extend, we always enter the mean interarrival time in the *Generator* block as shown in Figure 13.4.

## Entering the Queue

The *Queue, FIFO* block is found in the *Discrete Event.lix* library and the *Queues* submenu, and is used to place arriving customers into the queue. This block should now be put in the active model window to the right of the *Generator* block. Since each new arrival must enter the queue, we need to connect the *Generator* block to the *Queue, FIFO* block to move it. In Extend, we link the item out(put) connector of the *Generator* block to the item in(put) connector of the *Queue, FIFO* block. Position the *Queue, FIFO* block to the right of the *Generator* block, then place your cursor on the item out connector of the *Generator* block. Your cursor now turns into an inkwell. Move the inkwell to begin drawing a line, and connect this line to the item in connector of the *Queue, FIFO* block. You know that you have made a good connection when the line thickens. When item out connectors are correctly connected to item in connectors, there will be a thick double line. Think of this as a pipeline that the item moves through. Once the model is run, each arrival generated by the *Generator* block will now move to the *Queue, FIFO* block. The connected blocks are shown here.

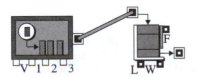

Customers enter and exit our banking queue based on a FIFO (first in, first out) rule. Often, when people are involved, a FIFO queue discipline is used, as assumed by the *Queue, FIFO* block. This block eliminates behavior such as a customer moving ahead of others in the queue because of maneuvering or priority. Other queue behaviors will be discussed in later examples. Extend sets the default for the Maximum queue length at 1000 (found in the Queue tab) as shown in Figure 13.6. At this time, the only purpose of this setting is to prevent excessive queue buildup.

Two important classes of statistics are reported in the *Queue, FIFO* block Results tab: line (queue) length and waiting time. Specifically, the average and maximum values

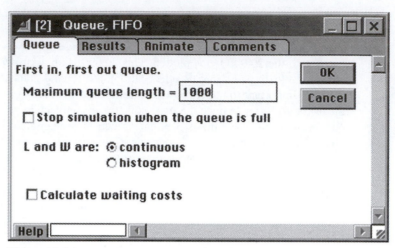

**Figure 13.6** Screen Shot of the Dialog Box for the *Queue, FIFO* Block after Selecting the Queue Tab

of these statistics are reported. We define LQ as the *average length of the queue* and WQ as the *average waiting time in the queue. Queue utilization*, the proportion of time that customers are in the queue, is also reported. Note that Extend uses L to refer to the current number of items in the line and W as the waiting time for items leaving the queue, as can be seen by looking at the value output connectors of the *Queue, FIFO* block. We will have more to say about the Results tab after running our banking simulation.

## Receiving Service

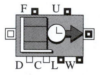

The *Activity, Multiple* block found in the *Discrete Event.lix* library and the *Activities* submenu is used to provide service. Connect the item out connector of the *Queue, FIFO* block to the item in connector of the *Activity, Multiple* block to move the items from the queue into service as shown here.

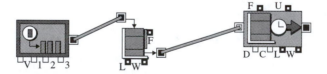

Remember that customers in our FIFO queue are served on a first in, first out (FIFO) basis. To specify the number of tellers, enter a 1 in the box labeled Maximum number in activity (Activity tab) as shown in Figure 13.7. If the service time is constant, such as in an automated car wash, simply enter the fixed service time value into the Delay location (Activity tab) also shown in Figure 13.7. Service time can be thought of as "delaying" a customer from moving through the bank and exiting.

Similar to our discussion about interarrival times, service times are often random and represented by probability distributions. However, random service times *cannot* be set

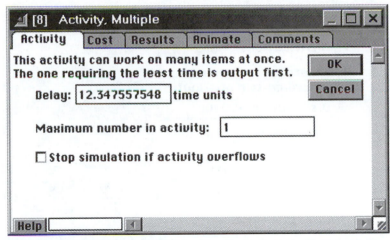

**Figure 13.7** Screen Shot of the Dialog Box for the *Activity, Multiple* Block after Selecting the Activity Tab

within the *Activity, Multiple* dialog box. An additional block called *Input Random Number* found in the *Generic.lix* library and the *Input/Ouputs* submenu must be used. The parameters for the probability distribution are set through the Distributions tab. Click in the Distribution box to select the desired probability distribution and to specify the parameters in the indicated boxes.

A random service time must be generated for each customer as it enters the *Activity, Multiple* block. In Extend, first position the *Input Random Number* block below the *Activity, Multiple* dialog block. Then link the value output connector of the *Input Random Number* block to the Delay (labeled D) value input connector of *Activity, Multiple* block as shown. The D value input connector passes the random service time to the *Delay* box (Activity tab) contained in the *Activity, Multiple* dialog block. This value overrides any Delay value that previously may have been entered in the dialog box of the *Activity, Multiple* block.

This process is a powerful way that Extend uses to pass information between blocks. Connecting the *Input Random Number* block to the *Activity, Multiple* using the value in and value out connectors is different from connecting the *Generator* and *Queue, FIFO* blocks with the item in and item out connectors. In the first case, we are passing information between blocks (a solid, single line). In the second case, we are moving an item between blocks (a double line).

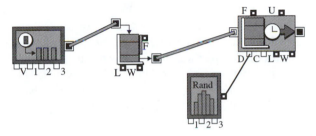

The process of choosing a service time distribution and its parameters is the same as that described for the *Generator* block. That is, service time data must be collected and then fitted to a probability distribution using Stat::Fit. In our banking simulation, we will assume that our service time data can be fitted to an *Erlang distribution*. This distribution

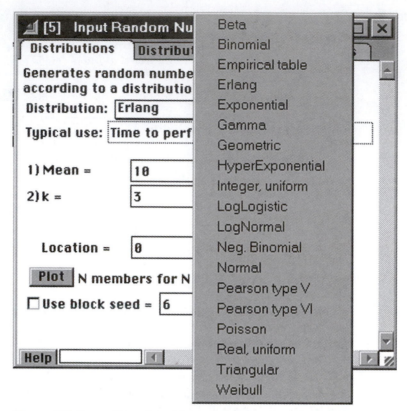

**Figure 13.8** Screen Shot of the Dialog Box for the *Input Random Number*
Block after Selecting the Distributions Tab and Distribution

is often used to describe the variability of service times. Two parameters are needed
to specify an Erlang distribution: the mean service time (Mean) and an integer shape
parameter (k). The Erlang can approximate a variety of distributions depending upon parameter values. For example, a k value of 1 causes the Erlang to become an exponential
distribution, whereas larger k values tend to make the Erlang look more like a normal distribution. We assume that service time follows an Erlang distribution with a mean of 10
and a k value of 3. Note that in practice, these parameters would be provided by Stat::Fit
after it evaluates sample data that was provided. These values should be entered into
the appropriate boxes in the *Input Random Number* block (Distributions tab) as shown in
Figure 13.8.

Now we can plot our service time distribution as shown in Figure 13.9. As in the plot
of interarrival time data previously shown, this plot is based on 20,000 randomly generated service times. This plot was obtained by setting the N items for N = location to 20000
and clicking the Plot button in the *Input Random Number* block (Distributions tab). Figure 13.9 shows that this Erlang distribution looks somewhat like a skewed normal distribution, since the k value is 3. As mentioned earlier, for larger k values, the graph will look
even more normal.

Just as we found that there is a relationship between the mean interarrival time and
the mean arrival rate, there also is a relationship between the *mean service time* and the
*mean service rate*. Using an argument similar to the one made for the arrival process, the
mean service rate ($\mu$) is the reciprocal of the mean service time ($1/\mu$). In our example,

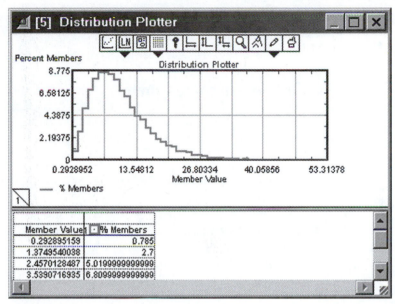

**Figure 13.9**  Screen Shot of an Erlang Service Time Distribution Plot with a Mean of 10 and Shape Parameter (k) of 3 Based on 20,000 Randomly Generated Values, from the *Input Random Number* Block Distributions Tab

the mean service time is ten minutes, so our mean service rate is six customers per hour. Continuing with the analogy, we can also measure the average number of customers in service (LS) and the average waiting time (WS) for our service facility (*Activity, Multiple* block, Results tab). Extend uses L to refer to the number of items in service, and W to refer to the waiting time for items leaving the service area as can be seen by looking at the value output connectors of the *Activity, Multiple* block. Extend also measures the *service utilization*, defined as the percent of time that the single teller is busy. We will have more to say about the Results tab after running our banking simulation.

## Exiting the System

The *Exit* block is found in the *Discrete Event.lix* library and the *Routing* submenu, and is used to remove items from the simulation. Connect the item out connector of the *Activity, Multiple* block to the item in connector of the *Exit* block to remove the items that have completed service from the simulation as shown.

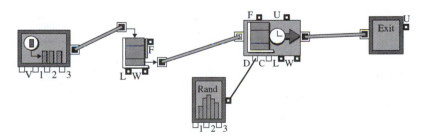

The box labeled Exited (Exit tab) reports the number of items that exited during the simulation run as shown in Figure 13.10.

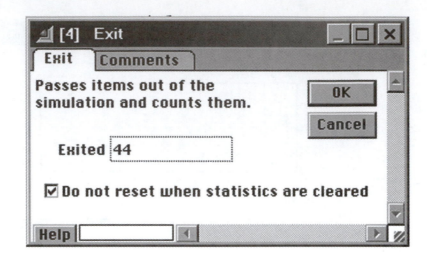

**Figure 13.10** Screen Shot of the Dialog Box for the *Exit* Block after Selecting the Exit Tab

## Keeping Time

The *Executive* block found in the *Discrete Event.lix* library (no submenu) creates a clock and manages time during the simulation. This block must be placed to the left of all other blocks in every discrete event Extend model as shown.

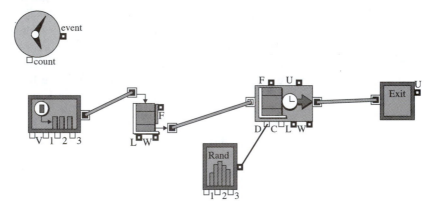

Generally you will have no reason to change anything in the dialog box shown in Figure 13.11.

## Plotting the Results

The *Plotter, Discrete Event* block is found in the *Plotter.lix* library (no submenu) and offers a flexible plotter that can be used in your models. It provides both a table and a graph of the numerical values. We recommend plotting L and W from the *Queue, FIFO* block,

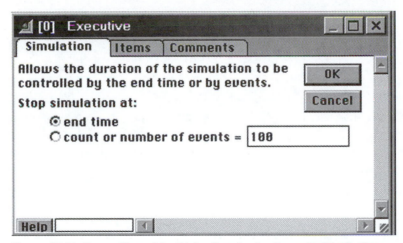

**Figure 13.11** Screen Shot of the Dialog Box for the *Executive* Block after Selecting the Simulation Tab

although you may need to plot other outputs such as the number of customers that exit the simulation. To plot L and W, connect the value out connector labeled L of the *Queue, FIFO* block to the second (red) connector of the *Plotter, Discrete Event* block. Similarly, connect the value out connector labeled W to the top (blue) connector as shown.

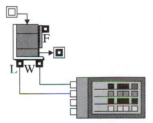

Opening the dialog box of the *Plotter, Discrete Event* block displays a set of plotter tools that can be used to customize your plots. The three most important tools are Trace properties, Open Dialog, and Auto Scale XY. Figure 13.12 displays the locations of these tools.

The Trace properties command brings up a window shown as Figure 13.13 that allows the user to specify which Y-axis will be used for each plot (Y1/Y2 option). If two plots are to appear on the graph, simply click the Y1/Y2 option for either one of the plots and it will switch from the default Y1 axis (left) to the Y2 axis (right).

The Open Dialog tool opens a dialog box that allows the user to control when the graph is displayed and also to automatically scale the Y-axis. As shown in Figure 13.14, we recommend selecting Show plot at end of simulation. Also click on the box in the lower left-hand corner of this dialog box and change the No Autoscaling option to Autoscale at end of simulation. If you do not change to Autoscale at end of simulation, you will have to click on the Auto Scale XY tool after running the simulation (see Figure 13.12 for the location of this tool).

## Running the Complete Model

Our banking simulation model is now complete and is given as Figure 13.15 and in a file called BANK1T.mox. Before running our simulation we must specify the length of time our simulation will be run and the number of simulation runs we wish to make. From

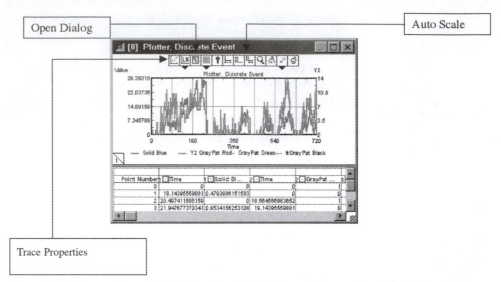

**Figure 13.12** Screen Shot of the Dialog Box for the *Plotter, Discrete Event* Block Showing Three Useful Plotting Tools

the main Extend menu, select *Run, Simulation Setup,* and the Discrete event tab. If we want to simulate our bank for an eight-hour day and express time in minutes, enter 480 in the box labeled End simulation at time, as shown in Figure 13.16. Multiple simulation runs can improve the accuracy of your estimates of such factors as LQ and WQ. For example, to simulate 365 days, enter 365 in the Number of runs box in Figure 13.16. Details about the impact of making multiple runs will be discussed later when we cover confidence intervals. For now, we will run our model for one 480-minute day.

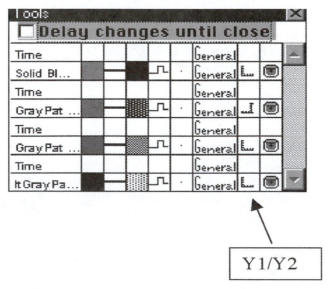

**Figure 13.13** Screen Shot of Y1\Y2 Option from the Dialog Box of the *Plotter, Discrete Event* Block

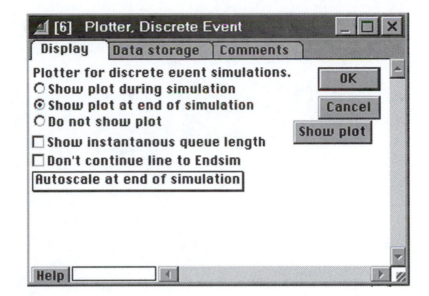

**Figure 13.14** Screen Shot of the Dialog Box of the Open Dialog Option of the *Plotter, Discrete Event* Block after Selecting the Display Tab

The user also has the option to set a generic time unit in the simulation model. This can be set using the Time units tab within *Simulation Setup.* Remember to use the same time units for entering the mean interarrival, mean service, and end simulation times.

There are several ways to run the simulation model. For example, the model can be run by using the Run Now button that is found in the *Simulation Setup* dialog box shown in Figure 13.16. If the *Simulation Setup* options have been previously set, the *Run* and

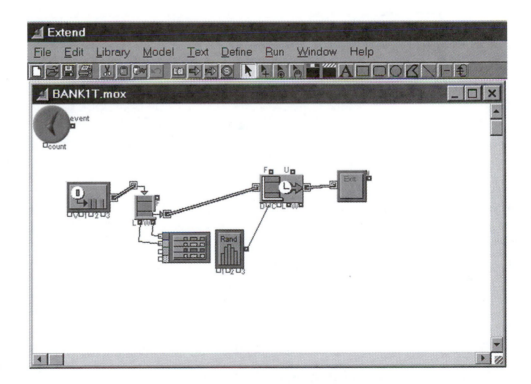

**Figure 13.15** Screen Shot of the Complete Banking Simulation Model (BANK1T.mox)

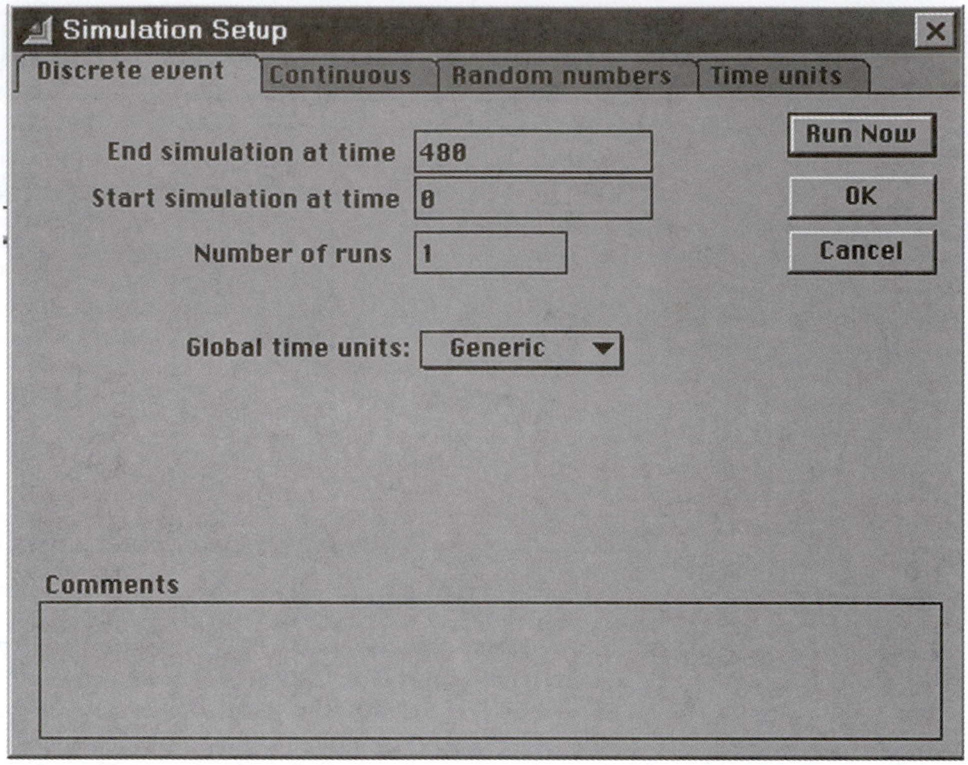

**Figure 13.16** Screen Shot of the *Run*, *Simulation Setup* Dialog Box after Selecting the Discrete Event Tab

*Run simulation* commands can be used or the user can simply click on the green right arrow on the toolbar (to the immediate right of the notebook icon; (see Figure 13.15). After running the model we recommend printing the entire model along with the Results tabs of selected dialog boxes, including *Queue, FIFO* and *Activity, Multiple*.

Extend also has the capability for animation. To have the same icon move throughout the model, open the *Generator* dialog box, click on the Animate tab, and select the desired icon by clicking on the box next to Items will appear as. To have different icons appear, open the dialog box of the desired block, click on the Animate tab, select the desired icon, and click on the button Change all pictures to. To animate select Run and Show Animation.

### Interpreting the Model's Results

The plot of queue length and waiting time during the simulation best summarizes the results of running BANK1T.mox as shown in Figure 13.17. This plot shows that queue length is increasing rapidly, reaching 103 customers in line by the end of the simulation. That's quite a long line! The results for waiting time are just as disturbing, since it reaches 319.1419 minutes or 5.32 *hours* by the end of the simulation. Remember that we are simulating random events, so if you run BANK1T.mox the results will be similar, but not exactly the same.

More detailed results can be found by viewing the Results tabs of the *Queue, FIFO* and *Activity, Multiple* blocks and the Exit tab of the *Exit* block shown in Figures 13.18 through 13.20, respectively. The queue output in Figure 13.18 shows the same maximum

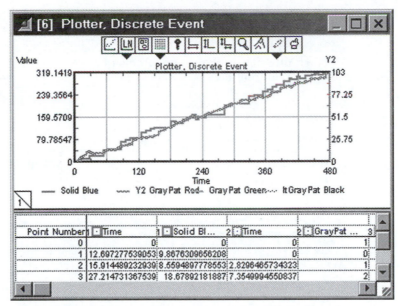

**Figure 13.17** Screen Shot of *Plotter, Discrete Event* Dialog Box after Running BANK1T.mox

values for line length and waiting time found on the plot, but also reports that LQ is 51.33 customers and WQ is 168.91 minutes. In addition, Figure 13.18 shows that 148 customers entered the queue and only 45 exited, leaving 103 customers still in line at the end of the simulation (the latter result is seen on the plot). The queue was busy nearly all of the time as the 99.4% utilization result indicates.

It is useful to compare the actual number of arrivals during the simulation with the expected number. Remembering that the average interarrival time is 3 minutes, we expect about 480 minutes/(3minutes/customer) = 160 arrivals per day. The difference between 160 and 148 is sufficiently close, and is due to randomness.

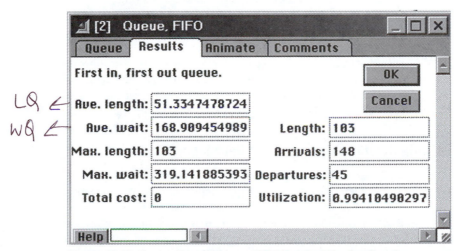

**Figure 13.18** Screen Shot of *Queue, FIFO* Results Tab after Running BANK1T.mox

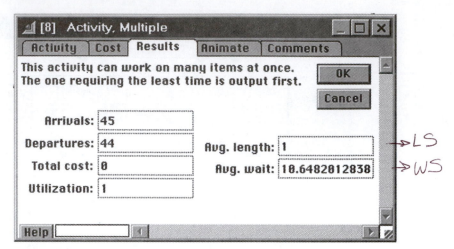

**Figure 13.19** Screen Shot of *Activity, Multiple* Results Tab after Running BANK1T.mox

Where did the 45 customers who exited the queue go? As Figure 13.19 indicates, they went to the *Activity, Multiple* block to receive service. All but one exited the service block, with one customer in service at the end of the simulation.

It is useful to compare the average service time during the simulation with the expected. As shown in Figure 13.19, the average waiting time in service (WS) was 10.65 minutes, very close to the average service time of 10 minutes that we entered. Also, the average number of customers in service (LS) is 1, meaning that the server is constantly handling customers with no breaks during the simulation. This latter result is confirmed by noting that the utilization of the server is 1. Finally, the 44 customers who completed service exited the simulation as shown in Figure 13.20.

Based on our results, we can determine the average total waiting total time (WT) and the average number of customers (LT) in our simulated bank. WT is simply the sum of the average time waiting in the queue (WQ) and the average time waiting for the service to be completed (WS). Similarly, the average number of customers in our simulated bank (LT) is the sum of the average number waiting in the queue (LQ) and the average number in service (LS). From Figures 13.18 and 13.19 and the results previously discussed, we see that WT = 168.91 + 10.65 = 179.56 minutes, and LT = 51.33 + 1 = 52.33 customers.

In summary, the results of running BANK1T.mox show that the single server cannot keep up with the number of arriving customers. Line lengths and waiting times are mushrooming and out of control. Clearly, additional servers are required—but how many? The next section will discuss an important relationship that will help to answer this question.

### An Important Queuing Relationship: $\lambda$, $\mu$, and the Number of Servers

There is an important relationship between $\lambda$, $\mu$, and the number of servers that should be considered before running any queuing simulation. Remember that in our banking simulation, $1/\mu$ is 10 minutes/customer, so that $\mu$ is 6 customers/hour. Therefore, if the average arrival rate of customers to our bank is up to, but not including, 6 customers per hour, the single teller could theoretically keep up with demand on average. Continuing with this argument, if $\lambda$ is up to, but not including, 12 customers/hour then at least two

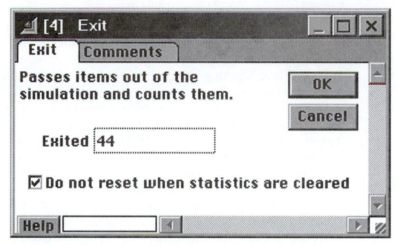

**Figure 13.20**  Screen Shot of _Exit_ Block in Exit Tab after Running
BANK1T.mox

tellers are needed to keep up with demand on average. In our case, $1/\lambda = 3$ minutes/customer, so that $\lambda$ is 20 customers/hour. Therefore, at least 4 tellers are needed to keep up with demand and prevent queue length and waiting time from continuing to grow during the simulation.

We define N as the _minimum number of servers_ to prevent an ever-expanding queue. In particular, N can be defined as the smallest integer greater than $\lambda/\mu$. In our example, $\lambda/\mu = (20$ customers/hour)/(6 customers/hour) $= 3.33$, so N is 4 servers. Since we usually estimate $1/\lambda$ and $1/\mu$, and not $\lambda$ and $\mu$, an algebraically equivalent approach for determining N is to divide the average service time $(1/\mu)$ by the average interarrival time $(1/\lambda)$ and raise the result to the next highest integer [note that $(1/\mu)/(1/\lambda) = \lambda/\mu$]. That is:

$$N = \text{the smallest integer greater than } (1/\mu) / (1/\lambda)$$

In our example, $(1/\mu) = 10$ and $(1/\lambda) = 3$. Therefore, $(1/\mu) / (1/\lambda) = 10/3 = 3.33$, so N is 4 servers. This is the same result as the one already found since the two formulae are equivalent. We recommend using the latter equation since $1/\mu$ and $1/\lambda$ are known and entered into Extend.

Note that if $(1/\mu) / (1/\lambda)$ is exactly an integer, we still set N as the _next highest_ integer because the variation in arrival and service times will otherwise still lead to an unstable situation.

Obviously, if the number of servers is set to a value larger than N, WQ and LQ will decrease. This point leads to a fundamental trade-off between the cost of providing service and the cost of waiting, which we will discuss in a later chapter. For now, we wish to demonstrate the impact of increasing the number of servers on the performance of our banking simulation.

## Running the Banking Simulation with Additional Servers

We now assume that a single queue feeds all four tellers, and that the person at the front of the line goes to the first available teller. The advantage of the previous formula is that we do not have to even try two or three servers since we know that a minimum of four servers is needed. To run our banking simulation with four servers, simply change the Maximum number in activity box from 1 to 4 in the Activity tab of the *Activity, Multiple* block. The results are in a file called BANK4T.mox. Figure 13.21a shows the impact of increasing the number of servers to 4 on a plot of queue length and waiting time during the simulation. Note that both of these measures are not continually growing during the simulation as in our previous run. Also, the maximum queue length is a much shorter 10 customers, and the maximum waiting time is reduced to 28.50 minutes.

The *Queue, FIFO* block output in Figure 13.21b shows that LQ is a low 2.16 customers and WQ is a respectable 5.99 minutes. In addition, Figure 13.21b shows that 173 customers entered the queue and all of these exited, with no one in line at the end of the simulation. The queue was busy a bit more than half of the time, as the 57.3% utilization result indicates.

Figure 13.22 shows that 169 of the 173 customers who entered the *Activity, Multiple* block received service and then exited. The remaining four were in the process of being served at the end of the simulation. When there are multiple servers, the utilization of the service area is computed as the average percentage of the server capacity that is used over the simulation. Another way of obtaining this result is to divide the average number of customers in service (3.52) by the total number of available servers (4) to obtain the 88.0% result (see Figure 13.22). This high utilization indicates that the tellers remain very busy throughout the simulation.

Interestingly, we can estimate the service area utilization *before* running our simulation by first remembering that each server can handle $\mu = 6$ customers/hour on average. Since we have four servers, our service facility can handle 24 customers/hour on average. Since on average $\lambda = 20$ customers arrive per hour, we expect our service facility utilization to be $100 * (20/24) = 83.3\%$. The difference in results is due to randomness and the (relatively) short length of our simulation run.

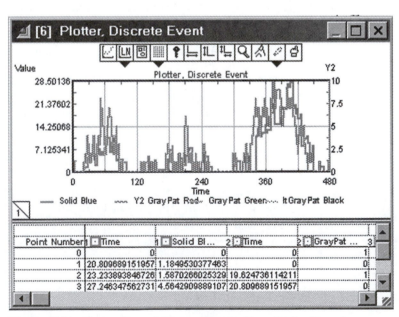

**Figure 13.21a** Screen Shot of *Plotter, Discrete Event* Dialog Box after Running BANK4T.mox

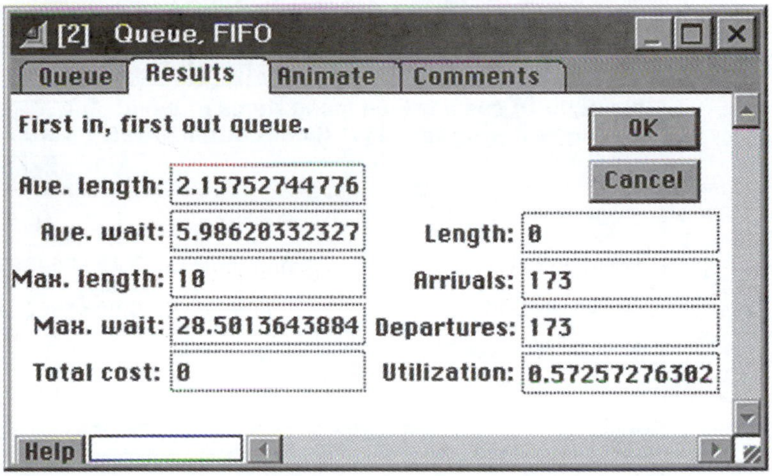

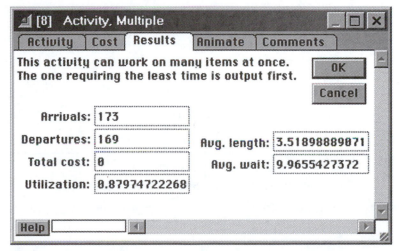

**Figure 13.21b** Screen Shot of *Queue, FIFO* Results Tab after Running BANK4T.mox

An interesting question is the extent to which the utilization of the service facility and the performance of the queue improve if we add an additional teller to our banking simulation. Using the approach already discussed, we can estimate that service facility utilization should be in the neighborhood of $100 * (20/5 * 6) = 66.7\%$. Figure 13.23 shows in fact that service facility utilization dropped to 62.0% in a five-server simulation run, which is close to our expectation. Figure 13.24 shows that LQ and WQ dropped to very low levels of 0.13 customers and 0.42 minutes, respectively. In addition, the maximum line length is only 3 customers, and the maximum wait is 5.39 minutes. Also, the queue is only busy 10% of the time. Further results of running the five-server simulation can be found in a file called BANK5T.mox.

**Figure 13.22** Screen Shot of *Activity, Multiple* Results Tab after Running BANK4T.mox

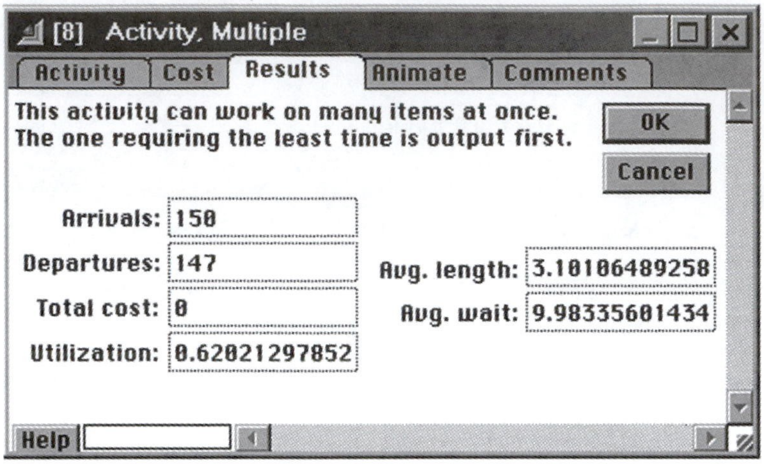

**Figure 13.23** Screen Shot of *Activity, Multiple* Results Tab after Running BANK5T.mox

Taken together, the results indicate that a significant performance improvement occurs with the addition of the fifth teller. However, remember that this improvement comes at the cost of scheduling an additional teller. One approach on deciding how many servers to schedule requires minimizing the cost of scheduling servers plus the cost of customer waiting time. This approach is appropriate when the cost of customer waiting time is known, such as the cost of drivers waiting for their trucks to be unloaded. Since it is often difficult to measure the cost of waiting in consumer situations, an alternate approach is to set the number of servers so that customer waiting time will never exceed an established maximum time. In many service businesses, this is the approach that is followed. We will have more to say about these issues in a later chapter. To complete the description of the output of our banking simulation models, we wish to present another important queuing relationship.

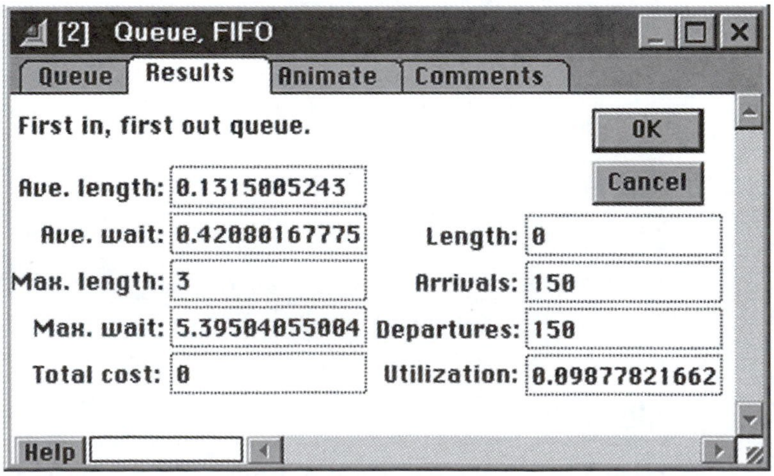

**Figure 13.24** Screen Shot of *Queue, FIFO* Results Tab after Running BANK5T.mox

## Little's Law

There is an important relationship between LQ and WQ that is sometimes called the fundamental theorem of queuing or Little's Law (after John D. C. Little). It is simply this:

$$\text{Little's Law: LQ} = \lambda(\text{WQ}).$$

This relationship is independent of the number of servers and the probability distributions describing the arrival and service processes. We fondly refer to Little's Law as the "$E = mc^2$ of queuing." Just as the square of the speed of light is the proportionality constant between energy and matter, the arrival rate is the proportionality constant between average queue length and average waiting time.

In running a simulation model, the empirical results will closely approximate Little's Law if the simulation has been run for a "long enough" period of time so that the behavior of the simulated system is stable. We call this stability condition *steady state*.

To demonstrate Little's Law, recall that LQ equals 2.16 customers and WQ is 5.99 minutes in our four-server simulation run. Since WQ is expressed in minutes, we need to express $\lambda$ in minutes. Since $1/\lambda = 3$ minutes, $\lambda = 1/3$ customers/minute. Applying Little's Law would lead us to predict that LQ = (1/3) * 5.99 = 2.00, which is close to our simulated result of 2.16. You might try simulating BANK4T.mox for a very long period of time to become convinced that the closeness of these results is no accident.

We will provide a simple illustration (not a proof) of why Little's Law works (for a proof see Little (1961)). Suppose $\lambda = 2$ arrivals per minute. Assume that there is no random variation in the arrival rate, so that two customers arrive *every* minute. Further assume that each person who enters the queue waits exactly the *same* amount of time in the queue, say three minutes. This is equivalent to assuming that WQ = 3 minutes.

Now consider what happens to the queue length during the 10th minute as shown in Figure 13.25. The two people who arrived during minute 10 enter the queue and remain in the queue for minutes 11 and 12. The two people who arrived during minute 9 are still in the queue, as are the people who arrived during minute 8. Therefore, there are a total of six people in the queue during minute 10. The same argument holds for every minute except the first two, since "steady state" does not occur until minute 3. This argument shows that LQ = $\lambda$(WQ), that is, 6 = 2(3), assuming no randomness. Note that

| | | | Queue length by minute | | | | | | |
|---|---|---|---|---|---|---|---|---|---|
| 2 arrivals during minute | ... | 10 | 11 | 12 | 13 | 14 | 15 | ... |
| 8 | | 2 | – | | | | | |
| 9 | | 2 | 2 | – | | | | |
| 10 | | 2 | 2 | 2 | – | | | |
| 11 | | | 2 | 2 | 2 | – | | |
| 12 | | | | 2 | 2 | 2 | – | |
| 13 | | | | | 2 | 2 | 2 | |
| 14 | | | | | | 2 | 2 | |
| 15 | | | | | | | 2 | |
| Total number in queue | ... | 6 | 6 | 6 | 6 | 6 | 6 | ... |

**Figure 13.25** Illustration of Little's Law Assuming No Randomness

Little's Law also holds for the service area and the complete system. That is, LS = $\lambda$(WS), and LT = $\lambda$(WT).

## Statistics and Confidence Intervals

### Confidence Intervals

As we mentioned earlier in this chapter, it is important to make multiple runs of a simulation model to improve the estimates of key queuing statistics such as the average number of people waiting in line and the average amount of time people wait in line. In practice, confidence intervals should also be computed to clarify the interpretation of simulation output data. Using point estimates can be misleading if confidence intervals are very wide relative to the size of the point estimates. As a result decision makers must consider how values within this range affect their decisions. All of these objectives can be accomplished by adding the *Queue Stats* block from the *Statistics.lix* library (no submenu) to any Extend model. This block is not connected to any other block in the simulation and can be placed anywhere in the model. Statistics from any type of queuing block will automatically appear as output in the dialog box. You must select the Append new updates and Update at end of simulation options in the dialog box to produce the desired results.

Suppose we want to make 25 runs of BANK4T.mox and compute 95% confidence intervals for LQ and WQ. The Number of runs location in the *Run, Simulation Setup* window is set to 25. This model is shown as Figure 13.26 and in a file called BANK4TSTATS.mox. The two differences between BANK4T.mox and BANK4TSTATS.mox are that the *Queue Stats* block appears in BANK4TSTATS.mox and the number of runs is 25 in BANK4TSTATS.mox.

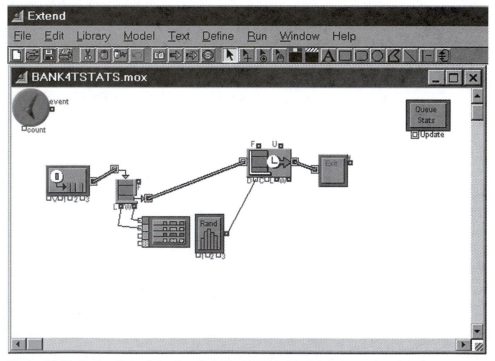

**Figure 13.26** Screen Shot of the Complete Banking Model with a *Queue Stats* Block (BANK4TSTATS.mox)

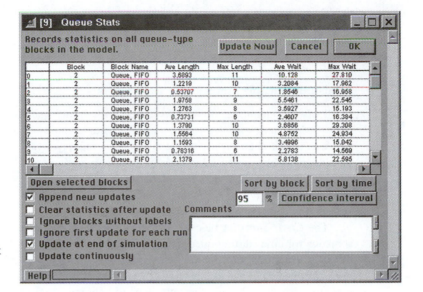

**Figure 13.27** Screen Shot of the Dialog Box for the *Queue Stats* Block Showing the Results of the Individual Runs

After running the simulation, double click on the *Queue Stats* block to see the results of each individual run. The average and maximum number of people in line and the average and maximum wait in line results of the first 11 runs (run number 0 through 10) are shown in Figure 13.27. Click on Confidence Interval to produce a confidence interval for each statistic. A 95% confidence interval for LQ is 1.91 +/− 0.87 (Figure 13.28), and indicates in our example there is a 95% probability that the true population value for LQ is between 1.04 and 2.78.

Clearly, increasing the number of runs will reduce the width of the confidence interval since we will have more sample data and will thus be more confident in the results. Increasing the confidence level from 95% to 99% will increase the width since the interval must be wider for us to be more confident in the results. For example, if we change

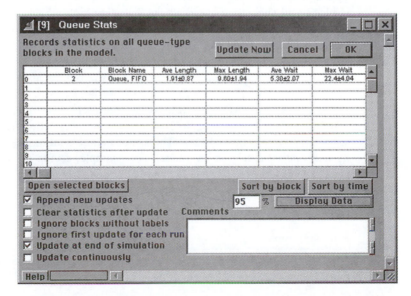

**Figure 13.28** Screen Shot of the Dialog Box for the *Queue Stats* Block Showing the 95% Confidence Intervals

the 95% confidence interval to a 99% confidence interval in the *Queue Stats* block and select Display Data and then Confidence Interval we see that the 99% confidence interval for LQ is 1.91 +/− 1.18. This means that there is a 99% probability that the true population value for LQ is between 0.73 and 3.09.

### Adjusting Queuing Statistics for Cold Starts

In all of our queuing examples we started with empty queues and empty service facilities. The problem with this is that the first customer did not have to wait in line since no one was in the queue when they arrived. As a matter of fact, the first few customers of the day probably waited a little less in line than customers who arrived later in the day. As a result, we may not want to include statistics from the first few customers in line since they may not be typical. To address this issue, we can start computing statistics after the system has been operating for a period of time.

The *Clear Statistics* block from the *Statistics.lix* library (no submenu) will adjust our statistics for cold starting queues. The *Clear Statistics* block is not connected to any other block in the model. If you want to start computing statistics after 30 minutes of operation, simply set the Clear statistics at time location to 30. The queuing statistics should now increase since the first few customers did not have to wait as long in the queue. However, if you simulate for a long enough period of time, this adjustment should not make much of a difference in the statistics. Our purpose here is to show how this issue can be addressed if desired.

## Hierarchical Models

Extend has the capability of grouping blocks hierarchically so that a simplified overview of a model can be shown. This is particularly useful when making a presentation to anyone who is not interested in the details of the model, but they may be interested in the general flow of the model. In Extend, building a hierarchical block is accomplished by highlighting a set of blocks, and selecting the *Model* and *Make Selection Hierarchical* commands. A dialog box asks if you wish to name the block and to click on the Make H-block button to confirm. Extend will then replace the highlighted blocks with an empty square with the proper connections to other blocks in the model. Double clicking on the H-block will show the Extend blocks that were highlighted.

After highlighting a hierarchical block, select *Model* and *Open Hierarchical Block Structure* to modify the H-block as can be seen in Figure 13.29. The user can expand the window in the upper left-hand corner of Figure 13.29 and replace the box with another shape or graphic and add text and color as desired. A disadvantage of using photographic images is that the size of the file can get very large.

BANK4THIERARCHICAL.mox is a representation of BANK4T.mox that has a hierarchical block for each of the major activities—generate arrivals, wait in line, receive service, and exit (Figure 13.30). The use of hierarchical blocks further improves the clarity and understanding of the model. For example, seeing a customer at the door of the bank should indicate that this hierarchical block is used to generate arrivals.

## Model Input and Output

### The Notebook

Extend has many features that are used to improve on the presentation of model input and output. The first one that we will discuss is an option called Notebook where model pa-

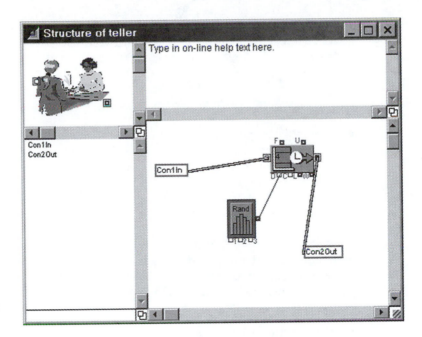

**Figure 13.29** Screen Shot of Service H-Block of the Bank Model

rameters, text, and graphics can be placed. To access the notebook feature, select the _Model_ and _Open Notebook_ commands to open a notebook window. The notebook is valuable for summarizing and presenting model input and output. The _cloning_ feature is used to capture items that can be placed into the notebook.

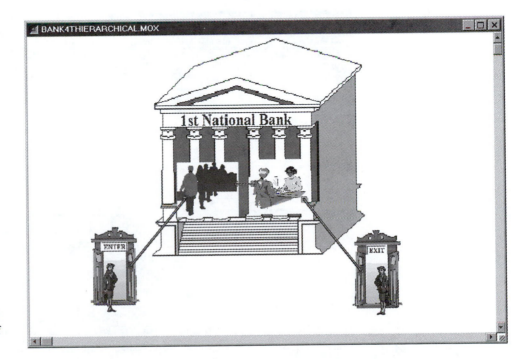

**Figure 13.30** Screen Shot of the Hierarchical Block Representation of the Bank Model

For example, suppose we want to place the mean interarrival time value into the notebook. First, open the *Generator* dialog box, then select the cloning tool from the menu toolbar:

Next, drag the average interarrival time clone (a "boxed" 3) from the dialog box to the notebook. Other cloned items can be added in a similar fashion. To add text to the notebook, remember to click on the main cursor:

To move text or resize a text box in the notebook, the main cursor must be active. To move or resize a cloned item in the notebook, the cloning tool must be active. An example of using the notebook is shown in BANK4TNOTE.mox. A screen shot of the complete model and notebook is given in Figure 13.31.

### Excel Spreadsheet Interface

Extend allows the user to send output to a spreadsheet. We can modify BANK4TSTATS.mox and send the 25 WQ values to a spreadsheet. This is accomplished by first connecting the WQ output connector from *Queue, FIFO* to the input connector of the *Mean & Variance* (*Generic.lix*, *Statistics*) block. This block will compute the WQ value for each simulation run. Next, connect the M output connector (the WQ value) of the *Mean & Variance* block to the input connector of *Data Send* (*Ipc.lix*, none).

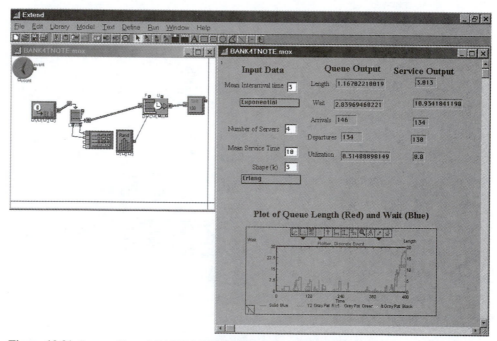

**Figure 13.31** Screen Shot of BANK4TNOTE.mox Illustrating the Notebook

As shown in Figure 13.32, the name and location of the Excel spreadsheet in the Spreadsheet File Name box must be specified within the dialog box of *Data Send* (Data Send tab). Our Excel file is called bank4toutput.xls and is assumed to reside in the same folder as our Extend file. Note that this file must be open when running the simulation. The Send data to: Row and Column values are both 1, meaning that the output from the first run will be sent to the row 1 and column 1 cell in the spreadsheet. We also checked the box: If neither row nor column connector are used increment row every, and changed this setting from step to run since we want the WQ value for each run to be sent to the spreadsheet. The WQ results from the 25 runs will be sent to column 1 and rows 1 through 25, respectively. These results also appear in the *Queue Stats* block. The complete model is shown in Figure 13.33 and is in a file called BANK4TEXCEL.mox.

### Extend's Report Generating Feature

Extend also allows the user to send output to a text file instead of a spreadsheet. First select the *Run* and *Generate Report* commands, and then highlight the blocks whose information should be included in the report. We will send the information from the *Queue, FIFO*

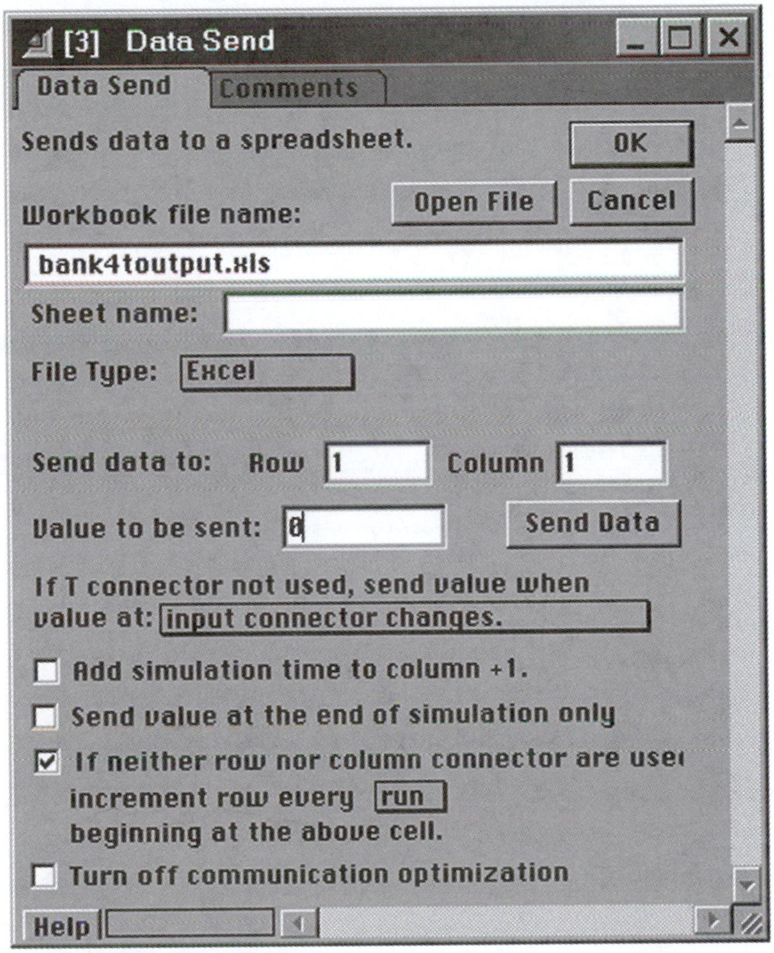

**Figure 13.32** Screen Shot of the Dialog Box of the *Data Send* Block after Selecting the Data Send Tab

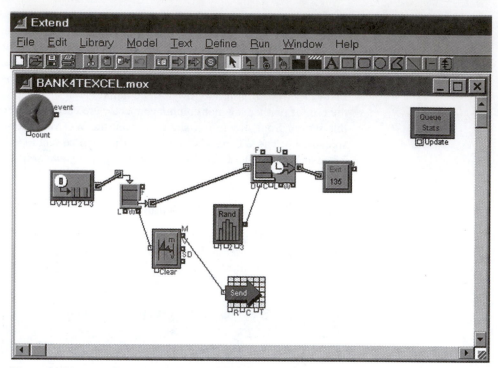

**Figure 13.33** Screen Shot of the BANK4TEXCEL.mox Model

```
Text File "report.txt"
Extend Statistics Report - 7/10/2001 3:39:27 PM
Run #0


QUEUES_____
Block Label    Number Name        Depart  Arrive  AvgLeng AvgWait MaxLeng MaxWait Renege  Util    Cost
-------------- ------ ----------- ------- ------- ------- ------- ------- ------- ------- ------- -------
               2      FIFO        179     184     4.00315 10.5974 11      30.262          0.81299


*************************************************************


Extend Statistics Report - 7/10/2001 3:39:28 PM
Run #1


QUEUES_____
Block Label    Number Name        Depart  Arrive  AvgLeng AvgWait MaxLeng MaxWait Renege  Util    Cost
-------------- ------ ----------- ------- ------- ------- ------- ------- ------- ------- ------- -------
               2      FIFO        170     176     2.96753 7.77338 13      26.4711         0.56377


*************************************************************


Extend Statistics Report - 7/10/2001 3:39:28 PM
Run #2


QUEUES_____
Block Label    Number Name        Depart  Arrive  AvgLeng AvgWait MaxLeng MaxWait Renege  Util    Cost
-------------- ------ ----------- ------- ------- ------- ------- ------- ------- ------- ------- -------
               2      FIFO        159     174     3.03894 6.96255 16      35.4679         0.54068
```

**Figure 13.34** Screen Shot of the Report Results for three runs of a Sample Model

block to the report. After this block is highlighted, simply select the *Run* and *Add Selected to Report* commands. We also recommend that you select the *Show Reporting Blocks* command. This will list the reporting blocks in the model. If you are only interested in reporting the statistics, then select the *Run*, *Report Type*, and *Statistics* commands. After the model is run, the results will be sent to a file whose default name is report.txt. Figure 13.34 shows partial results from a sample report.

## SUMMARY

In this chapter we have seen how simulation with Extend enables the modeling of situations where one or more of the factors are probabilistic. We have illustrated the process of building queuing simulations that model the processes of generating arrivals, entering the queue, servicing the arrivals, and exiting them from the system. We have demonstrated how arrival data can be collected and fitted to a probability distribution. Two important queuing relationships have also been described. The first is the relationship between the arrival and service rates that determine the minimum number of servers necessary to prevent continual buildup in the queue. The second is Little's Law that shows how the average queue length and average waiting time in the queue are related through the arrival rate. The importance of fully understanding and correctly interpreting the results of a simulation analysis was also introduced and will be more fully explored in future chapters. Confidence intervals and cold start concepts have also been discussed. We have also shown how models could be represented hierarchically. Model input and output features, specifically, the notebook feature, interfacing with Excel spreadsheets, and Extend's report generating feature were also introduced. In the next chapter, we will present many model variations and explain how Extend can be used to simulate these situations. You will once again see the concept of the building block approach in action as we expand on the basic banking example.

## HOMEWORK PROBLEMS

**1.** The LAWN and garden center has a basic queuing system in which customers arrive, wait in line, receive service, and exit. The average interarrival time is 75 seconds and the average service time is 135 seconds. Assume that interarrival times are exponentially distributed and service times are Erlang distributed with a k value of 5. Also, assume a FIFO queue discipline.

**(a)** Determine the minimum number of servers needed to stop the line from continually increasing.

**(b)** Using the minimum number of servers from part a, simulate this queuing system for an eight-hour workday. Record the values of WQ, LQ, and server utilization that you obtained.

**2.** The Super MART grocery store has a basic queuing system in which customers arrive, wait in line, receive service, and exit. The average interarrival time is 18 seconds and the average service time is three minutes. The interarrival time distribution is exponential and the service time distribution is Erlang with a k value of seven. Assume a FIFO queue discipline.

**(a)** Determine the minimum number of servers needed to stop the line from continually increasing.

**(b)** Using the minimum number of servers from part a, simulate this queuing system for a one-hour period. Record the values of WQ, LQ, and server utilization that you obtained.

**(c)** Show that the simulated results closely approximates Little's Law LQ = λ(WQ).

**3.** The PLEX Movie Theatre has a basic queuing system in which customers arrive, wait in line, receive service, and exit. They have gathered and analyzed arrival and service time data. The average interarrival time is 12 seconds and the average service time is 38 seconds. The interarrival time distribution is exponential and the service time distribution is Erlang with a k value of 2. Assume a FIFO queue discipline.

**(a)** Determine the minimum number of servers needed to stop the line from continually increasing.

**(b)** Using the minimum number of servers from part a, simulate this queuing system for a one-hour period. Record the values of WQ, LQ, and server utilization that you obtained.

**(c)** Create a notebook for this model that has similar information as BANK4TNOTE.mox.

**4.** The BURGER Barn has a basic queuing system where customers arrive, wait in line, receive service, and exit. The average interarrival time is 2 minutes and the average service time is 5.1 minutes. The interarrival time distribution is exponential and the service time distribution is Erlang with a k value of 3. Assume a FIFO queue discipline.

**(a)** Determine the minimum number of servers needed to stop the line from continually increasing.

**(b)** Using the minimum number of servers from part a, simulate this queuing system for an eight-hour period and repeat for 25 runs. Show 95% and 99% confidence intervals for WQ.

**(c)** Can you state with 95% confidence that the true population value for WQ is less than four minutes? Explain.

## REFERENCES

Geer Mountain Software Corporation, Stat::Fit, South Kent, CT, 2002.

Gross, D. and C. M. Harris, *Fundamentals of Queueing Theory*, 3rd ed., New York, Wiley, 1997.

Imagine That, Inc., *Extend*, San Jose, CA, 2001.

Law, A. M. and W. D. Kelton, *Simulation Modeling & Analysis*, 3rd ed., New York, McGraw-Hill, 2000.

Little, J. D. C. "A proof for the queueing formula $L = \lambda W$," *Operations Research*, Vol. 9, No. 3, pp. 383–387, 1961.

*New York Times*, *"Conquering Those Killer Queues*, by N. R. Kleinfield, 25 September 1988.

Washington Post, "Clues on Queues: What's in Our Minds About Those Lines?" by M. Gladwell, 14 December 1992.

# Chapter 14

# Process Simulation Extensions Using Extend

## INTRODUCTION

In the previous chapter we introduced Extend through a basic motivating example set in a bank. We now illustrate the value of the building block approach by presenting several extensions of this example. Each of these extensions introduces additional issues in process simulation that can be modeled in Extend, and which in turn can be combined or adapted to form additional models. Although we use a bank as the context for our discussion, many of the ideas and models can be easily adapted to other situations. For additional examples of process simulation applications, the reader is referred to Bayus et al. (1985), Brigandi et al. (1994), Dean et al. (1994), Landauer and Becker (1989), Martin (1998), and Saltzman and Mehrotra (2001).

## EXTENSIONS OF THE BANKING SIMULATION MODEL

The basic banking model described in the previous chapter shows that simulation can be a powerful tool to help solve problems related to items waiting in lines. However, there are often other characteristics of a queuing environment that need to be considered in practice. Simulation modeling can address these needs when applied to additional variations of our basic banking models. In general, we will not discuss the results of the models, but explain how additional blocks can be used to take advantage of the power of Extend to model these situations (Imagine That, Inc. 2001).

### Reneging

From experience we know that most customers will not wait in a line indefinitely. Suppose that we have observed that any customer will leave the bank if they wait more than four minutes in the queue. In queuing parlance, this behavior is called *reneging*. The *Queue, FIFO* block does not allow the customer to renege. However, we can model this situation if the *Queue, FIFO* block is replaced by the *Queue, Reneging* block found in the *Mfg.lix* library and the *Queues* submenu. Set the *Renege time* to 4 in the *Queue, Reneging* dialog box (Queue tab, Figure 14.1). Since customers who renege leave the bank, we attach an additional *Exit* block to the left item out connector to keep track of the customers who renege. This model is shown as Figure 14.2 and in a file called BANK4TFR.mox. The FR in the file name stands for fixed reneging, since the renege time is four minutes for all customers.

In reality, we know that everyone does not have the same attitude about waiting, so it is unrealistic to assume that the renege time is the same for everyone. It is probably

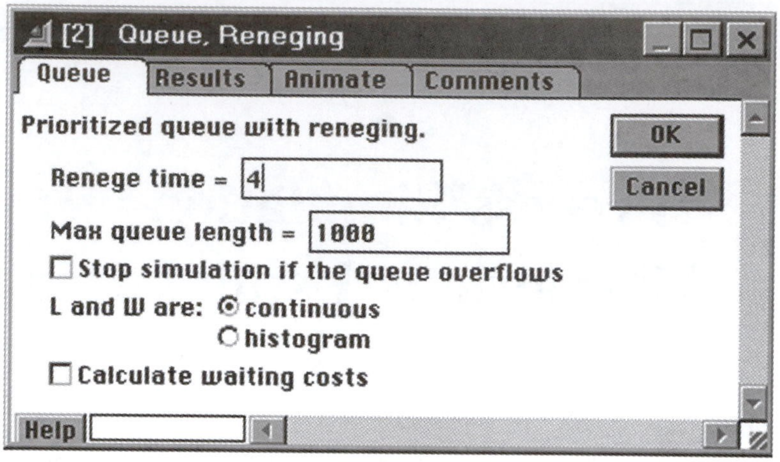

**Figure 14.1** Screen Shot of the Dialog Box for the *Queue, Reneging* Block after Selecting the Queue Tab

more realistic to assume that renege time is random. Suppose we gathered renege time data for (say) 50 people, analyzed the data in Stat::Fit, and found that renege time is exponentially distributed with a mean of four minutes. It is relatively easy to modify the model just developed to accommodate this change. As a matter of fact, based on work that was done earlier with random service times, you may have already figured out how to make this change. Simply connect an *Input Random Number* block (exponential

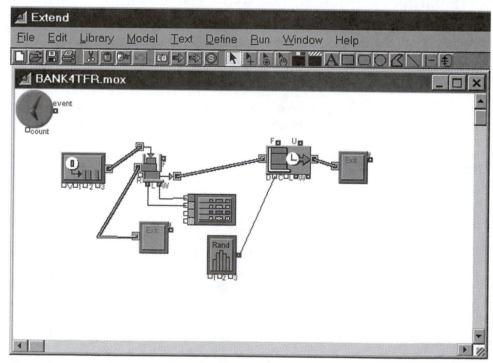

**Figure 14.2** Screen Shot of the Complete Banking Model with Fixed Reneging, BANK4TFR.mox

distribution with a mean of four) to the value in connector labeled <u>R</u> in the *Queue, Reneging* block.

It is probably becoming clearer that the connectors are used to override any preset values in a dialog box and that this greatly adds to the power of Extend. This model is shown as Figure 14.3 and in the file called BANK4TRR.mox. Here RR stands for random reneging.

More reneging is expected in the random reneging model than the fixed reneging model even though the average values are the same. Since the exponential distribution is skewed to the right in the random reneging case, there is a greater chance that the reneging time will be *less* than four minutes leading to *more* reneging. By checking the dialog boxes of the *Exit* blocks that are connected to the *Queue, Reneging* blocks in the two reneging models, you will see that 10 people reneged in the fixed reneging model and 25 reneged in the random renege model.

## Balking

As we saw in the previous section, customers may choose to leave the line if they wait too long. In addition, they may refuse to join the queue in the first place if the line is too long. This latter behavior is called *balking*. In similar style to the reneging case, we will develop fixed balking and random balking models. That is, first assume that any customer will balk when there are five people already in line; then allow balking to be random with a mean of five.

To develop an Extend model for fixed balking (*without reneging*), simply use the *Prioritizer* block found in the *Discrete Event.lix* library and the *Routing* submenu. This block is placed between the *Generator* and the *Queue, FIFO* blocks. There are five output

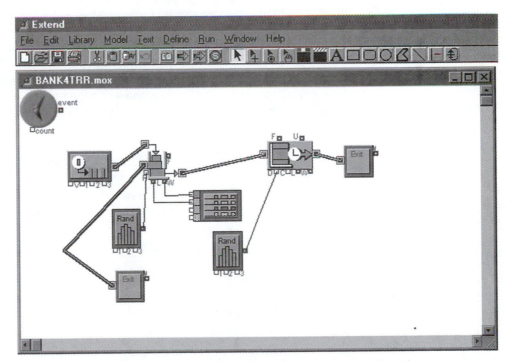

**Figure 14.3** Screen Shot of the Complete Banking Model with Random Reneging, BANK4TRR.mox

connectors on the right side of the *Prioritizer* block that are used to route the customer to up to five different locations, depending on the priority values (a through e) in the dialog box (the Prioritizer tab). These priority values correspond to the five output connectors on the right side of the block. We use the a and b default priority values of 1 and 2, respectively, as shown in Figure 14.4. The customer will be sent to the top connector (which goes to *Queue, FIFO*) if that block accepts the customer, and otherwise to the second connector to exit. Since balking always occurs when there are five customers in the queue, set the Maximum queue length = 5, in the *Queue, FIFO* dialog box (Queue tab). If there are five items in the queue, the *Queue, FIFO* block sends the customer back to the *Prioritizer* block where the customer moves to the second connector, balks, and then exits. This model is shown as Figure 14.5 and in the file called BANK4TFB.mox. Here FB stands for fixed balking.

It should be obvious that the maximum length of the queue in this situation is five since balking will always occur if there are five people in the queue. This result can be seen in the dialog box of the *Queue, FIFO* block (Results tab) as shown in Figure 14.6 (see Max. length).

As we saw with the reneging model, everyone does not have the same attitude about waiting. This means that balking is different for different people and is probably random. Some people are more patient, others are less patient—and you know who you are! Let's talk about how we could determine the shape of the balking distribution in practice. In the reneging example, we simply observed people reneging and then analyzed that data. However, there is no way to estimate the probability that a customer will balk by direct observation. For example, a customer might balk when the line length is eight, but would that customer have balked if the line length were seven or lower? Observation, in conjunction with a consumer survey is probably needed.

Assume that we did the proper analysis and found that the random balking threshold is fitted to an Erlang distribution with a mean of five and a k value of five. We then modify BANK4TFB.mox by first replacing the *Prioritizer* block with the *Select DE Output* block found in the *Discrete Event.lix* library and the *Routing* submenu. In the dialog box of this block (the Select Output tab), select Chooses an output based on "select" value. Then enter 0 in the box labeled Top output is chosen by "select" = (Figure 14.7). If the value of "select" is 0, the customer will go to the block connected to the top output. In this case, it is the *Exit* block, meaning that the customer balked. If the value of "select" is 1 (that is,

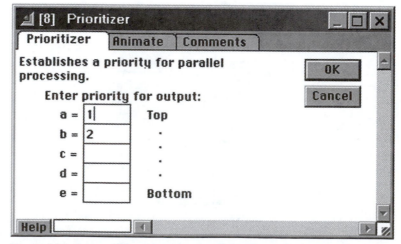

**Figure 14.4** Screen Shot of the Dialog Box for the *Prioritizer* Block

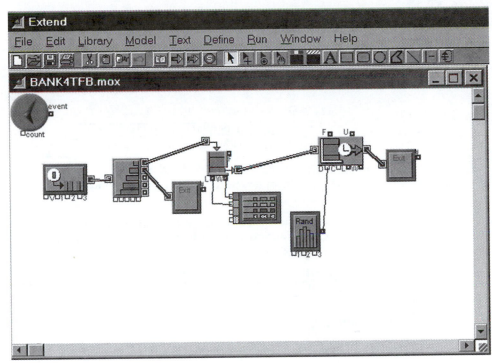

**Figure 14.5** Screen Shot of the Complete Banking Model with Fixed Balking, BANK4TFB.mox

1 more than 0), the customer will go to the block connected to the bottom output. In this case, the customer moves to *Queue, FIFO*, indicating that the customer enters the queue.

Next, we must determine the value of "select." Here we use the *Decision* block from the *Generic.lix* library and the *Decisions* submenu. This block provides the logic needed to make the balking decision. The balking decision is made by comparing the random threshold balking value (from the Erlang distribution) to the number of people currently in line (L). We connect the value output connector labeled L in the *Queue, FIFO* block to the value in connector labeled A in the *Decision* block. We also connect an *Input*

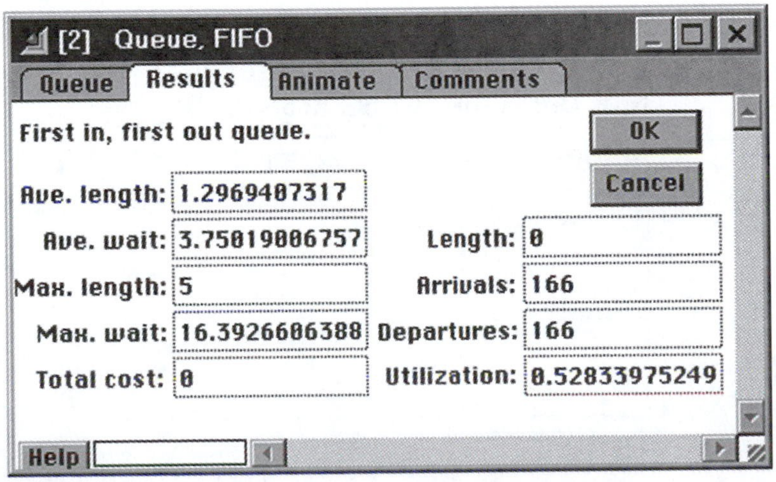

**Figure 14.6** Screen Shot of the *Queue, FIFO* Results Tab

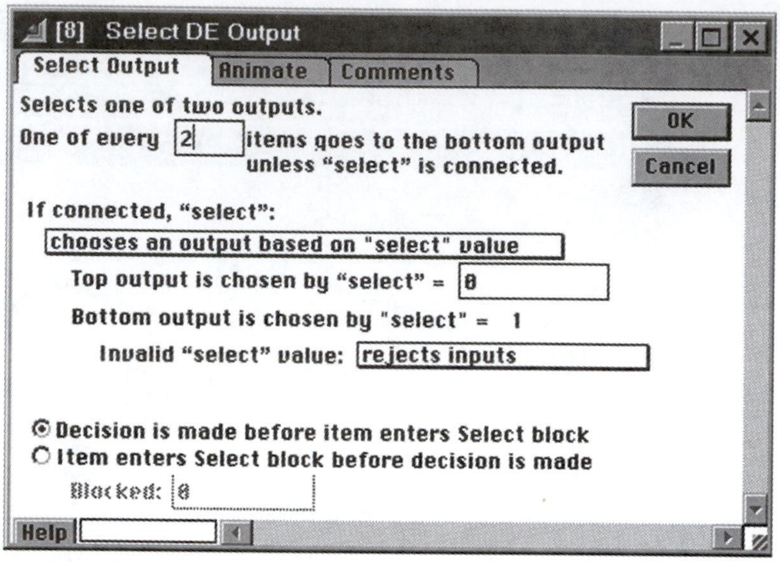

**Figure 14.7** Screen Shot of the Dialog Box for the *Select DE Output* Block

*Random Number* block generating the balking value to the value in connector labeled B in the *Decision* block. In the dialog box of the *Decision* block, select the option If input A < B (Figure 14.8). This means that if A < B, then Y = 1, and this value is passed from the Y value output connector of the *Decision* block to the "select" value input connector of the *Select DE Output* block. Otherwise, "select" remains as 0. In simple English, if A (the current line length) is less than B (the balking threshold), a 1 is passed from Y to the Select connector, otherwise "select" remains as 0. Remember that a "select" value of 0 means that balking occurs and a "select" value of 1 means that no balking occurs.

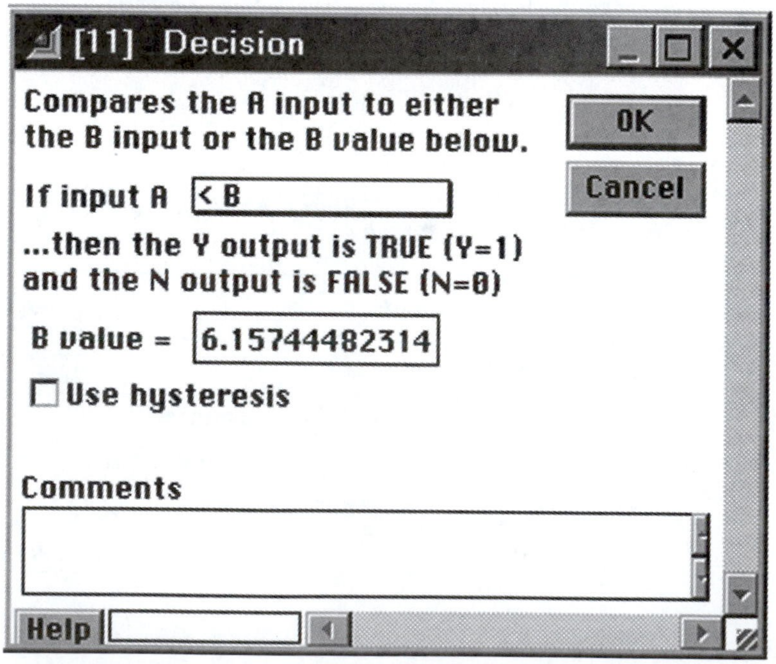

**Figure 14.8** Screen Shot of the Dialog Box for the *Decision* Block

As shown in Figure 14.8, the next customer entering the bank balks if 6.15 or more customers are in the queue. If the number of customers in line (or A) is 4, select is 1 and balking does not occur (bottom output in *Select DE Output*). However, if A were 7 and the random threshold value were 6.15, then select is 0 and balking does occur (top output in *Select DE Output*). The random balking model is shown as Figure 14.9 and in the file called BANK4TRB.mox. Here RB stands for random balking.

Instead of directly connecting the L connector of the *Queue, FIFO* block to the A connector of the *Decision* block, we use a named connection. Select the Text tool on the toolbar (A), click where you want to insert a named connection, type in the desired text, such as length, and click anywhere else in the model when finished. Click on the black arrow to the right of the red stop button on the toolbar to return to normal use. The benefit of using named connections is that you can eliminate the need to connect blocks with lines. As a result, models do not look as cluttered and are easier to comprehend when named connections are used.

## Interarrival Times Change During the Simulation

Another common occurrence in many waiting systems is that the interarrival times change during the course of the simulation. That is, certain times of the day or certain days of the week, month, or year are busier than others. As we will see, Extend can easily handle this situation.

Suppose interarrival time data for customers coming to our bank was collected in two-hour increments. During the course of a workweek, 100 interarrival times between the hours of 9:00 and 11:00 A.M. and an additional 100 interarrival times between the hours of 11:00 and 1:00 P.M. was collected. Figure 14.10 provides a plot of both sets of observed interarrival times. Note that the pattern of interarrival times is quite different

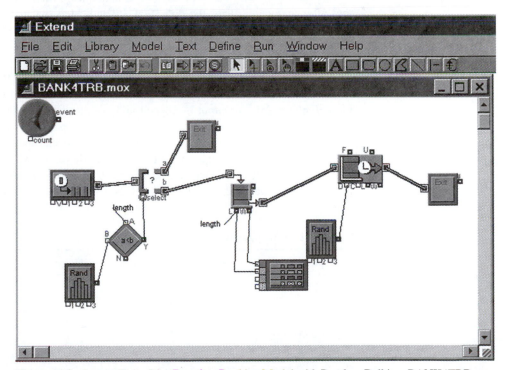

**Figure 14.9**  Screen Shot of the Complete Banking Model with Random Balking, BANK4TRB.mox

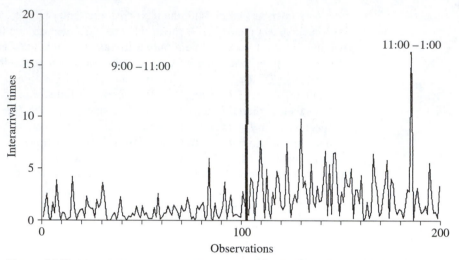

**Figure 14.10** Plot of 100 Interarrival Times from Two Different Time Periods

over the two time periods. Specifically, the interarrival times are generally lower during the first two-hour period compared to the second two-hour period, which implies that there are more customers arriving during the first two-hour period. As a result, it would be incorrect to fit all 200 observations to one probability distribution. Instead, analyze each set of 100 observations separately using Stat::Fit, since it is quite likely that each time period will have different parameters and possibly even different probability distributions.

Stat::Fit reveals that the data over both time periods fit the exponential distribution; however, the mean for the first time period is 1.00, and the mean for the second period is 3.00. Continuing with this process, collect data during the remainder of the day. Suppose that after analyzing all of the data, Stat::Fit indicated that the average interarrival time varies during a typical Friday (from 9:00 A.M. to 9:00 P.M.) as shown in Table 14.1.

We can easily incorporate this information into an Extend model by using the *Input Data* block from the *Generic.lix* library and the *Inputs/Outputs* submenu. The dialog box is set up as a table (Input Data tab), with the times placed in the Time column and the average interarrival time appearing in the Y output column (Figure 14.11). Also, keep the default setting as Output is stepped and *not* interpolated. This implies that the mean interarrival time remains constant during each time period. Note that the interval times are set at the left endpoint of the interval. It is critical that the final time in the Time column be greater than or equal to the time the simulation ends.

The value output connector of the *Input Data* block is connected to the 1 value input connector (that is, the mean or $1/\lambda$) of the *Generator* block. As usual, the value passed

**Table 14.1** Changing Average Interarrival Times During a Workday

| Time period | Time (minutes) | $1/\lambda$ (minutes) |
| --- | --- | --- |
| 9:00–11:00 | 0–120 | 1 |
| 11:00–1:00 | 120–240 | 3 |
| 1:00–3:00 | 240–360 | 1 |
| 3:00–5:00 | 360–480 | 3 |
| 5:00–9:00 | 480–720 | 1 |

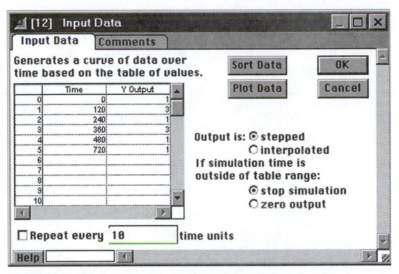

**Figure 14.11** Screen Shot of the Dialog Box for the *Input Data* Block

from the *Input Data* block overrides any preset value appearing in the mean of the dialog box of the *Generator* block. This model is shown as Figure 14.12 and in the file called BANK4TIC.mox. Here IC stands for interarrivals changing. By simply one block to the basic banking model, we have greatly added to its power and value.

After running the model, the plotter provides valuable information about the wait in line and the line length, as shown in Figure 14.13. During the peak periods, $1/\lambda = 1$

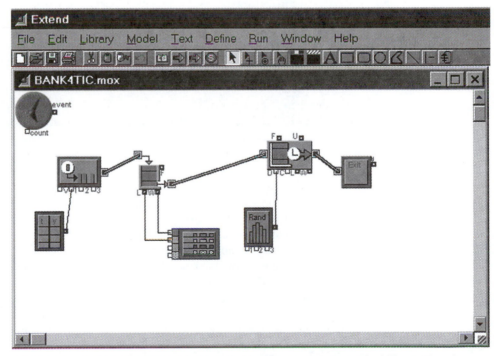

**Figure 14.12** Screen Shot of the Complete Banking Model with Interarrival Times Changing, BANK4TIC.mox

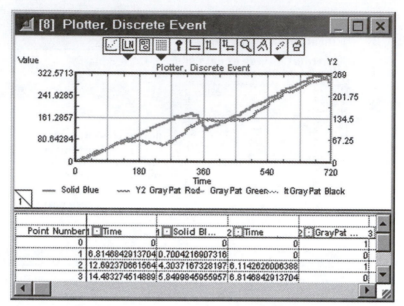

**Figure 14.13** Screen Shot of Plotter for Banking Model with Changing Interarrival Times

minute per customer, while $1/\mu = 10$ minutes per customer. Remember the formula that we use to determine the minimum number of servers needed to prevent an ever-expanding queue is N = the smallest integer greater than $(1/\mu)/(1/\lambda)$. The implication is that we need 11 and *not* 10 tellers during the first two hours. As a result, the queue will build since we only have four tellers during this peak period. As expected, we see in Figure 14.13 that the queue builds during the first two hours. After the peak period the queue declines a little because $1/\lambda = 3$ minutes per customer, so we need at least N = 4 tellers during the off-period, which is the number of servers available. The solution to this problem is pretty clear: we need at least 11 tellers during the peak periods and four tellers during the off-peak periods.

BANK4TIC.mox can be modified to allow the number of tellers to change over time by using another *Input Data* block. The output connector of this block is linked to the C connector (capacity) of the *Activity, Multiple* block since this connector determines the number of servers available. The dialog box for the *Input Data* block (Figure 14.14) shows that we have 11 tellers during peak periods and four servers during off-peak periods. The model is shown in Figure 14.15 and in the file called BANKITC.mox. Here ITC stands for interarrival times and capacity changing.

Some companies do not change the number of servers at specific times of the day, but have a policy to adjust the number of servers based on the number of people waiting in line. Suppose our bank has decided to have four tellers open when the queue length is less than or equal to four and 11 tellers otherwise. This policy can be accomplished using the *Conversion Table* block from the *Generic.lix* library and the *Math* submenu. The dialog box is set up as a table, with L values (from *Queue, FIFO*) placed in the x in column and the number of tellers placed in the y out column (Figure 14.16). We end the table with an LQ value of 100 to cover all possibilities (although this is not shown in the table). The table indicates that if zero through 4 people are in line then four tellers will be used; however, if five or more people are in line then 11 tellers will be used.

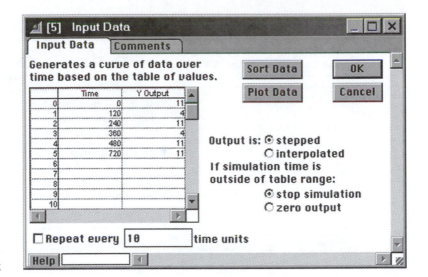

**Figure 14.14** Screen Shot of the Dialog Box for the *Input Data* Block

The L value out connector from *Queue, FIFO* is connected to the value input connector of the *Conversion Table*, whereas the value output connector of the *Conversion Table* is connected to the C value input connector of the *Activity, Multiple* block. Remember that since the C value represents the number of servers, this model checks the number of people in line (L) and makes a decision about the number of servers to have open. This model is shown as Figure 14.17 and in the file called BANKITCL.mox. Here ITCL stands for interarrival times and capacity changing based on the number of people in line (L).

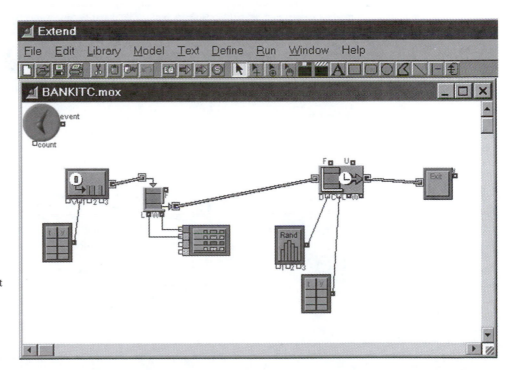

**Figure 14.15** Screen Shot of the Complete Banking Model with Interarrival Times and Number of Servers Changing, BANKITC.mox

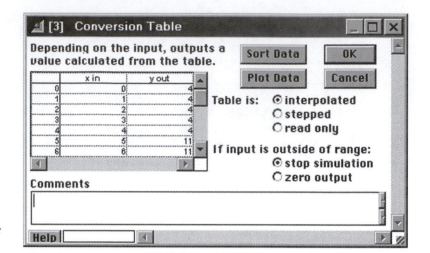

**Figure 14.16** Screen Shot of the Dialog Box for the *Conversion Table* Block

## Computing Service Levels

There are situations where a manager might want to know what percentage of customers waited in line more than a specified period of time. For example, suppose that in our basic banking model we would like to know the percentage of customers who had to wait more than 10 minutes in line. This is referred to as a measure of *service level* and is computed by dividing the number of customers who waited more than 10 minutes (found in the *Holding Tank* block, *Generic.lix* library, and *Holding* submenu) by the total number of customers (found in *Count Items* block, *Discrete Event.lix* library, and *Information* submenu) that arrived. Specifically, the numerator of this ratio is determined by identifying

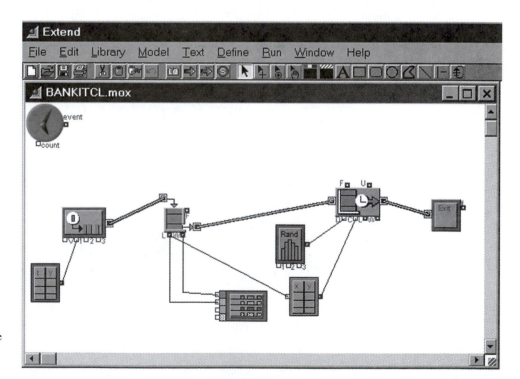

**Figure 14.17** Screen Shot of the Complete Banking Model with Changing Interarrival Times and Number of Servers Dependent on the Number of People in Line, BANKITCL.mox

(*Decision* block) and then accumulating *Holding Tank*) those customers who waited more than 10 minutes. The result is divided by the total number of customers that arrived (*Count Items* block). The percentage for each run is sent to an Excel spreadsheet called SERVLEV.xls.

In this example, we assume that Stat::Fit returns an exponential interarrival time distribution with a mean of 3, but the location parameter is 1.00. That is, the first parameter from Stat::Fit is 1 instead of the usual 0.00, which simply means that the minimum interarrival time is 1.00 and not 0.00. In a sense, this is an exponential distribution that is shifted to the right. Figure 14.18 shows a graph for this distribution. Notice that the x axis starts at 1 rather than 0.

The *Generator* block does not have a location parameter in its dialog box; however the *Input Random Number* block does. In this situation we should choose the constant distribution within the *Generator* block and the exponential distribution with a mean of 3 and a location parameter of 1 within the *Input Random Number* block. The complete model is shown as Figure 14.19 and in the file called BANKSL.mox.

## Batch Arrivals and Cycling

Suppose that a branch of our bank is situated at a corner where a bus depot is also located. As a result, this bank has noticed that customers sometimes arrive in batches after a bus has pulled into the depot. After gathering and analyzing data in Stat::Fit it was found that the interarrival time is exponentially distributed with a mean of three minutes between arrivals, and that 80% of the time there is one arrival; 15% of the time there are two arrivals; and 5% of the time there are three arrivals.

Interarrival times are generated according to an exponential distribution with a mean of three minutes by using the Generator block, as usual. To determine the *number* of arrivals in a batch, use an *Input Random Number* block choosing an *empirical table* with appropriate probabilities and values (that is, 80% 1's, 15% 2's, and 5% 3's). These values are then passed to the Value (V) connector of the *Generator* block. Next, use a *Queue, FIFO* block to create individual customers so they can be processed, then use the *Set*

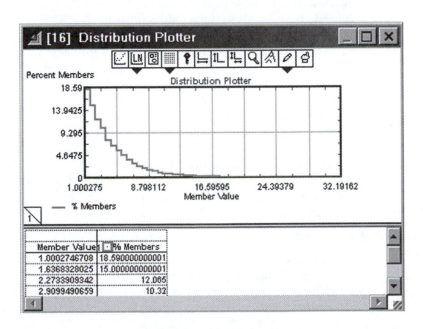

**Figure 14.18** Screen Shot of Plotter for BANKSL.mox Model

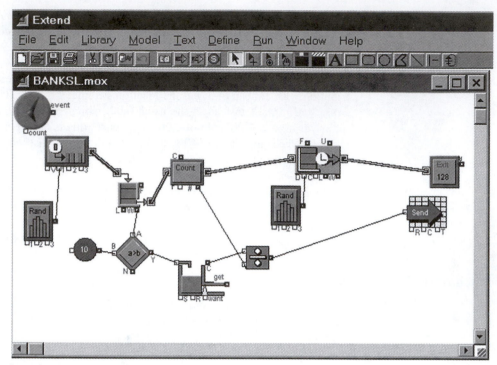

**Figure 14.19** Screen Shot of the Complete Banking Model that Computes Service Level, BANKSL.mox

*Priority* block from *Discrete Event.lix* and *Attributes* submenu to make all customers a priority 2. We will see later why this is needed. Customers then go into a *Queue, Priority* (*Discrete Event.lix*, *Queues* submenu) where they wait for service. This block orders the customers by priority, that is, all priority 1s in the front of the line and priority 2s at the end of the line. Why are priorities needed?

Suppose that after being served, 10% of the customers require a second type of banking service and 90% of the customers exit the bank. This is modeled using an *Input Random Number* block with probabilities entered through an empirical table and a *Select DE Output* block. If a customer receives this second type of service, the customer cycles back to the front of the *Queue, Priority* to receive the first service again. These customers have their priority changed to a 1 so that they go to the front of the priority queue. Both groups of customers are fed into the same queue using the *Combine* block from *Discrete Event.lix* and the *Routing* submenu. Service times for the first type of service follow an Erlang distribution with a mean of 7 and a k value of 3; the second type of service follows an Erlang with a mean of 4 and a k value of 3. This model is shown as Figure 14.20 and in the file called BANKCYCLE.mox.

## Banking Simulation with Resources

Now we model a situation where more than one type of resource may be needed to provide service. For example, consider a customer service desk at a bank where associates are available to process certain types of transactions. Unlike tellers, who must have a terminal, customer service associates share terminals since they can only process transactions

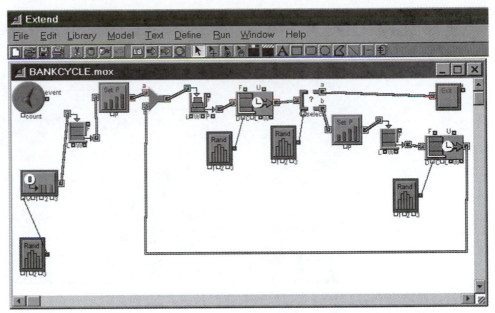

**Figure 14.20** Screen Shot of the Complete Banking Model with Batch Arrivals and Cycling, BANKCYCLE.mox

in which cash is not involved. This means that the bank does not have to provide a terminal for every associate, which is a cost-saving measure.

Suppose that customers arrive at the service desk, on average, every minute (exponential distribution); however, 70% of the customers require a service that needs an associate and a computer, and 30% require a service that only needs an associate. The average service time for customers who need an associate only is 3.5 minutes (Erlang distribution with a k value of 4). The average service time for customers that need an associate and a computer is 1.4 minutes (Erlang distribution with a k value of 3).

This bank currently has three associates and two computers. Since these resources are limited, this problem is different from all of the others that we discussed so far. For example, if a customer is first in line and requires an associate and a computer, but two associates are already busy working with the two computers, the third associate cannot help this individual since all computers are busy.

First we must define the available resources using a *Resource Pool* block from the *Discrete Event.lix* library and the *Resources* submenu. This block is not connected to any other block in the model and simply identifies the available resources. Since we have two resources for this problem—associates and computers—we need two *Resource Pool* blocks. The dialog box for the associates is shown in Figure 14.21a. We have called the resource pool "associates," and specified that initially there are three associates available. A similar block is needed to define the computer resource.

Once arrivals are generated we must determine whether they need an associate or an associate and a computer. This is accomplished with an *Input Random Number* block and a *Set Attribute* block. Think of an attribute as a customer characteristic. Alternatively, think of an attribute as a tag on a customer's back that shows one or several characteristics about that customer (gender, eye color, spending habits, etc.). In our example, we will put a 0 on the tag to indicate a customer who needs an associate only (30%) and a 1 to indicate a customer who needs an associate and a computer (70%).

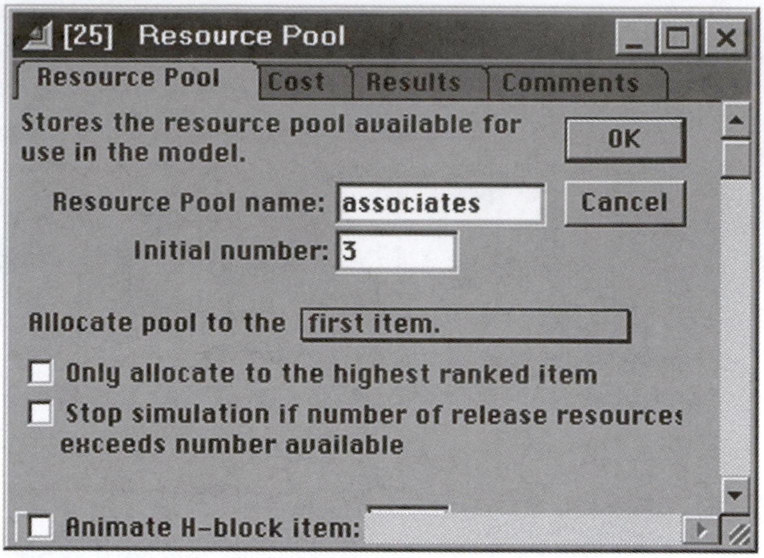

**Figure 14.21a** Screen Shot of the Dialog Box for the *Resource Pool* for Associates

As shown in Figure 14.21b, we have named the first attribute in the dialog box of the *Set Attribute* block as type (Attribute tab). To randomly determine the customer type according to the probabilities indicated, select empirical table from the Distribution box in the dialog box of an *Input Random Number* block (Distribution tab). To specify the distribution, enter 0 and 1 in the Value column of the table and .3 and .7 in the Probability column. Next, link the out connector of the *Input Random Number* block to the value in connector labeled A of the *Set Attribute* block so that the randomly generated type value is set for the arriving customer.

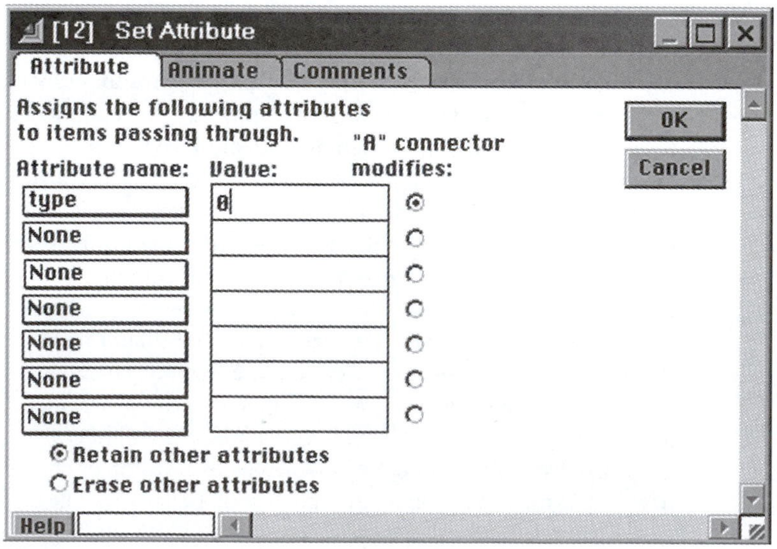

**Figure 14.21b** Screen Shot of the *Set Attribute* block after Setting Type as an Attribute

The customer then enters the *Queue,FIFO* block tagged as an associate and computer customer (1) or an associate only customer (0). Once the customer is ready for service, retrieve the attribute value and route the customer to a queue that requires an associate only (top queue) or a queue that requires an associate and a computer (bottom queue). This decision is made with a *Select DE Output* block based on the attribute value, which is why we need to use the *Get Attribute* block before we select the path with the *Select DE Output* block. The *Get Attribute* block retrieves the attribute value. This value is passed from the value out connector of the *Get Attribute* block to a value in connector labeled "select" of the *Select DE Output* block so that the customers are routed to the correct queue. It is critical to connect the A (attribute) value out connector of the *Select DE Output* block to the select connector of the *Get Attribute* block so that the attribute value is passed between blocks. Within the *Select DE Output* block select chooses an output based on "select" value. The top output is chosen by "select" equal to 0 and bottom output is chosen by "select" equal to 1.

Instead of using a *Queue, FIFO* block we need a *Queue, Resource Pool* block from the *Discrete Event.lix* library and the *Queues* submenu. This block manages the resources by allowing a customer to start service only if the resources that they need are available. If the resources are not available the customer continues to wait. The dialog box for the *Queue, Resource Pool* for customers that require an associate and a computer is shown as Figure 14.22. Notice that we chose All of the above resource pools are required and we specified that one computer and one associate are required.

Next, service must be provided with an *Input Random Number* block and an *Activity, Multiple* block. Once service is complete, we make the resources available for another customer by using a *Release Resource Pool* block from the *Discrete Event.lix* library and the *Resources* submenu. In the dialog box, you must specify which resource is being made available. Figure 14.23 shows the dialog box releasing the associates. The final step of this model is to use an *Exit (4)* block from the *Discrete Event.lix* library and the *Routing* submenu. This will keep track of the customers requiring each type of service. The complete model is shown as Figure 14.24 and in a file called BANKCUSTSERV.mox.

## Scheduled Arrivals

Sometimes arrivals are not random but scheduled, as shown in the following example. Suppose a bank offers an investment service where a counselor provides financial advice to

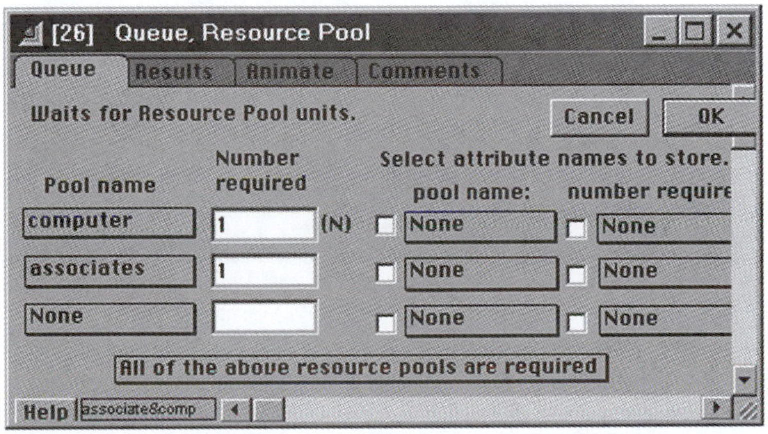

**Figure 14.22** Screen Shot of the Dialog Box for the Queue, Resource Pool

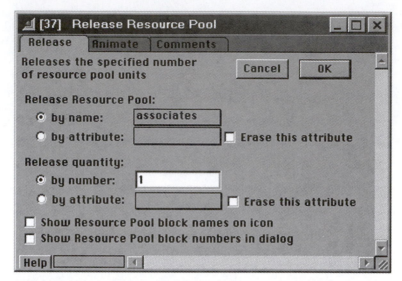

**Figure 14.23**  Screen Shot of the Dialog Box for the Release Resource Pool for Associates

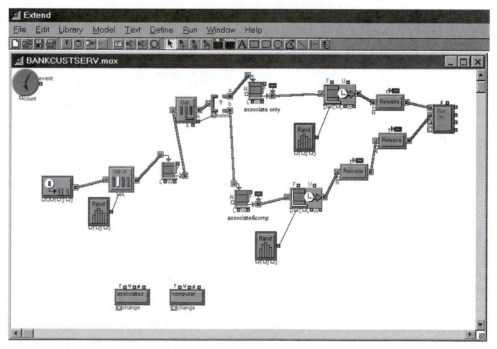

**Figure 14.24**  Screen Shot of the Complete Banking Customer Service Model, BANKCUSTSERV.mox

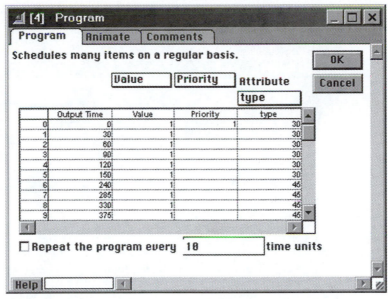

**Figure 14.25** Screen Shot of the Dialog Box for the *Program* Block

clients. For simplicity, assume that the counselor schedules existing clients every 30 minutes in the morning to review their portfolio and schedules potential clients every 45 minutes in the afternoon so that she can explain the bank's services. The *Program* block from the *Discrete Event.lix* library and the *Generators* submenu is used to generate scheduled arrivals. In the dialog box of the *Program* block, the *Output Time* is the time the client is scheduled to arrive, the Value indicates how many clients arrive at each output time (in our case 1), and our Attribute, labeled type, indicates the client's expected service time (Figure 14.25). Notice that the first six clients are existing customers (expected service time is 30 minutes) and the next five clients are potential customers (expected service time is 45 minutes). Because of the size of the window, the last client does not appear in the dialog box, but can be seen by using the scroll bar.

We know from experience that clients do not always arrive when scheduled. Suppose that 50% arrive as scheduled, 30% arrive five minutes late, and 20% arrive 10 minutes late. We use the *Input Random Number* block with an empirical table to determine this delay. This value is then sent to the D connector of the *Activity, Multiple* block. In this case, the *Activity, Multiple* block is used to delay a customer rather than to provide service. This delay coupled with the scheduled arrival time determines the actual arrival time.

Even though we plan on a 30-minute service time for existing clients, the average service time is 20 minutes (10 minutes less). This service time is assumed to follow an Erlang distribution with a mean of 20 minutes and a k value of 5. Similarly, the service time for potential clients is Erlang with a mean of 35 minutes (10 minutes less than the 45 minutes planned) and a k value of 5. Since both service times are 10 minutes less than their scheduled times, we subtract (*Subtract* block from the *Generic.lix* library and the *Math* submenu) 10 minutes (*Constant* block from the *Generic.lix* library and the *Inputs/ Outputs* submenu) from the scheduled service time (the type Attribute). This value is sent to the mean input connector of an *Input Random Number* block, which determines a random service time that is passed to the delay connector of *Activity, Multiple*. This model is shown as Figure 14.26 and in the file called BANKINVEST.mox.

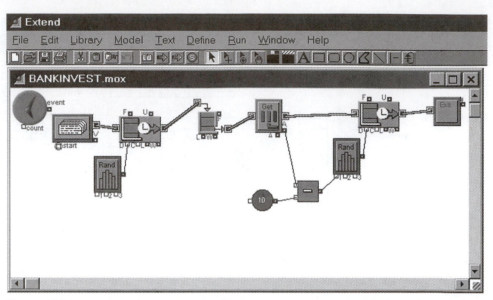

**Figure 14.26** Screen Shot of the Complete Bank Investment Model, BANKINVEST.mox

## Lines Behind Each Server: A Bank Drive-Through Window

In our basic banking model (BANK4T.mox) all of the tellers served customers from one common line, but in a bank drive-through window a line forms behind each server. We consider a drive-through bank where a customer enters the shortest of three lines. Assume that two servers are experienced and both have an average service time of seven minutes; however, the third server is new and has an average service time of 10 minutes. Further assume that all service time distributions are Erlang with a k of 4. Suppose arrival data were analyzed by Stat::Fit and we found that the average interarrival times are exponential with a mean of three minutes.

Before an arrival joins the shortest line, we must know how many customers are in each line and what servers are busy. A subtlety exists that needs to be considered. Suppose that two lines both have zero customers in them. We might assume that a customer would arbitrarily choose one of the two lines since there is a tie. This could be incorrect since the server may be busy for one line while the server may be idle for the other line. In this case the customer would choose the line where the server is idle. Therefore, customers must make their decision based on the number of people in each line *plus* the number of people receiving service in each line.

For each queue, use an _Add_ block from the _Generic.lix_ library and the _Math_ submenu to sum the number of people in line (L from _Queue, FIFO_) and the number of people receiving service (L from _Activity, Multiple_). Since we have three queues, we send these three values to three connectors (a, b, and c, respectively) on the bottom of the _Prioritizer_ block. The _Prioritizer_ block then makes the routing decision for the customer. The dialog box for the _Prioritizer_ block is shown as Figure 14.27 and indicates that at this time, for the three queues, there are three, one, and two people, respectively, waiting in line and receiving service. Therefore, the _Prioritizer_ block would send the next customer to queue 2 since this has the least number of people in line and receiving service. The complete model is shown as Figure 14.28 and in the file called BANKDRIVETHRU1.mox.

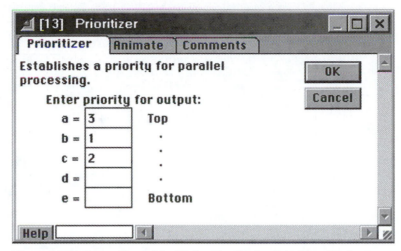

**Figure 14.27** Screen Shot of the Dialog Box for the *Prioritizer* Block

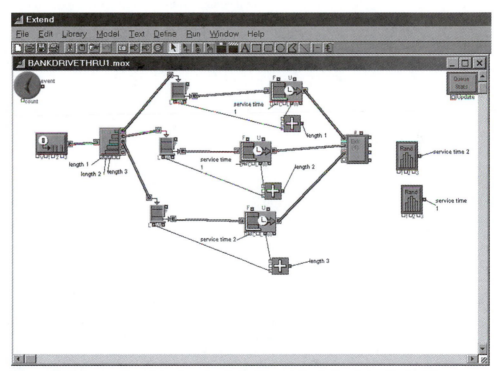

**Figure 14.28** Screen Shot of the Complete Drive-Through Bank Simulation Having Three Servers, BANKDRIVETHRU1.mox

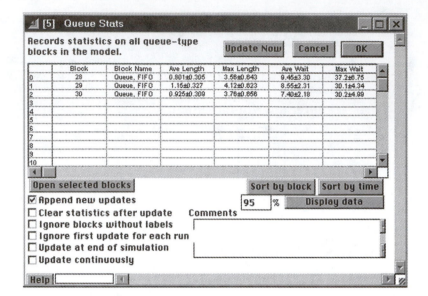

**Figure 14.29** Screen Shot of the Dialog Box for the *Queue, Stats* Block for the Drive-Through Bank

After running the simulation 25 times, the *Queue Stats* block shows the 95% confidence intervals for the key queuing statistics (Figure 14.29). Note that Extend labels all of the blocks in a given model. Block 28 is the queue for the slower server, while blocks 29 and 30 are for the top and middle servers, respectively. Figure 14.29 shows, as expected, that WQ for the slower server is larger than the WQ values for the faster servers.

Since the *Prioritizer* only has five connectors, if more than five lanes (servers) are open, then several *Prioritizer* blocks as well as other blocks are required. An example of this situation can be found in a file called BANKDRIVETHRU2.mox, which will not be discussed in detail but is available if needed.

## SUMMARY

In this chapter, we have applied the building block approach by presenting several extensions or variations of the basic banking model introduced in the previous chapter. We began by modeling situations where balking or reneging could occur. The impact that changing interarrival times can have on customer waiting times at a bank were studied. Specifically, we have shown how simulation could be used to determine the appropriate number of servers needed during busy and slow periods. We then developed a model to determine the percentage of customers waiting in line more than a specified period of time (service level). Also introduced was a model where arrivals occur in batches and customers receive service but may cycle back to repeat service. We have also simulated a bank where customer arrivals are scheduled and have modeled a bank with two limited resources—associates and computers. The final model studied the effects of having a line form behind each server as opposed to providing service from one central line.

The benefit of discussing all of these models is to illustrate how a basic model can be modified to capture important features of a realistic situation. We could not present models for every conceivable variation that could occur in practice. Our intention is to show how these variations can be modeled so that a modeler would develop an ability to handle variations that are of interest to them.

Now that we have learned how to use Extend to model many different types of situations, we need to analyze the simulation results in order to make decisions. This is the subject of the next chapter and is obviously very important. Although it is necessary to know how to model, the most important part of the decision making process is to use this information to help make good decisions. It is time to turn our attention to redesigning a process in order to improve the efficiency and effectiveness of service.

# HOMEWORK PROBLEMS

**1.** Consider the banking examples that we have discussed in class. Assume that a bank in HOLTON has an interarrival time distribution that is identical to the one given in BANK4TIC.mox. Also assume that service time is Erlang distributed with a mean of 10 minutes and a k value of 3. Suppose that balking occurs according to the BANK4TRB.mox model and reneging occurs according to the BANK4TRR.mox model. The bank is open for business twelve hours per day.

**(a)** Using 25 simulation runs, compute 95% and 99% confidence intervals for WQ and LQ when 4 and 11 tellers are used during slow and peak periods, respectively. Save the model in a file called HOLTON411.mox. How do these confidence intervals differ?

**(b)** Using 25 simulation runs, compute 95% confidence intervals for LQ and WQ when 5 and 12 tellers are used during slow and peak periods, respectively. Save the model in a file called HOLTON512.mox. What differences do you observe in the 95% confidence intervals computed in parts a and b?

**2.** TICKETS for Sure sells tickets to all sorts of events. People call the agency and are placed on hold if an agent is not available. Calls are then answered on a first-come-first-serve basis. Tickets for Sure is open for business eight hours a day. Data has been gathered that indicates that there are three distinct periods of demand during the day. The average time between calls from 9:00 A.M. until 11:00 A.M. is three minutes; the average time between calls from 11:00 A.M. until 3:00 P.M. is two minutes; and the average time between calls from 3:00 P.M. until 5:00 P.M. is three minutes. The interarrival time distribution, for all three time periods during the day, is believed to be exponential. Data has also been gathered to determine the average service times. The data indicated that the average service time is 22 minutes per call and follows an exponential distribution.

**(a)** How many people, on average, are expected to call Tickets for Sure each day?

**(b)** What is the minimum number of servers that must be available during each of the three periods?

**(c)** Suppose that Tickets for Sure wants the average queue time during the day to be less than six minutes. Design and run a simulation that can help Tickets for Sure determine the minimum number of agents to have available during the day that will satisfy their average queue time requirement. Using 25 simulation runs, develop the appropriate 95% confidence interval to support your staffing plan.

**3.** Consider a SUPER Fields grocery store that has the following key assumptions: The interarrival times for customers follow an exponential distribution with a mean of 0.75 minutes. A line forms behind each checker. No balking, reneging, or jockeying (moving from one line to another) is allowed. The number of items purchased by a customer follows the integer, uniform distribution, with a minimum of 2 and a maximum of 30 items.

The average service time is related to the number of items purchased. Assume that the service time distribution for all checkers is Erlang with a k value of 4. However, the mean of the Erlang distribution is equal to 0.1 minutes times the number of items purchased. Super Fields should be simulated over a 14-hour day.

**(a)** Based on the above assumptions, determine the minimum number of checkers that are needed to insure that long lines do not always form.

**(b)** Create an Extend model for this problem and save your file as SUPER1.mox. Compute 95% confidence intervals for WQ for each queue based on the results of 25 runs.

**(c)** Suppose that management is considering changing their layout so that all checkers service one line. Assume that all other aspects of the problem from part b do not change. Create an Extend model for this problem and save your file as SUPER2.mox. Compute a 95% confidence interval for WQ based on the results of 25 runs.

**(d)** Compare the results obtained in parts b and c above. Are the confidence intervals for WQ significantly different between the two systems? What would be your recommendation for Super Fields? Use appropriate analysis to support your answer.

**4.** Consider a bank in the thriving metropolis of LEBANON Valley with the following assumptions. The interarrival times for customers follow an exponential distribution with a mean of 30 seconds that does not change during the day. 75% of the customers visit the tellers and 25% of the customers must see one of two managers. Assume that the same customer will not visit the tellers and the managers. (You can alternatively assume that if the same person needs to see the tellers and the managers, he or she is considered a new customer each time.)

For security purposes, all arriving customers must walk through a single door where a camera takes their picture. This takes one second for all customers and the time does not vary. After passing through the security door, each customer proceeds to either the teller queue or the manager queue. The tellers service customers from one central queue. The managers service customers from one central queue. There are two separate queues for the tellers and the managers. No balking or reneging is allowed. The average service time for the tellers is 255 seconds. The service time distribution is Erlang with a k value of 2. The average service time for the managers is 180 seconds. The managers' service time distribution is Erlang with a k value of 3. The bank should be simulated for an eight-hour day.

**(a)** At least seven tellers are needed to ensure that long lines do not form. Explain.

**(b)** The managers at the bank have decided that they want the average WQ for the teller's queue to be less than 90 seconds and the average WQ for the manager's queue to be less than 300 seconds. Determine the minimum number of tellers and managers needed to satisfy these requirements. Create an Extend model for this problem and save your file as LEBANON1.mox. Compute 95% confidence intervals for WQ for each queue based on the results of 25 runs.

**(c)** Suppose that management is considering installing ATM machines to replace some tellers. Data gathered at other branches indicates that 80% of the customers will use the ATM machines, while 15% will see a teller, and 5% will visit a manager. The average service time at an ATM is 60 seconds. These times follow an Erlang distribution with a k value of 4. Assume that the service times for the tellers and managers are the same as in part b. Also assume that the average WQ for the customers that visit the ATM machines and the tellers must be less than 90 seconds, whereas the average WQ for the manager's queue must be less than 300 seconds. Determine the minimum number of ATM machines, tellers, and managers needed to satisfy these requirements. Create an Extend model for this problem and save your file as LEBANON2.mox. Compute 95% confidence intervals for WQ for each queue based on the results of 25 runs.

**(d)** Compare the results obtained in parts b and c above. What would be your recommendation for the bank? Use appropriate analysis to support your answer.

**5.** Consider the FARM Fresh produce stand with the following key assumptions: The interarrival times for customers follow an exponential distribution with a mean of 2.5 minutes. After entering the store, each customer enters a line to retrieve a basket. It takes one second (that is, $1/60 = 0.0167$ minutes) to get the basket. Assume that this time is constant for each customer. After shopping for produce, a line forms behind each checker. No balking, reneging, or jockeying (moving from one line to another) is allowed. The number of items purchased by a customer follows the integer, uniform distribution, with a minimum of one item and a maximum of 45 items. The average service time is related to the number of items purchased. Assume that the service time distribution for all checkers is Erlang with a k value of 7. However, the mean of the Erlang distribution is equal to 0.25 minutes times the number of items purchased. Farm Fresh should be simulated over a 12-hour day.

**(a)** Based on the above assumptions, determine the minimum number of checkers that are needed to insure that long lines do not always form.

**(b)** Create an Extend model for this problem that uses the minimum number of checkers found in part a, and save your file as FARM1.mox. Compute 95% confidence intervals for WQ for each queue based on the results of 25 runs.

**(c)** Suppose that management is considering changing their layout by converting one of the existing checkers to an express checkout lane. Assume that a customer *will* always go to the express checkout if they have 15 or fewer items. Also assume that a customer will *not* go to the express checkout line if they have more than 15 items, but will choose the shortest "regular" line. Assume that all other aspects of the problem from part b do not change. Create an Extend model for this problem and save your file as FARM2.mox. Compute a 95% confidence interval for WQ based on the results of 25 runs.

**(d)** Compare the results obtained in parts b and c above. Are the confidence intervals for WQ significantly different between the two systems? Which of the two layouts that you evaluated would you recommend for Farm Fresh? Provide a reason to support your recommendation.

These are more challenging questions that may involve using blocks that were not covered in any previous models. They will provide good practice in modeling with Extend.

**6.** In BANKCYCLE.mox the probability that a customer needs a second type of service is 10%. This probability does not change after a customer has been through the second service. In other words, if a customer requires a second service, they go back to receive the first service. After this, we use the 10% probability to decide if the customer needs the second service again, which may not be realistic. Modify BANKCYCLE.mox so that the probability that a customer needs a second type of service is 10% the first time through but changes to only 1% thereafter. Save this model as BANKCYCLE2.mox.

**7.** Modify BANKCYCLE2 so that if a customer needs the second type of service, they always exit after going back to receive the first service again. Save this model as BANKCYCLE3.mox.

**8.** Modify SUPER1.mox from problem 3 so that a customer chooses a line based on the number of items in the baskets of the people in line. Specifically, assume that when a customer chooses a line, he or she counts the number of items in all of the baskets in each line and then chooses the line with the least number of items. Save this model as SUPER3.mox. You will need many blocks that we did not cover. This is a challenging question but will be beneficial for you to try to solve.

**9.** Modify SUPER1.mox from problem 3 to allow jockeying. To simplify, assume that the last customer in any line will always jump to the shortest line if the shortest line has two less customers than the line that the customer is currently in. *Hint*: You need to use a *Process, Preemptive* block (*Mfg.lix*, *Activities*) to model jockeying.

# REFERENCES

Bayus, B. L., R. L. Banker, S. K. Gupta, and B. H. Stone, "Evaluating Slot Machine Placement on the Casino Floor," *Interfaces,* Vol. 15, No. 2, pp. 22–32, 1985.

Brigandi, A. J., D. R. Dargon, M. J. Sheehan, and T. Spencer, "AT&T's Call Processing Simulator (CAPS) Operational Design for Inbound Call Centers," *Interfaces,* Vol. 24, No. 1, pp. 6–28, 1994.

Dean, B. V., R. L. Salstrom, J. Feidler, B. Molnar, and K. Haake, "Statistical and Simulation Analysis Assists Santa Clara Valley Water District Planning," *Interfaces,* Vol. 24, No. 6, pp. 82–99, 1994.

Imagine That, Inc., *Extend,* San Jose, CA, 2001.

Landauer, E. G., and L. C. Becker, "Reducing Waiting Time at Security Checkpoints," *Interfaces,* Vol. 19, No.5, pp. 57–65, 1989.

Martin, E., "Centralized Bakery Reduces Distribution Costs Using Simulation," *Interfaces,* Vol. 28, No. 4, pp. 38–46, 1998.

Saltzman, R. M., and V. Mehrotra, "A Call Center Uses Simulation to Drive Strategic Change," *Interfaces,* Vol. 31, No. 3, pp. 87–101, 2001.

# Chapter 15

---

# Process Redesign Using Extend

## INTRODUCTION

In the previous chapter we illustrated the power of Extend by showing many extensions of the basic banking model. While being able to develop useful models in Extend is important, we cannot lose sight of the fact that the most important skill is using these models to help make decisions. The purpose of this chapter is to show how the output from simulation models can be used to improve the decision-making process. In general, the models in this chapter will be similar to those previously covered, since the focus is not on modeling but on analysis.

We will begin with an example of how simulation can be used to redesign a process for better efficiency. We will use simulation for cost and service level analysis to support decision making. This chapter concludes by demonstrating an important feature of Extend—optimization. This powerful option has the ability to optimize decision variables automatically. The reader interested in other examples of process redesign and cost analysis is referred to Everett (1996), Fincke and Vaessen (1988), and Lee and Elcan (1996).

## PROCESS REDESIGN USING EXTEND: A CAR WASH EXAMPLE

### One Wash-Only Bay

A series of car wash models follow that illustrate how simulation can identify issues that lead to process redesign. We begin with a car wash with one bay that just washes cars during an eight-hour day. Interarrival times are exponential with a mean of four minutes and service time is a *constant* at six minutes. Note that this problem is similar to BANK1T.mox, except that the *Input Random Number* block is not needed, since service time is constant. Therefore, we set the Delay box to six in the *Activity, Multiple* block (Activity tab). The complete model is in the file called CARWASH1.mox and is given as Figure 15.1.

Based on our discussion in Chapter 13 about the minimum number of servers, we find that N equals 2 since it is the smallest integer greater than 6/4. Therefore, since we only have one server, we expect LQ and WQ to continually build throughout the simulation. After running the simulation we find out that our expectations are correct, as shown in Figure 15.2.

### Adding a Second Bay: Wash-Only

Based on these results, add a second wash-only bay to reduce the queue length and waiting time. To simulate the effect of this design modification, simply change the Maximum number in activity box in the *Activity, Multiple* block (Activity tab) from 1 to 2 in CARWASH1.mox. The revised model is found in a file called CARWASH2.mox.

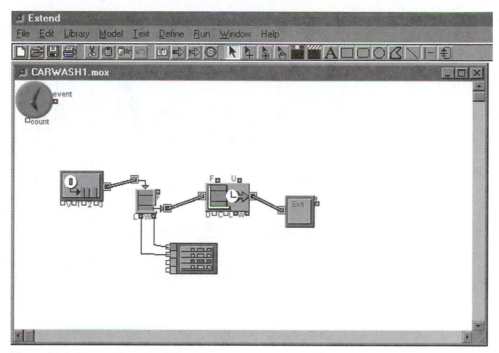

**Figure 15.1** Screen Shot of a Car Wash Simulation Model with One Wash-Only Bay

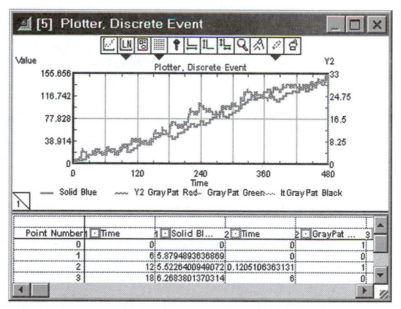

**Figure 15.2** Screen Shot of *Plotter, Discrete Event* Dialog Box after
Running CARWASH1.mox

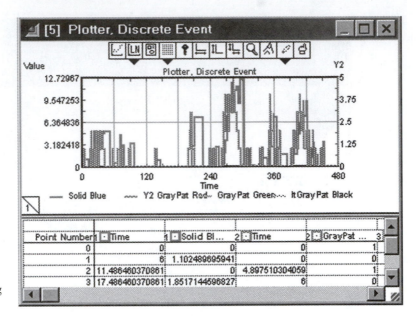

**Figure 15.3** Screen Shot of *Plotter, Discrete Event* Dialog Box after Running CARWASH2.mox

After running the simulation we find again that our expectations are correct, as shown in Figure 15.3.

## Adding a Second Bay: Wash-and-Wax

The car wash models just presented are not detailed enough since the customer usually has other options, for example, having wax applied after the wash. As in the BANKCUSTSERV.mox model in Chapter 14, this situation can be modeled by setting an attribute (*Set Attribute*) to the cars coming from the *Generator* block, then getting that attribute (*Get Attribute*) as the car gets washed so that a routing decision can be made.

We will assume that 75% of the cars require no wax, that is, they have an attribute value of 0; and 25% require wax, having an attribute value of 1. Once again the *Input Random Number* block (Distribution tab) with an empirical table is used to specify these probabilities. The customer then enters the *Queue,FIFO* block tagged as a wax (1) or no wax (0) customer. Once the customer is ready for service, we must retrieve the attribute value since our car wash has one bay for wash-only (top bay) and one bay for wash-and-wax (bottom bay). The *Get Attribute* block retrieves the attribute value, and passes it to a value in connector labeled select of the *Select DE Output* block so that the cars are routed to the correct bay.

We assume that the service time for wash-only is six minutes and the service time for wash-and-wax is eight minutes. The delay boxes in the *Activity, Multiple* blocks must be set accordingly. The Extend model is in the file called CARWASH3.mox and is given as Figure 15.4. As shown in Figure 15.5, line length and waiting time continue to grow during the simulation.

An alternate approach for modeling the generation of wash-only and wash-and-wax customers is to use a *Generator* block for each arrival process. Since the mean interarrival time is four minutes, over a 16-minute time interval there will be three wash-only arrivals and one wash-and-wax arrival on average. Viewing the arrival processes separately, this observation translates into a mean interarrival time of $16/3 = 5.33$ minutes for wash-only

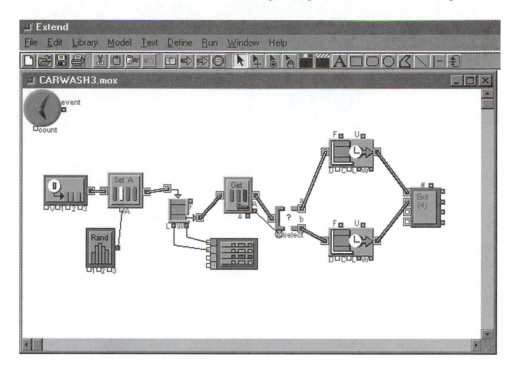

**Figure 15.4** Screen Shot of the Car Wash Simulation with One Wash-Only Bay and One Wash-and-Wax Bay

customers, and $16/1 = 16$ minutes for wash-and-wax customers. Once an arrival is generated, we set its attribute type as either 0 or 1. A *Combine* block (*Discrete Event.lix*, *Routing*) is used to merge the two arrival streams for entrance into the *Queue FIFO* block. The rest of the model is the same as CARWASH3.mox as shown in Figure 15.6.

As shown in Figure 15.7, line length and waiting time continue to grow during the simulation. This pattern is similar to the one found in Figure 15.5.

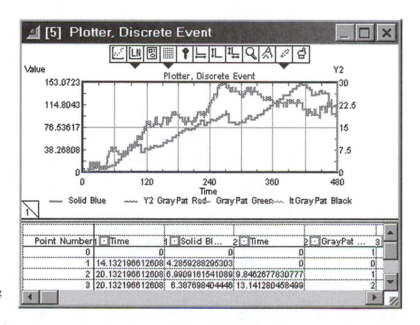

**Figure 15.5** Screen Shot of *Plotter, Discrete Event* Dialog Box after Running CARWASH3.mox

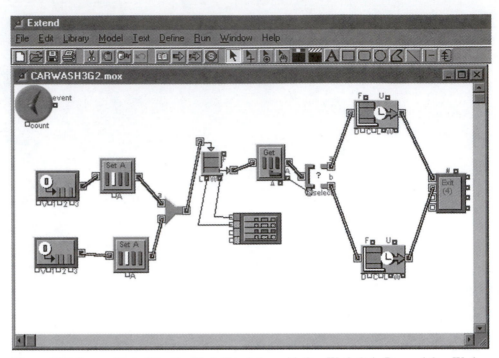

**Figure 15.6** Screen Shot of the Car Wash Simulation with One Wash-Only Bay and One Wash-and-Wax Bay Using Two *Generator* Blocks

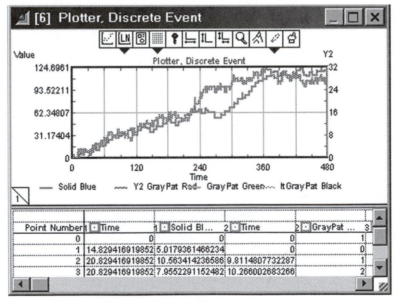

**Figure 15.7** Screen Shot of *Plotter, Discrete Event* Dialog Box after Running CARWASH3G2.mox

## Converting Both Bays to Wash-and-Wax

One might think that two bays should be enough to prevent a constantly growing queue and that our average service time is $(.75)(6) + (.25)(8) = 6.5$, so that N should equal 2 according to our formula. But this formula for computing N does not hold in the present circumstance because of how our queue operates. For example, suppose the second customer in line wants a wash-only and the first customer wants a wash-and-wax. If the wash-only bay is available and the wash-and-wax bay is occupied, then the second customer must wait until the first customer begins service. This example points out a major flaw in this car wash design. The operation of the car wash can be improved by providing both bays with the capability to wash-only or wash-and-wax. This redesign requires an investment that can only be justified if the additional profit generated will cover the cost of modifying the bays over a reasonable period of time.

The simulation model representing the redesigned process is given in the file called CARWASH4.mox. As shown as Figure 15.8, this model is similar to CARWASH1.mox, except that in the dialog box of the *Activity, Multiple* block (Activity tab) we set the Maximum number in activity box to 2. Through the *Input Random Number* block with an empirical table, we also specify that 75% of the time service time is six minutes (wash-only) and 25% of the time service time is eight minutes (wash-and-wax). As shown in Figure 15.9, line length and waiting time are now stabilized during the simulation.

## Economic and Service-Level Analysis

### Cost Analysis Using an Unloading Facility Example

Earlier we mentioned that simulation could study the fundamental trade-off between the cost of providing service and the cost of waiting. We will now use an example to illustrate how Extend can support this analysis.

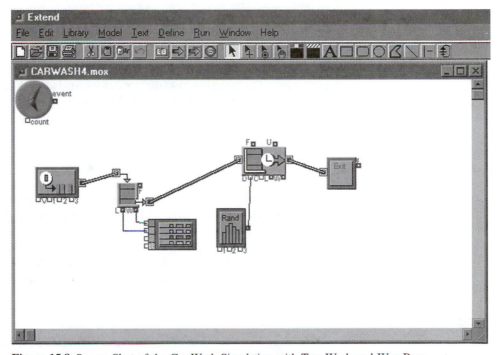

**Figure 15.8** Screen Shot of the Car Wash Simulation with Two Wash-and-Wax Bays

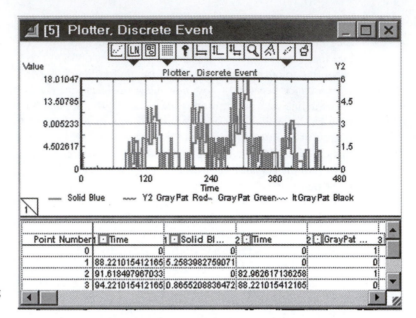

**Figure 15.9** Screen Shot of *Plotter, Discrete Event* Dialog Box after Running CARWASH4.mox

An integrated petroleum company is considering expansion of its one unloading facility at its refinery. Due to random variations in weather, loading delays, and other factors, ships randomly arrive at the refinery to unload crude oil. The interarrival time follows an exponential distribution where the mean interarrival time is one day. Service time is Erlang distributed with a mean service time of 0.5 days with a k value of 6. The company currently rents a loading berth at a cost of $1,000 per day and can rent additional berths at the same cost. The service time for the new berths follows the same assumptions as the existing berth. In addition, we estimate that a ship's waiting time is worth $5,000 per day and that this cost is assessed both when a ship is waiting for service and while it is being serviced.

Simulation can help to determine the number of loading berths that this company should have. The structure of the model needed for this problem is identical to BANK1T.mox but with the following modifications. In the *Generator* block (Cost tab), we enter $5,000 in the Waiting cost per time unit location. We also check the box Calculate waiting costs in the *Queue, FIFO* block (Queue tab). In the *Activity, Multiple* block (Cost tab), we again enter $5,000 in the Waiting cost per time unit location. To charge only for time spent waiting in line, you would not enter a cost value in the *Activity, Multiple* block. We add the *Cost Stats* block from the *Statistics.lix* library and no submenu to compute the average cost to wait in line and the average cost to wait during service.

Essentially, Extend keeps track of the amount of time (in days) that each ship spends in the queue and multiplies that by $5,000. These results are summed for all ships. A similar process is used to compute the average service cost. The results of a single server model are in LOADING1.mox; the dialog box for the *Queue Stats* block appears in Figure 15.10. These results show that over 50 years, the average waiting cost in the queue is $536,600 and the average waiting cost during service is $912,700 for an average total waiting cost of $1,449,300 per year. Since berths are being rented for $1,000 per day, the average total cost (ATC) is also $1,814,300 per year.

The results of a two-server model are in LOADING2.mox. These results show that over 50 years, the average waiting cost in the queue has dropped dramatically to $41,640.

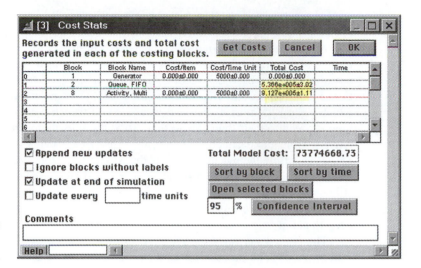

**Figure 15.10** Screen Shot of the *Cost Stats* Dialog Box for LOADING1.mox

The average cost during service is, as expected, roughly the same, $911,800 for an average total waiting cost of $953,440 per year. The berth rental costs are $2,000 per day. Therefore, the ATC per year = $953,440 + 2 * 1000 * 365 = $1,683,440.

The results of a three-server model are in LOADING3.mox. These results show that over 50 years, the average waiting cost in the queue has continued to drop to $4,715. Again, the average waiting cost during service is, as expected, roughly the same—$911,300 for an average total waiting cost of $916,015 per year. In fact, the exact value for the expected average waiting cost during service is 365(1/2)(5000) = $912,500. We must spend $3,000 per day to rent two berths. Therefore, the ATC per year = $916,015 + 3000 * 365 = $2,011,015.

The cost summary of the three models is

ATC per year (1 berth)  = $1,814,300;

ATC per year (2 berths) = $1,683,440;

ATC per year (3 berths) = $2,011,015

Based on this analysis, it is recommended that 2 berths be used. After thinking about these results, we can see that it is unnecessary to run the analysis for three berths. In LOADING2.mox, the average waiting cost in the queue is $41,640. Even if this number would drop to zero when a third berth is added, we would still incur $365,000 ($1,000 * 365) for renting the additional berth. This amount is far greater than the potential savings in waiting cost. Insights like this can save time and effort.

### A Service Level Analysis Using a Subway Toll Booth Example

In many situations it may not be possible to estimate the waiting cost for customers. For example, we know that customers are inconvenienced when they wait in a line in a supermarket, but it may be difficult to estimate an exact cost for waiting. As an alternative, companies sometime look at service levels for their customers. Earlier we showed how Extend could be used to compute the percentage of customers who waited more than 10 minutes in line, which is a service-level measure. The following example illustrates a service-level measure where a manager wants the average amount of time a customer waits in line (WQ) to be less than five seconds.

A new subway system uses computerized turnstiles to collect fares. Passengers buy up to $10.00 worth of riding credits from automated machines at each station. Each card has a strip on its back that records the value of the card. Passengers proceed to the entrance turnstiles that provide access to the trains. They insert their cards into the machines, which record the time of day and location, and then the cards are returned. Passengers then proceed to their train, where they board the subway for the ride to their destination. After leaving the destination station, they insert their cards into the exit turnstiles once again. This time the machine deducts the correct fare from the value of the card. For example, if a ride costs $0.75 and the passenger had purchased a $10.00 card, the exit turnstile would make the deduction and print $9.25 as the remaining value on the card. If the card has only $0.75 left on its credit, the turnstile would open, but the machine would keep the card.

The typical subway station has six turnstiles, each of which can be controlled by the station manager to be used for either entrance or exit, but never for both. The manager must decide at different times of the day just how many turnstiles to use for entering and exiting passengers. If five turnstiles are set for entering riders and only one for exiting, then entering passengers will probably experience virtually no delays. Exiting passengers, however, may be caught in a lengthy queue.

Between 7:00 and 9:00 A.M. at the Paoli Station, the interarrival times for entering and exiting passengers are exponentially distributed with means of 0.714 and 1.25 seconds, respectively. Service time is always Erlang with a mean of 2 seconds per customer and a k of 4, regardless of direction. Assume that riders form a common queue at both entry and exit and then proceed to the first available turnstile. We can use our formula for N (*minimum number of servers*) to gain insight into this problem.

*For Entering Customers:* $1/\lambda = 0.714$ seconds per customer and $1/\mu = 2$ seconds per customer, therefore N = the smallest integer greater than $2/0.714 = 2.80$ or 3. This means that we need at least three entering turnstiles.

*For Exiting Customers:* $1/\lambda = 1.25$ seconds per customer and $1/\mu = 2$ seconds per customer, therefore N = the smallest integer greater than $2/1.25 = 1.60$ or 2. This means that we need at least two exiting turnstiles.

The two models that we need for this problem (one for entering and one for exiting customers) are virtually identical to BANK1T.mox with changes to some of the dialog boxes. We simulated the two-hour study time for 10 days. The entering model is in a file called SUBENT3.mox, and the results show that the 95% confidence interval for WQ is 5.48 +/− 0.913 seconds. In other words, we are 95% confident that the population WQ is between 4.567 and 6.393. This result indicates that it is quite probable that the true population value for WQ will be more than five seconds, so more than three turnstiles are needed in the entering direction. The results of the four-server model are in SUBENT4.mox and show that the 95% confidence interval for WQ for the 10 runs is between 0.4148 and 0.4812 seconds. These results are acceptable and we now know that four turnstiles are needed in the entering direction.

We found earlier that we need at least two turnstiles in the exiting direction. The results of the two-server model are in SUBEXIT2.mox, and show that the 95% confidence interval for WQ is between 2.004 and 2.256 seconds, and is acceptable. Therefore, four turnstiles are needed in the entering direction and two in the exiting direction.

We should also mention that we made a few simplifying assumptions in this problem. First, we assumed that someone would never have a fare that is for more money than is available on their card. If this happens they would probably have the card returned to them and would have to go stand in another line to pay to have more money put on their card. Although we are not considering such situations, with attributes (similar to CARWASH3.mox) and cycling (similar to BANKCYCLE.mox) they can be modeled in Extend.

We also assumed that arrivals occurred independently and do not occur in batches. Often in this situation, batch arrivals do occur as groups of passengers are delivered in batches to trains from other trains and buses. As a result we must model not only the time between arrivals, but also the number of arrivals in each batch. In Chapter 14, we showed how batch arrivals could be modeled in the BANKCYCLE.mox model. A third variation is that the station probably has a queue behind each turnstile and reneging and balking may occur. The BANK4TRR.mox, BANK4TRB.mox, and BANKDRIVETHRU1.mox models can be used for these types of variation.

## OPTIMIZATION WITH EXTEND

In the first example in the previous section we performed cost analysis to determine the ideal number of loading berths. We analyzed the total cost of waiting and renting assuming one, two, and three berths were available. An alternate approach is to use the optimization feature in Extend to automatically evaluate different numbers of berths to find the one that minimizes total cost.

Extend's optimization works by running the model with different parameters until the best solution has been found. It is important to note that Extend does not guarantee to find the optimal answer since we are dealing with uncertainty; however, for many problems it is preferred to the brute force trial-and-error method that we used in the last section. In the *Evolutionary Optimizer* (*Optimizationl.lix*, no submenu), the help screen provides a cautionary warning, "Optimization is not fool-proof! Any optimizer can converge to a sub-optimum solution, especially if it is not run long enough. It is recommended that at least 100 generations are used, and the case should be run several times with convergence to the same or near solution before that solution is actually used." One additional problem with optimization is that it may take a long time for the optimizer to finish.

You can add the *Evolutionary Optimizer* block to any model. An objective function is entered, and may represent cost, profit, or some other measure to be optimized. In addition, Extend allows constraints to be entered in the optimization model. The way that the optimizer works is that the model is run several times and the results are averaged and sorted for one particular solution. This process is repeated for other solutions, and the best solutions are then used to evaluate slightly different solutions, called *generations,* that might be better. There are built-in rules that are used to stop the process when there are probably no better solutions.

Here is a brief overview of the steps required to run the optimizer.

1. Open a model that you want to optimize.
2. Place the *Evolutionary Optimizer* (*Optimizationl.lix*, no submenu) anywhere in the model.
3. Define an objective function as a profit or cost equation.
4. Drag the variables that you need from any block and drop them into the closed *Evolutionary Optimizer* block.
5. Set any limits for these variables in the Optimizer's Variable table.
6. Enter the objective function into the Optimizer's dialog.
7. Enter constraints, if needed.

8. Select Quicker Defaults, Random Model or Better Defaults, Random Model in the Optimizer Parameters tab of the *Evolutionary Optimizer* block.

9. Click on the Results tab of the *Evolutionary Optimizer* block.

10. Select the Run Optimization button (to the right of the green Run simulation button on the toolbar).

## Optimization for the Loading Berth Problem

We now demonstrate the optimization feature of Extend (Imagine That, Inc. 2000) for the loading example from the previous section (see LOADINGOPT.mox). Following the above steps we opened LOADING1.mox and placed the *Evolutionary Optimizer* in the model. For this problem we want to minimize the total cost, which is computed as the total waiting cost ($5,000 per day for each ship) plus the cost for the loading berths ($1,000 per day for each berth). The computation for the cost for the loading berths is easy. We simply multiply 1,000 by the number of berths to determine our cost per day. The computation of the waiting cost is not as straightforward. Remember that the waiting cost is assessed for waiting in the queue plus waiting for service. You might think that we multiply (WQ + WS) by 5,000, but we really want to multiply (LQ + LS) by 5,000. The following example will help to explain why this is so. Suppose for the first three days we have 3, 2, and 4 ships in the queue, respectively. This means that we incur $15,000 in waiting costs in the queue during the first day (3(5,000)), $10,000 during the second day, and $20,000 during the third day. The same logic can be applied for waiting cost while ships are being serviced.

We are now ready to place the necessary variables in the optimizer block. We must place the average length value from the *Queue, FIFO* block (Results tab) and the average length value from the *Activity, Multiple* block (Results tab) into the optimizer so that the total cost can be computed. We also must place the Maximum number in activity value from the *Activity, Multiple* block (Activity tab) into the optimizer since this is the value that we want to vary to find the minimum cost solution. To enter these values into the optimizer you must use the clone tool and drag and drop the values onto the closed *Evolutionary Optimizer* block. If we entered the values into the optimizer in the order that they have been discussed, then var0 is LQ, var1 is LS, and var2 is the number of berths.

Once these values are entered, we must specify the objective function. We can either mincost or maxprofit. Obviously in this example we want to mincost and it is equal to 5,000 * (var0 + var1) + 1,000 * var2. The first term represents the cost of waiting in the queue (var0) plus the cost of waiting for service (var1), while the second term represents the cost of the loading berths (var2). We must also tell the optimizer what values it can change to try to find the best solution. This is accomplished by entering Min Limit and Max Limit values for the number of loading berths (var2). We will set Min Limit to 1 and Max Limit to 3. Do not use decimal points since only integer solutions for the number of loading berths are wanted. All of the information that has been entered appears in Figure 15.11.

The information at the bottom of the Set Cost tab (Value, Convergence, etc.) appears after the model is run. To run the model, select Quicker Defaults, Random Model or Better Defaults, Random Model in the Optimizer Parameters tab. The latter will take longer to run. The results of the run appear in the Results tab of the optimizer block and are shown as Figure 15.12.

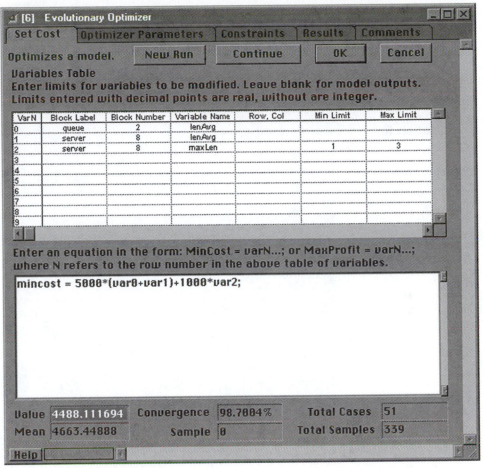

**Figure 15.11** Screen Shot of the *Evolutionary Optimizer* Block Showing Variables and Objectives Function

The best results found appear in the top row of the Result tab. We see that the best number of berths is 2 (var2 in row 0). The total cost is $4,488.11 per day or $1,638,160.15 per year (365(4,488.11)). Remember that when we used trial and error for this problem in the last section, we found that two loading berths should be used and the total cost was $1,683,440 per year. We see that these two results are very close and, as usual, the differences are due to the randomness. Extend also automatically changes the number of servers in the *Activity, Multiple* block to two. Since we could not change var0 (LQ) or var1 (LS), the entries in the var0 and var1 column are blank.

## Optimization for a Toll Booth Problem

We now turn our attention to analyzing waiting time at a toll booth on a turnpike. The interarrival time for customers follows an exponential distribution with a mean of seven seconds and does not change during the two-hour time period from 4:00 P.M. to 6:00 P.M. The turnpike commission decided to implement the EZ Pass system that many cities now use. Drivers receive a device that they place on the windshield of their car. This device

**[6] Evolutionary Optimizer**

| Set Cost | Optimizer Parameters | Constraints | **Results** | Comments |

| New Run | Continue | OK | Cancel |

**Population**
**Best at row 0**

| | Var0 | Var1 | Var2 | MinCost | samples | ±error |
|---|---|---|---|---|---|---|
| 0 | | | 2 | 4488.11169358 | 5 | 156.8 |
| 1 | | | 2 | 4488.62742891 | 5 | 56.51 |
| 2 | | | 2 | 4517.22574789 | 5 | 162.3 |
| 3 | | | 2 | 4525.95674587 | 5 | 120 |
| 4 | | | 2 | 4527.06047873 | 5 | 67.06 |
| 5 | | | 2 | 4532.98444511 | 5 | 73.03 |
| 6 | | | 2 | 4634.03008882 | 5 | 98.97 |
| 7 | | | 2 | 4537.39671322 | 5 | 112.5 |
| 8 | | | 2 | 4546.81897633 | 5 | 90.96 |
| 9 | | | 2 | 4663.4488798 | 5 | 108.9 |
| 10 | | | | | | |
| 11 | | | | | | |
| 12 | | | | | | |
| 13 | | | | | | |
| 14 | | | | | | |
| 15 | | | | | | |
| 16 | | | | | | |
| 17 | | | | | | |
| 18 | | | | | | |
| 19 | | | | | | |
| 20 | | | | | | |
| 21 | | | | | | |
| 22 | | | | | | |
| 23 | | | | | | |
| 24 | | | | | | |
| 25 | | | | | | |

**Current convergence metrics: mean**

| | | | | | |
|---|---|---|---|---|---|
| **Value** | 4488.111694 | **Convergence** | 98.7004% | **Elapsed time** | 00:00:52 |
| | | | | **Total Cases** | 51 |
| **Mean** | 4663.44888 | **Sample** | 0 | **Total Samples** | 339 |

**Help**

**Figure 15.12** Screen Shot of the Results from *Evolutionary Optimizer* Block

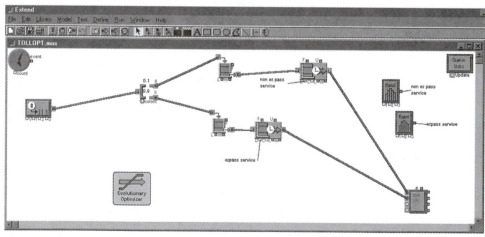

**Figure 15.13** Screen Shot of the Toll Booth Simulation (TOLLOPT.mox)

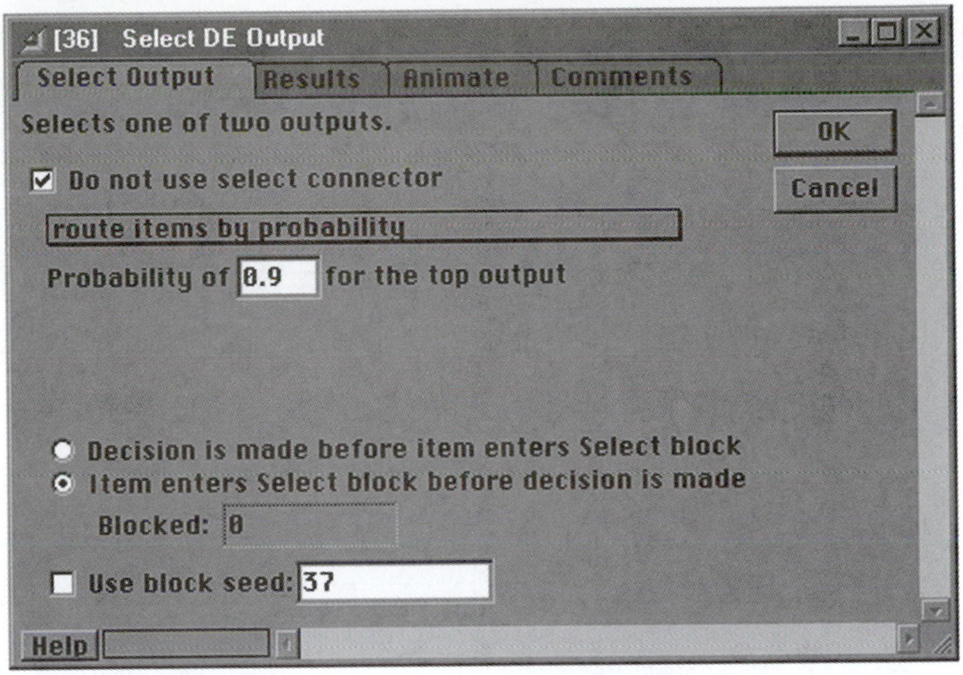

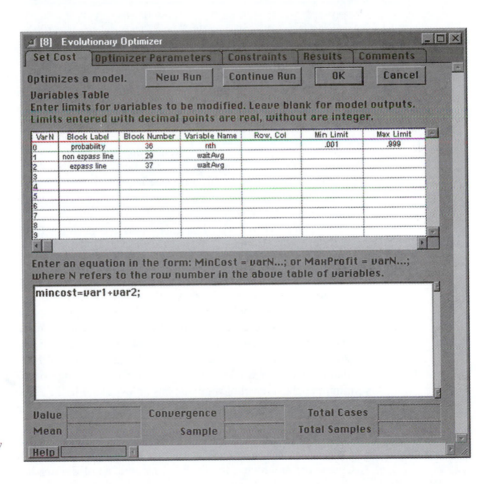

**Figure 15.14** Screen Shot of the Dialog Box for the *Select_DE Output* Block

**Figure 15.15** Screen Shot for the *Evolutionary Optimizer* Block

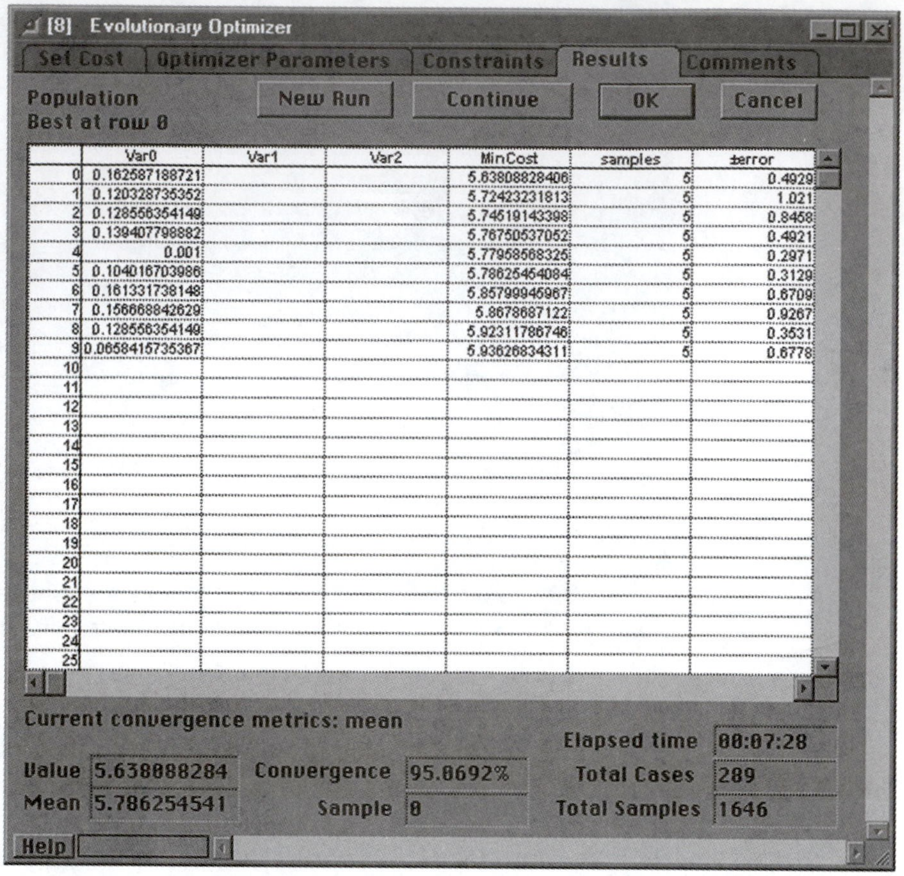
[8] Evolutionary Optimizer
Set Cost
Optimizer Parameters
Constraints
Results
Comments
Population
Best at row 0
New Run
Continue
OK
Cancel
Var0 Var1 Var2 MinCost samples ±error
0 0.162587188721 5.63808828406 5 0.4929
1 0.120328735352 5.72423231813 5 1.021
2 0.128556354149 5.74519143398 5 0.8458
3 0.139407798882 5.76750537052 5 0.4921
4 0.001 5.77958568325 5 0.2971
5 0.104016703986 5.78625454084 5 0.3129
6 0.161331738148 5.85799945967 5 0.6709
7 0.156668842629 5.8678687122 5 0.9267
8 0.128556354149 5.92311786746 5 0.3531
9 0.0658415735367 5.93626834311 5 0.6778
Current convergence metrics: mean
Elapsed time 00:07:28
Value 5.638088284
Convergence 95.0692%
Total Cases 289
Mean 5.786254541
Sample 0
Total Samples 1646
Help

**Figure 15.16** Screen Shot of the Results from *Evolutionary Optimizer* Block

allows them to drive their car through special lanes that detect the device. The customer is billed through their credit card. The benefit of the EZ Pass is that the driver only needs to slow down instead of coming to a complete stop to pay the toll and does not need to look for money when going through the toll booth.

Assume that EZ Pass customers always choose the EZ Pass lanes and that non-EZ Pass customers always pay their tolls using the regular lanes. Suppose that historical data indicates that the service time distribution with the EZ Pass system is Erlang with a mean of 2 seconds and a k value of 5. The average service time for non-EZ Pass customers is also Erlang but the mean is 28 seconds with a k value of 5.

The turnpike commission realizes that it is important to know the percentage of EZ Pass customers because that will impact the amount of time customers will wait in line. Their goal is to minimize the amount of time that customers spend in the EZ Pass and non-EZ Pass lines; however, they only want one lane of each type. Therefore, the turnpike commission would like to identify the percentage of EZ Pass customers that will minimize the amount of time that customers spend in the EZ Pass and non-EZ Pass lines. The model for this problem (TOLLOPT.mox) appears in Figure 15.13.

The interarrival time process is entered in the *Generator* block; the service time information is entered in the two *Input Random Number* blocks; and the EZ Pass and non-EZ Pass servers are entered in the top and bottom *Activity, Multiple* blocks, respectively. Customers are routed to the EZ Pass and non-EZ Pass lanes through the *Select DE*

*Output* block. We are using this block in a slightly different manner. Figure 15.14 shows the dialog box for this block. Notice that we clicked Do not use select connector and selected route items by probability. We arbitrarily entered a probability of .9. This means that initially 90% of the customers will go to non-EZ pass and 10% will go to EZ Pass.

We are now ready to enter the necessary information into the *Evolutionary Optimizer*. Figure 15.15 shows the dialog box for this block. Using the cloning tool we entered the probability for the non-EZ Pass line (var0) and the WQ values for the non-EZ Pass line (var1) and the EZ Pass line (var2). Since our decision variable is the percentage of customers using the non-EZ Pass line, we put limits on this value of .001 and .999. The objective is to mincost var1 and var2. This will minimize the sum of the waiting times in both lines. The results of running the optimization are shown in Figure 15.16. We see that the ideal probability of non-EZ Pass customers is 0.162 and the percentage of EZ Pass customers is 0.838. The total waiting time in both lines is 5.63 minutes.

## SUMMARY

We have shown in this chapter that there is more to simulation than building models: the goal is to use the information obtained from the model to help make decisions. This chapter focused on how we use the results to improve the decision-making process. We began with a car wash example that showed how simulation could be used to redesign a process for better efficiency. We also presented a loading berths example to illustrate how cost analysis can be used to help make decisions. We then studied the waiting time of people going through turnstiles in a subway and used a service-level measure to analyze this system. The last part of this chapter demonstrated the use of optimization within simulation modeling. A powerful option in Extend offers the ability to optimize decision variables automatically. After describing how to use this feature, we applied it to our loading example and a toll booth waiting time problem.

## HOMEWORK PROBLEMS

**1.** TOOLCRIB is a production shop of a large industrial corporation that services skilled workers. Attendants dispense tools on a first-come-first-serve basis to the skilled workers who need tools during an eight-hour workday. Recently, the vice president of production has been receiving complaints of excessively long waiting lines for the skilled workers. A subsequent study indicates that approximately 30 workers per hour arrive at the tool crib, yet an attendant can service only approximately 20 workers per hour. Assume that the arrival time distribution is exponential and the service time distribution is Erlang with a k value of 3. The company has found that it costs $30.00 per hour for each attendant. They also have found that it costs $45.00 per hour to have their skilled workers wait in the queue. (In assessing this cost, they have decided that the service time should not be included in the waiting cost.)

**(a)** What is the minimum number of attendants that must be hired?

**(b)** Perform an analysis to determine the number of attendants that are needed to minimize average total cost. You can use either trial and error or optimization.

**2.** The ARMSTRONG Wholesale Grocery Company owns a small distribution center in one of the cities it serves. The single server loading dock can accommodate only one truck at a time to be loaded or unloaded and operates weekdays for eight hours a day. The average interarrival time for the trucks is 16 minutes and the interarrival time distribution is exponential. Currently, the company employs two workers to load and unload the trucks. The loading time is Erlang distributed with an average service time of 12 minutes per truck and a k value of 3. The company can employ additional persons in the loading crew. This will result in the average service time being reduced as new people are hired. Assume that the average service time drops by one minute for each additional loading crew employee up to a maximum crew size of five.

The company estimates that the cost of an idle truck anywhere in the system is $18.00 per hour, and the company pays $14.00 per hour (including fringe benefits) for each employee in the loading crew.

Perform an analysis to determine the number of crewmembers that are needed to minimize average total cost. You can use either trial and error or optimization.

**3.** FIRST FEDERAL is running a special credit card promotional program and is experiencing a high demand level. They process the applications by phone and have made the following assumptions about the peak period from 9 A.M. to 10 A.M.

The interarrival times for customers follow an exponential distribution with a mean of 3.0 seconds. There are three steps in the process to apply for a credit card that every customer must complete in order. First, the customer must wait in a line to see an informational clerk who enters all customer information into the computer. There are 475 informational clerks working during this one-hour period. The informational service time follows an Erlang distribution with a mean of 600 seconds and a k value of 4. Next, the customer must wait to see a verification clerk who reviews the application for accuracy. There are 27 verification clerks. The verification service time follows an Erlang distribution with a mean of 150 seconds and a k value of 4. Finally, the customer must wait to see a decision clerk who informs the customer about whether they have been approved or not. There are 226 decision clerks. The decision service time follows an Erlang distribution with a mean of 675 seconds and a k value of 4. No balking or reneging is allowed and all lines are first-come-first-serve.

**(a)** Create an Extend model for this problem and save your file as credit1.mox. Compute 95% confidence intervals for WQ for each queue based on the results of 25 runs.

**(b)** Long waits often occur at the verification clerks' section but there are virtually no waits in the queue for the decision clerks. Explain why this is happening and recommend changes that will resolve this problem. Your recommendation should also consider the cost impact. (Do not change the design. That is, you must use informational, verification, and decision clerks.) Create an Extend model and save as credit2.mox. Compute 95% confidence intervals for WQ for each queue based on the results of 25 runs.

**(c)** In reviewing the output for credit2.mox, the manager had some general questions.

1. What does the utilization result mean in the *queue* block for informational clerks?
2. What does the utilization result mean in the *activity* block for informational clerks?
3. Should these results be the same? Explain your answer.

**(d)** The office is considering redesigning the process. If all clerks are retrained then a customer can see a clerk who performs all three functions. The time to do this is simply the sum of the times from part a, that is, assume that service time is Erlang with a mean of 1425 and a k value of 4 in this design.

They would like to use as few clerks as possible, but they do not want the average total waiting time to increase compared to the results obtained in part b. Through experimentation with Extend, determine how many clerks would be required to satisfy their requirements under this new design.

Create an Extend model for this redesigned process using the minimum number of clerks that does not increase total waiting time and save your file as credit3.mox. Compute a 95% confidence interval for WQ based on the results of 25 runs. Comment on whether the design from part b or part d is preferred. Also, explain why the recommended system works better.

**(e)** If desired, the office cannot implement this new redesign for six months due to the training that is required. Therefore, the office must take the model from part b and consider an issue that was previously ignored. When the application is being reviewed for accuracy, it is possible that the application has errors. If this occurs, the customer must wait for a correction clerk to help fix the errors in the application. After seeing the correction clerk the application goes to the decision clerk. There is money in the budget for only five correction clerks and their service time follows an Erlang distribution with a mean of 120 seconds and a k value of 4. They would like the average waiting time at the correction clerk to not exceed five seconds. They would like to determine the minimum percentage of customers that correctly complete the application and do not need to see the correction clerk that would satisfy their waiting time requirement. Modify credit2.mox to handle this change. Create an Extend model for this modified process and save your file as credit4.mox.

**4.** RAPID OIL wants to study the process of their customers purchasing gas. They have made the following key assumptions.

The interarrival times for customers follow an exponential distribution with a mean of 2.5 minutes and do not change during the day. There are three gasoline pumps that customers can use and lines form behind each pump. A customer will always choose the shortest line. No balking, reneging, or jockeying is allowed. The average service time follows an Erlang distribution with a mean of 6 minutes and a k value of 5. RAPID is open for business 12 hours each day.

**(a)** Based on this information, explain why three pumps are needed to insure that long lines do not always form.

**(b)** Create an Extend model for this problem and save your file as RAPID1.mox. Compute 95% confidence intervals for WQ for each queue based on the results of five runs. Record these confidence intervals.

**(c)** Rapid is always trying to stay ahead of the competition when it comes to providing better service to its customers. As a result, Rapid is considering implementing a new system for some of its customers. If a customer registers for this new program, called IndyPass, they will be given a sticker to attach to their rearview mirror. The customer has the ability to choose the grade of gasoline they want and the amount of gasoline they want to purchase. When the customer pulls up to a special pump, sensors automatically read coded information on their sticker, approve the sale, sense where the fuel tank door is located, open the fuel tank door, unscrew the fuel cap, dispense gas, replace the fuel cap, charge the customer's credit card, and provide a receipt. All of this occurs without the customer leaving their car. Assume that if a customer registers for IndyPass, they will always use it when buying gas at Rapid. Preliminary tests indicate that the service time distribution with this new system is still Erlang, but the mean is reduced to 3.5 minutes with a k value of 5.

Rapid is considering converting one of their three pumps

to IndyPass. Customers with IndyPass would form a single line to use the special pump. Assume that cars without IndyPass would never try to use the special pump. Also assume that all non-IndyPass customers choose the shorter of the two regular pumps.

Rapid realizes that it is important to know the percentage of customers who will register for IndyPass because that will impact the amount of time customers will wait in line. Initially, Rapid estimates that 10% of their customers will register for IndyPass.

Create an Extend model for this problem and save your file as RAPID2.mox. Compute 95% confidence intervals for WQ for each queue based on the results of five runs.

**(d)** Rapid executives have asked you to review the confidence intervals for WQ obtained in parts b and c. They do not want the average waiting time to increase if the IndyPass system is used. If 10% of their customers use IndyPass, should Rapid have one IndyPass pump and two non-IndyPass pumps? If yes, state your reason. If no, state your reason and offer a recommendation concerning another option that should be investigated. Do not create a new model to support this recommendation.

**(e)** Rapid expects the percentage of customers who register for IndyPass to increase over time. They want to analyze the situation where 70% of the customers use IndyPass. Create an Extend model for this problem and save your file as RAPID3.mox. Compute 95% confidence intervals for WQ for each queue based on the results of five runs. Record these confidence intervals.

**(f)** Rapid executives have asked you to review the confidence intervals for WQ obtained in parts b and e. As stated, they do not want the average waiting time to increase if the IndyPass system is used. If 70% of their customers use IndyPass, should Rapid have one IndyPass pump and two non-IndyPass pumps? If yes, state your reason. If no, state your reason and offer a recommendation concerning another option that should be investigated. Do not create a new model to support this recommendation.

## REFERENCES

Everett, J. E., "Iron Ore Handling Procedures Enhanced Export Quality," *Interfaces,* Vol. 26, No. 6, pp. 82–94, 1996.

Fincke, U. and W. Vaessen, "Reducing Distribution Costs in a Two-Level Inventory System at Ciba-Geigy," *Interfaces,* Vol. 18, No. 6, pp. 92–104, 1988.

Imagine That, Inc., *Extend*, San Jose, CA, 2001.

Lee, Y. and A. Elcan, "Simulation Modeling for Process Reengineering in the Telecommunications Industry," *Interfaces,* Vol. 26, No. 3, pp. 1–9, 1996.

# Chapter 16

# Financial Simulation
# Using Extend*

## INTRODUCTION

There are many application areas in finance that are subject to random behavior and uncertainty. In these instances it may be beneficial to simulate the financial process so that alternatives can be evaluated and recommendations made. Financial models can be simulated in Extend (Imagine That, Inc. 2000) by using the continuous modeling approach. The reader interested in additional examples of financial simulation beyond those covered in this chapter is referred to Ben-Dov et al. (1992), Holmer (1994), Russell and Hickle (1986), and Trippi (1996).

## CONTINUOUS SIMULATION WITH EXTEND: A FINANCIAL MODEL

### Introduction

You recall from the introductory simulation chapter that in continuous modeling, time is stepped in fixed increments and is not advanced based on the occurrence of the next event. For this reason, the *Executive* block is not used in continuous simulation.

Consider the following simplified financial analysis example. Suppose we are considering an investment in inventory of a product (let's say inexpensive sunglasses) that we will resell. We wish to simulate the performance of this investment over a five-year time horizon. We are interested in computing the mean and variance of the present value of the investment's returns using a 7% discount rate. In addition, we also wish to determine the probability distribution of the investment's present values to more fully understand the possible variation in returns.

We make the following simplified assumptions for our financial analysis model:

1) Annual sales (number of units sold) are uniformly distributed on the interval (100, 200);

2) Product price is constant at $5.00 per unit;

3) Variable cost (in dollars) per unit is uniformly distributed on the interval (.50, 1.00); and,

4) Fixed cost is $50 per year.

---

*Substantial contributions to this chapter were made by Jeannette Kelley.

We begin by setting the appropriate options under *Run*, *Simulation Setup*. Extend considers each year of our financial simulation to be a *step*. Since we are simulating over a period of five years, each simulation run consists of five steps. Therefore, in the *Simulation Setup* dialog box (Continuous tab) set Start simulation at time to 1, End simulation at time to 5, and Number of steps to 5. Since we wish to make 25 runs of our simulation, set number of runs to 25.

The Extend model for this problem completes the following activities:

1. For each step in the run, compute the cash flow, the discount factor, and the discounted cash flow.

2. Accumulate the discounted cash flows and total them over the five steps to obtain the present value of the run.

3. Send the present value of the run to a spreadsheet and to a block for computing the mean and variance of the discounted cash flows.

4. Repeat numbers one through three for each of the 25 runs.

5. Compute the mean and variance of the present values over the 25 runs.

6. Graph the probability distribution of present values in a spreadsheet.

We will consider each activity in turn. The Extend model is in the file called Shades.mox.

## Cash Flow Computations

### Computing the Cash Flow

Extend has all of the required mathematical operators to do the calculations required to obtain the needed outputs. An *Input Random Number* block (Distributions tab) is used to randomly generate variable cost per unit sales at the current step using a Real, Uniform probability distribution with Min = 0.5, Max = 1.0. Since product price is fixed, Constant value = is set to 5 in the dialog box of the *Constant* block (*Generic.lix*, *Math*). The constant price is sent to the top input connector, and the randomly generated variable cost is sent to the lower connector of the *Subtract* block (*Generic.lix*, *Math*). The output of this block is the contribution margin for the current step.

An *Input Random Number* block is used to randomly generate sales, where Min = 100, Max = 200 in a Real, Uniform distribution. The randomly generated sales value is passed to the upper input connector, and the contribution margin obtained is passed to the lower connector of the *Multiply* block (*Generic.lix*, *Math*). In the dialog box of a second *Constant* block, the Constant value = is set to 50 to account for the fixed cost. This fixed-cost value is passed to the lower input connector, and the result of the *Multiply* block is sent to the upper connector of a second *Subtract* block. The output from this *Subtract* block is the cash flow for the current step. The blocks required for completing this portion of the model are given here.

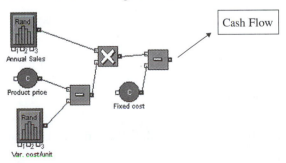

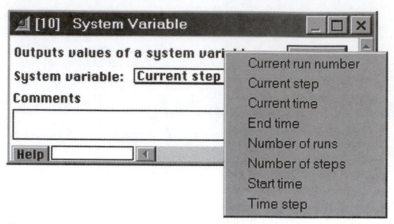

**Figure 16.1** Screen Shot of the Dialog Box of the *System Variable* Block

### Computing the Discount Factor

Next, we need to compute the discount factor for the current step. Mathematically, this factor would seem to be $(1 + \text{interest rate})^{\text{step}}$. We begin by setting another *Constant* block to 1.07. As shown in Figure 16.1, the *System Variable* block (*Generic.lix*, *Inputs/Outputs*) provides certain factors that describe the status of the simulation model while it is running. In the *System Variable* dialog box, select the current step option from the System Variable box. In Extend, step numbering begins with 0 and not 1. Therefore, add 1 to the current step number to make the necessary adjustment, since we are using end-of-period discounting in our example. To accomplish this, set another *Constant* block to 1 and send it to the lower connector of the *Add* block (*Generic.lix*, *Math*), while the output connector of the *System Variable* block is sent to the upper connector.

Now we are ready to compute the discount rate for the current step. We pass the output of the *Add* block (current step plus one) to the input connector labeled y, and the output of the *Constant* block (1.07) to the input connector labeled x of the *Exponent* block (*Generic.lix*, *Math*). The *Exponent* block raises the input x to the power of the input y. The output of the *Exponent* block is the discount factor for the current step. The blocks required for completing this portion of the model are given here.

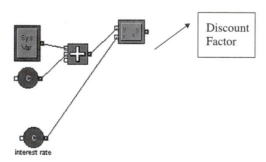

### Computing the Discounted Cash Flow

We can now compute the discounted cash flow for the current step. We connect the cash flow output from the *Subtract* block to the upper input connector, and the discount factor output from the *Exponent* block to the lower input connector of the *Divide* block (*Generic.lix*, *Math*) as shown. The output of the *Divide* block is the discounted cash flow for the current step.

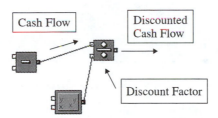

Computing the discounted cash flow in Extend does require using several blocks, but the operations are fairly straightforward. The power of Extend is that it is easy to modify these operations to reflect other factors or changes in assumptions. The discounted cash flow outputs from the five steps of a run are passed to the input connector of the *Holding Tank* (*Generic.lix*, *Holding*) for this purpose.

## Model Ouput

Connect the C output connector from *Holding Tank* to the input connector of *Mean & Variance* (*Generic.lix*, *Statistics*). You must check Calculate for multiple simulations in *Mean & Variance*. Also, connect the C output connector of *Holding Tank* to the input connector of *Data Send* (*Ipc.lix*, none). As shown in Figure 16.2, the name and location of the Excel spreadsheet in the Spreadsheet File Name box must be specified within the dialog box of *Data Send* (Data Send tab). Our Excel file is called pvshades.xls and must be open when running the simulation. The other default settings are correct for our application.

We wish to place the present values of the 25 runs into the first column of the spreadsheet. The *Data Send* block needs to know that the present values will be placed in the spreadsheet row number corresponding to the run number. Like the numbering of steps, Extend begins numbering runs with 0, not 1. We follow the same convention used in BANK4TEXCEL.mox to send the output to the spreadsheet. This portion of the model is shown here.

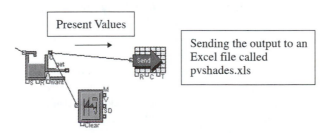

The complete model is shown in Figure 16.3. As shown in Figure 16.4, the simulation model produced a mean present value of $2,459.64. Since we are using a simple example, we can compute the actual expected present value and compare it to our results. Since sales are uniformly distributed across the interval (100, 200) the mean of the sales distribution is 150. Using a similar argument the mean variable cost is $.75. So expected profit per year is $150 * (5.00 - .75) - 50.00 = $587.50$. The present value of $587.50 a year for five years at 7% equals $2,408.87, which is close to our simulated result.

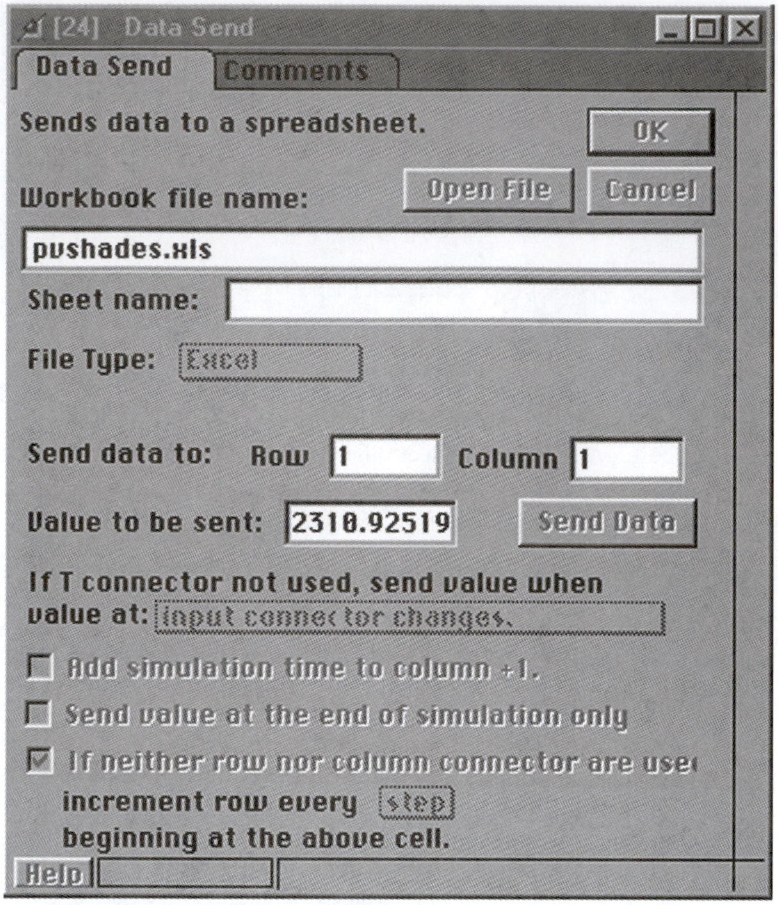

**Figure 16.2** Screen Shot of the Dialog Box of the *Data Send* Block after Selecting the Data Send Tab

Figure 16.4 also shows that the standard deviation of our present value results is fairly large at $223.16, or about 9.1% of the mean.

Using the results in pvshades.xls, we can create a graph shown in Figure 16.5 that displays the probability that the present value will be at a given level or greater. Note that since we made 25 runs, the result of each run had a 0.04 probability of occurring. This graph is contained in a spreadsheet called pvgraph.xls. If a new set of runs is made, simply copy the 25 values from pvshades.xls to cells A6 through A30 in pvgraph.xls and sort in descending order.

The graph in Figure 16.5 provides a risk profile of our investment. That is, it shows the likelihood of very high or very low present values as compared to the average. Risk profiles of competing investments can be compared to determine the degree to which one investment dominates another.

## A Hierarchical Model

ShadesH.mox is a hierarchical representation of Shades.mox that directly corresponds to the approach used to build the original model (Figure 16.6). The use of text boxes and color further improves the clarity of the model. Such higher level representations are extremely useful in enhancing and documenting the model and in communicating

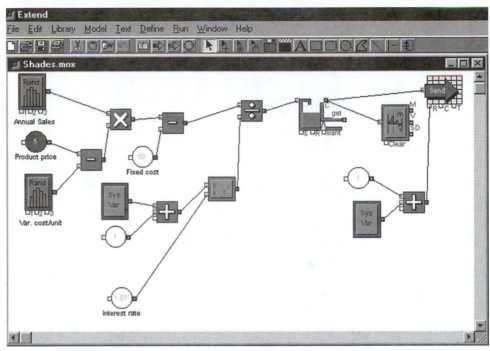

**Figure 16.3** Screen Shot of the Complete Financial Simulation Model

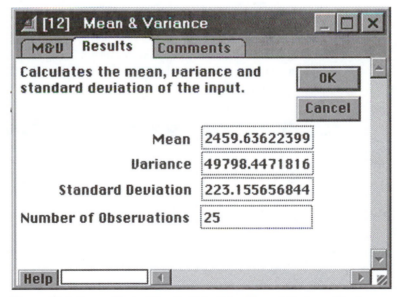

**Figure 16.4** Screen Shot of Results Tab of the *Mean & Variance* Block

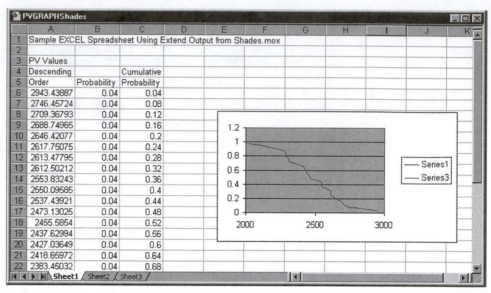

**Figure 16.5** Screen Shot of a Risk Profile Graph of Simulated Investment Using Excel

the essential ideas of a simulation model to management. Additional details on building hierarchical models in Extend can be found in Chapter 13.

## BUILDING AN ENHANCED FINANCIAL MODEL

### Introduction

As in discrete event simulation, using a tool such as Extend provides the flexibility to build models with increased levels of detail and realism without the need to abandon the initial model. In the same way, we can now take this beginning financial model, relax our assumptions, and use a building-block approach to describe the more complex situation we now wish to model.

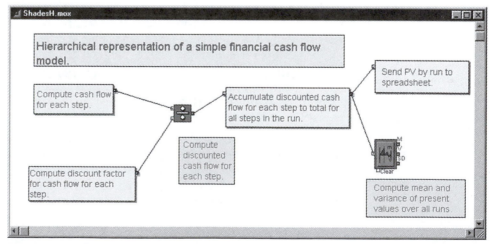

**Figure 16.6** Screen Shot of the Hierarchical Block Representation of the Financial Simulation Model

We are still considering an investment in marketing sunglasses, but are now considering a larger business with much higher revenue levels and selling prices. More variables need to be incorporated into our model to account for the various expenses that could occur. We are considering purchasing a business, Shades Inc., that already markets expensive designer sunglasses and that had annual revenue last year of $20 million. We now have projections that predict sales growth for the next five years. Each year's projected revenue level is a function of the previous year's revenue, plus or minus some percentage of anticipated sales growth. In years one through three, we have a 20% chance of sales growing between 0% and 3%, a 70% chance of sales growing between 3% and 6%, and a 10% chance of sales growing between 6% and 9%. In years four and five we have a 70% chance of sales varying between a decline of 3% to an increase of 3%, and a 30% chance of sales increasing between 3% and 8%. Within each sales growth interval, the percentages are uniformly distributed.

Furthermore, the profit margin we can generate is also a function of sales growth. If demand is strong (positive sales growth), we have a better chance of achieving a higher margin. In these good years, there is a 10% chance of a 34–37% margin, a 50% chance of a 37–40% margin, and a 40% chance of a 40–43% margin. But if sales are weak (negative sales growth) our expected margins will decline to a 60% chance of 34–37%, a 30% chance of 37–40%, and a 10% chance of 40–43%.

Also, to better represent our real anticipated net revenue, we need to adjust for Selling, General & Administrative (SG&A) expenses, taxes, and other factors. Our SG&A expense will be $4 million if sales growth is strong but will increase to $4.4 million if sales growth is weak and we need to do more advertising and promotion. Assume that we pay 34% of our income in taxes.

## Developing the Model

We add these enhancements to the model in the following manner: Our simulation setup is similar to Shades.mox by having five steps representing the five years and we will make 25 runs. Annual sales growth is represented by an *Input Random Number* block where we choose between two of these, depending on whether the model is simulating years one through three or years four or five. Within each block is an empirical table that represents our probabilities of achieving the various sales growth percentages. The dialog box of one of these blocks is given in Figure 16.7.

Note that we changed the Empirical values are field from the default Discrete to Stepped. By choosing Stepped here, we are able to establish an empirical table that outputs values from *within* ranges, rather than individual specific values. For example, by putting 0 and 0.03 in the first two cells in the value column and then .2 in the first cell in the probability column, we are telling Extend to generate values uniformly distributed between 0 and 0.03, 20% of the time. We continue this convention in the rest of the table, with the probability listed in any given row being the chance of generating a value between the one that is listed in the same row and the one that is in the next row. We also need to enter one additional bin (with 0 probability) at the end of our table, in order to define the upper range of our distribution. So even though our highest projected sales growth rate is 9%, we have one additional bin of 9–12% sales growth, with 0 probability. Note that if we do not remember to add this bin, but do specify that empirical values are Stepped, Extend will add the extra bin for us. If we leave empirical values as Discrete, the *Input Random Number* block will not generate values within the ranges. It will instead output only the exact numbers that are listed in the values column, which is not what we want for this model.

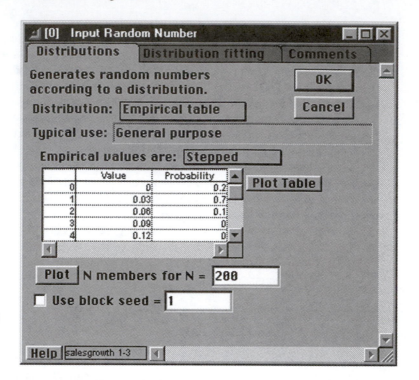

**Figure 16.7** Screen Shot of the Dialog Box of the *Input Random Number* Block

The logic for choosing which of the two *Input Random Number* blocks will be used is contained in a *Decision* block. If the current step, or year (plus 1, just like in Shades.mox, since Extend starts its step numbering with 0) is greater than or equal to 4, then the *Decision* block sends a 1 (Y = 1) to a *Select Input* (*Generic.lix, Decisions*) block. Otherwise, the *Decision* block sends a 0 (Y = 0). This means that Y = 0 for years 1 through 3 and Y = 1 for years 4 and 5.

When the *Select Input* block receives this value as its T value, it is compared to the critical value (CV) contained in this block. Figure 16.8 shows the default critical value is 0.5, which is very useful for making logical decisions. If you are familiar with the concepts of Boolean or binary logic, then you can probably see the value of this. If we assume that 0 = False and 1 = True, we can then model decisions easily using combinations of Extend blocks that generate these Boolean values (such as *Decision*) and others that

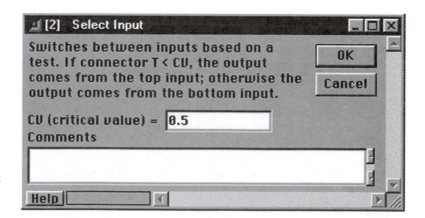

**Figure 16.8** Screen Shot of the Dialog Box of the *Select Input* Block

receive them (such as *Select Input*). You may think of the *Select Input* block as a "gate" that opens either the top or the bottom track, based on the message it receives at its switch, to allow either the top value or the bottom value to flow through and become the output. When the model is run with animation on, you can see this gate opening and closing within the block's icon.

For our example, the *Select Input* block chooses the top input if T is less than the CV (0.5) and chooses the bottom input if T is greater than or equal to the CV. So for years 1 through 3 (T = 0), the top *Input Random Number* is used since T < CV, and for years 4 and 5, the bottom one is used since T >= CV.

So for years 1 through 3, the top *Input Random* Number is used, and for years 4 and 5, the bottom one is used. This portion of the model is given here.

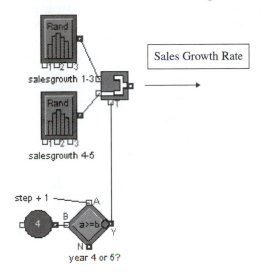

If you have reason to do so, you can also change the critical value to a different number. For example, in this portion of the model, you could change the CV to 3.5 (or any number between 3 and 4). If you did this, the decision about which *Input Random Number* block would be chosen would be made within the *Select Input* block. You could connect step + 1 to the T connector of *Select Input*, then, if the current step represented one of the years between 1 and 3, the step + 1 value would be less than the critical value, so the top input would be chosen within *Select Input*. Likewise, if the current step + 1 equals 4 or 5, that number would be greater than the critical value, so the bottom input would be selected. This is meant only as an example of the flexibility of Extend and to emphasize that there is often more than one way to model a process.

Next, we need to multiply the sales growth rate (plus 1) by the previous year's revenue to generate this year's revenue. In year 1, we use the initial revenue of $20 million. This value is transferred to a *Select Input* block via a named connection. In years 2 through 5, we transfer the previous year's revenue to the *Select Input* block from a *Global Array* block (*Generic.lix, Arrays*). The choice between initial and subsequent year's revenue is accomplished with another combination of a *Decision* block and a *Select Input* block.

The *Global Array Manager* (*Generic.lix, Arrays*) block is used to define a global array and is not connected to any other block in the model. The *Global Array* block functions like an internal spreadsheet within Extend and can accept data from, or transmit data to, other blocks. To create a global array, open the dialog box of the *Global Array Manager* block and click on the Manage tab, select the New real array button and specify its name (Revenue in this problem) and dimensions (number of rows and columns).

In this example, the *Global Array* named Revenue appears twice in this model: once to receive revenue and once to transmit revenue.

Some additional logic is needed to select the appropriate value of revenue from the *Global Array* block for years 2 through 5. In this example, we use an *Equation* block (*Generic*, *Math*) for this purpose. Here the *Equation* block passes a value to the r (or row) connector of the *Global Array* block to determine which revenue value to pass to the *Select Input* block. If the current step is 0 (year 1), we will not draw the revenue from the *Global Array* block but will use the initial revenue of $20 million. However, the *Equation* block passes a zero value that is not used. For years 2 through 5, or current steps one through four, the *Equation* block passes values of zero through three, respectively. For example, for year 3 we must retrieve the revenue from year 2, which is found in row one of the *Global Array* block. Note that again Extend's numbering convention comes into play: the first row of the *Global Array* block is labeled as row zero. The dialog box of the *Equation* block shows the "if, then, else" logical structure entered by the user to pass the appropriate row value:

```
if(currentStep == 0) result = 0;
    else result = currentStep - 1;
```

The product of the current year's sales growth rate (plus one) times the previous year's revenue is the current year's revenue. It is sent to a named connection called "this year's revenue," which will be used again later in the model. It is also sent via a *Data Send* block to an Excel spreadsheet named shadesincrevenue.xls. This sheet retains the values for each year's annual revenue. In addition, "this year's revenue" is also sent to another *Global Array* block named Revenue, for use in determining next year's revenue, as previously discussed. Note that the r connector of the *Global Array* block is the current step from the *System Variable* block. This portion of the model appears below.

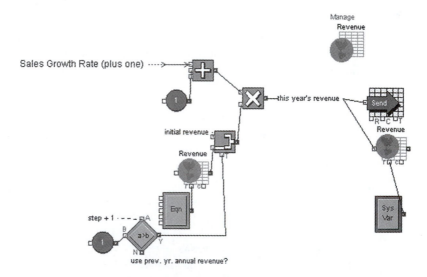

The sales growth rate (plus one) is also used to determine this year's profit margin. Another *Decision* block is used to determine whether the growth rate (plus one) is positive. The result is passed to another *Select Input* block to select the appropriate *Input Random Number* block to generate this year's profit margin. As with the sales growth rates, both of these blocks contain empirical tables that represent the probabilities of the various profit margins. Again, empirical values are stepped and an extra bin (in this case,

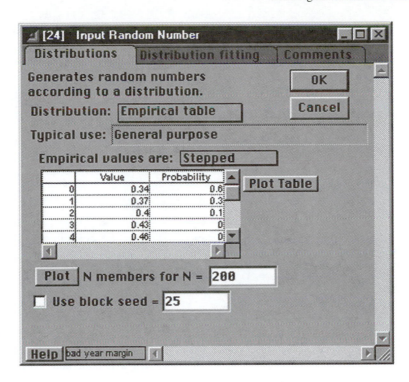

**Figure 16.9** Screen Shot of the Dialog Box of the *Select Input* Block for Profit Margin

profit margin between 43% and 46%) with 0 probability is added to put an upper bound on the probability distribution (Figure 16.9). The current year's profit margin is multiplied by "this year's revenue" to determine gross profit.

Next, the same *Decision* block that we used to evaluate if sales growth (plus one) was positive sends a message to another *Select Input* block. This message tells the block to choose between our lower SG&A expense (if growth is positive) or our higher SG&A expense (if we will have higher promotional costs to combat the slower sales). This yields Earnings Before Taxes (EBT).

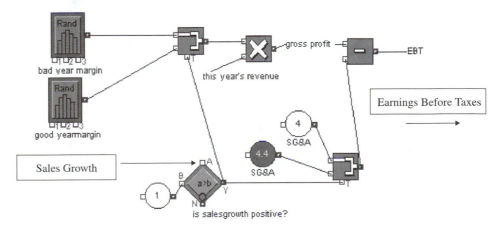

We then multiply our EBT by our tax rate, and then subtract this result from EBT to yield Free Cash Flow (FCF). Next we use the same blocks as in Shades.mox to calculate the present value. Note that we could also have used the hierarchical block that performs this function (from ShadesH.mox). Extend not only allows us to build hierarchical blocks,

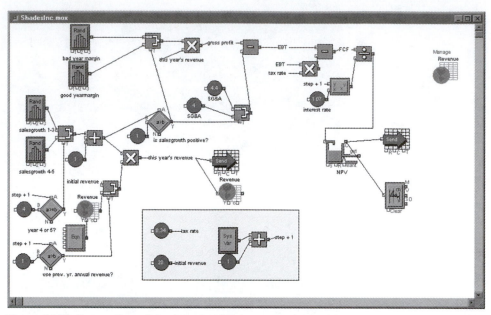

**Figure 16.10** Screen Shot of the Completed Enhanced Financial Model

but also to store them so that they are available later for reuse in similar modeling circumstances.

## Model Output

As in the Shades model, we send the results of each simulation run to a *Holding Tank* to accumulate the present values for the five years of simulated cash flows. We also transmit these values for each run, via a *Data Send* block, to an Excel spreadsheet (pvshadesinc.xls). The completed model is shown in Figure 16.10 and in a file called ShadeInc.mox.

Toward the bottom of the model is a worksheet that holds several additional blocks. This effect is generated simply by using Extend's Draw Rectangle tool, selecting a background color with the palette, and placing the desired blocks in the rectangle. A good reason to establish a separate area such as this is to isolate blocks that have inputs that you (or another user of the model) might wish to change for future runs of this model. In the image here we have placed our constant blocks for tax rate and initial sales. Another reason to establish a separate area is to segregate blocks that are needed in multiple places within the model or whose use in the model might be confusing to someone who is viewing the model for the first time (or who does not desire to know all the details of how it operates). In this case we have also placed our use of the *System Variable* block to compute "step + 1".

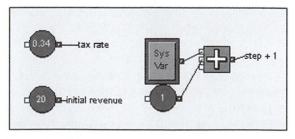

Our results from the *Mean and Variance* block show us an average over the 25 runs of about $10 million in present value, generated over five years. If the asking price is $8 million, should we purchase the firm? We may decide that we now have enough information to make this decision about our relatively small sunglasses company. However, based on the type of industry, the risk we are willing to take, and so forth, we may decide that we need to build more detail into our model. Examples of what could be added are: R&D costs, other investments and expenses, effects of debt and interest payments, resulting working capital, possibility of liability exposure, variation in tax rates, tax write-offs due to losses, and the likely terminal value of the company if we wished to sell it after five years. You can probably think of more. Most of these factors will be probabilistic in nature and can have important, even surprising, effects on our results. Because we are simulating the effects of all of these probabilistic variables on each other and on the final result, we obtain a more realistic representation of the eventual success of our business than we would obtain using static, spreadsheet-based calculations.

## MODEL VALIDATION

In several previous models in earlier chapters, we have looked at the results generated by Extend and have compared them either to real observations or to mathematical calculations in order to verify that our results were reasonable. It is critical with all modeling to not become so enamored of the process (which can be fun) that we focus too much on model building and not enough on model validation. One way to be assured of building a good model is to have frequent consultation with experts who know the details of the process being modeled. But we must also check to make certain that the model is functioning properly and that it really represents what we think it does. Even though we present this material here in our discussion of continuous simulation, it also applies to discrete-event simulation.

One way of validating a model is to input historical data and then to determine if the model's results closely approximate the actual historical results. Another validation technique is to use animation to check our work. In discrete-event models, it is relatively easy for us to see if items are moving through the system properly or if they are instead blocked due to an error in our modeling efforts. With continuous models, in which we are simulating values instead of things, it is harder for us to see these possible errors.

A tool that can be useful for this is the *ReadOut* block (from *Generic.lix, Inputs/Outputs*). *ReadOut* simply displays the value sent to its input connector; it does not perform an operation upon it.

You may have found in your discrete-event models that you could *not* connect an item output to more than one item input, since an item cannot be divided (at least not with the blocks we used in those models). In continuous simulation, however, we are looking at values, not things, so we *can* connect an output value from one block to the inputs of two or more blocks. If we have one or several stages in our model where calculations are being performed or decisions being made and we want to know what value is being generated, we can connect the input of a *ReadOut* block at that point. When the simulation is run, the values are displayed in the *ReadOut* block.

The last value displayed in this block is the value that was generated on the last step of the final run of the simulation. Use the displayed values from these blocks to trace the simulation and evaluate whether the model appears to be acting properly. An example of the ShadesInc model with several *ReadOut* blocks is shown below.

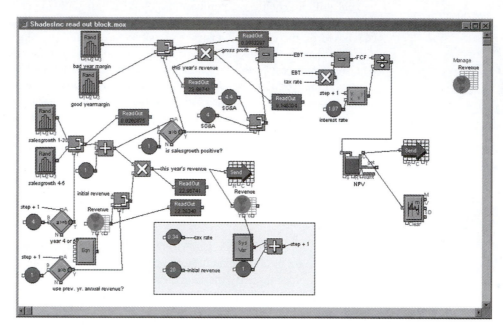

Since this is a representation of the last year of the simulation, we proceed logically through the model and check to make sure that the values displayed in the *ReadOut* blocks make sense to us for year 5. Starting with the leftmost *Select Input* block, we see that it displays a value of approximately 0.026. This represents the sales growth value generated by the salesgrowth 4–5 *Input Random Number* block for that run. We are confident that the value came from that lower block because the lower track in the *Select Input* block is the one that is open. If this value of about 0.026 was not within the prescribed ranges for our sales growth percentages, we would have reason to go back into the *Input Random Number* block and search for an error. Likewise, if we ran the model several times and the *ReadOut* block always displayed the same value or only the discrete values that were input into the empirical table, we would know there was something wrong. Following the model down and to the right, we see two *ReadOut* blocks that help us verify that the annual sales levels being generated are correct. The first of these two *ReadOut* blocks tells us that the value being generated for "this year's revenue" is approximately 22.97. We are happy to verify that 22.97 equals the previous year's sales being received at the *Global Array* block (22.38) plus the sales growth percentage we read earlier.

Moving upward and to the right from the sales growth portion of the model, we have three additional *ReadOut* blocks to check our model logic and output values. Knowing that sales growth in that year was about 0.026, which is positive, we are happy to see that the *Decision* block acted correctly. The red dot next to the Y in this block tells us that a 1 was sent to the next *Select Input* block. We would therefore expect the next *ReadOut* block to display a plausible value for good year margin, which it does. The additional *ReadOut* blocks confirm that the correct this-year's-revenue value is being read and that it is being multiplied by the margin to achieve a value of approximately 9.15 for gross profit. Following this approach, we can continue adding *ReadOut* blocks anywhere that we wish to check the values in our model.

Note that the *ReadOut* blocks would generally be removed after this validation and debugging process. However, in presentations to management it may be helpful to include this block at certain places in the model to help explain or document the model's activities.

## SUMMARY

This chapter explains how simulation can be used to model financial applications. We have provided examples of continuous simulation models that point out the differences between discrete-event and continuous simulations. A basic financial model was constructed then enhanced with additional modeling constructs to more thoroughly reflect a full financial analysis. We have also discussed the importance of model validation for both continuous and discrete-event models and described some methods of model validation. Financial modeling is an important application area for simulation as the financial ramifications of a decision can have a significant impact on a company.

## HOMEWORK PROBLEMS

**1.** A major pharmaceutical company has completed preliminary development of SUNDROPS, a revolutionary type of eyedrop that automatically adjusts the pupil's diameter according to the brightness of the sun. This product has the potential to replace some people's use of sunglasses.

Initial estimates are that 120 million people are potential users of this product. The annual growth rate of this market is expected to be between 0% and 5%, uniformly distributed. However, there is a 25% chance that a competitor will enter this market; if so, the market available is expected to shrink by 5% to 15%. The company's marketing department estimates that market penetration will be normally distributed with a mean of 8% and a standard deviation of 2%. It is further estimated that annual profit generated per customer will be $10.

Costs include the $20 million already invested in this project, as well as further testing costs and marketing expenses. Testing costs are expected to be uniformly distributed with a minimum of $9 million and a maximum of $15 million. Marketing costs are estimated by a triangular distribution, whose most likely value is $48 million, but could vary from $36 million to $54 million. Testing costs will occur only during the first year, but marketing costs will continue every year.

**(a)** Using Extend, estimate the net profit after one year and also after five years. Use at least 25 runs and establish a 95% confidence interval for each.

FDA approval of SunDrops is not assured. To be approved, a one-year controlled test on a sample of 100 patients must meet or exceed the FDA's minimum threshold of 75 patients receiving significant benefit from SunDrops without significant side effects. The company's preliminary tests indicated a success rate of 80%. If SunDrops is not approved, the company will suffer a loss, since gross profit will be $0, and the initial investment plus the testing costs (but not the marketing costs) will still be incurred.

**(b)** Taking into account the probability of FDA approval, determine the range of likely net profit values and the mean, after one year. (*Hint*: since we are talking about success vs. failure in the testing process, use the binomial distribution.) Given the multi-million dollar nature of this investment, use 1,000 simulation runs. Use either the *Histogram* block (*Plotter.lix*) or Excel's Data Analysis, Histogram tool to establish and evaluate the shape of the probability distribution. Analyze the risk of the investment.

**2.** The SANDALS Company is considering expanding its product offerings by adding one of two possible new lines, Flip and Flop. Only one can be added to Sandals' product mix.

For each year in the next five years, sales of either product are expected to grow according to the following probability distribution: 30% chance of growth between 0% and 10%, 50% chance of growth between 10% and 20%, and 20% chance of growth between 20% and 30%. The past year's sales of similar products at a competing company was $10 million for a product like Flip and $9 million for a product like Flop.

Expected profit margins for Flip are between 45–50% (50% chance), between 50–55% (40% chance), and between 55–60% (10% chance). Expected margins for Flop are between 45–50% (20% chance), between 50–55% (70% chance), and between 55–60% (10% chance).

If Flip is produced, SG&A costs and interest expense are expected to be $1 million and $240,000 respectively. However, less would be invested in Flop, if produced, so SG&A costs and interest expense would be $500,000 and $120,000 respectively.

**(a)** Assuming a tax rate of 34% and a discount rate of 9%, calculate the present values of the two products over 25 runs for the five-year horizon.

**(b)** Is Flop a flop?

## REFERENCES

Ben-Dov, Y., L. Hayre, and V. Pica, "Mortgage Valuation Models at Prudential Securities," *Interfaces,* Vol. 22, No. 1, pp. 55–71, 1992.

Holmer, M. R., "The Asset-Liability Management Strategy System at Fannie Mae," *Interfaces,* Vol. 24, No. 3, pp. 3–21, 1994.

Imagine That, Inc., *Extend*, San Jose, CA, 2001.

Russell, R. A. and R. Hickle, "Simulation of a CD Portfolio," *Interfaces,* Vol. 16, No. 3, pp. 49–54, 1986.

Trippi, R. R., "The AIM Game: Learning Investment Management Principles Through Monte Carlo Simulation," *Interfaces,* Vol. 26, No. 3, pp. 66–76, 1996.

# Chapter 17

# Project Scheduling Using Microsoft Project 2000

## INTRODUCTION

Projects and operations are ways that organizations can perform work. Operations are *ongoing* and *repetitive* whereas projects are *temporary* and *unique*. For example, an assembly line that continually produces cars according to defined specifications during a model year is an operation. However, the work required to modify the assembly line so that it can be used to produce cars during the next model year is a project. This latter effort requires a series of separate jobs or tasks performed by a variety of departments, such as engineering, operations, quality assurance, and product design. Some of these tasks must be performed in a specified sequence, such as making certain equipment changes prior to running a production test. Other tasks may be performed in parallel, such as documenting work procedures and completing final testing. This effort is unique to some extent, since the modifications required differ from one year to the next. Careful attention to scheduling, resource allocation, and coordination of the various tasks is necessary to achieve the goal of the project: completion of all project tasks on time and within budget. From this discussion note that:

- A project is a temporary endeavor undertaken to create a unique product or service.
- Projects are comprised of a set of logically related activities or *tasks* that lead toward a common goal.

In this chapter we will develop the theory and methods of project scheduling by using a warehouse construction example. Project resource and cost analysis will be considered in the next chapter. Throughout these chapters we will demonstrate how to build a project schedule using Microsoft Project 2000. With an installed user base of over five million (www.microsoft.com), MS Project 2000 is the world's most popular project management software package. Research has shown that MS Project 2000 is the project management software package most used by project management professionals (Pollack-Johnson and Liberatore 1998). An additional reference on the use of MS Project 2000 is Friedrichson and Bunin (2000).

## Examples

The use of projects to perform work has accelerated as organizations have become leaner and flatter and teams have replaced functional departments. There are many examples of work that is performed as projects:

**Building:** a warehouse, a ship, a satellite, an oilrig, a nuclear plant.

**Developing:** computer programs, an advertising campaign, a political campaign, a new product, a new process, software, training materials.

**Implementing:** new technologies and work procedures.

The field of project management has expanded rapidly to help individuals and organizations achieve project goals. The Project Management Institute (PMI) has established a body of knowledge in this field (PMI 2000) and has developed a certification program (www.pmi.org). Project management includes planning, organizing, staffing, directing, and controlling project tasks. There are many good texts that address project management such as Meredith and Mantel (2000), Mantel, Meredith, Shafer, and Sutton (2001), Cleland (1999), Kerzner (2000), and Gray and Larson (2000).

Specifically, in this chapter we will consider:

- The earliest time to complete the project.
- The earliest and latest start and finish times for each task.
- Which tasks must be completed exactly as scheduled to keep the project on schedule.
- Which tasks can be delayed if necessary, and by how much, without increasing the project completion time.

## CPM and PERT

The development of modern project scheduling methods can be traced back to two important and independent developments that occurred during the 1950s. The U.S. Navy with the assistance of the consulting firm Booz-Allen Hamilton and the Lockheed Corporation developed the Program Evaluation and Review Technique (PERT) for the Polaris submarine and missile project. The focus of PERT was determining the probability that a project could be completed by a specified date. It required optimistic, most likely, and pessimistic time estimates for the completion of each task and made certain assumptions about the probability distributions associated with individual task time estimates and the time to complete the entire project.

Researchers at E. I. du Pont de Nemours & Company and Remington-Rand developed the critical path method (CPM) to improve the planning, scheduling, and reporting of the company's engineering projects, including plant maintenance and construction. CPM used deterministic task times and assumed that a task time could be shortened at an additional expense. The focus of CPM was to analyze the time/cost tradeoffs in a project; that is, determining the least costly approach to expedite the completion of the project. Both methods had much in common, including determining the earliest completion date of the project and the amount of time a task could be delayed without delaying project completion. Over time both methods merged and today the two names are often used interchangeably or combined into the single acronym PERT/CPM.

## STRUCTURING THE PROJECT

### Required Task Information

Every project is composed of a set of interrelated activities or *tasks*. The following information is needed to define a project:

**1. Task Duration** The amount of time required to complete each task is called its *duration*. We assume that all task durations are deterministic; that is, there is no uncertainty associated with these times. If there is uncertainty, we recommend the use of Monte Carlo simulation to analyze the project schedule (See Chapter 12 for a discussion of Monte Carlo simulation.) Other approaches for addressing uncertainty such as the PERT three-estimate approach are discussed in Hillier and Lieberman (2001), Anderson,

Sweeney, and Williams (2000), Meredith, Mantel, Shafer and Sutton (2001), and Meredith and Mantel (2000).

**2. Immediate Predecessors**   To represent the interdependence between tasks (for example, a market survey precedes a product launch), we specify the *immediate predecessors* of each task. A task's immediate predecessors are those tasks that must be completed before the given task can begin.

**3. Start and Finish Tasks**   Every project has a *start task* and a *finish task*. The start task has no immediate predecessors and has zero duration. Analogously, the finish task has zero duration and no immediate *successors*. Start and finish tasks are used so that the project has unique beginning and ending tasks.

Consider the following example of a small office supply company that wishes to conduct a critical path analysis for the construction of a new warehouse. After a series of meetings with members of the executive committee and distribution management, the facilities manager prepares the task, duration, and immediate predecessor information for the project as shown in Table 17.1.

## Using MS Project 2000

### Setup

To enter the information contained in Table 17.1 into MS Project 2000 we must first set up a new project. After launching MS Project 2000, click on the *New* button on the standard tool bar, or *File, New* from the main menu, and then click *OK*. From the main menu, click *Project, Project Information* and then enter the project *Start date:* and click *OK*. (The current date is the default start date.) So that your results match those presented here, enter 10/1/01 as the project start date. Click on the *Save* icon, type in a name for your project and then click *OK*. A screen shot of the *Project Information* dialog box is given as Figure 17.1. The completed model is found in a file called construction.mpp. Note that

**Table 17.1**   Task, Duration, and Immediate Predecessor Information for Construction Project

| Task | Description | Immediate predecessors | Duration (weeks) |
|------|-------------|------------------------|------------------|
| 1 | START | — | 0 |
| 2 | Excavate and Pour Footers | 1 | 3 |
| 3 | Pour Concrete Foundation | 2 | 1 |
| 4 | Erect Rough Wall & Roof | 3 | 4 |
| 5 | Install Siding | 4 | 6 |
| 6 | Install Plumbing | 4 | 3 |
| 7 | Install Electrical | 4 | 4 |
| 8 | Install Wallboard | 6,7 | 5 |
| 9 | Lay Flooring | 8 | 6 |
| 10 | Do Interior Painting | 8 | 3 |
| 11 | Install Interior Fixtures | 9,10 | 3 |
| 12 | Install Gutters & Downspouts | 5 | 2 |
| 13 | Do Grading & Landscaping | 12 | 3 |
| 14 | FINISH | 11,13 | 0 |

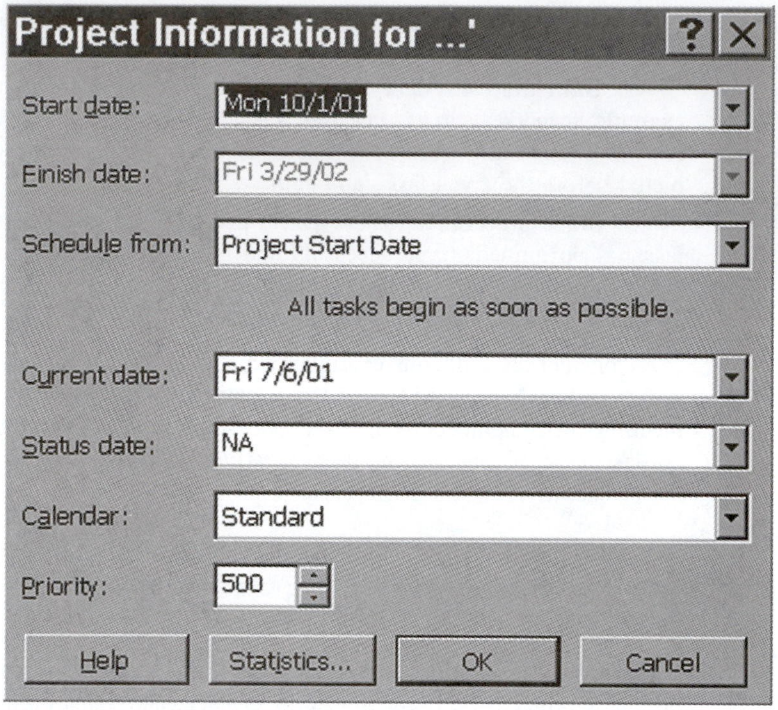

**Figure 17.1** Screen Shot of the Project Information Dialog Box

the finish date shown in Figure 17.1 will only be different from the start date if the project task, duration, and predecessor information has been entered.

We wish to make a few changes to customize the settings for our project. From the main menu, click *Tools, Change Working Time* to make adjustments as necessary to the project calendar, such as hours worked per day and holidays. Throughout our presentation we will use the default settings. Next, click *Tools, Options*, and then click on the Schedule tab. Here three changes are necessary. First, select Weeks in the Duration is entered in: location. Next, make sure that the New tasks are effort driven box is *not checked* and Default task type: is Fixed Duration. The later changes are very important especially when resources are added and leveled. Click *Set as Default*, then *OK*. Figure 17.2 is a screen shot of the updated Schedule tab.

**Entering Task Information**

MS Project 2000 offers a variety of modes or *views* to display and work with project information. The default view is *Gantt Chart,* which displays an Entry table on the left portion of the screen and the corresponding Gantt Chart on the right. The Gantt Chart consists of bars for each task that graphically depicts start and finish dates; it will be discussed in more detail later. Note that the blue *i* icon or indicator column in the Entry table is used to represent information for a specific task or resource, such as notes, hyperlinks, and constraints.

Enter the data from Table 17.1 into the appropriate fields on the left portion of the screen. Move the vertical line dividing the screen to the right so that all columns in the table are visible. In the first row of the Task Name field, type in START, then press

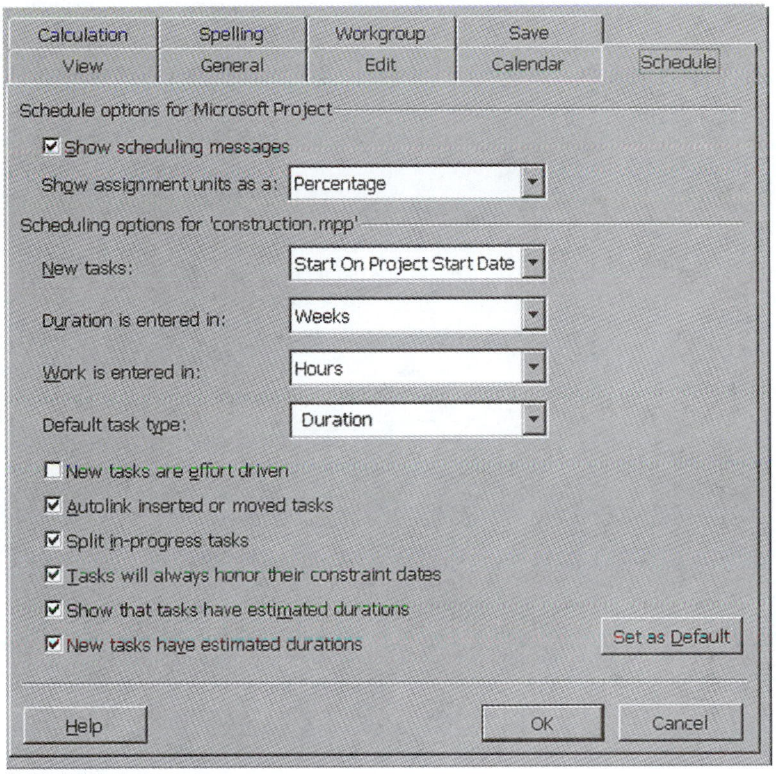

**Figure 17.2** Screen Shot of the Tools, Options, Schedule

the Tab key and enter 0 under Duration. The rows, and therefore the tasks, are numbered from 1 to 14, and start and finish dates are listed. MS Project 2000 assumes that a workweek consists of five working days. Repeat the data entry process for the remaining tasks and their durations as given in Table 17.1. MS Project 2000 uses the following abbreviations for entering task duration (not counting non-working time): months = mo, weeks = w, days = d, hours = h, and minutes = m.

There are several methods for entering the precedence relationships. The most direct method is to enter the task numbers of the predecessors for a given task in the Predecessors field. Since task 1 has no predecessors, its predecessor cell is left blank. For task 2 enter a 1 in the Predecessors field, for task 3 enter a 2, and so on. MS Project 2000 automatically computes start and finish dates for each task using the predecessor information. The use of the critical path method to perform these calculations will be discussed in succeeding sections. A screen shot of the completed *Entry* table portion of the Gantt Chart view is given as Figure 17.3.

If you have not made a predecessor list for each task in your project, you can use a different approach to link tasks. To select adjacent tasks for linking, click on the predecessor task in the Task Name field, hold down the *SHIFT* key, and then click on the successor task in the same field. To select non-adjacent tasks, click on the predecessor task, hold down the *CTRL* key, and then click on the successor task. To finish making the link in either situation, click the *Link Tasks* icon on the standard toolbar, or click *Edit, Link Tasks* from the main menu. To unlink tasks, use *SHIFT* or *CTRL* as mentioned, but then click the *Unlink Tasks* icon on the standard toolbar, or click *Edit, Unlink Tasks* from the main menu.

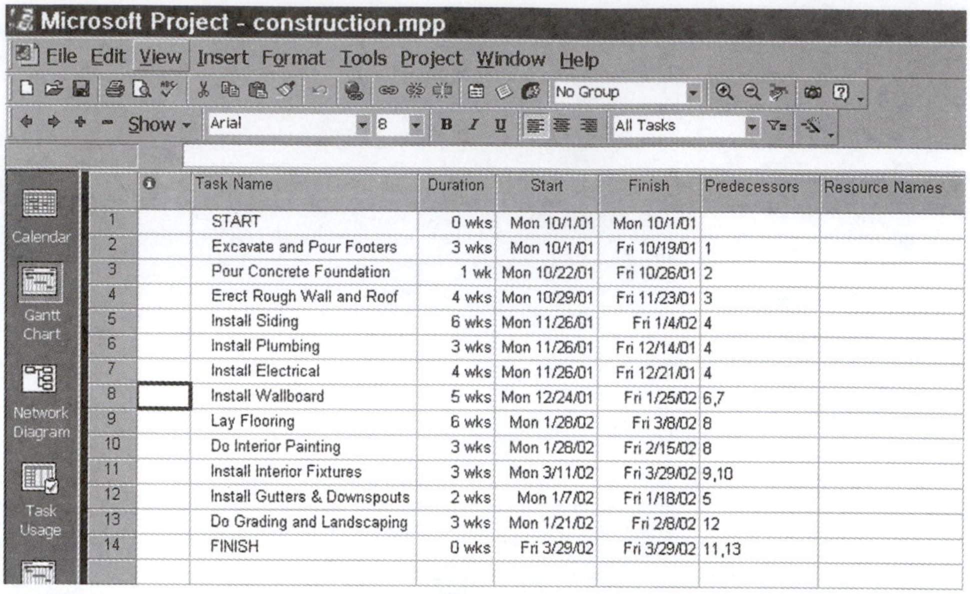


| | Task Name | Duration | Start | Finish | Predecessors | Resource Names |
|---|---|---|---|---|---|---|
| 1 | START | 0 wks | Mon 10/1/01 | Mon 10/1/01 | | |
| 2 | Excavate and Pour Footers | 3 wks | Mon 10/1/01 | Fri 10/19/01 | 1 | |
| 3 | Pour Concrete Foundation | 1 wk | Mon 10/22/01 | Fri 10/26/01 | 2 | |
| 4 | Erect Rough Wall and Roof | 4 wks | Mon 10/29/01 | Fri 11/23/01 | 3 | |
| 5 | Install Siding | 6 wks | Mon 11/26/01 | Fri 1/4/02 | 4 | |
| 6 | Install Plumbing | 3 wks | Mon 11/26/01 | Fri 12/14/01 | 4 | |
| 7 | Install Electrical | 4 wks | Mon 11/26/01 | Fri 12/21/01 | 4 | |
| 8 | Install Wallboard | 5 wks | Mon 12/24/01 | Fri 1/25/02 | 6,7 | |
| 9 | Lay Flooring | 6 wks | Mon 1/28/02 | Fri 3/8/02 | 8 | |
| 10 | Do Interior Painting | 3 wks | Mon 1/28/02 | Fri 2/15/02 | 8 | |
| 11 | Install Interior Fixtures | 3 wks | Mon 3/11/02 | Fri 3/29/02 | 9,10 | |
| 12 | Install Gutters & Downspouts | 2 wks | Mon 1/7/02 | Fri 1/18/02 | 5 | |
| 13 | Do Grading and Landscaping | 3 wks | Mon 1/21/02 | Fri 2/8/02 | 12 | |
| 14 | FINISH | 0 wks | Fri 3/29/02 | Fri 3/29/02 | 11,13 | |

**Figure 17.3** Screen Shot of the Entry Table from the Gantt Chart View

## Drawing the Project Network

The project network is a visual depiction of the interdependencies between tasks. There are two approaches that are used to draw project networks: *activity-on-arc* (AOA) and *activity-on-node* (AON). We will use the AON method since this approach is used by nearly all project management software. In the AON method, numbers contained within circles denote the activities or tasks, while directed-line segments (lines with an arrow on one end) between tasks depict precedence relationships.

Using the information given in Table 17.1, we can draw the network for the construction project as shown in Figure 17.4. The project network begins with START (task 1) since it has no immediate predecessors. The first task requiring actual construction work is task 2, since its immediate predecessor is task 1, as indicated by the directed-line segment connecting tasks 1 and 2. In a similar fashion there are directed-line segments connecting tasks 2 and 3 and tasks 3 and 4. Next, notice from Table 17.1 that tasks 5, 6, and 7 all have the same immediate predecessor, namely task 4. For this reason there are three directed-line segments originating at task 4 and ending at tasks, 5, 6, and 7, respectively. Since task 8 has tasks 6 and 7 as its immediate predecessors, there are directed arcs leaving from tasks 6 and 7 and ending at task 8. Tasks 9 and 10 have the same immediate predecessor, which is task 8, so there are two directed-line segments starting at task 8 and ending at tasks 9 and 10, respectively. Task 11 has as its immediate predecessors tasks 9 and 10, so there are directed arcs leaving from tasks 9 and 10 and ending at task 11. Task 12 has task 5 as its only immediate predecessor, so there is a directed line segment starting at task 5 and ending at task 12. Similarly, there is a directed line segment from task 12 to task 13. Tasks 11 and 13 are not immediate predecessors to any tasks that require construction work. For this reason, the actual project work is completed once tasks 11 and 13 are completed. Therefore, we draw directed-line segments starting at both tasks 11 and 13 and ending at FINISH (task 14).

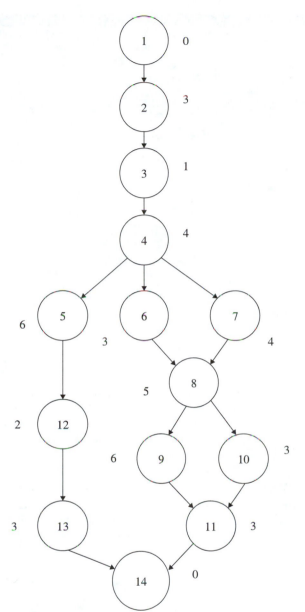

**Figure 17.4** Project Network for Construction Project

In general there may be one or more tasks requiring work that have no immediate *predecessors*, and one or more tasks requiring work that have no immediate *successors*. In *all* of these cases we will include START and FINISH nodes with zero duration for the purposes of clarity.

The project network can be seen in MS Project by changing the view from Gantt Chart to Network Diagram. Simply click on the *Network Diagram* icon in the panel on the extreme left-hand side of the *Entry* table in the Gantt Chart view, or from the main menu, click on *View, Network Diagram*. The tasks are shown as being linked from left to

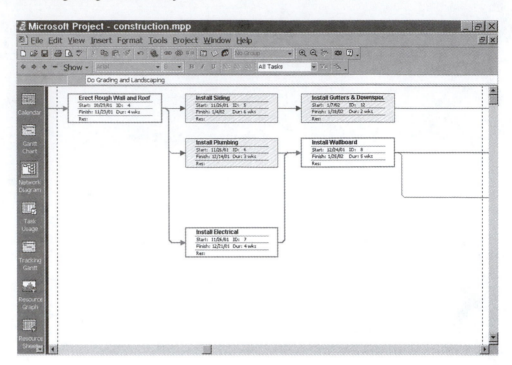

**Figure 17.5** Screen Shot of the Project Network View

right on your screen. The zoom in and zoom out icons (indicated by magnifying glasses with + and − within them, respectively) can be used to focus on any part of the network. Figure 17.5 provides a screen shot of a portion of the network. Once the task, duration, and predecessor information is entered into MS Project 2000, the critical path analysis is automatically completed. The shaded boxes represent the critical tasks that can be delayed without delaying the project completion, as will be described later in this chapter.

The Gantt Chart is another way of depicting the interdependencies between tasks. Figure 17.6 is a screen shot of the Gantt Chart view with the screen adjusted so that the full task names are shown on the left and the complete Gantt Chart is shown on the right. The length of the bars relates to the duration of the tasks, and the directed arrows linking

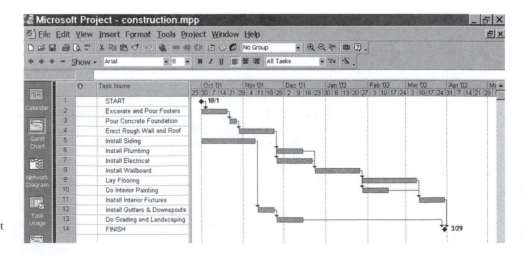

**Figure 17.6** Screen Shot of the Gantt Chart View

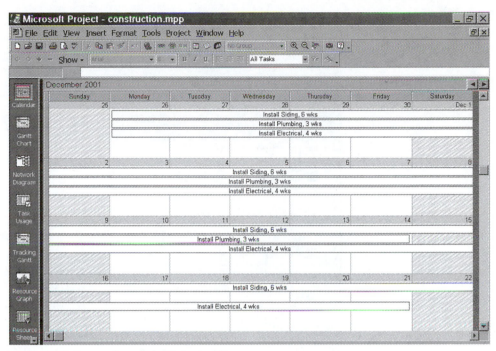

**Figure 17.7** Screen Shot of the Calendar View

the bars denote precedence. Another option for displaying the project schedule is the *Calendar* view shown for the month of December in Figure 17.7.

## Milestones

The START and FINISH tasks in Figure 17.6 are shown as diamonds. MS Project 2000 assumes that any task that has zero duration is a *milestone*. Other tasks can be added as milestones if desired. The choice of milestones depends on such factors as approval procedures, payment agreements, logical groupings of activities, and project decision points. Milestones serve several useful purposes, including target events directing project team effort, check points for overall management, and reporting items for management above the project.

In our construction project, a new task called Under Roof could be inserted as a milestone after the completion of task 4 to indicate that internal and external finish work can begin. Click on Install Siding (task 4) in the Task Name column. From the main menu click on *Insert, New Task*, then type in "Under Roof" as the task name. Enter 0 for the duration and Erect Rough Wall and Roof as its immediate predecessor. Set Under Roof as the immediate predecessor of Install Siding, Install Plumbing, Install Electrical. The revised Entry table in the Gantt Chart view is shown as Figure 17.8 and the revised construction project is given in the file called constructionMS.mpp.

## Accessing Task Information

To access all information about a particular task, highlight the task name, and then click *Project, Task Information* from the main menu or the *Task Information* icon. Figure 17.9 is a screen shot of the Predecessors tab of *Task Information*. Notice that duration and

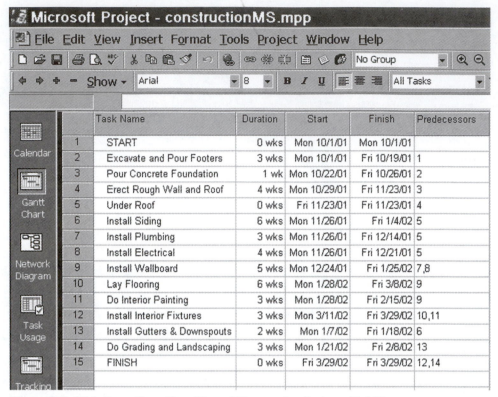

**Figure 17.8** Table Entry Gantt Chart View of Construction Project with Milestone

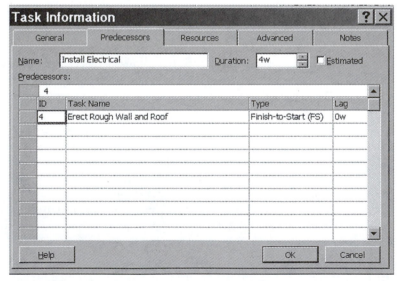

**Figure 17.9** Screen Shot of Predecessors Tab of Task Information

predecessor information can be entered or adjusted here. All of the predecessor relationships used in our example are finish–start (FS). Other types of relationships are possible, including finish–finish, start–start, start–finish. Positive and negative lags can be added to a precedence relationship in order to further adjust when the successor activity can start. These and other aspects of precedence diagramming are discussed in Meredith and Mantel (2000). If you wish to mark a task as a milestone, select the General tab and check the appropriate box. Tasks that do not have zero duration also can be marked as milestones.

## Summary Tasks

MS Project 2000 also allows you to add summary tasks to better organize your work. Returning to construction.mpp and reviewing the task list, we might organize the work into three phases: Structure, Interior, and Exterior. We can insert these as new tasks with zero duration. In the Gantt Chart view, place the Structure summary task between tasks 1 and 2, move current task 5 (Install Siding) between current tasks 11 and 12, place the Exterior summary task before the moved Install Siding task, and place the Interior summary task before the current task 6 (Install Plumbing). Since Excavate and Pour Footers, Pour Concrete Foundation, and Erect Rough Wall and Siding are part of the Structure task, they must be *indented*. Click on Excavate and Pour Footers in the Task Name column, and then click on the *indent* icon (thick arrow point to the right) from the toolbar to indent this task. Repeat this for the other tasks. The summary tasks must be *outdented* (thick arrow point to the left) and appear in bold. All tasks have been renumbered. The black bars on the Gantt Chart show the start and finish of summary tasks. The revised Gantt Chart view is shown in Figure 17.10 and the model is found in constructionS.mpp.

## Work Breakdown Structure

MS Project 2000 also allows the user to assign special Work Breakdown Structure (WBS) codes for all project tasks. A WBS is a categorized list of all project tasks that must be

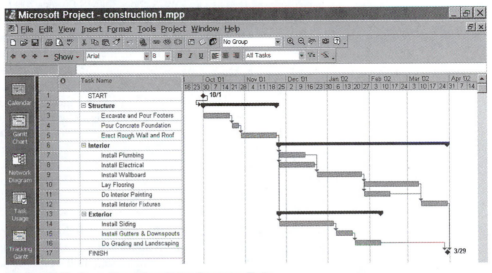

**Figure 17.10** Gantt Chart View Using Summary Tasks

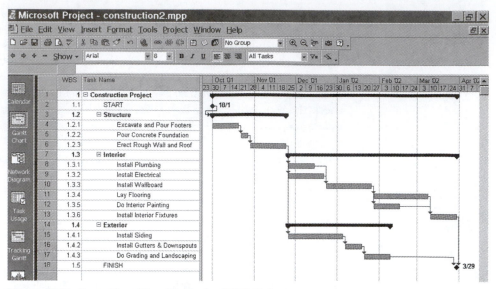

**Figure 17.11** Gantt Chart View Displaying WBS Codes

conducted in order to complete a project. The summation of all elements at one level of the WBS must be the sum of all work at the next lower level. The WBS can be organized into as many levels as desired using summary tasks. It is important to remember that each element of work should be assigned to one WBS level. More details on the use of WBS can be found in Meredith and Mantel (2000).

In constructionS.mpp add a new summary task, called Warehouse Construction, above the START task that is the sum of *all* the work in the project. The start and finish times for this task are those for the entire project. Once this new summary task is added, we need to indent the Structure, Interior, and Exterior summary tasks. With these changes we now have three WBS levels: project, phase (including START and FINISH), and task. (In other applications these three levels might be called project, task, and work package.)

We are now ready to add WBS codes. In MS Project 2000 the default WBS codes consist of the task numbers. Here we will illustrate how to assign new WBS codes. Click on *Project, WBS, Define Code*, then click on *sequence*, select numbers (ordered), press Enter, then continue to select numbers (ordered) for the second and third WBS levels. In the Gantt Chart view, click on the Task Names column, then click *Insert*, *Column* . . . , and within *Field name*, choose *WBS* to display WBS codes within the Gantt Chart view. The revised Gantt Chart view is shown in Figure 17.11 and the model is found as constructionWBS.mpp. In the following section on critical path analyis we will use construction.mpp without summary tasks and work breakdown structure in order to focus on the ideas presented.

## CRITICAL PATH ANALYSIS

### Introduction

The purpose of a critical path analysis is to determine the earliest date that the project can be completed. One might initially think that summing the durations of all project tasks will yield the earliest completion time. From Table 17.1 we see that the sum of all task durations is 43 weeks. Will our construction project take 43 weeks to complete assuming no delays? We will see that this is not the case because this line of reasoning ignores the precedence relationships in the network.

Looking at Figure 17.4, notice tasks 1 through 4 must be done in sequence, so it will take 8 weeks to complete them assuming no delays. Note that once task 4 is completed we can begin to *simultaneously* work on tasks 5, 6, and 7. Since the durations of these three tasks are 6, 3, and 4 weeks, respectively, after a total elapsed time of 14 (8 + 6) and *not* 21 (8 + 6 + 3 + 4) weeks we can complete tasks 1 through 7 assuming no delays. This example shows that we must take the precedence relationships into account in order to determine the earliest project completion time. An important assumption we are currently making is that all needed resources to complete the various tasks are available. The impact of resource limitations will be discussed in the next chapter.

## Path Enumeration

To determine the project completion date (also called the *project duration*) we must look at the length of each path through the project network. A *path* is a route through the project network that begins at the first node or START task and ends at the last node or FINISH task. The *critical path* is the longest path in the project network. The length of the critical path is the project duration. The various paths and their lengths for the construction project are summarized in Table 17.2. We see that path 1-2-3-4-7-8-9-11-14 is the longest path and has a length of 26 weeks. Therefore, the earliest that the project can be completed is 26 weeks after it is started. The *critical tasks* along this path cannot be delayed without delaying the project completion.

Once the task, duration, and predecessor information is entered into MS Project 2000, the critical path is computed automatically. Returning to construction.mpp and as shown in Figure 17.12, clicking on the *Project, Project Information,* and the *Statistics . . .* buttons shows that the duration of the critical path is 26 weeks. Assuming our start date of 10/1/01 and a five-day workweek, the project will be completed on 3/29/02.

Why is the longest path in the network the critical path? Since the tasks along any given path must be done one after another to finish them as soon as possible, the project duration cannot be *shorter* than that given path length. But the project duration can be *longer*, because tasks that have more than one immediate predecessor must wait for their predecessors to be completed before they can start. The implication of this point when determining the project duration is now shown.

From Table 17.2, we see that all paths contain tasks 1 through 4 since these tasks can be done in sequence. As mentioned previously, once task 4 is completed, tasks 5, 6, and 7 can start and be worked on in parallel. Tasks 6 and 7 are immediate predecessors of task 8. Since the duration of task 7 is greater than that of task 6, task 8 must wait until task 7 is completed before it can start. This shows that the sub path 1-2-3-4-7-8 has more effect

**Table 17.2**  Paths and Path Lengths for the Construction Project

| Path | Length |
|------|--------|
| 1-2-3-4-5-12-13-14 | 0 + 3 + 1 + 4 + 6 + 2 + 3 + 0 = 19 weeks |
| 1-2-3-4-6-8-9-11-14 | 0 + 3 + 1 + 4 + 3 + 5 + 6 + 3 + 0 = 25 weeks |
| 1-2-3-4-6-8-10-11-14 | 0 + 3 + 1 + 4 + 3 + 5 + 3 + 3 + 0 = 22 weeks |
| 1-2-3-4-7-8-9-11-14 | 0 + 3 + 1 + 4 + 4 + 5 + 6 + 3 + 0 = 26 weeks* |
| 1-2-3-4-7-8-10-11-14 | 0 + 3 + 1 + 4 + 4 + 5 + 3 + 3 + 0 = 23 weeks |

*critical path

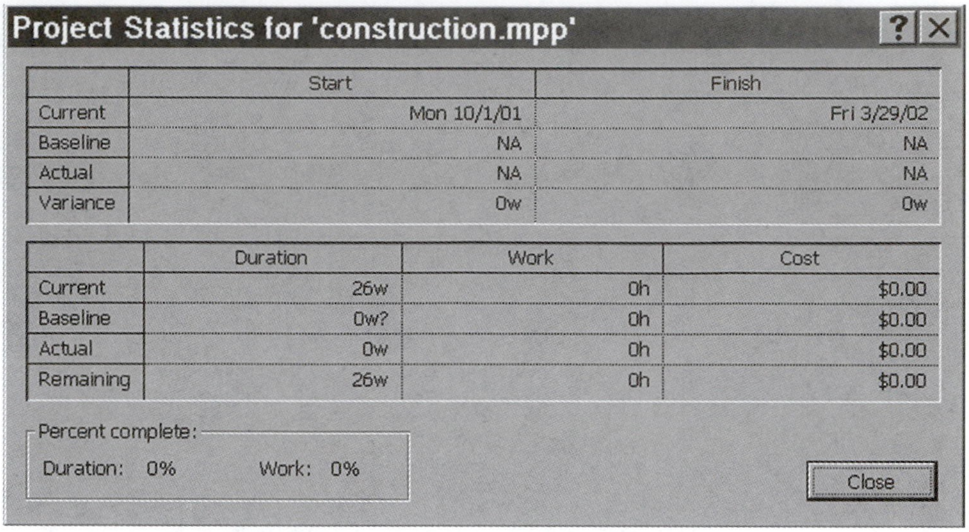

**Figure 17.12** Screen Shot of Project, Project Information, and Statistics

in controlling the project duration than the sub path 1-2-3-4-6-8. Similarly, once task 8 is completed, tasks 9 and 10 can start. Tasks 9 and 10 are immediate predecessors of task 11. Since task 9's duration is longer than that of task 10, task 11 must wait until task 9 is completed. This shows that sub path 1-2-3-4-7-8-9-11 has more effect in controlling the earliest project completion than sub path 1-2-3-4-7-8-10-11. Note that once task 4 is completed tasks 5, 12, 13 can follow sequentially, yielding a sub path 1-2-3-4-5-12-13. Now once tasks 11 and 13 are completed task 14 (finish) can start. The length of sub path 1-2-3-4-7-8-9-11 is 26 and the length of sub path 1-2-3-4-5-12-13 is 19. Therefore, task 14 has to wait until the sub path 1-2-3-4-7-8-9-11 is completed. Therefore, the longest path in the network, 1-2-3-4-7-8-9-11-14, is the critical path or the shortest project duration. Simply enumerating the lengths of all paths is an easier way of obtaining the results.

For small project networks, enumerating all paths and identifying the longest path is a convenient way to determine the critical path. However, this is not an efficient procedure for large projects. There is a more efficient method that involves determining a series of start and finish times for each task. This method is the basis of most computer software approaches, including MS Project 2000, and will be discussed in the next few sections.

## Early Start and Finish Times

In developing a project schedule, we often would like to determine the times that each task will start and finish. If we assume that all tasks are completed as soon as possible, we then would compute the *earliest start* and *earliest finish* times for each task. The approach for computing these times is similar in concept to our discussion in the previous section and relies on two basic ideas:

*The earliest a task can start is just after all of its immediate predecessor tasks have finished as early as possible.*

*The earliest a task can finish is the sum of its earliest start time and its duration.*

The application of these two ideas to our construction problem follows. We let ES and EF represent the earliest start and earliest finish times, respectively.

**Task 1:** Since task 1 has no immediate predecessors, $ES(1) = 0$. Since its duration is 0, $EF(1) = ES(1) = 0$.

**Task 2:** Since task 2 has one immediate predecessor, task 1, $ES(2) = EF(1) = 0$. Since task 2 has a duration of 3, $EF(2) = ES(2) + 3 = 0 + 3 = 3$.

Since tasks 3 through 7 each have one immediate predecessor, the ES-EF calculations are similar to those for task 2. That is, the ES of these tasks is simply the EF of the task's immediate predecessor.

**Task 3:** Since task 3 has one immediate predecessor, task 2, $ES(3) = EF(2) = 3$. Since task 3 has a duration of 1, $EF(3) = ES(3) + 1 = 3 + 1 = 4$.

**Task 4:** Since task 4 has one immediate predecessor, task 3, $ES(4) = EF(3) = 4$. Since task 4 has a duration of 4, $EF(4) = ES(4) + 4 = 4 + 4 = 8$.

**Task 5:** Since task 5 has one immediate predecessor, task 4, $ES(5) = EF(4) = 8$. Since task 5 has a duration of 6, $EF(5) = ES(5) + 6 = 8 + 6 = 14$.

**Task 6:** Since task 6 has one immediate predecessor, task 4, $ES(6) = EF(4) = 8$. Since task 6 has a duration of 3, $EF(6) = ES(6) + 3 = 8 + 3 = 11$.

**Task 7:** Since task 7 has one immediate predecessor, task 4, $ES(7) = EF(4) = 8$. Since task 7 has a duration of 4, $EF(7) = ES(7) + 4 = 8 + 4 = 12$.

Note that tasks 5, 6, and 7, have the same ES values, since all three have the same immediate predecessor task.

**Task 8:** Since task 8 has *two* immediate predecessors, tasks 6 and 7, both of these must be finished before it can start. Since the EF's for tasks 6 and 7 are 11 and 12, respectively, the larger or *maximum* of these values becomes the ES(8). That is, $ES(8) = Max[EF(6), EF(7)] = Max(11, 12) = 12$. Since task 8 has a duration of 5, $EF(8) = ES(8) + 5 = 12 + 5 = 17$.

**Task 9:** Since task 9 has one immediate predecessor, task 8, $ES(9) = EF(8) = 17$. Since task 9 has a duration of 6, $EF(9) = ES(9) + 6 = 17 + 6 = 23$.

**Task 10:** Since task 10 has one immediate predecessor, task 8, $ES(10) = EF(8) = 17$. Since task 10 has a duration of 3, $EF(10) = ES(10) + 3 = 17 + 3 = 20$.

Note that tasks 9 and 10 have the same ES values, since both have the same immediate predecessor task.

**Task 11:** Since task 11 has two immediate predecessors, tasks 9 and 10, both of these must be finished before it can start. Since the EF's for tasks 9 and 10 are 23 and 20, respectively, $ES(11) = Max[EF(9), EF(10)] = Max(23, 20) = 23$. Since task 11 has a duration of 3, $EF(11) = ES(11) + 3 = 23 + 3 = 26$.

**Task 12:** Since task 12 has one immediate predecessor, task 5, $ES(12) = EF(5) = 14$. Since task 12 has a duration of 2, $EF(12) = ES(12) + 2 = 14 + 2 = 16$.

**Task 13:** Since task 13 has one immediate predecessor, task 12, $ES(13) = EF(12) = 16$. Since task 13 has a duration of 3, $EF(13) = ES(12) + 3 = 16 + 3 = 19$.

> **Task 14:**   Since task 14 has two immediate predecessors, tasks 11 and 13, both of these must be finished before it can start. Since the EF's for tasks 11 and 13 are 26 and 19, respectively, $ES(14) = Max[EF(11), EF(13)] = Max(26, 19) = 26$. Since task 11 has a duration of 0, $EF(14) = ES(14) = 26$.

The EF of the FINISH task (14) is the project duration, or 26 weeks, the same result obtained using path enumeration. These results are summarized in Table 17.3.

## Late Start and Finish Times

The computation of the ES and EF for each project task enabled us to determine the project completion and a task schedule. However, it does not identify the tasks along the critical path and does not indicate how much non-critical path tasks can be delayed without delaying the project completion. To obtain these additional important results, we need to determine the latest start (LS) and latest finish (LF) times for each task. The approach for computing the LS and LF for project tasks is similar in concept to the approach described for ES and EF except that it is in some sense the *reverse*. That is, in computing ES and EF we begin with the START task and move *forward* through the network until we reach the FINISH task, first computing the ES and then the EF for each task. Here we begin with the FINISH task and move *backward* through the network until we reach the START task, first computing the LF and then the LS for each task. The rules for LF and LS are also in a sense the reverse of those for the ES and EF:

> *The latest a task can finish is just before all of its immediate successor tasks have started as late as possible.*
>
> *The latest a task can start is the difference of its latest finish time and its duration.*

The application of these two ideas to our construction problem follows.

> **Task 14:**   Since task 14 has no immediate successors, the latest it can finish is the project completion or $LF(14) = 26$. Since its duration is 0, $LS(14) = LF(14) = 26$.
>
> **Task 13:**   Since task 13 has one immediate successor, task 14, $LF(13) = LS(14) = 26$. Since task 13 has a duration of 3, $LS(13) = LF(13) - 3 = 26 - 3 = 23$.

Since tasks 12 through 9 each have one immediate successor, the LF–LS calculations are similar to those for task 13. That is, the LF of these tasks is simply the LS of the task's immediate successor.

> **Task 12:**   Since task 12 has only one immediate successor, task 13, $LF(12) = LS(13) = 23$. Since its duration is 2, $LS(12) = LF(12) - 2 = 23 - 2 = 21$.
>
> **Task 11:**   Since task 11 has one immediate successor, task 14, $LF(11) = LS(14) = 26$. Since its duration is 3, $LS(11) = LF(11) - 3 = 26 - 3 = 23$.

Note that tasks 11 and 13 have the same LF since they have the same immediate successor.

> **Task 10:**   Since task 10 has one immediate successor, task 11, $LF(10) = LS(11) = 23$. Since its duration is 3, $LS(10) = LF(10) - 3 = 23 - 3 = 20$.
>
> **Task 9:**   Since task 9 has one immediate successor, task 11, $LF(9) = LS(11) = 23$. Since its duration is 6, $LS(9) = LF(9) - 6 = 23 - 6 = 17$.

Note that tasks 9 and 10 have the same LF since they have the same immediate successor.

**Task 8:**  Since task 8 has *two* immediate successors, tasks 9 and 10, it must finish before both of these can start. Since the LS's for tasks 9 and 10 are 17 and 20, respectively, the smaller or *minimum* of these values becomes the LF(8). That is, LF(8) = Min[LS(9),LS(10)] = Min(17,20) = 17. Since task 8's duration is 5, LS(8) = LF(8) − 5 = 17 − 5 = 12.

**Task 7:**  Since task 7 has one immediate successor, task 8, LF(7) = LS(8) = 12. Since its duration is 4, LS(7) = LF(7) − 4 = 12 − 4 = 8.

**Task 6:**  Since task 6 has one immediate successor, task 8, LF(6) = LS(8) = 12. Since its duration is 3, LS(6) = LF(6) − 3 = 12 − 3 = 9.

Note that tasks 6 and 7 have the same LF since they have the same immediate successor.

**Task 5:**  Since task 5 has one immediate successor, task 12, LF(5) = LS(12) = 21. Since its duration is 6, LS(5) = LF(5) − 6 = 21 − 6 = 15.

**Task 4:**  Since task 4 has *three* immediate successors, tasks 5, 6, and 7, it must finish before these three tasks start. Since the LS's for tasks 5, 6, and 7 are 15, 9, and 8, respectively, LF(4) = Min[LS(5),LS(6),LS(7)] = Min(15,9,8) = 8. Since task 4's duration is 4, LS(4) = LF(4) − 4 = 8 − 4 = 4.

**Task 3:**  Since task 3 has one immediate successor, task 4, LF(3) = LS(4) = 4. Since its duration is 1, LS(3) = LF(3) − 1 = 4 − 1 = 3.

**Task 2:**  Since task 2 has one immediate successor, task 3, LF(2) = LS(3) = 3. Since its duration is 3, LS(2) = LF(2) − 3 = 3 − 3 = 0.

**Task 1:**  Since task 1 has one immediate successor, task 2, LF(1) = LS(2) = 0. Since its duration is 0, LS(1) = LF(1) = 0.

These results are also summarized in Table 17.3. Figure 17.13 shows a Gantt Chart that highlights the critical path. The screen was adjusted to show the full task names on the left and the full chart on the right. Click *View, More Views . . . , Detail Gantt,* and then click on *Apply*. The red bars on the right side of the screen denote the critical path tasks.

**Table 17.3**  Start and Finish Times and Slack

| Task | Duration | ES | EF | LS | LF | TF | FF |
|------|----------|-----|-----|-----|-----|-----|-----|
| 1 | 0 | 0 | 0 | 0 | 0 | 0 | 0 |
| 2 | 3 | 0 | 3 | 0 | 3 | 0 | 0 |
| 3 | 1 | 3 | 4 | 3 | 4 | 0 | 0 |
| 4 | 4 | 4 | 8 | 4 | 8 | 0 | 0 |
| 5 | 6 | 8 | 14 | 15 | 21 | 7 | 0 |
| 6 | 3 | 8 | 11 | 9 | 12 | 1 | 1 |
| 7 | 4 | 8 | 12 | 8 | 12 | 0 | 0 |
| 8 | 5 | 12 | 17 | 12 | 17 | 0 | 0 |
| 9 | 6 | 17 | 23 | 17 | 23 | 0 | 0 |
| 10 | 3 | 17 | 20 | 20 | 23 | 3 | 3 |
| 11 | 3 | 23 | 26 | 23 | 26 | 0 | 0 |
| 12 | 2 | 14 | 16 | 21 | 23 | 7 | 0 |
| 13 | 3 | 16 | 19 | 23 | 26 | 7 | 7 |
| 14 | 0 | 26 | 26 | 26 | 26 | 0 | 0 |

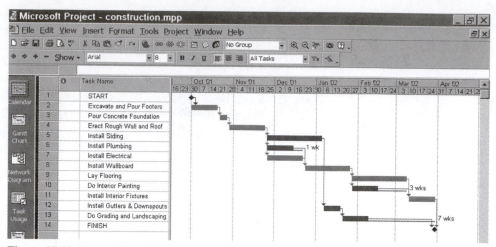

**Figure 17.13** Screen Shot of Detail Gantt Chart Showing Critical Path

## Total Slack

Using the results of the earliest and latest start and finish calculations, we can easily identify the critical tasks. But first we must compute the difference between a task's latest finish (LF) and earliest finish (EF) times. This difference is called *total slack (TS)* or *total float.* That is,

$$TS = LF - EF$$

Since $LF - EF = LS - ES$, either difference can be used to calculate TS.

If a task's LF and EF are the same, this means that no delay in completing this task is possible if we wish to complete the entire project in the minimum amount of time. Therefore, *tasks that have a TS of zero are on the critical path.* For example, task 3 is on the critical path, since $TS(3) = LF(3) - EF(3) = 4 - 4 = 0$, and $LS(3) - ES(3) = 3 - 3 = 0$. The calculations for TS for all tasks are included in Table 17.3. Note that tasks 1, 2, 3, 4, 7, 8, 9, 11, and 14 have TS values of zero, and are therefore on the critical path. This is the same result that we obtained using path enumeration (Table 17.2).

Now consider a task that is not on the critical path, such as task 5. Using the formula for TS we find $TS(5) = LF(5) - EF(5) = 21 - 14 = 7$. This result indicates that if the completion of task 5 is delayed up to 7 weeks the project can still be completed in 26 weeks. Why is this possible? Suppose task 5 is delayed 7 weeks and is completed at its LF of 21. Task 12 could then start at its LS of 21 and finish at its LF of 23, task 13 could begin at its LS of 23 and finish at its LF of 26, and task 14 (FINISH) could start and end at 26, the project duration.

An inspection of Table 17.3 shows that tasks 5, 12, and 13 all have TS values of 7. Does this mean that *each* of these tasks can be delayed by up to 7 weeks and the project will still finish on time? Again suppose that task 5 is delayed 7 weeks and is completed at the end of week 21 as before. If we now delay the start of task 12 by 7 weeks to week 28, we find that task 12 will be completed at week 30, already past our desired project completion of 26 weeks.

Looking at Figure 17.4 or Table 17.2 we see that tasks 5, 12, and 13 lie on path 1-2-3-4-5-12-13-14, which has a length of 19 weeks. The difference between 26 and 19 is the total slack of this path. Since tasks 5, 12, and 13 are the non-critical tasks on this path, these tasks *together* can be delayed at most 7 weeks without delaying the project completion. For example, as shown, if task 5 is delayed by 7 weeks, then tasks 12 and 13 would have to follow without delay. Another possibility for completing the project on time is to delay task 5 by 4 weeks, delay task 12 by 3 weeks, and then start task 13 without any delay. An inspection of Figure 17.13 shows that TS values are given on the *Detail Gantt* chart. The TS value of 7 is shown at the end of sub path 5-12-13.

Since task 6 is not on the path that contains tasks 5, 12, and 13, it can be delayed by its TS of 1 week and task 5 can be delayed by its TS of 7 weeks without delaying the project completion. These examples show that without a more careful inspection of the project network we can only safely use the full TS of one task and be certain that we will not delay the project completion.

## Free Slack

If we delay the completion of task 5 by 7 weeks and complete it after 21 weeks have elapsed, task 12, its immediate successor, could not start at its ES of 14 but would have to start at 21 weeks. That is, whenever task 5 uses any or all of its TS it delays the start of task 12 by that amount, reducing the available TS of task 12. Thus, we say that the TS of task 5 is not *free*. *Free slack (FS)* for a task is the amount of TS that can be used without delaying the start of any immediate successor tasks. Free slack can be computed using the following rule:

*Free slack (FS) of a task is the difference between the smallest of the ES's of the task's immediate successors and the task's EF.*

This rule may seem complex at first, but is easy to apply:

**Critical Tasks 1, 2, 3, 4, 7, 8, 9, 11, and 14:** Since FS is a portion of TS, we know the FS of all critical path tasks is zero. This result can be verified by applying the

| | Task Name | Start | Finish | Late Start | Late Finish | Free Slack | Total Slack |
|---|---|---|---|---|---|---|---|
| 1 | START | Mon 10/1/01 | Mon 10/1/01 | Mon 10/1/01 | Mon 10/1/01 | 0 wks | 0 wks |
| 2 | Excavate and Pour Footers | Mon 10/1/01 | Fri 10/19/01 | Mon 10/1/01 | Fri 10/19/01 | 0 wks | 0 wks |
| 3 | Pour Concrete Foundation | Mon 10/22/01 | Fri 10/26/01 | Mon 10/22/01 | Fri 10/26/01 | 0 wks | 0 wks |
| 4 | Erect Rough Wall and Roof | Mon 10/29/01 | Fri 11/23/01 | Mon 10/29/01 | Fri 11/23/01 | 0 wks | 0 wks |
| 5 | Install Siding | Mon 11/26/01 | Fri 1/4/02 | Mon 1/14/02 | Fri 2/22/02 | 0 wks | 7 wks |
| 6 | Install Plumbing | Mon 11/26/01 | Fri 12/14/01 | Mon 12/3/01 | Fri 12/21/01 | 1 wk | 1 wk |
| 7 | Install Electrical | Mon 11/26/01 | Fri 12/21/01 | Mon 11/26/01 | Fri 12/21/01 | 0 wks | 0 wks |
| 8 | Install Wallboard | Mon 12/24/01 | Fri 1/25/02 | Mon 12/24/01 | Fri 1/25/02 | 0 wks | 0 wks |
| 9 | Lay Flooring | Mon 1/28/02 | Fri 3/8/02 | Mon 1/28/02 | Fri 3/8/02 | 0 wks | 0 wks |
| 10 | Do Interior Painting | Mon 1/28/02 | Fri 2/15/02 | Mon 2/18/02 | Fri 3/8/02 | 3 wks | 3 wks |
| 11 | Install Interior Fixtures | Mon 3/11/02 | Fri 3/29/02 | Mon 3/11/02 | Fri 3/29/02 | 0 wks | 0 wks |
| 12 | Install Gutters & Downspou | Mon 1/7/02 | Fri 1/18/02 | Mon 2/25/02 | Fri 3/8/02 | 0 wks | 7 wks |
| 13 | Do Grading and Landscapir | Mon 1/21/02 | Fri 2/8/02 | Mon 3/11/02 | Fri 3/29/02 | 7 wks | 7 wks |
| 14 | FINISH | Fri 3/29/02 | Fri 3/29/02 | Fri 3/29/02 | Fri 3/29/02 | 0 wks | 0 wks |

**Figure 17.14** Screen Shot of the Schedule Table from the Gantt Chart View

rule. For example, task 8 has two immediate successors, tasks 9 and 10. The ES of tasks 9 and 10 are both 17, so the minimum of these values is also 17. The EF(8) is 17, so FS(8) = 17 − 17 = 0.

**Task 5:**    Since task 5 has only one immediate successor, task 12, FS(5) = ES(12) − EF(5) = 14 − 14 = 0, as previously determined.

**Task 6:**    Since task 6 has only one immediate successor, task 8, FS(6) = ES(8) − EF(6) = 12 − 11 = 1. This result indicates that if task 6 finishes 1 week later than its earliest finish time, task 8 still can start at its earliest start time.

**Task 10:**    Since task 10 has only one immediate successor, task 11, FS(10) = ES(11) − EF(10) = 23 − 20 = 3. This shows that all of the TS for task 10 is free.

**Task 12:**    Since task 12 has only one immediate successor, task 13, FS(12) = ES(13) − EF(12) = 16-16 = 0.

**Task 13:**    Since task 13 has only one immediate successor, task 14, FS(13) = ES(14) − EF(13) = 26 − 19 = 7. This shows that all of the TS for task 10 is free.

These results are summarized in Table 17.3.

Taken together, these results indicate that, if necessary, task 6 can be delayed by 1 week, task 10 can be delayed by 3 weeks, and task 13 can be delayed by 7 weeks and the project can still be completed on time. An important application is delaying tasks within their free slack in order to reduce resource peaks without extending the project duration, as will be discussed in the next chapter.

MS Project 2000 can display the results shown in Table 17.3. In the main menu from the *Gantt Chart* view, click on *View*, select *Table: Entry*, and then click on *Schedule*. Figure 17.14 is a screen shot of the resulting table portion of the Gantt Chart view. Using the information about slack, the start and finish times for each task can be adjusted as necessary to create a project schedule. In the next chapter we will investigate the impact of limited resources on the project schedule.

## SUMMARY

In this chapter we have discussed the creation of a project schedule. We began by differentiating projects from other forms of work and providing examples of work typically organized as projects. We have discussed how the project planning process begins by organizing a project into tasks, estimating task durations, and identifying precedence relationships. Using this information we create a project network using the activity-on-node method to visually depict the interrelationships among project tasks. Here the tasks are represented as circles and precedence is denoted as directed-line segments between nodes. We showed how to create a project schedule using Microsoft Project 2000, and illustrated several useful features for organizing work, including milestones, summary tasks, and work breakdown structure codes. We also showed different views for displaying project and task information.

Next we discussed the concept of the critical path within a project network. The critical path is the longest path in the project network, and its length is the earliest project completion time. Tasks along the critical path cannot be delayed without delaying the project completion. We have demonstrated why and how path enumeration can identify the critical path. We then showed how to compute the earliest and latest start and finish times for each task to create a project schedule. We also showed how to compute total slack and free slack for non-critical path tasks, and explained the difference between these two measures. Throughout this discussion we have shown how to obtain and display information about the critical path using Microsoft Project 2000.

## HOMEWORK PROBLEMS

**1.** ARMANT is developing a plan for the production of a low budget film. Task and precedence information are:

| Task | Description | Immediate Predecessors | Duration (Days) |
|---|---|---|---|
| 1 | START | — | 0 |
| 2 | Edit Script | 1 | 2 |
| 3 | Casting | 1 | 1 |
| 4 | Special Effects | 2 | 2 |
| 5 | Build Sets | 2 | 3 |
| 6 | Horror Scenes | 3,4 | 3 |
| 7 | Other Scenes | 3,5 | 1 |
| 8 | Previews | 6 | 1 |
| 9 | Edit Film | 6,7 | 2 |
| 10 | FINISH | 8,9 | 0 |

Enter this information into MS Project 2000. Assume the project starts on 10/1/01.

**(a)** Can the project be completed in 10 working days or less?

**(b)** Which tasks have a positive amount of total slack?

**(c)** Would the project still be completed in 10 working days or less if "Build Sets" took 2 days longer than expected to complete?

**2.** DOLAND plans and coordinates assertiveness training programs for various clients. Task and precedence information for a current project are:

| Task | Description | Immediate Predecessors | Duration (Weeks) |
|---|---|---|---|
| 1 | START | — | 0 |
| 2 | Plan Topic | 1 | 2 |
| 3 | Obtain Speakers | 2 | 3 |
| 4 | List Locations | 1 | 2 |
| 5 | Select Location | 4 | 2 |
| 6 | Plan Travel | 3,5 | 1 |
| 7 | Check Speakers | 6 | 2 |
| 8 | Prepare Brochure | 3,5 | 4 |
| 9 | Take Reservations | 8 | 4 |
| 10 | Last Minute Details | 7,9 | 2 |
| 11 | FINISH | 10 | 0 |

Enter this information into MS Project 2000. Assume the project starts on 10/1/01.

**(a)** What is the earliest project completion date?

**(b)** What are the critical path tasks?

**(c)** What are the total slack (TS) and free slack (FS) times for each task?

**(d)** What is the project schedule by task, assuming all tasks start on their earliest start (ES) time?

**3.** EASTWICK has won a contract for a systems development and implementation project. Task and precedence information are:

| Task | Description | Immediate Predecessors | Duration (Days) |
|---|---|---|---|
| 1 | START | — | 0 |
| 2 | Evaluate Hardware | 1 | 4 |
| 3 | Evaluate Software | 1 | 3 |
| 4 | Discuss Needs with Users | 2,3 | 5 |
| 5 | Develop Data Flow Diagrams | 4 | 6 |
| 6 | Develop Screen Designs | 4 | 2 |
| 7 | Review Screens with Users | 6 | 3 |
| 8 | Revise Requirements | 5,7 | 4 |
| 9 | Select Users for Initial Training | 7 | 2 |
| 10 | Code System | 8 | 10 |
| 11 | Testing | 10 | 5 |
| 12 | Install Software | 10 | 2 |
| 13 | Develop Training Materials | 10 | 3 |
| 14 | Train Selected Users | 9,13 | 3 |
| 15 | Develop Documentation | 11 | 2 |
| 16 | FINISH | 12,14,15 | 0 |

Enter this information into MS Project 2000. Assume the project starts on 10/1/01.

**(a)** What is the earliest project completion date?

**(b)** What are the critical path tasks?

**(c)** The project manager feels that Code System should be an immediate predecessor of Train Selected Users. What impact does this change have on the project schedule? Explain.

**(d)** Add at least two milestone tasks to help direct the project. Justify your choices.

**4.** SILEX is developing a plan to promote a new product. Task and precedence information are:

| Task | Description | Immediate Predecessors | Duration (Days) |
|---|---|---|---|
| 1 | START | — | 0 |
| 2 | Budget approval | 1 | 3 |
| 3 | Develop media plan | 2 | 15 |
| 4 | Draft print materials | 3 | 20 |
| 5 | Review/revise print materials | 4 | 5 |
| 6 | Agency develops TV commercials | 3 | 25 |
| 7 | Internal review TV commercials | 6 | 4 |
| 8 | Focus group review of TV commercials | 6 | 10 |
| 9 | Finalize TV commercials | 7,8 | 6 |
| 10 | Train marketing personnel | 5 | 5 |
| 11 | Management approval | 5,9 | 2 |
| 12 | Release ads to print media | 10,11 | 5 |
| 13 | Release commercials to networks | 11 | 3 |
| 14 | FINISH | 12,13 | 0 |

Enter this information into MS Project 2000. Assume the project starts on 10/1/01.

**(a)** Will the project be completed before the end of 2001?

**(b)** What are the critical path tasks?

**(c)** Identify the free slack for all tasks.

**(d)** Add at least two summary tasks for this project. Justify your choices.

## REFERENCES

Anderson, D. R., D. J. Sweeney, and T. A. Williams, *An Introduction to Management Science: Quantitative Approaches to Decision Making*, 9th ed., Cincinnati, OH, South-Western Publishing, 2000.

Cleland, D. I., *Project Management: Strategic Design and Implementation*, 3rd ed., New York, McGraw-Hill, 1999.

Friedrichsen, L. and R. B. Bunin, *New Perspectives on Microsoft Project 2000—Introductory*, Cambridge, MA, Course Technology, 2000.

Gray, C. F. and E. W. Larson, *Project Management: The Managerial Process*, New York, Irwin McGraw-Hill, 2000.

Hillier, F. S. and G. J. Lieberman, *Introduction to Operations Research*, 7th ed., New York, McGraw-Hill, 2001.

Kerzner, H., *Project Management: A Systems Approach to Planning, Scheduling, and Controlling*, 7th ed., New York, Wiley, 2000.

Mantel, S. J. Jr., J. R. Meredith, S. M. Shafer, and M. M. Sutton, *Project Management in Practice,* Wiley, New York, 2001.

Meredith, J. R. and S. J. Mantel, Jr., *Project Management: A Managerial Approach*, 4th ed., Wiley, New York, 2000.

Pollack-Johnson, B. and M. J. Liberatore, "Project Management Software Usage Patterns and Suggested Research Directions for Future Developments," *Project Management Journal,* Vol. 29, No. 2 (June 1998), 19–28.

Project Management Institute, *A Guide to the Project Management Body of Knowledge,* 2000.

# Chapter 18

# Project Resource and Cost Analysis Using Microsoft Project 2000

## INTRODUCTION

In this chapter we consider how the availability and usage of resources affect the development of the project schedule. In the previous chapter we developed a project schedule under the implicit assumption that all resources are available as needed. However, in many situations there are limitations on resources such as workers, equipment, and materials. In some cases we must explicitly consider differences in worker skill level during schedule development. For example, the project manager may need to consider computer programmers and financial analysts as two separate resources. In addition, workers may not be available over certain time periods because of vacations or commitments to other projects or operations. From a financial perspective we may wish to avoid heavy spending early in the project, or to smooth out our expenditures over the course of the project. These examples point out the importance of considering resources in the preparation of a project schedule. Since consuming resources incurs costs, finalizing the schedule will then enable the project manager to prepare a budget.

Of course we must not forget that time is also an important resource in projects. Completing a project later may offer the advantage of reducing peak resource needs, but it may delay realizing the benefits from a completed project. For example, suppose that a project produces an output that generates a new revenue stream or reduces costs, such as a new product or process, respectively. Delaying the completion of the project can delay the realization of these financial benefits. In other situations opportunity costs are incurred, since a delay may result in forestalling work on other promising opportunities.

Clearly there is a trade-off between the time required to complete the project and the associated costs. In some situations there may be an incentive to complete the project earlier than indicated by the length of the critical path. For example, construction contractors are often given incentives for completing a project early. Also, releasing a new version of a software program earlier in a highly competitive market may lead to an increased cash flow through additional sales. In such situations the project manager must balance the cost of expediting tasks to compete the project earlier with the incentives resulting from an earlier completion.

Here we develop the theory and methods of project resource and cost analysis using the construction example that was introduced in the previous chapter. In particular we consider the effect of limited resources on the project schedule and the benefits and costs of faster project completion. We will demonstrate how to conduct these resource and costing analyses using Microsoft Project 2000.

## RESOURCE ANALYSIS

### Entering Resource Information

We begin by creating a chart that summarizes all of the information that we will need for our resource analysis. After opening construction.mpp, click *View, Gantt Chart* (or use the *Gantt Chart* icon on the left panel of your screen), click *View, Table,* and then select *Entry.* This table contains all of the necessary information except for slack. Now click on the Resources Names column, click *Insert, Column,* then in the Field Names location select Free Slack. Repeat the latter process to insert Total Slack. A screen shot of the revised table view is shown as Figure 18.1. Note that the start and finish times shown in Figure 18.1 are the early start (ES) and early finish (EF) times, respectively.

Suppose that a construction crew consisting of at most seven workers can be assigned to complete the tasks shown in Figure 18.1. To track and manage the allocation of workers to this project, we begin by creating a resource within Microsoft Project 2000. From the main menu click on *View, Resource Sheet* (or use the *Resource Sheet* icon on the left panel of your screen), and then enter workers in the Resource Name column. Next, tab over to the Max. Units column and enter 700% to indicate that we have 7 workers. MS Project 2000 uses percentages to allow portions of resources to be allocated to projects and tasks. For example, a resource might be defined as an individual who might be assigned only half time or 50% to a particular project. In the Std. Rate column enter $30.00/hour, and keep all other columns at their default settings. A screen shot of the completed Resource Sheet is shown as Figure 18.2.

Microsoft Project 2000 allows the user to change the amount of resource units available over time. For example, in the Resource Sheet view, double-click on workers to open the Resource Information screen. The amounts and timing of resources can be specified using the Available From, Available To, and Units fields.

Next, we estimate the number of workers needed to accomplish the tasks shown in Figure 18.1. For example, suppose six workers are needed for the Excavate and Pour Footers task. Since the duration of this task is three weeks, we assume that six workers will be required to work continuously during the three weeks to complete this task, for a

| | Task Name | Duration | Start | Finish | Predecessors | Free Slack | Total Slack | Resource Names |
|---|---|---|---|---|---|---|---|---|
| 1 | START | 0 wks | Mon 10/1/01 | Mon 10/1/01 | | 0 wks | 0 wks | |
| 2 | Excavate and Pour Footers | 3 wks | Mon 10/1/01 | Fri 10/19/01 | 1 | 0 wks | 0 wks | |
| 3 | Pour Concrete Foundation | 1 wk | Mon 10/22/01 | Fri 10/26/01 | 2 | 0 wks | 0 wks | |
| 4 | Erect Rough Wall and Roof | 4 wks | Mon 10/29/01 | Fri 11/23/01 | 3 | 0 wks | 0 wks | |
| 5 | Install Siding | 6 wks | Mon 11/26/01 | Fri 1/4/02 | 4 | 0 wks | 7 wks | |
| 6 | Install Plumbing | 3 wks | Mon 11/26/01 | Fri 12/14/01 | 4 | 1 wk | 1 wk | |
| 7 | Install Electrical | 4 wks | Mon 11/26/01 | Fri 12/21/01 | 4 | 0 wks | 0 wks | |
| 8 | Install Wallboard | 5 wks | Mon 12/24/01 | Fri 1/25/02 | 6,7 | 0 wks | 0 wks | |
| 9 | Lay Flooring | 6 wks | Mon 1/28/02 | Fri 3/8/02 | 8 | 0 wks | 0 wks | |
| 10 | Do Interior Painting | 3 wks | Mon 1/28/02 | Fri 2/15/02 | 8 | 3 wks | 3 wks | |
| 11 | Install Interior Fixtures | 3 wks | Mon 3/11/02 | Fri 3/29/02 | 9,10 | 0 wks | 0 wks | |
| 12 | Install Gutters & Downspouts | 2 wks | Mon 1/7/02 | Fri 1/18/02 | 5 | 0 wks | 7 wks | |
| 13 | Do Grading and Landscaping | 3 wks | Mon 1/21/02 | Fri 2/8/02 | 12 | 7 wks | 7 wks | |
| 14 | FINISH | 0 wks | Fri 3/29/02 | Fri 3/29/02 | 11,13 | 0 wks | 0 wks | |

**Figure 18.1** Screen Shot of Modified Gantt Chart Table View

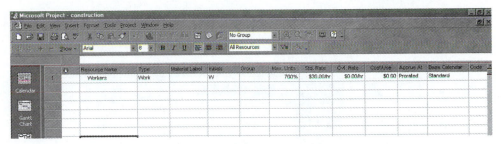

**Figure 18.2** Screen Shot of Resource Sheet View

total of 18 (3 * 6) worker-weeks. Similar estimates are made for the other tasks as shown in Figure 18.3.

There are several ways of entering resource data into MS Project 2000. Perhaps the easiest is selecting the _Gantt Chart, Table: Entry_ view, clicking on _Window_ on the main menu, and then selecting _Split_. To enter six workers for the Excavate and Pour Footers task, first click on this task name in the upper portion of your screen, then click on the open space immediately below the Resource Name column and select Workers. Next, click on the space immediately below the Units column and enter 600%, and then click the _OK_ button in the lower right-hand section of your screen. To enter the number of workers for the next task, simply click on the _Next_ button in the lower right-hand section of your screen. A screen shot of the completed process for the Excavate and Pour Footers task is shown as Figure 18.4. Note that Workers (600%) has now been automatically entered in the Resource Names column and in the Gantt Chart in the upper half of the split screen.

There are other methods for entering resource data in MS Project 2000. Again select the _Gantt Chart, Table: Entry_ view, and in the Task Name field, click on the Excavate and Pour Footers task. Next, click _Tools, Resources, Assign Resources,_ or use the _Assign Resources_ icon. A dialog box now appears on your screen. Since we have one resource, only workers appears in the Name field. In the Units column enter 600% and then click _Assign_. A check mark to the left of the Name column indicates that the resource is assigned to the selected task. Click on the next task to continue assigning resources, and click on

| Task | Description | Number of Workers |
|------|-------------|:-----------------:|
| 1 | START | — |
| 2 | Excavate and Pour Footers | 6 |
| 3 | Pour Concrete Foundation | 6 |
| 4 | Erect Rough Wall & Roof | 6 |
| 5 | Install Siding | 4 |
| 6 | Install Plumbing | 4 |
| 7 | Install Electrical | 2 |
| 8 | Install Wallboard | 2 |
| 9 | Lay Flooring | 4 |
| 10 | Do Interior Painting | 3 |
| 11 | Install Interior Fixtures | 2 |
| 12 | Install Gutters & Downspouts | 2 |
| 13 | Do Grading & Landscaping | 4 |
| 14 | FINISH | — |

**Figure 18.3** Workers Required by Task

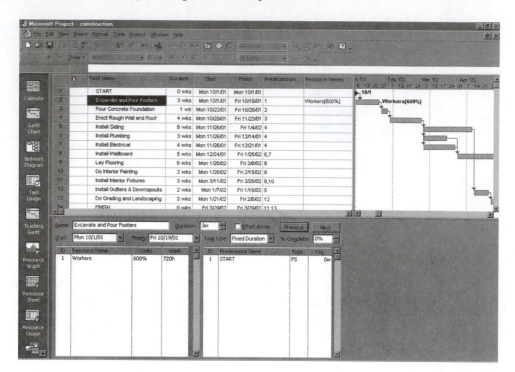

**Figure 18.4** Screen Shot of Split Gantt Chart View for Entering Resource Data

*Close* when you are finished. A screen shot of the completed process for the Excavate and Pour Footers task is shown as Figure 18.5. Clicking on the *Task Information* icon, and then clicking on the Resources tab can also enable resources to be assigned. Figure 18.6 is a screen shot of the Gantt Chart Table Entry View with all worker data entered. This information is found in the file called constructionRES.mpp.

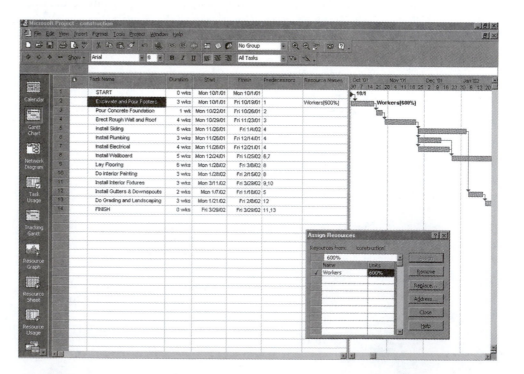

**Figure 18.5** Screen Shot of Gantt Chart View with Assign Resources Dialog Box for Entering Resource Data

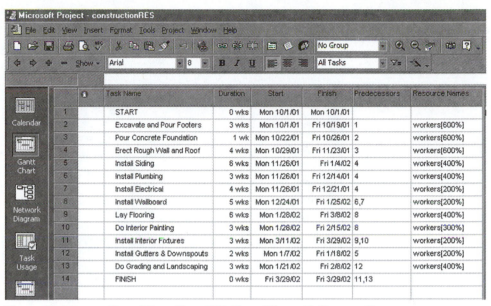

**Figure 18.6** Screen Shot of Gantt Chart Table Entry View with Resource Data

## Resource Loading

Once workers are allocated to all tasks we can prepare a resource loading chart. This chart indicates the number of units of a resource such as workers that are required during each time period over the course of the project. We begin by creating and manipulating resource loading charts in Excel rather than in MS Project 2000 in order to illustrate the methods used in resource analysis.

Initially, resource loading charts are prepared assuming all tasks start at their earliest start (ES) times. Using the start and finish dates for each task given in construction-RES.mpp (these are the ES and EF times) and the number of assigned workers given in Figure 18.6 we can build a resource loading chart on a week-by-week basis in Excel as shown in Figure 18.7. This chart is found in the file called construction resource loading1.xls. For each task (row) we enter the number of required workers during each week the task is scheduled, and then sum the number of workers over each week (column) to determine the load. An examination of Figure 18.7 shows that the number of required workers exceeds our maximum of seven during weeks 9–11 and 18–19, and trails off to low levels during the latter stages of the project.

## Resource Leveling

Smoothing or *leveling* the resource load during the course of the project offers many advantages for the project manager. Resource leveling attempts to minimize the period-to-period variations in resource use. Human resource management issues such as morale, motivation, and coordination are generally improved if the project work force is not constantly changing. Using equipment at constant levels for longer periods of time makes for more efficient use, and ordering materials at constant rates rather than in periodic large quantities can reduce inventory costs.

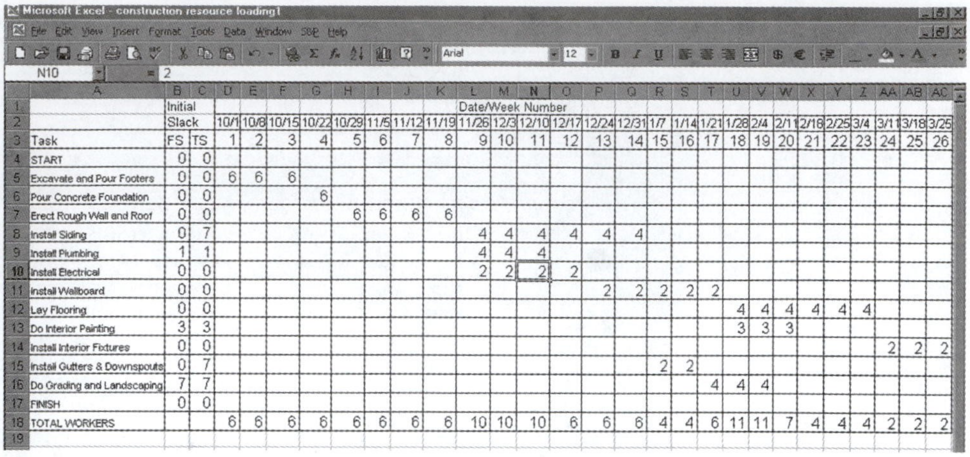

| Task | FS | TS | 1 10/1 | 2 10/8 | 3 10/15 | 4 10/22 | 5 10/29 | 6 11/5 | 7 11/12 | 8 11/19 | 9 11/26 | 10 12/3 | 11 12/10 | 12 12/17 | 13 12/24 | 14 12/31 | 15 1/7 | 16 1/14 | 17 1/21 | 18 1/28 | 19 2/4 | 20 2/11 | 21 2/18 | 22 2/25 | 23 3/4 | 24 3/11 | 25 3/18 | 26 3/25 |
|---|---|---|---|---|---|---|---|---|---|---|---|---|---|---|---|---|---|---|---|---|---|---|---|---|---|---|---|---|
| START | 0 | 0 | | | | | | | | | | | | | | | | | | | | | | | | | | |
| Excavate and Pour Footers | 0 | 0 | 6 | 6 | 6 | | | | | | | | | | | | | | | | | | | | | | | |
| Pour Concrete Foundation | 0 | 0 | | | | 6 | | | | | | | | | | | | | | | | | | | | | | |
| Erect Rough Wall and Roof | 0 | 0 | | | | | 6 | 6 | 6 | 6 | | | | | | | | | | | | | | | | | | |
| Install Siding | 0 | 7 | | | | | | | | | 4 | 4 | 4 | 4 | 4 | 4 | | | | | | | | | | | | |
| Install Plumbing | 1 | 1 | | | | | | | | | 4 | 4 | 4 | | | | | | | | | | | | | | | |
| Install Electrical | 0 | 0 | | | | | | | | | 2 | 2 | 2 | 2 | | | | | | | | | | | | | | |
| Install Wallboard | 0 | 0 | | | | | | | | | | | | | 2 | 2 | 2 | 2 | 2 | | | | | | | | | |
| Lay Flooring | 0 | 0 | | | | | | | | | | | | | | | | | | 4 | 4 | 4 | 4 | 4 | 4 | | | |
| Do Interior Painting | 3 | 3 | | | | | | | | | | | | | | | | | | 3 | 3 | 3 | | | | | | |
| Install Interior Fixtures | 0 | 0 | | | | | | | | | | | | | | | | | | | | | | | | 2 | 2 | 2 |
| Install Gutters & Downspouts | 0 | 7 | | | | | | | | | | | | | | | 2 | 2 | | | | | | | | | | |
| Do Grading and Landscaping | 7 | 7 | | | | | | | | | | | | | | | | | | 4 | 4 | 4 | | | | | | |
| FINISH | 0 | 0 | | | | | | | | | | | | | | | | | | | | | | | | | | |
| TOTAL WORKERS | | | 6 | 6 | 6 | 6 | 6 | 6 | 6 | 6 | 10 | 10 | 10 | 6 | 6 | 8 | 4 | 4 | 6 | 11 | 11 | 7 | 4 | 4 | 4 | 2 | 2 | 2 |

**Figure 18.7** Screen Shot of Excel Resource Loading Chart (construction resource loading1.xls)

## Constrained Resource Scheduling

### Background

In situations such as our construction example we have a limitation or *constraint* on the amount of a resource that is available during the course of the project. Leveling resource usage may or may not drop the resource peaks below the maximum available. The goal of *constrained resource scheduling* is to adjust the project schedule so that the resource limitation is not exceeded. There are several solution approaches that can be applied to this problem. See Wiest and Levy (1977) for a mathematical programming formulation, and Moder, Phillips, and Davis (1983) for an illustration of the branch and bound method (Chapter 2 provides a branch and bound example). However, in practice constrained resource scheduling problems are often difficult to solve using these methods, due to the large number of combinations of possible task start times that must be considered.

As a result, heuristic procedures are frequently used in practice to solve such combinatorial problems. A *heuristic* is sometimes called a "rule of thumb" since it is drawn from experience in solving a particular class of problems. Heuristics do not always find the optimal solution, but experience or computational testing demonstrate that good heuristics often find good solutions with a minimum of effort. There are a variety of heuristic techniques that have been proposed for resource constrained scheduling in situations of single or multiple resources. See Meredith and Mantel (2000) for additional discussion.

A good heuristic for the constrained single-resource problem involves the use of *slack time* to delay tasks that contribute to the resource overallocations. Here we must make the important distinction between the use of free slack and total slack to reschedule the project. Recall from the previous chapter that *total slack (TS)* is the amount of time a task can be delayed without delaying the project completion. *Free slack* (FS) for a task is the amount of total slack that can be used without delaying the start of any immediate successor tasks. Therefore delaying the start of a task by up to its amount of FS has no impact on the start times of other tasks in the network. However, if a task is delayed by its TS and it is not free, *successor* tasks must be delayed by the same amount. Otherwise the precedence relationships in the project network will be violated. Software programs such as MS Project 2000 incorporate the use of slack in their resource constrained heuristic procedures. Interestingly, MS Project 2000 calls its schedule adjustment procedure resource leveling and not constrained resource scheduling.

**Heuristic Method**

The constrained resource scheduling heuristic that we will illustrate is as follows:

**1.** Starting at the beginning of the project, inspect the resource loading chart to determine the first instance when the resource constraint is violated.

**2.** Identify those tasks having positive TS values that are scheduled during the time identified in step 1.

**3.** Of those tasks identified in step 2, select the task that has the largest TS value and move its start date forward to reduce the resource level. If the constraint is violated over several consecutive periods, continue moving the task forward within the available slack as necessary. Update the TS and FS values for the task moved. If the slack used is not free, move the start date(s) of immediate successor task(s) forward by the same amount. If the overallocation is eliminated go to step 5.

**4.** Repeat step 3 using the task that has the next largest TS value, and continue until the overallocation is eliminated. If the overallocation cannot be eliminated, go to step 6.

**5.** Identify the next overallocation of the resource constraint (if any), return to step 2 above, and continue until all overallocations have been addressed.

**6.** Extend the project completion date by one additional time unit, re-compute the TS and FS for each task, and return to step 1. Continue until all overallocations of the resource constraint are eliminated.

Other variations of this heuristic are possible, such as considering the amount of resources used as well as the TS value of the task identified in step 3. Our purpose here is to illustrate the basic ideas of using slack in resource-constrained scheduling.

*Application of the Heuristic*    We now apply the heuristic to our construction example.

*Step 1:* The first overallocation occurs during weeks 9–11 when 10 workers are needed (see Figure 18.7).

*Step 2:* The tasks contributing to this overallocation include Install Siding (FS = 0, TS = 7), Install Plumbing (FS = 1, TS = 1), and Install Electrical (FS = 0, TS = 0).

*Step 3:* Install Siding has the largest TS of the tasks identified in step 2, so its start date is moved forward by three weeks. Since Install Siding's slack is not free, its immediate successor, Install Gutters and Downspouts, must also have its start date moved forward by three weeks. This in turn triggers moving Do Grading and Landscaping forward by three weeks, since the slack of Install Gutters and Downspouts is not free. The adjusted schedule over weeks 9–11 satisfies the resource constraint. Note that three days of slack have been used from each of the three tasks whose schedules have been modified. The adjusted schedule is given as Figure 18.8 and is found in a file called construction resource loading2.xls. Since the overallocation is eliminated, go to step 5.

*Step 5:* The next overallocation occurs during weeks 18–22 where 9, 9, 11, 8, and 8 workers, respectively, are needed (see Figure 18.8). Return to step 2 to address this overallocation.

*Step 2:* The tasks contributing to this overallocation in week 18 include Lay Flooring (FS = 0, TS = 0), Do Interior Painting (FS = 3, TS = 3), and Install Gutters and Downspouts (FS = 0, TS = 4).

*Microsoft Excel - construction resource loading2*

**Figure 18.8** (Revised Slack: FS, TS — Date/Week Number)

| Task | FS | TS | 10/1 (1) | 10/8 (2) | 10/15 (3) | 10/22 (4) | 10/29 (5) | 11/5 (6) | 11/12 (7) | 11/19 (8) | 11/26 (9) | 12/3 (10) | 12/10 (11) | 12/17 (12) | 12/24 (13) | 12/31 (14) | 1/7 (15) | 1/14 (16) | 1/21 (17) | 1/28 (18) | 2/4 (19) | 2/11 (20) | 2/18 (21) | 2/25 (22) | 3/4 (23) | 3/11 (24) | 3/18 (25) | 3/25 (26) |
|---|---|---|---|---|---|---|---|---|---|---|---|---|---|---|---|---|---|---|---|---|---|---|---|---|---|---|---|---|
| START | 0 | 0 | | | | | | | | | | | | | | | | | | | | | | | | | | |
| Excavate and Pour Footers | 0 | 0 | 6 | 6 | 6 | | | | | | | | | | | | | | | | | | | | | | | |
| Pour Concrete Foundation | 0 | 0 | | | | 6 | | | | | | | | | | | | | | | | | | | | | | |
| Erect Rough Wall and Roof | 0 | 0 | | | | | 6 | 6 | 6 | 6 | | | | | | | | | | | | | | | | | | |
| Install Siding | 0 | 4 | | | | | | | | | | | | 4 | 4 | 4 | 4 | 4 | 4 | | | | | | | | | |
| Install Plumbing | 1 | 1 | | | | | | | | | 4 | 4 | 4 | | | | | | | | | | | | | | | |
| Install Electrical | 0 | 0 | | | | | | | | | 2 | 2 | 2 | 2 | | | | | | | | | | | | | | |
| Install Wallboard | 0 | 0 | | | | | | | | | | | | | 2 | 2 | 2 | 2 | 2 | | | | | | | | | |
| Lay Flooring | 0 | 0 | | | | | | | | | | | | | | | | | | 4 | 4 | 4 | 4 | 4 | 4 | | | |
| Do Interior Painting | 3 | 3 | | | | | | | | | | | | | | | | | | 3 | 3 | 3 | | | | | | |
| Install Interior Fixtures | 0 | 0 | | | | | | | | | | | | | | | | | | | | | | | | 2 | 2 | 2 |
| Install Gutters & Downspouts | 0 | 4 | | | | | | | | | | | | | | | | | | 2 | 2 | | | | | | | |
| Do Grading and Landscaping | 4 | 4 | | | | | | | | | | | | | | | | | | | | 4 | 4 | 4 | | | | |
| FINISH | 0 | 0 | | | | | | | | | | | | | | | | | | | | | | | | | | |
| TOTAL WORKERS | | | 6 | 6 | 6 | 6 | 6 | 6 | 6 | 6 | 6 | 6 | 6 | 6 | 6 | 6 | 6 | 6 | 6 | 9 | 9 | 11 | 8 | 8 | 4 | 2 | 2 | 2 |

Note: Move Install Siding ahead by 3 weeks, requiring Install Gutters and Do Grading also to move ahead by 3 weeks

**Figure 18.8** Screen Shot of Excel Resource Loading Chart after Resource Overallocation During Weeks 9–11 Are Eliminated (construction resource loading2.xls)

*Step 3:* Install Gutters and Downspouts has the largest TS of the tasks identified in Step 2, and so its start date is moved forward by three weeks. Its immediate successor, Do Grading and Landscaping, must also be moved forward by three weeks. The adjusted schedule over weeks 18–20 satisfies the resource constraint. Note that three additional days of slack have been used from each of the two tasks whose schedules have been modified. The adjusted schedule is given as Figure 18.9 and is found in the file called construction resource loading3.xls.

*Step 5:* The overallocation occurring during the week 23 where eight workers are needed must now be addressed (see Figure 18.9).

*Step 2:* The tasks contributing to this overallocation include Lay Flooring (FS = 0, TS = 0) and Do Grading and Landscaping (FS = 1, TS = 1).

*Microsoft Excel - construction resource loading3*

**Figure 18.9** (Revised Slack: FS, TS — Date/Week Number)

| Task | FS | TS | 10/1 (1) | 10/8 (2) | 10/15 (3) | 10/22 (4) | 10/29 (5) | 11/5 (6) | 11/12 (7) | 11/19 (8) | 11/26 (9) | 12/3 (10) | 12/10 (11) | 12/17 (12) | 12/24 (13) | 12/31 (14) | 1/7 (15) | 1/14 (16) | 1/21 (17) | 1/28 (18) | 2/4 (19) | 2/11 (20) | 2/18 (21) | 2/25 (22) | 3/4 (23) | 3/11 (24) | 3/18 (25) | 3/25 (26) |
|---|---|---|---|---|---|---|---|---|---|---|---|---|---|---|---|---|---|---|---|---|---|---|---|---|---|---|---|---|
| START | 0 | 0 | | | | | | | | | | | | | | | | | | | | | | | | | | |
| Excavate and Pour Footers | 0 | 0 | 6 | 6 | 6 | | | | | | | | | | | | | | | | | | | | | | | |
| Pour Concrete Foundation | 0 | 0 | | | | 6 | | | | | | | | | | | | | | | | | | | | | | |
| Erect Rough Wall and Roof | 0 | 0 | | | | | 6 | 6 | 6 | 6 | | | | | | | | | | | | | | | | | | |
| Install Siding | 0 | 4 | | | | | | | | | | | | 4 | 4 | 4 | 4 | 4 | 4 | | | | | | | | | |
| Install Plumbing | 1 | 1 | | | | | | | | | 4 | 4 | 4 | | | | | | | | | | | | | | | |
| Install Electrical | 0 | 0 | | | | | | | | | 2 | 2 | 2 | 2 | | | | | | | | | | | | | | |
| Install Wallboard | 0 | 0 | | | | | | | | | | | | | 2 | 2 | 2 | 2 | 2 | | | | | | | | | |
| Lay Flooring | 0 | 0 | | | | | | | | | | | | | | | | | | 4 | 4 | 4 | 4 | 4 | 4 | | | |
| Do Interior Painting | 3 | 3 | | | | | | | | | | | | | | | | | | 3 | 3 | 3 | | | | | | |
| Install Interior Fixtures | 0 | 0 | | | | | | | | | | | | | | | | | | | | | | | | 2 | 2 | 2 |
| Install Gutters & Downspouts | 0 | 1 | | | | | | | | | | | | | | | | | | | | | 2 | 2 | | | | |
| Do Grading and Landscaping | 1 | 1 | | | | | | | | | | | | | | | | | | | | | | | 4 | 4 | 4 | |
| FINISH | 0 | 0 | | | | | | | | | | | | | | | | | | | | | | | | | | |
| TOTAL WORKERS | | | 6 | 6 | 6 | 6 | 6 | 6 | 6 | 6 | 6 | 6 | 6 | 6 | 6 | 6 | 6 | 6 | 6 | 7 | 7 | 7 | 6 | 6 | 8 | 6 | 6 | 2 |

Note: Move Install Gutters ahead by 3 weeks, requiring moving Do Grading ahead by 3 weeks

**Figure 18.9** Screen Shot of Excel Resource Loading Chart after Resource Overallocation During Weeks 18–20 Are Eliminated (construction resource loading3.xls)

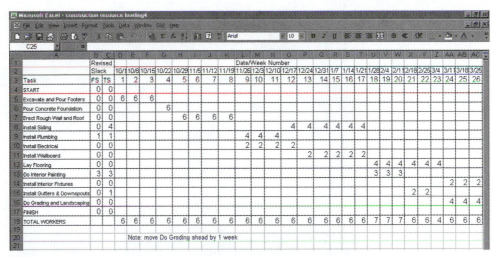

**Figure 18.10** Screen Shot of Excel Resource Loading Chart after Resource Overallocation During Week 23 Is Eliminated (construction resource loading4.xls)

*Step 3:* The start date of Do Grading and Landscaping is moved forward by one week. Since this slack is free (in this case because this task has no immediate successors requiring work) no additional schedule changes are required. Note that the final day of slack for this task has now been used. The final adjusted schedule is given as Figure 18.10 and is found in a file called construction resource loading4.xls.

## Constrained Resource Scheduling Using MS Project 2000

### Manual Schedule Adjustment

The resource-loading chart given as Figure 18.7 can be obtained in MS Project 2000 using constructionRES.mpp. Click *View, Resource Graph* (or the *Resource Graph* icon on the left panel of your screen), and then use the zoom buttons to adjust the view to weeks. Right-click on the chart and select Peak units to calibrate the resources into percentages. The horizontal black line represents the constraint of seven workers. A screen shot providing a partial view of this chart is given as Figure 18.11.

MS Project 2000 enables the user to identify those tasks contributing to resource overallocations. Click *View, Resource Usage* (or the *Resource Usage* icon on the left panel of your screen), and then use the zoom buttons to adjust the view to weeks. A useful feature (especially in the multi-resource case) is to click on the Filter list arrow (the menu box currently displaying All Resources) and select Overallocated Resources. Click on the expand button to the left of Workers in the Resource Names column to display all of the project tasks. Move the display to the right until you see three entries of 400h in red, indicating that 400 hours, or 10 workers, are needed during weeks 9–11 (November 26– December 10, 2001). The tasks contributing to this overallocation are now shown in the entries below the weekly totals as shown in a screen shot of the *Resource Usage* view given as Figure 18.12.

At this point, the user can return to the Gantt Chart view, select *Table: Schedule*, view the available slack for the tasks contributing to the overallocation, and then *manually* adjust the start dates of tasks as desired. This feature is useful for those users who are not satisfied with the results of MS Project 2000's automatic resource leveling feature (to be described shortly) or who wish to investigate alternative schedules.

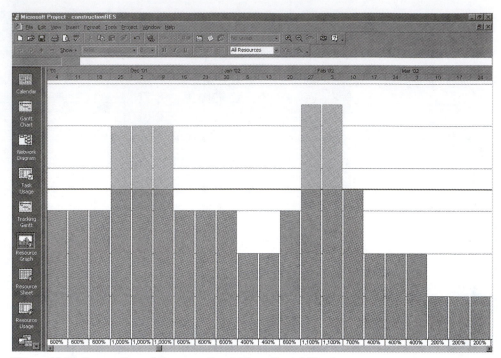

**Figure 18.11** Screen Shot of Resource Graph View (Partial View)

The manual adjustment of the start dates of those tasks contributing to the overallocations proceeds as follows. First, the start date of the Install Siding task is moved three weeks forward from November 26, 2001 (week 9) to December 17, 2001 (week 12). This adjustment triggers a message in MS Project 2000 relating to the links, or predecessor-successor relationships, in the network. Select the option Move the task (Install Siding) to start on Mon Dec 17, '01 and keep the link. MS Project 2000 then adjusts the start and finish dates of Install Gutters and Downspouts and Do Grading and Landscaping as desired since these are immediate successors of Install Siding. The total and free slack values for all tasks are also adjusted. Returning to the *Resource Usage* view will show that an overallocation no longer exists for weeks 9–11.

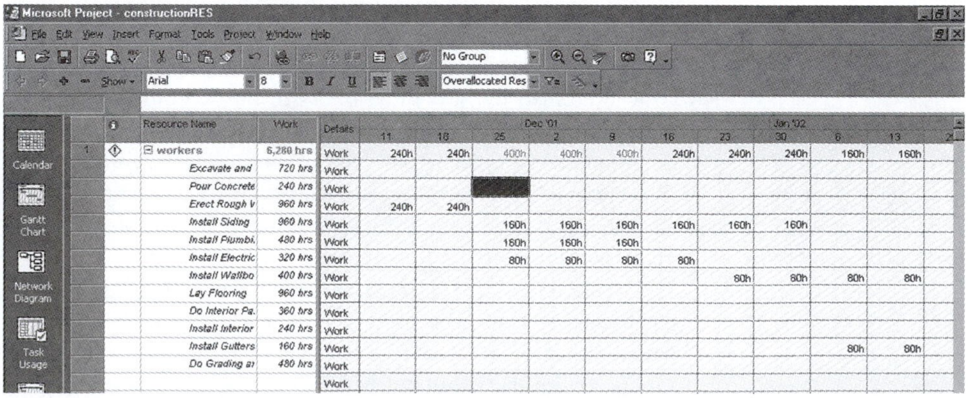

**Figure 18.12** Screen Shot of Resource Usage View (Partial View)

Next we can move the start of Install Gutters and Downspouts three weeks forward to start on February 18, 2002, and then move the start of Do Grading and Landscaping one additional week forward to start on March 11, 2002. Figure 18.13 shows a screen shot of the modified Gantt Chart view after all of these changes have been made. The modified project is saved in the file called constructionRES-M.mpp. Changing the view to *Resource Graph* shows that the results obtained match those displayed in Figure 18.10.

### Automatic Schedule Adjustment

MS Project 2000 can automatically adjust start and finish dates using its resource leveling option. Within the software, the term *leveling* means eliminating overallocation of resources. Returning to constructionRES.mpp, click on *Tools, Resource Leveling . . .* , select Manual, check Clear values before leveling and Level only within available slack, and *un*check Leveling can adjust individual assignments on a task and Leveling can create splits in remaining work. After making these changes, click the Level Now button. A screen shot of the Resource Leveling dialog box is given as Figure 18.14. The results are given in the file called constructionRES7MAX.mpp.

The Resource Graph view (not shown here) of constructionRES7MAX.mpp shows that MS Project produces the same resource loadings as those given in Figure 18.10. A screen shot of the *Gantt Chart Table: Schedule* view given as Figure 18.15 shows that the start and finish dates of the adjusted tasks are the same as those found in Figure 18.10. However, the values for TS in this figure are listed as 0 for Install Siding, and Install Gutters and Downspouts, in contrast to the values of 4 and 1, respectively, shown in Figure 18.10. Remember that these are two of the three tasks whose start dates were modified. Care must be exercised if further schedule adjustments are made. For example, manually adjusting the start date of Install Siding one week forward to December 24, 2001

| | | Task Name | Start | Finish | Late Start | Late Finish | Free Slack | Total Slack |
|---|---|---|---|---|---|---|---|---|
| | 1 | START | Mon 10/1/01 | Mon 10/1/01 | Mon 10/1/01 | Mon 10/1/01 | 0 wks | 0 wks |
| | 2 | Excavate and Pour Footers | Mon 10/1/01 | Fri 10/19/01 | Mon 10/1/01 | Fri 10/19/01 | 0 wks | 0 wks |
| | 3 | Pour Concrete Foundation | Mon 10/22/01 | Fri 10/26/01 | Mon 10/22/01 | Fri 10/26/01 | 0 wks | 0 wks |
| | 4 | Erect Rough Wall and Roof | Mon 10/29/01 | Fri 11/23/01 | Mon 10/29/01 | Fri 11/23/01 | 0 wks | 0 wks |
| | 5 | Install Siding | Mon 12/17/01 | Fri 1/25/02 | Mon 1/14/02 | Fri 2/22/02 | 0 wks | 4 wks |
| | 6 | Install Plumbing | Mon 11/26/01 | Fri 12/14/01 | Mon 12/3/01 | Fri 12/21/01 | 1 wk | 1 wk |
| | 7 | Install Electrical | Mon 11/26/01 | Fri 12/21/01 | Mon 11/26/01 | Fri 12/21/01 | 0 wks | 0 wks |
| | 8 | Install Wallboard | Mon 12/24/01 | Fri 1/25/02 | Mon 12/24/01 | Fri 1/25/02 | 0 wks | 0 wks |
| | 9 | Lay Flooring | Mon 1/28/02 | Fri 3/8/02 | Mon 1/28/02 | Fri 3/8/02 | 0 wks | 0 wks |
| | 10 | Do Interior Painting | Mon 1/28/02 | Fri 2/15/02 | Mon 2/18/02 | Fri 3/8/02 | 3 wks | 3 wks |
| | 11 | Install Interior Fixtures | Mon 3/11/02 | Fri 3/29/02 | Mon 3/11/02 | Fri 3/29/02 | 0 wks | 0 wks |
| | 12 | Install Gutters & Downspout | Mon 2/18/02 | Fri 3/1/02 | Mon 2/25/02 | Fri 3/8/02 | 0 wks | 1 wk |
| | 13 | Do Grading and Landscapin | Mon 3/11/02 | Fri 3/29/02 | Mon 3/11/02 | Fri 3/29/02 | 0 wks | 0 wks |
| | 14 | FINISH | Fri 3/29/02 | Fri 3/29/02 | Fri 3/29/02 | Fri 3/29/02 | 0 wks | 0 wks |

**Figure 18.13** Screen Shot of Gantt Chart Table: Schedule View with Adjusted Start Dates of Selected Tasks

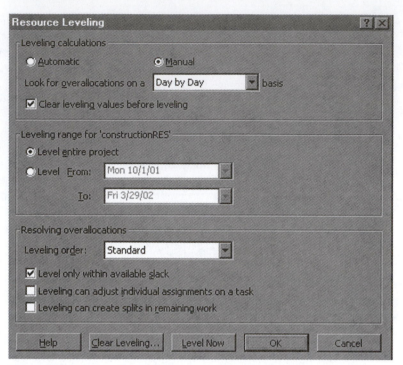

**Figure 18.14** Screen Shot of Resource Leveling Dialog Box

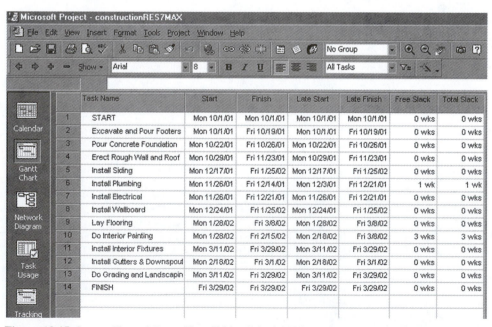

**Figure 18.15** Screen Shot of Gantt Chart Table: Schedule View after Resource Leveling

triggers the start dates of its immediate successor Install Gutters and Downspouts, and the latter's immediate successor, Do Grading and Landscaping, to move one week forward as well. As a result of these changes, the project will be completed one week late. Therefore, using the start dates and slack information *prior* to leveling along with the results of the leveling analysis is required if further changes are desired.

The original and leveled schedules can be seen using the Leveling Gantt chart view. From the main menu, click *View, More Views . . .* , and then select Leveling Gantt. A screen shot of this chart is given as Figure 18.16. For each task, the green bar shows the pre-leveled schedule, the open bar indicates the leveling delay, and the blue bar depicts the leveled schedule. The amount of the leveling delay by task is shown in the table on the left side of Figure 18.16.

MS Project 2000 does not consider the three-week delays to the start of Install Gutters and Downspouts and Do Grading and Landscaping that resulted from the delay of their Install Siding to be caused by leveling (see Figure 18.8). These changes are viewed as having resulted from the enforcement of links, or predecessor-successor relationships. Following this logic, only the three weeks that the start of Install Gutters and Downspouts was delayed in the second stage of leveling (Figure 18.9), and the one week that Do Grading and Landscaping was delayed in the third stage of leveling (Figure 18.10) are considered leveling delays by MS Project 2000.

### Further Schedule Adjustments

The final schedule (Figure 18.10) illustrates that resource usage is nearly constant throughout the project at six workers, with seven being required during weeks 18–20 and only four during week 23. A question that naturally arises is whether the number of workers can be reduced from seven to six for further cost savings. The heuristic given in the section Heuristic Method can once again be applied, starting with the results given in Figure 18.10.

*Step 1:* The first overallocation occurs during weeks 18–20 where 7 workers are needed.

*Step 2:* The tasks contributing to this overallocation include Lay Flooring (FS = 0, TS = 0), and Do Interior Painting (FS = 3, TS = 3).

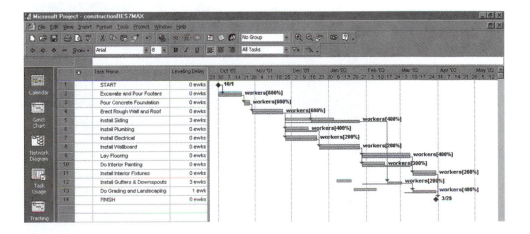

**Figure 18.16** Screen Shot of Leveling Gantt Table: Delay View

**Figure 18.17** Screen Shot of Excel Resource Loading Chart after Resource Overallocation During Weeks 18–20 is Eliminated (construction resource loading5.xls)

| Task | FS | TS | 10/1 | 10/8 | 10/15 | 10/22 | 10/29 | 11/5 | 11/12 | 11/19 | 11/26 | 12/3 | 12/10 | 12/17 | 12/24 | 12/31 | 1/7 | 1/14 | 1/21 | 1/28 | 2/4 | 2/11 | 2/18 | 2/25 | 3/4 | 3/11 | 3/18 | 3/25 |
|---|---|---|---|---|---|---|---|---|---|---|---|---|---|---|---|---|---|---|---|---|---|---|---|---|---|---|---|---|
| *(Week Number)* | | | 1 | 2 | 3 | 4 | 5 | 6 | 7 | 8 | 9 | 10 | 11 | 12 | 13 | 14 | 15 | 16 | 17 | 18 | 19 | 20 | 21 | 22 | 23 | 24 | 25 | 26 |
| START | 0 | 0 | | | | | | | | | | | | | | | | | | | | | | | | | | |
| Excavate and Pour Footers | 0 | 0 | 6 | 6 | 6 | | | | | | | | | | | | | | | | | | | | | | | |
| Pour Concrete Foundation | 0 | 0 | | | | 6 | | | | | | | | | | | | | | | | | | | | | | |
| Erect Rough Wall and Roof | 0 | 0 | | | | | 6 | 6 | 6 | 6 | | | | | | | | | | | | | | | | | | |
| Install Siding | 0 | 4 | | | | | | | | | | | | 4 | 4 | 4 | 4 | 4 | | | | | | | | | | |
| Install Plumbing | 1 | 1 | | | | | | | | | 4 | 4 | 4 | | | | | | | | | | | | | | | |
| Install Electrical | 0 | 0 | | | | | | | | | 2 | 2 | 2 | 2 | | | | | | | | | | | | | | |
| Install Wallboard | 0 | 0 | | | | | | | | | | | | | 2 | 2 | 2 | 2 | 2 | | | | | | | | | |
| Lay Flooring | 0 | 0 | | | | | | | | | | | | | | | | | | 4 | 4 | 4 | 4 | 4 | 4 | | | |
| Do Interior Painting | 0 | 0 | | | | | | | | | | | | | | | | | | | | | 3 | 3 | 3 | | | |
| Install Interior Fixtures | 0 | 0 | | | | | | | | | | | | | | | | | | | | | | | | 2 | 2 | 2 |
| Install Gutters & Downspouts | 0 | 1 | | | | | | | | | | | | | | | | | | | | | 2 | 2 | | | | |
| Do Grading and Landscaping | 0 | 0 | | | | | | | | | | | | | | | | | | | | | | | | 4 | 4 | 4 |
| FINISH | 0 | 0 | | | | | | | | | | | | | | | | | | | | | | | | | | |
| TOTAL WORKERS | | | 6 | 6 | 6 | 6 | 6 | 6 | 6 | 6 | 6 | 6 | 6 | 6 | 6 | 6 | 6 | 6 | 6 | 4 | 4 | 4 | 9 | 9 | 7 | 6 | 6 | 6 |

Note: move Do Interior Painting ahead by 3 weeks

*Step 3:* The start date of Do Interior Painting is moved forward by three weeks. The adjusted schedule is given as Figure 18.17 and is found in the file called construction resource loading5.xls.

*Step 5:* The next overallocation occurs during weeks 21–23 where 9, 9, and 7 workers, respectively, are needed (see Figure 18.17).

*Step 2:* The tasks contributing to this overallocation during week 21 include Lay Flooring (FS = 0, TS = 0), Do Interior Painting (FS = 0, TS = 0), and Install Gutters and Downspouts (FS = 0, TS = 1).

*Step 3:* The start date of Install Gutters and Downspouts is moved forward by one week. The adjusted schedule is given as Figure 18.18 and is found in the file called construction resource loading6.xls.

*Step 4:* Since an overallocation still exists during week 21 (February 18, 2002), and since both tasks contributing to this overallocation have zero TS, we are unable to meet the resource constraint without extending the project completion date.

**Figure 18.18** Screen Shot of Excel Resource Loading Chart with Resource Overallocation Remaining During Week 21 (construction resource loading6.xls)

| Task | FS | TS | 10/1 | 10/8 | 10/15 | 10/22 | 10/29 | 11/5 | 11/12 | 11/19 | 11/26 | 12/3 | 12/10 | 12/17 | 12/24 | 12/31 | 1/7 | 1/14 | 1/21 | 1/28 | 2/4 | 2/11 | 2/18 | 2/25 | 3/4 | 3/11 | 3/18 | 3/25 |
|---|---|---|---|---|---|---|---|---|---|---|---|---|---|---|---|---|---|---|---|---|---|---|---|---|---|---|---|---|
| *(Week Number)* | | | 1 | 2 | 3 | 4 | 5 | 6 | 7 | 8 | 9 | 10 | 11 | 12 | 13 | 14 | 15 | 16 | 17 | 18 | 19 | 20 | 21 | 22 | 23 | 24 | 25 | 26 |
| START | 0 | 0 | | | | | | | | | | | | | | | | | | | | | | | | | | |
| Excavate and Pour Footers | 0 | 0 | 6 | 6 | 6 | | | | | | | | | | | | | | | | | | | | | | | |
| Pour Concrete Foundation | 0 | 0 | | | | 6 | | | | | | | | | | | | | | | | | | | | | | |
| Erect Rough Wall and Roof | 0 | 0 | | | | | 6 | 6 | 6 | 6 | | | | | | | | | | | | | | | | | | |
| Install Siding | 0 | 4 | | | | | | | | | | | | 4 | 4 | 4 | 4 | 4 | | | | | | | | | | |
| Install Plumbing | 1 | 1 | | | | | | | | | 4 | 4 | 4 | | | | | | | | | | | | | | | |
| Install Electrical | 0 | 0 | | | | | | | | | 2 | 2 | 2 | 2 | | | | | | | | | | | | | | |
| Install Wallboard | 0 | 0 | | | | | | | | | | | | | 2 | 2 | 2 | 2 | 2 | | | | | | | | | |
| Lay Flooring | 0 | 0 | | | | | | | | | | | | | | | | | | 4 | 4 | 4 | 4 | 4 | 4 | | | |
| Do Interior Painting | 0 | 0 | | | | | | | | | | | | | | | | | | | | | 3 | 3 | 3 | | | |
| Install Interior Fixtures | 0 | 0 | | | | | | | | | | | | | | | | | | | | | | | | 2 | 2 | 2 |
| Install Gutters & Downspouts | 0 | 0 | | | | | | | | | | | | | | | | | | | | 2 | 2 | | | | | |
| Do Grading and Landscaping | 0 | 0 | | | | | | | | | | | | | | | | | | | | | | | | 4 | 4 | 4 |
| FINISH | 0 | 0 | | | | | | | | | | | | | | | | | | | | | | | | | | |
| TOTAL WORKERS | | | 6 | 6 | 6 | 6 | 6 | 6 | 6 | 6 | 6 | 6 | 6 | 6 | 6 | 6 | 6 | 6 | 6 | 4 | 4 | 6 | 9 | 7 | 7 | 6 | 6 | 6 |

Note: move Install Gutters and Downspouts ahead by 1 week

The same result is obtained using MS Project 2000. Using constructionRES7MAX.mpp under the *Resource Sheet* view, change Max. Units from 700% to 600%, click on *Tools, Resource Leveling . . . ,* select the same options as chosen previously *except un*check Clear leveling values before leveling so that we begin this analysis from the same starting point. MS Project 2000 is also unable to meet the resource constraint, and sends the following message: Microsoft Project cannot resolve the overallocation of workers on Mon 2/18/02.

The solution to this problem requires extending the project completion date as indicated by our heuristic. For every unit of time the project completion date is extended, an additional unit of TS is given to each task. An inspection of Figure 18.18 shows that the workers are overallocated in weeks 21–23, as previously mentioned. The two tasks contributing to this overallocation are Lay Flooring and Do Interior Painting. The start of Lay Flooring would have to be moved forward by six weeks to eliminate the overallocation. However, if the start of Do Interior Painting is moved forward by three weeks, and if its successor, Install Interior Fixtures, is also moved forward by three weeks, these overallocations are eliminated at the expense of increasing the project completion by three weeks. Therefore, the latter change is accepted. These adjustments in turn lead to overallocations in weeks 24–26, which can be eliminated by moving Do Grading and Landscaping forward by three weeks. A screen shot of the adjusted schedule given in Excel is shown as Figure 18.19 and is found in the file called construction resource loading7.xls.

The same results can be obtained using the MS Project 2000 Resource Leveling feature. Returning to constructionRES7MAX.mpp, again click on *Tools, Resource Leveling,* use the same settings as in the previous analysis except *un*check Level only within available slack. A screen shot of the Resource Leveling dialog box is given as Figure 18.20. Making this change will allow MS Project 2000 to extend the project completion date as needed. After making these changes, click the Level Now button. The results are given in a file called constructionRES6MAX.mpp. A screen shot of the *Leveling Gantt Table: Delay* view is given as Figure 18.21.

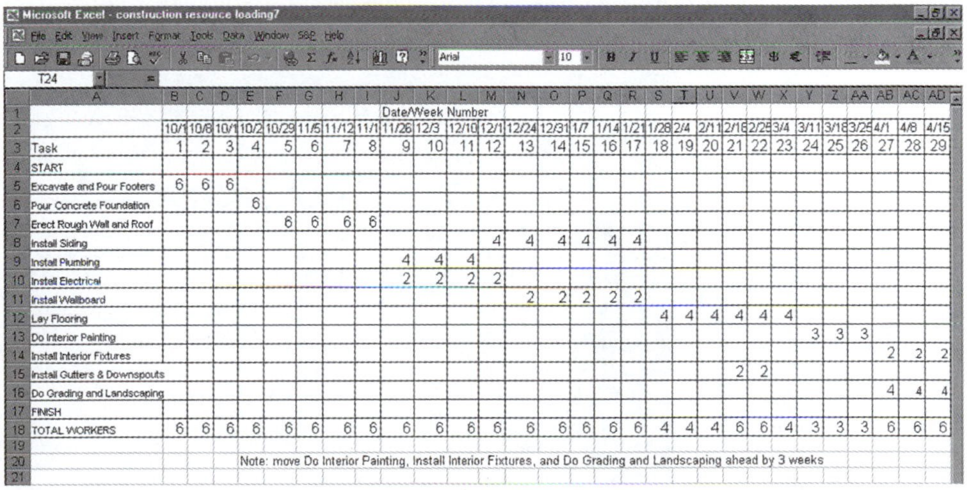


| | | | | | | | | | | | | | | | | | | | | | | | | | | | | | |
|---|---|---|---|---|---|---|---|---|---|---|---|---|---|---|---|---|---|---|---|---|---|---|---|---|---|---|---|---|---|
| | | | | | | | | | Date/Week Number | | | | | | | | | | | | | | | | | | | | |
| | 10/1 | 10/8 | 10/1 | 10/2 | 10/29 | 11/5 | 11/12 | 11/1 | 11/26 | 12/3 | 12/10 | 12/1 | 12/24 | 12/31 | 1/7 | 1/14 | 1/21 | 1/28 | 2/4 | 2/11 | 2/1 | 2/2 | 3/4 | 3/11 | 3/1 | 3/2 | 4/1 | 4/8 | 4/15 |
| Task | 1 | 2 | 3 | 4 | 5 | 6 | 7 | 8 | 9 | 10 | 11 | 12 | 13 | 14 | 15 | 16 | 17 | 18 | 19 | 20 | 21 | 22 | 23 | 24 | 25 | 26 | 27 | 28 | 29 |
| START | | | | | | | | | | | | | | | | | | | | | | | | | | | | | |
| Excavate and Pour Footers | 6 | 6 | 6 | | | | | | | | | | | | | | | | | | | | | | | | | | |
| Pour Concrete Foundation | | | | 6 | | | | | | | | | | | | | | | | | | | | | | | | | |
| Erect Rough Wall and Roof | | | | | 6 | 6 | 6 | 6 | | | | | | | | | | | | | | | | | | | | | |
| Install Siding | | | | | | | | | | | | 4 | 4 | 4 | 4 | 4 | 4 | | | | | | | | | | | | |
| Install Plumbing | | | | | | | | | 4 | 4 | 4 | | | | | | | | | | | | | | | | | | |
| Install Electrical | | | | | | | | | 2 | 2 | 2 | 2 | | | | | | | | | | | | | | | | | |
| Install Wallboard | | | | | | | | | | | | | 2 | 2 | 2 | 2 | 2 | | | | | | | | | | | | |
| Lay Flooring | | | | | | | | | | | | | | | | | | 4 | 4 | 4 | 4 | 4 | 4 | | | | | | |
| Do Interior Painting | | | | | | | | | | | | | | | | | | | | | | | | 3 | 3 | 3 | | | |
| Install Interior Fixtures | | | | | | | | | | | | | | | | | | | | | | | | | | | 2 | 2 | 2 |
| Install Gutters & Downspouts | | | | | | | | | | | | | | | | | | | | | 2 | 2 | | | | | | | |
| Do Grading and Landscaping | | | | | | | | | | | | | | | | | | | | | | | | | | | 4 | 4 | 4 |
| FINISH | | | | | | | | | | | | | | | | | | | | | | | | | | | | | |
| TOTAL WORKERS | 6 | 6 | 6 | 6 | 6 | 6 | 6 | 6 | 6 | 6 | 6 | 6 | 6 | 6 | 6 | 6 | 6 | 4 | 4 | 4 | 6 | 6 | 4 | 3 | 3 | 3 | 6 | 6 | 6 |

**Figure 18.19** Screen Shot of Excel Resource Loading Chart with Resource Overallocations Removed with the Extension of the Project Completion Date by Three Weeks (construction resource loading7.xls)

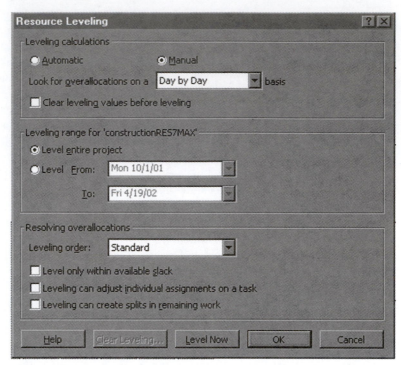

**Figure 18.20** Screen Shot of Resource Leveling Dialog Box Where the
Project Completion Date Can Be Extended

## Setting the Project Schedule and Budget

The project manager must decide whether to complete the project in 26 weeks with an
additional worker on staff for three weeks, or to complete the project in 29 weeks with a
maximum of six workers and a varying amount of workers required during the latter stages
of the project. In some situations it may be possible to complete the project in 26 weeks
with six workers through the use of overtime or temporary workers. The costs and bene-

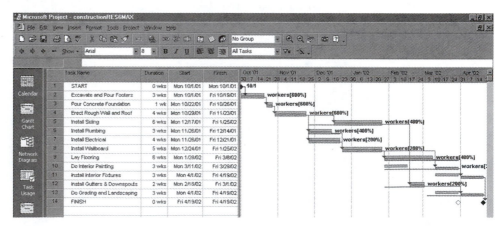

**Figure 18.21** Screen Shot of Leveling Gantt Chart Table: Delay View (Modified) after Reducing
Resource Usage to Six Workers

fits of the various options must be weighed to settle on a final schedule. The Analytic Hierarchy Process (Chapter 10) can also be used to address this problem. For this example, we assume that the project manager has decided that the project must be finished in 26 weeks and that a temporary worker can be employed for the three weeks when seven workers are needed at the $30.00/hour rate. Therefore, the schedule found in construction RES7MAX.mpp and in Figures 18.10 and 18.15 will be assumed to be final.

Once the project schedule is finalized a project budget can be prepared. MS Project 2000 calculates the cost of resources specified as work in the "type" field of the *Resource Sheet* view by multiplying the resource's hourly rate by the task duration. The project budget may also include non-labor costs such as materials and equipment. In particular, some projects may require materials costs that vary by task. For example, several tasks may require different amounts of conduit or wiring. In such cases an additional resource would be entered in the Resource Names field of the *Resource Sheet* view the term materials would be selected in the "type" field, and a cost per unit of the resource (such as $200 for a unit of 100 ft of conduit) would be entered in the Std. Rate field. The same approach previously used to assign workers to tasks would be used to assign units of this material to tasks. MS Project 2000 computes the cost of materials as the number of units of materials assigned to the task by the cost per unit.

In MS Project 2000 *fixed costs* can also be assigned to tasks. These are costs that are not driven by the number of resources assigned to a task. For example, Excavate and Pour Footers requires a fixed amount of concrete to complete this task. Some costs, such as equipment rental, could be entered either as a fixed amount or as a work type resource if costs are tracked on an hourly basis. A screen shot of the Gantt Chart: Cost Table view with fixed costs added to our project is shown as Figure 18.22. These data can be found in the file called constructionRES7MAX.mpp.

The project budget now consists of worker costs and fixed costs and can be viewed using an MS Project 2000 pre-developed report. From the main menu, click *View*,

| Task Name | Fixed Cost | Fixed Cost Accrual | Total Cost | Baseline | Variance | Actual |
|---|---|---|---|---|---|---|
| 1 START | $0.00 | Prorated | $0.00 | $0.00 | $0.00 | $0.00 |
| 2 Excavate and Pour Footers | $5,000.00 | Prorated | $26,600.00 | $0.00 | $26,600.00 | $0.00 |
| 3 Pour Concrete Foundation | $2,500.00 | Prorated | $9,700.00 | $0.00 | $9,700.00 | $0.00 |
| 4 Erect Rough Wall and Roof | $10,000.00 | Prorated | $38,800.00 | $0.00 | $38,800.00 | $0.00 |
| 5 Install Siding | $20,000.00 | Prorated | $48,800.00 | $0.00 | $48,800.00 | $0.00 |
| 6 Install Plumbing | $4,000.00 | Prorated | $18,400.00 | $0.00 | $18,400.00 | $0.00 |
| 7 Install Electrical | $3,000.00 | Prorated | $12,600.00 | $0.00 | $12,600.00 | $0.00 |
| 8 Install Wallboard | $1,500.00 | Prorated | $13,500.00 | $0.00 | $13,500.00 | $0.00 |
| 9 Lay Flooring | $4,500.00 | Prorated | $33,300.00 | $0.00 | $33,300.00 | $0.00 |
| 10 Do Interior Painting | $2,500.00 | Prorated | $13,300.00 | $0.00 | $13,300.00 | $0.00 |
| 11 Install Interior Fixtures | $6,500.00 | Prorated | $13,700.00 | $0.00 | $13,700.00 | $0.00 |
| 12 Install Gutters & Downspout | $1,500.00 | Prorated | $6,300.00 | $0.00 | $6,300.00 | $0.00 |
| 13 Do Grading and Landscaping | $2,000.00 | Prorated | $16,400.00 | $0.00 | $16,400.00 | $0.00 |
| 14 FINISH | $0.00 | Prorated | $0.00 | $0.00 | $0.00 | $0.00 |

**Figure 18.22**  Screen Shot of Gantt Chart Table: Cost View with Fixed Costs Added

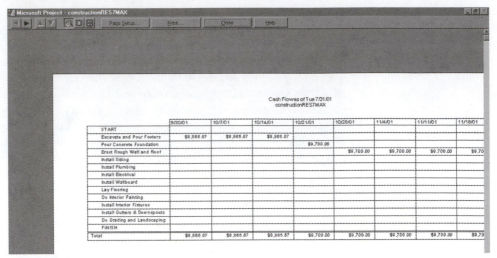

**Figure 18.23** Screen Shot of Cash Flow Report (Partial View)

*Reports . . . ,* select *Costs,* and then select *Cash Flow.* A screen shot of a partial view of this report is given as Figure 18.23. A value of $8,866.67 appears for each of the three weeks of the Excavate and Pour Footers task. This entry is computed as follows:

Worker cost per week = 6 workers * 40 hours/week * $30.00/hour = $7,200.00

Fixed cost allocation per week = $5,000/3 = $1,666.67

Total cost per week = $8,867.67

## Resource Analysis in Multiresource, Multiproject Environments

Additional complications arise in handling resource constraints in the presence of multiple resources and multiple projects. There are several heuristic approaches that can be applied to address multiple resource constraints. For example, if the resources can be prioritized, address the overallocations of the higher priority resource first. Then beginning with the adjusted schedule, address the overallocations in the second highest resource, and so on. Another heuristic approach is to move forward in time addressing each overallocation as it occurs. Of course, such approaches will not generally yield the optimal solution, and manual schedule adjustment may be required. MS Project 2000 addresses each resource in turn to address overallocations.

Resource constraints in the multiproject environment can be addressed by prioritizing projects and addressing the higher priority projects first. This approach is available as an option in MS Project 2000. Select *Project, Project Information,* and in the Priority field set the project priority as a number from 1 to 1,000—higher numbers having higher priority. Other approaches for scheduling and allocating resources in multiproject environments are discussed in Meredith and Mantel (2000).

## TIME-COST TRADE-OFF ANALYSIS

### The Time–Cost Trade-off Problem

Consider the project schedule without the resource constraint (600%) found in constructionRES.mpp and as shown in Figure 18.24. We now address a very different question

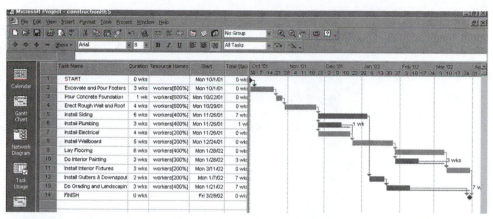

**Figure 18.24** Screen Shot of Detail Gantt Chart Table: Schedule View (Modified) without Resource Constraint

from the one discussed in the previous section. Suppose that the client for this construction project is not satisfied with the project's completion in 26 weeks and wishes to complete the project *sooner*. That is, the client is interested in expediting or *crashing* the completion of the project. As mentioned in the beginning of this chapter, the client may have an incentive to complete the project earlier than indicated by the length of the critical path. For example, construction contractors are often given incentives for completing a project early. Also, releasing a new product earlier in a highly competitive market may lead to an increased cash flow through additional sales. However, completing tasks in less time requires allocating additional resources with additional costs. In such situations the project manager must balance the cost of expediting tasks to complete the project earlier with the incentives resulting from an earlier project completion.

The goal of *time–cost trade-off analysis* is to adjust the project schedule by expediting selected tasks so that the project is completed by the desired date at the least cost. There are several solution approaches that can be applied to this problem. The reader is referred to Anderson, Sweeney, and Williams (2000) and Hillier and Lieberman (2001) for a mathematical programming formulation, and Mantel, Meredith, Shafer, and Sutton (2001) for a detailed example applying the Excel solver to this problem. Another approach, shown next, is to use a heuristic method in conjunction with project management software such as MS Project 2000.

## Time-Cost Trade-off Heuristic

### Normal and Crash Times and Costs

The *normal times* to complete tasks are those that we have used throughout this and the previous chapter. These are the times or durations that are required to complete the task using standard work methods and procedures. The *normal costs* for these tasks consist of the resource and fixed costs associated with completing the task in the normal time. The workers required for each task are those that we used in the previous section. The normal times, normal costs, and worker requirements by task are shown in Figure 18.24. Since the fixed costs are assigned by task and are unaffected by shortening task duration, they will not be considered in this analysis. For example, the normal time for Excavate and Pour Footers is three weeks, and six workers are required to complete this task. As discussed in the previous section the cost of a worker-week is $1,200.00 (40 hours/week ∗ $30.00/hour). Since 6 ∗ 3 = 18 worker-weeks are required to complete the Excavate and Pour Footers task, its normal cost is $21,600 (18 ∗ $1,200).

In general, the assignment of additional workers, materials, and/or equipment is required to reduce a task's duration. For ease of exposition, we limit consideration to the assignment of additional workers. In some cases a task cannot be expedited. For example, we assume that Excavate and Pour Footers and Pour Concrete Foundation cannot be expedited due to the nature of these tasks. However, the time to complete Erect Rough Wall and Roof can be reduced from four to three weeks if 11 workers are assigned to this task. That is, to reduce the completion of this task from four to three weeks, we must nearly double the number of assigned workers from six to 11. The cost of saving one week on the completion of this task is an increase in worker-weeks from 4 ∗ 6 = 24 to 3 ∗ 11 = 33 for a cost of (33-24) ∗ $1200 = $10,800. We refer to the reduced time of three weeks as the *crash* time and its associated cost as the *crash cost*. The normal and crash times and costs for all project tasks are summarized in an Excel spreadsheet called construction time-cost.xls, which is shown as Figure 18.25. The normal cost for the complete project is the sum of the normal costs of project tasks, and is $188,400 (Figure 18.25).

### The Heuristic

The normal and crash times and costs are essential components of a heuristic that will be presented for time–cost trade-off analysis. Assuming a linear relationship between the cost of crashing and the time saved, we can compute the critical value (K) for crashing a task as:

$$K = (CC - NC) / (NT - CT),$$

where CC = crash cost, NC = normal cost, NT = normal time, and CT = crash time. The K values for all tasks in the construction example are computed in Figure 18.25. For

**Microsoft Excel - construction time-cost**

C30 = 9000

| Task description | Task Number | Normal time | Normal workers | Normal cost | Crash time | Crash workers | Crash cost | K-Value | 1 | 2 | 3 | 4 | 5 | 6 | 7 | 8 |
|---|---|---|---|---|---|---|---|---|---|---|---|---|---|---|---|---|
| START | 1 | 0 | | | | | | | 0 | 0 | 0 | 0 | 0 | 0 | 0 | 0 |
| Excavate and Pour Footers | 2 | 3 | 6 | 21600 | | | | | 3 | 3 | 3 | 3 | 3 | 3 | 3 | 3 |
| Pour Concrete Foundation | 3 | 1 | 6 | 7200 | | | | | 1 | 1 | 1 | 1 | 1 | 1 | 1 | 1 |
| Erect Rough Wall and Roof | 4 | 4 | 6 | 28800 | 3 | 11 | 39600 | 10800 | 4 | 4 | 4 | 4 | 4 | 4 | 4 | (3) |
| Install Siding | 5 | 6 | 4 | 28800 | 3 | 12 | 43200 | 4800 | 6 | 6 | 6 | 6 | 6 | 6 | 6 | 6 |
| Install Plumbing | 6 | 3 | 4 | 14400 | 2 | 8 | 19200 | 4800 | 3 | 3 | 3 | (2) | 2 | 2 | 2 | 2 |
| Install Electrical | 7 | 4 | 2 | 9600 | 2 | 7 | 16800 | 3600 | 4 | 4 | (3) | (2) | 2 | 2 | 2 | 2 |
| Install Wallboard | 8 | 5 | 2 | 12000 | 4 | 3 | 14400 | 2400 | 5 | (4) | 4 | 4 | 4 | 4 | 4 | 4 |
| Lay Flooring | 9 | 6 | 4 | 28800 | 3 | 16 | 57600 | 9600 | 6 | 6 | 6 | 6 | (5) | (4) | (3) | 3 |
| Do Interior Painting | 10 | 3 | 3 | 10800 | 2 | 7 | 16800 | 6000 | 3 | 3 | 3 | 3 | 3 | 3 | 3 | 3 |
| Install Interior Fixtures | 11 | 3 | 2 | 7200 | | | | | 3 | 3 | 3 | 3 | 3 | 3 | 3 | 3 |
| Install Gutters & Downspouts | 12 | 2 | 2 | 4800 | 1 | 5 | 6000 | 1200 | 2 | 2 | 2 | 2 | 2 | 2 | 2 | 2 |
| Do Grading and Landscaping | 13 | 3 | 4 | 14400 | 2 | 8 | 19200 | 4800 | 3 | 3 | 3 | 3 | 3 | 3 | 3 | 3 |
| FINISH | 14 | 0 | | | | | | | 0 | 0 | 0 | 0 | 0 | 0 | 0 | 0 |
| TOTAL | | | | 188400 | | | | | | | | | | | | |

Iteration

| Paths | 1 | 2 | 3 | 4 | 5 | 6 | 7 | 8 |
|---|---|---|---|---|---|---|---|---|
| 1-2-3-4-5-12-13-14 | 19 | 19 | 19 | 19 | 19 | 19 | 19 | 18 |
| 1-2-3-4-6-8-9-11-14 | 25 | 24 | 24 | 23 | 22 | 21 | 20 | 19 |
| 1-2-3-4-6-8-10-11-14 | 22 | 21 | 21 | 20 | 20 | 20 | 20 | 19 |
| 1-2-3-4-7-8-9-11-14 | 26 | 25 | 24 | 23 | 22 | 21 | 20 | 19 |
| 1-2-3-4-7-8-10-11-14 | 23 | 22 | 21 | 20 | 20 | 20 | 20 | 19 |

| | | | | | | | | |
|---|---|---|---|---|---|---|---|---|
| Incremental Crash Cost | | 2400 | 3600 | 8400 | 9600 | 9600 | 9600 | 10800 |
| Total Crash Cost | | 2400 | 6000 | 14400 | 24000 | 33600 | 43200 | 54000 |
| Total Worker Cost | 188400 | 190800 | 194400 | 202800 | 212400 | 222000 | 231600 | 242400 |
| Incentive for Crashing | | 9000 | 18000 | 27000 | 36000 | 45000 | 54000 | 63000 |
| Net Gain from Crashing | | 6600 | 12000 | (12600) | 12000 | 11400 | 10800 | 9000 |

**Figure 18.25** Screen Shot of Excel Spreadsheet Used for Time–Cost Analysis

example, the data in this figure indicate that the time to complete the Install Siding task can be expedited by $6 - 3 = 3$ weeks if the cost is increased by $43,200 - \$28,800 = \$14,400$. The K value of $\$14,400/3 = \$4,800$ per day assumes that for *each* week that this task is expedited, up to a maximum of three weeks, there will be an increase in cost of $4,800. That is, the cost of reducing the task time from six to five weeks is the same as the cost of reducing the time from five to four weeks, and from four to three weeks. In many cases this is a good approximation of the rate at which costs increase. Other assumptions may be used as desired.

For example, if costs change in a nonlinear fashion, one approach is to assign specific K-values for each time unit the task is expedited, such as $2,000 for the first week, $3,500 for the second week, and so on. In other cases, there may only be two possibilities: completing the task in either the normal time *or* in the crash time. Both of these modifications can be incorporated into the heuristic with some adjustments. In our example, we will assume that the K-value is the same for each time unit the task is expedited up to the maximum possible.

One might be tempted to conclude that the least cost approach to crashing the completion of the construction project by one week is to expedite the project task that has the lowest K value. From Figure 18.25, we see that Install Gutters and Downspouts has the lowest K value, which is $1,200. However, an examination of Figure 18.24 shows that Install Gutters and Downspouts is not on the critical path and has a TS of seven weeks. Reducing its duration by one week will simply increase its TS to eight weeks and leave the project completion date unchanged. The reader can verify this by changing the duration of this task in contructionRES.ppt and observing the result. *Therefore, we should only expedite tasks that are on the critical path.* The heuristic can be expressed as follows.

> *If there is one critical path, expedite the task that has the lowest K value, the crash cost per time unit.*
>
> *If there are multiple critical paths, expedite that task or combination of tasks that reduces all critical paths at the lowest incremental crash cost.*
>
> *After each crashing iteration, check to see which path(s) are critical, and apply the two rules given above.*

Figure 18.25 summarizes the results of applying this heuristic. This spreadsheet can be found in a file called construction time-cost.xls. Note that the durations of all tasks are listed for each crashing iteration, enabling the computation of the lengths of all paths after the completion of each iteration. The first iteration reflects the results of the critical path analysis, and so no crashing costs are incurred here. Applying the heuristic in the second iteration, we see that task 8, Install Wallboard, has the lowest K value ($2,400) of all critical path tasks and so it is expedited by one week for a project completion of 25 weeks. Total worker costs are increased from the normal cost of $188,400 to $190,800.

Iteration 2 is complete once the lengths of all paths are recomputed. These results show that path 1-2-3-4-7-8-9-11-14 is still the only critical path. Since tasks 1, 2, 3, 11, and 14 cannot be crashed, and since task 8 cannot be crashed any further, we restrict our consideration to tasks 4, 7, and 9. The lowest K-value of these three tasks is $3,600 for task 7. Therefore, we crash task 7 by one week for a project completion of 24 weeks. With this change, crash costs increase to $2,400 + \$3,600 = \$6,000$, and total worker costs increase to $\$190,800 + \$3,600 = \$194,400$.

Iteration 3 is complete once the lengths of all paths are re-computed. As a result of crashing task 7, *two* paths are now critical: 1-2-3-4-7-8-9-11-14 and 1-2-3-4-6-8-9-11-14. As stated in the heuristic method, we must identify the least costly alternative to reduce the lengths of both paths from 24 to 23 weeks. Tasks 1, 2, 3, 8, 11, and 14 are unavailable for crashing, leaving consideration to tasks 4, 7, and 9 on the original critical path, and tasks 4, 6, and 9 on the new critical path. Since tasks 4 and 9 are on both paths they would appear to be attractive options for crashing. Another possibility is to crash task 7 by one more week in order to reduce the length of critical path 1-2-3-4-7-8-9-11-14 by one week, *and* to crash task 6 by one week to reduce the length of critical path 1-2-3-4-6-8-9-11-14 by one week. Comparing the crashing cost of these three options shows that crashing tasks 6 and 7 by one week each at a cost of $3,600 + $4,800 = $8,400 is cheaper than either crashing tasks 4 or 9 by one week at costs of $10,800 and $9,600, respectively. With this change, crash costs increase to $6,000 + $8,400 = $14,400, and total worker costs increase to $194,400 + $8,400 = $202,800.

Iteration 4 is complete once the lengths of all paths are re-computed. Paths 1-2-3-4-7-8-9-11-14 and 1-2-3-4-6-8-9-11-14 remain as the two critical paths. Since tasks 6 and 7 cannot be crashed any further, crashing options are limited to tasks 4 and 9. Task 9 is selected since it has the lower K value. The project is now scheduled for completion in 22 weeks. With this change, crash costs increase to $14,400 + $9,600 = $24,000, and total worker costs increase to $202,800 + $9,600 = $212,400. Paths 1-2-3-4-7-8-9-11-14 and 1-2-3-4-6-8-9-11-14 remain as the two critical paths, completing iteration 6.

Continuing to apply this heuristic we see that during iterations 7 and 8 we have the same options for crashing, namely tasks 4 and 9. Since task 9 can be crashed up to three weeks, it is crashed two additional weeks at a cost of $9,600 per week to reduce the project completion to 20 weeks. Total crash costs grow to $43,200 and total worker costs are now $231,600. However, at the end of iteration 8, *four* paths are now critical. Since tasks 1, 2, 3, 6, 7, 8, 9, 11, and 14 are unavailable for crashing, the only alternative for reducing the lengths of critical paths 1-2-3-4-6-8-9-11-14 and 1-2-3-4-7-8-9-11-14 is crashing task 4. Since task 4 lies on the other two critical paths, reducing task 4 by one week will reduce the project completion to 19 weeks. Since task 4 cannot be crashed further, the minimum completion time for the project is 19 weeks at a total crash cost of $54,000 and a total worker cost of $242,400.

After completing this analysis, the project manager must still decide whether or not to crash this project, and if so, by how many weeks. Suppose the client is willing to provide an incentive of $9,000 for every week the project is completed earlier than the original critical path length of 26 weeks. Returning to Figure 18.25, we compute the net gain

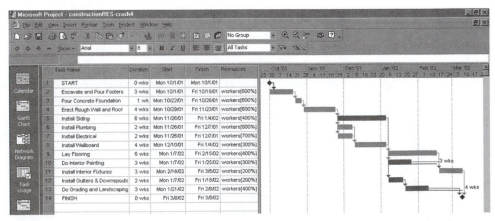

**Figure 18.26** Screen Shot of Detail Gantt: Table Delay (Modified) at Crashing Iteration 4

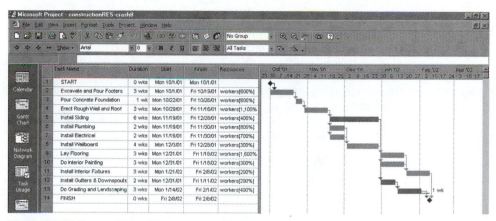

**Figure 18.27** Screen Shot of Detail Gantt: Table Delay (Modified) at Crashing Iteration 8

results from crashing at each iteration. The net gain is the difference between the incentive for crashing and the total crash cost. The results show that the net gain is maximized if the project is crashed three weeks for a completion in 23 weeks.

## Time–Cost Trade-off Using MS Project 2000

The time–cost heuristic also can be applied using MS Project 2000. The K values are computed as described previously. Once a task is selected for crashing, both its duration and number of assigned workers are manually changed in MS Project 2000. The Detail Gantt chart can be used to determine if additional paths become critical. Figure 18.26 shows a screen shot of the Detail Gantt Chart after making the required adjustments at the end of the fourth crashing iteration using the data contained in Figure 18.25. The results can be found in a file called constructionRES-crash4.mpp.

An examination of the right side of Figure 18.26 shows that tasks 6 and 7 are now critical, yielding two critical paths. The results of fully crashing the project at the completion of iteration 8 are shown in Figure 18.27. The results can be found in the file called constructionRES-crash8.mpp.

## SUMMARY

In this chapter we have considered how the availability and usage of resources affect the creation of the project schedule. We developed the theory and methods of project resource and cost analysis using the construction example that was introduced in the previous chapter. In particular, we have considered two important problems: the effect of limited resources on the project schedule and the benefits and costs of faster project completion. We began by developing a resource loading chart that displays the number of units of a resource that are required during each time period over the course of the project. Initially, resource loading charts were prepared assuming all tasks start at their earliest start (ES) times. We have shown how to create resources, assign them to tasks, and view resource loading charts in MS Project 2000.

Next we have discussed the methods of resource analysis. Resource leveling attempts to minimize the period-to-period variations in resource use. Since there is often a limitation on the maximum amount of resources available, we turned our attention to constrained resource scheduling. We have described and illustrated the application of a heuristic for the single constrained resource problem that involves the use of slack time to delay tasks that contribute to the resource overallocations. We have shown that if resource overallocations cannot be eliminated using slack, then the project due date must be extended. The application of this heuristic was then demonstrated using MS Project 2000. The automatic feature for constrained resource scheduling within MS Project 2000 (called resource leveling in the software) has also been discussed and demonstrated. We have also shown how to develop a project budget in MS Project 2000 using worker and fixed cost data once the project schedule is finalized. We completed this topic with a brief discussion of heuristic approaches that can be applied in situations having multiple resources and multiple projects.

We then turned our attention to situations where the client is interested in expediting or crashing the completion of the project. We began by developing the normal and crash costs and times for each task. Using this information, we have described and illustrated the application of a heuristic for the time–cost trade-off problem. The basis for this heuristic is crashing the critical path task that has lowest cost per time unit to expedite.

If multiple critical paths are present, then the lowest cost combination of expedited tasks is selected so that all critical paths are reduced. We have shown how to perform the crashing analysis step by step until the minimum project completion date was determined.

After completing this analysis, the project manager must still decide whether or not to crash this project, and if so, by how many time units. To help make this decision we have computed the net gain after each crashing iteration. The net gain is the difference between the financial incentive for crashing and the total crash cost. Our discussion of this topic is completed by showing how the crashing heuristic can be accomplished using MS Project 2000.

## HOMEWORK PROBLEMS

**1.** ARTHURSEN is planning to install a new financial reporting system for one of their clients. The necessary project information is defined in the table.

| Task | Time (days) | Predecessor | Workers Required |
|------|------------|-------------|------------------|
| A | 3 | – | 5 |
| B | 2 | – | 2 |
| C | 5 | A | 3 |
| D | 5 | B | 4 |
| E | 6 | C,D | 3 |
| F | 2 | C,D | 4 |
| G | 2 | F | 4 |

Enter this information into MS Project 2000. Assume the project starts on 10/1/01.

**(a)** What are the critical path tasks? What is the earliest date the project can be completed?

**(b)** Construct a resource loading chart using the Early Start (ES) dates for each task. Assuming worker costs of $40 per hour and a workday of eight hours, develop a budget for this project.

**(c)** Suppose only seven workers are available over the course of this project. Assuming no project completion delays are possible, can the project be rescheduled within this worker constraint?

**(d)** Suppose four of the seven available workers will be on vacation on October 11–12. Assuming no project completion delays are possible, can the project be rescheduled within this worker vacation constraint?

**2.** HEALY has prepared the information below to help manage a small construction project.

| Task | Time (weeks) | Predecessor | Workers Required |
|------|-------------|-------------|------------------|
| A | 2 | – | 3 |
| B | 4 | – | 2 |
| C | 3 | A | 4 |

| Task | Time (weeks) | Predecessor | Workers Required |
|------|-------------|-------------|------------------|
| D | 5 | A | 5 |
| E | 4 | B,C | 1 |
| F | 3 | B,C | 3 |
| G | 6 | E | 1 |
| H | 2 | D,F | 5 |

Enter this information into MS Project 2000. Assume the project starts on 10/1/01.

**(a)** What are the critical path tasks? What is the earliest date the project can be completed?

**(b)** Construct a resource loading chart using the Early Start (ES) dates for each task. Assuming worker costs of $800 per week/worker, develop a budget for this project.

**(c)** Suppose only six workers are available over the course of this project. Assuming no project completion delays are possible, can the project be rescheduled within this worker constraint? If not, what is the earliest project completion under this constraint?

**(d)** Now suppose only five workers are available. Can the project be rescheduled within this worker constraint? What is the earliest project completion under this constraint? Comment on the suitability of the revised schedule.

**3.** GRIFFIN has prepared the information below to help plan and manage the construction of a wooden deck and patio.

| Task | Immediate Predecessor | Time (days) |
|------|----------------------|-------------|
| A | – | 5 |
| B | A | 2 |
| C | A | 4 |
| D | B, C | 6 |
| E | C | 3 |
| F | D, E | 3 |

Enter this information into MS Project 2000. Assume the project starts on 10/1/01.

**(a)** What are the critical path tasks? What is the earliest date the project can be completed?

**(b)** Suppose the following normal and crash times and costs are provided.

| Task | Normal Time (days) | Crash Time | Normal Cost | Crash Cost |
|------|------|------|------|------|
| A | 5 | 2 | $ 500 | $ 800 |
| B | 2 | 1 | 300 | 375 |
| C | 4 | 2 | 900 | 1,000 |
| D | 6 | 3 | 1,100 | 2,000 |
| E | 3 | 1 | 200 | 250 |
| F | 3 | 2 | 800 | 1,200 |

Which activities should be crashed if Griffin wants the project to be completed within 15 working days? What additional costs for crashing will be incurred?

**4.** MECHANATRIX has been offered a contract to build and deliver nine extruding presses. The contract price is contingent upon meeting a specified delivery time, with a bonus offered for early delivery. The marketing department has established the following costs and time information.

| Task | Immediate Predecessor | Normal Time (wks) | Crash Time | Normal Cost | Crash Cost |
|------|------|------|------|------|------|
| A | – | 3 | 1 | $ 5,000 | $ 9,000 |
| B | A | 4 | 3 | 8,000 | 14,000 |

| Task | Immediate Predecessor | Normal Time (wks) | Crash Time | Normal Cost | Crash Cost |
|------|------|------|------|------|------|
| C | A | 3 | 2 | 4,000 | 6,000 |
| D | A | 8 | 7 | 5,000 | 6,000 |
| E | B | 4 | 2 | 3,000 | 5,000 |
| F | C | 6 | 4 | 2,000 | 3,600 |
| G | D | 5 | 4 | 10,000 | 14,000 |
| H | E,F | 3 | 1 | 7,000 | 10,600 |

The revenue for each delivery time is specified in the following table:

| Contract Time (wks) | Contract Amount |
|------|------|
| 18 | $52,750 |
| 17 | 58,500 |
| 16 | 62,000 |
| 15 | 62,500 |
| 14 | 65,000 |
| 13 | 70,000 |
| 12 | 72,500 |

**(a)** What are the critical path tasks? What is the earliest date the project can be completed? What is the normal cost for this project?

**(b)** Using the information provided, what completion time would you recommend?

# REFERENCES

Anderson, D. R., D. J. Sweeney, and T. A. Williams, *An Introduction to Management Science: Quantitative Approaches to Decision Making,* 9th ed., Cincinnati, OH, South-Western Publishing, 2000.

Friedrichsen, L. and R. B. Bunin, *New Perspectives on Microsoft Project 2000—Introductory,* Cambridge, MA, Course Technology, 2000.

Hillier, F. S. and G. J. Lieberman, *Introduction to Operations Research,* 7th ed., New York, McGraw-Hill, 2001.

Mantel, S. J., Jr., J. R. Meredith, S. M. Shafer, and M. M. Sutton, *Project Management in Practice,* New York, Wiley, 2001.

Meredith, J. R. and S. J. Mantel, Jr., *Project Management: A Managerial Approach,* 4th ed., New York, Wiley, 2000.

Moder, J. J., C. R. Phillips, and E. D. Davis, *Project Management with CPM, PERT and Precedence Diagramming,* 3rd ed., New York, Van Nostrand Reinhold, 1983.

Wiest, J. D. and F. K. Levy, *A Management Guide to PERT/CPM: with GERT/PDM, DCPM and other Networks,* 2nd ed., Englewood Cliffs, NJ, Prentice-Hall, 1977.

# Appendix A

# Statistical Concepts*

## INTRODUCTION

The purpose of this appendix is to provide background on statistical concepts used in this text, especially in Part 3, Computer Simulation. Our topics include: sampling, descriptive statistics, probability distributions, confidence interval estimation, and multiple comparison tests. We begin with sampling since the generation of random samples is the basis of Monte Carlo simulation. Descriptive statistics are discussed since they are used to summarize the results of a simulation analysis, while confidence interval estimation addresses the precision of these estimates, such as average waiting time. Probability distributions are used to represent those phenomena that are random in nature, such as interarrival and service times, while multiple comparison tests measure how well these distributions fit the observed data.

## STATISTICS OVERVIEW

Most individuals can associate statistics with the sports page of the newspaper. The statistician is the individual who compiles the shooting averages in basketball or the odds in a horse race. Although statisticians work with numerical data, it is usually for much more serious purposes such as calculating the unemployment rate, determining whether Product A is superior to Product B or running a test to determine if there is a link between alcohol and liver cancer. No matter what the business or organization, managers need to know how to use statistics to make informed and better business decisions.

Statistics is the systematic study of the collection, organization, analysis, and interpretation of data. Statistics is divided into two branches—descriptive and inferential. Descriptive statistics are those methods of collection and organization of data in the form of tables, graphs, and other visual arrangements for the purpose of describing some of the various features of the data set. Examples of descriptive statistics are a table showing the time between customer arrivals for car service and their relative frequency of occurrence (probability), or a pie chart showing the categories of company expenditures. In addition, the median weekly wages of garment workers or the mean monthly long-distance phone rate charged to commercial customers represent examples of the calculation of descriptive measures. Generally, in descriptive statistics there is little need of mathematical methods and reasoning since these charts, tables, means, and medians can easily be computed and/or constructed using basic arithmetic or software such as EXCEL.

Inferential statistics are those methods that make accurate, reliable estimates about characteristics of a population that cannot feasibly be obtained by direct measurement.

---

*This chapter was written by Professor Elaine Webster, Villanova University.

Conclusions are drawn from a limited amount of data taken from the population in the form of a sample. It is important to understand the following key terms:

- *Population:* an entire set of people or objects of interest to be studied.
- *Sample:* a proportion or subset of the population selected for a particular study.

Probability theory determines the likelihood that the sample results accurately reflect the population results. Two important areas of inferential statistics—confidence intervals and hypothesis testing—will be addressed later in more detail. Inferential statistics will answer such questions as whether the institution of a coffee break will increase the productivity of its workers or if there is a significant difference in the proportion of patients reporting a side effect of nausea between those using the new drug and those using the placebo. In addition to saving time, labor, and money by taking samples, inferential statistics is a powerful, economic tool for addressing business problems.

## SAMPLING

Sampling is one of the most important concepts in the study of statistics. It is basic to statistical theory and its applications. The population is all the units about which information is sought. Notice that, statistically, a population is never a set of objects, but always a set of measurements or counts obtainable from all objects in the study. A population may be finite (countable), such as the number of cars that are repaired per week, or infinite (not countable), such as the flipping of a coin an unlimited number of times. Generally, it is acceptable to treat a very large population, such as the number of TV sets in the world, as if it were infinite.

Since one can rarely investigate an entire population, one must draw conclusions about a population from samples selected from it. The relationship of a sample to a population is one of the most important problems in statistics since good estimates concerning a population necessitate good samples. A good sample is one that is closely representative of the population under study. Obtaining a good sample is not always easy, but generally it can be done. The specific statistical name for a good sample is a *random sample*.

- A *random sample* is a sample in which any one individual measurement in the population is as likely to be included as any other; in other words, each measurement has an equally likely chance to be picked.
- A *biased sample* is a sample in which certain individual measurements have a greater chance to be included than other ones.

When one selects a random sample, it is hoped that the sample is a reasonable representative of the population under study. However, correct sampling techniques occasionally display characteristics that deviate seriously from the corresponding ones of the population. For example, if one wishes to determine the sweetness of a cup of coffee in which the sugar has settled to the bottom, one could take a sip of the coffee and say the coffee is not sweet. The sip was not representative of the entire cup of coffee. One must stir the coffee first for a representative sample and then take a sip. As a result, a proper inferential statistical analysis will assign, using probability theory, a degree of "confidence" to the results of the analysis.

Since considerable references will be made to samples and populations, it is necessary to distinguish the terms and symbols related to each. Usually Greek letters are used for population measurements and Roman letters are used for sample measurements. A measurable characteristic of a population, such as its mean, is called the *population*

**Exhibit A.1**  Population and Sample Symbols

|  | Sample statistics | Population parameters |
|---|---|---|
| **Size** | n | N |
| **Mean** | $\bar{x}$ | $\mu$ |
| **Standard Deviation** | s | $\sigma$ |

*parameter*, or simply a *parameter*. A measurable quantity derived from a sample, such as the sample mean, is called the *sample statistic,* or simply a *statistic*. Note that the word statistics not only represents a systematic study of data, but also is used to represent a characteristic of the sample.

Parameters of a particular population are based on all the individual measurements of a variable; therefore, the parameters are fixed for that population. (Exhibit A.1 summarizes the symbols used to represent important sample statistics and population parameters.) However, since statistics are based on only part of the population, statistics will usually vary from one sample to another. For example, suppose the population mean number of minutes to complete a bank transaction is 5 minutes. However, one sample of 50 customers has a mean of 5.3 minutes and another sample of 50 different customers has a mean of 4.9 minutes. In order to use the sample mean, for instance, to make reliable statements about the population mean, statistical theory investigates the distribution of all possible sample means in order that one can make inferences about the population mean from just one sample. Inferential statistics studies the sample results so that conclusions can be drawn about the population.

## DESCRIPTIVE STATISTICS

Generally, in order to solve any business problem statistically, data are collected from the population in question. To obtain any meaningful information from the data, particularly with large sets of data, the measurements must be summarized in some fashion. The most common ways to summarize data are in tabular form or pictorial form:

- *Tabular Form:* data are arranged in columns and rows and include all information necessary for a complete understanding of the table.
- *Pictorial Form:* data are arranged in graphs or diagrams.

Reducing the data to tabular or pictorial form makes it easier to view the important characteristics of the data.

One important application of the tabular form and the pictorial form, respectively, is the *frequency distribution* and its *histogram*. The frequency distribution is a table that divides observed measurements into a set of classes and shows the number of observations falling in each class. Frequency distributions are particularly useful for simplifying large sets of data. Consider the raw data in Table A.1 that shows the time (in seconds) 30 customers wait in line at a bank. As raw, ungrouped data it is difficult to discern any useful information about the time customers spend waiting.

After the data are placed into a frequency distribution (Table A.2), it is easier to observe important characteristics of the data such as the fact that most customers (f = 10) wait between 120 but less than 180 seconds for service or only 6 of the 30 customers wait

**Table A.1** Time (in seconds) that 30 Randomly Selected Customers Spent in a Bank Line

| | | | | |
|---|---|---|---|---|
| 183 | 121 | 140 | 198 | 199 |
| 90 | 62 | 135 | 60 | 175 |
| 320 | 110 | 185 | 85 | 172 |
| 235 | 250 | 242 | 193 | 75 |
| 263 | 295 | 146 | 160 | 210 |
| 165 | 179 | 359 | 220 | 170 |

**Table A.2** Frequency Distribution for Time Spent in a Bank Line

| Time (in seconds) | Tally | Number of customers f |
|---|---|---|
| 60 and under 120 | ~~////~~ / | 6 |
| 120 and under 180 | ~~////~~ //// | 10 |
| 180 and under 240 | //// /// | 8 |
| 240 and under 300 | //// | 4 |
| 300 and under 360 | // | 2 |
| | | 30 |

240 seconds or more. The final frequency distribution is composed of the first column, Time, and the last column, Number of Customers (f).

In some situations, decision makers are interested in the percentage of measurements in each class or the number or percentage of measurements that lie below or above a certain value. An executive at the bank might want to know the percentage of people who wait 120 but less than 180 seconds or the cumulative percentage of people who wait less than 3 minutes. The frequency distribution must be adjusted to answer these questions. A *relative (percentage) frequency distribution* shows the proportion or percentage of measurements that fall within each class. Relative distributions are most useful when comparing two or more distributions, especially if they are unequal sizes; a comparison could not be done solely with frequency distributions. A *cumulative frequency distribution* shows the number of measurements less than a particular value. Table A.3 is a computer-generated frequency distribution of the bank example that includes a relative (percentage) frequency distribution in the third column and a relative cumulative frequency distribution in the last column. The number of people who wait 120 but less than 180 seconds to be helped is 33.3% and the cumulative percentage of people who wait less than 3 minutes is 53.3%.

Sometimes it is easier to describe data in a frequency distribution by using a graph. The most common graphical (pictorial) representation of a frequency or a relative frequency distribution is a *histogram.* A histogram is a vertical bar chart, with no space between the bars, such that each bar represents an individual class in the frequency distribution and the height of each bar represents the respective frequency of each class. The histogram for the bank example is shown in Figure A.1; it corresponds to the frequency distribution in Table A.2. Note that the histogram not only gives the class limits

**Table A.3** Frequency, Relative Frequency, and Cumulative Relative Frequency Distribution for Time Spent in a Bank Line

| | Time (in seconds) | | |
|---|---|---|---|
| Classes | Frequency | Relative (percentage) | Cumulative relative |
| 60 but less than 120 | 6 | 20.0% | 20.0% |
| 120 but less than 180 | 10 | 33.3% | 53.3% |
| 180 but less than 240 | 8 | 26.7% | 80.0% |
| 240 but less than 300 | 4 | 13.3% | 93.3% |
| 300 but less than 360 | 2 | 6.7% | 100.0% |
| Total | 30 | 100.0% | |

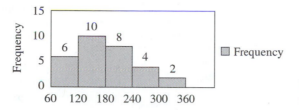

**Figure A.1** Histogram for Time Spent in a Bank Line

on the x-axis and frequencies on the y-axis, but also describes the shape of the distribution. In this example, the shape is not symmetrical but has a longer right tail than left tail.

Although the data may have been organized and presented in a suitable form, such as the frequency distribution and the histogram, it may not be sufficient to answer all questions about a particular study. In order to simplify the raw data further and address additional problems, certain measures that describe unique features of the raw data are needed. First it would be useful to have a tool that describes the central measurement in the data distribution. Although "central" can be defined differently depending on the situation, these tools will be called the *measures of central tendency*. The most common ones are the mean, median, and mode.

The *mean* is the arithmetic average of all the measurements in a given set of data. Notice that in this case central is defined as an average. The formulas for the population mean and the sample mean are given in Exhibit A.2. The mean is the most widely used and most reliable measure of central tendency. It takes every item into account and, since it can be calculated on any set of numerical data, it always exists and is unique. It is determined algebraically and amenable to algebraic operations. If the mean is affected by any extreme value or values, called outliers, it is no longer the most reliable measure of central tendency. These outliers pull the mean in the direction of the extreme number. As a result, the mean is distorted and should not be used as a measure of central tendency. In Table A.4 note that Stock Z has an extreme value of 20% that is generating a mean of 8%, well above the central measurement.

**Exhibit A.2**  Formulas and Examples for the Mean

| Population mean | Sample mean |
| --- | --- |
| $\mu = \dfrac{\sum X}{N}$ | $\bar{x} = \dfrac{\sum x}{n}$ |

Sample Mean Example

Raw Data: 10, 5, 9, 12, 6, 8

$$\bar{x} = \frac{\sum\limits_{i=1}^{n} x_i}{n} = \frac{x_1 + x_2 + x_3 + x_4 + x_5 + x_6}{6}$$

$$\bar{x} = \frac{10 + 5 + 9 + 12 + 6 + 8}{6}$$

$$\bar{x} = 8.33$$

**Table A.4**  Annual Return on Stock

|  | Stock X | Stock Y | Stock Z |
| --- | --- | --- | --- |
| **2001** | 10% | 17% | 20% |
| **2000** | 8 | −2 | 5 |
| **1999** | 12 | 16 | 5 |
| **1998** | 2 | 1 | 5 |
| **1997** | 8 | 8 | 5 |
|  | 40% | 40% | 40% |

Average Return on Stock = 40/5 = 8%

**Exhibit A.3**    Examples of Medians

| Even-sized sample | Odd-sized sample |
|---|---|
| Raw Data: 10, 5, 9, 6, 8 | Raw Data: 10, 5, 9, 12, 6, 8 |
| Ordered Array: 5, 6, 8, 9, 10 | Ordered Array: 5, 6, 8, 9, 10, 12 |
| $Median = 8$ | $Median = \dfrac{8 + 9}{2} = 8.5$ |

**Exhibit A.4**    Examples of Modes

**No Mode**
Raw Data: 11 5 9 13 8
**One Mode = 11**
Raw Data: 11 5 9 11 8
**More than One Mode = 9, 11**
Raw Data: 11 5 9 11 9

The *median* is the middle value in an ordered array of data. In this case, "central" represents the measurement such that 50% of the data are below it and 50% are above it. If there is an odd number of data points, a middle number can be found. If there is an even number of data points, an average of the two middle numbers in the array is used (Exhibit A.3). The median is unique, easy to understand, and always exists for numeric data. When there are extreme values in the data set, the median is preferred over the mean. Thus, in Table A.4 the median return for Stock Z is 5%, which is preferable to the mean of 8% since it gives a more accurate measure of central tendency for the distribution.

The third measure of central tendency is the *mode,* which is the value of the measurement that appears most often in the data set. "Central" here is defined as appearing the most. Although the mode is easy to understand, not affected by extreme values, and useful with both quantitative and qualitative problems, it is the least accurate of the measures of central tendency. There are no arithmetic properties and the data set may have no mode, one mode, or more than one mode (Exhibit A.4).

The mean, median and mode describe the central tendency of a set of values. In deciding which measure to use in a particular situation, one must consider the advantages and disadvantages of each as previously mentioned. The mean should not be used if extreme values are present in the data. Although the mode is less useful than the mean and median, there are circumstances where the mode is valuable. For example, when a shoe store owner decides how many of each size of a shoe to stock, it is more helpful to know the modal size than the average size. The average shoe size could be 8.232, which does not exist in a shoe size.

One useful application of the measures of central tendency is to describe the shape of the distribution of data. It is only necessary to compare the mean and the median to do this. If the mean equals the median, the distribution is *symmetrical*, such that the data is evenly distributed on each side of the mean. If the mean exceeds the median, the distribution of data is said to be *right* or *positively skewed.* The histogram in Figure A.1 is skewed to the right. On the other hand, if the median exceeds the mean, the distribution is *left* or *negatively skewed.* Generally an outlier in the data will cause the distribution to be skewed.

In addition to knowing the measures of central tendency, it is important to know the extent to which the measurements scatter or vary from the central point. In the Annual Return on Stock example in Table A.4, which stock, X or Y, is riskier? Both stocks have a mean of 8%. By itself, the mean does not give a clear picture of the spread of the values around 8%. Are the data closely packed around the central point or are the data values not near the central point but at the extremes? We need another measure to help identify this dispersion. The numerical values that determine the spread or scatter of the data about a central point are called the *measures of dispersion, or variability*. In this discussion we will address the most frequently used measures of dispersion: *the sample variance and the sample standard deviation*. Both measure the amount of variation around

**Exhibit A.5**   Measures of Dispersion

| Sample variance | Sample standard deviation |
|---|---|
| $$s^2 = \frac{\sum\limits_{i=1}^{n}(x_i - \bar{x})^2}{n-1}$$ | $$s = \sqrt{\frac{\sum\limits_{i=1}^{n}(x_i - \bar{x})^2}{n-1}}$$ |

*Where*

$\bar{x}$ = sample mean

n = sample size

$x_i$ = ith observation of the variable X

the mean. The sample variance ($s^2$) is the sum of the squared differences around the arithmetic mean divided by the sample size (n) minus 1. The sample standard deviation (s) is the square root of the sample variance. The formulas for both measures are given in Exhibit A.5.

Although the variance is widely used in statistical analysis, it is expressed in the squared units of the variable of interest. For many situations, it is desirable to have a measure expressed in the same units of the original data and its mean. As a result the standard deviation will be used here and addressed in more detail. When the standard deviation is close to 0, the measurements are closely grouped about the mean; when the standard deviation is large, the measurements are scattered farther away from the mean. If you have two sets of measurements with the same mean, such as the Annual Return on Stock example (Table A.4), the higher the standard deviation, the more variation around the mean, and therefore, the riskier the stock. By using the standard deviation we can answer the question posed earlier as to which was the riskier stock, X or Y? Referring to Table A.4. We compute the sample standard deviation for Stock X by applying the formula for the sample standard deviation. The sample standard deviation for the return on Stock X is 3.74%; notice the standard deviation is in the same units as the mean (see Table A.5).

Computed in the same way but not shown in Table A.5, the standard deviation for the return on Stock Y is 8.57%. Knowing that both stocks have the same mean of 8%, since Stock Y has a larger standard deviation than Stock X, one can conclude that it varies more than Stock X and is riskier (see Table A.6). Having completed our discussion of descriptive statistics, we now turn to a consideration of probability distributions.

**Table A.5**   Sample Standard Deviation of Stock X

|  | X | $\bar{X}$ | $(X - \bar{X})$ | $(X - \bar{X})^2$ |
|---|---|---|---|---|
| **2001** | 10 | 8 | 2 | 4 |
| **2000** | 8 | 8 | 0 | 0 |
| **1999** | 12 | 8 | 4 | 16 |
| **1998** | 2 | 8 | −6 | 36 |
| **1997** | 8 | 8 | 0 | 0 |
|  |  |  |  | 56 |

$$s = \sqrt{\frac{\sum(x - \bar{x})^2}{n-1}} = \sqrt{\frac{56}{4}} = \sqrt{14} = 3.74\%$$

**Table A.6**   Comparison of Stock X and Y

|  | Annual return on stock | |
|---|---|---|
|  | Stock X | Stock Y |
| **2001** | 10% | 17% |
| **2000** | 8 | −2 |
| **1999** | 12 | 16 |
| **1998** | 2 | 1 |
| **1997** | 8 | 8 |

Standard Deviation on Stock X = 3.74%

Standard Deviation on Stock Y = 8.57%

## SELECTED PROBABILITY DISTRIBUTIONS

In this section discussion is limited to those probability distributions that are most often used in simulation applications. When the events associated with an experiment can be described by numbers, the specific way of writing down all the events and their corresponding probabilities is called the *probability distribution*. For example, one roll of a fair die results in one of six events: 1, 2, 3, 4, 5, or 6, each having a probability of 1/6. If the *random variable*, x, is the numerical description of the outcome of an experiment, then x can take on any one of the integers from 1 to 6. In addition, for each of these numbers, there corresponds a positive probability, designated P(x). The probability distribution of x (the outcome of one roll of a fair die) is the listing of these outcomes and their probabilities as illustrated in Table A.7.

This table is an example of a discrete uniform distribution. For any probability distribution, it is required that

$$\sum_{i=1}^{n} P_i(x) = 1 \quad \text{and} \quad 0 \le P_i(x) \le 1.$$

A random variable is a variable whose outcomes occur by chance. Examples include the number of trucks sold, the daily levels of output, and the number of customers waiting in line. Random variables are classified as either *discrete* or *continuous*. A *discrete* random variable is one that can take on a finite or countable number of values. The number of snow blowers sold at the hardware store or the number of cars passing through the toll booth are examples of discrete random variables. Notice there are gaps in the observations; you cannot buy 1.3 snow blowers. On the other hand, a *continuous* random variable may take on any value over an interval. There are no gaps between the numbers because no matter how close two observations might be, a third can fall between them. For example, the number of pounds of sand a hardware store sells is continuous since one could sell 30, 30.0065 or 30.765 pounds of sand. Other examples of continuous variables include income, height, time between arrivals of customers, and customer service times.

### Discrete Probability Distributions

In a discrete probability distribution a table, graph, or equation describes the values of the random variable and the associated probabilities. Just as one can find the mean and variance of a data set, we can also find the mean and variance of a probability distribution.

The mean ($\mu$) of the random variable, x, is the sum of the products of the corresponding x's and their probabilities, P(x)'s; thus:

$$\text{Mean of x: } \mu = \sum_{i=1}^{N} [x_i P_i(x)]$$

Referring to Table A.7, the mean for the probability distribution of one roll of a fair die is:

$$\mu = 1(1/6) + 2(1/6) + 3(1/6) + 4(1/6) + 5(1/6) + 6(1/6) = 3.5$$

**Table A.7** Probability Distribution of One Roll of a Fair Die

| x | 1 | 2 | 3 | 4 | 5 | 6 |
|------|------|------|------|------|------|------|
| **P(x)** | 1/6 | 1/6 | 1/6 | 1/6 | 1/6 | 1/6 |

The variance ($\sigma^2$) of the random variable, x, is the sum of the products of the corresponding probabilities and the squares of the deviations from the mean; thus,

$$\text{Variance of x: } \sigma^2 = \sum_{i=1}^{N} [P_i(x)(x_i - \mu)^2]$$

Again referring to Table A.7, the variance for the probability distribution of one roll of a fair die is:

$$\sigma^2 = (1/6)(1 - 3.5)^2 + (1/6)(2 - 3.5)^2 + (1/6)(3 - 3.5)^2 + (1/6)(4 - 3.5)^2$$
$$+ (1/6)(5 - 3.5)^2 + (1/6)(6 - 3.5)^2 = 2.92$$

## Poisson Distribution

A special discrete probability distribution, which is highly useful in measuring the relative frequency of an event over a specified interval of time or space, is the *Poisson distribution*. It is often used to describe the number of arrivals of customers per hour, the number of defects in each square yard of material, or the number of defective electrical connections per mile of wiring. The Poisson probability function is:

### Poisson Probability Function

$$P(x) = \frac{\lambda^x e^{-\lambda}}{x!} \quad x \geq 0 \text{ else } P(x) = 0$$

*where*

$x$ = number of times (successes) the event occurs

$\lambda$ = mean occurrences in an interval of time or space

Note that $e$ is approximately equal to 2.71828, the base for natural logarithms. The two assumptions necessary for its application are: (1) the probability of the occurrence of an event is the same for any two intervals of equal length and (2) the occurrence of the event in any interval is independent of the occurrence in any other interval.

The Poisson distribution is really a family of distributions. Depending on the value of its mean, the shape of the probability distribution will vary considerably. Although the Poisson distribution is always positively skewed, it tends to become symmetrical as its mean becomes larger (see Figure A.2).

The mean and variance of the Poisson distribution are:

$$\text{Mean} = \lambda \qquad \text{Variance } \sigma^2 = \lambda$$

Observe that the larger the mean, the wider the spread from the mean.

## Binomial Distribution

The binomial distribution is typically used where a single trial is repeated many times, such as the tossing of a fair coin. There are two important assumptions: 1) each trial is assumed to be independent of all others, and 2) the probability of the event occurring, for example heads on a coin toss, is the same for each trial and is denoted as $p$. For a given number of trials ($n$), the binomial distribution gives the probability associated with each of the possible total number of successes that can occur. For example, if there are four trials, there can be 0, 1, 2, 3, or 4 successes. For a large number of trials, the binomial distribution may be approximated by the normal distribution (to be discussed later).

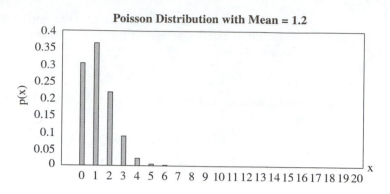

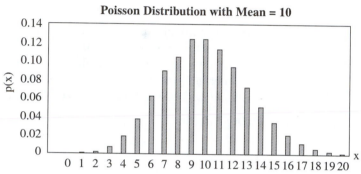

**Figure A.2** Graph of Two Poisson Distributions

## Binomial Probability Distribution

$$P(x) = \frac{n!}{x!(n-x)!}\, p^x\,(1-p)^{n-x}$$

*where*

$x =$ the number of successes over all trials

$n =$ number of trials

$p =$ the probability of a success

The binomial distribution can be skewed or symmetric depending on the values of its parameters. Whenever $p = 0.5$, the binomial distribution will be symmetrical regardless of the value of $n$. However, when $p$ is not equal to 0.5, the distribution will be skewed. The closer $p$ is to 0.5 and the larger the number of observations ($n$), the less skewed the distribution will be. Two binomial distributions, one that is skewed to the right and one that is symmetric are given as Figure A.3.

The mean and variance of the binomial distribution are:

$$\text{Mean} = np,\ \text{Variance} = np(1-p)$$

## Continuous Probability Distributions

Recall that for a continuous random variable, x takes on any value over an interval. The *probability density function* provides the value of the function at any particular value of x; it is a curve denoted f(x) such that f(x) $\geq$ 0. The exact probability of a particular value from a continuous distribution is 0; the density function can only find the probability of an interval. The area under the curve and above the x-axis over an interval is equal to the

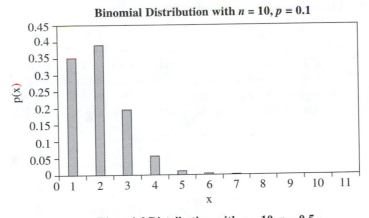

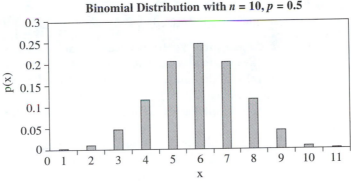

**Figure A.3** Graph of Two Binomial Distributions

probability that x will take on a value in that interval. All probability density functions are such that the total area under the curve is equal to 1. Since total area equals 1, the probability is simply equal to the area under the curve over the interval

$$\int_{-\infty}^{\infty} f(x)dx = 1 \quad \text{where } f(x) \geq 0$$

If we let A denote the probability that a random variable, x, assumes a value in the interval (a, b), then the probability is represented by the area A:

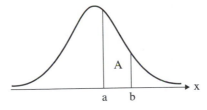

By rules of calculus, the area under the curve over a given interval is given as

$$P(A) = P(a \leq x \leq b) = \int_{a}^{b} f(x)dx$$

Unfortunately obtaining these probabilities or computing the means and variances for continuous functions require knowledge of integral calculus. However, statistical tables have been generated to eliminate these manual calculations for many common distributions.

**Uniform Continuous Probability Distributions**

The most straightforward of the continuous probability distributions is the *uniform distribution*. When minimal information is known about a task, the uniform distribution can be used to represent the time duration of the task; for instance, it can help determine that the time it takes a technician to service a mechanical device is uniformly distributed between two to seven minutes.

The continuous uniform probability density function (distribution) for x is

**Uniform Probability Density Function**

$$f(x) = \frac{1}{b - a} \quad \text{for } a \leq x \leq b, \text{ else } 0$$

*where*

    a = minimum value selected

    b = maximum value selected

The function outputs a real number between the minimum value a and the maximum value b inclusive. All values between a and b are equally likely to occur. The formula provides the height or value of the function at any particular value of x in the interval. The height is the same for each value of x. For a continuous random variable, probability is considered only in terms of the likelihood that a random variable has a value within a specified interval.

In a continuous uniform probability function, with $a \leq x \leq b$, the probability that x will be between a and b is

**Uniform Cumulative Distribution Function**

$$F(x) \begin{cases} 0 & \text{for } x \leq a \\ \dfrac{x - a}{b - a} & \text{for } a < x < b \\ 1 & \text{for } x \geq b \end{cases}$$

The uniform distribution is rectangular in shape as shown in Figure A.4. The formulas for the mean and variance of the uniform continuous probability distribution are:

$$\text{Mean} = \frac{(a + b)}{2} \qquad \text{Variance} = \frac{(b - a)^2}{12}$$

**Normal Probability Distribution**

One of the most important continuous probability distributions is the normal probability distribution. In addition to approximating other mathematical distributions, many business

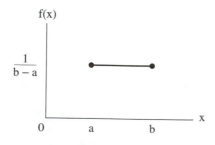

**Figure A.4** Graph of the Continuous Uniform Distribution

f(x)

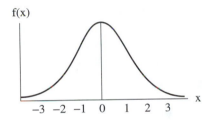

**Figure A.5** Graph of the Normal Distribution with $\mu = 0$, $\sigma = 1$ (also called the Standard Normal Distribution)

and economic variables approximate normal distributions such as the rate of return on stocks, the time it takes to perform a certain task, or the lengths of metal rods cut by a machine. The normal distribution is often used to measure various types of error and draw inferences from data sampling. For example, in receiving/inspection operations, calibrated instruments measure the dimensions of various components. These measurements are assumed to be normally distributed about the true dimensions of the component.

The probability density function for the normal probability distribution is

**Normal Probability Density Function**

$$f(x) = \frac{1}{\sqrt{2\pi}\sigma} e^{\frac{-(x-\mu)^2}{2\sigma^2}} \quad -\infty < x < \infty$$

*where*

$\mu$ = population mean

$\sigma$ = population standard deviation

$\pi$ = 3.14159

An example of a normal distribution is given as Figure A.5. The normal curve has two parameters, the mean and the standard deviation. They determine the location and shape of the distribution. Thus, there are families of normal distributions, each differentiated by its mean and standard deviation. The normal distribution is bell-shaped, symmetrical at the mean, and asymptotic to the x-axis in each direction. The mean equals the median equals the mode at the highest point of the curve. The standard deviation determines the spread of the distribution such that the larger the value, the more spread out is the distribution. Figure A.6 shows that although curve B has a greater mean, its standard deviation is smaller. Regardless of the shape of a particular normal curve, approximately 68% of the area is within one standard deviation of the mean, 95.5% is within two standard deviations of the mean, and nearly all (99.7%) is within three standard deviations.

Since normal distributions differ in shape, to avoid having to make different calculations for each shape, data can be standardized so that only one normal curve and table needs to be used. If one expresses any normal random variable as a deviation from its

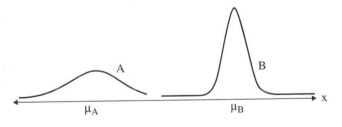

**Figure A.6** Graphs of Two Normal Distributions

mean and measures these deviations in units of its standard deviation, the result is called a *standard normal variable* and its continuous probability distribution is called the *standardized normal distribution* with a mean of 0 and a standard deviation of 1. Figure A.5 is also an example of the standardized normal distribution. By using the z-score (transformation) formula,

**The Z-Score Formula**

$$z = \frac{x - \mu}{\sigma}$$

*where*

z = number of standard deviations from the mean of 0

Any normal random variable, x, regardless of its mean and standard deviation can be converted into a standardized normal random variable, z. For example, the distribution of waiting times before the telephone is answered may follow a normal distribution where the mean waiting time is 20 seconds with a standard deviation of 2 seconds. You are interested in the probability that the waiting time will be between 16 to 24 seconds. Applying the z-score formula to standardize the data from seconds to deviations from the mean,

$$z = \frac{24 - 20}{2} = +2$$

$$z = \frac{16 - 20}{2} = -2$$

Therefore, the probability is 95.5% that the mean waiting time will be between 16 to 24 seconds since the area is within two standard deviations of the mean. Standard normal tables are available to compute probabilities for other z-scores.

The formulas for the mean and variance of the normal distribution are:

$$\text{Mean} = \mu \approx \bar{x}(n) = \frac{\sum_{i=1}^{N} x_i}{n} \qquad \text{Variance} = \sigma^2 \approx \frac{\sum_{i=1}^{N} (x_i - \bar{x}(n))^2}{n}$$

### Exponential Probability Distribution

The exponential probability distribution is a continuous probability distribution that is often useful in describing the interval of time or space it takes to get the first success or in describing the amount of time, space, or distance between occurrences of the event of interest. For example, it can be used to describe the length of time that must pass before the first incoming telephone call; the length of time between successive arrivals at a service counter; the length of time between failures of equipment; or the distance between defects in a bolt of cloth. It has widespread use in the management science topics of business processes, and queuing systems. If the number of arrivals per unit time (arrival rate) follows a Poisson distribution, the time between arrivals (interarrival time) follows an exponential distribution. The assumption that arrivals are independent from one another must hold.

The exponential probability density function is

**Exponential Probability Density Function**

$$f(x) = \mu e^{-\mu x} \quad \text{for } x \geq 0, \mu > 0$$

*where*

    x = length of the interval between occurrences

    $\mu$ = mean

The exponential distribution is a family of distributions, each differentiated by its mean (Figure A.7). It is very positively skewed, generally making it more likely that observed intervals between occurrences are shorter rather than longer (more likely that the values will be between 0 and the mean than between the mean and 2 times the mean). The mean and variance of the distribution are

$$\text{Mean} = \frac{1}{\mu} \qquad \text{Variance} = \frac{1}{\mu^2}$$

## Erlang Distribution

The Erlang distribution is a continuous probability distribution and a special case of the Gamma distribution. General applications include telephone traffic and queuing theory when an activity or service time is considered to occur in phases with each phase being exponentially distributed. It is common to use the Erlang distribution as a service time when you want to simplify a model by combining several similar steps into one representative step. The probability density function for the Erlang distribution is

**Erlang Probability Density Function**

$$f(x) = \frac{(\mu k)^k}{(k-1)!} x^{k-1} e^{-k\mu x} \quad \text{for } x > 0 \text{ else } 0; k > 0, \mu > 0$$

*where*

    k = any arbitrary positive integer

    $1/\mu$ = mean

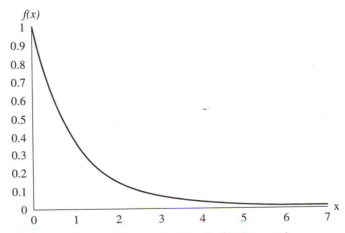

**Figure A.7** Graph of Exponential Distribution for $\mu = 1$

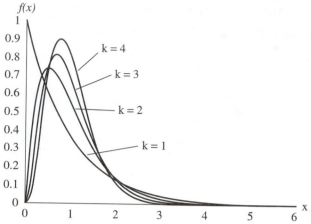

**Figure A.8** Graph of the Erlang Distribution

The Erlang distribution is a large family of distributions permitting only non-negative values as demonstrated in Figure A.8. It gives a value varying around the given mean, with a wide range of outcomes depending on the value of the second argument, k. The parameter k determines the dispersion of the distribution and is always a positive integer. The curve approximates other distributions depending on the value of its mean and especially the value of k. An Erlang distribution with a k of 1 reduces to the exponential distribution whereas large values of k tend toward a normal distribution. Overall the distribution tends to be skewed to the right. The mean and variance for the Erlang distribution are

$$\text{Mean: } = \frac{1}{\mu} \qquad \text{Variance: } = \frac{1}{k\mu^2}$$

## CONFIDENCE INTERVAL ESTIMATION

A major motivation of discussing confidence intervals is the accurate interpretation of the output of a computer simulation. While the sample mean represents our best point estimate of our population parameter, the confidence interval provides important information about the precision of our population parameter estimate. For example, the results of a computer simulation may provide information on customer waiting time. The sample mean waiting time generated in the computer simulation represents our best point estimate of the true population waiting time. The confidence interval provides information about the interval over which the true parameter can lie. Decisions have to be made in light of not only the point estimate, but also the confidence interval.

Statistical inference is the process of using statistics from a sample to draw conclusions about parameters of a population that are not initially known. The great strength of inferential statistics is that one can infer from the sample many important characteristics of the probability distribution of the population from which the sample is taken, even though the distribution of this population is unknown or inaccessible to us. One major technique of statistical inference is confidence interval estimation. For the purpose of this book, we shall confine the study of confidence interval estimation to population means; however, one should recognize that other population parameters, such as proportions and variances, can be applied.

We can estimate the mean of the population by examining the mean of a random sample taken from that population. This is an example of the way statistics functions in actual practice. A statement is made about the mean of the population based on the mean calculated from the random sample drawn from that population. The statistical statement is not usually exact, so we must assign a certain degree of confidence to the statement in order to give an indication of how much we can rely upon it. Consequently, the best we can do is establish limits within which the mean of the population will fall with a specified probability or confidence.

The range of values within which the actual value of the population parameter may fall is called the *interval estimate* (a < x < b) and the upper *b* and lower *a* values of the interval estimate are called the *confidence limits* for the parameter. The interval within which a population parameter is expected to occur with a specified degree of certainty is called the *confidence interval*. The confidence interval for the mean is expressed as (a < $\mu$ < b). The two confidence interval *levels* used extensively are the 95% and the 99%. The greater the specified confidence, the wider the confidence interval, all else held constant. The difference between the observed sample statistic and the actual value of the population parameter being estimated is referred to as the *sampling error*.

In general a 95% (99%) confidence interval estimate is interpreted as follows: for all possible samples of size n taken from a population, 95% (99%) of them will generate confidence intervals that contain the true population mean somewhere in the interval and 5% (1%) will not. In practice only one sample is selected. We are never sure that the confidence interval generated from our one sample includes the population mean or not. However, we can state that we are 95% (99%) confident that we chose a sample whose interval does contain the population mean, recognizing there is a 5% (1%) risk that the population mean is not in the interval. In other words, we are 95% (99%) confident that the true population mean value is contained within the interval. The formula for the confidence interval estimate for the mean when the population standard deviation ($\sigma$) is known is

**Confidence Interval for the Mean, $\sigma$ is Known**

$$\bar{x} \pm z \left( \frac{\sigma}{\sqrt{n}} \right)$$

*where*

$\bar{x}$ = sample mean

$\sigma$ = population standard deviation

n = sample size

z = z-score from normal distribution determined by the level of confidence desired
(Confidence level of 95% → z = 1.96)

The assumptions necessary to apply this formula are: (1) the population standard deviation is known, (2) the population is normally distributed or, if not normal, the sample size n is greater or equal to 30 by the Central Limit Theorem. The Central Limit Theorem states that for a population with a mean *u* and a standard deviation $\sigma$, the sampling distribution of the means of all possible samples of size n generated from the population will be approximately *normally distributed* with the mean $\mu_{\bar{x}} = \mu$ and the standard error $\sigma_{\bar{x}} = \sigma/\sqrt{n}$ assuming that the sample size is *sufficiently large* n $\geq$ 30. As the sample size n is increased, the sampling distribution will more closely approximate the normal distribution. The Central Limit Theorem is basic to the concept of statistical inference because

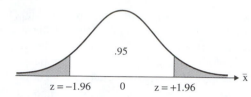

**Figure A.9** 95% Confidence Interval Graph, $\sigma$ is Known

it permits us to draw conclusions about the population based strictly on sample data, and without having any knowledge about the shape of the population distribution. An example of a 95% confidence interval for the mean with known standard deviation is given as Figure A.9.

For example, one might be interested in finding the 95% confidence interval for the true mean time spent in line at the bank before being helped. We will assume that the population standard deviation is 85 seconds and, from the sample data in Table A.1, the calculated sample mean is 179.9 seconds. Using the formula already given, the 95% confidence interval for the population mean time spent in line at the bank is

$$\bar{x} - z \cdot \frac{\sigma}{\sqrt{n}} \leq \mu \leq \bar{x} + z \cdot \frac{\sigma}{\sqrt{n}}$$

$$179.9 - 1.96 \cdot \frac{85}{\sqrt{30}} \leq \mu \leq 179.9 + 1.96 \frac{85}{\sqrt{30}}$$

$$149.48 \leq \mu \leq 210.32$$

Therefore, we are 95% confident that the true (population) mean time spent in line at the bank before being helped is between 149.48 to 210.32 seconds.

Usually if you do not know the population mean, you do not know the population standard deviation. It does happen that historical data is sometimes available on the population standard deviation, particularly in industrial processes. For example, you may not know the average height of a soldier today but the standard deviation of the heights has not changed through the generations. However it is more common that the population standard deviation is not known. In this case it is estimated by the sample standard deviations. The corresponding confidence interval uses a student's t-distribution instead of the normal z-distribution. The formula for the confidence interval estimate for the mean when the population standard deviation ($\sigma$) is unknown is

$$\bar{x} \pm t\left(\frac{s}{\sqrt{n}}\right)$$

*where*

    $\bar{x}$ = sample mean

    s = sample standard deviation

    n = sample size

    $\nu$ = degree of freedom = n − 1

    z = t-score from Student's t distribution corresponding to the level of confidence desired, with $\nu$ = n − 1 (e.g., t = 2.201 for 95% confidence level, n = 12, $\nu$ = 12 − 1 = 11)

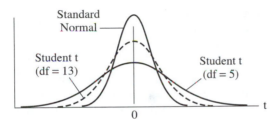

**Figure A.10** Student's t Distributions with the Normal Distribution

The assumptions are (1) the population standard deviation is unknown, (2) the t-distribution assumes the population is approximately normally distributed, but this is important only when the sample is small (n < 30).

The Student's t-distribution is a family of continuous, unimodal, bell-shaped distributions. The t-distribution is the probability distribution for the random variable

$$t = \frac{\bar{x} - \mu}{\dfrac{s}{\sqrt{n}}}$$

with a mean of zero. Its shape is determined by its degree of freedom ($\nu = n - 1$). The degree of freedom is the number of values that remain free to vary once some information about them is already known. The t-distribution is wider and flatter than the normal distribution as shown in Figure A.10. As the number of degrees of freedom increases, the t-distribution becomes increasingly similar to the normal distribution. For large degrees of freedom, they are essentially the same.

With respect to the bank problem from Table A.1, if the population standard deviation were unknown, then the sample standard deviation (73.66) calculated from the sample data is used with the t-distribution with a degree of freedom of 29.

$$\bar{X} - t \cdot \frac{s}{\sqrt{n}} \leq \mu \leq \bar{X} + t \cdot \frac{x}{\sqrt{n}}$$

$$179.9 - 2.05 \cdot \frac{73.66}{\sqrt{30}} \leq \mu \leq 179.9 + 2.05 \cdot \frac{73.66}{\sqrt{30}}$$

$$152.39 \leq \mu \leq 207.41$$

Therefore, we are 95% confident that the true mean time spent in line at the bank before being helped is between 152.39 to 207.41 seconds.

Extend has the capability of computing confidence intervals for all model output parameters such as average waiting time in queue. An example in the application and interpretation of confidence intervals using simulation output can be found in Chapter 13.

## HYPOTHESIS TESTING CONCEPTS

In order to understand the application of goodness-of-fit tests discussed in the next section, one must understand the concepts underlying *hypothesis testing*. In addition to confidence interval estimation, hypothesis testing is the other major technique used in inferential statistics. Whereas the confidence interval estimation begins with a sample statistic and builds an interval around the statistic to estimate the population parameter with a degree of confidence, the hypothesis test starts with a statement (null hypothesis) about the population parameter when its true value is unknown, then selects a sample from that population to use in determining whether the sample statistic supports or does not support the statement made in the null hypothesis. Because of the random nature of the sample, it is possible to reject the null hypothesis even though it is actually true. It is desired that this situation occur only 5% of the times the test is run. This typical value of 5% represents the risk of rejecting the null hypothesis when it is actually true and is called $\alpha$, *the level of significance*. This is the risk involved in using sample statistics to make decisions about population parameters.

Using the level of significance, the hypothesis test consists of determining a region of rejection for the null hypothesis. The *critical value* separates the region of rejection from the region of non-rejection. The size of the rejection region and location of the critical value is determined by the level of significance. If the test statistic falls into the region of non-rejection, the null hypothesis can not be rejected. If the null hypothesis is true, it is unlikely the statistic from the sample will fall within the region of rejection. However, if the null hypothesis is false, it is more likely the sample statistic will fall within the region of rejection. Therefore, if a value falls within the rejection region, we reject the null hypothesis because that value would be unlikely if the null hypothesis were true.

Either one or two regions of rejection are appropriate depending upon the application. If two regions of rejection are needed because of interest in both a very high and a very low result, it is called a two-tailed hypothesis test. Confidence intervals are an application of two-tailed tests. In confidence interval estimates, the confidence level of 95%, for example, determines the upper and lower values of the interval. Graphically the area (probability) above that confidence interval but under the curve is 95%. (Refer to Figure A.9.) We are 95% confident that the actual population parameter falls within the interval. Therefore, there is a 5% risk that it does not fall within the interval. The area in the two tails outside the confidence interval represents the risk and is called $\alpha$ (1 − confidence interval coefficient) = 1 − 95% = 5%). It represents the degree of certainty that the population parameter does not fall within the stated confidence interval.

If only one region of rejection is needed, it is referred to as a one-tailed hypothesis test. If the interest of the problem is in either a very low or a very high result (but not both), a one-tailed test is used. The Chi squared goodness-of-fit application discussed in the next section is a one-tailed test to the right.

## GOODNESS OF FIT TESTS

There are several goodness-of-fit tests used in practice. These include the Chi squared, the Kolmogorov Smirnov and the Anderson Darling tests. Depending on the circumstance, Stat::Fit uses two or more of these tests to evaluate how to fit data to a specific probability distribution. A detailed example using Stat::Fit is shown in Chapter 13. We now provide background to help understand the basic ideas that are used in two of these tests. Specifically, we include a description and example of the Chi squared test and the Kolmogorov Smirnov test.

### Chi Squared Goodness-of-Fit Test

The Chi squared distribution is a family of probability distributions, determined by the number of degrees of freedom. Recall that the degree of freedom is the number of values free to vary once some information about all of the values is already known. An important applications of the Chi squared distribution is the *goodness-of-fit* test. The Chi squared goodness-of-fit test is a statistical test that evaluates the closeness of a set of observed (empirical) frequencies to a corresponding set of expected (theoretical) frequencies. The result of the test is based on a Chi squared ($\chi^2$) value calculated from the observed data and a critical $\chi^2$ value found in a Chi squared table. Provided the expected frequencies in each category are greater than 5, a less complicated formula may be used to approximate the $\chi^2$ distribution given. The Chi squared formula is

**Chi Squared Formula**

$$\chi^2 = \sum_{i=1}^{k} \frac{(O_i - E_i)^2}{E_i}$$

*where*

O$_i$ = observed frequency in the ith category

E$_i$ = expected frequency in the ith category

k = total number of categories

m = the number of parameters that must be estimated from the sample data

$\nu$ = k − 1 − m = degree of freedom (need for critical $\chi^2$ table). For example, if the hypothesis is that the distribution is normal with a mean 8 and variance 5, the $\nu$ = k − 1; on the other hand, if the hypothesis is normal without knowing mean and variance, the $\nu$ = k − 1 − 2 = k − 3, since two items, the mean and variance, must be estimated.

The closer the expected values are to the observed values, the smaller will be the value of $\chi^2$. If $\chi^2$ is small, it can be concluded that the observed and expected data are a good fit. If the calculated value is less than the critical value (determined from the table), then the observed and expected distributions are compatible.

As an example, one might be interested in determining if the distribution of the time spent in line at the bank before being helped follows an exponential distribution. (Refer to Tables A.1 and A.2.) Table A.8 displays the calculation of the sample $\chi^2$ statistics for an exponential distribution, assuming seven classes with a class width of 60.

The hypothesized distribution is an exponential with a mean parameter of 179.9 seconds. The number of degrees of freedom is 5 ($\nu$ = k − 1 − m where k = 7 classes intervals with m = 1 for the estimated mean parameter). The calculated sample $\chi^2$ value is 28.894. In conjunction with the degree of freedom, the level of significance, $\alpha$, determines the critical $\chi^2$ statistic, the value that separates the region of rejection from the region of non-rejection. The critical $\chi^2$ ($\alpha$ = 5% and $\nu$ = 5) is 11.071. Since the sample $\chi^2$ is greater than the critical $\chi^2$, the result is significant and we will *reject* the hypothesized statement that the distribution of the waiting time at the bank does fit an exponential distribution. As mentioned, the expected frequencies should be greater than 5; note that the expected frequencies for five of the seven class intervals are less than 5; in actual practice, we would combine rows and intervals so that each expected frequency is at least 5.

**Kolmogorov Smirnov Test**

The Kolmogorov Smirnov Test (K-S) is a goodness-of-fit test to determine if two data sets differ significantly. Specifically, the K-S test evaluates the null hypothesis that a sample data set fits a *specified* (that is, all parameters are known) *continuous* distribution F(x). It is a non-parametric test and exact for all sample sizes (in contrast to the $\chi^2$ test, which

**Table A.8**   Goodness-of-Fit Chi Squared Test for an Exponential Distribution Time Between Arrivals of 30 Customers at a Bank

| | | Chi squared goodness-of-fit test for exponential distribution | | |
|---|---|---|---|---|
| Class intervals | Observed frequency $O_i$ | **Exponential distribution percentage factor $P(X<=x) = 1 - e^{-\mu x}$ | *Expected frequency $E_i$ | $\dfrac{(O - E)^2}{E}$ |
| 0 and under 60 | 0 | $P(X \le 60)$ $- P(X \le 0)$ $= 0.284$ | 8.52 | 8.520 |
| 60 and under 120 | 6 | $P(X \le 120) - P(X \le 60)$ $= 0.203$ | 6.09 | 0.001 |
| 120 and under 180 | 10 | $P(X \le 180) - P(X \le 120) = 0.145$ | 4.35 | 7.339 |
| 180 and under 240 | 8 | $P(X \le 240) - P(X \le 180) = 0.105$ | 3.15 | 7.467 |
| 240 and under 300 | 4 | $P(X \le 300) - P(X \le 240) = 0.074$ | 2.22 | 1.427 |
| 300 and under 360 | 2 | $P(X \le 360) - P(X \le 300) = 0.054$ | 1.62 | 0.089 |
| 360 or more | 0 | $P(X \le \infty)$   $- P(X \le 360) = 0.135$ | 4.05 | 4.050 |
| | | Calculated Chi squared value = summation of $(O_i - E_i)^2/E_i = \chi^2 = 28.894$ | | |

*Percentage factor multiplied by 30 total observations

**Calculated using cumulative exponential tables

relies on an adequate sample size for valid results). With large sample sizes, the $\chi^2$ test is probably better; however, with relatively small sample sizes, the K-S test is preferable.

The basis of the K-S procedure is the cumulative sample function, denoted S(x), which specifies for each value of x the proportion of sample values less than or equal to x. The sample cumulative distribution function for n observations, $X_1, \ldots, X_n$, is

$$S_n(x) = \begin{cases} 0 & x < X_1 \\ j/n & X_j \le x < X_{j+1} \quad j = 1, \ldots, n-1 \\ 1 & x \ge X_n \end{cases}$$

The K-S test compares the sample cumulative distribution function $S_n(x)$ with the hypothesized cumulative distribution function F(x) by using a statistic, denoted D, that is based on the maximum absolute vertical deviation between these two distributions. The test statistic is

$$D_n(x) = \max_{\text{all } x} |S_n(x) - F(x)|$$

*where*

F(x) = the hypothesized cumulative distribution function

$S_n(x)$ = the sample cumulative distribution function

One advantage of the K-S test is the distribution of the $D_n(x)$ statistic is independent of the underlying cumulative distribution function F(x). In applying this test, it is assumed that (1) the population is continuous and (2) the sample is a simple random one.

Figure A.11 represents a graphical display of how two sets of data may be distributed cumulatively and the location of D, the maximum absolute vertical deviation between $S_n(x)$ and F(x). For any number x, the cumulative fraction is the fraction of the data that is strictly smaller than x. For example, let S(x) be a sample data set with 12 data points sorted from lowest (2) to highest (30) such that the first three data points are 2, 3, and 6.

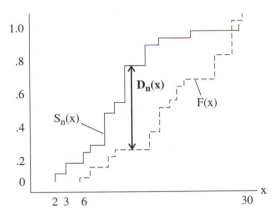

**Figure A.11** K-S Test Comparison Cumulative Fraction Plot

0% of the data lies below 2; 8.3% = .083 = 1/12 of the data lies below 3; 16.7% = .167 = 2/12 of the data lies below 6. This is how S is plotted in a cumulative fraction plot.

Unless the sample size is small, computers best handle the calculations for D. Most statistics texts compute the critical values $D_\alpha$ for a significance level $\alpha$ and sample size n. The null hypothesis that a sample data set fits a distribution F(x) is not rejected if $D_n(x) < D_\alpha$. Large values of $D_n(x)$ generally indicate that the observed data is significantly different and not representative of the expected distribution.

## SUMMARY

In this appendix we have provided information on statistical concepts that helps provide a fuller understanding of the material in this text, especially in Part 3, Computer Simulation. We began by describing the role of random sampling in statistics and how sample statistics are used to estimate population parameters. The generation of random samples is the basis of Monte Carlo simulation. We then discussed methods for summarizing data including frequency distributions and histograms. Important descriptive statistics, including measures of central tendency (mean, median, and mode) and measures of dispersion and variability of data (standard deviation and variance) were also presented. These statistics are often used to summarize the results of a simulation analysis. We then described those probability distributions that are most often used in simulation applications, including discrete probability distributions, such as the Poisson and binomial, and continuous distributions, such as the uniform, normal, exponential, and Erlang.

We then considered the theory of statistical inference, focusing on confidence interval estimation, which addresses the precision of the descriptive statistics obtained from the output of a simulation analysis. Here we discussed how the sampling distribution of the mean with known standard deviation is approximately normally distributed, based on the application of the central limit theorem. We also indicated that the student-t distribution instead of the normal should be applied when the population standard deviation is unknown. Next, we addressed the basic concepts of hypothesis testing, which is another form of statistical inference. Finally, we considered goodness of fit tests, which are used in simulation analysis to determine whether the observed data fit a specific probability distribution. Two of the most important of these tests, the Chi squared goodness-of-fit test, and the Kolmogorov Smirnov test were discussed.

# A Summary Description of All Extend Blocks Used

| Block Name | Library | Submenu | Explained in: | Description |
|---|---|---|---|---|
| Activity, Multiple | DE | Activities | Bank1t | Provides service for entering items |
| Add | Generic | Math | Bankdrivethru1 | Adds up to three numbers |
| Clear Statistics | Statistics | None | Bank4tstats | Clears statistics for selected blocks |
| Combine | DE | Routing | Bankcycle | Combines items into single stream |
| Constant | Generic | Inputs/Outputs | Banksl | Outputs a constant value |
| Conversion Table | Generic | Math | Bankitcl | Input determines output value |
| Cost Stats | Statistics | None | Loading1 | Computes costs for selected blocks |
| Count Items | DE | Information | Banksl | Counts items that pass this block |
| Data Receive | IPC | None | ShadesInc | Receives input from a spreadsheet |
| Data Send | IPC | None | Bank4texcel | Sends output to a spreadsheet |
| Decision | Generic | Decisions | Bank4trb | Makes decision based on comparison of inputs |
| Divide | Generic | Math | Shades | Divides two numbers |
| Equation | Generic | Math | ShadesInc | Outputs the result of an entered equation |
| Evolutionary Optimizer | Optimization | None | Loadingopt | Searches for the best solution |
| Executive | DE | None | Bank1t | Creates clock for discrete event simulation |
| Exit | DE | Routing | Bank1t | Removes items from model |
| Exit (4) | DE | Routing | Bankcustserv | Removes items from model and can track up to four exiting routes |
| Exponent | Generic | Math | Shades | Raises a number to a power |
| Generator | DE | Generators | Bank1t | Generates arrivals |
| Get Attribute | DE | Attributes | Bankcustserv | Reads attribute of an item |
| Global Array | Generic | Arrays | ShadesInc | Internal spreadsheet that accepts/transmits data |
| Global Array Manager | Generic | Arrays | ShadesInc | Creates a Global Array |
| Histogram | Plotter | None | Chapter 16, HWK1 | Creates a histogram of values received |
| Holding Tank | Generic | Holding | Banksl | Sums total of input values |
| Input Data | Generic | Inputs/Outputs | Bank4tic | Determines output based on time |
| Input Random Number | Generic | Inputs/Outputs | Bank1t | Generates random numbers |
| Mean & Variance | Generic | Statistics | Ban4texcel | Computes mean and variance |
| Multiply | Generic | Math | Shades | Multiplies two numbers |
| Plotter, Discrete Event | Plotter | None | Bank1t | Plots up to four variables |
| Prioritizer | DE | Routing | Bank4tfb | Establishes priority for parallel processing of items |
| Program | DE | Generators | Bankinvest | Generates scheduled arrivals |

| Block Name | Library | Submenu | Explained in: | Description |
|---|---|---|---|---|
| Queue, FIFO | DE | Queues | Bank1t | Creates a FIFO queue for items |
| Queue, Priority | DE | Queues | Bankcycle | Creates a priority queue for items |
| Queue, Reneging | MFG | Queues | Bank4tfr | Creates a reneging queue for items |
| Queue, Resource Pool | DE | Queues | Bankcustserv | Creates queue for items that need resources |
| Queue Stats | Statistics | None | Bank4tstats | Computes confidence intervals for any queuing block |
| ReadOut | Generic | Inputs/Outputs | ShadesInc | Displays values for debugging |
| Release Resource Pool | DE | Resources | Bankcustserv | Releases resources |
| Resource Pool | DE | Resources | Bankcustserv | Identifies resources |
| Select DE Output | DE | Routing | Bank4trb | Chooses one of two paths for item |
| Select Input | Generic | Decisions | ShadesInc | Chooses one of two input values |
| Set Attribute | DE | Attributes | Bankcustserv | Sets attribute of an item |
| Set Priority | DE | Attributes | Bankcycle | Sets the priority level for an item |
| Subtract | Generic | Math | Bankinvest | Subtracts one number from another |
| System Variable | Generic | Inputs/Outputs | Shades | Outputs values of system variables, such as run number |

# Index